Communications
in Computer and Information Science 56

T0189649

Dominik Ślęzak   Tai-hoon Kim
Alan Chin-Chen Chang   Thanos Vasilakos
MingChu Li   Kouichi Sakurai (Eds.)

Communication and Networking

International Conference, FGCN/ACN 2009
Held as Part of the Future Generation
Information Technology Conference, FGIT 2009
Jeju Island, Korea, December 10-12, 2009
Proceedings

 Springer

Volume Editors

Dominik Ślęzak
University of Warsaw & Infobright Inc., Poland
E-mail: slezak@infobright.com

Tai-hoon Kim
Hannam University, Daejeon, South Korea
E-mail: taihoonn@hnu.kr

Alan Chin-Chen Chang
National Chung Cheng University, Chiayi County, Taiwan
E-mail: ccc@cs.ccu.edu.tw

Thanos Vasilakos
University of Western Macedonia, West Macedonia, Greece
E-mail: vasilako@ath.forthnet.gr

MingChu Li
Tianjin University, China
E-mail: li_mingchu@yahoo.com

Kouichi Sakurai
Kyushu University, Fukuoka, Japan
E-mail: sakurai@csce.kyushu-u.ac.jp

Library of Congress Control Number: 2009940049

CR Subject Classification (1998): C.2, D.2, H.3.5, C.2.5, F.2.2, C.2.2, I.2.8

ISSN   1865-0929
ISBN-10   3-642-10843-1 Springer Berlin Heidelberg New York
ISBN-13   978-3-642-10843-3 Springer Berlin Heidelberg New York

springer.com

© Springer-Verlag Berlin Heidelberg 2009
Printed in Germany

Typesetting: Camera-ready by author, data conversion by Scientific Publishing Services, Chennai, India
Printed on acid-free paper   SPIN: 12805068   06/3180   5 4 3 2 1 0

Foreword

As future generation information technology (FGIT) becomes specialized and fragmented, it is easy to lose sight that many topics in FGIT have common threads and, because of this, advances in one discipline may be transmitted to others. Presentation of recent results obtained in different disciplines encourages this interchange for the advancement of FGIT as a whole. Of particular interest are hybrid solutions that combine ideas taken from multiple disciplines in order to achieve something more significant than the sum of the individual parts. Through such hybrid philosophy, a new principle can be discovered, which has the propensity to propagate throughout multifaceted disciplines.

FGIT 2009 was the first mega-conference that attempted to follow the above idea of hybridization in FGIT in a form of multiple events related to particular disciplines of IT, conducted by separate scientific committees, but coordinated in order to expose the most important contributions. It included the following international conferences: Advanced Software Engineering and Its Applications (ASEA), Bio-Science and Bio-Technology (BSBT), Control and Automation (CA), Database Theory and Application (DTA), Disaster Recovery and Business Continuity (DRBC; published independently), Future Generation Communication and Networking (FGCN) that was combined with Advanced Communication and Networking (ACN), Grid and Distributed Computing (GDC), Multimedia, Computer Graphics and Broadcasting (MulGraB), Security Technology (SecTech), Signal Processing, Image Processing and Pattern Recognition (SIP), and u- and e-Service, Science and Technology (UNESST).

We acknowledge the great effort of all the Chairs and the members of advisory boards and Program Committees of the above-listed events, who selected 28% of over 1,050 submissions, following a rigorous peer-review process. Special thanks go to the following organizations supporting FGIT 2009: ECSIS, Korean Institute of Information Technology, Australian Computer Society, SERSC, Springer LNCS/CCIS, COEIA, ICC Jeju, ISEP/IPP, GECAD, PoDIT, Business Community Partnership, Brno University of Technology, KISA, K-NBTC and National Taipei University of Education.

We are very grateful to the following speakers who accepted our invitation and helped to meet the objectives of FGIT 2009: Ruay-Shiung Chang (National Dong Hwa University, Taiwan), Jack Dongarra (University of Tennessee, USA), Xiaohua (Tony) Hu (Drexel University, USA), Irwin King (Chinese University of Hong Kong, Hong Kong), Carlos Ramos (Polytechnic of Porto, Portugal), Timothy K. Shih (Asia University, Taiwan), Peter M.A. Sloot (University of Amsterdam, The Netherlands), Kyu-Young Whang (KAIST, South Korea), and Stephen S. Yau (Arizona State University, USA).

We would also like to thank Rosslin John Robles, Maricel O. Balitanas, Farkhod Alisherov Alisherovish, and Feruza Sattarova Yusfovna – graduate students of Hannam University who helped in editing the FGIT 2009 material with a great passion.

October 2009   Young-hoon Lee
                                                                              Tai-hoon Kim
                                                                              Wai-chi Fang
                                                                              Dominik Ślęzak

Preface

We would like to welcome you to the proceedings of the 2009 International Conference on Future Generation Communication and Networking (FGCN 2009), which was organized as part of the 2009 International Mega-Conference on Future Generation Information Technology (FGIT 2009), held during December 10–12, 2009, at the International Convention Center Jeju, Jeju Island, South Korea.

FGCN/ACN 2009 focused on various aspects of advances in communication and networking with computational sciences, mathematics and information technology. It provided a chance for academic and industry professionals to discuss recent progress in the related areas. We expect that the conference and its publications will be a trigger for further related research and technology improvements in this important subject.

We would like to acknowledge the great effort of all the Chairs and members of the Program Committee. Out of 260 submissions to FGCN/ACN 2009, we accepted 82 papers to be included in the proceedings and presented during the conference. This gives roughly a 30% acceptance ratio. Seven of the papers accepted for FGCN/ACN 2009 were published in the special FGIT 2009 volume, LNCS 5899, by Springer. The remaining 75 accepted papers can be found in this CCIS volume.

We would like to express our gratitude to all of the authors of submitted papers and to all of the attendees, for their contributions and participation. We believe in the need for continuing this undertaking in the future.

We would also like to acknowledge Jun Zheng (New Mexico Institute of Mining and Technology, USA) and Yan Zhang (Simula Research Laboratory, Norway) for organizing the special session on Wireless Ad Hoc, Mesh, and Sensor Networks.

Once more, we would like to thank all the organizations and individuals who supported FGIT 2009 as a whole and, in particular, helped in the success of FGCN/ACN 2009.

October 2009

Dominik Ślęzak
Tai-hoon Kim
Alan Chin-Chen Chang
Thanos Vasilakos
MingChu Li
Kouichi Sakurai

Organization

Organizing Committee

General Chairs	Alan Chin-Chen Chang (National Chung Cheng University, Taiwan)
	Thanos Vasilakos (University of Western Macedonia, Greece)
	MingChu Li (Dalian University of Technology, China)
	Kouichi Sakurai (Kyushu University, Japan)
	Chunming Rong (University of Stavanger, Norway)
Program Chairs	Yang Xiao (University of Alabama, USA)
	Ch.Z. Patrikakis (National Technical University of Athens, Greece)
	Tai-hoon Kim (Hannam University, Korea)
	Martin Gilje Jaatun (SINTEF, Norway)
	Gansen Zhao (Sun Yat-sen University, China)
Advisory Board	Wai-chi Fang (National Chiao Tung University, Taiwan)
	Hsiao-Hwa Chen (National Sun Yat-Sen University, Taiwan)
	Han-Chieh Chao (National Ilan University, Taiwan)
	Gongzhu Hu (Central Michigan University, USA)
	Byeong-Ho Kang (University of Tasmania, Australia)
Publicity Chairs	Ching-Hsien Hsu (Chung Hua University, Taiwan)
	Houcine Hassan (Polytechnic University of Valencia, Spain)
	Yan Zhang (Simula Research Laboratory, Norway)
	Damien Sauveron (University of Limoges, France)
	Qun Jin (Waseda University, Japan)
	Irfan Awan (University of Bradford, UK)
Publication Chair	Maria Lee (Shih Chien University, Taiwan)

Program Committee

Aboul Ella Hassanien	Bogdan Ghita	Chu-Hsing Lin
Ai-Chun Pang	Byungjoo Park	Clement Leung
Andres Iglesias Prieto	Chao-Tung Yang	Damien Sauveron
Andrzej Jajszczyk	Chia-Chen Lin	Dimitrios D. Vergados
Antonio Lagana'	Christophe Fouqueré	Don-Lin Yang

Driss Mammass
Farrukh A. Khan
Gianluigi Ferrari
Hong Sun
Hui Chen
Huirong Fu
J. Vigo-Aguiar
Janusz Szczepanski
Jiann-Liang
Jieh-Shan George Yeh
Jiming Chen
Juha Roning
Kazuto Ogawa

Kin Keung Lai
Kwok-Yan Lam
Li Shijian
Luis Javier
Marc Lacoste
Matthias Reuter
Michel-Marie Deza
Mohammad Moghal
N. Jaisankar
Ning Gui
P.R. Parthasarathy
R. Yu-Kwong Kwok
Robert Goutte

Rui L. Aguiar
Shun-Ren Yang
Soon Ae Chun
Stephen Huang
Sun-Yuan Hsieh
Tae (Tom) Oh
Terence D. Todd
Victor C. M. Leung
Vincenzo De Florio
Weili Han
Witold Pedrycz

Table of Contents

A Dynamic Interval Scheduling and Congestion Control Scheme for Sensor Networks

Sun-Min Hwang, Seung-Min Han, Ga-Won Lee, and Eui-Nam Huh

Kyunghee University,
Internet Computing and Security Lab.
hsunny@icns.khu.ac.kr, hsm@icns.khu.ac.kr,
gawon@khu.ac.kr, johnhuh@ khu.ac.kr

Abstract. This paper introduces a novel interval scheduling and congestion control scheme in wireless sensor networks. Wireless sensor network is an event based system with several sensor nodes. Reliable event detection at the sink is based on collective information provided by sensor nodes. But due to the unreliable nature of wireless communication, it is hard to guarantee the end-to-end reliability and timeliness. Hence, we propose a novel dynamic congestion control scheme that ensures the reliable delivery of packets to a base station, and that minimizes congestion within sensor network. This solution includes a congestion control component that serves the purpose of minimizing congestion by burst traffic, data concentration, and link failure. And to achieve energy efficiency, reliability, and timeliness, we introduce the concept of dynamic interval scheduling algorithm that optimizes the data delivery ratio and energy usage for communication.

Keywords: Sensor network management, Congestion control, Sensor network duty cycle.

1 Introduction

WSNs have emerged as a new monitoring and control solution for various ubiquitous applications. Common sensor network applications are responsible for reporting conditions within a region where the environment suddenly changes due to an observed event, such as fire, flood, and earthquake. Sensor networks typically operate under light load and become active when an event is detected. This can result in the generation of large, sudden, correlated impulses of data that must be delivered to the sinks. Due to this feature, congestion easily occurs in sensor network. Thus, we propose congestion control scheme that provides reliable transmission minimizing delay, distortion and loss.

Also it is an important research issue for sensor applications to last a long life time with a limited energy supply. To prolong network life time with limited energy, it is necessary to reduce node communication and transmission duty cycles. In this paper, mainly we designed a novel interval scheduling algorithm that optimizes the sensor node`s data delivery ratio and communication energy consumption under unreliable sensor network environment.

D. Ślęzak et al. (Eds.): FGCN/ACN 2009, CCIS 56, pp. 1–8, 2009.

This paper is organized as follows: Section 2 introduces a well known congestion control algorithm CODA[1]; Section 3 describes the proposed idea; Performance evaluation is done and concluded in Section 4 and Section 5, respectively.

2 Related Works

In this section, we propose an energy efficient congestion control scheme for sensor networks called CODA (Congestion Detection and Avoidance)[1] that comprises three mechanisms:

- Congestion detection: CODA uses a combination of the present and past channel loading conditions, and the current buffer occupancy, to infer accurate detection of congestion at each receiver with low cost. Listening to the channel to measure local loading incurs high energy costs if performed all the time. Therefore, CODA uses a sampling scheme that activates local channel monitoring at the appropriate time to minimize cost while forming an accurate estimate. Once congestion is detected, nodes signal their upstream neighbors via a backpressure mechanism.
- Open-loop, hop-by-hop backpressure: In CODA a node broadcasts backpressure messages as long as it detects congestion. Nodes that receive backpressure signals can throttle their sending rates or drop packets based on the local congestion policy (e.g., packet drop, AIMD, etc.).
- Closed-loop, multi-source regulation: When the source event rate is less than some fraction of the maximum theoretical throughput of the channel, the source regulates itself. When this value is exceeded, however, a source is more likely contribute to congestion and therefore closed-loop congestion control is triggered. At this point a source requires constant, slow time-scale feedback (e.g., ACK) from the sink to maintain its rate. The reception of ACKs at sources serve as a self-clocking mechanism allowing sources to maintain their current event rates. In contrast, failure to receive ACKs forces a source to reduce its own rate.

3 Proposed Algorithm

In this section, we propose dynamic interval scheduling algorithm and congestion control scheme. In the proposed system, Tree-Routing Algorithm is adopted and designed to operate on event-driven network environment. After the topology construction phase, each node has one parent node and many child nodes. In the operation phase, Optimal transmission cycle is calculated and each node transmits data continuously at every calculated interval. Congestion control is also performed at operation phase.

3.1 Active Interval Scheduling Algorithm

When the sensors are deployed in the field, the manager first specifies about the event data and this information is included in the advertising packet. The manager broadcasts advertising packet through the sink node. After all the sensor nodes receive the advertising packet, each node finds out the information of event data.

In operation phase, each node transmits the sensing data, residual energy, and event occurring probability to the parent node at random interval. Event occurring probability is calculated from N sample sensing data.

When the node receives the data from child nodes, the node calculates the optimal data transmission interval based on child node's event occurring probability and its own event occurring probability. In this algorithm, we use two variable information P_{own}(event occurring probability), P_{avg}(average of received event occurring probabilities) , and three static information E_{tx}, E_{rx} and E_{idle} denoted to transmitting energy consumption, receiving energy consumption and energy consumption of sensor node itself, respectively.

Based on information about the probability of the event data and the sensor node power consumption, we create model to calculate the optimal data transmission interval. In the first phase, we suppose that 't' is the data transmission interval and 'p' is the event occurring probability. The probability of data transmission during 't' time can be calculated by Equation 1.

$$\sum_{i=0}^{t} pi = p\sum_{i=0}^{t} i = \frac{pt(t+1)}{2} \tag{1}$$

In the second phase, we can calculate the power consumption for data transmission during 't' time using the Equation 1 and energy consumption model of a radio transceiver[11-12] (as shown in Equation 2). E_{tx} means transmitting energy consumption and E_{rx} means receiving energy consumption. P_{own} means its own event occurring probability and P_{avg} means average of received event occurring probabilities, N_{node} means the number of child nodes.

$$\frac{P_{own} \cdot t(t+1)}{2} \cdot E_{tx} + \frac{P_{avg} \cdot t(t+1)}{2} \cdot E_{rx} \cdot N_{node} \tag{2}$$

In the third phase, we can calculate total energy consumption including energy consumption of sensor node itself. And the energy consumption per second can be calculated by dividing total energy consumption by 't' time (as shown in Equation 3).

$$\left\{ \left(\frac{P_{own} \cdot t(t+1)}{2} \cdot E_{tx} + \frac{P_{avg} \cdot t(t+1)}{2} \cdot E_{rx} \cdot N_{nocde} + E_{idle} \right\} / t \tag{3}$$

In the fourth phase, to calculate the optimal data transmission interval, we should find the 't' second which minimizes the energy consumption per second.

We can get simplified Equation expressing the optimal data transmission interval by differentiating Equation 3(as shown in Equation 4).

$$\frac{\partial C}{\partial t} = \frac{E_{tx} \cdot P_{own} + E_{rx} \cdot N_{node} \cdot P_{avg}}{2} - \frac{E_{idle}}{t^2} = 0$$

$$t_{opt} = \sqrt{\frac{2E_{idle}}{E_{tx} \cdot P_{own} + E_{rx} \cdot N_{node} \cdot P_{avg}}} \tag{4}$$

We can control the data transmission interval by calculating 'optimal t' based on Equation 4. After the optimal interval is calculated, each node transmits data to the parent node at the optimal interval.

3.2 Congestion Control Algorithm

As mentioned above, the event data occurred in the sensor network can cause large, sudden, unexpected traffic. In this section we propose congestion control algorithm that manages congestion derived from burst data, data concentration and link loss. When transmitting a packet, each node adds a field of hop count or time stamp to the packet. This information is used for recognizing *depth of congestion*. *Depth of congestion* indicates the number of hops that the congestion control message has traversed before a non-congested node is encountered. The depth of congestion is used by the routing protocol and interval regulation algorithm to help reduce the congestion. Detailed information will be covered later in this section.

This algorithm is consisted of two-phases, interval regulation and congestion avoidance. In the first phase, when congestion occurs, the node first finds out a packet with largest hop count in the packet queue. Hop count information is extracted from the packet and used to calculate T_{max}(as shown in Equation 5).

$$T_{max} = \alpha \cdot \text{hop\_count(time\_stamp)} \tag{5}$$

T_{max} value is included in backpressure beacon and congested node transmits backpressure beacon to upstream nodes as long as it detects congestion. Then backpressure beacons are propagated upstream toward the sources. Nodes that receive backpressure beacon increases their transmission interval if event occurring probability is less than P_{thresh}(as shown in equation 6). Hence, a node with high-probability maintains transmission interval for event reporting timeliness. If congestion is removed, interval is gradually restored to t_{opt}.

$$\text{interval} = t_{opt} \cdot 2^t \ (P_{event} \leq P_{thresh}) \tag{6}$$

Backpressure beacon has two fields, T_{max} and DoC(Depth of congestion). When the message is propagated to the congested nodes, DoC is incremented by 1 for each hop. In the second phase the node that received backpressure beacon calculates T_{thresh} using two variables, T_{max} and DoC(as shown in equation 7). 'df' is decreasing factor and 'df' makes the congested node close to source node have small T_{thresh}.

$$T_{thresh} = T_{max} \cdot df^{\alpha} \ (0.5 \leq df < 1, \ \alpha: \text{depth of congestion}) \tag{7}$$

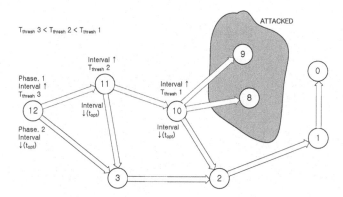

Fig. 1. Optimal data transmission interval

After T_{thresh} time, the node checks the packet queue and channel to figure out whether congestion is eliminated or not. If congestion is not eliminated, the node chooses another path in the routing table to avoid congestion(as shown in Fig. 1). According to the above formula, the congested node close to source node performs path selection earlier than other nodes. In summary, our congestion control scheme proposes transmission interval regulation to mitigate congestion derived from burst data and data concentration, and congestion avoidance algorithm to recover from persistent congestion by link loss.

4 Experimentation and Evaluation

In this section, we evaluated performance of our algorithm, interval scheduling and congestion control. We performed a packet-level simulation about our protocol on NS-2. Our algorithm exists in the transport layer of the Zigbee stack and is designed to work with any MAC protocol in the data-link layer with minor modification. Our solution is scalable and each sensor mote requires states (event occurring probability, congestion level) proportional to the number of its neighbors. We investigate the performance of algorithms using NS-2 simulations. We assumed that the maximum communication channel bit-rate is 250Kbps and each data packet is 128bytes. We further assumed that a node is only within range of its parent and children and there is no interference from nodes more than a hop away. We first placed sensor nodes in 10 * 10 grid and we assumed that sensors are fixed in first deployed position.

In subsection 3.2, we designed congestion control algorithm consisted of two phases, interval regulation and congestion avoidance. We performed a comparative analysis of our algorithm and existing congestion control algorithm, CODA[1].

We tested three cases:

- Case 1: no congestion control
- Case 2: transmission rate regulation (CODA)
- Case 3: transmission interval regulation and congestion avoidance (proposed algorithm)

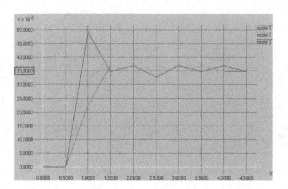

Fig. 2. Comparative analysis of throughput(Case1)

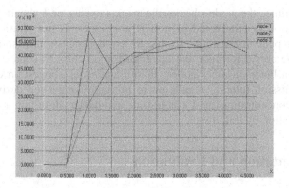

Fig. 3. Comparative analysis of throughput(Case2)

In the region where the event data occurs, the sensor nodes transmit data at short intervals. And this situation can cause burst traffic and congestion. We randomly select 3 sensor nodes(noted to node-1, node-2, node-3 in Fig.2) from the region where congestion has occurred and measured throughput at the sink node. Vertical axis represents data rate(Kbps) and horizontal axis represent time(second). Each node sends 128Kbytes to the sink node at different interval, and we measured data receiving rate at the sink node.

When congestion occurs, data receiving rate is 35Kbps at the sink node without congestion control and data throughput is reduced about 75%.

When transmission rate regulation(CODA) is applied, data receiving rate is 45Kbps at the sink node and the result shows 30% improvement compared to performance without congestion control.

At last, we applied our algorithm, interval scheduling and congestion avoidance, to the scenario(10*10 grid). Data receiving rate is 70Kbps at the sink node and we can figure out that our algorithm shows 65% improved throughput compared to CODA.

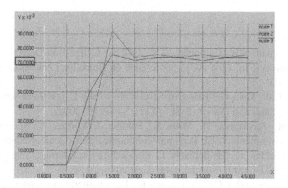

Fig. 4. Comparative analysis of throughput(Case3)

5 Conclusion

We proposed an transmission interval scheduling and congestion control scheme for lightweight sensor network considering an event-driven WSN. In sensor network environment, sensor nodes are battery powered and resource constrained. To extend the lifetime of sensor network, we have to minimize the energy consumption of each sensor node. The most energy-consuming element is communication between sensor nodes. Hence, we created interval scheduling algorithm to reduce data traffic.

The interval scheduling algorithm calculates the optimal data transmission interval based on local information, event occurring probability and energy consumption model of a radio transceiver. So, additional traffic for data gathering does not occur. If sensor nodes transmit data at optimal interval, we can reduce the loss factor of critical data and unnecessary network traffic. When the interval scheduling algorithm applied to the proposed routing algorithm, it shows good performance.

The event data occurred in the sensor network can cause large, sudden, unexpected traffic. To resolve the problem, we proposed congestion control algorithm in subsection 3.2. Our congestion control algorithm is consisted of two phases, interval regulation and congestion avoidance. Interval regulation algorithm adjusts the transmission interval calculated by Equation 4 to mitigate congestion. And congestion avoidance algorithm provides a solution to recover from persistent congestion by link loss. Our algorithm shows 65% improved performance compared to existing congestion control algorithm, CODA[1].

For the future work, we will perform larger scale experimentation comparing with other algorithms. And based on experiment results, we will modify our algorithms to improve the performance.

Acknowledgement

This work was supported by NIA(National Information Society Agency), KOREA under the KOREN program. (No. 2009-협약-위18)

References

1. Wan, C., Eisenman, S.B., Campbell, A.T.: CODA: Congestion Detection and Avoidance in Sensor Networks. In: First ACM conference on Embedded Networked Sensor Systems (November 2003)
2. Lindsey, S., et al.: Data Gathering in Sensor Networks Using the Energy Delay Metric. IEEE Trans. Parallel and Distrib. Syst., A(13), 924–935 (2002)
3. Badrinath, B.R., Srivastava, M., Mills, K., Scholtz, J., Sollins, K.: Special issue on smart spaces and environments. IEEE Personal Communications (October 2000)
4. Estrin, D., Govindan, R., Heidemann, J.: Embedding the Internet. Communications of the ACM 43(5), 39–41 (2000) (Special issue guest editors)
5. Lindsey, S., Raghavendra, C., Sivalingam, K.: Data gathering in sensor networks using the energy delay metric. In: International Workshop on Parallel and Distributed Computing: Issues in Wireless Networks and Mobile Computing, San Francisco, USA (April 2001)
6. Cao, Q., Abdelzaher, T.: Scalable logical coordinates framework for routing in wireless sensor networks. ACM Transactions on Sensor Networks 2(4) (November 2006)
7. Chang, J.-H., Tassiulas, L.: Maximum lifetime routing in wireless sensor networks. IEEE/ACM Transactions on Networking 12(4) (August 2004)
8. Sohrabi, K., Gao, J., Ailawadhi, V., Pottie, G.J.: Protocols for self-organization of a wireless sensor network. Personal Communications, IEEE 7(5) (October 2000)
9. Haas, Z.J., Halpern, J.Y., Li, L.: Gossip-based ad-hoc routing. IEEE/ACM Transaction on Networking 14(3), 479–491 (2006)
10. Kyasanur, P., Choudhury, R.R., Gupta, I.: Smart gossip: an adaptive gossip-based broadcasting service for sensor networks. In: IEEE International Conference on Mobile Ad-hoc and Sensor Systems (2006)

Game Theoretic Packet Scheduling in a Non-cooperative Wireless Environment

Zhen Kong[1] and Yu-Kwong Kwok[2]

[1] The University of Hong Kong, Pokfulam Road, Hong Kong
[2] Colorado State University, Fort Collins, CO 80523–1373, USA

Abstract. In many practical scenarios, wireless devices are autonomous and thus, may exhibit non-cooperative behaviors due to self-interests. For instance, a wireless cellular device may be programmed to report bogus channel information to gain resource allocation advantages. In this paper, we first analyze the impact of these rationally selfish behaviors on the performance of packet scheduling algorithms in time-slotted wireless networks. We further propose a novel game theoretic approach, where a user punishes the selfish user with a probability p, to enforce cooperation among selfish users. Through simulations, we can see the wireless users are scheduled more efficiently and fairly in this non-cooperative environment with our proposed approach.

Keywords: game theory, incentives, repeated game, Nash equilibrium, packet scheduling, wireless networks.

1   Introduction

In a centralized infrastructure based wireless network, packet scheduling is a very important issue to manage the precious radio resource while satisfying users' Quality-of-Service (QoS) requirements. Specifically, in a traditional downlink packet scheduling protocol, wireless users are required to report their channel conditions, such as signal-to-noise-ratio (SNR) or maximal achievable data rate, to the scheduler located at the base station (BS) or access point (AP). Then the scheduler can select some users' packets and allocate radio resources, such as power and frequency bandwidth, to these users for transmission according to some scheduling policies, such as maximum rate (MR) [8] and proportional fairness [3].

Usually, these scheduling algorithms are based on the assumption that the wireless users in the system will cooperate with each other, comply with the pre-defined scheduling algorithm, and honestly report their real channel conditions to the scheduler [4]. Then the wireless user will accept the scheduling results passively, and it will not affect the scheduling policy employed by the scheduler at all. However, in many practical scenarios, the wireless users are autonomous and thus, may exhibit non-cooperative behaviors due to self-interests.

In particular, in a typical wireless packet scheduling process, the scheduling policy is one of the major factors governing a user's data rate. Therefore, in a non-cooperative environment, a wireless user experiencing a bad channel condition

D. Ślęzak et al. (Eds.): FGCN/ACN 2009, CCIS 56, pp. 9–16, 2009.

might find out that if it honestly reports its channel condition to the scheduler, it may not be scheduled or just be assigned with a low data rate. Consequently, with a rationally selfish motivation, such user might report a bogus channel condition so as to get a higher probability to be scheduled for transmission or get a higher data rate. Though this non-cooperative behavior could increase the data rate for this selfish user, it may lead to inefficient resource utilization for the whole system. Due to the proliferation of open-source software technologies and software-defined radios, such non-cooperative behaviors are becoming more and more practicable because wireless devices could be easily programmed by users to behave in a selfish manner [1], [7]. Thus, whether the traditional packet scheduling algorithms are still effective in allocating resource in non-cooperative environment is in doubt and needs to be scrutinized carefully.

In our previous work [4], we have formulated this competitive wireless resource allocation problem as a non-cooperative packet scheduling (NPS) game, and proposed a repeated game theoretic method to punish selfish behavior and enforce cooperation among wireless users. But the condition in this method is too strong, where each user will punish the selfish user by transmitting at the highest rate; thus, the whole system is also penalized too much at the same time. Motivated by this observation, in this paper, we propose a new repeated game theoretic method, where a user only punishes the selfish user with a probability p. In this situation, the selfish user will also be punished while the whole system throughput will be less affected. Through simulations, we find that the proposed approaches based on repeated game can enforce cooperation among wireless users and increase the rate and fairness performances in a non-cooperative environment.

The remainder of this paper is organized as follows. In Section 2, we describe the system model, and discuss the impact of selfish behavior on system performance. In Section 3, we show that the performance can be improved via a repeated game strategy. We then demonstrate the performance in Section 4. Finally, we give some concluding remarks in Section 5.

2   Model

To study the impact of selfish users, we consider a time-slotted system with one BS serving N wireless users, where there are S selfish users deliberately deviating from the packet scheduling algorithm. The BS transmits in slots with fixed duration, and only one user can be scheduled in one time slot. All users are assumed to be either static or moving slowly and within the same communication range (i.e., each user can overhear any other users). We assume users always have packets to transmit. At the beginning of time slot t, each user i measures the downlink channel condition, and returns, via a feedback channel, a measured data rate $r_i(t)$ to the BS. Based on this information, the BS determines which user to transmit its packet in this time slot.

In our analysis, we assume adaptive modulation and ideal phase detection are used in a Rayleigh fading channel channel with bandwidth W, and no retransmission is considered. Typically, at time slot t, the maximal achievable symbol

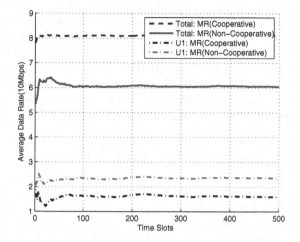

Fig. 1. The impact of selfish behavior on the average date rate of packet scheduling algorithm

rate $c_i^a(t)$ (bit/symbol) for user i can be decided by its current channel SNR $\gamma_i(t)$ and the required BER P_{ber}, then $c_i^a(t)$ can be expressed as [6]:

$$c_i^a(t) = \log_2(1 + \frac{-1.5}{\ln(5 \cdot P_{ber})} \cdot \gamma_i(t)) \tag{1}$$

We assume that the symbol rate belongs to the symbol rate set $C = \{c_i : 0 \le c_i \le M\}$, i.e., $c_i^a(t) \in C$, where M can be interpreted as the maximal modulation mode. Then the corresponding maximal achievable data rate is given by $r_i^a(t) = c_i^a(t) \cdot W$. Correspondingly we define the set of data rate as $R = \{r_i : 0 \le r_i \le r^M\}$, where $r^M = M \cdot W$ and $r_i^a(t) \in R$.

We assume that each $r_i(t)$ is an independent and stationary random variable, and let the reported $r_i(t)$ also belong to the set R, i.e., $r_i(t) \in R$. Within this framework, in the literature there are several well-known packet scheduling algorithms, such as the MR algorithm [8], which is designed to maximize the data rate at each slot, as well as the system aggregate data rate, by scheduling the user with the largest $r_i(t)$ for transmission.

These algorithms are optimal under their respective objectives with the assumption that every wireless user i will comply with the algorithms and report its maximum feasible rate $r_i^a(t)$ to the BS honestly. However, they do not have any consideration of the impact of selfish behavior on their predefined performance and objectives. For example, if a user knows it will not be scheduled for transmission if it reports its real channel condition, it could tell a bogus $r_i(t) > r_i^a(t)$ to the BS so as to increase its chance for transmission. Then the corresponding scheduling results may be totally different with what will be realized in cooperative environment. Of course, a higher assigned data rate $r_i(t)$ may result in a higher BER or lower PTSR under the same SNR $\gamma_i(t)$, making its actual achievable rate lower than the intended value. Nevertheless, a rationally selfish consideration is that the smaller realized rate may be compensated by the rate improvement induced by the increased transmission probability. Consequently, a non-cooperative device could still have the incentive to report a different data rate to the BS so as to increase its own potential payoff. This analysis is verified from the simulation result in Fig. 1. We can see the existence of selfish behavior in non-cooperative wireless networks could significantly degrade the data rate performance of packet scheduling algorithm.

3   Repeated Game Theoretic Striker Strategy

In [4], we have formulated this competitive wireless resource allocation problem as a non-cooperative packet scheduling game, and proposed a repeated game theoretic method to punish selfish behavior and enforce cooperation. But the condition in this method is too strong, where each user will punish the selfish user by transmitting at the highest rate; thus, the whole system is also penalized too much. To overcome this drawback, we modify it and present a new method as discussed below.

Here, we assume that the game is split up steps denoted by h. In each step, user i adjusts the rate according to its strategy. Furthermore, let us define the discounted average utility in $H_i < +\infty$ time steps as:

$$\overline{U_i}(H_i) = (1 - \omega) \cdot \sum_{h=0}^{H_i} U_i(h) \cdot \omega^h \tag{2}$$

where U_i is the utility function of user i and $0 < omega < 1$ is the discounting factor, which can be interpreted as the probability that the game ends in the next step. We assume ω is identical for all users in our model.

In [4], we have found that the selfish users are in an inefficient equilibrium when they all play Nash equilibrium(NE) strategy, whereas the maximal data rate can be achieved by using a cooperative strategy. From Folk Theorem [5], we know that in an infinitely repeated game, any feasible outcome that gives each player better payoff than the NE can be obtained. We can now determine the conditions that enable the users to enforce cooperation, and prove that they can do better by applying a strategy called *Striker*, as detailed below.

Definition 1. *A wireless user i is said to employ the Striker strategy if it plays r_i^a in the first time step, and for any subsequent time steps, it plays:*

- r_i^a *in the next time step if the other player j played r_j^a in the previous time step, or*
- r^M *with probability p_i for the next H_i time steps, if the other played anything else.*

The punishment interval H_i defines the number of time steps for which a player punishes the selfish player [2]. To simplify our analysis, we assume that the overall channel conditions remain relatively unchanged. Then, r_i^a over each step in the repeated game is similar. However, our simulation results show that our analysis still holds in wireless fading situations. Consequently, cooperation can be enforced using the *Striker* strategy as formalized in the following proposition.

Proposition 1. *An efficient Nash equilibrium can be enforced by the Striker strategy.*

Proof. We set user i's utility in terms of cooperative and non-cooperative situations as U_i^{COP} and U_i^{NCOP}, respectively. We consider the *Striker* strategy, and suppose user i adhere to it and choose r_i^a. If user $j \neq i$ uses the same strategy, then the outcome is (U_i^{COP}, U_j^{COP}) in every step, so that it obtains the stream of payoffs, which gives a discounted average of $(1 - \omega) \cdot \sum_{h=0}^{H_i} U_i(h) \cdot \omega^h = (1 - \omega^{H_i+1}) \cdot U_i^{COP}$.

If user j adopts a rate r_j^X so as to get a larger utility $U_j^{NCOP} > U_i^{NCOP}$ in all subsequent steps, user i will chooses r^M with probability p_i since user j's choice of r_j^X triggers the punishment. Then, in an attempt to maintain its own benefit, the selfish user j will have to choose r^M in every subsequent step with payoff U_j^M. Consequently, it obtains the stream of payoffs with discounted average utility:

$$
\begin{aligned}
&(1 - \omega) \cdot (U_j^{NCOP} + U_j^M + \omega \cdot (U_j^M) + \cdots + \omega_i^H \cdot (U_j^M)) \\
=&(1 - \omega) \cdot U_j^{NCOP} + (1 - \omega^{H_i+1} \cdot U_j^M)
\end{aligned}
\tag{3}
$$

Thus, user j can not increase its utility by deviating if and only if:

$$
(1 - \omega) \cdot U_j^{NCOP} + (1 - \omega^{H_i+1} \cdot U_j^M) < (1 - \omega^{H_i+1}) \cdot U_j^{COP}
\tag{4}
$$

Thus,

$$
\omega^{H_i+1} < 1 - (1 - \omega) \cdot \frac{U_j^{NCOP}}{U_j^{COP} - U_j^M}
\tag{5}
$$

The inequality cannot be fulfilled if the right side is negative, and therefore:

$$
(1 - \omega) \cdot \frac{U_j^{NCOP}}{U_j^{COP} - U_j^M} < 1
\tag{6}
$$

When this condition holds, since $\omega < 1$, we have:

$$
H_i \geq log_\omega((1 - \omega) \cdot \frac{U_j^{NCOP}}{U_j^{COP} - U_j^M}) - 1
\tag{7}
$$

Because the user's utility is highly related to its average data rate, we rewrite the above H_i as

$$
H_i \geq log_\omega((1 - \omega) \cdot \frac{R_j^{NCOP}}{R_j^{COP} - R_j^M}) - 1
\tag{8}
$$

Because when the selfish behavior is detected, each user i other than j will chooses r^M with probability p_i to punish user j. We can derive R_j^M as

$$R_j^M = \frac{1}{1 + \prod_{i \neq j}(p_i)} \cdot R_0^M \tag{9}$$

Here R_j^{NCOP} and R_j^{COP} are the average data rates in terms of non-cooperative and cooperative situations, respectively. R_0^M is the average data rate when all users in the network report r^M to AP, we simply estimated it by $R_0^M = \frac{1}{N}\sum_{t=1}^{t=T_H} r^M \cdot \alpha(r^M, r_j^a(t))$. Specifically, when all $p_i = 100\%$, the scheduler is just Round-Robin, and $R_j^M = \frac{1}{N} \cdot R_0^M$. Thus when the discounting factor is chosen as in (6) and punishment interval is set according to (8), the selfish user j will be forced to cooperate with user i such as to get higher payoff by *Striker* strategy. Correspondingly, an efficient NE is achieved.

4 Performance Analysis

To demonstrate the effect of *Striker* algorithm, we set up simulations for 20 users. We also let $\beta = 20\%$, $K = 10$ and $T_H = 10$ here. The performance results shown are averaged over 100 channel and location realizations.

We first analyze the data rate performance under *Striker* strategies with different Striker probability p. In the beginning, all wireless users perform honestly, and the individual average data rate is about $8Mbps$, which is also used as a threshold to detect deviation. At time slot 100, user 1 begins to deviate from the cooperative action. As shown in Fig. 2, its average rate increases up to $14.8Mbps$ dramatically. This abnormal deviation is soon detected by others, and then punished by the other users, which then make the data rate of this selfish user decrease dramatically. Then the data rate returns to the cooperative state. Thus, a more efficient equilibrium is achieved as well as the scheduling performance is optimized in a non-cooperative wireless network.

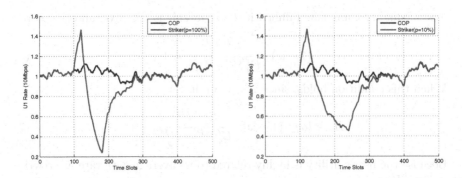

Fig. 2. U1 date rate under Striker strategies with different Striker probability p. (a) p = 100%; (b) p = 10%;

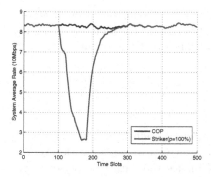 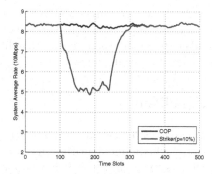

Fig. 3. System date rate under Striker strategies with different Striker probability p. (a) p = 100%; (b) p = 10%;

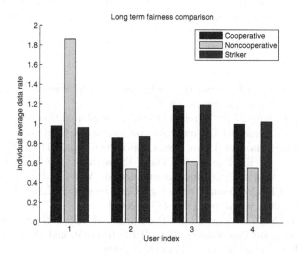

Fig. 4. Fairness comparison

Another important observation is that a lower Striker probability p will make less decrease of system rate during the period of punishment, as shown in Fig.3. This is because the system aggregate rate will suffer more loss when there are more users who increase their rate to penalize the selfish user. However, when p is larger, the punishment becomes much severer and the system will return to cooperative situation more quickly. Thus, the Striker probability p can be used to strike a balance between punishment interval and system rate. If we want to punish the selfish behavior more greatly and force the selfish user to behave cooperatively soon, a higher p is preferable.

We further show the average individual throughput over the whole 500 time slots for 4 users to investigate the long-term fairness in Fig. 4, where only user 1 is selfish and $p = 70\%$. The results illustrate that the fairness performance is much worse in a non-cooperative situation because selfish user 1 consumes large part of radio resources by lying to the BS. With the introduction of *Striker* algorithm, the impact of selfish behavior is restricted and then the users are more likely to report their channel conditions honestly. Consequently, the users are scheduled in a fairer manner.

5   Conclusions

In this paper we investigate the impact of rationally selfish behaviors on wireless packet scheduling algorithm in a non-cooperative wireless network. We find that the existence of selfish behavior indeed makes the data rate performance of MR packet scheduling algorithm decrease greatly. Based on this observation, we further propose a *Striker* strategy based on a repeated game to enforce cooperation among users and achieve a more desirable Nash equilibrium, in which the data rate performance can be increased efficiently. Furthermore, users can be scheduled in a fairer manner with our proposed *Striker* approach.

References

1. Buttyan, L., Hubaux, J.P.: Security and Cooperation in Wireless Networks. Cambridge University Press, Cambridge (2007)
2. Felegyhazi, M., Hubaux, J.P.: Wireless Operators in Shared Spectrum. In: Proceedings of the 25th Annual IEEE Conference on Computer Communications (INFOCOM 2006), Barcelona, Catalunya, Spain, April 2006, pp. 1–11 (2006)
3. Jalali, A., Padovani, R., Pankai, R.: Data Throughput of CDMA-HDR a High Efficiency-High Data Rate Personal Communication Wireless System. In: Proceeding of the 51th IEEE Vehicular Technology Conference (VTC2000 Spring), Tokyo, Japan, January 2001, vol. 3, pp. 1854–1858 (2001)
4. Kong, Z., Kwok, Y.-K., Wang, J.: On the Impact of Selfish Behaviors in Wireless Packet Scheduling. In: Proceedings of the IEEE International Conference on Communications (ICC 2008), Beijing, China (May 2008)
5. Osborne, M.J.: An Introduction to Game Theory. Oxford University Press, New York (2004)
6. Qiu, X., Chawla, K.: On the Performance of Adaptive Modulation in Cellular Systems. IEEE Transactions on Communications 47(6), 884–895 (1999)
7. Radosavac, S., Baras, J.S., Koutsopoulos, I.: A Framework for MAC Protocol Misbehavior Detection in Wireless Networks. In: Proceedings of the 4th ACM workshop on Wireless security (ACM WiSec 2005), Cologne, Germany, September 2005, pp. 33–42 (2005)
8. Tsybakov, B.S.: File Transmission Over Wireless Fast Fading Downlink. IEEE Transactions on Information Theory 48, 2323–2337 (2002)

Security Authentication for U-Health Application Services

Byeong Ho Ahn[1], Jinkeun Hong[2], and Donghoon Lee[1]

[1] Graduate School of Information Management and Security/
Center for Information Security Technologies, Korea University
1, 5-ka, Anam-dong, Sungbuk-Gu, Seoul, 136-701, South Korea
bhahn2@ensec.re.kr, donghlee@korea.ac.kr
[2] Division of information & Communication Baekseok University, 115 Anseo-dong,
Dongnam-Gu, Cheonan-si, Chnumnam, 330-704, Korea
jkhong@bu.ac.kr

Abstract. This paper reviews RFID health authentication scheme based on location in the hospital. The designed handheld care system is implemented that are RFID reader/tag, an embedded Visual C++4.0, Pocket PC2003 software development kit (SDK) in an 802.11 wireless network. We are confident that the research provides sufficient proof of the usefulness of this ubiquitous health system for the collection of care information. The proposed system consists of a care management module for health diagnosis, a personal record module, a data transport module, and an image information management module for the clinic. System uses an applied security mechanism for critical data, and presents RFID authentication scheme, is accessed and controlled according to the location in the hospital.

Keywords: Health care, RFID, ubiquitous.

1 Introduction

Ubiquitous health services have connected a new creation including an increasing amount of service, and research area across, rather than within, the boundaries of standard organizations [1-2]. Establishing information is obtained from driving activities within the health services as well as in other areas, but understanding the unique demands in the preparation of healthcare, guidelines are presented that may be of benefit to those involved in rising relationships, and networks. Ubiquitous computing technologies can be used to provide better solutions for healthcare of elderly persons at home or in the hospital. Also, information fusion from multiple sensors shows itself as having the capability to originate a system of better monitoring of persons. In this paper, we present details of the security implementation of a ubiquitous healthcare system, one that is based on location, and which is managed by patients, nurses, managers, and doctors, for emergency and health condition management. Alexander Berler et al [2] in Greece presented the idea of a roadmap

D. Ślęzak et al. (Eds.): FGCN/ACN 2009, CCIS 56, pp. 17–24, 2009.
© Springer-Verlag Berlin Heidelberg 2009

toward healthcare information systems interoperability; this is a system with a focus on terminologies and standards, on interoperability and information systems sustainability, on clear goals and system metrics, on people and what they have to say. Stergiani Spyrou, et al [3] review a methodology for reliability analysis in health networks, [4] which led to the idea of an authenticated key establishment protocol for the home health care system. A Bluetooth 2.1 based emergency data delivery system in health net is reviewed by Seung Hoon Lee, et al [5]. Nilmini Wickramasi and Elie Geisler present conceptual domains and applications of knowledge management in health care [6]. Toshiyo Tamura et al have presented ideas of home healthcare with an ad hoc network system [7]. Chiu, et al [8] review secure and RFID authentication and search protocol, and Weis, et al[9] researched about security and privacy aspects of RFID. In this paper, we review an efficient mechanism that can access or protect secession from the boundary of ranges, which is applied to a location management concept in the client mobile terminal for secure patient care information. Also, we review authentication scheme in the implementation of a ubiquitous healthcare system, one that contains RFID reader based on location, and which is managed by patients, nurses, managers, and doctors, for emergency and health condition management. In a ubiquitous environment, the principal service among health care services and patient management services must be supported centering on the patient. Hence, in the point of authentication based on RFID system for emergencies in a secure healthcare network, and its security characteristic is analyzed. The remainder of this paper is organized as follows. In the next section, detailed descriptions of the framework of the healthcare system based on the location are given. In section 3, the designed authentication system of RFID healthcare system is illustrated. Security analysis of prototype implementation and security is presented in section 4, and concluding remarks are provided in section 5.

2   The Framework of Healthcare System

Each hospital may maintain its own electronic database of patient information accessible by PDA. These local data bases can then be connected via the Internet for data transmission, so that a doctor at one hospital may review a patient's information from the information server. Patients' personal privacy becomes an issue of concern when extra personal information is collected besides IP and position for enhanced health content personalization. The healthcare portal solutions provide the foundation for more reasonable and efficient information sharing, enabling healthcare professionals to work together more effectively, react more quickly, and deliver higher quality care in a wireless environment. If the software does detect an emergency state, the hospital information manager will be notified and warned, the doctor and nurse will be sent to examine the patient based on the information, and they will then decide on the best course of action. The PDA is used to give feedback to the patient and his family about the condition of the patient's body, as well as about the status of the sensors.

3 Design of Authentication Scheme on RFID System

We review that the designed authentication scheme on RFID system. In writing process, server manager writes b, RID, DBID, TID, (Rx, Ry), (Tx, Ty), and RoundT values in DB and tag. Identification means that a person is described by identifiers such as name, date of birth, address and etc.

3.1 Location Process

(Rx, Ry) is reference position values of longitude and latitude of reader, (Tx, Ty) is reference position values of longitude and latitude of tag, and RoundT is reference returned time from reader and tag. First reader is connected with PC and knows its location. The location information is written at first stage and then is written at predefined time after authentication. Initial tag's location (Rx, RY) is written by the manager and then its location value according to location movement is stored in tag. Where, location movement value (Tx, Ty) is calculated with the received power of RSSI, time delay from received tag, and direction of antenna.

$$(Tx, Ty) = \text{optimizing value \{distance (received power of RSSI), time delay from received tag\}, direction of antenna\}} \qquad (1)$$

3.2 Authentication Process

In step1, reader broadcasts challenge and random number u to tag in Fig. 1. In step2, tag computes and transmits to reader values such as, X, Y, A, B. In this step, hID is $f(TID)$, a is $hID(+)u(+)b(+)(Rx,Ry)(+)(Tx,Ty)(+)RoundT$, A is $f(a)$, B is $f(b)$. Here, TID is a field for the temporary identification value of RF tag T. $f( )$ is mixed random number component(rng) and chaos function. $f(TID)$ is a mixed value of random

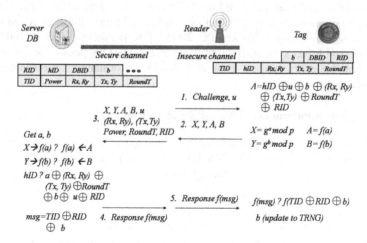

Fig. 1. The process diagram to authenticate of patient, nurse, doctor, information manager

component(rng) and chaos function of tag ID. (+) is exclusive-or(XOR) function. Reader sends *u* to the tag. Receiving *u* from the reader, tag calculates *a, X, Y, A, B* and then sends them to the reader. Server DB gets *a* and *b*, and checks if *hID* is validate. After validating the *hID*, server DB responds *f(msg)* to the reader. Reader sends *f(msg)* to the tag and then finally tag checks if *f(msg)* is validate.

In step3, the reader transmits to server DB values such as, *X, Y, A, B, u, (Rx, Ry), (Tx, Ty), RoundT, RID*. In step4, the server computes and verifies transmitted data and DB data. First, let be get a, b. In server, there compute and verify *f(a), f(b)* and *a, b* are computed from which is stored data in DB, and transmitted *X(=f(a))*, and *Y(=f(b))*. Also a, b are derive by doing decryption of *X, Y*.

Table 1 show that it is presented security characteristics in according to authentication schemes and the proposed scheme is guaranteed major security characteristics, and can be controlled access of device through position tracking in particular.

Table 1. Security Characteristics in each scheme

Scheme	Anonymity	Forward secrecy	Replay attack	DoS attack	Position tracking
Hash locking(Weis)[9]	X	X	X	O	X
Randomized hash locking (Weis)[9]	X	X	X	O	X
Varying ID locking (Henrici)[10]	O	X	X	O	O
Mutual Auth(Yang)[11]	X	X	O	O	X
Proposed scheme	O	O	O	O	O

4   Implementation and Security Analysis

The tool that is used is an HP iPAQ hx4705 Pocket PC handheld model and the client prototype is implemented in a Windows mobile edition 2003 second edition OS, embedded Visual C++4.0, Pocket PC 2003 SDK platform, window 2003 server, oracle DB, and RFID system. In algorithm2, if a patient happens to be set outside of the location boundary, patient is warned by the information system according to his/her identity and duty.

4.1   Sufficient Randomness of Mixed Random Function

It is applied the mixed random number function(rng) and logistic chaos function. To generate the random stream of logistic function, which is the discrete chaos map, it is applied for the randomized process, as follows:

$$X_{n+1} = -\alpha X_n (1 - X_n) \tag{2}$$

where the range of α is $0 \le \alpha \le 4$, and the range of the initial value X_0 is $0 \le X_0 \le 1$. The value of X_{n+1} is derived from the previous state value X_n. Inversely, given X_{n+1}, X_0 has resolved the two values of the solution in an equation of the second degree.

The logistic map has the characteristic of irreversibility, and α is the sensitivity parameter that determines the dependence of the next value derived from the initial value. For the condition $\alpha < 1$, when the process of X_n is performed recursively, the value of X_n converges to 0. For the convergence to the direction of the chaos domain, which continues to infinity, the value of α must be $\alpha > 3.56$. However, the distribution of the output bit stream of the chaos function has an independent and uniform distribution, and is an integral number between [0, d-1]. To apply the random number generator, the integral number between [0, 1] is distributed uniformly by the tent transformation function. By the tent function $x' = h(x)$, the non-linear value of the discrete chaos function becomes a linear value.

$$x' = h(x) = \sin^2(\pi x / 2) \tag{3}$$

Let y_0 be x'_0, it is driven the equation $y_1 = f(y_0)$, $y_2 = f^2(y_0)$ $\cdots\cdots$ $y_k = f^k(y_0)$. From the f function and T function, it can be driven as follows:

$$f^k(h(x)) = h(T^k(x)) \tag{4}$$

where k is 0, 1, 2, ..., . The non-linear value of the x' axis by the tent function is transformed to a linear value of the x axis, which has a uniform distribution. In the evaluation of randomness, the bit steam during one period (U) is set at 200,000 bits. The mixed stream of random number generation component and the chaos function is satisfied conditions of randomness, as shown in Table2.

Table 2. Results of security randomness evaluation (at chaos function with transform + random generation component)

Test item	Degree of freedom(v)	Threshold value($a<0.05$)	Results
Frequency test	29	42.557	25.623
Permutation test	23	35.172	17.981
Gap test	11	19.675	12.961
Run test	6	12.591	3.953

The information system consists of a DB based on device IP address, ID information, and location mapped data. The query and reply from the system server is executed periodically to check.

In table 3, it is reviewed the efficiency in according to authentication scheme. As shown in Table 2, proposed scheme has 5 rounds, $T_{rng^\wedge chaos}(4)$ time(tag) value, $T_{TRNG}(1)$ and $T_{GPS}(1)$ time(reader) value, and $T_{TRNG}(1)$, $T_{rng^\wedge chaos}(1)$ and $T_{GPS}(1)$ time(server).

Extremely sensitive data communications among manager, doctor, patient, and nurse must be considered as extremely sensitive because in these communications, the possibility of exchanging patient's information that is extremely sensitive is very high. Also, the health care information should be protected against threats and loss, and disclosed only to authorized users such as doctors, patients, and the nurse in charged.

Table 3. The Efficiency in each scheme

Scheme	Round	Time(tag)	Time(Reader)	Time(Server)
Hash locking (Weis)	6	0	-	0
Randomized hash locking (Weis)	5	$T_{Hash}/T_{PRF}(1)$, $T_{RNG}(1)$	-	$T_{Hash}(n)/T_{PRF}$
Varying ID locking (Henrici)	5	$T_{Hash}(3)$	$T_{RNG}(1)$	$T_{Hash}(2)$
Mutual Auth(Yang)	5	$T_{Hash}(2)$	$T_{RNG}(1)$	$T_{Hash}(2n)$
Proposed scheme	5	$T_{rng^\wedge chaos}(4)$	$T_{TRNG}(1)$, $T_{GPS}(1)$	$T_{rng^\wedge chaos}(1)$, $T_{TRNG}(1)$, $T_{GPS}(1)$

Any disclosure to other users must follow the patient's consent. Health care information is the patient's personal information, medical history, diagnosis, test result, and current treatment. We define and analysis security requirements as follows: Theorem1 ~Theorem5.

4.2   Theorem 1 (Anonymity) Proof

In step2 and 4, we will emphasis that it is supported encryption process and difficult to estimate data by the attacker. In step 2, we can present that it can not made an inference a by any attacking, a is g^a mod p, where a is $hID(+)u(+)$ $b(+)(Rx,Ry)(+)(Tx,Ty)(+)RoundT$, and it cannot solved hID due to the mixed rng and chaos function property. In step4, from response $f(msg)$, we can show that $f(msg)$ is processed by the rng and chaos function. Where $f(msg)$ is $TID(+)RID(+)b$. So we can be proved about anonymity property.

4.3   Theorem 2 (Forward Secrecy) Proof

If it tries to leak out data on tag by attacker, the previous data cannot be inference from the presented data.

An attacker controlling all but one reader in a RFID network should not be able to recover TID, b, hID, b, X, Y, h(x), f(msg) shared between the reader/server and the tag. There are no relationships between the current value b and previous value b', between the current value a and the previous value a'. Check a = hID(+) u(+) b(+) (Rx,Ry)(+)(Tx,Ty)(+)RoundT ? a' = hID (+)u'(+)b'(+) (Rx,Ry) (+)(Tx',Ty') (+) RoundT.

Check f(msg) is TID(+)RID(+)b ? f(msg') is TID(+) RID(+)b'. Therefore, we show that it cannot be induced a and b from a'and b'.

4.4   Theorem 3 (Replay Attack) Proof

During transmission, attacker intercepts RFID data, and the captured data is transmitted by the attacker after a certain time.

The reader send original values u and (Tx,Ty), and new values u' and (Tx,Ty)'. Check a = hID(+)u(+)b(+)(Rx,Ry)(+)(Tx,Ty)(+)RoundT ? a' = hID(+)u'(+) b(+)

(Rx,Ry)(+)(Tx,Ty)'(+)RoundT. f(msg) is TID(+)RID(+)b ? Check f(msg') is TID (+)RID(+)b'. Therefore, we show that it cannot be replayed to attack a', b' and f(msg').

4.5 Theorem 4 (DOS Attack) Proof

DOS is kinds of attacks such as, jamming and interference on physical layer, blocking and disrupting the operation of RFID reader and server.

If secret value shared between tag and sever can not be synchronized, response messge f(msg) is failed. But in Server DB, previous value b is stored, and f(msg') (is TID(+)RID(+)b') send to reader, and tag. In the tag, to authenticate, it requires TID, RID, and updated b'. Against dos attack, it can be guaranteed msg' from mixed rng and chaos function f( ).

4.6 Theorem 5 (Position Tracking) Proof

If the access of communication connection between the tag and the reader/server can be controlled, the link will be guaranteed. If attacker, which is distinguished, will be tried the access of the reader and the server, it can be traced the attacking tag. $A_r(x, y)$ *is included in (Rx, Ry) reference of x coordinates (longitude) and y coordinates (latitude). RoundT' is new access time for round trip between reader and tag. When the location of tag and reader decides, the reference values are RoundT and power(received power, which is between reader and tag). If* $(Rx', Ry') \in A_r(x, y)$, *it can be accessed the reader. If RoundT < RoundT' and (Rx,Ry) < (Rx',Ry'), tag cannot be accessed in reader.*

Location of tag is estimated from reader location (Rx,Ry), power and length, which is estimated as followed.

$$\text{Tag(x, y)} = \text{(Rx,Ry)} + \text{Avg(Length(RoundT/2), Power)} \qquad (2)$$

Where avg( ) is a function of ( )., check a = hID(+)u(+)b(+) (Rx,Ry)(+)(Tx,Ty) (+) RoundT ? a' = hID(+) u(+)b(+)(Rx',Ry')(+)(Tx,Ty)(+)RoundT'.

Therefore, we show that it can be accessed in case of a, otherwise, cannot be access in case of a'.

5 Conclusion

The proposed system is consists of care management module for health diagnosis, personal record module, data transport module, image information management module for clinic, is applied on security mechanism for critical data, and accessed, controlled in according to the location in the hospital. Recently, health care applications have been issued in ubiquitous computing services. In this paper, it is presented to the authentication scheme, which is RFID based on location in the hospital and health care center. When we are compared proposed scheme with the conventional scheme in RFID network, it takes robust characteristics in respect of position tracking.

References

1. Kim, M.-K., Park, J.-H., Jee, K.-Y.: Demand Analysis and Market Strategies of u-Health. In: Proceedings of ICACT 2007, pp. 12–14 (2007)
2. Berler, A., Tagaris, A., Angelidis, P., Koutsouris, D.: A roadmap towards healthcare information systems interoperability in Greece. Journal of Telecommunications and information Technology 2 (2006)
3. Spyrou, S., Barnidis, P.D., Maglaveras, N., Pangalos, G., Pappas, C.: A Methodology for Reliability Analysis in Health Networks. IEEE transactions on Information Technology in Biomedicine 12(3), 377–386 (2006)
4. Singh, K., Muthukkumarasamy, V.: Authenticated Key Establishment Protocols for a Home Health Care System. In: Proceedings of ISSNIP2007, 3rd, pp. 3–6 (2007)
5. Lee, S.-H., Jung, S., Chang, A., Cho, D.-K., Gerla, M.: Bluetooth 2.1 based Emergency Data Delivery System in HealthNet. In: Proceedings of WCNC 2008, March 31-April 3 (2008)
6. Wickramasinghe, N., Geisler, E.: Care Conceptual Domain and Applications of Knowledge Management (Km) in Health Care. In: Proceedings of PICMET 2007, pp. 5–9 (2007)
7. Tamura, T., Kawada, T., Sekine, M.: The home health care with the ad-hoc network system. In: Proceedings of SICE annual conference 2007, pp. 17–20 (2007)
8. Tan, C.C., Sheng, B., Li, Q.: Secure and Serverless RFID Authentication and Search Protocols. IEEE Transactions on Wireless Communication 7(4), 1400–1407 (2008)
9. Weis, S.A., Sarma, S.E., Rivest, R.L., Engels, D.W.: Security and privacy aspects of low-cost radio frequency identification systems. In: Hutter, D., Müller, G., Stephan, W., Ullmann, M. (eds.) Security in Pervasive Computing. LNCS, vol. 2802, pp. 201–212. Springer, Heidelberg (2004)
10. Henrici, A.D., Mauller, P.: Hash-based enhancement of location privacy for radio frequency identification devices using varying identifiers. In: IEEE PerCom 2004, pp. 149–153 (2004)
11. Yang, J., Park, J., Lee, H., Ren, K., Kim, K.: Mutual authentication protocol for low cost RFID. In: Encrypt Workshop on RFID and Lightweight Crypto (2005)

Priority Early Frame Discard Algorithm for TCP-Based Video Streaming

Kai-Fu Chan[1], Wen-Jyi Hwang[1,*], Chih-Peng Lin[2], and Tun-Hao Yu[1]

[1] Department of Computer Science and Information Engineering,
National Taiwan Normal University, Taipei, 116, Taiwan
ivy_ckf@hotmail.com, whwang@ntnu.edu.tw, 697470559@ntnu.edu.tw
[2] Department of Electronic Engineering,
National Taiwan University of Science and Technology, Taipei, 106, Taiwan
lcpe6969@ms11.hinet.net

Abstract. This paper presents novel adaptive frame discard algorithms for TCP-based video streaming over IP networks. The proposed algorithms, termed Priority Early Frame Discard (PEFD) algorithms, reduce the long playback delay for heterogeneous clients having insufficient network bandwidth and/or decoding speed. They discard frames at the server side in accordance with the network bandwidth and computational capabilities associated with the clients. The algorithms have low computational complexity, and can be easily implemented in digital surveillance systems such as IP cameras with only limited computational capacity for realtime video broadcast.

1 Introduction

The goal of this paper is to present novel network-adaptive algorithms for video streaming over IP networks. The particular problem considered in this paper consists of a digital surveillance and broadcast system where video is streamed to a variety of heterogeneous clients, such as PDAs, notebooks or workstations. The surveillance system is based on an IP camera (IP CAM) [4], which is a stand alone system containing an embedded processor and a video codec circuit. No external computer is required to encode the captured video.

The surveillance systems transmit video bit streams using HTTP/TCP through the internet. HTTP over TCP has congestion control mechanism and is supported by most network devices. It is also convenient for users to browse these video streaming via a user-friendly interface. Another alternative for video delivery is based on RTP/UDP. However, RTP/UDP has no congestion control mechanism. Since bandwidth is not shared fairly, starvation is possible for some host. Further, RTP/UDP flows may not be supported by network routers or firewalls. The TCP-based video streaming then is the major focus of our design.

Although HTTP/TCP is suitable for surveillance system, there is no QoS (Quality of Service) guaranteed for video transmission over the Internet. QoS is

---

* Corresponding author.

D. Ślęzak et al. (Eds.): FGCN/ACN 2009, CCIS 56, pp. 25–32, 2009.

important to assure a proper delivery of real-time video with strict delay and bandwidth. There are two approaches to obtain better performance of the IP networks. One approach is to enhance network devices such as routers or gateways by making them QoS-aware, but it requires modification on existing infrastructures. Another approach is to make the sender has the ability to implement QoS [5]. The sender must be capable of monitoring network conditions and adjusting its transmission rate. The second approach mitigates the effects on the network devices without QoS functionalities and hence is adopted in our design. This paper therefore aims to enhance QoS of surveillance system using IP CAMs.

It should be noted that IP CAM broadcast with a unified QoS may not be suitable for heterogeneous network environments and hosts. Insufficient network bandwidth and stream-decoding speed may result in a full queue and transmission delay. When a receiving queue is full, certain encoded frames will be discarded by IP CAM. Thus, the receiver will receive incomplete video bit streams. Moreover, some features of TCP including retransmission and variations in delay [1] may influence the efficiency of IP CAM. In some real-time applications, long delayed packets are not favored. If the network congestion situation becomes more critical, the surveillance system would not be able to provide real-time information and fail its job.

In order to apply a flexible QoS on TCP-based video streaming, we propose novel algorithms termed PEFD (Priority Early Frame Discard). The PEFD algorithms are based on rate shaping via server-side selective frame-discarding. The algorithms consider the network bandwidth and devices' computational capabilities. They actively discard necessary frame and effectively control the frame rate in IP CAM. Moreover, they keep the quality of video streaming and ensure the bit streams can be delivered to receivers in time. By taking both the network constraints and client computational capability into account, the proposed PEFD algorithms are well suited for the IP CAM broadcast in the surveillance systems, where TCP-based realtime video delivery over heterogeneous network environments is desired.

2   Surveillance System Architecture

For an IP CAM based surveillance system, an IP CAM usually acts as a server and the surveillant would be clients. The clients connect to the IP CAM for browsing the video streaming. The receiver could browse the video streaming on a web browser or any type of HTTP-based camera-monitoring software which supports video coding standards such as MPEG-4 [3]. Although the accessing flow is simple, it may cause excessive end-to-end delay which results from TCP retransmission mechanism and insufficient computational capacity of the receiver side.

In a typical IP CAM, the encoded video frames produced by a video hardware encoder are sent to the the input buffer. The frames in the input buffer are first segmented to packets, and then are delivered to the TCP send queue for the TCP-based video streaming. In a receiving client, the TCP receive queue is used for

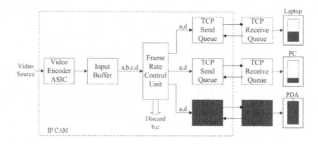

Fig. 1. A simple frames discarding architecture of the surveillance system

holding the received packets. The packets in the TCP receive queue are then re-assembled to frames, which are then sent to the decoding buffer for video playout. Consequently, when a client does not have sufficient computational capacity, frames at the decoding queue may accumulate rapidly. When the decoding queue becomes full, packets in the TCP receive queue start to accumulate as well. Consequently, a full decoding queue may result in a full TCP queue at both receiver side and sender side. As a result, large number of new encoded frames may be discarded in IP CAM. This may severely degrade the performance of the surveillance system.

Figure 1 shows a typical example based on the simple frame discard. The architecture assumes that IP CAM transmits video streaming to three differ-ent receivers at the same time. Although each receiver has its own TCP link, they share the same video bit streams. In this architecture, PDA has low decod-ing speed because of its insufficient computational capability. As a result, the decoding queue and the TCP queues are nearly full.

Because all receivers share the same video bit streams, if the system discards frames in order to eliminate full queue, each receiver will receive the same in-complete bit streams. As shown in Figure 1, assume that the system has to discard frame b and frame c to reduce the queue length of PDA. Consequently, the notebook and PC could only receive the frame a and frame d instead of the complete bit streams.

In order to solve the problems, this paper proposes a new architecture for alleviating TCP full queue and playback delay as shown in Figure 2. In this architecture, each connection is associated with its own frame discarding mech-anism. The proposed architecture only discards frame c and frame d for PDA when its queues are full, but not discards any frame for laptop and PC.

The frame rate control unit is built in the application layer in the proposed architecture, as shown in Figure 3. Since each client is associated with one frame rate control unit, only one client is considered in the figure for sake of brevity. The frame control unit for a client does not operate alone. Its operation is based on the the network transmission time of a frame and the waiting time of various queues for adaptively regulating the frame rate to that client. These measurements are obtained from the application or transport layers. The details of algorithms based on the proposed system architecture would be presented in next section.

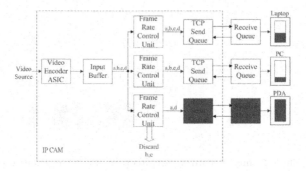

Fig. 2. The proposed architecture for alleviating TCP full queue and playback delay

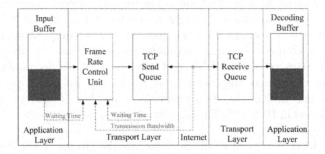

Fig. 3. Frame rate control unit in the proposed architecture

3   The Proposed Algorithm

There are 5 PEFD algorithms presented in this section. The first algorithm (termed PEFD Algorithm 1) is a simple frame discarding method. The system discards frames when detecting a full input buffer regardless of frame types. Note that the encoded video frames don't have the same priority. In the MPEG standards [3], I-Frame and first P-Frames are the reference frames of subsequent P-Frames for compression in a group of picture (GOP). It implies that I-Frame and first P-Frames have higher priority than subsequent P-Frames. Therefore, the fragmented GOPs received at receiver side may result in failure of reconstructing lower priority frames.

The PEFD Algorithm 2 can be used for solving the fragmented GOP problem. When the input buffer is full, in addition to removing the current frame, the PEFD Algorithm 2 will further discard all the subsequent frames in the current GOP. The problem of delivering undecodable frames therefore can be solved. However, the PEFD Algorithm 2 doesn't take the transmission and playback delay into account. The algorithm is not well-suited for surveillance applications where realtime delivery and playback are desired.

The PEFD Algorithm 3 is a timing-aware algorithm. It discards frames when these frames cannot be played back at the receiving client on time. Assumes that IP CAM encodes video frames 30 frames per second (fps). Thus, the time between two adjacent frames is $T = 1/30$ sec. The time injected to input buffer for initial bit streams (i.e. 0th frame) is t_0, and the time at the i-th frame injected to input buffer would be $t_0 + iT$. The waiting time in the input buffer for the i-th frame is denoted by $T_{i,S}$. The waiting time in the TCP queue is $T_{i,TCP}$, and the network transmission delay is $T_{i,N}$. Let E_i be the injection time to the decoding queue of the i-th frame at the client. Therefore,

$$E_i = t_0 + iT + T_{i,S} + T_{i,TCP} + T_{i,N}. \tag{1}$$

The i-th frame will be displayed at time epoch P_i based on frame rate 30 fps on receiver side. The time epoch P_i becomes $P_i = P_0 + iT$, where P_0 is the playback time of the initial frame at the client. Thus P_0 can be written as $P_0 = t_0 + T_{0,N} + T_B$, where T_B is the buffering time in the decoding buffer at the client. To ensure that the i-th frame can be play back on time at the client, it then follows that

$$E_i \leq P_i \tag{2}$$

Based on eq.(2), it can be derived that

$$T_{i,S} \leq T_B - (T_{i,N} - T_{0,N}) - T_{i,TCP} \tag{3}$$

The PEFD Algorithm 3 performs adaptive frame discard based on eq.(3). Because the frame rate control unit locates behind the input buffer, as shown in Figure 3, the waiting time $T_{i,S}$ in the input buffer is known to the unit before the frame discard operations. In addition, the buffering time T_B at the client is a constant, and is also known prior to the frame discard operations. Consequently, in PEFD Algorithm 3, it is only necessary to estimate $T_{i,TCP}$ and $\Delta_i = (T_{i,N} - T_{0,N})$ in eq.(3). The $T_{i,TCP}$ could be estimated by size of the i-th frame divided by average throughput of TCP queue. The size of i-th frame after video compression can be known prior to the computation of $T_{i,TCP}$. The throughput of the TCP queue can be obtained from operating system kernel.

Because $\Delta_i = (T_{i,N} - T_{0,N})$, estimation of Δ_i requires the estimations of $T_{i,N}$ and $T_{0,N}$. Note that $T_{i,N}$ and $T_{0,N}$ are the transmission delays, which can be estimated by round trip time (RTT) [2] of the packets carrying the i-th frame and the initial frames, respectively. The RTT of a packet is computed as the difference between the time the packet is sent and the time an ACK for that particular packet is received.

Table 1 shows the pseudo code of PEFD Algorithm 3. Only the frames being able to be played back on time will be delivered to the client. However, the algorithm is not priority-aware. Undecodable frames may be delivered to clients. The PEFD Algorithm 4 is a simple extension of PEFD Algorithm 3 so that it can be both timing-aware and priority-aware. In PEFD Algorithm 4, when a frame is decided to be discarded according to eq.(3), all the remaining frames in the GOP will be discarded, as shown in Table 2.

Although PEFD Algorithm 4 is effective, further improvements may still be necessary to preserve resource for higher priority frames when the available bandwidth decreases or the receiver has insufficient computational capacity. The PEFD Algorithm 5 is designed for this purpose.

Table 1. The pseudo code for PEFD Algorithm 3

Given a frame i inside a GOP,
If (($T_{i,S} \leq T_B - (T_{i,N} - T_{0,N}) - T_{i,TCP}$))   Admit();
else   Discard();

Table 2. The pseudo code for PEFD Algorithm 4

Given a frame i inside a GOP,
If (((frame $i == I$-Frame) && ($T_{i,S} \leq T_B - (T_{i,N} - T_{0,N}) - T_{i,TCP}$))) {
Admit(); }
else If ((frame $i == P_k$-Frame) && ($T_{i,S} \leq T_B - (T_{i,N} - T_{0,N}) - T_{i,TCP}$) &&
(the I-Frame and P_n-Frame, $n=1, ..., k-1$ of the GOP are not discarded) {
Admit(); }
else   Discard();

Table 3. The pseudo code for PEFD Algorithm 5

Given a frame i inside a GOP,
If (average $\Delta\rho_i < 0$ for n consecutive frames) {
If ((frame $i == I$-Frame) && ($T_{i,S} \leq T_B - (T_{i,N} - T_{0,N}) - T_{i,TCP}$)) {
Admit(); }
else if ((frame $i == P_k$-Frame) && ($T_{i,S} \leq T_B - (T_{i,N} - T_{0,N}) - T_{i,TCP} - qkT$) &&
the I-Frame and P_n-Frame, $n = 1, ..., k-1$ of the GOP are not discarded)) {
Admit(); }
else   Discard(); }
else {   If ((frame $i == I$-Frame) && ($T_{i,S} \leq T_B - (T_{i,N} - T_{0,N}) - T_{i,TCP}$))
Admit(); }
else if ((frame $i == P_k$-Frame) && ($T_{i,S} \leq T_B - (T_{i,N} - T_{0,N}) - T_{i,TCP}$) &&
The I-Frame and P_n-Frame, $n = 1, ..., k-1$ of the GOP are not discarded)) {
Admit(); }
else   Discard(); }

Let $\rho_i = T_B - (T_{i,N} - T_{0,N}) - T_{i,TCP} - T_{i,S}$. We can view ρ_i as available resource in the network for video delivery. Eq.(3) holds when $\rho_i > 0$, implying that the system has enough network resources to transmit the i-th frame. Otherwise, the system resource is not available. Let $\Delta\rho_i$ be the variation of available resources. That is, $\Delta\rho_i = \rho_i - \rho_{i-1}$. The system forecasts that the available resource will decrease if there are n consecutive $\Delta\rho_i$'s smaller than 0. In this case, the k-th P-frame, P_k-frame, in a GOP will be discarded if $T_{i,S} \leq T_B - (T_{i,N} - T_{0,N}) - T_{i,TCP} - kqT$, where q is a constant. The priority of the P_k-frame decreases with increasing k. Therefore, the P_k-frame is likely to be discarded for larger k values. The I-frame discarding is still based on eq.(3), as shown in Table 3. This is beneficial for preserving the network resources for higher priority frames for internet video streaming.

Table 4. The output bandwidth (bytes/second) of various PEFD algorithms

Rate Control Algorithms	Output bandwidth				
Algorithm 1	18,143				
Algorithm 2	18,438				
Algorithm 3	18,008				
Algorithm 4	18,241				
Algorithm 5	$(n=4)$	$(n=3)$	$(n=2)$	$(n=1)$	$(n=0)$
	17,229	16,596	15,138	13,102	11,535

4 Experimental Results

In our experiments, the proposed algorithms are implemented in an IP CAM. The client is a PDA. In addition, all the video sequences captured by the IP CAM are transmitted over wireless network. The IP CAM contains an MPEG-4 ASIC for encoding video sequences. The frame size is in CIF format with frame rate 30 fps. There are only two types of frames: I-frame and P-frame. Each GOP contains one I-frame and 29 P-frames. Both the IP CAM and PDA support IEEE 802.11b, and are able to access wireless network.

Three performance measures are considered in the experiments: good frame throughput rate, output bandwidth and playback latency. The good frame throughput rate is the ratio of numbers of decoded frames to numbers of frames delivered by the IP CAM. The output bandwidth is the number of bytes delivered by the IP CAM per second. The playback latency is the average time required for the playback of each frame i. It is the sum of $T_{i,S}$, $T_{i,TCP}$, $T_{i,N}$, and T_B.

We first compare the good frame throughput rate of various PEFD algorithms. Algorithms 1 and 3 are not priority-aware, therefore their good frame throughput rate are only 75.1 % and 87.2 %, respectively. On the contrary, Algorithms 2, 4 and 5 are able to attain 100 % good frame throughput rate because of the employment of priority-aware frame discard policy.

Table 4 shows the output bandwidth of various PEFD algorithms. It can be observed from the table that Algorithms 1, 2, 3 and 4 have similar bandwidth. The bandwidth of Algorithm 5 varies for different n values. To reserve the network resources for higher priority frames, the Algorithm 5 will discard more lower priority frames as n becomes lower. The output bandwidth therefore reduces with the decreasing n, as shown in Table 4.

Figure 4 depicts the latency-bandwidth performance for various PEFD algorithms. From Figure 4, it can be observed that the playback latency can be reduced by lowering the output bandwidth in Algorithm 5. Moreover, Algorithm 5 has lower playback latency as compared with other algorithms given the same output bandwidth. Therefore, in addition to providing flexibility for selecting different playback latencies and bandwidth, Algorithm 5 also attains best latency-bandwidth performance for TCP-based video streaming. All these facts demonstrate the effectiveness of Algorithm 5.

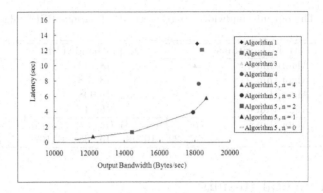

Fig. 4. The latency-bandwidth of various PEFD algorithms

5 Concluding Remarks

The proposed PEFD algorithm 5 has been found to be effective for TCP-based video streaming. The algorithm is both priority-aware and timing-aware. In addition, the algorithm can actively preserve network resources for higher priority frames when it forecasts decreasing network resources. Physical measurements reveals that the algorithm has superior latency-bandwidth performance over the other PEFD algorithms for the applications with limited bandwidth and computational resources.

References

1. Chebrolu, K., Rao, R.R.: Selective Frame Discard for Interactive Video. In: IEEE International Conference on Communications, June 2004, vol. 7, pp. 4097–4102 (2004)
2. Comer, D.E.: Internetworking With TCP/IP: Principles Protocols, and Architecture, 5th edn., vol. 1. Prentice-Hall, Englewood Cliffs (2006)
3. Richardson, I.E.G.: H.264 and MPEG-4 Video Coding. Wiley, Chichester (2003)
4. Tung, Y.C., Ou, C.M., Hwang, W.J., Wu, W.D.: Service Discovery of IP Cameras Using SIP and Zeroconf Protocols. In: Rong, C., Jaatun, M.G., Sandnes, F.E., Yang, L.T., Ma, J. (eds.) ATC 2008. LNCS, vol. 5060, pp. 388–402. Springer, Heidelberg (2008)
5. Vaz, R.N., Nunes, M.S.: Selective Frame Discard for Video Streaming over IP Networks. In: Proceedings of the 7th Conference on Computer Networks, Leiria, Portugal (October 2004)

CDN-Based Video Streaming Using Dynamic Bandwidth Allocation

Chih-Peng Lin[2], Chia-Yi Jan[1], Wen-Jyi Hwang[1,*], and Tun-Hao Yu[1]

[1] Department of Computer Science and Information Engineering,
National Taiwan Normal University, Taipei, 116, Taiwan
chiayi.jan@gmail.com, whwang@ntnu.edu.tw, 697470559@ntnu.edu.tw
[2] Department of Electronic Engineering,
National Taiwan University of Science and Technology, Taipei, 106, Taiwan
lcpe6969@ms11.hinet.net

Abstract. A novel dynamic bandwidth allocation algorithm for archived video delivery is presented in this paper. It adopts the generalized Brieman, Friedman, Olshen, and Stone (BFOS) algorithm for optimizing the rate-distortion performance for image delivery. Without feedback from clients, the algorithm is able to find the convex hull in the rate-distortion plane with low computational complexity. It is therefore well-suited for CDN-based media streaming applications with high client variations.

1 Introduction

A server for media streaming applications usually pre-stores compressed media data, and transports it on demand to a client for playback in realtime. Many streaming servers provide only unicast service. Because of limited bandwidth capacity associated with a server, simple server-client model may only support a small number of clients for media streaming. A content delivery network (CDN) [5] can be used for alleviating the problem. In a CDN, content from a provider is distributed to multiple servers in the network, and a client request is served by a nearest server. Although the CDN technique is effective, bandwidth consumption is still an important concern. A number of server allocation and placement algorithms [1,2] based on the distribution of clients have been proposed for balancing load of each server in the CDN. However, as the client distribution is time-varying, it is difficult to avoid excessive bandwidth consumption for each server in the CDN.

One way to control the bandwidth consumption is to employ a bandwidth allocation algorithm, which will be activated as the total bandwidth consumption exceeds a pre-specified threshold. The algorithm may lower the transmission rate of some clients for reducing the total bandwidth consumption. Moreover, the transmission rates will be restored as the total bandwidth consumption falls below the threshold. Many existing dynamic bandwidth allocation algorithms

---

* Corresponding author.

D. Ślęzak et al. (Eds.): FGCN/ACN 2009, CCIS 56, pp. 33–40, 2009.

[4] are based on online video encoding. These algorithms, therefore, are not well-suited for media streaming application, where the media data are stored off-line.

This paper a novel dynamic bandwidth algorithm optimizing rate-distortion performance for CDN-based media streaming applications. We assume that each archived video in a server is pre-encoded by two or more encoding rates independently. Each client subscribing to the video can select one of these encoding rates in accordance with its own processing capacity and/or network bandwidth. As the number of clients varies, the algorithm may be activated periodically for maintaining the optimal rate-distortion performance for media streaming. Based on the set of available encoding rates, the proposed algorithm then select video sequence with optimal encoding rate for each client minimizing the average distortion over all the clients subject to the pre-specified bandwidth constraint.

Although a simple full-search algorithm can be adopted for optimal dynamic bandwidth allocation, its computational complexity may be very high. The proposed algorithm is based on the generalized Brieman, Friedman, Olshen, and Stone (BFOS) algorithm [3] to facilitate the dynamic bandwidth allocation. The BFOS algorithm is able to find the lower boundary of convex hull in the rate-distortion plane with significantly lower computational complexity. The algorithm can be simplified further by assuming the video sequences have convex rate-distortion performance. In this case, only simple table lookup is required for online bandwidth allocation. Experimental results reveal that the proposed algorithm is an effective alternative for the CDN-based media streaming applications for bandwidth and network traffic control.

2   The Proposed Algorithm

Consider a CDN system consisting of a video content provider and a number of servers. Each video sequence in the content provider is pre-encoded with K different bit rates $(R_1,...,R_K$ bits per second(bps)) independently. Assume that $R_1 \leq R_2 \leq ... \leq R_K$. Clients can brow and subscribe video sequences with bit rates well-suited to their own bandwidth and/or processing capacity. The closest servers then cache and deliver the video sequences with the specified transmission rates.

Depending on the distribution of clients, servers cache different number of video sequences. Each server performs bandwidth allocation independently. Without loss of generality, only the bandwidth control of a single server is considered. Suppose the server caches C video sequences for media streaming. Note that C is not a constant. It may vary as the clients join or leave the CDN system.

Let $B_{i,j}$ be the set of clients associated with the server subscribing the video sequence i with rate $r_{i,j} \leq R_j$, where $1 \leq i \leq C$ and $1 \leq j \leq K$. That is, $r_{i,j}$ take value only from the set $\{R_1, ..., R_j\}$. In this scenario, each client specifies only the highest possible bandwidth (i.e., R_j for all the clients in set $B_{i,j}$). The actual allocated bandwidth $r_{i,j}$ may be lower than the specified one. Let $n_{i,j}$ be the number of clients in the set $B_{i,j}$. Therefore, the total bandwidth consumed by the server, denoted by R, is given by

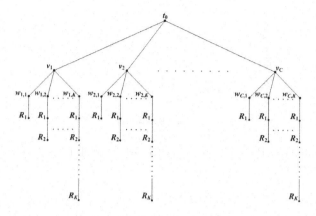

Fig. 1. The tree model for generalized BFOS algorithm for fast dynamic bandwidth allocation

$$R = \sum_{i=1}^{C} \sum_{j=1}^{K} n_{i,j} r_{i,j}. \tag{1}$$

Let $d_i(r_{i,j})$ be the average distortion of the video sequence i encoded with rate $r_{i,j}$. Consequently, D, the average distortion of the video sequence reconstructed at each client's site assuming no delivery error, is given by

$$D = \frac{1}{\sum_{i=1}^{C} \sum_{j=1}^{K} n_{i,j}} \sum_{i=1}^{C} \sum_{j=1}^{K} n_{i,j} d_i(r_{i,j}). \tag{2}$$

In many media streaming applications, the total bandwidth consumed by the server is an important concern for the service provider. It is usually desired that R is less than a bandwidth constraint R_T. Consequently, the goal of the bandwidth allocation is to find $r_{i,j}, i = 1, ..., C, j = 1, ..., K$, minimizing average distortion D subject to $R \leq R_T$.

The clients can join or leave the system any time. Therefore, the algorithm is activated periodically for maintaining the optimal rate-distortion performance for media streaming. Computational complexity for the bandwidth allocation is then an important concern. Although full-search for finding the optimal solution is possible, it can be shown that the search complexity is $O((K!)^C)$.

Our algorithm adopts the generalized BFOS algorithm [3] for fast dynamic bandwidth allocation. As depicted in Figure 1, a CDN server can be modeled as a tree in which the root t_0 has C children $v_1, ..., v_C$ (one for each video sequence). Each v_i has K children $w_{i,1}, ..., w_{i,K}$. The subtree rooted at $w_{i,j}$, denoted by $T_{i,j}$, is unary.

Let T be the complete tree shown in Figure 1. Let S be a subtree of T that share the same root node of $T_{i,j}, i = 1, ..., C, j = 1, ..., K$, (denoted $S \prec T$), in addition to t_0 and $v_1, ..., v_C$. The bandwidth of S, denoted by $R(S)$, can be computed by eq.(1), where $r_{i,j}$ is the leaf node of the $T_{i,j}$. Similarly, the

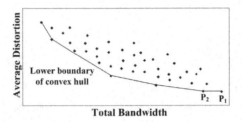

Fig. 2. An example of the set of points $(D(S), R(S))$ of all the subtrees S of T in the rate-distortion plane

average distortion of S, denoted by $D(S)$, can be computed by eq.(2), where $d_{i,j}$ is obtained by measuring the average distortion of the reconstructed video sequence i encoded with rate $r_{i,j}$.

The largest S is T. In this case each $B_{i,j}$ obtains maximum bit rate R_j (i.e., $r_{i,j} = R_j$). The smallest S, denoted as S_0, contains only root node of $T_{i,j}, i = 1, ..., C, j = 1, ..., K$, (i.e., $w_{i,j}, i = 1, ..., C, j = 1, ..., K,$) in addition to t_0 and $v_1, ..., v_C$. In this case each $B_{i,j}$ obtains only minimum bit rate R_1.

Consider the set of points $(D(S), R(S))$ of all the subtrees S of T in the rate-distortion plane. Figure 2 shows an example of plots of such points. The generalized BFOS algorithm find the optimal points that lies on the lower boundary of convex hull. It can be shown that the points on the convex hull corresponds to a series of nested subtrees. Since the complete tree is always on the convex hull, it is possible to start with T and prone back to S_0, producing a list of nested subtrees, which trace out the vertices of the convex hull.

The generalized BFOS algorithm operates as follows. It starts with $\mathbf{p}_1 = (D(T), R(T))$ (corresponding to the right most point in rate-distortion plane in Figure 2). The magnitude of slope λ is computed for each line connecting $(D(T), R(T))$ to every other point in the plane. The point $\mathbf{p}_2$ whose slope is the smallest of the computed slopes is the next point to the left on the convex hull, as shown in Figure 2. The $\mathbf{p}_2$ will then becomes the point from which new slopes are computed. The same process is repeated until $(D(S_0), R(S_0))$ (corresponding to the left most point in rate-distortion plane in Figure 2) is reached.

The generalized BFOS algorithm was designed for binary trees in [3]. Nevertheless, in our design, the trees $T_{i,j}$ rooted in $w_{i,j}, i = 1, ..., C, j = 1, ..., K$, are actually unary. Therefore, the generalized BFOS may further be simplified. To illustrate this fact in more detail, let $\Delta_i(n, k)$ be the slope of increase in distortion of video sequence i when rate is reduced from R_n to $R_k, 1 \le k < n \le K$. That is, $\Delta_i(n, k) = \frac{d_i(R_k) - d_i(R_n)}{R_n - R_k}$.

Suppose now we get the next rate allocation by pruning the unary tree $T_{i',j'}$, where $1 \le i' \le C, 1 \le j' \le K$. Assume $r_{i',j'} = R_n, 1 < n \le j'$ before pruning, and $r_{i',j'} = R_k$ afterward. In addition, let S and S' be the tree representing the whole rate allocation before and after pruning, respectively. Define the slope $\lambda_{i',j'}(n, k) = \frac{D(S') - D(S)}{R(S) - R(S')}$. That is, $\lambda_{i',j'}(n, k)$ is the bandwidth-distortion slope of the overall system by pruning $T_{i',j'}$ from R_n to R_k. It then can be proved that $\lambda_{i',j'}(n,k) = \frac{1}{\sum_{i=1}^{C}\sum_{j=1}^{K} n_{i,j}}\Delta_{i'}(n,k)$. Consequently, $\lambda_{i,j}$ is determined from Δ_i.

For streaming media applications, the video sequences are pre-stored. Therefore, $\Delta_i, i = 1, ..., C$, can be computed offline. The computational complexity can be further lowered when the rate-distortion function of each video sequence is convex. Given rates $R_1, ..., R_K$, video sequence i is said to have convex rate-distortion function if $\Delta_i(K, K-1) < \Delta_i(K-1, K-2) < ... < \Delta_i(2,1)$. It is then necessary to prune only one node at a time for each unary tree. Based on the convex assumption, the generalized BFOS is then stated as follows.

Algorithm I

1. Initialization:
   Assume there are C video sequences with $R_1, ..., R_K$, and $n_{i,j}, i = 1, ..., C, j = 1, ..., K$.
   Set $q(i,j) = j$ and $r_{i,j} = R_{q(i,j)}$ for $i = 1, ..., C, j = 1, ..., K$.
   Compute $\lambda_{i,j}(k, k-1)$ for $i = 1, ..., C, j = 2, ..., K, k = 2, ..., j$.
2. Tree Pruning:
   Find the set $B_{i,j}$ for which slope $\lambda_{i,j}(q(i,j), q(i,j)-1)$ is the smallest. Assume it is $B_{i',j'}$ (if there is more than one set having the minimum slope λ, choose all the sets), set $q(i',j') = q(i',j') - 1$.
3. Bandwidth and Distortion Measurement:
   Calculate the new total bandwidth and average distortion of the system using eqs.(1) and (2), where $r_{i,j} = R_{q(i,j)}$.
4. Check for Stop:
   Stop if $r_{i,j} = R_1 \ \forall i, j$. Otherwise, goto Step 2.

The steps 1 and 2 can be further simplified for reducing the computational complexity. We first observe that, the K unary trees $T_{i,1}, ..., T_{i,K}$, are based on the same video sequence i. Consequently, when pruning each tree from rate R_k to R_{k-1}, we have $\lambda_{i,k}(k, k-1) = ... = \lambda_{i,K}(k, k-1) = \frac{1}{\sum_{i=1}^{C}\sum_{j=1}^{K} n_{i,j}}\Delta_i(k, k-1)$. The search for minimum slope therefore can be based on $\Delta_i(k, k-1), i = 1, ..., C, k = 2, ..., K$. The simplified algorithm is shown below.

Algorithm II

1. Initialization:
   Assume there are C video sequences with $R_1, ..., R_K$ and $n_{i,j}, i = 1, ..., C, j = 1, ..., K$.
   Set $q(i,j) = j$ and $r_{i,j} = R_{q(i,j)}$ for $i = 1, ..., C, j = 1, ..., K$.
   Set $p_i = K, i = 1, ..., C$.
   Compute $\Delta_i(k, k-1)$, for $i = 1, ..., C, k = 2, ..., j$.
2. Tree Pruning:
   Find video sequence i such that $\Delta_i(p_i, p_i - 1)$ is the smallest.
   Assume it is i', set $p(i') = p(i') - 1, q(i',j) = q(i',j) - 1. \ \forall j > p(i')$.

3. Bandwidth and Distortion Measurement:
   Calculate the new total bandwidth and average distortion of the system using eqs.(1) and (2), where $r_{i,j} = R_{q(i,j)}$.
4. Check for Stop:
   Stop if $r_{i,j} = R_1$ $\forall i, j$. Otherwise, goto Step 2.

It can be shown that there are $(K - 1)C$ prunes. In the Algorithm II, the tree pruning process is based only on $\Delta_i(k, k - 1)$. Because $\Delta_i(k, k - 1)$, $i = 1, ..., C, k = 2, ..., j$, are computed offline, the order of unary trees to be pruned can be determined offline as well. Let $A(m)$ be the set of unary trees to be pruned at the m-th tree prune,$m = 1, ..., (K - 1)C$. We can store $A(m)$ in a table for fast online bandwidth allocation, as shown below.

Algorithm III

1. Initialization:
   Assume there are C video sequences with $R_1, ..., R_K$, and $n_{i,j}, i = 1, ..., C, j = 1, ..., K$.
   Set $q(i, j) = j$ and $r_{i,j} = R_{q(i,j)}$ for $i = 1, ..., C, j = 1, ..., K$.
   Set $p_i = K, i = 1, ..., C$, and $m = 1$.
   Compute $\Delta_i(k, k - 1)$, $i = 1, ..., C, k = 2, ..., j$.
   Find and store $A(1), ..., A((K - 1)C)$ based on $\Delta_i(k, k - 1)$, $i = 1, ..., C, k = 2, ..., j$.
2. Tree Pruning:
   Find the index of video sequence contained in $A(m)$.
   Assume it is i', set $p(i') = p(i') - 1$, $q(i', j) = q(i', j) - 1$. $\forall j > p(i')$.
3. Bandwidth and Distortion Measurement:
   Calculate the new total bandwidth and average distortion of the system using eqs.(1) and (2), where $r_{i,j} = R_{q(i,j)}$.
4. Check for Stop:
   Stop if $m = (K - 1)C$. Otherwise, set $m = m + 1$,and goto Step 2.

The algorithm III requires $(K - 1)C$ computations of average rates and average distortions for identifying the entire convex hull. Therefore, the complexity of the online bandwidth control is only $O(KC)$.

3   Experimental Results

This section presents some experimental results of the proposed algorithm. Only the algorithm III is implemented because it has lowest complexity. Figure 3 shows the rate-distortion performance of all the bandwidth allocations of two video sequences "Twy" and "Missa" (i.e., $C = 2$) in a CDN server. Each video sequence is pre-coded with three rates (R_1=400k, R_2=800k, and R_3=1200k bps) independently. Consequently, the clients in this experiments are divided into 6 sets: $B_{i,j}, i = 1, 2, j = 1, 2, 3$. The number of clients associated with $B_{i,j}, i = 1, 2, j = 1, 2, 3$, are given by $n_{1,1} = 12$, $n_{1,2} = 108$, $n_{1,3} = 37$, $n_{2,1} = 59$,

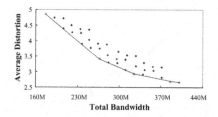

Fig. 3. The rate-distortion performance of all the bandwidth allocations of two video sequences in a server

$n_{2,2} = 74$, and $n_{2,3} = 152$, respectively. Frame size of the video sequences are in CIF format. The video compression is based on H.264. Because $C = 2$ and $K = 3$, there are 36 different bandwidth allocations. Both the video sequences have convex rate-distortion performance. The proposed algorithm is then able to find the lower boundary of the convex hull, as depicted in the figure.

Given the same video sequences as those for the performance measurement in Figure 3, the lower boundary of convex hull for two sets of $\{n_{i,j}, i = 1, 2, j = 1, 2, 3\}$ are revealed in Figure 4. It can be observed from Figure 4 that the number of vertices on the convex hull is independent of the values of $n_{i,j}, i = 1, 2, j = 1, 2, 3$. This result is not surprising because the convex hulls are identified by the same table $A(m)$, which is independent of the number of clients. This advantage is useful for data streaming applications because it is not necessary to update table $A(m)$ as the clients join or leave the streaming systems.

Figure 5 shows the results of bandwidth allocation for two non-convex video sequences. Each video sequence is pre-coded with four rates (R_1=300k, R_2=600k, R_3=900k, R_4=1200k bps) independently. From the figure, we observe that the

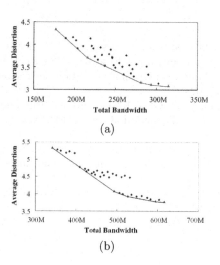

(a)

(b)

Fig. 4. The lower boundary of convex hull for two sets of $\{n_{i,j}, i = 1, 2, j = 1, 2, 3, \}$

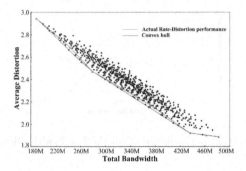

Fig. 5. The rate-distortion performance of all the bandwidth allocations of two non-convex video sequences

rate-distortion performance of the proposed algorithm is very closed to the convex hull. When total bandwidth is 380 Mbps, the gap in average distortion is only 0.13. All these facts demonstrate the effectiveness of the proposed algorithm.

4   Concluding Remarks

The proposed algorithm has low computational complexity for online bandwidth allocation for CDN-based media streaming applications. The algorithm extends the generalized BFOS algorithm so that dynamic bandwidth allocation can be accomplished by a simple table lookup process. The table is invariant to the number of clients. The algorithm therefore is effective for media streaming applications, in which clients are free to join or leave CDN servers at any time.

References

1. Bektasa, T., Oguza, O., Ouveysi, I.: Designing cost-effective content distribution networks. Computers and Operations Research, 2436–2449 (2007)
2. Cidon, I., Kutten, S., Soffer, R.: Optimal allocation of electronic content. Computer Networks, 205–218 (2002)
3. Chou, P.A., Lookabaugh, T., Gray, R.M.: Optimal Prunning with Applications to Tree-Structured Source Coding and Modeling. IEEE Trans. Inform. Theory 35, 299–315 (1989)
4. Chakareski, J., Girod, B.: Rate-distortion optimized video streaming with rich acknowledgments. In: Proc. Visual Communications and Image Processing, San Jose, CA (January 2004)
5. Pallis, G., Vakali, A.: Insight and perspectives for content delivery networks. Communications of ACM, 101–106 (2006)

2-Layered SOA Test Architecture Based on BPA[*]-Simulation Event[**]

Youngkon Lee

e-Business Department, Korea Polytechnic University,
2121 Jeongwangdong, Siheung city, Korea
yklee777@kpu.ac.kr

Abstract. This paper presents an implementation case study for business-centric SOA test framework. The reference architecture of SOA system is usually layered: business process layer, service layer, and computing resource layer. In the architecture, there are so many subsystems to affect system performance, moreover they relate with each other. As a result, in the respect of overall performance, it is usually meaningless to measure each subsystem's performance separately. In SOA system, the performance of the business process layer with which users keep in contact depends on the summation of the performance of the other lower layers. Therefore, measuring performance of the business layer includes indirect measurement of the other SOA system layers. We devised a business-centric SOA test framework in which activities and control primitives in business process managers are simulated to invoke commands or services in a test scenario. That is, in the test framework, a real business process scenario can be replaced to a mimicked business process test scenario, which is executed in a test proxy based on event mechanism. In this paper, we present the concept of BPA simulation, 2-layered test suites model, and reference architecture.

Keywords: SOA, QoS, BPA, Event-Driven Architecture.

1 Introduction

Service Oriented Architecture (SOA) is generally defined as a business-centric IT architectural approach that supports integrating businesses as linked, repeatable business tasks, or services [1]. SOA enables to solve integration complexity problem and facilitates broad-scale interoperability and unlimited collaboration across the enterprise. It also provides flexibility and agility to address changing business requirements in lower cost and time to market via reuse.

SOA has a lot of promises of interoperability, however, at the cost of: lack of enterprise scale QoS, complex standards which are still forming, lack of tools and framework to support standards, and perform penalty. Recently, as SOA has been

---

[*] BPA: Business Process Activity.
[**] This test framework has been implemented in an e-Government project sponsored by KIEC(Korea Institute of Electronic Commerce).

D. Ślęzak et al. (Eds.): FGCN/ACN 2009, CCIS 56, pp. 41–50, 2009.

widely adopted in business system framework, performance issues in SOA are raised continuously from users and developers.

SOA system is generally composed of various subsystems, each of which relates intimately with others. Therefore, if performance issues are raised, it's very difficult to find out clearly what's the reason. For example, if a business process in SOA system has longer response time than before, there could be various reasons: cache overflow in a business processor, wrapping overhead in service interface, or exceptions in computing resources, etc. One thing clear is that the performance of business process layer depends on the lower layer and measuring the performance of business layer includes indirect measuring the performance of all the lower layers. But, most test frameworks developed until now focus on measuring SOA messaging performance, as we present in section 2. They almost adopt batch-style testing where all the test cases are executed in a sequence.

OMG published a standard SOA reference model, MDA (Model Driven Architecture) [2]. It is widely adopted in real world because it presents normative architecture and enables SOA system to be implemented in a business-centric approach. In the MDA, a business process is designed firstly in a way for satisfying business requirements and later services are bounded to the activities in the business process. Business processes are described in a standardized language (e.g. WSBPEL) and they are executed generally on a business process management (BPM) system.

For testing SOA systems implemented according to the MDA reference model in business-centric way, test harness should have business process simulation functionality so that it may behave as BPM and at the same time test overall performance. This means that the test harness can execute business process, perform tests, and gather metric values.

We devised a new SOA test harness, BOSET , focusing on business process layer. It adopts a proxy mechanism, in which business processes and activities are simulated and executed to invoke events. The events initiate the service invocation so that the test system can gather the metric of the service performance. For the business-centric test execution, we also designed test suite, which is a document including structured and standardized test script. The test suite enables test harness to change its configuration flexibly according to the change of test target.

In section 2, we present some related works. Section 3 provides the principle requirement for test suite. In section 4, we describe the principle of test suite design. Section 5 presents briefly event-driven execution model and section 6 shows reference architecture for SOA test framework. Conclusions are presented in last section.

2 Related Works

There are various test frameworks and script languages developed or proposed for testing Web services systems, business processes, or business applications. This section briefs representative test systems and scripts.

2.1 Web Services Quality Management System

This system has been developed by NIA(National Information Agency in Korea) in order to measure Web services quality on the criteria of WSQM (Web Services

Quality Model) quality factors [3]: interoperability, security, manageability, performance, business processing capability, and business process quality. This system contributes to consolidate the quality factors of SOA. However, it requires expanding its architecture to apply SOA system, because it targets to only Web services system.

2.2 ebXML Test Framework

This framework has been implemented by NIST and KorBIT for testing ebXML system according to OASIS IIC Specification [4]. It could test packaging, security, reliability, and transport protocol of ebXML messaging system implemented by ebMS specification [5]. The main purpose of it is to test conformance and interoperability of ebXML messaging system, so it is not proper to test service oriented systems. Besides, it cannot test ad hoc status resulting from various events, because it is not event-driven but batch-style test framework.

2.3 JXUnit and JXU

JXUnit [6] and JXU [7] is a general scripting system (XML based) for defining test suites and test cases aimed at general e-business application testing. Test steps are written as Java classes. There is neither built-in support for business process test nor support for the event-driven features. However, as a general test scripting platform that relies on a common programming language, this system could be used as an implementation platform for general e-business test.

2.4 ATML (Automatic Test Mark-Up Language)

In its requirements, this specification provides XML Schemata and support information that allows the exchange of diagnostic information between conforming software components applications [8]. The overall goal is to support loosely coupled open architectures that permit the use of advanced diagnostic reasoning and analytical applications. The objective of ATML is focusing on the representation and transfer of test artifacts: diagnostics, test configuration, test description, instruments, etc.

2.5 Test Choreography Languages

These are standards for specifying the orchestration of business processes and/or transactional collaborations between partners. Although a markup like XPDL [9] is very complete from a process definition and control viewpoint, it is lacking the event-centric design and event correlation / querying capability required by testing and monitoring exchanges. Also, a design choice has been here to use a very restricted set of control primitives, easy to implement and validate, sufficient for test cases of modest size. Other languages or mark-ups define somehow choreographies of messages and properties: ebBP[10], WS-BPEL[11], WS-Choreography[12]. The general focus of these dialects is either the operational aspect of driving business process or business transactions, and/or the contractual aspect, but not monitoring and validation. Although they may express detailed conformance requirements, they fall short of covering the various aspects of an exhaustive conformance check e.g. the generation of intentional errors or simulation of uncommon behaviors. In addition, the focus of these languages is mainly on one layer of the choreography – they for instance ignore lower-level message exchanges entailed by quality of service concerns such as reliability, or binding patterns with the transport layer.

3   Requirements for Test Suite

Because SOA system is very complex and variable and has a number of heterogeneous subsystems, test suites including test logic and test cases should satisfy following requirements.

Event-driven and time-independent execution model: The test script must be executable either for real-time verification or as off-line (deferred) validation over a log of the interaction. Test cases also must be able to react to all sorts of events, and correlate past events. For these reasons, all input must be captured in the form of events and wrapped into a standard event (XML) envelope. The coordination of test-case executions within a test suite is also event-driven. The state of the test case workflow is also represented as events so that no additional persistence mechanism is required by a recoverable test engine.

Protocol-agnostic and platform-ubiquitous: Test script logic and control are abstracted from SOA protocols; it is versatile for messaging, business process, and business content testing regardless of technologies. Hence it can be used with either ebXML AS2 or Web Services message profiles. Of course a test case script that verifies business headers in ebXML may not apply to Web service messages, but a change in event-adapter should be the only modification needed to adapt a test script focused on verifying business transaction and payloads, from one message protocol to the other.

Adaptable interface: In our approach, the SOA test framework should have proxy which is delegated to replace temporarily BPM system. As a result, test framework has facilities to interface seamlessly services, functions, and components. For example, we implemented a service adapter, which transforms service appearance for adapting services. There could be plug-in systems which enable module or components to be easily connected and service wrappers which encompass functions in legacy systems into service types.

Extensible coverage of BPA simulated: BPA set simulated in test framework should be extensible to cope with the change of BPM systems which could be test target. Each BPA simulated should follow a standardized interface for connecting services.

4   Test Suite Design

Test suite means a document which describes the test target and test procedures. Test target is usually extracted from SOA standard specification. Test procedure could be used to control test flows. For making it easy, we designed 2-layered model for test suites: abstract test suites (ATS) and executable test suites (ETS) as shown in Fig 1.

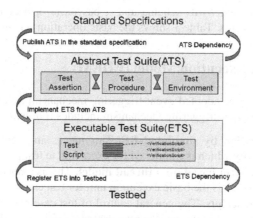

Fig. 1. BOSET Test Suit Structure

ATS describes test metadata of target expressed in test assertions and procedure and ETS describes executable test steps in the format of test execution language.

A test assertion is a testable or measurable expression for evaluating the adherence of part of an implementation to a normative statement in a specification. There is always a need to make explicit the relationship between a test assertion and the precise part of the specification to which it applies.

Test procedure describes test flow composed of a series of test activities which are simulated to business process activities. It is used in a test proxy, which is delegated as a process controller for test on replace of a BPM system. Test environment is a configuration description of a test harness.

ETS is a script for presenting each test step (in the other words, test case). It is independent from the SOA standard specification and domain environment but depends on the test execution model. For supporting machine and human readability, its

Table 1. Basic Operations in ETS

Operation type	Operation name	Description
Event operation	*post*	generate an event
	find	select event(s) from EventBoard
	mask	mask or unmask some past events to a monitor instance
Monitor flow Control	*start*	start a new instance of a monitor
	set	assign a value or an XML infoset
	sleep	suspend an instance of a monitor
	cad	check-and-do operation.
	jump	pursue the execution thread at another (labelled) test step inthe monitor
External resources	*call*	invoke either an event-adapter or an evaluation-adapter
Test case control	*actr*	dynamically activate a trigger
	exit	terminate the current test case

format follows predefined XML schema and it has basic operation sets to initiate, control, and process events. Table 1 shows the basic operation sets in ETS.

5   Event-Driven Execution Model (EDEM)

For invoking services, we adopted event-triggering mechanism according to business process activity. The event-triggering mechanism includes following concepts:

- **Event invocation by simulated BP.** This means an event invocation by a business activity which is mimicked for execution in test proxy.
- **Workflow control based on a thread model.** This is embedded in the notion of Monitor, which is the basic execution unit for test cases.
- **Event-driven scripts.** The general control of test case execution within a test suite and of the test suite itself is represented by Triggers which define under which conditions and events an execution takes place. (Fig. 2)
- **Event logging and correlation.** Event management, central to BOSET, is supported by an entity called Event Board. The Event Board normally suffices for mediating all inputs to a test case, as well as outputs.
- **Messaging gateways.** Message traffic expected in all e-Business applications, is mapped to and from events. Event-Adapters perform these mappings, allowing for abstracting test cases from communication protocol aspects.
- **Semantic test plug-ins.** Agile verifications on business documents, ranging from schema validation to semantic rules over business content, are delegated to Evaluation-Adapters.

While these features may themselves be potentially complex, it has been possible in BOSET to identify a minimal set of controls sufficient for SOA testing. For example, workflow control only makes use of the simplest control primitives that have proved sufficient for test cases, not pretending to replicate the full range of workflow operators. Event correlation and querying rely on simple selection expressions based on XPath. Based on the main concepts, the test execution model requires following components (Fig. 3):

Monitor: This represents the logic of a test case. A test case may use several monitors in its definition, and a test case instance may engage the concurrent or sequential execution of several monitor instances. A monitor is a script that specifies the steps and workflow of the test case. A monitor instance is always created as the result of a start operation executed either by another monitor or by a trigger. The first monitor started for a test case (i.e. Started by a Trigger) is called root monitor for the test case. There is always a trigger at the origin of monitor(s) execution (directly or indirectly). A monitor instance can start another monitor instance concurrently to its own execution, and can activate another trigger. The outcome of a test case (pass / fail / undetermined) is determined by the final outcome of the monitor(s) implementing this test case. The execution of a monitor produces a trace that can be posted as an event.

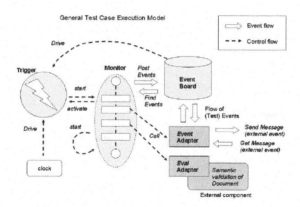

Fig. 2. Event-Driven Execution Model

Trigger: The trigger is a script that defines the event or condition that initiates the execution of the test case, i.e. the execution of a monitor. A trigger can be set to react to an event (event-watching) or to a date (clock-watching), and is associated with one or more monitors. Because a trigger initiates the execution of a test case, it is usually not considered as part of the test case itself, but part of the test suite that coordinates the execution of several test cases. A trigger is active when ready to react to events for which it has been set, and ready to trigger its associated monitors. When a trigger starts a test case, a case execution space (CES) is allocated, within which the created monitor instance as well as all subsequent dependent instances will execute. The CES defines a single scope of access to events and to other objects referred to by variables. When activated, a trigger is given to a context object, which will be part of the CES of the monitor(s) the trigger will start.

Test Suite: A test suite is a set of test cases, the execution of which is coordinated in some way. This coordination may be represented by a monitor, that will either directly start the monitors that represent individual test cases, or that will instead activate triggers that control these monitors. For example, a test suite may serialize the execution of test cases TC1 and TC2 by setting a trigger for TC2 that reacts to the event posted by TC1 at the end of its execution. Or, the test suite may set a trigger that will initiate the concurrent execution of several test cases. The following figure illustrates the structure of a test suite:

Event (or Test Event): An event is a time-stamped object that is managed by the Event Board. Events are used to coordinate the execution of a test case, and to communicate with external entities. For example an event may serve as a triggering mechanism (in event-driven triggers) for test cases, as a synchronization mechanism (e.g. a test step waiting for an event) or as a proxy for business messages, in which case the mapping between the event representation and the business message is done by an event adapter. Some events are temporary, which means they are only visible to monitors from the same test case execution (CES) and are automatically removed from the event board at the end of the CES they are associated with.

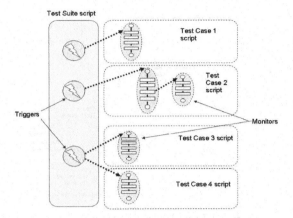

Fig. 3. Test Case Triggering

Event Board (EB): The event board provides event management functions. Events can be posted to the board, or searched. An event board can be seen as an event log that supports additional management functions. The event board is the main component with which a monitor interacts during its execution.

Event Adapter: An event adapter is a mediator between the external world and the event board. It maps external events such as message sending/receiving, to test events and vice versa. For example, an event adapter will interface with an SOA gateway so that it will convert received business messages into a test event and post it on the event board. Conversely, some events posted on the event board by a monitor can be automatically converted by the adapter into business messages submitted for sending. An event adapter can also be directly invoked by a monitor. Whether the adapter is designed to react to the posting of an event on the board or is directly invoked by the monitor, is an implementation choice. In both cases, it would convert a test event into an external action.

Evaluation Adapter: An evaluation adapter is implementing – or interfacing with an implementation of - a test predicate that requires specific processing of provided inputs that is not supported by the script language. Typically, it supports a validation check, e.g. semantic validation of a business document. An evaluation adapter is always invoked by a monitor. On invocation, an evaluation adapter returns an XML infoset summarizing the outcome, which can be evaluated later in the monitor workflow.

6   Reference Architecture

For testing SOA systems that have various components and flexible architecture, test requirement and the change in a test target should be rapidly applicable on a test harness. Thus, the test harness should reuse easily test components and be reconfigurable.

BOSET is composed of a test component part and a test interface part (Fig. 4). The test components include modules defined in EDEM, which are classified as stationary

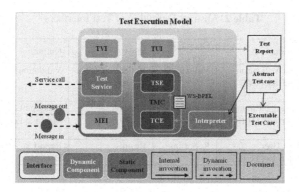

Fig. 4. Reference Architecture for EDEM

and non-stationary. Stationary module is static independent of any specific standard and/or test environment. Non-stationary module could be changed dynamically according to standards or test suite designs.

Stationary test components is composed of **TMC**(Test Main Component, Test Driver) and **TCE**(Test Configuration Engine). TMC orchestrates other test components and interfaces, and consequently drives the execution of test. TCE dynamically sets up test components in accordance with a configuration profile. **TSE**(Test Sequence Engine) interprets and drives executable test steps and interacts with test other components and interfaces.

Non-stationary test components include a test service module and an interpreter. Test Service stimulates target **SUT**(System Under Test) with pre-defined actions, which include instructions at the test state. The actions could be modified or created for the test specifics. Interpreter reads the test case and then parses it into test procedure, test assertions, and configuration information. Interpreter could be modified according to test suite design.

For interaction with SUTs, test drivers, and test users, BOSET has following interfaces:

- **MEI** (Messaging Engine Interface): delivers messages to/from SUTs based on the message protocol used. i.e., ebMS engine, SOAP engine, etc.
- **TVI** (Test Validation Engine): validates messages according to verification script. i.e, Xpath, Schematron, Xquery, JESS, OWL, etc.
- **TUI** (Test User Interface): provides user-interface using web or intranet. i.e, IIC web UI, WS-I UI, etc.

For interface model for Service Description, we adopted WSDL (Web Service Description Language), a standard specification. TCE discoveries and dynamically deploys interface modules in the Universal Test Module Repository. Configuration document could be registered in a registry implemented according to UDDI (Universal Description, Discovery and Integration) specification. TSE orchestrates deployed test component and interface modules. For dynamic invocation, WS-BPEL (Web Service Business Process Execution Language) primitives could be used.

Table 2. Abstract Definition of Test Interfaces

Interface	Operation Name	Input	Output
Test Validation Interface(TVI)	Validation	Validation script and target messages	Validation result
Message Engine Interface(MEI)	Sending	Message	Message Log
	Query (Receiving)	Query Script	Message Log
Test User Interface(TUI)	Reporting	Results	Report Document

7 Conclusion

We presented a SOA test framework, which has been implemented in Korea government side for testing public SOA systems. The framework facilitates to test SOA systems by introducing the concept of business activity simulated event proxy. For the framework, we also devised 2-layered test suites: abstract test suite and executable test suite. The abstract test suite describes test workflow based on a business process. The executable test suite represents test operations in detail for test case execution. This model decouples test procedure and test cases; as a result it enhances the reusability of test components. We also provide reference architecture for SOA test framework, which will be a guideline to later implementation of business-centric test framework.

References

1. Nickul, D.: Service Oriented Architecture (SOA) and Specialized Messaging Patterns., Adobe technical paper (December 2007)
2. Miller, J., Mukerji, J.: MDA Guide Version 1.0.1., OMG (June 2003), http://www.omg.org/docs/omg/03-06-01.pdf
3. Lee, Y., et al.: Web Services Quality Model 1.1. OASIS WSQM TC (October 2008)
4. Durand, J., et al.: ebXML Test Framework v1.0. OASIS IIC TC (October 2004)
5. Wenzel, P., et al.: ebXML Messaging Services 3.0. OASIS ebMS TC (July 2007)
6. Java XML Unit (JXUnit), http://jxunit.sourceforge.net
7. JUnit, Java for Unit Test, http://junit.sourceforge.net
8. ATML, Standard for Automatic Test Markup Language (ATML) for Exchanging Automatic Test Equipment and Test Information via XML, IEEE (December 2006)
9. XPDL: XML Process Definition Language (Workflow Management Coalition) Document Number WFMC-TC-1025: Version 1.14, October 3 (2005)
10. OASIS, Business Process Specification Schema 1.0.1, May 2001 and ebBP, v2.0.4 (October 2006)
11. OASIS, Web Services Business Process Execution Language 2.0 (committee draft in review phase) (August 2006)
12. Web Services Choreography Description Language (WSCDL), Version 1.0 (candidate recommendation) (November 2005)

Impacts of Power Ramping for ARQ-Aided Downlink Time Switched Transmit Diversity in the WCDMA LCR-TDD System

Ri-A. Ma, Cha-Eul Jeon, and Seung-Hoon Hwang

Dept. of Electronics Engineering
Dongguk University, Seoul, Korea
shwang@dongguk.edu

Abstract. In this paper, we investigate the performance of the ARQ-aided downlink Time Switched Transmit Diversity (TSTD) in the WCDMA LCR-TDD system, when power ramping is applied. Proposed scheme ramps up the transmission power and then retransmits the data, when the receiver sends the response signal (ACK or NACK signal) to the transmitter and the response signal is NACK signal. Simulation results demonstrate that the proposed scheme yields about 0.7dB performance gain in terms of average Eb/N0, compared with the conventional ARQ-aided TSTD when a mobile speed is 3km/h and a frame error rate (FER) is 1%, respectively. In addition, 2.5% of throughput gain is achieved when the average Eb/N0 is equal to 0dB.

Keywords: TSTD, automatic repeat request (ARQ), transmit diversity, WCDMA, LCR-TDD, Power Ramping.

1 Introduction

The 3GPP UMTS standard one of the third generation of mobile communication standards, includes two kinds of transmit diversity, namely open-loop transmit diversity and closed-loop transmit diversity [1]. The open loop schemes does not need feedback information related to the channel condition from the mobile station (MS), which includes Space Time Transmit Diversity (STTD) as a simple coding scheme, as well as Time Switched Transmit Diversity (TSTD) as a transmit antenna alternately changing scheme. Both STTD and TSTD have an additional transmit antenna to a single transmission antenna system. The STTD is a technique which sends the same data through two or four transmit antennas with different coding and modulation and then receives to combine the data [2]. The TSTD is a downlink transmit diversity for WCDMA Low Chip Rate (LCR)- Time Division Duplex (TDD) which transmits data through two transmit antennas alternatively switched over regular time interval [3],[4].

The TSTD transmission scheme yields a considerable gain, compared with a non-diversity mode system, by simply adding switching components in front of the transmitting antennas, and it requires only one switch and one additional RF/IF block in the base station (BS), and no additional components in the MS because the channel estimation and modulation for each slot is performed on a slot by slot basis [3],[4].

D. Ślęzak et al. (Eds.): FGCN/ACN 2009, CCIS 56, pp. 51–57, 2009.
© Springer-Verlag Berlin Heidelberg 2009

Therefore, the TSTD scheme is known as a simple and effective transmit diversity method that can increase the downlink capacity in the WCDMA LCR-TDD systems [5]. In the UMTS standard of the 1.28 Mcps TDD, the TSTD makes antenna alternatively switched every sub-frame of 5ms. Figure 1 shows the TSTD system structure defined as a 3GPP UMTS standard [1].

Packet data service employ an Automatic Repeat request (ARQ) method in order to guarantee a reliable data transmission, in which the same redundancy bits for error correction are transmitted repeatedly when a negative acknowledgement (NACK) is obtained. The acknowledgement signaling may be utilized as a channel quality indicator, which shows whether the channel is good or bad. Basically, the receiver transmits acknowledgement (ACK) or NACK to the transmitter, if the receiver transmits ACK signal, the transmitter come to the conclusion that transmitted packet is received correctly. If the receiver transmits NACK signal, the transmitter come to the conclusion that transmitted packet is received not correctly and then the transmitter retransmit error data packet. The physical ARQ scheme is included in high speed packet access (HSDA) physical layer specifications [6].

In a similar approach for highly reliable packet data transmission, the physical ARQ scheme was simply combined with the TSTD scheme in [7]. Therefore, the ARQ-Aided TSTD system was proposed where ACK/NACK signal was employed as closed loop channel quality indicator, and its improved performance was investigated in terms of FER (frame error rate) and throughput for various Eb/N0 and mobile speeds. However, it is still necessary to have additional link adaptive method in order to improve the overall system throughput and reduce the number of retransmissions.

To achieve high capacity and acceptable quality of service, the effect of fading and propagation loss are generally mitigated through the use of power control. In [8], a power ramping method was introduced for UMTS random access retransmission. Similarly, the power ramping was modified for the ARQ in the WCDMA downlink to overcome the poor channel conditions in [9]. In this paper, we propose a novel ARQ-aided power ramping TSTD system, under retransmissions designed for reliable and energy efficient data transmissions. The system performances are evaluated in terms of frame error rate (FER) and throughput. The impacts of mobile speed are also analyzed.

In this paper, it is assumed that the ARQ scheme is operated in the TSTD systems. Figure 2 shows the antenna switching pattern for ARQ-aided TSTD systems. After the transmitter sends the sub-frame2 by ANT 2, it receives a NACK signal for the

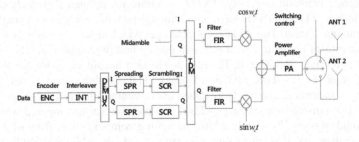

Fig. 1. The TSTD system structure defined in 3GPP UMTS standard

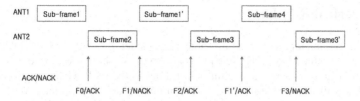

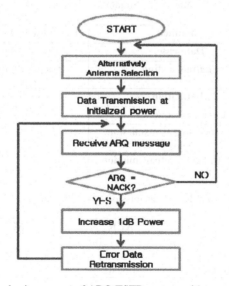

Fig. 2. Antenna switching pattern for ARQ-aided TSTD systems

sub-frame1 (F1/NACK), which means failure of the transmission of the sub-frame1. When the F1/NACK signal is received, the transmitter sends a retransmission of sub-frame1 (sub-frame1') by ANT 1. Then, the sub-frame3 is transmitted by ANT 2 and a sub-frame4 by ANT 1. In this figure, it is assumed that both the ACK/NACK decisions and transmissions cause delays of one sub-frame.

2 Proposed Power Ramping for ARQ-Aided TSTD

Figure 3 represents a flow chart for ARQ-aided TSTD with power ramping under retransmissions. The proposal has performance gain through selectively increasing the retransmission power in the ARQ method. When the ACK signal is received at the transmitter, the transmit power is initialized as the first transmission power. Meanwhile, when the NACK signal is received, the transmitter increases the power with a predetermined amount (e.g., 1dB). In this paper, such power ramping scheme is combined with the ARQ-aided TSTD and its results are compared with a conventional ARQ-aided TSTD system in [7].

Fig. 3. The basic concept of ARQ TSTD system with power ramping

3   Numerical Results

Simulation parameters are listed in Table 1. Consider 1.28Mcps LCR-TDD as a system model [5], since the TSTD scheme is deployed for the PDSCH in the standard. A 10ms radio frame consists of two 5ms sub-frames in the LCR-TDD system. Input data is encoded with the 1/3 code rate convolutional code, block-interleaved, and then QPSK-modulated. A one path Rayleigh channel model is assumed and it is also assumed that an error free feedback channel is considered, from the BS to the MS in the ARQ-aided TSTD system. The time delay related to the ARQ processing and transmission is set to be a sub-frame size of 5ms. The maximum number of retransmissions that are allowed is five. Mobile velocity is 3km (pedestrian velocity).

The system performance is evaluated in terms of the FER for varying average $Eb/N0$. For TSTD transmission, two spatially separated antennas are alternatively used to transmit the subframe units where the data rate is assumed to be 12.2kbps, and the carrier frequency is 2GHz. Therefore two antennas transmit 100 sub frames per second. The FER performances for average $Eb/N0$ are shown in Figure 3, when the mobile speed is 3km/h. Average $Eb/N0$ is defined as the average value of the transmitted $Eb/N0$ over several retransmissions with boost-up power, since it may show the fair performance comparison on the aspect of energy efficiency.

For a conventional TSTD, the average $Eb/N0$ means a static $Eb/N0$ value. Meanwhile, for the proposed TSTD, the transmit power increases 1dB under the retransmissions. When the maximum number of retransmissions are allowed to be five, the transmit power may be summed up to five times. However, note that the retransmission can be finished before the fifth transmission. Transmission power parameters are listed in Table 2.

Table 1. The Simulation Parameters

Channel	1-path Rayleigh fading
Data rate	12.2 kbps
Channel coding	1/3 convolutional coding
Modulation	QPSK
Carrier frequency	2GHz
ARQ processing transmission delay	5ms
Max. Number of retransmission	5

Table 2. Transmission Power Parameter

	ACK	NACK
TSTD(ARQ)	Initial Eb/N0	
Proposed TSTD(ARQ)	Reset to initial Eb/N0	+1dB

From the Figure 4, it is observed that the ARQ-aided TSTD system may be improved by power ramping. In order to acquire the FER of 1%, the conventional system is required to maintain average 3dB Eb/N0 but power ramping system is required to maintain average 2.3dB Eb/N0. That is, applied power ramping needs to less average Eb/N0 in case of NACK.

In Figure 5, the required average Eb/N0 is shown at various mobile speeds, when the target FER is equal to 1%. MS speeds are required from 1km to 120km. We can see the required Eb/N0 decreases as the mobile speed increases. This is due to the interleaving gain. For the low mobile speed, it is shown that the power ramping is more influential to improve the performances than the conventional TSTD. For example, the average 5dB Eb/N0 is required at 1km/hr in the conventional ARQ-aided TSTD scheme. With the consideration of power ramping, 4dB is needed. Hence, the performance gain of 1dB is obtained by the power ramping.

Furthermore, it is seen that the performance gain is still maintained when the MS speed increases. For example, for 120km/hr mobile speed, an average 0dB Eb/N0 is needed in the conventional TSTD scheme. Meanwhile, an average -2dB Eb/N0 is needed in the proposed power ramping TSTD scheme. Proposed power ramping TSTD compare to conventional TSTD, It has gain regardless of the mobile speed. Because power ramping has gain regardless of mobile speed.

The throughput performances are presented in Figure 6 when the mobile speed is 3km/h. As the average Eb/N0 increases, the throughput performances improve. However, for high average Eb/N0 region, the throughput performance differences decrease. Because, no ARQ gain and nearly 100% throughput in high Eb/N0. But, in

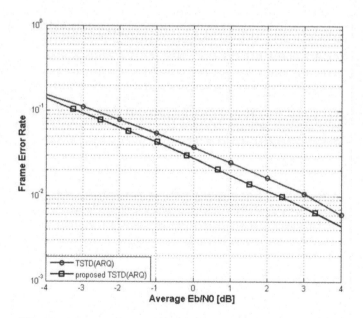

Fig. 4. The basic concept of ARQ TSTD system with power ramping

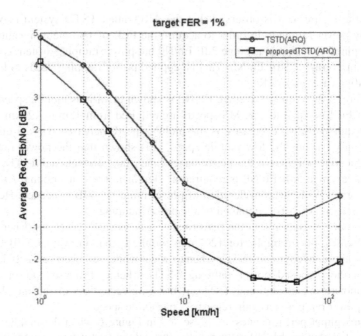

Fig. 5. The basic concept of ARQ TSTD system with power ramping

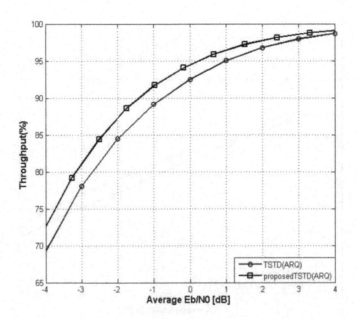

Fig. 6. The basic concept of ARQ TSTD system with power ramping

case of properly Eb/N0, there is difference of throughput performance each TSTD system. For example, when the Eb/N0 is 0dB, a improved throughput performance of 2.5% is obtained in the proposed TSTD with power control. Therefore, we can say that the proposed power ramping TSTD scheme is more effective in the low average Eb/N0 region to improve the throughput performances.

4 Conclusion

In this paper, the ARQ-aided TSTD with power ramping for WCDMA LCR-TDD systems was proposed and its performances were investigated. Numerical results show that the ARQ-aided TSTD system may be improved by power ramping. In summary, 0.7dB of improvement performance is shown when 1% FER, 2.5% of throughput gain is shown when average Eb/N0 is equal to 0dB. Therefore, the performance of ARQ-aided TSTD system with power ramping may be further improved significantly from the view point of energy efficiency. Future work will be continued to enhance the performance of the ARQ-aided power ramping TSTD system with other schemes such as turbo codes and the use of hybrid ARQ.

References

1. 3GPP TS25.224, Physical layer procedures (TDD), `ftp://ftp.3gpp.org/`
2. Yangxin, Y.X.: Performance Analysis of Space-Time Transmit Diversity for Wideband CDMA. In: Proceding of IEEE Vehicular Technology Conf., Spring, vol. 3, pp. 2006–2008 (2001)
3. Lee, H.-W., Kim, S.-J., Sung, D.-K.: Performance analysis of downlink time switched transmit diversity in the WCDMA LCR-TDD system. IEICE Trans. Commun. E86-B(6), 2028–2031 (2003)
4. Lee, H.W., Yeom, J.H., Sung, D.K.: Performance of down link time switched transmit diversity in W-CDMA mobile radio. In: Proceeding of IEEE PIMRC, pp. 1139–1143 (1999)
5. 3GPP TR25.928, 1.28Mcps Functionality for UTRA TDD Physical Layer, `ftp://ftp.3gpp.org/`
6. Holma, H., Toskala, A.: HSDPA/HSUPA for UMTS. Wiley, Chichester (2006)
7. Jeon, C.-E., Ma, R.-A., Baek, J.-H., Hwang, S.-H.: Downlink time switched transmit diversity systemn with ARQ scheme. In: The 11th International Conference on Advanced Communication Technology, Phenix park, Korea, February 15-18 (2009)
8. 3GPP, TS25.214: Physical layer procedures, `ftp://ftp.3gpp.org/`
9. Hwang, S.: Effect of the power ramping under retransmission in an ARQ for the WCDMA downlink in one path rayleigh fading channel. IEICE Trans. Commun. E89-B(3), 1024–1026 (2006)

Active Worm Propagation in Hierarchical Peer-to-Peer Network Management Systems: Modeling and Analysis

Zahra Zohoor Saadat[1], Saleh Yousefi[2], and Mahmood Fathy[3]

[1] Islamic Azad University – Pardis Branch
[2] Computer Engineering Department, Urmia University
[3] Iran University of Science and Technology
zohoorsaadat@gmail.com, s.yousefi@urmia.ac.ir,
mahfathy@iust.ac.ir

Abstract. Hierarchical peer to peer Network Management Systems are attracting a surge of interest in recent years. However, due to their special characteristics, they are more vulnerable to active worm propagations in comparison to current network management systems. In this paper, we study the speed of active worm propagation in a typical hierarchical P2P based network management system from an analytical point of view. Numerical study of the proposed model then is invoked to analyze the propagation process and study the impact of different factors including system size, node type and connection degree.

Keywords: P2P systems, Network Management Systems, Active Worms.

1 Introduction

Currently there is a growing belief that using hierarchical Peer-to-Peer (P2P) approach leads to noticeable improvement in the performance of Network Management Systems (NMSs) [1, 2]. However they can be potential vehicle for active worms which can spread in all manager peers in a short time. In [3] we used a simulation approach to study the speed of active worm propagation in a typical hierarchical P2P NMS (proposed in [1, 2]). This paper is an analytical framework which provides more solid basis for studying the impact of different factors on the speed of active worm propagation. To the best of our knowledge there is no other study on propagation process of active worms in hierarchical P2P NMSs. However many people have studied modeling and analysis of propagation of P2P active worms for several years. Tao Li, Zhihong Guan and Xianyong in [4] introduced two different scanning strategies of P2P active worms. Wei Yu modeled three active worm attack strategies in [5], and presented an analytical approach to analyze the propagation of active worms under pre-defined attack models. Jie Ma, Xinmeng Chen, Guangli Xiang in [6] modeled passive worm propagation in P2P systems and gave numerical results. Guanling Chen, Robert S. Gray in [7] identified three strategies that a non-scanning worm may use to propagate through P2P systems. They provided a workload-driven simulation framework for worms and identified the parameter influencing the worm propagation. Yu Yao, Xingrui Luo, Fuxiang Gao, Songling Ai in [8] presented a potential worm propagation model for pure P2P principle.

D. Ślęzak et al. (Eds.): FGCN/ACN 2009, CCIS 56, pp. 58–64, 2009.
© Springer-Verlag Berlin Heidelberg 2009

The rest of the paper is organized as follows. In Section 2 a typical hierarchical model is introduced for P2P based network management systems. In Section 3 a P2P active worm attack model is proposed. In Section 4, the proposed model is studied numerically. Finally in Section 5, the paper is concluded along with some directions for future works.

2 Network Management System Architecture

In this paper, we study active worm attacks to the hierarchical P2P network management architecture proposed in [1, 2]. The proposed architecture includes 3 levels of managers: top level manager (TLM), mid level manager (MLM), and low level manager (LLM). TLM reacts to human operator requests, communicates with other managers in order to accomplish a management task, while MLM reacts to TLMs' or other MLMs' requests, finally LLMs access to Network elements and react to MLMs' requests.

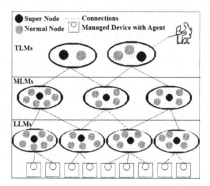

Fig. 1. Network Manager Architecture

As shown in the Fig.1, there is a super manager node (black nodes) in each group by which the hierarchical layers are connected. In other words the communication channel between two different layers goes through super manager nodes, which are indeed part of management message path. The grouping topology of manager peers (gray nodes) is Chord [9].

3 Analytical Model

In this paper we study a P2P-based attack strategy: online P2P-based approach (OPS). In OPS, the attack starts from the time the worm is entered to the system at time unit 0. The worm infected manager initiates an attack against its P2P neighbors with its full attack capacity. At the same time, the worm infected manager can also attack its neighbors in the hierarchical structure in case the worm infected manager is a super manager node. The detailed algorithm is presented in [3].

Table 1. Notations in this paper

T	Total nodes in the system
S	Scan rate of infected nodes
M_0	Initial infected nodes in the 'P2P' system at the system's initial time
M'_0	Initial infected nodes in the 'super-P2P' system at the system's initial time
P_1	Probability of nodes in the 'super-P2P' system to be vulnerable
P_2	Probability of nodes in the 'P2P' system to be vulnerable, where $P_1 \leq P_2$
R	The number of 'super-P2P' system nodes
θ	Topology degree of 'P2P' system
r_j	Number of connections between the infected super node of group j and other super nodes in the 'super-P2P' system (at step i)
n_j	Number of infected super node's neighbors belonging to group j in the 'P2P' system (at step i)
$M(i)$	Number of infected nodes at step i in the whole system
$N(i)$	Number of vulnerable nodes at step i in the whole system
$E(i)$	Number of newly infected nodes added at step i in the whole system $(E(0)=0)$
$M(i,X)$	Number of infected nodes at step i, where $M(i,0)$ is the infected nodes in the 'P2P' system and $M(i,1)$ is the infected nodes in the 'super-P2P' system $(M(0,0)$ is the initial infected nodes in the 'P2P'system and $M(1,0)$ is the initial infected nodes in the 'super-P2P' system)
$N(i,X)$	Number of vulnerable nodes at step i, where $N(i,0)$ is the vulnerable nodes in the 'P2P' system and $N(i,1)$ is the vulnerable nodes in the 'super-P2P' system $(N(0,0)$ is the initial vulnerable nodes in the 'P2P'system and $N(1,0)$ is the initial vulnerable nodes in the 'super-P2P' system)
$E(i,X)$	Number of newly infected nodes added at step i, where $E(i,0)$ is the newly infected nodes added at step i in the 'P2P' system and $E(i,1)$ is the newly infected nodes added at step i in the 'super-P2P' system

We assume that there are two logical systems: one is called 'super-P2P' system in which every group's super node is represented as a single node in the three-level hierarchical architecture. The other is called 'P2P' system, which represents the P2P managers in each group. In both 'super-P2P' system and 'P2P' system, we assume that a number of nodes are vulnerable. As our analysis considers the average case, we assume that each manager in 'super-P2P' or 'P2P' system has the certain probability to be vulnerable and this vulnerable probability in 'super-P2P' is certainly less than 'P2P' system for importance of sensibility of hierarchical structure. In the sequel we introduce new terms to distinguish between worm propagation in 'P2P' and 'Super-P2P' systems: OPPS (Online P2P-based scan for P2P system Strategy) and OPSPS (Online P2P-based scan for Super P2P system Strategy) respectively represent online P2P-based attacks in the 'P2P' and 'Super-P2P' Systems. In the following we adopt the epidemic dynamic model [5] for worm propagation in the two aforementioned cases. Table 1 lists all parameters and notations in this paper.

Theorem 1: In OPPS approach, with $M(i,0)$ and $N(i,0)$ at time i, the next tick will have following equation:

$$E\left(i+1,0\right)=\left(N\left(i,0\right)-M\left(i,0\right)\right)\left[1-\left(1-\frac{1}{T-R}\right)^{(\min(\theta,S)*(E(i,0)+E(i,1)))}\right]. \quad (2)$$

Where $M(0,0)=0$ or M_0, $N(0,0)=T*P_2- R*P_1$. We have also recursive formulas as follows:

$$M(i+1,0)=M(i,0)+E(i+1,0).$$
$$N(i+1,0)=N(i,0) - E(i+1,0). \quad (3)$$

Theorem 2: In OPSPS approach, with $M(i,1)$ and $N(i,1)$ at time i, the next tick will have equation:

$$E\left(i+1,1\right)=\left(N\left(i,1\right)-M\left(i,1\right)\right)\left[1-\left(1-\frac{1}{R}\right)^{\sum_{j=1}^{E(i,1)}\min(r_j,S)+\sum_{j=1}^{E(i,0)}n_j}\right]. \quad (4)$$

Where r_j is total of input and output connections of each infected super manager node (at step i) in a specific level of the hierarchical structure, n_j is the number of infected super manager node's neighbors (at step i) in group j, $M(0,1)=0$ or M'_0, $N(0,1)=R*P_1$. We have also recursive formulas as below:

$$M(i+1,1)=M(i,1)+E(i+1,1).$$
$$N(i+1,1)=N(i,1) - E(i+1,1). \quad (5)$$

Note that Regarding to theorem 1 and theorem 2, one can easily results in $M(i)=M(i,0)+M(i,1)$, $N(i)=N(i,0)+N(i,1)$ and $E(i)=E(i,0)+E(i,1)$. We assume there is the same probability that initial infected nodes are chosen from both super manager nodes and normal manager nodes. Note that $(E(i,0)+E(i,1))$ * $\min(S, \theta)$ is the number of normal manager nodes are scanned by both infected super manager nodes and normal manager nodes, thus $\left(1-\frac{1}{T}\right)^{(E(i,0)+E(i,1))*\min(S,\theta)}$ is probability of not being among scanned normal manager nodes. As it follows from equation (2), we can understand that $E(i+1,0)$ is increased if S, θ and/or T are increased.

Moreover, note that $\sum_{j=1}^{E(i,1)} \min(r_j, S)$ is the number of super manager nodes that are scanned by infected super manager nodes in the hierarchical structure (we do not consider θ in comparison with S) and $\sum_{j=1}^{E(i,0)} n_j$ is the number of super manager nodes which are scanned by infected normal manager nodes. Therefore, $\left(1-\dfrac{1}{R}\right)^{\sum_{j=1}^{E(i,1)} \min(r_j,S)+\sum_{j=1}^{E(i,0)} n_j}$ is probability of not being among scanned super nodes. As it follows from equation (4), $E(i+1,1)$ is increased if S, r_j, n_j and/or R are increased.

4 Numerical Study

To study the model numerically, we need to obtain $\sum_{j=1}^{E(i,1)} \min(r_j,S)+\sum_{j=1}^{E(i,0)} n_j$. For this purpose we simulate a sample instance of a NMS. It contains 20 groups organized in 3 TLM groups, 8 MLM groups and 9 LLM groups. The system has 529 manager nodes which are divided into groups of 2 managers in TLM and maximum 32 managers in MLM and LLM. Then we make use of theorem 1 and theorem 2 (see section 3). In the figures appearing below we measure infection ratio (defined as: the ratio of accumulated number of infected nodes to the number of all vulnerable nodes) in terms of time (i.e., time steps).

First we investigate the effects of node type on the speed of worm propagation. For this purpose we assume that a normal node (or a super node) is infected. Then using the simulated instance of the architecture we obtain $\sum_{j=1}^{E(i,1)} \min(r_j,S)+\sum_{j=1}^{E(i,0)} n_j$ for each step $i+1$ from step i information. We also use equations (2) and (4) for obtaining $E(i)=E(i,0)+E(i,1)$ and depicting Fig.2. As follows from the figure, if the initial infected node is a super node, then the speed of worm propagation grows faster. The reason is that active worm can be propagated on several levels of the architecture's backbone. Therefore super manager nodes have important role from the viewpoint of defense policies.

In the second step, we investigate the impact of system size. We varied the number of manager members in both mid and low levels. The worm attack is initialized with one infected super manager node. As shown in Fig. 3 although the number of

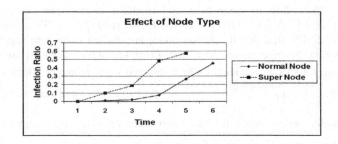

Fig. 2. Effect of node type on the speed of worm in the whole system

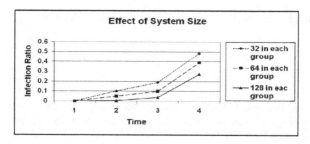

Fig. 3. Effect of system size on the speed of worm in the whole system

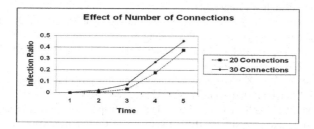

Fig. 4. Effect of number of connections on the speed of worm in the whole system

manager nodes is increased by factors of 2 and 4, it does not increase the speed of propagation with the same degrees (i.e., 2 and 4 times). This fact can be justified in that manager nodes are divided into many groups and thus in each group we have only slight increase in the number of neighbors. It should be recalled that the speed of worm propagation is decreased by increasing the number of managers inside of each group.

In the third experiment, we varied the number of connections (denoted by r_j in equation (4)) between groups in different levels of hierarchy (i.e., TLM, MLM, LLM; see Fig. 1). One may increase the number of connections in order to improve the availability of network management systems. Fig. 4 shows the result for 20 and 30 connections. We concluded that more connections lead to faster worm propagation. This issue suggests that the number of connections in the model plays a critical role in the NMS design because increasing the number of connections improves availability but from the other side makes the NMS more vulnerable to worm attacks.

5 Conclusion

We proposed a propagation model for active worm propagation in hierarchical P2P network management systems. The proposed analytical model is then used to study the impact of node type, system size and number of connections on the speed of worm propagation. The results of this paper are complementary to and in agreement with the simulation results in [3]. In the future works we intend to design effective defense systems against P2P based active worm attacks.

Acknowledgment. This work is supported by the Iran Telecommunication Research Center (ITRC).

References

1. Granville, L.Z., da Rosa, D.M., Panisson, A., Melchiors, C., Almeida, M.J.B., Tarouco, L.M.R.: Managing computer networks using peer-to-peer technologies. IEEE Communications Magazine 43, 62–68 (2005)
2. Arozarena, P., Frints, M., Collins, S., Fallon, L., Zach, M., Serrat, J., Nielsen, J.: Madeira: a peer-to-peer approach to network management. In: Proceedings of the Wireless World Research Forum, Shanghai, China (2006)
3. Saadat, Z.Z., Yousefi, S., Fathy, M.: Active Worm Propagation inHierarchical Peer-to-Peer Network Management Systems. In: Proceeding of the Second International Conference on Communication Theory, Reliability, and Quality of Service, France, pp. 52–57. IEEE computer society, Los Alamitos (2009)
4. Lia, T., Guan, Z., Wu, X.: Modeling and analyzing the spread of active worms based on P2P systems. Computers and Security 26(3), 213–218 (2007)
5. Yu, W., Boyer, C., Chellappan, S., Xuan, D.: Peer-to-peer system-based active worm attacks: modeling and analysis. In: IEEE International Conference, vol. 1(16-20), pp. 295–300 (2005)
6. Ma, J., Chen, X., Xiang, G.: Modeling Passive Worm Propagation in Peer-to-Peer System. In: 2006 International Conference on Computational Intelligence and Security, vol. 2(3-6), pp. 1129–1132 (2006)
7. Chen, G., Gray, R.S.: Simulating non-scanning worms on peer-to-peer networks. In: ACM International Conference Proceeding Series: Proceedings of the 1st international conference on Scalable information systems, vol. 152, Article No. 29 (2006)
8. Yao, Y., Luo, X., Gao, F., Ai, S.: Research of a Potential Worm Propagation Model based on Pure P2P Principle. In: ICCT 2006, International Conference Proceeding Series: Proceedings of the 1st international conference on Computer, pp. 1–4 (2006)
9. Stoica, I., Morris, R., Liben-Nowell, D., Karger, D.R., Kaashoek, M.F., Dabek, F., Balakrishnan, H.: Chord: a scalable peer-to-peer lookup protocol for internet application. IEEE/ACM Transactions on Networking (TON) 11(1), 17–32 (2003)

Security Enhancement on an Improvement on Two Remote User Authentication Scheme Using Smart Cards

HanCheng Hsiang[1], TienHo Chen[2], and WeiKuan Shih[2]

[1] Department of Information Management, Vanung University, Taiwan, R.O.C
[2] Department of Computer Science, National Tsing Hua University, No. 101, Kuang Fu Rd,
Sec. 2, 300 HsingChu, Taiwan, ROC
{shc,riverchen,wshih}@rtlab.cs.nthu.edu.tw

Abstract. In 2004, Ku et al. proposed an improved efficient remote authentication scheme using smart cards to repair the security pitfalls found in Chien et al.'s scheme, in which only few hashing operations are required. Later, Yoon et al. presented an enhancement on Ku et al.'s scheme. Recently, Wang et al. showed that both Ku et al.'s scheme and Yoon et al.'s scheme are still vulnerable to the guessing attack, forgery attack and denial of service (DoS) attack. Then, proposed an efficient improvement over Ku et al.'s and Yoon et al.'s schemes with more security. In this paper, we state that Wang et al.'s scheme is vulnerable to the impersonation attack and parallel session attack. A modification to enhance the security of Wang et al.'s scheme is proposed. Our scheme is suitable for applications with high security requirement.

Keywords: Authentication; cryptography; password; impersonation attack; parallel session attack.

1 Introduction

Remote user authentication scheme allows a server to check the authenticity of a remote user through insecure communication channel. Password-based authentication schemes have been widely deployed to check the validity of the login message and authenticate the user. In 1981, Lamport [1] proposed the first well-known password based remote user authentication scheme without using encryption techniques. Since then, some schemes [2, 3] have been proposed to improve security, cost or efficiency. These schemes suffer from the risk of a modified verifier table and the cost of protecting and maintaining the verifier table on remote system. If the verification table is stolen by the adversary, the system will be partially or totally broken.

Owing to the low cost, the cryptographic capacity and the portability, smart cards have been widely adopted in remote authentication schemes [4–5, 8-14]. In 2000, Hwang and Li [11] developed a password based remote user authentication scheme by using smart cards. However, Hwang and Li's scheme was only to maintain a secret key without storing a password table in the system. The scheme could not only withstand an impersonation attack [12], but also the user can not freely change his password. In 2000, Sun [13] proposed an efficient password based remote user

D. Ślęzak et al. (Eds.): FGCN/ACN 2009, CCIS 56, pp. 65–73, 2009.

authentication scheme by using smart cards. Sun's scheme requires only several hash operations instead of the costly modular exponentiations. However, Sun's scheme does not provide mutual authentication. Furthermore, the user also has to remember a pseudo-random number as his password and can not change his password [13]. In 2002, Chien et al. [4] proposed an efficient password based remote user authentication scheme, and claimed that their scheme has the merits of providing mutual authentication, freely choosing password, no verification table, and involving only few hashing operations. Later, Ku-Chen [5] showed that Chien et al.'s scheme is vulnerable to a reflection attack [6], insider attack [7] and is not reparable [8] when a users permanent secret is compromised. An improved scheme [5] was given to prohibit the weaknesses of Chien et al.'s scheme. But, the improved scheme is still susceptible to parallel session attack and is insecure for changing the user's password in password change phase. Hence, Yoon et al. [9] presented an enhancement to resolve such problems. Recently, Wang et al. [10] showed that both Ku et al.'s scheme and Yoon et al.'s scheme are still vulnerable to the guessing attack, forgery attack and denial of service (DoS) attack. To remedy these flaws, they proposed an efficient improvement over Ku et al.'s and Yoon et al.'s schemes with more security.

However, we found that Wang et al.'s scheme is still vulnerable to the impersonation attack [12] and parallel session attack [5]. We propose an enhancement of Wang et al.'s scheme to resolve the problems. The proposed scheme not only inherits the merits of their scheme but also enhances the security of their scheme.

The rest of this paper is organized as follows. In Section 2, a brief review of Wang et al.'s scheme is given. Section 3, describes a cryptanalysis of Wang et al.'s scheme. Our enhanced scheme is proposed in Section 4. The security analysis of the proposed improved scheme is presented in Section 5. Finally, some concluding remarks are included in the last section.

2   Review of Wang et al.'s Scheme

The notations used throughout this paper can be summarized as follows:

- U: the user.
- ID: the identity of U.
- PW: the password of U.
- S: the remote server.
- x: the permanent secret key of S.
- h ( ): a cryptographic unkeyed hash function.
- h_p ( ): a cryptographic keyed hash function with secret s.
- $\Rightarrow$: a secure channel.
- $\rightarrow$: a common channel.
- ‖: string concatenation operation

In this section, we briefly review Wang et al.'s scheme [10]. There are four phases in Wang et al.'s scheme, namely: registration, login, verification and password change. Different phases work as follows:

2.1 Registration Phase

This phase is invoked whenever U initially registers or reregisters to S. The following steps are involved in this phase.

1. U selects a random number b and computes $h\,(b \oplus PW)$.
2. $U \Rightarrow S$: ID, $h\,(b \oplus PW)$.
3. S performs the following computations:
   $P = h(ID \oplus x)$
   $R = p \oplus h(b \oplus PW)$
   $V = h_p\,(h(b \oplus PW))$
4. $S \Rightarrow U$: a smart card containing V, R, and $h\,(\ )$.
5. U enters b into his smart card.

Note that U's smart card contains V, R, b, $h_p(\ )$, and $h\,(\ )$.

2.2 Login Phase

Whenever U wants to login S, the following operations will perform:

1. U inserts his smart card into the smart card reader, and then enters ID and PW.
2. U's smart card performs the following computations:
   $p = R \oplus h(b \oplus PW)$ and checks whether $h_p(h(b \oplus PW))? = V$ holds or not. If not, smart card terminates this session.
3. Smart card generates a random number r, and performs the following computations:
   $C_1 = p \oplus h\,(r \oplus b)$.
   $C_2 = h_p(h(r \oplus b) \oplus T_U)$, where T_U denotes U's current timestamp.
4. $U \to S$: $C = \{ID, C_1, C_2, T_U\}$.

2.3 Verification Phase

After the message C is received, remote server S and the smart card execute the following operations.

1. If either the format of ID is invalid or $T_U = T_S$, where T_S is the current timestamp of S, then S rejects U's login request. If $(T_S - T_U) > \Delta T$, where ΔT denotes the expected valid time interval for transmission delay, then S rejects the login request.
2. S computes $p = h(ID \oplus x)$, $C_1' = p \oplus C_1$, and $C_2' = h_p(C_1' \oplus T_U)$. If the computed result C_2' equals the received C_2, S accepts U's login request and computes $C_3 = h_p(C_1' \oplus T_S)$, where T_S denotes S's current timestamp. Otherwise, S rejects U's login request.
3. $S \to U$: T_S, C_3.
4. Upon receiving the message $\{T_S, C_3\}$, U verifies either T_S is invalid or $T_S = T_U$, U terminates this session. Otherwise, U computes $C_3' = h_p(h\,(r \oplus b) \oplus T_S)$ and then compares the result C_3' to the received C_3. If they are equal, U successfully authenticates S, otherwise U terminates the operation. In addition, since r is randomly generated in each login phase, $C_1' = h(r \oplus b)$ shared between U and S can be used as the session key for the subsequent private communication.

2.4 Password Change Phase

This phase is invoked whenever U wants to change his password PW with a new one, say PW_{new}.

1. U inserts his smart card into the smart card reader, enters ID and PW, and requests to change password.
2. U's smart card computes $p^* = R \oplus h\,(b \oplus PW)$ and $V^* = h_p^*(h\,(b \oplus PW))$.
3. U's smart card verifies V^* and stored V (in smart card).
4. If they are equal, then U selects new password PW_{new}, otherwise the smart card rejects the password change request.
5. U's smart card computes $R_{new} = p^* \oplus h\,(b \oplus PW_{new})$ and $V_{new} = h_p^*(h\,(b \oplus PW_{new}))$, and then replaces R, V with R_{new}, V_{new}, respectively. Now, new password is successfully updated.

3   Cryptanalysis of Wang et al.'s Scheme

In this section, we will show that the scheme of Wang et al. [10] is still vulnerable to impersonation attack [12, 14], and parallel session attack [5, 9]

3.1   Impersonation Attack

Assume that an adversary has intercepted one of the legal users U_i's previous login message $\{ID_i,\ C_1,\ C_2,\ T_U\}$. If the adversary attempts to impersonate U_i to login S at time T^* $(>T_U)$, an impersonation attack can be performed as given below:

Step A1.   The adversary computes $\Delta t = T_U \oplus T^*$ and $C_1^* = C_1 \oplus \Delta t$.

Step A2.   Adversary $\to S$: $\{ID_i,\ C_1^*,\ C_2,\ T^*\}$.

Step A3.   Since T^* is valid, S will proceed to compute $p = h(ID \oplus x)$, $C_1' = p \oplus C_1^*$ $(= p \oplus p \oplus h\,(r \oplus b) \oplus \Delta t)$, which will yield $h\,(r \oplus b) \oplus \Delta t$.

Step A4. S computes $C_2' = h_p(C_1' \oplus T^*)$ $(= h_p(h\,(r \oplus b) \oplus \Delta t \oplus T_U \oplus \Delta t)$, which will yield $h_p(h\,(r \oplus b) \oplus T_U)$. Since the computed result C_2' equals the received C_2, S accepts the adversary's login request.

By generalizing the above attack, the adversary can easily imitate any user to login S at any time.

3.2   Parallel Session Attack

An adversary without knowing user's passwords want to masquerade as a legal user U by creating a valid login message from the eavesdropped communication between remote server S and U. The adversary applies the following steps can successfully make a valid login request to masquerade as the legal user U: Intercepts the login message $C = \{ID,\ C_1,\ C_2,\ T_U\}$ which is sent by the user U to S. If $\{ID,\ C_1,\ C_2,\ T_U\}$ is valid, the identification of U is authenticated and S responses $\{C_3,\ T_S\}$ to U, where T_S is the current time stamp. Intercepts the response message $\{C_3,\ T_S\}$.

Once the adversary intercepts the messages, he masquerades as the legal user U to starts a new session with the S. The adversary sends a fabricated login message $C_f = \{ID, C_1, C_2^*, T_U^*\}$, where $C_2^* = C_3$ and $T_U^* = T_S$. After receiving the adversary's login request, the S performs the following steps.

1. Check the valid of ID and T_S, and $T_U^* = T_S^*$, where T_S^* denotes S's current time-stamp. Because of the transmission delay or the adversary delay on purpose, the T_U^* is not equal to T_S^*. The S will continue process the following steps.
2. S computes $p = h(ID \oplus x)$, $C_1' = p \oplus C_1 = p \oplus p \oplus h(r \oplus b) = h(r \oplus b)$, and $C_2' = h_p(C_1' \oplus T_U^*) = h(h(r \oplus b) \oplus T_S)$. As receiving U_i's login request, the login message $\{ID, C_1, C_2^*, T_u^*\}$ will pass the user authentication of the Wang et al.'s scheme because $C_2^* = C_3 = h(h(r \oplus b) \oplus T_S)$, the computed result C_2' equals the received C_2^*.

Finally, S responses the message $\{C_3^*, T_S^*\}$ to U, where $C_3^* = h(h(r \oplus b) \oplus T_S^*)$ and T_S^* is S's current timestamp. The adversary intercepts and drops this message.

Most recently, an advanced collision attack on iterative hash algorithms have showed [15–17], such as the widely used SHA, MD4, MD5 etc. Wang et al. [10] pointed out that the security of Ku et al.'s scheme completely relied on the one way property of hash function. Thus the Ku et al.'s scheme suffers from the potential risk of off-line attack and the adversary can impersonate U to login anytime. When the secret information $h(EID \oplus x)$ is revealed, the system secret key x may also be broken under the advanced collision attack due to the fact that EID and $h(EID \oplus x)$ are known to the adversary and both of them keep invariant in each login request. To overcome the security flaws, Wang et al.'s scheme provides two-variant hashing operations for resisting guessing attack, forgery attack and advance hash collision attacks[15–17] , even if all the information stored in smart card or transmitted via insecure channel is extracted by adversary. Unfortunately, we found that Wang et al.'s scheme [10] is still vulnerable to the impersonation attack [12, 14] and parallel session attack [5, 9] where the adversary can easily impersonate any user to login the server at any time. The security of Wang et al.'s scheme is still not enough.

4   Our Enhanced Scheme

In this section, we propose an enhancement to Wang et al.'s scheme that can withstand the security flaws described in previous sections. Our improved scheme enhances the security of Wang et al.'s scheme; the proposed scheme performs as follows.

4.1   Registration Phase

This phase is invoked whenever U initially registers or reregisters to S. The following steps are involved in this phase.

1. U selects a random number b and computes $h(b \oplus PW)$.
2. $U \Rightarrow S: ID, h(b \oplus PW)$.
3. S performs the following computations:

$P = h(ID \oplus x)$

$R = p \oplus h(b \oplus PW)$

$V = h_p(h(b \oplus PW))$

4. $S \Rightarrow U$: a smart card containing V, R, and $h(\ )$.
5. U enters b into his smart card.

Note that U's smart card contains V, R, b, $h_p(\ )$, and $h(\ )$.

4.2 Login Phase

Whenever U wants to login S, the following operations will perform:

1. U inserts his smart card into the smart card reader, and then enters ID and PW.
2. U's smart card performs the following computations: $p = R \oplus h(b \oplus PW)$ and checks whether $h_p(h(b \oplus PW))?=V$ holds or not. If not, smart card terminates this session.
3. Smart card generates a random number r, and performs the following computations:

    $C_1 = p \oplus h(r \oplus b)$.

    $C_2 = h_p(h(r \oplus b) \| T_U)$, where T_U denotes U's current timestamp.
4. $U \rightarrow S$: $C = \{ID, C_1, C_2, T_U\}$.

4.3 Verification Phase

After the message C is received, remote server S and the smart card execute the following operations.

1. If either the format of ID is invalid or $T_u = T_s$, where Ts is the current timestamp of S, then S rejects U's login request. If $(T_s - T_u) > \Delta T$, where ΔT denotes the expected valid time interval for transmission delay, then S rejects the login request.
2. S computes $p = h(ID \oplus x)$, $C_1' = p \oplus C_1$, and $C_2' = h_p(C_1' \| T_U)$. If the computed result C_2' equals the received C_2, S accepts U's login request and computes $C_3 = h_p(C_1' \oplus T_S \| p)$, where T_S denotes S's current timestamp. Otherwise, S rejects U's login request.
3. $S \rightarrow U$: T_S, C_3.
4. Upon receiving the message $\{T_S, C_3\}$, U verifies either T_S is invalid or $T_S = T_U$, U terminates this session. Otherwise, U computes $C_3' = h_p(h(r \oplus b) \oplus T_S \| p)$ and then compares the result C_3' to the received C_3. If they are equal, U successfully authenticates S, otherwise U terminates the operation. In addition, since r is randomly generated in each login phase, $C_1' = h(r \oplus b)$ shared between U and S can be used as the session key for the subsequent private communication.

4.4 Password Change Phase

This phase is invoked whenever U wants to change his password PW with a new one, say PW_{new}.

1. U inserts his smart card into the smart card reader, enters ID and PW, and requests to change password.
2. U's smart card computes $p^* = R \oplus h\,(b \oplus PW)$ and $V^* = h_p{}^*(h\,(b \oplus PW))$.
3. U's smart card verify V^* and stored V in smart card.
4. If they are equal, then U select new password PW_{new}, otherwise the smart card rejects the password change request.
5. U's smart card compute $R_{new} = p^* \oplus h\,(b \oplus PW_{new})$ and $V_{new} = h_p{}^*(h\,(b \oplus PW_{new}))$, and then replaces R, V with R_{new}, V_{new}, respectively. Now, new password is successfully updated.

5 Security Analysis

The enhanced scheme is a modified form of the original scheme: Wang et al.'s scheme. The security analysis has been already discussed and demonstrated in [10]. Therefore, this section will only discuss the enhanced security features of the proposed scheme.

5.1 Impersonation Attack Resistance

An adversary attempts to intercept one of the legal users U_i's previous login message $\{ID_i, C_1, C_2, T_U\}$, if the adversary attempts to impersonate U_i to login S at time T^* ($>T_U$), then computes $\Delta t = T_U \oplus T^*$ and $C_1{}^* = C_1 \oplus \Delta t$. The adversary sends the modified login message $C = \{ID_i, C_1{}^*, C_2, T^*\}$ to S. After the message C is received, this impersonation attempt will fail in the step 2 of the authentication phase, because S computes $p = h(ID \oplus x)$, $C_1{}' = p \oplus C_1 (= p \oplus p \oplus h\,(r \oplus b) \oplus \Delta t)$, and $C_2{}' = h_p((C_1{}' \oplus p) \parallel T_U) = h_p((h\,(r \oplus b) \oplus \Delta t) \parallel T_U)$. Because the computed result $C_2{}'$ doesn't equal the received $C_2 = h_p(h\,(r \oplus b) \parallel T_U)$, then S rejects U's login request.

5.2 Parallel Session Attack Resistance

In the Wang et al.'s scheme, because C_2 and C_3 are all using the same function $h_p(h\,(r \oplus b) \oplus T)$, an attacker can always send (C_3, T_s) to fabricated login request after intercepting the communication between S and U. The proposed scheme can prevent the parallel session attack in Wang et al.'s scheme because C_2 and C_3 use the different function. An attacker without knowing user's passwords want to masquerade as a legal user U by creating a valid login message from the eavesdropped communication between remote server S and U. The attacker applies the following steps cannot successfully make a valid login request to masquerade as the legal user U:

The attacker intercepts the login message $\{ID, C_1, C_2, T_U\}$ and the response message $\{T_S, C_3\}$. Starts a new session with the S by sending a fabricated login message $\{ID, C_1, C_3, T_S\}$. After receiving the login request, S checks the valid of ID and T_S. Then computes $p = h(ID \oplus x)$, $C_1{}' = p \oplus C_1$, and $C_2{}' = h_p(C_1{}' \parallel T_S) (= h_p(h\,(r \oplus b) \parallel T_S))$. Because $C_3 = h_p(C_1{}' \oplus T_S \parallel p)$, $C_2{}' \neq C_3$, S rejects the login request.

6 Conclusion

In this paper, we reviewed some secure schemes which have been proposed for user authentication based on smart cards. Wang et al's scheme is more flawless among the related user authentication schemes. However, we found that Wang et al's scheme is vulnerable to the impersonation attack and parallel session attack. The two flaws can cause the scheme unsecured, because the attacker can successfully impersonate to be the legal user to login and use the server resources. Hence, we proposed an enhancement of Wang et al.'s scheme. The proposed scheme is still completely based on cryptographic hash functions, and does not maintain any verification table on the remote server. The proposed scheme not only inherits the merits of their scheme but also enhances the security of their scheme. Moreover, the impersonation attack and parallel session attack are completely solved without raising any computation cost.

References

1. Lamport, L.: Password authentication with insecure communication. Communications of the ACM 24(11), 770–772 (1981)
2. Lennon, R.E., Matyas, S.M., Mayer, C.H.: Cryptographic authentication of time-invariant quantities. IEEE Transactions on Communications 29(6), 773–777 (1981)
3. Yen, S.M., Liao, K.H.: Shared authentication token secure against replay and weak key attack. Information Processing Letters, 78–80 (1997)
4. Chien, H.Y., Jan, J.K., Tseng, Y.M.: An efficient and practical solution to remote authentication smart card. Computers and Security 21(4), 372–375 (2002)
5. Ku, W.C., Chen, S.M.: Weaknesses and improvements of an efficient password based remote user authentication scheme using smart cards. IEEE Transactions on Consumer Electronics 50(1), 204–207 (2004)
6. Mitchell, C.: Limitations of challenge-response entity authentication. Electronic Letters 25(17), 1195–1196 (1989)
7. Ku, W.C., Chen, C.M., Lee, H.L.: Cryptanalysis of a variant of Peyravian-Zunic's password authentication scheme. IEICE Transactions on Communication E86-B(5), 1682–1684 (2003)
8. Hsu, C.L.: Security of Chien et al.'s remote user authentication scheme using smart cards. Computer Standards & Interfaces 26(3), 167–169 (2004)
9. Yoon, E.J., Ryu, E.K., Yoo, K.Y.: Further improvement of an efficient password based remote user authentication scheme using smart cards. IEEE Transactions on Consumer Electronics 50(2), 612–614 (2004)
10. Wang, X.M., Zhang, W.F., Zhang, J.S., Khan, M.K.: Cryptanalysis and improvement on two efficient remote user authentication scheme using smart cards. Computer Standards & Interfaces 29, 507–512 (2007)
11. Hwang, M.S., Li, L.H.: A new remote user authentication scheme using smart cards. IEEE Transactions on Consumer Electronics 46(1), 28–30 (2000)
12. Chan, C.K., Cheng, L.M.: Cryptanalysis of a remote user authentication scheme using smart cards. IEEE Transactions on Consumer Electronics 46(4), 992–993 (2000)
13. Sun, H.M.: An efficient remote user authentication scheme using smart cards. IEEE Transactions on Consumer Electronics 46(4), 958–961 (2000)

14. Ku, W.C., Chang, S.T.: Impersonation attack on a dynamic ID based remote user authentication using smartcards. IEICE Transaction on Communication 88–b (5), 2165–2167 (2005)
15. Wang, X., Guo, F., Lai, X., Yu, H.: Collisions for Hash Functions MD4,MD5, HAVAL-128 and RIPEMD, Rump Session of Crypto 2004 and IACR Eprint Archive (2004)
16. Wang, X., Yin, Y.L., Yu, H.: Finding collisions in the full SHA1 (2005),
    http://www.infosec.sdu.edu.cn/paper/
    sha1-crypto-auth-new-2-yao.pdf
17. Wang, X., Yu, H.B.: How to break MD5 and other hash functions. In: Cramer, R. (ed.) EUROCRYPT 2005. LNCS, vol. 3494, pp. 19–35. Springer, Heidelberg (2005)

Improving the Performance of Beacon Safety Message Dissemination in Vehicular Networks Using Kalman Filter Estimation

Mohammadreza Armaghan[1], Mahmood Fathy[2], and Saleh Yousefi[3]

[1] Department of Computer Engineering, Islamic Azad University, Tehran-South Branch, Tehran, Iran
[2] Iran University of Science and Technology, Tehran, Iran
[3] Computer Department, Faculty of Engineering, Urmia University, Iran
mohammadreza.armaghan@gmail.com, mahfathy@iust.ac.ir,
s.yousefi@urmia.ac.ir

Abstract. This paper proposed an estimation method based on Kalman filter to decrease the number of disseminated beacon safety messages in Vehicular Ad-Hoc Networks (VANETs). The ultimate goal is to reduce the number of packet collisions which in turn results in fresher information to be available for vehicles. The proposed method is implemented in application layer and thus applicable to any MAC layer including IEEE 802.11p (the MAC of DSRC standard). In the proposed algorithm, each vehicle estimates its location ahead for several intervals and sends them out along with actual current position. During the time that estimated information is available, there are no fresh transmissions unless some estimation error is detected. Also adaptive parameters exist in the algorithm. Results of extensive simulation study show that the proposed algorithm significantly improves the QoS of the beacon safety application which leads to increasing safety level in vehicular networks.

Keywords: safety applications, inter-vehicle communications, DSRC, Kalman filter.

1 Introduction

During the last decades, prevention of traffic causalities has been of great importance.

VANET does not need any infrastructure and connection links between nodes are established when their distance is less than a vehicle's transmission range. VANETs are based on short-range wireless transmission (e.g., IEEE 802.11). The Federal Communications Commission (FCC) has allocated 75 MHz of spectrum in the 5.9 GHz band for Dedicated Short Range Communication (DSRC) to enhance the safety and productivity of the nation's transportation system [1]. DSRC ruling has permitted both safety and non-safety (commercial) applications, provided safety messages are accorded priority. As a part of DSRC standard, IEEE 802.11p [2] improves IEEE 802.11 to deal with vehicular environment which includes data exchange between high-speed vehicles, and between vehicles and the roadside infrastructure. VANETs

D. Ślęzak et al. (Eds.): FGCN/ACN 2009, CCIS 56, pp. 74–82, 2009.

tend to be very challenging and a comprehensive survey about communication challenges is provided in [3]. Although many decisions in this field have not been made yet, according to FCC frequency allocation we can categorize two main classes of applications for vehicular ad hoc networks: comfort and safety. In comfort applications, the goal is to improve passenger comfort and traffic efficiency. In safety applications, the goal is to improve the safety level of passengers by exchanging safety relevant information between vehicles. Some examples are: cooperative forward collision warning, left/right turn assistant, lane changing warning, stop sign movement assistant and road-condition warning. The safety massages can be classified in two categories: alarm and beacon, which have different dissemination policies and roles in safety improvement. Alarm messages are issued by vehicles to announce others about the already happened events in a specific point of a road, like a car crash, icy surface, etc. Whereas, beacon messages are issued periodically. Using the received beacons, vehicles try to inhibit possible events (not already occurred) such as erroneous lane changing, forward collisions, wrong left/right turning, alarm for unsafe distance, etc.

However, due to DSRC standard suggested for VANETs, collisions between simultaneous transmissions are inevitable. This is indeed because the MAC layer is IEEE 802.11p and has CSMA/CA nature. This issue causes sever challenge for safety application which demands a high degree of certainty. This paper proposed an estimation method based on Kalman filter [4] to decrease the number of issued messages and thus reducing the number of collisions. The proposed method is implemented in application layer and thus applicable to any MAC layer including IEEE 802.11p (i.e., DFRC). In this method, each vehicle estimates its location for several intervals and sends them out along with actual current position. The estimation is done based on the previous history and record of the vehicle's location. During the time that estimated information is available, there are no fresh transmissions unless some estimation error is detected. Therefore, the number of message transmissions is decreased. In other words, the vehicle transmits only if the error between its current actual location and the estimated location (which is already transmitted) is more than a threshold. In this method two adaptive parameters exist: the number of estimation and the estimation error threshold which are adjusted optimally to increase the safety performance. Since each vehicle keeps only one Kalman estimator, the algorithm requires low processing power and memory usage which sufficiently match the capabilities of equipment inside vehicles. Note that our simulation done with FleetNET [5] movement patterns shows the significance of using Kalman estimation as the number of successful estimations remain acceptable during the simulation time. Moreover the average estimation error stays quite low after a short time from the beginning. The above issue leads to decreasing the number of packet (beacon message) collisions which results in increase of information availability, i.e., the amount of correct and precise information about neighbouring vehicles. It is obvious that the success of any safety application depends directly on the degree of information availability.

The rest of this paper is organized as follows. Section 2 reviews related work. In section 3, the proposed method is described. In section 4, simulations framework is introduced. In section 5, the results of simulations are presented along with some discussion. Finally the paper is concluded in section 6.

2 Related Work

Beacon safety message dissemination tends to be very challenging. In [6] the authors used extensive simulation study in order to study the related challenges. The paper suggests that in order to achieve high QoS in beacon message dissemination, one way is to decrease the number of transmitted messages (i.e., increasing the transmission interval). However, this may lead to deteriorating the safety level which may be provided. This paper proposed a way to achieve this goal while the safety level is preserved in an acceptable level.

Using Kalman filter for location estimation in vehicular ad hoc networks is studied in few work. In [7] the authors presented a location management protocol, call MALM (Mobility-Assisted Location Management), to provide location service to vehicles in VANETs. In MALM, a vehicle calculates the current location of other vehicles by using Kalman filtering based on the historical location information of other nodes. Theoretical analysis is provided to show that MALM is able to achieve high location information availability in the network. Performance evaluation of MALM coupled with a geographical routing protocol in VANETs showed via extensive simulations.

The most related works in the literature to our work is probably the works presented on [8], [9]. There, the authors described a communication scheme for Cooperative Active Safety System (CASS). CASS uses information communicated from neighboring vehicles via wireless communication in order to actively evaluate driving situations and provide warnings or other forms of assistance to drivers. The paper suggests that the CASS could be enabled by broadcasting messages, as little as once every 500 msec. In the proposed scheme, each vehicle manages three location estimators based on extended kalman filter including Self estimator, Neighbor estimator (for all the neighboring vehicles) and Remote estimator. A vehicle's decision to communicate or not communicate at any instant of time is made based on the differences between the outputs of estimators. However our work is different from this work in the following cases. Firstly, we use one estimator in each vehicle due to the low capacity of processing and memory usage in corresponding to VANET equipment inside vehicle, whereas in [8], [9] the number of estimators equal to the number of neighbors which could be very large in a dense traffic. Secondly, in [8], [9] the simulation is focused on estimation part of the work and the communication part is not studied. Therefore, the lost packets caused due to communication between vehicles are not taken into account. However, in our work we simulated the VANET formed between vehicles using GloMosim simulator along with realistic movement patterns.

3 Proposed Method

We assume that each vehicle periodically observes its location in each 100 milliseconds. This number has been found out to be reasonable in previous research [10]. The location information is accessible through the GPS. Then a Kalman filter algorithm is implemented in each vehicle to estimate the longitudinal and lateral location of the vehicle. The Kalman filter is a set of mathematical equations that provides an efficient

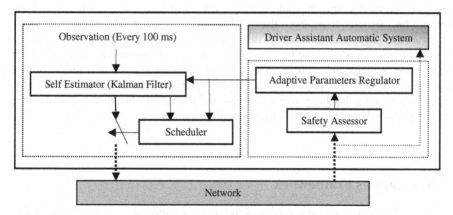

Fig. 1. Method Block Diagram

computational (recursive) means to estimate the state of a process, in a way that it minimizes the mean of the squared error. The filter is very powerful in several aspects: it supports estimations of past, present, and even future states, and it can do so even when the precise nature of the modeled system is unknown [4]. The parameters of Kalman filter algorithm has been adjusted through plenty of simulation experiments to obtain the best estimation (less error rate and suitable training time).

As demonstrated in the block diagram of Fig.1, in this method only one estimator in each vehicle is performed. This estimator calculates next location information for several steps (each step is 100 ms). The Scheduler block determines if any transmission is necessary or not. In each 100 milliseconds, the scheduler allows the transmission if the error of previous transmitted location (obtained by estimation) from the actual location is more than a threshold. Fresh transmission is also done if no estimations are available (i.e., after estimation steps). In other words, when neighbours are informed about vehicle location properly, no transmission is done.

In each transmitted packet (beacon message), actual location information, actual speed and estimated longitudinal and lateral locations for next intervals are available. The threshold of lateral and longitudinal location estimation error and the number of estimation steps (number of next locations will be estimated by estimator for next time intervals that each interval or step is 100 ms) are of adaptive parameters which are very important and critical in the success of the safety application. In this paper we propose the following procedure for this purpose. When a packet (beacon message) is received by a vehicle, the distance and the relative speed between transmitter and the receiver (i.e., the vehicle) is calculated (location and speed of transmitter exist in each packet). By considering these two factors, the safety or unsafely state of the situation is recognized. The main goal of aforementioned adaptive parameters (i.e., error threshold and number of estimation steps) is to provide a safe situation for the vehicle and its neighbours. If the distance between two vehicles (meter) is less than absolute value of relative speed (meter/second), receiver vehicle recognizes an unsafe state. Hence adaptive parameters of that vehicle are adjusted in the following way: the threshold of longitudinal and lateral estimation error respectively decreases to 1 meter and 0.5 meter, and the number of estimation steps reduces to 2. Otherwise if the state is considered as safe, the threshold of longitudinal estimation error increases to 2 meters and lateral estimation error raises to 1 meter and the number of estimation steps increases to 9. For more attention in distance (denoted with d) and relative speed (denoted with v) comparison, the maximum longitudinal estimation error of the transmitted location, which equals with 2 meters, has been added to absolute value of relative speed. For raising the safety, another constant quantity can be added through safety experts viewpoints that here, it denoted with s. In other words, when the relationship (1) is established then the safety situation will be gained.

$$(|v| + 2 + s) < d. \tag{1}$$

4   Simulations Framework

In order to evaluate the effectiveness of the proposed approach, we made use of Glomosim 2.03 [11] network simulator. The above described blocks have been coded completely in the simulator. All possible efforts have been done in order to make the implementation as realistic as possible. Thus the codes can be implemented in a real-life environment easily. To have a more precise simulation, we used the movement patterns published by European project FleetNet [5]. The particular movement pattern which is used in this simulation includes 270 vehicles with the speed 24 to 44 meters/second in a unidirectional highway with three lanes which have been distributed with the traffic density of 6 vehicles in each kilometre in each lane. Table 1 shows the detailed simulation parameters.

A typical one-hop broadcast algorithm was implemented and the functionality of the algorithm was examined. It is basically because the results of our preliminary simulation showed that multi-hop transmission for beacon messages lead to large number of collisions. Thus, the performance deteriorates severely and it is not a good option. Therefore, we continued our work with single-hop transmissions. This finding is also in agreement with [10] which suggests single-hop transmission for many safety

Table 1. Simulation setting parameters

Parameter	Value
Propagation model	Two-ray-ground
Radio range (m)	500
MAC type	IEEE 802.11 (the base for DSRC standard)
Channel bandwidth (Mbps)	6
Traffic type	CBR (UDP)
Message payload size (byte)	512
Number of vehicle	270
Speed (m/s)	24, 44
Traffic density (vehicle/km/lane)	6
Number of lanes	3
Simulation time (s)	60
Observation period (ms)	100
Number of estimation steps	adaptively set (mentioned in the text)
Longitudinal and lateral error threshold	adaptively set (mentioned in the text)

applications including beacon based safety applications. Furthermore, according to [10] many safety applications require beacon messages to be sent with transmission ranges from 50 to 300 m. Thus, vehicles' transmission is set to 500 meters.

As mentioned in the previous section, the actual transmission is conditional and the condition is checked every 100 milliseconds. Thus the interval of message propagation is not constant but it varies from 100 to 900 milliseconds (an integer scale of 100ms). The execution interval of the Kalman filter program is 100 milliseconds. Since the estimator works is based on the previous history of the vehicle's location, it needs some initial warm-up time to be tuned properly. The simulation showed that the warm-up time required for accurate estimation (i.e., the estimation with error less than threshold) varies between 4 to 8 seconds.

5   Results and Discussions

In this section, we present the most important results of our simulation study. The goal is to evaluate different aspects of the proposed algorithm.

First, we show how much the proposed algorithm is successful in decreasing the number of disseminated beacons. Based on the discussion of previous section, it is expected that the number of sent packets (beacon messages) is decreased markedly. Simulation results confirm this expectation.

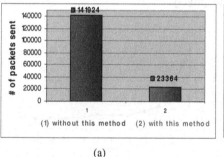
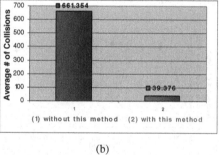

| (a) | (b) |

Fig. 2. a. Number of packets (beacon messages) disseminated from all vehicles, (1) without this method, (2) with this method **b.** Average number of packet (beacon message) collisions for all vehicles, (1) without this method, (2) with this method

As illustrated in Fig.2.a, the number of disseminations has decreased extremely in presence of our proposed algorithm. In other words, the dissemination time interval for beacon messages dissemination has increased. Note that this interval varies between 100ms to 900ms depending on the estimation error.

Therefore, channel load has decreased which in turn leads to decreasing the number of collisions. Fig.2.b shows this phenomenon. As the figure shows, the salient decrease of packet (beacon messages) collision is observable. This issue results in increase of information availability, i.e., the amount of correct and precise information about neighbouring vehicles. It is obvious that the success of any safety application depends directly on the degree of information availability.

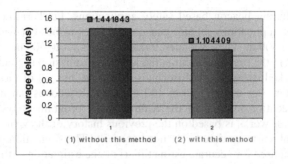

Fig. 3. Average end-to-end delay for all vehicles (in disseminated beacon messages), (1) without this method, (2) with this method

Moreover, another result of decreasing the channel load is decreasing delay. As Fig.3 shows, the average delay improved or decreased after implementation of the new method in application layer in each vehicle. This finding is also important due to criticality of delay in safety applications.

Next we show whether the Klaman filter estimation matches special characteristics of vehicle movements. For this purpose, we use real-life movement patterns published by FleetNet project [5]. As mentioned before, the Kalman estimator calculates a number of next steps based on the previous history of vehicle's movement. The number of steps is not pre-determined and is adjusted adaptively.

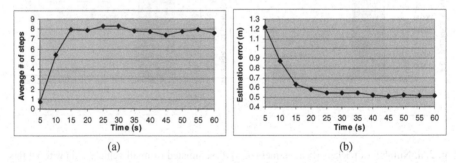

(a)   (b)

Fig. 4. a. Average number of steps (number of estimated location for next time intervals that was corrected. Thus, neighboring vehicles used them) for all vehicles **b.** Average longitudinal estimation error for all vehicles.

We show in Fig.4.a the average number of steps that the estimator is used during the time. As the figure shows, Kalman estimation is quite successful as the number of steps remains around 8 most of the time. This finding confirms that using Kalman estimation is quite successful in estimation of vehicle's movement and thus improving the safety of beacon based safety application.

Advantage of using Kalman filter
In order to estimate, extrapolation methods, neural network models, and classic mathematical methods are studied. Neural network models are not sufficiently fast for

safety applications, also extrapolation methods and classic mathematical methods are not optimum and applicable for this purpose. Extended Kalman filter and particle filter have more computational overhead than the Kalman filter while in this situation and specially to estimate the longitudinal location, its accuracy is not equal to incurrence computational overhead.

Finally, we evaluate the longitudinal estimation error. For this purpose, we investigate the estimated information available to each neighbouring vehicle and calculate the error it has in comparison with exact information (i.e., position) available from observation. As Fig.4.b shows the average longitudinal estimation error decreases to around 0.5 m after warm-up time of estimator and remains almost in the same value during the simulation time. This issue again supports our idea in this paper for using Kalman estimation in beacon message dissemination.

6 Conclusions

In this paper we showed that using Kalman filter estimation is beneficial in improving the performance of beacon safety message dissemination in vehicular networks. The result of simulations with real-life traffic patterns suggests that the estimated locations are often correct. Thus, new beacon disseminations is prohibited. Therefore the number of collisions is reduced and reception rate is increased. As a result, the safety level which is provided by beacon message dissemination is improved noticeably.

References

1. Federal Communications Commission, FCC 03-324. FCC Report and Order (February 2004)
2. IEEE, IEEE Standard 802.11p. Draft Amendment: Wireless Access in Vehicular Environments (WAVE). Draft 1.0 (2004)
3. Yousefi, S., Siadat Mousavi, M., Fathy, M.: Vehicular Adhoc NETworks (VANETs): Challenges and Perspectives. In: Proc. 6th Int. Conf. on ITS Telecommunications, pp. 761–766 (2006) doi:10.1109/ITST.2006.289012
4. Welch, G., Bishop, G.: An Introduction to the Kalman Filter. Technical Report. UMI Order Number: TR95-041, University of North Carolina at Chapel Hill (1995)
5. The FleetNet Project, http://www.et2.tu-harburg.de/fleetnet/, The patterns are publicly,
   http://www.informatik.uni-mannheim.de/pi4.data/content/projects/hwgui/
6. Yousefi, S., Fathi, M., Benslimane, A.: Performance of beacon safety message dissemination in Vehicular Ad hoc NETworks (VANETs). J. Zhejiang Univ. Sci. A., 1990–2004 (2007) doi:10.1631/jzus.2007.A1990
7. Zhaomin, M., Hao, Z., Makki, K., Pissinou, N.: Mobility-Assisted Location Management for Vehicular Ad Hoc Networks. In: Proc. IEEE Wireless Communications and Networking Conference, pp. 2224–2228 (2008) doi:10.1109/WCNC.2008.393
8. Rezaei, S., Sengupta, R., Krishnan, H.: Reducing the Communication Required By DSRC-Based Vehicle Safety Systems. In: Proc. IEEE Intelligent Transportation Systems Conference, pp. 361–366 (2007)

9. Rezaei, S., Sengupta, R., Krishnan, H., Guan, X., Bhatia, R.: Tracking the position of neighboring vehicles using wireless communications. Transport. Res. Part C (2009) doi:10.1016/j.trc.2009.05.010

10. Crash Avoidance Metrics Partnership (CAMP), Identify Intelligent Vehicle Safety Applications Enabled by DSRC. Vehicle Safety Communications Project, Task 3 Report, Public Document (2004)

11. GloMoSim Network Simulator, http://pcl.cs.ucla.edu/projects/glomosim/

Media-Oriented Service Overlay Network Architecture over Future Internet Research for Sustainable Testbed

Sungwon Lee[1], Sang Woo Han[2], Jong Won Kim[2], and Seung Gwan Lee[1]

[1] Department of Computer Engineering, Kyung Hee University,
1 Seocheonding, Giheunggu, Yonginsi, Gyeonggido, 446-701, Korea
{drsungwon,leesg}@khu.ac.kr
[2] Gwangju Institute of Science and Technology (GIST), Korea

Abstract. The Future Internet Research for Sustainable Testbed (FIRST) is an experimental project in South Korea aimed at creating future internet platforms and investigating innovative ideas on developed platforms. The primary goal of the project is research and development for a media-oriented service overlay network architecture. From 2009 to 2014, dynamic media-oriented service composition technologies using virtualized network environments will be constructed, and results will be shared globally. In this paper, we explained the motivation for the FIRST project, and introduced the project itself.

Keywords: SOA, Future Internet, Network Virtualization, GENI, OMF.

1 Introduction

The "Future Internet Research for Sustainable Testbed (FIRST)" started in 2009 as a five-year project. Participating members are Chungnam National University (CNU), Electronics and Telecommunications Research Institute (ETRI), Gwangju Institute of Science and Technology (GIST), Kyung Hee University (KHU), and Pohang University of Science and Technology (POSTECH). The goal of the project is to identify key internet technologies and to investigate their feasibilities in an experimental system. Expected results of the FIRST project are new platforms (including software and hardware), experimental infrastructure and new internet services. Two platforms are being considered. One is the FIRST@ATCA platform which uses a commercial off-the-shelf (COTS) system for its telecom grade platform, and the other is the FIRST@PC platform for use in academic and experimental developments. Based on these platforms, innovative and creative ideas for future network infrastructures and services will be designed and implemented using a service overlay network architecture.

2 Service Overlay Network Architecture

The service overlay network architecture (SONA) concept was proposed for efficient control and management of the FIRST platforms. SONA is currently under development with FIRST@PC platforms. The scope of SONA includes management and control of virtualized network elements such as networking service components,

D. Ślęzak et al. (Eds.): FGCN/ACN 2009, CCIS 56, pp. 83–88, 2009.
© Springer-Verlag Berlin Heidelberg 2009

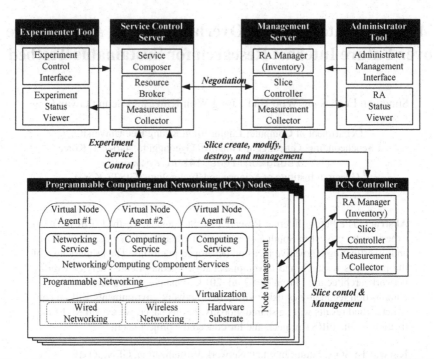

Fig. 1. Various components of the service overlay network architecture based on FIRST@PC

computing service components, slices, and experimental services. The design philosophy of SONA is "media and media service oriented". Thus, SONA's key features are proposed to support dynamic media-oriented service composition with scalability, easy-programmability, and flexibility. SONA's core network elements and its interfaces are depicted in Fig. 1.

2.1 Experimenter Tool

Experimenter Tool provides a consistent programming model of service composition for experimenters. By using the 'Experiment Control Interface,' experimenters are able to define a process description which defines and describes the required resources and procedures and initiates an experiment service. Experimenters can monitor the status of the testbed through 'Experiment Status Viewer'.

2.2 Service Control Server

The Service Control Server is a real-time controller for media service composition processes. The 'Service Composer' provides service synthesis, which maps a requested process description to the available network resources; service discovery to request services or appropriate replacements; service selection to determine the best matched service among the candidate services; and service execution, which executes a service based on desired requirements such as QoS and efficiency of resources.

'Resource Broker' negotiates with 'Slice Controller' of the management server to obtain available slice resources during a service synthesis period.

2.3 Management Server

Management Server manages all of the resource aggregators (RAs) in a testbed network via 'RA Manager.' An RA is a logical view of the resources in the virtualized testbed network and is physically implemented by the Programmable Computing and Networking (PCN) nodes. The 'RA Manager' provides control and management services over the PCN nodes such as inventory management and real-time resource status monitoring of the RAs. 'Slice Controller' allocates and controls the RAs for incoming service requests which are generally requested by the Service Control Server.

2.4 Administrator Tool

The Administrator Tool provides the operation and management tools for administrators. Using this tool, operators can monitor and manage the virtualized testbed network.

2.5 PCN Nodes

PCN Nodes provide networking and/or computing component services. The node virtualization framework and the programmable open interfaces are employed in addition to wireless and wire-line networking infrastructures. Through the node virtualization framework, multiple networking and/or computing service components can operate independently in the same PCN Node. Also, through the programmable open interfaces, experimenters and/or administrators can configure and control the networking devices for their experimental purposes.

2.6 PCN Controller

The PCN Controller takes charge of each RA consisting of PCN Nodes. Based on coordination with the Management Server, the PCN Controller monitors the resources of the PCN Nodes and the slices.

3 Hierarchical Architecture of SONA

SONA is a hierarchical architecture of the physical network layers and multiple logical network layers, as depicted in Fig.2.

3.1 Physical Network

The Physical Network consists of several programmable routers that support valuable services and provide open application programming interfaces (APIs) to control and manage the services. Thus, higher layers can configure and control physical networks for their own purposes.

3.2 Networking Service Candidates

Networking Service Candidates are sets of networking service instances, which are defined as pre-configured functional relationships between programmable routers based on the capability of the programmable routers and their networking connection status. Each networking instance supports single or multiple network transport services such as a forwarding service, replication service, NAT/firewall traversal service, prioritized transmission service, encryption service, or a decryption service,.

3.3 Composite Services

Composite Services are single or converged multiple multimedia services including media producer service, media consumer service, trans-coding service, video composition service, video tiling service and video resolution resizing service. Functional dependency graphs and/or workflows are used for composite and control services. For service composition control, multimedia services are characterized by service name, service code, pre-conditions, post-conditions, and execution time.

3.4 Media Applications and Users

As previously explained, several media-oriented services can be designed and implemented over the FIRST@PC testbed using SONA. Experimenters can enter their own

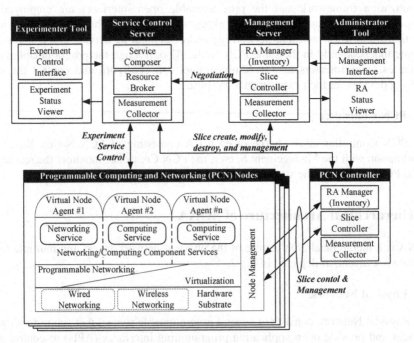

Fig. 2. The hierarchical layering in SONA. The physical network consists of programmable routers with open APIs. Logical layers such as network service candidates and composite services are mapped to the physical network. Based on composite services, users experience media application services.

service description in the Experiment Tool. Based on the requested service description, the Service Control Server controls and manages the FIRST@PC testbed to enable the service compositions requested by the experimenters. In this way, users can easily experience their own media applications.

4 SONA-Based Media Composition Service Example

Experimental services have been designed and developed based on the FIRST@PC testbed and SONA. Figure 3 shows a media composition service for heterogeneous devices with various processing capabilities, display resolutions and network bandwidths. The first device is mobile with relatively low processing power, low resolution, and limited wireless bandwidth. The second device is the Note-PC, and the third is the tiled multi-monitor display. Our goal was to simultaneously send both on-demand content and live-streaming content with all three devices. For this, SONA provided various network services via PCN Nodes to optimally deliver the contents. Based on the experimenter's request, the Service Control Server initiated control of SONA via PCN Controllers. The PCN Controller configured PCN Nodes to satisfy the requested service requirements.

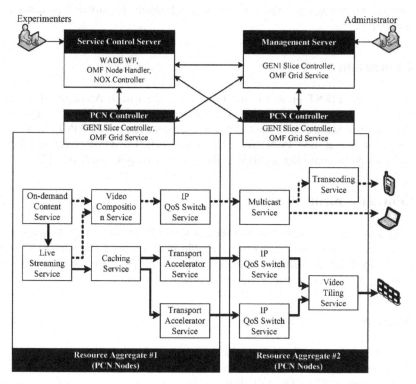

Fig. 3. A media composition service example scenario using SONA. The On-demand content server and Live-streaming server send content over the FIRST@PC-based network for various devices such as mobile phones, Note-PCs and tiled multiple-monitor displays.

4.1 Media Service for Limited-Capability Devices

When supporting mobile devices and Note-PCs, the On-demand Content Server/ Service and Live-Streaming Server/Service send multimedia content to the Video Composition Server/Service independently. Both multimedia sources are mixed to reduce bandwidth and required processing power in mobile devices and Note-PCs.

Quality of service at the wire-line network is guaranteed via IP QoS Switch Services for networking services. The Multicast Service transmits multimedia content via a multicast feature for efficient use of network bandwidth. Finally, SONA enables the Trans-coding Server/Service to optimize the required bandwidth and processing power for mobile devices.

4.2 Media Service for High-Capability Devices

With a tiled multi-monitor display, higher resolution is a key service requirement. For this, a Caching Server/Service is supported for reliability and network efficiency. High resolution content is divided into multiple pieces by a Live Streaming Server/Service based on the requirements of multiple monitors at the destination. Transport Accelerator Servers/Services are enabled to increase the transmission speed for divided streams. The Video Tiling Server/Service at the destination network provides coordination and synchronization functionality for divided contents to be synchronized.

5 Conclusion

The goal of the FIRST project is not to reinvent the wheel. As depicted in Fig. 2, SONA uses slice control from the Global Environment for Network Innovation (GENI) and grid service from the Orbit Management Framework (OMF) between the Management Server and PCN Node Controller [1]. The OMF node handler and OpenFlow's NOX controller are used in the Service Composition Server [2].

Acknowledgement

This paper is one of results from the project (2009-F-050-01), "Development of the core technology and virtualized programmable platform for Future Internet" that is sponsored by MKE and KCC. I'd like to express my gratitude for the concerns to spare no support for the research and development of the project.

References

1. Global Environment for Network Innovation (GENI), http://www.geni.net
2. OpenFlow, http://www.openflowswitch.org,
   http://www.ncbi.nlm.nih.gov

Monotonically Increasing Bit Vector for Authenticated Anonymous Routing

Roman Schlegel and Duncan S. Wong

Department of Computer Science
City University of Hong Kong
sschlegel2@student.cityu.edu.hk, duncan@cs.cityu.edu.hk

Abstract. Anonymous routing where data packets can be routed efficiently while hiding the topology of the network from all nodes is a crucial part of achieving anonymity in an efficient anonymous network. Traditional routing protocols leak network topology information to nodes while existing anonymous routing protocols do not provide authentication for routing information. A malicious node can arbitrarily reduce the path cost value carried in an anonymous route announcement message for the purpose of negatively influencing routing efficiency or facilitating launching various attacks such as eavesdropping or man-in-the-middle attacks. In this paper we propose a generic scheme and a concrete instantiation to transform a routing protocol into an authenticated one in the sense that the path cost cannot be reduced by a malicious node.

1 Introduction

Consider an anonymous network in which there are L nodes, each one of them has a unique address (which is not necessarily a real IP address but a virtual address and might already be providing some degree of anonymity to the underlying node). Apart from knowing its neighbors, a node does not have any additional information about the topology of the network. In other words, each node only knows how to reach its neighbors; but has no idea on how other nodes are connected in the network. A network of this type is typically referred to as an anonymous network [16,15,12].

One fundamental problem in an anonymous network is to find out how to route data packets from one node to another efficiently while maintaining the anonymity of the network, that is, without leaking any significant network topology information. Flooding is possible but neither scalable nor efficient.

In [16,15,12], several anonymous routing protocols have been proposed. These protocols can ensure that when a node receives a routing announcement, it can only learn via which of its neighbors a particular destination can be reached with the smallest path cost. Apart from an estimated path cost (number of hops, latency, etc.), no additional information about the network topology is leaked. These protocols can create routes efficiently and also prevent routing loops.

D. Ślęzak et al. (Eds.): FGCN/ACN 2009, CCIS 56, pp. 89–96, 2009.

(*Lack of Authentication*) However, in these protocols, there is no *authentication*. They assume that nodes are honest and do not maliciously alter the path cost when updating a routing announcement. In fact, if any node in their networks is malicious, the node can arbitrarily reduce the path cost value carried by a route announcement message. By doing this, this malicious node may be able to act as a sink in the network and route all the traffic to itself. This may help the node to launch various attacks such as eavesdropping or man-in-the-middle attacks.

Some non-anonymous routing protocols, such as S-BGP [5], soBGP [14] and psBGP [13] support authentication so that any malicious reduction of path cost value of a traversing route announcement message can be detected by other nodes in the network. However, these routing protocols inherently leak the network topology information.

A natural question to ask is whether it is possible to transform an existing anonymous routing protocol into an authenticated version so that it not only maintains the anonymity property, but also ensures that no malicious node can reduce the path cost value of any route announcement message when the message is traversing the node.

Our Results.

In this paper, we propose a solution which can be used to convert distance-vector based anonymous routing protocols such as [16,15,12] to authenticated ones so that the path cost of routing messages cannot be reduced maliciously. At the same time, the anonymity of these protocols is maintained so that there is no leakage of network topology information due to using this new solution.

We first propose a generic solution which is relying on signature schemes. By using elliptic curve and bilinear pairing, we then construct an efficient concrete scheme with low memory requirement.

Paper Organization. The rest of the paper is organized as follows: section 2 discusses related work and section 3 describes the attack model considered in our scheme. We then present the a solution based on signature schemes in section 4. This is followed by a performance evaluation of size and computational complexity in section 5 and in section 6 we conclude.

2   Related Work

Route authentication has especially been discussed in recent years concerning BGP [11], the inter-domain routing protocol used in the Internet. BGP works by exchanging routing information with peers, but this information is not authenticated which makes it akin to listening to and trusting *hearsay*.

There are a number of other acknowledged vulnerabilites of BGP [8] and several proposals like S-BGP [5,6], psBGP [13] and soBGP [14] have been made to remedy this situation. These three proposals have in common that they try to fix routing problems because of misconfiguration or possibly malicious rerouting of traffic by *authenticating* all routing information. To achieve this, AS numbers are certified, as are address ranges (to ensure that entities are authorized to announce a specific prefix), and, depending on the proposal, BGP speakers (to ensure that only authorized speakers can participate). The proposals differ mainly in the way these certifications are made.

The three protocols ([5,13,14]) all leak information about the nodes in the network. For an anonymous network outlined in Sec. 1, on the other hand, this is not desirable. In order to ensure authentication while providing anonymity to the network, we emphasize that the secure anonymous routing protocol should make sure that the cost along a path cannot be maliciously reduced by any malicious node along a route and *at the same time* the origin of every single route announcement message should be authenticated. This prevents a node from positioning itself as a sink and from advertising a destination other than itself.

Anonymous routing, on the other hand, has been studied especially in connection with mobile ad-hoc networks (MANET). Protocols like [16,3,10,2,9,15] are all focused on MANETs and use on-demand routing. These protocols try to preserve anonymity when establishing routes but the type of anonymity they achieve and the assumptions they make for the correct functioning of the protocol differ.

The anonymous routing protocol described in [12] fulfills the requirements of establishing routes without leaking information about the topology of the network, but it is also vulnerable to a malicious node which arbitrarily reduces the path cost when forwarding a route announcement. Our solution below can be applied directly to this protocol for solving the path-reduction problem.

3 Attack Model

Before proposing our solution we discuss the adversarial capabilities of a malicious network in more detail in this section.

As introduced in Sec. 1, we consider a typical network of L nodes where each node is connected to a few neighbors. Each node knows the address of its neighbors, but other than that it has no information about how other nodes in the network are connected. By running a distance-vector based routing protocol, efficient routes can be establisehd. We refer readers to [12] for a recently proposed anonymous routing protocol which is distance-vector based.

Figure 1 shows an example of a network where $L = 9$. The shaded node denoted by S initiates an announcement, with an initial path cost of 1 (for example as the hop count), which is then increased by each node and forwarded.

In this example, suppose all the nodes are honest. If node D wants to send data to node S, it will forward it to node A.

Now assume node M is malicious and tries to re-route traffic by leaving the path cost value carried by a route announcement message unchanged. D would still choose A as the next hop. However, if M succeeded in reducing the path cost, say by two (which our solution will prevent), this would make B to be chosen as the next hop by D and B would choose M as the next hop and so on.

To prevent malicious node M from reducing the path cost value carried by a route announcement message when forwarding it to node D, one idea is to

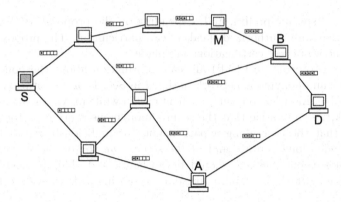

Fig. 1. An example network where the shaded node broadcasts an announcement. Each node increases the path cost value of the corresponding route announcement message by one and forwards it.

add some authentication mechanism to each route announcement message so that the next node (i.e. node D) can verify whether the path cost value in the receiving route announcement message has been maliciously reduced.

As discussed above, we target to convert existing anonymous routing protocols such as those in [16,15,12] *without* modifying any of their routing mechanisms. Our solution would only modify the path cost value. To achieve this, we introduce an authentication mechanism so that the path cost value carried by their route announcement messages cannot be maliciously reduced. Also, this additional authentication mechanism does not leak any information about the network topology. The advantages of this authentication approach is that the solutions can be applied directly to various anonymous routing protocols and also help maintain the anonymity properties of the anonymous routing protocols.

4   Generic Scheme

Our idea stems from the creation of a binary vector of length n bits: $\boldsymbol{v} = (b_1 b_2 \dots b_n)$. The value n denotes the maximum possible value the path cost of a route announcement may reach. The Hamming weight of this binary vector $\boldsymbol{v}$ is the path cost. A node who wants to increase the path cost by 1 picks a zero bit on $\boldsymbol{v}$ and flips it to one, that is, it increases the Hamming weight of $\boldsymbol{v}$ by one. Our solution below will introduce mechanisms to ensure that the Hamming weight of $\boldsymbol{v}$ can only be monotonically increased (i.e. either leave it unchanged or increase it, but it cannot be reduced). The binary vector $\boldsymbol{v}$ also does not need to be sent explicitly but can instead be generated from the authentication mechanism introduced in our solution. Hence we refer to $\boldsymbol{v}$ as an 'imaginary' n-bit binary vector in the remaining part of this paper.

For generating a path cost of 0 (i.e. all the n bits of $\boldsymbol{v}$ are zeros) in a route announcement, the route initiator prepares the following tag:

$$PathCostTag = < S, V_1, V_2, \mathsf{Sign}_\mathsf{S}(S, T, V_1) > \tag{1}$$

where S is the address of the source (e.g. node S in Fig. 1), T is a timestamp (for preventing replay attacks) and $Sign_S(S, T, V_1)$ is the signature over (S, T, V_1) generated by the source. This signature is to prevent a malicious node from replacing V_1. (V_1, V_2) is a data structure which realizes v.

Let $SIG = (Gen, Sig, Ver)$ be a signature scheme. On input a security parameter $k \in \mathbb{N}$, the probabilistic polynomial-time algorithm (PPT) $Gen(k)$ generates a signing/verification key pair (sk, vk). On input a signing key sk and a message $m \in \{0, 1\}^*$, $Sig(sk, m)$ generates a signature σ. On input a verification key vk, a message m and a signature σ, $Ver(vk, m, \sigma)$ outputs 1 if the signature is valid with respect to vk on m; otherwise it outputs 0. For security, we require SIG to be existentially unforgeable against chosen message attack [4].

In the generic scheme, we use the structure of $PathCostTag$ as shown in (1). V_1 is composed of the collection of verification keys vk_i $(1 \leq i \leq n)$ and V_2 contains the corresponding signing keys sk_i $(1 \leq i \leq n)$. Each pair of the keys are generated independently using Gen. Additionally, V_1 contains a message M. Without loss of generality, we assume that the message space of SIG is $\{0, 1\}^k$. M in V_1 is chosen uniformly at random from $\{0, 1\}^k$.

Now suppose that we want to increase the path cost by 1, for example, by flipping the first bit of the 'imaginary' n-bit binary vector v from zero to one, we compute $y_1 \leftarrow Sig(sk_1, M)$ and replace sk_1 in V_2 by y_1. Thus the updated V_2 becomes $V_2 = (y_1, sk_2, \cdots, sk_n)$. To check whether the first bit of v is flipped or not, we run $Ver(vk_1, M, y_1)$ and determine if its output is 1, where vk_1 is obtained from V_1. If so, we conclude that the first bit is flipped.

In the following, we describe an instantiation of the generic scheme above. It is based on a short signature constructed from bilinear pairing.

4.1   BLS Short Signature Based

The short signature by Boneh, Lynn and Shacham (BLS) [1] can be used to implement the generic scheme above, with the advantage that each component in V_1 and V_2 is quite small. The signature uses bilinear pairing which is reviewed as follows.

Let $\mathbb{G}_1$, $\mathbb{G}_2$ and $\mathbb{G}_T$ be cyclic groups of prime order p, let g_1 a generator of $\mathbb{G}_1$ and g_2 a generator of $\mathbb{G}_2$. $e : \mathbb{G}_1 \times \mathbb{G}_2 \to \mathbb{G}_T$ is a bilinear pairing if the following properties are satisfied: (1) **Bilinear**: for all $P \in \mathbb{G}_1$, $Q \in \mathbb{G}_2$ and $a, b \in \mathbb{Z}_p$, $e(P^a, Q^b) = e(P, Q)^{ab}$; (2) **Non-degenerate**: $e(g_1, g_2) \neq 1$; and (3) **Computable**: $e(P, Q)$ can be computed efficiently for all $P \in \mathbb{G}_1$ and $Q \in \mathbb{G}_2$. When practically implementing bilinear pairing, different types of pairings can be used with different speed and size characteristics. The types we refer to (A, D, F) will be further explained in Sec. 5.2.

In BLS, a signing key sk is a random element in $\mathbb{Z}_p$, a verification key vk is computed as $vk = g_2^{sk}$. For a message $M \in \{0, 1\}^*$, the signature is computed as $y \leftarrow H(M)^{sk}$ where $H : \{0, 1\}^* \to \mathbb{G}_1$ is a hash function. The verification is done by checking that $e(\sigma, g_2) = e(H(M), vk)$.

Optimization through Aggregation. In [1], Boneh et al. also suggested a method to aggregate the BLS short signatures. By applying aggregation, we can further reduce the size of $PathCostTag$ by aggregating the signatures in V_2 (i.e. those flipped bits of the 'imaginary' n-bit binary vector v). Without loss of generality, suppose that the first l bits of v have been flipped, that is, V_2 would become $V_2 = (y_1, \cdots, y_l, sk_{l+1}, \cdots, sk_n)$ where $y_j = H(M)^{sk_j}$ for all j, $1 \leq j \leq l$. Instead of sending V_2 in this form, we can aggregate all the l short signatures into one single signature and the next V_2 would become $V_2^{new} = (y_{agg}, sk_{l+1}, \cdots, sk_n)$ where $y_{agg} = \prod_{j=1}^{l} y_j \in \mathbb{G}_1$. This aggregated signature can be verified by checking that $e(y_{agg}, g_2) = e(H(M), \prod_{j=1}^{l} vk_j)$. Note that not only has the size of the $PathCostTag$ (specifically, the size of V_2) been reduced, but we also reduced the computational complexity of the verification from $2l$ number of pairing evaluations to just two pairing evaluations.

5   Performance Evaluation

5.1   Size

Table 1 shows the size requirements depending on the signature scheme and the type used. In the comparison, we consider a 'imaginary' n-bit binary vector v of length 100 bits (i.e. $n = 100$). We only consider the size of the elements themselves for a security level of 80 bits and do not include the invariant parameters.

In the table, *Empty Vector* refers to the initial state of v where all the bits are zero, while *Full Vector* means that all the n bits of v have been flipped, so that it represents the maximum path cost supported. In other words, the sizes shown in Table 1 in the *Empty Vector* column indicate the lower bound for the size of each instantiation and under the *Full Vector* column the upper bound for the size of each instantiation is given.

Table 1. Size Comparison

Instantiation	Empty Vector	Full Vector
BLS (Type A)	2 KB	12.5 KB
BLS (Type D)	2 KB	8.3 KB
BLS (Type F)	2 KB	5.9 KB
BLS (aggr., Type A)	2 KB	6.3 KB
BLS (aggr., Type D)	2 KB	6.2 KB
BLS (aggr., Type F)	2 KB	**3.9 KB**

5.2   Computational Complexity

To test the computational complexity of our scheme, we performed benchmarks for typical operations in the different schemes. We used the Pairing Based Cryptography Library from Stanford University [7]. Once again, we consider 80-bit level security.

Table 2. Benchmark results for different instantiations

Scheme	Gen. Priv. Keys	Gen. Pub. Keys	Transf. Elem.	Verify Elem.
BLS (Type A)	$1601ms$	$524ms$	$524ms$	$1150ms$
BLS (Type D)	$1601ms$	$1925ms$	$163ms$	$2935ms$
BLS (Type F)	$1601ms$	$405ms$	$163ms$	$18754ms$
BLS agg. (Type A)	$1598ms$	$524ms$	$526ms$	$14ms$
BLS agg. (Type D)	$1595ms$	$1922ms$	$163ms$	$39ms$
BLS agg. (Type F)	$1602ms$	$402ms$	$163ms$	$188ms$

The benchmark consists of performing key generation, element transformation and element verification. For the tests we set $n = 100$, i.e. a vector contains 100 elements. All tests were done on a computer running Mac OS X 10.5.7 on an Intel Core 2 Duo 2.4 GHz processor. The computation time required for the different operations was determined using the getrusage() system call.

The PBC library [7] supports different types of bilinear pairings with different characteristics. For the BLS signature schemes we used types A, D and F. Type F has smaller elements, but is much slower than type D. Type A is the fastest for the pairings but has a larger element size than the other two types.

5.3 Discussions

Looking at tables 1 and 2 we can see that there is a distinct trade-off to be made between size and computational complexity depending on the type of bilinear pairing used.

The most important operation is the verification of elements of a vector received by a neighbor, because it is the most frequently done operation. Schemes where the verification is fast are therefore more desirable. A good compromise between size and computational complexity is the BLS aggregate signature with pairing of type A. Using type D or F would decrease the size further, at a slightly higher verification cost.

6   Conclusion

We proposed a scheme and a concrete instantiation which can be used to generically convert distance-vector based anonymous routing protocols such as [16,12] to authenticated ones so that the path cost of routing messages cannot be reduced maliciously. At the same time, the anonymity of these protocols is maintained so no network topology information is leaked due to using these new solutions. An interesting question which remains is how to further reduce the size of these schemes without introducing any significant computational burden to network nodes or making many assumptions on the nodes which may undermine the anonymity of the underlying network.

References

1. Boneh, D., Lynn, B., Shacham, H.: Short signatures from the weil pairing. In: Boyd, C. (ed.) ASIACRYPT 2001. LNCS, vol. 2248, pp. 514–532. Springer, Heidelberg (2001)
2. Boukerche, A., El-Khatib, K., Xu, L., Korba, L.: A novel solution for achieving anonymity in wireless ad hoc networks. In: Ould-Khaoua, M., Zambonelli, F. (eds.) PE-WASUN, pp. 30–38. ACM Press, New York (2004)
3. El-Khatib, K., Korba, L., Song, R., Yee, G.: Secure dynamic distributed routing algorithm for ad hoc wireless networks. In: International Conference on Parallel Processing Workshops (ICPPW 2003), pp. 359–366 (2003)
4. Goldwasser, S., Micali, S., Rivest, R.: A digital signature scheme secure against adaptive chosen-message attack. SIAM J. Computing 17(2), 281–308 (1988)
5. Kent, S., Lynn, C., Seo, K.: Secure Border Gateway Protocol (S-BGP). IEEE Journal on Selected Areas in Communications 18(4), 582–592 (2000)
6. Kent, S.T., Lynn, C., Mikkelson, J., Seo, K.: Secure Border Gateway Protocol (S-BGP) - Real World Performance and Deployment Issues. In: NDSS (2000)
7. Lynn, B.: PBC Library, http://crypto.stanford.edu/pbc/
8. Murphy, S.: BGP Security Vulnerabilities Analysis. RFC 4272 (Informational) (January 2006)
9. Papadimitratos, P., Haas, Z.: Secure routing for mobile ad hoc networks. In: SCS Communication Networks and Distributed Systems Modeling and Simulation Conference (CNDS 2002), San Antonio, TX, pp. 01–27 (2002)
10. Rajendran, T., Sreenaath, K.V.: Secure anonymous routing in ad hoc networks. In: Shyamasundar, R.K. (ed.) Bangalore Compute. Conf., p. 19. ACM Press, New York (2008)
11. Rekhter, Y., Li, T., Hares, S.: A Border Gateway Protocol 4 (BGP-4). RFC 4271 (Draft Standard) (January 2006)
12. Schlegel, R., Wong, D.S.: Low Latency High Bandwidth Anonymous Overlay Network with Anonymous Routing. Cryptology ePrint Archive, Report 2009/294 (2009), http://eprint.iacr.org/
13. Wan, T., Kranakis, E., Van Oorschot, P.C.: Pretty Secure BGP (psBGP). In: NDSS (2005)
14. White, R.: Securing BGP through secure origin BGP (soBGP). Business Communications Review 33, 47–53 (2003)
15. Zhang, Y., Liu, W., Lou, W.: Anonymous communications in mobile ad hoc networks. In: INFOCOM, pp. 1940–1951. IEEE, Los Alamitos (2005)
16. Zhu, B., Wan, Z., Kankanhalli, M., Bao, F., Deng, R.: Anonymous Secure Routing in Mobile Ad-Hoc Networks. In: 29th Annual IEEE International Conference on Local Computer Networks, 2004, pp. 102–108 (2004)

Avoid Unnecessary Handovers
in a High Dense Environment

Ara Cho[1], Navrati Saxena[1], Abhishek Roy[2], Swades De[3], and Hari M. Gupta[3]

[1] Sungkyunkwan University
ara44.cho@samsung.com, navrati.saxena@ece.skku.edu
[2] Samsung Eletronics
abhishek.roy@samsung.com
[3] Indian Institute of Technology Delhi
swadesd@ee.iitd.ac.in, hmgupta@ee.iitd.ac.in

Abstract. In this paper we propose a new efficient handover algorithm across overlapped macro and home eNodeBs in emerging LTE systems. More home eNodeBs are anticipated so it is important to find out a good handover algorithm in a high dense environment. Our algorithm focuses on maximizing cell duration. Our implementation and simulation results show that the proposed strategy reduces the number of handover as well as keeps suitable signal level.

Keywords: home eNodeB, macro eNodeB, handover, cell duration, measurement window size, rate of change of SINR, handover threshold, LTE.

1 Introduction

As shown in Fig.1, LTE (Long Term Evolution) of 3GPP cellular systems visualizes multiple home base stations, also referred to as home eNodeBs, overlapped with the current macro eNodeBs to increase system capacity and satisfy service demand. The number of home eNodeB rapidly increases because not only do network operators install home eNodeBs but also individual customers can setup them. Closed home eNodeB came out to satisfy private service demand. UEs (User Equipment) with no access right will not be served by closed home eNodeB. The swift increase in the number of home eNodeBs and arbitrarily deployment makes the system inefficient to configure and manage handover.

Handover is a process of redirection from its current cell and its used channel to a new cell and a new channel during a call in progress. LTE systems support hard handover. Hard handover means that UE is linked to no more than 1 eNodeB at a given time. UE keeps measuring RSS (Received Signal Strength) and SINR (Signal-to-noise-interference) and reports to a serving eNodeB periodically.

Our contribution is to reduce the number of handover in an environment where lots of eNodeBs are distributed. In Section 2, we see some related works about handover algorithms. To introduce our algorithm, we describe the basic framework in Section 3. In Section 4, simulation results demonstrate the efficiency of our solution to reduce handovers in the LTE system.

D. Ślęzak et al. (Eds.): FGCN/ACN 2009, CCIS 56, pp. 97–104, 2009.

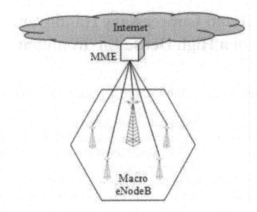

Fig. 1. Entities in LTE systems

2 Related Works

The seamless handover has been discussed as standardization in 3GPP systems in [1]. Recent simulation experiments [2] have revealed the optimal handover parameters required for a suitable compromise between average number of handovers and average uplink SINR. What makes handover decision function complex lie in the fact that home eNodeBs are not controlled by network operator and are enormous. This motivates us to investigate the handover problem in a high dense environment.

The handover decision is mainly based on RSS and SINR. Handover may begin when signal strength at the UE received from serving eNodeB is less than that of other eNodeBs. This causes many handovers while it keeps good signal. A better idea, threshold and hysteresis margin were proposed. Threshold is used not to make handover if signal is tolerable. Hysteresis margin helps to reduce the handover rate by initiating handover process when the difference of RSS between new eNodeB and serving eNodeB is greater than hysteresis margin. In an overlaid environment, umbrella concept was designed to handle remarkably fast UEs. Umbrella idea is that fast UEs connect to macro eNodeBs and slow UEs to home eNodeBs.

3 Smooth Handover

In this paper we propose a handover decision algorithm which focuses on selecting an eNodeB where UE stays longest. Our algorithm avoids switching to a nearby eNodeB because it causes another handover. The goal is to stay in a new target eNodeB for a long time. Our algorithm postpones handover using handover threshold which is used not to make handover if SINR is tolerable.

3.1 Concept of Longer Cell Duration

We postulate ideal circumstance that the number of home eNodeBs is infinite and UE directs to a point for a certain time. If a serving eNodeB knows UE's trajectory, the

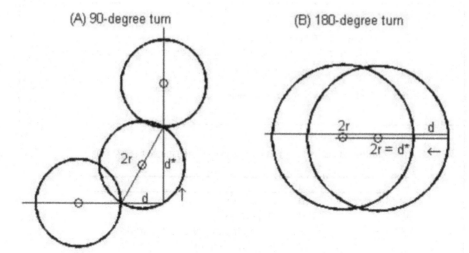

Fig. 2. Finding the best eNodeB on turning

```
algorithm GetHandoverOccurrenceOfLongerCellDuration
// Coverage, HandoverMargin are constant
// Queue has Out and IsEmpty method.

int GetHandoverOccurrenceOfLongerCellDuration (Queue
Path){
    int HandoverOccurrence = 0;
    int HandoverOccurrenceSum = 0;
    double r, d, d*;
    double theta;
    Position CurPos; // current position of UE
    Position TargetPos; // next target position of UE

    r = Coverage - HandoverMargin;
    d* = 0;
    CurPos = Path.Out();

    while(!Path.IsEmpty()) {
        TargetPos = Path.Out();
        theta = GetRadian(CurPos, TargetPos);
        d = GetDistance(CurPos, TargetPos) - d*;

        HandoverOccurrence = floor(d/2/r);
        d = d - HandoverOccurrence 2 r;

        if ( d > 0 ){
        HandoverOccurrence++;
        // calculate d* using equation in the Table 1;
        d* = GetTurningDistance(d, r, theta);
        }
```

```
        else d* = 0;

        CurPos = TargetPos;
        HandoverOccurrenceSum += HandoverOccurrence;
    }

    return HandoverOccurrenceSum;
}
```

Table 1. d* calculation (d* = GetTurningDistance (d, r, Θ))

Θ	d*
$0 < \Theta < \pi/2$	$d* = 2r \cdot \cos \Theta$
$\Theta = \pi/2$	$d* = \sqrt{((2r)^2 - d^2)}$
$\pi/2 < \Theta < \pi$	Let α is an angle between 2r and d
	$2r \cdot \sin \alpha = d* \cdot \sin \Theta$
	$\cos \alpha = ((2r)^2 + d^2 - d*^2)/(2 \cdot 2r \cdot d)$
	$\cos^2\alpha + \sin^2\alpha = 1$
$\Theta = \pi$	$d* = 2r$

eNodeB is able to calculate how many times handover happens using longer cell duration concept. Fig. 2 shows two scenarios of finding the best target eNodeB when UE changes its direction. Our solution is to select an eNodeB which cover d before changing direction and maximize d* after turning direction. Fig. 2 (A) exemplifies a situation that UE changes its direction 90-degree. It induces the equation of the 2nd row in Table 1. Fig. 2 (B) illustrates a scenario which UE changes its direction 180-degree and is indicated by the equation of the 4th row in Table 1. Overlapping area is necessary to communicate serving eNodeB and target eNodeB and to avoid network loss. We call it handover margin. Cell coverage and handover margin correlates to cell duration.

3.2 Framework of Smooth Algorithm

Fig. 3 provides a close look at the general SINR changes. As UE approaches an eNodeB, SINR increases. When UE is in close proximity to an eNodeB, SINR maximizes. After peaking out, SINR recedes as UE become more distant. SINR variation informs UE's movement from an eNodeB. SINR of near neighbors like B in Fig. 3 turns decreasing in a short time while SINR of far neighbors like C, D and E in Fig. 3 is still increasing.

Though instant SINR variation is useful, SINR variation pattern leads to selecting an eNodeB with longer cell duration. Measurement window is introduced in order to keep track of the change of SINR. SINR is collected and measurement window is updated every measurement report. When handover decision function is called, count from the latest measurement window so long as SINR variation is positive. We call it the rate of change of SINR; how long UE approaches to the eNodeB. Our algorithm uses not absurd value of change of SINR but sign of it for the rate of change of SINR

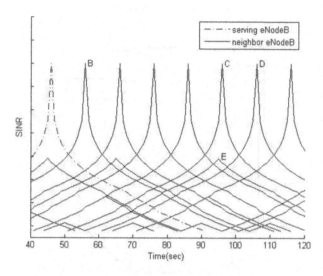

Fig. 3. SINR variation with time

because value of SINR is unpredictable if various home eNodeBs with different antenna height and Tx power are deployed.

Measurement window size is an additional part to reduce handover count whereas cell coverage is a major part. Cell coverage is directly related to threshold which is a deciding factor of handover initiation. If the path is same and there is unlimited time for movement in an ideal circumstance, handover rate is independent of speed.

Our algorithm uses the rate of change of SINR to extract candidate group which have biggest rate. If SINR variation is negative, it is too closed to be chosen as a target eNodeB. To keep from selecting neighbors at hand as a target eNodeB, the rate of change of SINR is useful. Among candidate group, our algorithm decides a target eNodeB which has best SINR. In a high dense environment, there are a few candidates whose rate of change of SINR is same. ENodeB with sufficiently good SINR does not cause subsequent handover in a short time.

4 Simulation

Fig. 4 shows deployment of eNodeBs in an ultra-high dense environment. The layout of macro eNodeBs follows seven-cell clusters. Home eNodeBs are distributed randomly. Table 2 describes deployment parameters. The number of home eNodeB is 150 times that of macro eNodeB. The ratio of closed home eNodeB versus open home eNodeB is 1:2. Path loss model as well as interference model, antenna height and other parameters are from IEEE Evaluation Methodology [3]. Though Evaluation Methodology depicts cell-to-cell distance, cell-to-cell distance is not used in the simulation because lots of home eNodeBs are populated by uniform distribution. UE's trajectory follows a space graph proposed by Jardosh [4]. Bounding area is extended to 5km x 5km as shown Fig. 4.

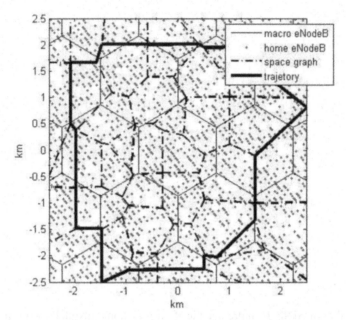

Fig. 4. Deployment of eNodeBs and trajectory of UE

Table 2. Deploy parameters

	Macro eNodeB	Open home eNodeB	Close home eNodeB
Number	37	2700	1350
Distribution	Hexagonal	Uniformly distributed	Uniformly distributed
Cell coverage	1.5km	0.3km	0.3km
Path loss model	COST231	LOS	LOS

Simulation results are captured from a specific run using UE's speed is 100kmph and window size is 20. Fig. 5 shows SINR, uplink delay and downlink delay. UE moves 15.001 km and data of 10.35Mbytes is sliced and is sent and the same amount is received. 31 handover happens and there is no handover to a macro eNodeB. Macro eNodeBs are available to handle very fast moving UEs whose speed is more than 200kmph. Uplink and downlink delay are in inverse proportion to SINR. When handover occurs, delay becomes larger but it is not too big to lose network.

The following simulation results are based on an average observation on 100 different runs. The parameters and their values are same as the one in Fig. 5. Fig. 6 and Table 3 compares smooth algorithm to deferred method. Defer handover decision function and smooth way is common in that they use threshold to decide when to initiate handover. Deferred algorithm does not consider the rate of change of SINR but selects an eNodeB with the best SINR. Fig. 6 illustrates that smooth algorithm is beneficial about 6.57%. If the path is known, the benefit goes up to 24.5%. Table 3 shows that smooth algorithm has merit in data delay as well as handover occurrence. The reason for better performance of our smooth algorithm over deferred algorithm is due to the fact that longer cell duration induces less handover.

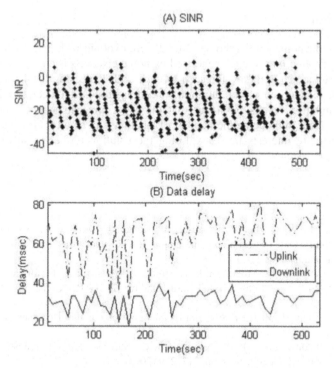

Fig. 5. Smooth algorithm - Simulation results

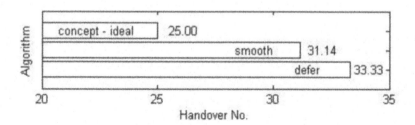

Fig. 6. Handover occurrence according to algorithm

Table 3. Comparison smooth to deferred method

	Deferred	Smooth
SINR (dBm)	-34.754388	-34.746834
Uplink delay (msec)	66.437929	64.063545
Downlink delay (msec)	31.896733	31.238003

5 Conclusion

It is a common phenomenon that home eNodeBs are overlaid with macro eNodeBs in LTE systems. Though interference generated by home eNodeBs is a major issue to be solved, more home eNodeBs are foreseen to cope with increasing local traffic or to cover the private area. Longer cell duration concept is proposed to decrease the handover rate. Simulation results point out that our algorithm can achieve more than 6.57% improvement in reducing the number of handovers in an ultra high dense environment. Our future interests lie in exploring the solution further to solve vertical handover in LTE systems.

References

1. Emmelmann, M., Wiethoelter, S., Koepsel, A., Kapler, C., Wolisz, A.: Moving toward seamless mobility: state of the art and emerging aspects in standardization bodies. Wireless Personal Communications 43(3), 803–816
2. Anas, M., Calabrese, F.D., Mogensen, P.E., Rosa, C., Pedersen, K.I.: Performance Evaluation of Received Signal Strength Based Hard Handover for UTRAN LTE, pp. 1046–1050 (2007)
3. I.B.W.A.W. Group : Draft IEEE 802.16m Evaluation Methodology Document, August 16 (2007)
4. Jardosh, A., Belding-Royer, E.M., Almeroth, K.C., Suri, S.: Towards realistic mobility models for mobile ad hoc networks, pp. 217–229 (2003)
5. 3rd Generation Partnership Project: 3GPP TS 36.300 V8.5.0. 2008-05

Adaptive Beamforming in Wireless Sensor Network in the Presence of Interference Sources

Husnain Naqvi[1], Muhammad Sulayman[2], and Mehwish Riaz[2]

[1] Department of Electrical and Computer Engineering,
The University of Auckland, New Zealand
snaq002@aucklanduni.ac.nz
[2] Department of Computer Science, The University of Auckland, New Zealand
msu1028@aucklanduni.ac.nz, mria007@aucklanduni.ac.nz

Abstract. In adaptive beamforming, the beam produced by sensor network is cumulative result of all sensor nodes in that network. To use beamforming in sensor network, phase synchronization and delay synchronization are the parameters that need to be addressed. In this paper we propose an adaptive algorithm that helps to achieve phase synchronization in order to produce collaborative beamforming in the presence of noise and interference in sensor network. The results show that adaptive filter is computationally efficient, works in the presence of noise and operates in such an environment where the actual beam pattern is known at the receiver side. It has also been noted that the filter produces output which is very close to its optimum value. It has further been shown that when the number of sensors increases, the noise power at the receiver decreases and that the interference power depends upon the ratio between the number of sensors and the number of interference sources.

Keywords: Adaptive filter, Beamforming, Node, Sensor network, Cooperative communication, Collaborative communication, Signal power, Interference power.

1 Introduction

Sensor networks, due to important properties such as low cost, small size and low power consumption, got significance in modern communication systems. The communication problems in sensor networks have been discussed addressed in literature e.g., [1] and [2]. Initially beamforming was used on the receiver side in sensor network but in [3], distributed transmit beamforming involving multiple cellular base stations to improve SNR is presented. However, the synchronization for beamforming has not been addressed in this work. These issues have been discussed in [4] which propose master slave architecture for information transfer where slave nodes find their phase from master node for beamforming. In these model nodes in the network cooperatively transmit the data to the remote receiver and spatial diversity and redundancy available in the sensor network is used to achieve energy efficient communication [4]. The challenge is in devising protocols to coordinate the

D. Ślęzak et al. (Eds.): FGCN/ACN 2009, CCIS 56, pp. 105–113, 2009.
© Springer-Verlag Berlin Heidelberg 2009

transmissions of individual sensors in a distributed fashion [4]. This challenge has been addressed in [5] where Least Mean Square (LMS) algorithm is used for distributed beamforming. In approach, each cluster head (Reference) node has perfect knowledge of its own position and the position of the secondary nodes within the sensor cluster prior to beamforming [5]. Angle of arrival (AOA) of the desired signal is also known to the all sensor in cluster prior to beamforming [5].

Diversity such as time, frequency and antenna is the key factor in the communication systems and recent work has focused on it for cooperative communication. The diversity problems of cooperative communication in cellular networks have been discussed in [6]. Multiple cooperating relays between transmitter and receiver allow distributed coding, decoding and forward or amplify and forward strategy that can achieve maximum gain [7]. In distributed beamforming, synchronization between nodes is considered more important than distributed diversity [8] and synchronization can also be a limiting factor for some classes of distributed diversity schemes [8-11]. Distributed beamforming offers the possibility of achieving power efficiency in wireless ad-hoc networks. It has also been discussed in [8-11] that even partial phase synchronization leads to significant increase in network performance. Energy efficient communication is a fundamental problem in wireless ad-hoc and sensor networks. Feasibility of a distributed beamforming approach for energy efficient communication in wireless ad-hoc network, with a cluster of distributed transmitters emulating a centralized antenna array so as to transmit a common message signal coherently to a distant Base Station, is proposed in [12]. In [9], a collaborative beamforming method is presented with the assumption that the positions of the sensors are known to the base station but the factors of noise and interference are not considered. Distributed beamforming presented in [4] and [12] focus on phase synchronization but the position of sensors are assumed deterministic and noise and interference have also been taken into consideration.

We propose a beamforming approach in the presence of noise and interference and have considered completely deterministic position of the sensors. Our assumption is that the position of sensors is known however, there could be some placement error that translates into phase error. Therefore, we estimate the phase between the reference sensor and other sensors. In this paper an adaptive algorithm that synchronizes the phase is proposed. The phase synchronization achieved by this algorithm is used for collaborative beamforming to transfer the data. The algorithm is analyzed for different number of sensors and it also work in the presence of interference and noise sources.

The remainder of the paper is organized as follows: section 2 describes the system model, mathematical derivation and adaptive beamforming algorithms that are used for beamforming. Section 3 presents the analysis and results followed by conclusions in section 4.

2   System Model

Let $g_i(t)$ be the transmitted signal by the ith sensor, the received signal at the receiver is given by $\text{Re}(g_i(t)e^{jwt+\theta_i})$, where w is the carrier frequency and Θ_i is the phase. To detect the original signal, the carrier frequency w and phase should be known to the

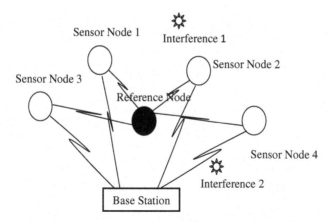

Fig. 1. Geometry of sensor Nodes and other sources

receiver. Carrier frequency can be estimated easily but phase is not as easy to estimate due to the reason that noise and interference produce distortion in phase. We are, therefore, using adaptive filter for phase estimation. Beamforming produces gain in SNR, therefore, we are using the adaptive beamforming algorithm for weight and angle (phase) optimization. It is well known that phase synchronization within cluster of sensor network is cheaper and convergence is faster than phase synchronization between sensors and the receiver [12].

For adaptive beamforming in a sensor network in the presence of noise and interference, we have considered a model with $N \geq 1$ sensors and one receiver with different noise and interference sources. The receiver is static and is fixed but the noise and interference sources are random and non-static. This model is elaborated in the Figure 1.

The block diagram of beam former at receiver is shown in Figure 2 and Adaptive filter to update weights is shown in Figure 3 and Figure 4. The same type of filter is used for angle (phase) adjustment.

In beamformer block diagram presented in Figure 2, the source transmits the known signal $g_i(t)$ where i represents each sensor number with $i \leq N$. Beamformer produces beam steering vector $F_i(\Theta_i(t))$ with n values to get the signal. Noise and interference is also added in the signal. The Steering Vector Formulation block shown in Figure 2 produces the steering vector. Weight adjustment and Angle adjustment is done by Minimum Mean Square Estimation (MMSE) filter which produces the weights and angle $\Theta_i(t)$. Weights adjustment and Angle adjustment blocks shown in Figure 2 represent the MMSE filter whose details are shown in Figure 3 and Figure 4.

Each sensor has a beamformer to transmit the signal but it does not perform angle synchronization. The weights adjustment is done at transmitter which uses the weights calculated at receiver. This means that Figure 2 becomes transmitter beamformer block diagram if Angle adjustment block and steering vector formulation block are removed.

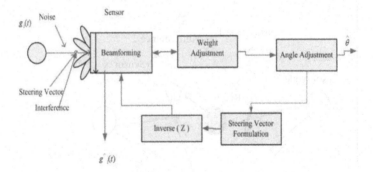

Fig. 2. Block Diagram of System Model at Receiver

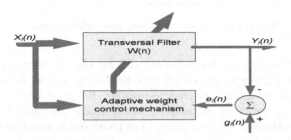

Fig. 3. Block Diagram of Adaptive Weight Adjustment Filter

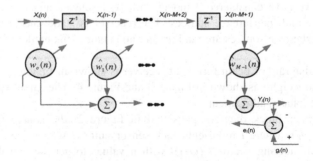

Fig. 4. Structure of Adaptive Filter

The weights and steering vectors are updated recursively. In the first iteration weights are updated by fixing the steering vector. In the next iteration the updated weights are used to update the steering vector. Figure 3 shows the block diagram for adaptive filter to update the weights that are used by beamformer. These weights are updated recursively and a linear transversal filter is used for this purpose. The signal transmitted by transmitter is known to the user and the filter optimizes its weights to detect the optimal value of the signal by taking steering vector constant. The detail of this transversal filter is shown in Figure 4.

Figure 3 and Figure 4 represents the block diagram and transversal filter for weight adjustments, the same block diagram and transversal filter is used for angle (phase) adjustment by changing weights with angle (phase).

2.1 Mathematical Model

The beamformer will produce the steering vector $F_i(\Theta_i(t))$ to detect the signal. The received signal by beamformer is given by

$$X_i(t) = g_i(t)F_i(\theta_i(t)) + n + \gamma, \tag{1}$$

where n is the AWGN Noise and γ is the interference.
   The output of the beamformer is given by

$$Y_i(t) = X_i(t)W_i(t)^{\mathrm{T}}, \tag{2}$$

where $W_i(t)$ is the weight vector and T represents the Transpose.
   In is shown in the literature that the initial weight vector selection leads towards the fast convergence of adaptive filter [11]. As the initial positions of the sensors are known to the reference sensor, the initial weights (when filter start operation) can be calculated as follows instead of initializing it by 1 [11].

$$W_i(t) = \frac{F_i(\theta_i(t-1))}{F_i(\theta_i(t-1))F_i^{\mathrm{H}}(\theta_i(t-1))}, \tag{3}$$

where H represents the Hermition (complex conjugate and transpose).
   The signal $g_i(t)$ transmitted by the transmitter is known to the receiver and it is the desired response.

$$D_i(t) = g_i(t). \tag{4}$$

If the output of the beamformer and desired response are equal then the weights and angle (phase) are optimized. The difference between equation 2 and equation 4 is known as error and is calculated as

$$e_i(t) = D_i(t) - Y_i(t). \tag{5}$$

This error needs to be minimized in order to obtain optimized weights and angle (phase). It is shown in block diagram (Figure 3) that two filters are used to optimize Weights $W_i(t)$ and angle $F_i(\Theta_i(t))$. A recursive procedure is used by applying $F_i(\Theta_i(t))$ to find $W_i(t+1)$ which is then used to find $F_i(\Theta_i(t+1))$.
   For minimization of the error given in equation 5, value of error is squared and its expected value is taken, this is then differentiated w.r.t $W_i(t)$ by keeping $F_i(\Theta_i(t))$ constant and equating it to zero, the $W_i(t)$ then achieve its optimized value as follow

$$e_i^2(t) = E[(D_i(t) - Y_i(t))(D_i(t) - Y_i(t))^{\mathrm{H}}]. \tag{6}$$

For minimized value:

$$\partial(e_i(t)^2)/\partial W_i(t) = 0.   \tag{7}$$

After a simple calculation, the above equation gives the following results.

$$\Rightarrow -2E[D_i(t)X_i(t)] + 2E[X_i(t)X_i(t)^H]W_i(t) = 0,   \tag{8}$$

$$\Rightarrow E[X_i(t)X_i(t)^H]W_i(t) = E[D_i(t)X_i(t)].   \tag{9}$$

The above procedure is used to find the optimal weights; the same procedure as above is used for angle (Phase) optimization. The results are calculated as

$$\Rightarrow E[X'_i(t)X'_i(t)^H W_i(t)W_i^H(t)]F_i(\theta_i(t)) = E[D_i(t)X'_i(t)W_i^H(t)]   \tag{10}$$

where $X'_i(t)$ is the derivative of $X_i(t)$ w.r.t $F_i(\Theta_i(t))$.

From equation 10, the angle (phase) can be found which leads towards the recursive relation for calculating value of $F_i(\Theta_i(t))$.

3   Analysis and Results

We have simulated the above model in MATLAB by considering only one sensor and one transmitter both of which are fixed, their position is known, and there are no noise and interference sources. The initial beam matrix is calculated and is shown in Figure 5. This analysis clearly shows that if position of the sensors is known, collaborative beamforming produces good results.

In Figure 5, there is only one sensor (transmitter) and one receiver and their positions are known to each other. No noise and signal interference is assumed and full power (100 db) is provided to the single sensor. Figure 5 shows that side lobes are very few and their power is very less.

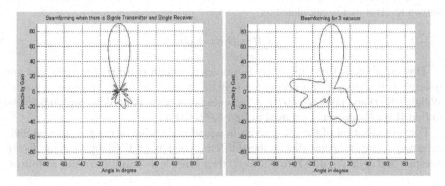

Fig. 5. Beamforming for one transmitter   **Fig. 6.** Beamforming for 3 sensors

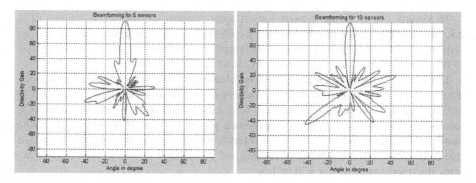

Fig. 7. Beamforming for 5 sensors   **Fig. 8.** Beamforming for 10 sensors

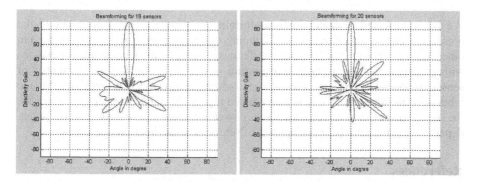

Fig. 9. Beamforming for 18 sensors   **Fig. 10.** Beamforming for 20 sensors

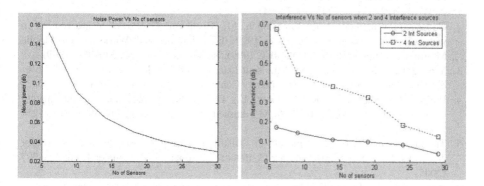

Fig. 11. Noise power vs. No of sensors   **Fig. 12.** Interference power vs. No of sensors

In figures 6, 7, 8, 9 and 10 there are 3, 5, 10, 18 and 20 sensors, respectively with two interference sources. It is noticed that for small number of sensors compared to the interference sources the side lobes have more power and the half-power beam-width gain is not significant.

In Figure 11, the noise power for different number of sensors is shown. It is noticed that the noise power reduces exponentially by increasing the number of sensors. The signal to noise ratio will also increase as number of sensors will increase. In this figure we have not considered any interference sources.

In Figure 12, the interference power is calculated for different number of sensors. There are two and four interference sources in addition to one noise source. It is noticed that the interference power will also reduced when the number of sensors is increased. It is also noticed that interference power is reduced if the ratio between number of sensors and the number of interference sources is increased. This means that if the ratio between number of sensors and the number of interference sources are high, the interference power will be low.

4 Conclusions

We have presented a model for beamforming in wireless sensor networks in the presence of noise and interference assuming one sensor and receiver are static and other sensors, noise sources and interference sources can change their positions without enhancing the network transmitting power. It is shown that as number of sensors is increases than half-power, beam-width significantly improves and the side lobes decrease significantly. It is also noticed that as the number of sensors increases, the noise power and the interference power decreases. The interference power depends upon the ratio between number of sensors and the interference sources.

References

1. Ananthasubramaniam, B., Madhow, U.: Virtual radar imaging for sensor networks. In: Proc. 3rd International Symposium on Information Processing in Sensor Networks (IPSN 2004), April 26–27, pp. 294–300 (2004)
2. Gomez, J., Campbell, A.T., Naghshineh, M., Bisdikian, C.: Power aware routing in wireless packet networks. In: Proc. 1999 IEEE International Workshop on Mobile Multimedia Communications (MOMUC 1999), November 15–17, pp. 380–383 (1999)
3. Yipeng Tang, M., Valenti: Coded transmit macro diversity: block space-time codes over distributed antennas. Vehicular Technology Conference 2, 1435–1438 (2001)
4. Barriac, G., Mudumbai, R., Madhow, U.: Distributed beamforming for information transfer in sensor networks. IEEE/ACM Transactions on Networking (TON) 14(SI), 2725–2748 (2006)
5. Tummala, M., Chee, C., Vincent, P.: Distributed beamforming in wireless sensor Networks. In: Thirty-Ninth Asilomar Conference, October 28 - November 1, pp. 793–797 (2005)
6. Sendonaris, A., Erkip, E., Aazhang, B.: User cooperation diversity. part i. system description 51, 1927–1938 (November 2003)
7. Laneman, J., Wornell, G.: Distributed space-time-coded protocols for exploiting cooperative diversity in wireless networks 49, 2415–2425 (October 2003)
8. Mudumbai, R., Barriac, G., Madhow, U.: Spread-spectrum techniques for distributed space-time communication in sensor networks. In: Proc. 38th Asilomar Conference on Signals, Systems and Computers (Asilomar 2004), Pacific Grove, CA, November 7–10 (2004)

9. Ochiai, H., Mitran, P., Poor, H.V., Tarokh, V.: Collaborative beamforming in ad hoc networks. IEEE Trans. Signal Processing 53(1053-1058), 4110–4124 (2005)
10. Mudumbai, R., Hespanha, J., Madhow, U., Barriac, G.: Scalable Feedback Control for Distributed Beamforming in Sensor Networks. In: Proc. 2005 IEEE International Symposium on Information Theory (ISIT 2005), Adelaide, Australia (September 2005)
11. Mc Whirter, J.G., Shepherd, T.J.: Systolic Array Processor for MVDR Beamforming. IEE Proceedings for Radar and Signal Processing 136(2), 75–80 (1989)
12. Mudumbai, R., Barriac, G., Madhow, U.: On the feasibility of distributed beamforming in wireless networks. IEEE Trans. on Wireless Commun. 6(5), 1754–1763 (2007)
13. Albowicz, J., Chen, A., Lixia, Z.: Recursive position estimation in sensor networks. In: Ninth International Conference on Network Protocols, November 11-14, pp. 35–41 (2001)

Performance Analysis of Collaborative Communication with Imperfect Frequency Synchronization and AWGN in Wireless Sensor Networks

Husnain Naqvi, Stevan Berber, and Zoran Salcic

Department of Electrical and Computer Engineering,
The University of Auckland, New Zealand
snaq002@ec.auckland.ac.nz, s.berber@auckland.ac.nz,
z.salcic@auckland.ac.nz

Abstract. Collaborative communication produces high power gain, if the frequency and phase synchronization is achieved. In this paper a novel architecture is proposed for a collaborative communication system in the presence of AWGN and frequency offsets. The mathematical expressions are derived and verified through simulation for received power and bit error rate (BER) of the system. It is analyzed that using this collaborative communication model, the significant power gain and reduction in BER can be achieved even though the system is with imperfect frequency synchronization. The analysis of the model is performed using the parameters of off-the-shelf products. The analysis revealed that power gain decreases and BER increases as the frequency offsets (errors) are increases.

Keywords: Sensor Network, AWGN, Collaborative Communication, Raleigh Fading, Frequency offsets, Bit Error Rate, Signal to Noise Ratio (SNR).

1 Introduction

Due to limited power of sensor nodes, an energy efficient transmission is the key requirement in sensor networks [1-2]. In collaborative communication, a number of wireless transmitters collaboratively transmit the same message signal to the common target receiver [2-3]. Despite that none of the transmitter can directly reach the receiver with required received power, it was reported in [2-3] that, if the transmitted signal from each individual transmitter can be coherently combined, a large power gain N^2 (where N is the number of collaborative nodes) can be achieved the target receiver. By coherent combination, it means that the phase angles, the frequencies, and the transmission delays of signals from multiple transmitting nodes are expected to be positively constructed in the receiver [2-3]. In collaborative communication the synchronization between nodes is considered more important than distributed diversity [4] and it is also shown that this synchronization can be a limiting factor for some classes of distributed diversity schemes. In [4] it is shown that even partial phase synchronization leads to significant increase in network performance. The directivity patterns achieved through random array are studied in [5].

D. Ślęzak et al. (Eds.): FGCN/ACN 2009, CCIS 56, pp. 114–121, 2009.

Master-slave architecture that achieves phase synchronization by assuming that local communication within the cluster is less expensive and with minimal communication between nodes in cluster and base station is proposed in [2-3]. It is also considered that base station transmit an un-modulated carrier signal to all slave nodes, slave nodes demodulate the signal and estimate the channel coefficients. It is assumed that using these estimated channel coefficients slave nodes pre-amplify the signal to be transmitted, and channel effect (fading) is mitigated. It has been shown that collaborative communication systems produce high gain over traditional single transmission system [6-9] if perfect synchronization among transmitters is achieved. The algorithms and bounds for standard synchronization are also found in [3, 4]. The Cramer-Rao bounds for frequency offset in collaborative communication system is derived and verified by simulation is presented in [10].

One of the major contributions of this paper is the new mathematical model of collaborative communication system that includes the influence of the frequency error and AWGN. The considered figures of merit are received power and BER. Other major contributions are derivations of theoretical expression for the received power as the function of number of sensor nodes and BER as a function of signal to noise ratio (SNR). The simulation results confirmed over theoretical findings. Results show that total received power decreases and BER increases as the frequency error increases. As the number of sensor nodes increases, the received power increases the BER decreases significantly.

The paper is organized as follows. Section 2 describes the system architecture and theoretical model for received power and probability of error calculation in the AWGN channel. Section 3 presents the analysis of theoretical and simulation results and Section 4 presents the conclusions.

2 System Model

To perform collaborative transmission in wireless sensor networks, frequency, time and phase synchronization needs to be achieved. We are proposing a more general architecture in which data is exchanged between the nodes and all the nodes in the network may transmit the data at the same time towards common receiver (base station) as shown in Fig. 1.

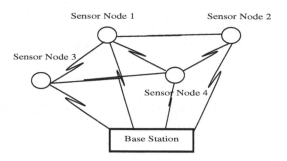

Fig. 1. Geometry of sensor Nodes

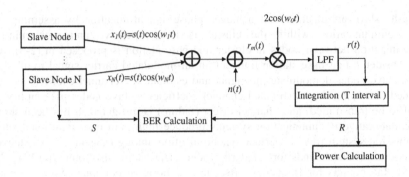

Fig. 2. Theoretical Model of the System

As the sensor nodes have their own oscillators that may cause frequency mismatch among the transmitted signal. The proposed collaborative communication model can achieve high signal to noise ratio gain reduction in BER with imperfect phase synchronization.

2.1 Theoretical Model

Theoretical model of the system is shown in Fig. 2. Let N sensor nodes make a network to transfer the information from master node to the base station. Let $s(t)$ is the information data to be transmitted to the base station.

The signal transmitted by the ith sensor node is given by

$$x_i(t) = s(t)\cos(w_i t),\tag{1}$$

where $w_i = w_0 + \Delta w_i$, w_0 is the carrier frequency and Δw_i is the frequency offset.

The received signal at the base station is the sum of all the signals transmitted by sensor nodes and the noise and is given by

$$r_m(t) = \sum_{i=1}^{N} s(t)\cos(w_i t) + n(t),\tag{2}$$

where $n(t)$ is zero-mean AWGN.

$$r(t) = \sum_{i=1}^{N} s(t)\cos(\Delta w_i t) + n(t).\tag{3}$$

$$R = \sum_{i=1}^{N} S \frac{\sin(\Delta w_i T)}{\Delta w_i T} + n,\tag{4}$$

where $S = \pm\sqrt{E_b}$ is the signal amplitude and n is the noise amplitude at time T.

Power of received signal R is given by

$$P_R = \left| \sum_{i=1}^{N} S \frac{\sin(\Delta w_i T)}{\Delta w_i T} + n \right|^2.\tag{5}$$

As Δw_i and n are the random variables, so we have to calculate the mean value of received power.

$$E[P_R] = E\left[\left|\sum_{i=1}^{N} S \frac{\sin(\Delta w_i T)}{\Delta w_i T} + n\right|^2\right]. \tag{6}$$

As Δw_i and n are the independent random variables and n is zero-mean random variable, after some mathematical derivation the above equation can be written as

$$E[P_R] = \sum_{i=1}^{N} S^2 E\left[\left(\frac{\sin(\Delta w_i T)}{\Delta w_i T}\right)^2\right] + \sum_{\substack{i=1 \\ i \neq j}}^{N}\sum_{j=1}^{N} S^2 E\left[\frac{\sin(\Delta w_i T)}{\Delta w_i T}\frac{\sin(\Delta w_j T)}{\Delta w_j T}\right] + \sigma_n^2, \tag{7}$$

where σ_n^2 is the variance of noise.

As all Δw_i are i.i.d random variables having uniform distribution from $\{-w_e$ to $w_e\}$ for all i, then $E[\Delta w_i] \approx E[\Delta w]$. The equation (7) can now be written as

$$E[P_R] = NS^2 E\left[\left(\frac{\sin(\Delta w T)}{\Delta w T}\right)^2\right] + N(N-1)S^2 E\left[\frac{\sin(\Delta w T)}{\Delta w T}\right]E\left[\frac{\sin(\Delta w T)}{\Delta w T}\right] + \sigma_n^2. \tag{8}$$

Using the values of equation (A.1) and (A.2) equation (8) becomes

$$E[P_R] = NS^2\left[1 + \frac{(w_e T)^4}{180} - \frac{(w_e T)^2}{9}\right] + N(N-1)S^2\left[1 - \frac{(w_e T)^2}{18}\right]^2 + \frac{N_0}{2}. \tag{9}$$

The results obtained from equation (9) and Monte Carlo simulation is discussed in section 3.

2.2 Probability of Error Distribution

Suppose that the data is sent using BPSK. The received signal R depends upon random variables Δw_i and n. The input of the decision circuit is given in equation (4). For BPSK the probability of error in the system [11] is given by

$$P_e = 0.5 erfc\left(\frac{\mu_R}{\sqrt{2\sigma_R^2}}\right). \tag{10}$$

We can represent $R = g + n$ (sum of two random variables), where $g = \sum_{i=1}^{N} S \frac{\sin(\Delta w_i T)}{\Delta w_i T}$. Due to statistical independence of the two random variables we may have and using equation (A.1) and $\mu_n = 0$, we have

$$\mu_R = NS\left[1 - \frac{(w_e T)^2}{18}\right]. \tag{11}$$

Variance of R that is a sum of two independent random variables and using equation (A.3), we have

$$\sigma_R^2 = NS^2 \frac{(w_e T)^4}{405} + \frac{N_0}{2} \tag{12}$$

Because g is a sum of i.i.d random variables, according to the central limit theorem, its distribution tends to Gaussian when N is sufficiently large. Then the sum of g and n is also Gaussian. If we insert (11) and (12) into (10) we may find the probability of error as

$$P_e = 0.5 erfc \left(\frac{NS\left[1 - \frac{(w_e T)^2}{18}\right]}{\sqrt{2\left(NS^2 \frac{(w_e T)^4}{405} + \frac{N_0}{2}\right)}} \right) \tag{13}$$

As $S^2 = E_b$, Equation (13) can be written as

$$P_e = 0.5 erfc \left(\left[1 - \frac{(w_e T)^2}{18}\right] \sqrt{\frac{N^2(E_b/N_0)}{\left(\frac{2N(E_b/N_0)(w_e T)^4}{405} + 1\right)}} \right) \tag{14}$$

If there is no frequency error i.e. $w_e = 0$, the equation (14) is reduced to

$$P_e = 0.5 erfc \left(\sqrt{N^2(E_b/N_0)} \right) \tag{15}$$

3 Analysis and Results

We have simulated the above system in SIMULINK and MATLAB. In our analysis we have considered the parameters of two off-the-shelf products i.e. CC2420 and AT86RF212. Figures 3 and 4 show the analytical and simulation results in the presence of frequency errors for received power at the base station for CC2420 and AT86RF212 respectively. The transmitted signal power by each sensor node is considered 1W and noise power is 0.1W. Results show that analytical results match to the simulation results. It is observed that high power gain can be achieved using collaborative communication in the presence of frequency errors.

Results in Fig. 3 shows that by considering the parameters of CC2420, $0.97\ N^2$, $0.92\ N^2$ and $0.85\ N^2$ power gain can be achieved for frequency errors 150 KHZ, 250 KHz and 350 KHz respectively. Results in Fig. 4 shows by considering the parameters of AT86RF212, $0.95\ N^2$, $0.86\ N^2$ and $0.80\ N^2$ power gain can be achieved for frequency errors 35 KHZ, 55 KHz and 86 KHz respectively.

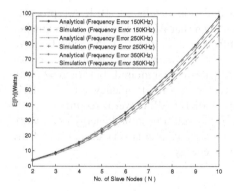

Fig. 3. Received Power for CC2420 with data rate 250Kbps

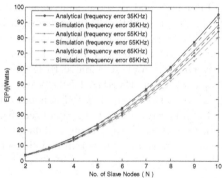

Fig. 4. Received Power for AT86RF21 with data rate 40Kbps

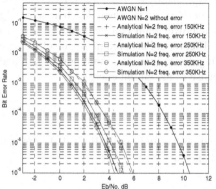

Fig. 5. BER for CC2420 with transmitted power NE_b and data rate 250Kbps

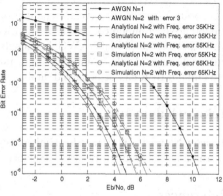

Fig. 6. BER for AT86RF212 with transmitted power NE_b and data rate 40Kbps

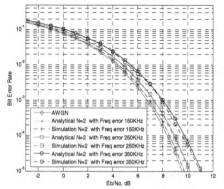

Fig. 7. BER for CC2420 with transmitted power E_b/N and data rate 250Kbps

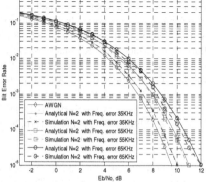

Fig. 8. BER for AT86RF212 with transmitted power E_b/N and data rate 40Kbps

Figures 5 and 6 show analytical and simulation results for BER for products CC2420 and AT86RF212 respectively. It is shown that BER decreases as the number of transmitter increases, which is the confirmation of the fact that collaborative communication produces SNR gain. From Figure 5 it is analyzed that for (number of sensor nodes) $N=1$, to achieve BER 10^{-3}, 7dB power is required, but for $N=2$, with frequency error 150KHz 1.5dB power is required, with frequency error 250KHz 1.7dB power is required, with frequency error 350KHz 2dB power is required.

From Figures 7 and 8 it is analyzed that if the total transmitted energy of network is decreased by N, BER using collaborative communication is very close to the BER for single transmitter transmitting N times more energy.

4   Conclusions

We have presented collaborative communication model for sensor networks with imperfect frequency synchronization in the presence of AWGN. The theoretical model of the system is presented and the expression for received power and the probability of error for AWGN channel are derived. It is concluded that by using collaborative communication (1) a significant power gain can be achieved and (2) BER can be reduced in the AWGN channels. Theoretical and simulation results match with each other. As the number of transmitting nodes increase, more power gain and reduction in BER can be achieved on the expanse of the circuit energy.

Acknowledgments

Husnain Naqvi is supported by Higher education Commission (HEC), Pakistan and International Islamic University, Islamabad, Pakistan.

References

1. Karp, P., Kung, H.T.: Greedy perimeter stateless routing (gpsr) for wireless networks. In: 6th ACM/IEEE International Conference on Mobile Computing and Networking (MOBICOM), pp. 243–254 (2000)
2. Barriac, G., Mudumbai, R., Madhow, U.: Distributed beamforming for information transfer in sensor networks. In: 3rd International Symposium on Information Processing in Sensor Networks (IPSN 2004), pp. 81–88 (2004)
3. Barriac, G., Mudumbai, R., Madhow, U.: On the feasibility of distributed beamforming in wireless networks. IEEE Trans. Wireless Comm. 6(5), 1754–1763 (2007)
4. Barriac, G., Mudumbai, R., Madhow, U.: Spread-spectrum techniques for distributed space-time communication in sensor networks. In: Proc. 38th Asilomar Conference on Signals, Systems and Computers, Asilomar 2004 (2004)
5. Ochiai, H., Mitran, P., Poor, H., Tarokh, V.: Collaborative beamforming for distributed wireless ad hoc sensor networks. IEEE Trans. on Signal Process 53(1053-587X), 4110–4124 (2005)
6. Ochiai, H., Mitran, P., Tarokh, V.: Space-time diversity enhancements using collaborative communications. IEEE Trans. Inf. Theory, 2041–2057 (June 2005)
7. Morelli, M., Mengali, U.: Carrier-frequency Estimation for transmissions over selective channels. IEEE Trans. Commun., 1580–1589 (September 2000)

8. Schmidl, T.M., Cox, D.C.: Robust frequency and timing synchronization for OFDM. IEEE Trans. Commun. 45(12), 1613–1621 (1997)
9. Sendonaris, A., Erkip, E., Aazhang, B.: User cooperation diversity – parts I and II. IEEE Trans. Commun. 51(11), 1927–1948 (2003)
10. Parker, P.A., Bliss, D.W., Mitran, P., Tarokh, V.: Distributed Computing Systems Workshops, 2007. ICDCSW 2007. 27th International Conference, June 2007, p. 82 (2007)
11. Blumenfeld, D.E.: Operations Research Calculations. Crc Press, N.W. Corporate Blvd, Boca Raton, Florida (2000)

Appendix

Let Δw_i is uniformly distributed over $\{-w_e \sim w_e\}$. From the parameters of off-the-shelf products like CC2420 and AT86RF212, the product of Δw_i and T is small.

Mean value of $\dfrac{\sin(\Delta wT)}{\Delta wT}$

$$E\left[\frac{\sin(\Delta wT)}{\Delta wT}\right] = \int_{-w_e}^{w_e} \frac{1}{\Delta wT}\left(\Delta wT - \frac{(\Delta wT)^3}{3!} + \frac{(\Delta wT)^5}{5!} - \frac{(\Delta wT)^7}{7!} + \dots\right)\frac{1}{2w_e}d\Delta w$$

As the $\Delta w_i T$ is small, we can ignore higher order terms.

$$= 1 - \frac{(w_e T)^2}{18} \tag{A.1}$$

Mean value of $\left[\dfrac{\sin(\Delta wT)}{\Delta wT}\right]^2$

$$E\left[\left(\frac{\sin(\Delta wT)}{\Delta wT}\right)^2\right] = \int_{-w_e}^{w_e}\left\{\frac{1}{\Delta wT}\left(\Delta wT - \frac{(\Delta wT)^3}{3!} + \frac{(\Delta wT)^5}{5!} - \frac{(\Delta wT)^7}{7!} + \dots\right)\right\}^2 \frac{1}{2w_e}d\Delta w$$

As the $\Delta w_i T$ is small, we can ignore higher order terms.

$$E\left[\left(\frac{\sin(\Delta wT)}{\Delta wT}\right)^2\right] = 1 - \frac{(w_e T)^2}{9} + \frac{(w_e T)^4}{180} \tag{A.2}$$

Variance of $\dfrac{\sin(\Delta wT)}{\Delta wT}$

$$Var(\frac{\sin(\Delta wT)}{\Delta wT}) = E\left[\left(\frac{\sin(\Delta wT)}{\Delta wT}\right)^2\right] - \left(E\left[\frac{\sin(\Delta wT)}{\Delta wT}\right]\right)^2$$

Using equation (A.1) and equation (A.2) above equation becomes

$$= \left[1 - \frac{(w_e T)^2}{9} + \frac{(w_e T)^4}{180}\right] - \left(1 - \frac{(w_e T)^2}{18}\right)^2 = \frac{(w_e T)^4}{405} \tag{A.3}$$

The Performance Improvement of Searching a Moving Vehicle on Fisheye CCTV Image Using Inverse Diffusion Equation

In-Jung Lee

Computer Engineering, Hoseo University,
BaybangMyun, Asan City, ChungNam, South Korea
leeij@office.hoseo.ac.kr

Abstract. When we are collecting traffic information on CCTV images, we have to install the detect zone in the image area during pan-tilt system is on duty. An automation of detect zone with pan-tilt system is not easy because of machine error. So the fisheye lens attached camera or convex mirror camera is needed for getting wide area images. In this situation some troubles are happened, that is a decreased system speed or image distortion. This distortion is caused by occlusion of angled ray as like trembled snapshot in digital camera. In this paper, we propose two methods of de-blurring to overcome distortion, the one is image segmentation by nonlinear diffusion equation and the other is deformation for some segmented area. As the results of doing de-blurring methods, the de-blurring image has 15 decibel increased PSNR and the detection rate of collecting traffic information is more than 5% increasing than in distorted images.

Keywords: De-blurring, Deformation, Fisheye Image, Nonlinear Diffusion Equation.

1 Introduction

Closed Circuit Television(CCTV) systems have been extensively deployed to monitor freeways in urban areas. While CCTVs have proven to be very effective in monitoring traffic flows and supporting incident management, they simply provide images that must be interpreted by trained operators[1]. These large and expensive video systems have, however, limited functionality. Recently, the university or scientific transportation institution have been researching to extend the CCTV functionality for the most part of detection system via CCTV images, for example integrating CCTV surveillance with video image vehicle detection system(VIVDS) [1,2,3] and detection weather or road surface condition using CCTV[4]. Almost all of CCTV surveillance system must have a pan, tile and zoom(PTZ) drive by reason that CCTV system cannot be displayed bidirectional or more wide area of traffic flow simultaneously. If operators want to view the 360 degree all round area extremely at the same time, four CCTV cameras or convex-mirror [18] or fisheye lens are needed.

D. Ślęzak et al. (Eds.): FGCN/ACN 2009, CCIS 56, pp. 122–132, 2009.
© Springer-Verlag Berlin Heidelberg 2009

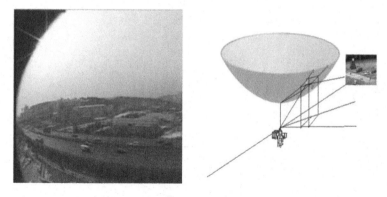

Fig. 1. Fisheye view or convex mirror view

Fig. 2. The blurring is occurred because small size image of fisheye view is spread out to larger size of de-warped image

And if an operator has a single camera when PTZ is on, the detect zone has to install in the CCTV images, this installing system is not easy because of machine error. When we use an improved CCTV added fisheye lens or convex mirror which has a more widely view than ordinary CCTV system, fisheye view is not a familiar image in human eye, distortion across the hemispherical field of view shown as Fig.1.

Then operators in Traffic Management Center (TMC) cannot be monitoring the traffic situation via naked CCTV image with fisheye. But, as in [17], traffic information can be collected within convex image. So the tracking of moving object can be detected, but the speed of vehicle is not properly adaptive in this situation. Also we have to need a transformation algorithm fisheye view into de-warped image.

And when fisheye image spread out in transformation of fisheye view into de-warped image, the blurring occurred because small size image of fisheye view is spread out to larger size of de-warped image shown as Fig.2.

Let a point p(x,y,z) be in the fisheye image and a corresponding point q(a,b) be in flat image as Fig.3. Then we can transform p(x,y,z) to q(a,b) through the equation 1,2, where r is a radius of fish-eye image. So the de-warped image is shown by this transform in Fig.4.

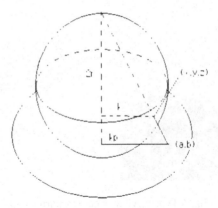

Fig. 3. A matching from one point (x,y,z) on a sphere to the point (a,b) on disc

Fig. 4. A transformed image from a fish-eye image applying equation 1,2

$$a = \frac{2xr}{2r-z} \tag{1}$$

$$b = \frac{2yr}{2r-z} \tag{2}$$

In the paper [14], the de-blurring transformation algorithm with nonlinear equation and shift expansion method such that the de-warped image have to be restored according to expansion of DOV and backward solution[9,10,11,12,13] of wave equation by the reflection and interference of light. But, this method has large number of calculation. In this paper, we propose nonlinear diffusion equation and deformation method in section II. Also we shall show performance of moving vehicle detection performed with de-blurring image in section III.

2 Nonlinear Diffusion Equation and Deformation

In this section, we introduce a discontinuous force function, resulting in a system as equation 3, that has discontinuous right-hand side(RHS)[15].

$$\frac{\partial u_n}{\partial t} = \frac{1}{m_n}\left(F(u_{n+1} - u_n) - F(u_n - u_{n-1})\right) \; n = 1,2,3,\dots N \tag{3}$$

where u_n is a discredited signal and F is a force function.

Such equations received much attention in control theory because of the wide usage of relay switches in automatic control systems. More recently, deliberate introduction of discontinuities has been used in control applications to drive the state vector onto lower-dimensional surfaces in the state space. As we will see, this objective of driving a trajectory onto a lower-dimensional surface also has value in image analysis and in particular in image segmentation. Segmenting a signal or image, represented as a high-dimensional vector, consists of evolving it so that it is driven onto a comparatively low-dimensional subspace which corresponds to a segmentation of the signal or image domain into a small number of regions. The type of force function of interest to us here is illustrated in Fig.5.

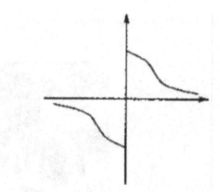

Fig. 5. Force function for a stabilized inverse diffusion equation

More precisely, we wish to consider force functions which satisfy the following properties equation 10 such as

$$F'(v) \le 0 \text{ for } v \ne 0,$$

$$F(0^+) > 0 \tag{4}$$

$$F(v_1) = F(v_2) \text{ if and only if } v_1 = v_2$$

However, because of the discontinuity at the origin of the force function in Fig.5, there is a question of how one defines solutions of equation 4 for such a force function. Indeed, if equation 4 evolves toward a point of discontinuity of its RHS, the value of the RHS of equation 4 apparently depends on the direction from which this point is approached, making further evolution non-unique. We therefore need a special definition of how the trajectory of our evolution proceeds at these discontinuity points. For this definition to be useful, the resulting evolution must satisfy well-posedness properties, that is the existence and uniqueness of solutions, as well as stability of solutions with respect to the initial data. Viewed as a segmentation algorithm, our evolution can be summarized as follows.

1) Start with the trivial initial segmentation: each sample is a distinct region.
2) Evolve equation 5 until the values in two or more neighboring regions become

$$\frac{\partial u_{n_i}}{\partial t} = \frac{1}{m_{n_i}} \left(F\left(u_{n_{i+1}} - u_{n_i}\right) - F\left(u_{n_i} - u_{n_{i-1}}\right) \right)$$

$$u_{n_i} = u_{n_i+1} = \cdots = u_{n_i+m_{n_i}-1}$$

(5)

where

$$i = 1,2,3,\dots p, 1 = n_1 < n_2 \dots < n_{p-1} < n_p \leq N \, n_{i+1} = n_i + m_{n_i}$$

3) Merge the neighboring regions whose values are equal.
4) Go to step 2.

Applying this algorithm to a 256*256 gray image, we obtain a result image as follows Fig.6.

Fig. 6. A result image is right image by applying segmentation algorithm to left image

Nevertheless, we can not find segmented face area which is vary important region for de-blurring. Under the same stability of Eq.5, we propose a parameter α such as

$$\frac{\partial u_{n_i}}{\partial t} = \frac{1}{m_{n_i}} \left(F\left(u_{n_{i+1}} - u_{n_i}\right) - \alpha F\left(u_{n_i} - u_{n_{i-1}}\right) \right)$$

$$u_{n_i} = u_{n_i+1} = \cdots = u_{n_i+m_{n_i}-1}$$

(6)

where

$$i = 1,2,3,\dots p, 1 = n_1 < n_2 \dots < n_{p-1} < n_p \leq N \, n_{i+1} = n_i + m_{n_i}$$

Fig. 7. A result image applied by Eq6

Fig. 8. A de-blurring image is obtained at right from blurring image at left

Applying this Eq6. to a 256*256 gray image, we obtain a result image as follows Fig.7.

In this segmented area, the deformation method is used to get de-blurring image[16]. The deformation equation is defined by equation 7, let a surface be Ω,

$$\frac{\partial \Omega}{\partial t} = \alpha(s,t)T + \beta(s,t)N$$
$$\Omega(s,0) = \Omega_0(s) \tag{7}$$

where T is a tangent and N is a normal vector, α and β are arbitrary function. From this equation 7, we define a curvature deformation equation. Let a function of surface be

$$z = \varphi(x,y,t),$$
$$\frac{\partial \Omega}{\partial t} = -KN$$
$$\Omega(s,0) = \Omega_0(s) \tag{8}$$
$$K = \frac{(\varphi_{xx}\varphi_y^2 - 2\varphi_{xy}\varphi_x\varphi_y + \varphi_{yy}\varphi_x^2)}{(\varphi_x^2 + \varphi_y^2)^{\frac{2}{3}}}$$

Where

Applying equation 8 at a segmented area, we obtain a de-blurring image as Fig.8.

So we apply the CCTV image, we have a de-blurred image as in Fig.9. For evaluation of de-blurring effectiveness, we can choose one line of image in Fig.10, and compute the cross section in Peek Signal To Noise Rate(PSNR), Equation 9, of this data.

$$PSNR = 20 \log_{10} {(\frac{255}{\sigma})}$$ (9)

Where, σ is mean squared errors. The Fig.11 shows the difference of PSNR about 20 decibels with or without de-blurring.

Fig. 9. Blurred image and their de-blurring image

(a) The cross section of blurring image of one line

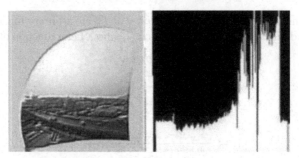

(b) The cross section of de-blurring image with diffusion equation and deformation

Fig. 10. The cross section of blurring image of one line (a) and the de-blurring image with diffusion equation and deformation

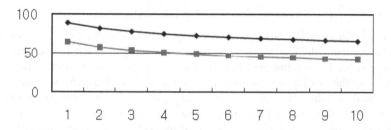

Fig. 11. The blue line is PSNR with de-blurred image and red line is without de-blurring

3   Performance of Moving Vehicle Detection

We transform a fish-eye image to flat image in order to collecting traffic information and then we install the detection zone on the transformed flat image as in Fig.12.

Fig. 12. The detection zone of collecting traffic information in a flat image

But, because of image distortion arising transform process, some trouble has happened for finding a vehicle speed or calculating vehicle numbers amount per properly chosen times as about 3 seconds. So as section II, de-blurring is applied to flat image in order to performance of recognition. Actually, the tracking vehicle is doing as in Fig.13 by using difference image and its binary image. In order to get some information from the binary difference image, we decide the area rectangle of moving vehicle as the fig.14. And we use the equation 10 as for a set R of one line-segment along ① or ②, a binary function OccFlaggs : R → {0, 1} by

$$\text{OccFlags}(x) = \begin{cases} 1 & \text{if } x > \lambda \\ 0 & \text{otherwise} \end{cases} \tag{10}$$

Where $x = \frac{1}{N}\sum_{i}^{N-1} p_{i,j}$ along ② and $x = \frac{1}{N}\sum_{j}^{N-1} p_{i,j}$ along ① $p_{i,j}$ is 0 or 1 that is a value of binary pixel and λ is a deciding factor. The factor λ is obtained by experimental data which is about 20%. But, in this situation we miss the correct line and misread for blurred image, hence get more wide area than real area. Because of this reason, the traffic information is not correct. In Fig. 15, we show some experimental results of vehicle speed compared blurring image arising flat transformation and de-blurring image and fish-eye free camera image. Those experimental processes are played 20th from the same saved video file images. We show that de-blurring image has 5% increasing performance than blurring image. In spite of de-blurring, the performance of flat transformed image is not better than fish-eye free camera image. In this experimental process, almost every speed data is in the interval 2-σ distance from the mean, it is evidence that this experimental system is stable.

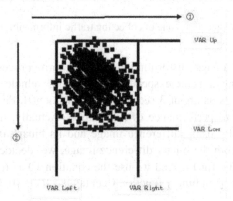

Fig. 13. The detection zone for tracking vehicle

Fig. 14. The area rectangle of moving vehicle

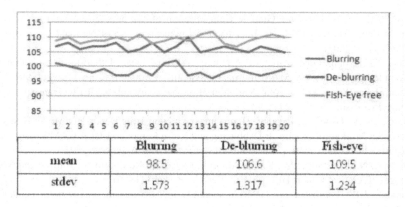

	Blurring	De-blurring	Fish-eye
mean	98.5	106.6	109.5
stdev	1.573	1.317	1.234

Fig. 15. The vehicle speed of blurring, de-blurring and fish-eye free camera image 20th experiments from the same video file

4 Conclusion

An automation of detect zone with pan-tilt system is not easy because of machine error. So the fish-eye lens attached camera or convex mirror camera is needed for getting wide area images. In this situation some troubles are happened, that is a decreased system speed or image distortion. This distortion is caused by occlusion of angled ray as like trembled snapshot in digital camera. In this paper, we propose two methods of de-blurring to overcome distortion, the one is image segmentation by nonlinear diffusion equation and the other is deformation for some segmented area. As the results of doing de-blurring methods, the de-blurring image has 15 decibel increased PSNR and the detection rate of collecting traffic information is more than 5% increasing than in distorted images.

References

1. Namkoong, S., Tanikella, H., Smith, B.: Design and Field Evaluation of a System Integrating CCTV Surveillance with Video Image Vehicle Detection Systems (VIVDS). Paper submitted for presentation at the 2005 Annual Meeting of the Transportation Research Board and publication in the Transportation Research Record, p. 7 (2004)
2. Pack, M.L.: Automatic Camera Repositioning Techniques for Integrating CCTV Traffic Surveillance Systems With Video Image Vehicle Detection Systems. Masters Thesis in Engineering, University of Virginia, Charlottesville, VA (2002)
3. Lee, I.J., Min, J.Y.: Development of an Algorithm for Automatic Installation of Detection Area in CCTV Image on Highways. In: Proc. of the International Conference on Image Science, Systems and Technology, June 26-29, pp. 381–386 (2000)
4. Kenichi, W., et al.: A Study on Sensing System for Running Road Surface Conditions in ITS. In: Proceedings of 10th World Congress on Intelligent Transport Systems, Madrid, Spain (November 2003)

5. Jung, S.H.: A Study on the Graphic Compensation of Warping Image Induced to Wide Angle Lens. Masters Thesis in Industry and Engineering, Seoul National University of Technology (2003)
6. Chan, T.F., Golub, G.H., Mulet, P.: A Nonlinear Primal-Dual Method for Total Variation-Based Image Restoration. SIAM Journal on Scientific Computing 20(6), 1964 (1999)
7. Chan, T.F., Wong, C.K.: Total Variation Blind De-convolution. IEEE Transactions on Image Processing 7(3), 370 (1998)
8. Marquina, A., Osher, S.: Explicit Algorithms for a New Time Dependent Model Based on Level Set Motion for Nonlinear Deblurring and Noise Removal. UCLA CAM Report 99-5, Department of Mathematics, University of California, Los Angeles (1999)
9. Moayeri, N., Konstantinides, K.: An Algorithm for Blind Restoration of Blurred and Noisy Images. Technical Report HPL-96-102, Hewlett-Packard (1996)
10. Dupont, T.L.: Estimates for Galerkin methods for second-order hyperbolic equations. SIAM J. Numer. Anal. 10, 392–410 (1973)
11. Canuto, C., Yousuff, M., Alfio, H., Thomas, Q., Zang, A.: Spectral Methods in Fluid Dynamics. Springer, Heidelberg (1988)
12. Truginy, Y.: Product approximation for nonlinear Klein Gordon equations. IMA journal of Numerical Analysis 9, 449–462 (1990)
13. Lee, I.-J.: Numerical Solution for Nonlinear Klein-Gordon Equation by Using Lagrange Polynomial Interpolation with a Trick. The KIPS Transactions Part A 11-A(7), 571–576 (2004)
14. Lee, I.J., Namkoong, S.J., Min, J.Y.: Expanding Degree of View of CCTV Camera Video Image and De-blurring with Nonlinear Equation. In: Proceedings of 10th World Congress on Intelligent Transport Systems, October 9-12, pp. 485–489 (2007)
15. Pollak, I., Willsky, A.S.: Image Segmentation and Edge Enhancement with Stabilized Inverse Diffusion Equations. IEEE Transactions on Image Processing 9(2), 256–266 (2000)
16. Kimia, B.B., Siddiqi, K.: Geometric Heat Equation and Nonlinear Diffusion of Shapes and Images. Computer Vision and Image Understanding 64(3), 305–322 (1996)
17. Yamazawa, K., Yokoya, N.: Detecting Moving Objects from Omnidirectional Dynamic Images Based on Adaptive background Subtraction. In: ICIP 2003, pp. 210–215 (2003)
18. Huang, H., Hong, H.: Estimation of Omnidirectional Camera Model with One Parametric Projection. LNCIS, vol. 345, pp. 827–833. Springer, Heidelberg (2006)

Scheduling Algorithm for Beacon Safety Message Dissemination in Vehicular Ad-Hoc Networks

Vahid Sadatpour[1,*], Mahmood Fathy[2], Saleh Yousefi[3], Amir Masoud Rahmani[1], Eun-suk Cho[4], and Min-kyu Choi[4]

[1] Department of Computer, Science & Research Branch,
Islamic Azad University, Tehran Iran
{vsadatpour,rahmani}@srbiau.ac.ir
[2] Computer Engineering Faculty,
Iran University of Science and Technology
mahfathy@iust.ac.ir
[3] Computer Engineering Department, Urmia University
s.yousefi@urmia.ac.ir
[4] Dept. of Multimedia, Hannam University 133 Ojeong-dong, Daedeok-gu, Daejeon, Korea
eunsukk@empal.com, freeant7@naver.com

Abstract. Beacon safety message dissemination in Vehicular Ad-hoc Networks (VANETs) suffers from poor reliability especially in congested road traffics. The main origin of this problem is CSMA nature of Dedicated Short Range Communications (DSRC) in MAC layer. In this paper, a scheduling algorithm in the application layer is proposed to alleviate the problem. We first divide the road into a number of geographical sections. In each section, we form a cluster between moving vehicles. Then we perform a scheduling algorithm including two levels. In the first level, nonadjacent clusters can transmit at the same time. While the second level of scheduling deals with inside of each cluster in which we implement a TDMA-like approach. Simulation results show that the proposed algorithm improves the reliability in beacon message dissemination. Moreover, the accuracy of the information which each vehicle can obtain from its neighboring vehicles is significantly increased. Thus the proposed scheduling scheme leads to considerable enhancement of the safety level provided by Beacon Safety Messages (BSMs).

Keywords: beacon message dissemination, safety, scheduling, VANET.

1 Introduction

Dissemination of alarm safety messages as well as comfort messages has been widely investigated in recent literature [1-3], but there are few studies about BSM. In [4] performance of BSM dissemination is studied. The authors conclude that reliability is the most fundamental challenge in disseminating BSM. Since DSRC standard is based on IEEE 802.11, it runs a CSMA-like MAC policy which does not possess any scheduling provision in the medium access. To mitigate this problem, we propose a

---

* Corresponding author.

D. Ślęzak et al. (Eds.): FGCN/ACN 2009, CCIS 56, pp. 133–140, 2009.
© Springer-Verlag Berlin Heidelberg 2009

scheduling algorithm implemented in the application layer. The algorithm will be based on cluster networking.

We adopt the concept of Space Division Multiple Access (SDMA) presented in [5] in which it is assumed that the road has been already subdivided into a series of discrete sections and any vehicle is permitted to access the channel only at the time slot corresponding to the section in which it is located. In [6] and [7], the same concept of SDMA has been represented. In contrast to the existing SDMA scheme, [8] subdivides the road on demand which any section is covered by a cluster of network. The scheduling algorithm of this paper can be implemented among vehicles for sending BSM using method [8].

In this paper, we divide the road into a series of sections in which only nonadjacent sections transmit the beacon message simultaneously. Inside each section we subdivide the section into several subsections where only one vehicle can be placed in each subsection. Furthermore, only one subsection can transmit at the same time.

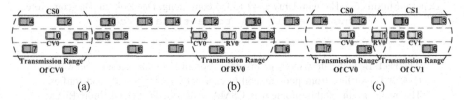

Fig. 1. Cluster formation (a) generation of CV_0; (b) generation of RV_0 (c) generation of CV_1

2 Proposed Scheduling Algorithm

2.1 Cluster Formation

In this step, the network is subdivided into a series of contiguous clusters arranged along the length of the road. The details of this step are as follows. The network configuration is implemented using a Request Message (RM) containing the following control fields.

MT (1-bit): This 1-bit field determines whether the received RM has been broadcasted by a Cluster-head Vehicle (designated as CV) or a Relay Vehicle (designated as RV). If the MT is 0, the message is originated from a CV; otherwise it comes from an RV.

CV-ID (several bits): This field contains the identification number of the current CV.

MD (1-bit): The message direction field. This field indicates the direction of RM transmission with respect to traffic flow. '0' means downstream direction, '1' means upstream direction.

GP (several bits): GPS position field. This field records the GPS position of the CV (or RV) which issued the RM.

The process of cluster formation is depicted in Fig.1. As the figure shows, it is assumed that vehicle number 0 becomes CV_0 with ID_0 (CV-ID = 0), therefore CV_0

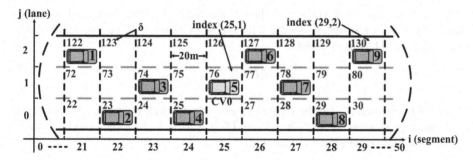

Fig. 2. Road block partitions and time-slot label assignment for $M=3$ and $N=50$

forms cluster space 0 (designated as CS_0). The scope of CS_0 is equal to the transmission range of the CV_0. CV_0 sets the control fields of RM, for example MT = '0', CV-ID = '0', MD = '0' and the GP by its current position and then broadcasts it. In Fig. 1(a), vehicles 4, 0, 7, 2, 9, 1 are within the transmission range of CV_0 thus they receive the RM and become members of CS_0. Furthermore vehicles 2, 9, 1 recognize that they are located in front of CV_0 by checking the GP field of the received RM and their own GPS information and also the MT field of the received RM. To find the vehicle at the head of the scope, each vehicle sets a timer whose initial value is inversely proportional to its distance with the RM's sender, currently the CV. Thus, the timer of the farther vehicle will expire first and it will become RV. For instance, in fig.1 (a) the vehicle number 1 is the farthest from CV_0 among vehicles in the CS_0. Consequently, its timer expires earlier and it'll win the competition. Thereafter, it issues Winner Message (WM) to announce its victory to the others (i.e. vehicles 2, 9). Finally, vehicle 1 takes the role of the relay vehicle and becomes RV_0 (see Fig. 1 (b)). Next, it modifies some specific fields of the RM including MT and GP fields (e.g. MT = '1', GP = the GPS information of RV_0) and rebroadcasts it. As shown in Fig. 1 (b), vehicles 0, 1, 2, 5, 8, 9, 10 are within the scope of RV_0, thus they receive RM, yet vehicles 8 becomes CV among vehicles in front of RV. Note that the vehicles which are behind CV or RV do not participate in the competition and hence ignore the RM.

2.2 BSM Transmission

During the cluster formation step, a series of contiguous clusters are arranged along the road so that any cluster has a unique CV. In order to indicate termination of the cluster formation step, the CV_0 puts the time T in a field of RM. T is sent consecutively by CV_is and RV_is. Finally, all CVs will be aware of T to know when the network clustering is to be terminated. After the end of the cluster formation, each CV broadcasts a Hello Message (HM) to announce its current position to the other vehicles in its corresponding CS. Then in order to transmit the BSM free of collisions, a kind of Time Division Multiple Access (TDMA) mechanism is employed. To reach this goal, each CS is subdivided into N segments

$$N = \frac{2R}{L_s} \qquad (1)$$

where R is the transmission range of the CV and the Ls is the minimum allowed distance of two vehicles. Recall that 2R is the length of each CS. If the road has M lane, there are B road blocks in each CS

$$B = M \times N \qquad (2)$$

where only one vehicle can be located in each block. Each road block is identified with index (i, j) where $0 \leq i \leq N - 1$ and $0 \leq j \leq M - 1$. As shown in Fig. 2, each road block is assigned a time-slot label as:

$$\delta = i + j \times N + 1 \qquad (3)$$

Then each vehicle sends its BSM in accordance with its own road block therefore each vehicle should be able to identify its own block. For this purpose, it should be able to determine the index (i, j). We assume that each vehicle is equipped with digital maps and it can use its own Global Position System (GPS) receiver to recognize its lane, thus j can be identified for any vehicle. Furthermore, each vehicle can determine i using the following formula:

$$Segment\ (i) = \left\lfloor \frac{R}{Ls} \right\rfloor + \left\lfloor \frac{Xv - Xcv}{Ls} \right\rfloor \qquad (4)$$

where x_v and x_{cv} are x-coordinate of the vehicle and CV_i, respectively. For example, Fig. 2 shows a part of CS_0, supposing R=500m, Ls=20m, vehicle 9 can identify index (i, j) using its own GPS receiver and (4) (x_{cv} has been already received by HM). Thus it can obtain δ using (3) and send its message at the $130t+T_{hello}$ ($x_{cv} = 20 \times 25$, $x_v = 20 \times 29$), where t is the duration of sending message and T_{hello} is when HM was issued. As shown in Fig. 3, collisions may happen if vehicles belonging to adjacent CSs send BSMs simultaneously.

To avoid this problem, the even-numbered CVs will send HM at T_{hello} and the odd-numbered CVs will send it at $T_{hello}+\Delta$, where

$$\Delta = B \times t \qquad (5)$$

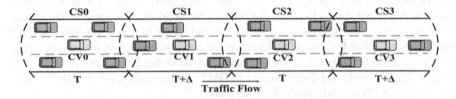

Fig. 3. Clusters synchronization

3 Performance Evaluation

Performance evaluation of the proposed scheduling algorithm is done by GloMoSim library 2.03 [11]. We used IEEE 802.11 (which is the base of DSRC standard) as a MAC layer protocol and Two-ray-ground as a radio model. We also made use of realistic movement patterns published by European FleetNet [10] Project. We have assumed that each vehicle sends a BSM with size 512 bytes every 500ms [4]. In order to compare the performance of our algorithm, we also simulated a scenario in which no scheduling is applied. For this case we send information with 10% jitter in the transmission starting time. Simulations were performed with following 3 scenarios:

1) Traffic density is 2 veh/km/lane and the number of vehicles is 86.
2) Traffic density is 6 veh/km/lane and the number of vehicles is 271.
3) Traffic density is 11 veh/km/lane and the number of vehicles is 473.

In the following, we have compared performance of beacon message transmission in the above-mentioned scenarios with and without the proposed scheduling algorithm. Three performance metrics are considered as follows: number of collisions, beacon messages reception rate and the accuracy of neighbor information. The first two metrics are intended to measure the QoS of the BSM transmission while the aim of the

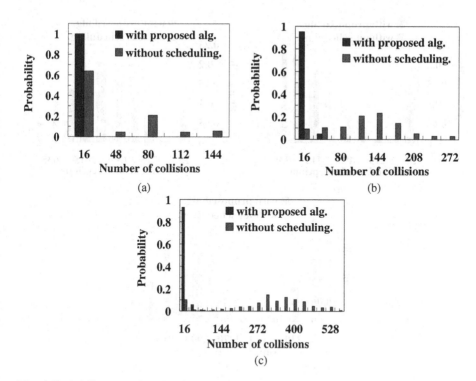

Fig. 4. Probability mass function for number of collisions in (a) scenario 1 (b) scenario 2 (c) scenario 3

third one is to quantify the success level of beacon safety dissemination application. Note that the ultimate goal of any beacon message dissemination algorithm is to provide exact information for each vehicle about its neighboring vehicles. Thus having a metric that evaluate this factor is of great importance. To the best of our knowledge this metric is firstly defined in this paper. We compute the accuracy of adjacent list information as follows. First, we calculate the distance between any vehicle and its neighbors from the following well known equation:

$$d_i^j = \sqrt{(y_i - y_j)^2 + (x_i - x_j)^2} \tag{6}$$

where (x_i, y_i) are coordinates of vehicle i, and (x_j, y_j) are coordinates of vehicle j in the neighboring list of vehicle i. This distance is computed once really from the movement file, denoted by d_{i-real}^j.

Then it is obtained another time from the information which vehicles i has in its neighboring list during the simulation, denoted by d_{i-sim}^j. Afterward, the relative error in distance between vehicle i and one of its neighbors (i.e. vehicle j), is calculated as:

$$E_i^j = \frac{d_{i-real}^j - d_{i-sim}^j}{d_{i-real}^j} \tag{7}$$

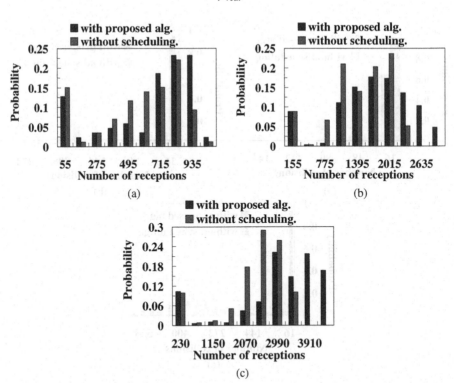

Fig. 5. Probability mass function for number of message receptions in (a) scenario 1 (b) scenario 2 (c) scenario 3

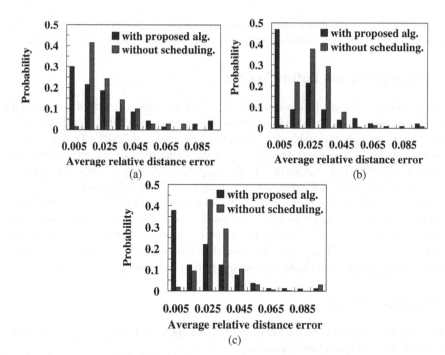

Fig. 6. Probability mass function for average distance errors in (a) scenario 1 (b) scenario 2 (c) scenario 3

Then we take the average by (8) to obtain the error of vehicle i, where n is the number of neighbors of vehicles i.

$$E_i = \sum_j E_i^j \Big/ n \qquad (8)$$

We consider some grouping and judge the average value of each group as its designated value (shown in X-axis). The Y-axis in the probability of events related to each group.

Fig. 4 shows probability mass function for the number of collisions in three aforementioned scenarios. In this figures, each group contains 32 values (e.g.,[0, 31], [32, 64] ...). The horizontal axis is designated of each group (e,g, designated of goup [0, 31] is 16).

As can be concluded from the figure, the probability of large number of collisions are considerably lower in the presence of the proposed scheduling algorithm. In addition, by comparison between 3 aforementioned scenarios, one can easily find out that as the traffic becomes denser, the number of collisions increases. These results are expected due to CSMA nature of the MAC layer. Fig. 5 shows the probability mass function for the number of received beacon message. If a vehicle obtains more messages, it will have more updated information about its neighbors. As shown, there is larger number of vehicles with higher received messages in presence of proposed scheduling algorithm. Moreover, Fig. 6 illustrates probability mass function for the average relative distance error to all member of adjacent list. As the figure suggests, the probability of large average distance errors is considerably lower in presence of proposed scheduling algorithm. As we know when the average distance error is lower, then each vehicle has more accurate information about its neighbors. In other words, the adjacent list accuracy increases in presence of proposed scheduling algorithm.

4   Conclusions and Future Works

Beacon safety message dissemination by all vehicles causes saturated medium and thus the reliability is deteriorated noticeably. The main cause of this is collision in the MAC layer which is inevitable due to CSMA-like nature of DSRC. To alleviate the problem, in this paper, we proposed a scheduling algorithm in the application layer aiming at increasing the reliability. In the proposed algorithm, vehicle disseminates their beacon messages in a pre-determined time slots. Thus collisions are avoided except for few vehicles mainly because of dynamic nature of traffic. The results of our simulation show that the proposed algorithm decreases the number of collisions and increase the reception rate as well as the accuracy of vehicle's information about their neighboring vehicles. The latter, give us a direct sense on the benefits of our algorithm in provisioning an acceptable level of safety for vehicles.

Acknowledgement

This work was supported by the Security Engineering Research Center, granted by the Korea Ministry of Knowledge Economy.

References

1. Benslimane, A.: Optimized dissemination of alarm messages in Vehicular Ad-hoc NETworks (VANETs). In: Mammeri, Z., Lorenz, P. (eds.) HSNMC 2004. LNCS, vol. 3079, pp. 655–666. Springer, Heidelberg (2004)
2. Wischhof, L., Ebner, A., Rohling, H.: Information dissemination in self-organizing intervehicle networks. IEEE Trans. On Intell. Transp. Syst (2005)
3. Adler, C., Eigner, R., Schroth, C., Strassberger, M.: Context-adaptive Information Dissemination in VANETs –Maximizing the Global Benefit. In: Proc. 5th IASTED Int. Conf. on communication System and Networks, pp. 7–12 (2006)
4. Yousefi, S., Fathy, M., Benslimane, A.: Performance of beacon safety message dissemination in vehicular Ad-hoc NETworks (VANETs). Journal of Zhejiang University Science A 8(12), 1990–2004 (2007)
5. Bana, S.V., Varaiya, P.: Space Division Multiple Access (SDMA) for Robust Ad Hoc Vehicle Communication Networks. In: Proc. IEEE ITS, pp. 962–967 (2001)
6. Blum, J., Eskandarian, A.: Adaptive Space Division Multiplexing: An Improved Link Layer Protocol for Inter-Vehicle Communications. In: Proc. IEEE ITS, pp. 455–460 (2005)
7. Blum, J., Eskandarian, A.: A Reliable Link-Layer Protocol for Robust and Scalable Intervehicle Communications. IEEE Trans. On ITS 8(1), 4–13 (2007)
8. Chang, W.R., Lin, H.T., Chen, B.X.: TrafficGather: An Efficient and Scalable Data Collection Protocol for Vehicular Ad Hoc Networks. In: Proc. IEEE CCNC (2008)
9. HWGui and HighwayMovement Homepage,
   http://www.informatik.uni-mannheim.de/pi4/projects/HWGui
10. Glomosim library 2.03 Simulator,
   http://pcl.cs.ucla.edu/projects/glomosim

Influence of Low-Pass Filtering on Perceived Quality of Asymmetrically Coded Stereoscopic Images

Xu Wang, Mei Yu, You Yang, and Gangyi Jiang

Institute of Circuits and Systems, Ningbo University, Ningbo 315211, China

Abstract. Measurement of visual quality is of fundamental importance for numerous stereoscopic image and video processing applications. The effect of distortions on the perceived stereoscopic images quality already been investigated. But few works focus on the weight preference between distortion types. This paper firstly analyzed the weight preference of stereoscopic images between distortion types. The results show that human rating on quality of stereoscopic image will be insensitive, when the quality of left view image keep constant and the right view is Gaussian blurred. Secondly, this paper investigates whether low-pass filtering on JPEG compressed stereoscopic image can enhance the stereoscopic perceptual quality. The results of the experiments show that low-pass filtering may be used to enhance the perceived quality of stereoscopic images in which the right view image is JPEG compressed at an extent of distortion. Furthermore, the enhancement is image content dependent.

Keywords: Quality Enhancement, Quality Assessment, Stereoscopic Perceptual Quality.

1. Introduction

Stereoscopic image processing is getting public attentions these days, and it will be a promising entertainment implementation for customers [1]. Compared to monoscopic images, stereoscopic images contain more perceptual details with the same spatial resolution [2], which has created a widespread interest in designing and standardizing technologies for production[3], coding[4], and viewer of Three-Dimensional television(3DTV) [5]. However, image distortion and unwanted side effects of current 3DTV system have hampered development of 3DTV. For example, stereoscopic coding approach may result in blockiness[6, 7] and cause eye-strain. Therefore, quality assessment and improvement of stereoscopic images is an important issue in research.

Quality assessment of monoscopic image can be categorized as subjective and objective approaches. Subjective tests can be performed in order to find the factors that can affect human psychologically. Objective approach can predict perceived image quality automatically and is employed to benchmark image processing algorithms widely [9]. But these contributes in monoscopic image quality assessment can not be applied to stereoscopic image directly, since the stereoscopic image contains depth information and typical stereoscopic distortions are not incorporated with monoscopic image. Before the stereoscopic image quality can be modeled, a

D. Ślęzak et al. (Eds.): FGCN/ACN 2009, CCIS 56, pp. 141–148, 2009.
© Springer-Verlag Berlin Heidelberg 2009

deeper understanding is needed of the relationship between the physical system parameters and the perceptual factors contributing perceived stereoscopic image quality [8]. Some significant subjective quality assessment experiments concerning on concrete stereoscopic image or video processing had already been made. To research the response of the human visual system to compressed and mixed-resolution stereoscopic video, Stelmach applied a different compression ratio on the left and right views of a stereo sequence using MPEG-2(introducing blockiness) [10] and low-pass filtering (introducing blur)[11]. The results showed that the subjective image quality of a stereo image sequence fell approximately midway between the qualities of the left- and right-eye views when MPEG-2 coding was used. Seuntiëns analyzed the effects of symmetric and asymmetric JPEG coding and camera separation [12] to show that the relationship between perceived image quality and average bit-rate is not straightforward. To improve the performance of stereoscopic video compression or virtual images rendering, Tam had conducted a series of experiments to understand human perception of stereoscopic images [13, 14, 15]. However, few works focus on the weight preference between distortion types.

In this paper, the weighting preference between different distortion types is discussed. Then we investigate the influence of low-pass filtering on stereoscopic image quality where the right view is JPEG compressed.

This paper is organized as follows. Section 2 will discuss the weighting preference between different distortion types and then, experimental detail and results will be given in section 3. Finally, in section 4, we will discussion the results and give a short outlook on our future work.

2   Weighting Preference between Distortion Types

In our previous investigation [17], ten test stereoscopic images are selected from Middlebury Stereo Vision Lab stereo image dataset [18,19] as listed in Fig.1. These images are rectified and radial distortion has been removed. Therefore, these calibrated images are crystal clear and qualified for quality evaluation. The right view of stereoscopic images was processed with different distortion types. Total 370 distorted stereoscopic images have been evaluated by participants in the experiments. The controllable distortion can be manually added on images with specific parameters, and these distortions include JPEG2000 compression, JPEG compression, white noise and Gaussian blur.

The results show the relationships between distortion parameters and perceived quality of stereoscopic images are different for distortion types. Human rating on stereoscopic image quality will be insensitive, when left view image keep constant quality and right view is Gaussian blurred. Quality rating will be more sensitive, when left view image keep constant quality and right view is JPEG compressed. In other words, weighting preferences from different participants in the procedure of stereoscopic image quality experiments directly affect the final perceived quality score. The preference shows that the score will be different even though the right views are with the same subjective quality when participants are assessing the quality of two different distorted type stereoscopic images. There will be no obvious weighting preference for different distortion types in the quality assessment of

Fig. 1. Images used in the experiments. (a) *Art* (b) *Bowling1* (c) *Computer* (d) *Dolls* (e) *Drumsticks* (f) *Dwarves* (g) *Laundry* (h) *Mobius* (i) *Reindeer* (j) *Rocks1*.

monoscopic images. So far, few works notice the weight preference between distortion types. In this section, we choose the Peak Signal-to-Noise Ratio (PSNR) value and Measurement of Structural Similarity (SSIM) index [20] as the quality index of right view images to investigate the weight preference between distortion types, respectively. We choose the Bowling1 and Drumsticks test images for examples, where the quality rating data is provided from [17]. For distortion types JPEG coding and Gaussian blurring, Figs. 2(a) and 2(b) show the mean score and its 95% confidence interval when PSNR is changed, respectively. Figs. 2(c) and 2(d) show the mean score and its 95% confidence interval when SSIM index is changed, respectively. The dotted curves in both figures give similar trends and indicate that DMOS value will decrease when the volume of distortion becomes smaller. On the other hand, Gaussian blurred images will have the minimal DMOS value in both examples if all distortion with same PSNR or SSIM index. The JPEG compression distortion will have the maximal DMOS value in this kind of comparison. In other words, participants will tend to give weighting preferences on blurred images. Based on this, we conduct a subjective experiment to investigate whether the Gaussian blurring (low-pass filtering) can improve the quality of impaired stereoscopic image with JPEG compression. The experiment detail and result will be described in Section-3.

3   Experimental Details and Results

The subjective human trial, based on the ITU-R Recommendation 500, assess the quality of distorted stereoscopic images relative to the originals. The double-stimulus continuous quality-scale (DSCQS) method [16] for stereoscopic image assessment is followed. The DSCQS method is cyclic, in which the participants will view a pair of pictures of the same image, the compressed and uncompressed original ones, and will be asked to assess the quality of both. The assessors will be presented with a series of

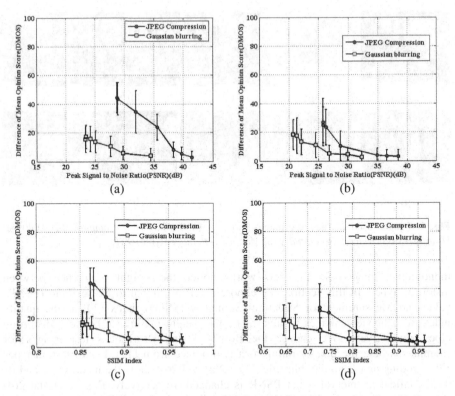

Fig. 2. Comparative results of distortion types JPEG coding and Gaussian blurring. (a) Results of *Bowling1* vs. PSNR value. (b) Results of *Drumsticks* vs. PSNR value. (a) Results of *Bowling1* vs. PSNR value. (b) Results of *Drumsticks* vs. PSNR value.

stereoscopic image pairs in random order, with compression amounts covering all required combinations. Then the mean scores for each distortion type and image will be calculated.

3.1 Display and Viewing Conditions

Polarization-multiplexed display method is used in the experiments. Stereoscopic images are played back through a duality stereoscopic projection system where two BenQ P8265 DLP projectors are used as front projectors. The duality projection system is used in conjunction with the DELL real-time 3D graphics workstations to provide a complete stereoscopic production and replay system. The size of stereoscopic projection screens is 150 inches. Polarized glasses are worn in order to separate left and right images on a single screen to the appropriate eyes. The experiments are conducted in a special room that ambient illumination, color temperature and ambient sound can be controlled over according to the requirements in ITU-R Recommendation 500.

3.2 Test Stereoscopic Images Generation

We choose Bowling1 and Drumsticks in Fig.1 as the original images. Based on the results of our previous work, we first generate the distorted images by compressing the right images (full color) with JPEG at four different compression levels. The implementation used was the imwrite function in MATLAB [9]. Table 1 gives the PSNR value, SSIM index and Compression Level of each stereoscopic image. Then each JPEG compressed images is impaired by Gaussian blurring. The standard deviation σ is 3 and 10 pixels where the window size is 45 pixels, respectively. The three color components of the right image were blurred using the same kernel. Thus in total, 2 scenes, 4 compression levels of JPEG compression, 3 blurring levels are used in this Phase. The number of test images is 2×4×3=24.

Table 1. PSNR value, SSIM index and quality level of test images

Compression Level	Bowling1		Drumsticks	
	PSNR(dB)	SSIM index	PSNR(dB)	SSIM index
2	28.772	0.8615	25.77	0.7268
5	31.995	0.8788	28.683	0.8092
10	35.569	0.9138	34.905	0.9283
30	39.718	0.9530	36.511	0.9468

3.3 Participants

There are 20 participants be recruited in campus, whose age varies from 20 to 24 with a mean of 23 years. All participants of the experiment meet the minimum criteria of acuity of 20:30 vision, stereo-acuity at 40 sec-arc, and passed the color vision test. All of them are non-expert, in that they are not directly concerned with image quality in their normal work, and are not experienced image assessors. Participants are not aware of the purpose of the experiment, or that one of the stereoscopic images is origin.

Before the start of the experiment, subjects received instructions and completed a practice trial of the stereo display. The trial contains 4 sets of stereo images viewed and rated in the same ways as for those in the later experiments, but these practice trials are not included in the experiment analyses.

3.4 Grading Scale and Processing of Raw Data

1) In each trial the images are rated on a sliding scale of Excellent, Good, Fair, Poor and Bad. Participants are asked to assess the overall image quality of each stereo pair by writing in the answer sheet. In the data processing stage, the difference mean opinion scores (DMOS) will be evaluated using the recommendations adapted from ITU-R Recommendation BT.500 16 on a scale of 0-100.

For calculation of DMOS scores, the raw scores are first converted to raw quality difference scores as

$$d_{ij} = r_{iref(j)} - r_{ij} \tag{1}$$

where r_{ij} is the raw score for the i-th subject to j-th stereoscopic image pair, and $r_{iref(j)}$ denotes the raw quality score assigned by the i-th subject to the reference image corresponding to the j-th distorted image. Then, raw difference scores d_{ij} were converted into DMOS which is the mean of the raw difference scores.

2) Outlier Detection and Subject Rejection [9]: A simple outlier detection and subject rejection algorithm are chosen. Raw difference score for an image is considered to be an outlier if it was outside a 95% confidence interval of the mean score for that image. All quality evaluations of a subject will be rejected if more than 10% of his evaluations in that phase are outliers. In this experiment, the number of rejected subjects is 3.

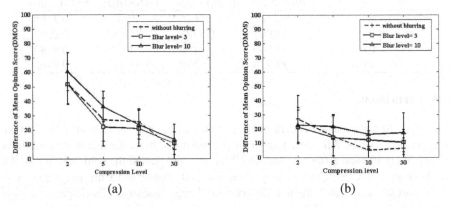

(a)   (b)

Fig. 3. Error bar for image quality for the scenes *Bowling1* and *Drumsticks*. (a) Results of *Bowling1*. (b) Results of *Drumsticks*.

3.5 Experimental Results

Fig.3 (a) and Fig.3 (b) shows the mean quality score, and 95% confidence interval for the scenes *Bowling1* and *Drumsticks,* respectively. Their x-axis represent the compression level of JPEG coded images. The three curves in the figures represent three levels of Gaussian blurring with different standard deviation, unimpaired, 3, 10 pixels. The quality scores show that when the DMOS value between 20 and 30, the low-pass filtering will enhance the quality of JPEG compressed images. when the DMOS value is low than 20 or higher than 30, low-pass filtering on JPEG compressed images will increased the DMOS value (the perceived quality will decrease). This fact can be explained that low-pass filter can smooth the blockiness artifact caused by JPEG compression in some cases.

4 Discussions

In this paper, investigating on the experiments data in our previous work shows that there exists weighting preference of distortion types when participants quality rating. Given a right view image is distorted by JPEG compression and Gaussian blurring but with the same PSNR value or SSIM index, respectively. The quality rating of stereoscopic images with Gaussian blurring will be better than that of JPEG compressed. This phenomenon is meaningful for objective quality metric designing.

The results of subjective experiments show that Gaussian blurring may be used to enhance the perceived quality of stereoscopic images in which the right view image is JPEG compressed at an extent of distortion. Furthermore, the enhancement is image content dependent.

In the near future, we will try to investigate the stereoscopic image quality perception more precisely, and design a new objective quality metric for stereoscopic images which is distortion type independent.

Acknowledgements

This work was supported by the Natural Science Foundation of China (grant 60672073, 60872094), the Program for New Century Excellent Talents in University (NCET-06-0537), and Natural Science Foundation of Ningbo (grant 2007A610037).

References

1. Kalva, H., Christodoulou, L., Mayron, L., et al.: Challenges and opportunities in video coding for 3DTV. In: IEEE International Conference on Multimedia and Expo, pp. 1689–1692. IEEE Press, New York (2006)
2. Hakkinen, J., Kawai, T., Takatalo, J., et al.: Measuring stereoscopic image quality experience with interpretation based quality methodology. In: Proceedings of SPIE-IS&T Electronic Imaging, SPIE, vol. 6808, 68081B. SPIE Press, San Jose (2008)
3. Alatan, A.A., Yemez, Y., Güdükbay, U., et al.: Scene representation technologies for 3DTV - A survey. IEEE Transactions on Circuits and Systems for Video Technology 17, 1587–1605 (2007)
4. Karlsson, L.S., Sjostrom, M.: Region-of-interest 3D video coding based on depth images. In: 3DTV Conference: The True Vision - Capture, Transmission and Display of 3D Video, pp. 141–144. IEEE Press, Los Alamitos (2008)
5. Jiang, G.Y., Fan, L.Z., Yu, M., et al.: New view generation method for free-viewpoint video system. WSEAS Transactions on Computers 7, 589–598 (2008)
6. Smolic, A., Mueller, K., Stefanoski, N., Osteraiann, J.A., et al.: Coding algorithms for 3DTV - A survey. IEEE Transactions on Circuits and Systems for Video Technology 17, 1606–1620 (2007)
7. Tam, W.J., Stelmach, L.B., Meegan, D., et al.: Bandwidth reduction for stereoscopic video signals. In: Proc. SPIE, vol. 3957, pp. 33–40. SPIE Press, San Jose (2000)
8. Meesters, L.M.J., Jsselsteijn, W.A., Seuntiens, P.J.H.: A survey for perceptual evaluations and requirements of three-dimensional TV. IEEE Transaction on Circuits and Systems for Video Technology 14, 381–391 (2004)

9. Sheikh, H.R., Sabir, M.F., Bovik, A.C.: A statistical evaluation of recent full reference image quality assessment algorithms. IEEE Transactions on Image Processing 15, 3440–3451 (2006)
10. Stelmach, L.B., Tam, W.J.: Stereoscopic image coding: Effect of disparate image-quality in left- and right-eye views. Signal Processing: Image Communication, Special Issue on 3D Video Technology 14, 111–117 (1998)
11. Stelmach, L.B., Tam, W.J., Meegan, D.V., et al.: Stereo image quality: Effects of mixed spatio-temporal resolution. IEEE Transactions on Circuits and Systems for Video Technology 10, 188–193 (2000)
12. Seuntiëns, P., Meesters, L., IJsselsteijn, W.: Perceived quality of compressed stereoscopic images: Effects of symmetric and asymmetric JPEG coding and camera separation. ACM Transactions on Applied Perception 3, 95–109 (2006)
13. Tam, W.J., Alain, G., Zhang, L., et al.: Smoothing depth maps for improved stereoscopic image quality. In: Proc. SPIE, vol. 5599, pp. 162–172. SPIE Press, San Jose (2004)
14. Tam, W.J., Zhang, L.: Non-uniform smoothing of depth maps before image-based rendering. In: Proc. SPIE, vol. 5599, pp. 173–183. SPIE Press, San Jose (2004)
15. Zhang, L., Tam, W.J.: Stereoscopic image generation based on depth images for 3D TV. IEEE Transactions on Broadcasting 51, 191–199 (2005)
16. ITU-R Recommendation. BT.500-10.: Methodology for the subjective assessment of the quality of television pictures. Geneva (June 2000)
17. Wang, X., Yu, M., Yang, Y., et al.: Research on subjective stereoscopic image quality assessment. In: Proceedings of SPIE-IS&T Electronic Imaging, SPIE, vol. 7255, 725509. SPIE Press, San Jose (2009)
18. Scharstein, D., Pal, C.: Learning conditional random fields for stereo. In: IEEE Computer Society Conference on Computer Vision and Pattern Recognition. IEEE Press, New York (2007)
19. Hirschmüller, H., Scharstein, D.: Evaluation of cost functions for stereo matching. In: IEEE Computer Society Conference on Computer Vision and Pattern Recognition. IEEE Press, New York (2007)
20. Wang, Z., Bovik, A.C., Sheikh, H.R., et al.: Image quality assessment: From error visibility to structural similarity. IEEE Transactions on Image Processing 13, 600–612 (2004)

Module-Based Finite Automata: A Scalable and Memory-Efficient Architecture for Multi-pattern Matching in Deep Packet Inspection[*]

Junchen Jiang[1], Yi Tang[1], Xiaofei Wang[2], and Bin Liu

[1] Department of Computer Science and Technology, Tsinghua University China PRC
[2] Department of Computer Science and Technology, Dublin City University, Ireland
livejc@gmail.com

Abstract. Multi-pattern matching is a critical technique for building high performance Network Intrusion Detection Systems (NIDS) and Deep Packet Inspection System (DPIS). Given a set of signature database, multi-pattern matching compares packet against patterns to detect the known attacks. Deterministic Finite Automaton (DFA) is widely used for multi-pattern matching in NIDS for its constant matching speed even in the worst case. Existing DFA-based works have claimed to achieve a high speed throughput at expenses of extremely high memory cost and logic complexity, so it fails to meet the memory space requirements of embedded system or high performance routers. In this paper, we propose a novel a memory-efficient multi-pattern matching acceleration scheme called Module-based Finite Automata (MB-FA) which could achieve a great acceleration with little memory duplication. The basic idea of MB-FA is to store the original DFA in independent modules with a delicate algorithm so that inter-flow parallelism can be exploited to its largest scale. A full systematic design of MB-FA is presented, and support for rule update is also introduced. Evaluation experiments show that without any optimization, MB-FA can achieve an average speed-up of 20 times when the memory cost is almost the twice of original DFA.

Keywords: deterministic finite automata (DFA), deep packet inspection (DPI).

1 Introduction

Network Intrusion Detection/Protection Systems (NIDS/NIPS) are widely deployed to safe-guard the security of network. Since that most of the known attacks can be represented with pattern (string), multi-pattern matching becomes one of the key components in NIDS design. Meanwhile, more and more application requiring high throughput will be performed on network processor (such as embedded system and

[*] This work is supported by NSFC (60625201, 60873250, 60903182), the Cultivation Fund of the Key Scientific and Technical Innovation Project, MoE, China (705003), the Specialized Research Fund for the Doctoral Program of Higher Education of China (20060003058), 863 high-tech project (2007AA01Z216,2007AA01Z468) and national innovation experiment program for university students.

D. Ślęzak et al. (Eds.): FGCN/ACN 2009, CCIS 56, pp. 149–156, 2009.
© Springer-Verlag Berlin Heidelberg 2009

high speed routers) where memory resource is very limited for high throughput. Therefore high speed pattern matching with compact memory is an urgent challenge to meet real world application.

Deterministic Finite Automaton (DFA) is widely used for multi-string matching in NIDS for its constant matching speed even in worst case. However, its throughput of one-character-per-cycle based matching algorithms is strictly proportional to the memory access frequency. For example, an NIDS dealing with 10 Gb/s requires a memory access frequency of at least 1.2 GHz, for 8-bit data bus, which is impractical with the current technologies.

Parallel matching is a promising solution to accelerate matching speed. Approaches utilizing intra-flow parallelism consume multiple characters in single flow per cycle. However, the throughput increases at the cost of an unbearable huge extra memory cost and hardware logic, which greatly restrains their scalability. Alternatively, inter-flow parallelism, from our investigation, is a promising approach to enhance throughput. In this paper, we propose our matching model on the basis of an analysis and observation on the structure of DFA and utilization of inter-flow parallelism to enhance throughput. Our major contributions in this work are highlighted below:

- We analyze the DFA structure from a novel view, and problem of memory access conflict in parallelism system is further studied.
- Motivated by the analysis, we propose a new DFA-based matching algorithm (called BM-FA). The formal architecture of BM-FA is further introduced. In a network processor environment, it can exploit inter-flow parallelism to its largest scale, so that large acceleration can be achieved.
- Our architecture is easy to be updated when new patterns (strings) are added.
- The algorithm has no conflict with other work, which means that our architecture can be further optimized (in space and time) by other techniques used on DFA.

The rest of paper is organized as follows. Section 2 gives a brief review of the related work on multi-pattern matching. In Section 3, we first analyze DFA structure and describe our observation. Section 4 gives the idea and design of BM-FA. Experimental evaluations are offered in section 5. Finally, conclusions and further studies are drawn in section 6.

2   Related Work

Multi-pattern matching is one of the well studied problems in last decades [1-5]. Some well-known algorithms such as Aho-Corasick[6] and Commentz-Walter[7] algorithms have been already implemented in famous NIDS like Snort[8] and Bro[9]. However, most of classical multi-string matching algorithms are suitable only for software implementation and therefore suffering from throughput limitations.

Single Character Multiple String Matching
Recently, many hardware-based algorithms have been proposed for network security, among which some solutions are based upon reconfigure logic FPGA and commodity search devices such as BCAM, TCAM. Tan et al. [14] proposed an approach that splits each character into multiple slices and building a DFA for each of them. This can compress overall memory usage because of a significant reduction in the fanout of the

DFA states. Jan v. Lunteren [13] gave an architecture based on B-FSM with string set partitioning to achieve the goal. Yu et al. proposed a TCAM-based scheme [15] that can successfully deal with complex patterns such as arbitrarily long patterns, correlated patterns, and patterns with negation. The major concern is that to process one character requires one TCAM access on average.

These methods focus on single character multi-string matching. Because of the well-known "byte alignment problem", single character multi-string matching can hardly exploit the parallelism of hardware device and the throughput threshold is not easy to break through. Even with an 800 MHz TCAM employed [15], the capacity upper bound is limited to 6.4 Gb/s.

Multiple Character String Matching
In multiple characters multi-string matching, many algorithms [11,12,16,17] were proposed to improve throughput with tradeoffs between memory and bandwidth. With Bloom-filter implemented on on-chip memory, Dharmapurikar et al. presented a scheme [12] that can process multiple characters per clock cycle and attain average throughput up to multi-gigabit with moderate memory consumption. However, the proposed schemes are vulnerable to malicious attacks since in the worst case they must frequently access the far slow off-chip SRAMs to launch exact string comparisons. In [16], Nan et al. introduced a variable-stride method to deal with string matching rule set. The variable-stride can enhance the matching performance. However, this method is sensitive to rule set and input string. The variable-stride would be greatly reduced when input is not suitable for its splitting algorithms. In [11], Lu et al. proposed a multiple character approaching architecture consisting of multiple parallel DFAs. The use of BCAM/TCAM as its search engine to store transitions. CAM's violently parallel searching can definitely reduce the memory storage, however, at the high cost of using large size CAM circuit.

In our paper, we propose a novel method of utilizing multiple flows parallel by investigating the essence of DFA-based approach, and further develop a new DFA-based algorithm which is not only well supported in theoretical level and but also in hardware implementation. Compared with previous work on traditional DFA, the searching engine based on our algorithm gains a high speedup with low memory.

3 Motivation and Basic Idea

3.1 Revisiting DFA

In multi-pattern matching problem, we are given a pattern set P of n strings $S_i = c_{i,1}c_{i,2}...c_{i,l_i}, i = 1,2,...n$ and an input stream text $T = t_1 t_2 ...t_m ...$. We seek to find all the occurrences of any string in P in T. We make the following definitions first. The string patterns set {*institution, stimulation, animal*} is used as example.

Definition 1: In a string matching DFA F, we define $STR_F (V)$[1] for every state V as the shortest string on the path from initial state to V. (e.g. in Fig. 1, of state 8, STR(8) is "*in*").

---

[1] STR (V) for simplicity if $V \in F$.

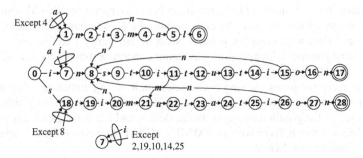

Fig. 1. DFA for the example of {*institution, stimulation, animal*}

Definition 2: after reading a string text *T*, the longest suffix of *T* which is also a prefix of some rules in rule set, is called *LS*.

The essence of DFA matching is that its current state always records the *LS* (e.g. after reading "*sabteni*", *LS* is "*eni*", and the DFA is at state 3 and STR(3)= "*eni*"). It can be observed that transitions from in DFA can be classified into four categories:

- Basic transitions are those successfully accept some pattern from initial state (state 0). Such as the transition from 0 to 1 through character '*a*' and 1 to 2 through character '*n*'. They can be seen as the backbone of the DFA.
- Cross transitions are those transfer from one pattern to another. They are used because the suffix of some pattern is also the prefix of some other. Such as the transition from 11 to 21 through character '*m*'.
- Restartable transitions transfer current state to the next state of initial state. They restart the matching, such as transition from 3 to 8 through character '*n*' which restarts new matching.
- Failure transitions transfer current state to initial state 0, which represents failure of the matching. Transition from 7 to 0 through character '*x*' belongs to this category.

3.2 Motivation

In a general parallel matching system, the main factor diminishing the acceleration is the access conflicts on the same parallel module. When storing DFA in multiple instances, one natural thought is simply to copy DFA in instances which would essentially prevent access conflicts. However, it is impractical when compared with state-of-the-art.

To store DFA in several modules can be a potential solution. Given several input streams, it is identical to give an active state to each of them. And if these active states always access different modules, we can largely exploit the inter-flow parallelism. So the problem explicitly described as follow: To find a separating memory scheme in order to minimize the access conflicts.

3.3 Idea of MB-FA

Memory access conflict occurs when two active states are transferred to states stored in the same module. So if we store every transition in the modules once, the problem of memory conflicts would be solved only when there is no two transitions that linking to states in same module.

It can be observed that in Fig. 1, only basic transitions are necessary for the matching of a certain pattern, and other three categories is used to guarantee to a constant throughput. So it is reasonable to store same states on basic transitions in one module. However, through observation on Fig. 1, most of the transition going to initial state, which means that the module storing the initial state (called initial module for simplicity) will be accessed very frequently. Thus, to achieve a fully parallelism system, we should store the module storing initial state for more than one time. And to avoid wasting of memory cost, memory for the initial state should be small. To sum up, the model of MB-FA should meet two requirements:

1. There should be no transitions from states in different modules going to the states in the same module except the initial module.
2. Storage cost for the initial module is as small as possible.

4 MB-FA

4.1 MB-FA Design

We introduce the design of MB-FA with the same illustrating example {*institution, stimulation, animal*} in section 3.1.

Firstly, the number of modules (except initial module) should be set before building modules, and we denote it as E. In the example, we let $E = 2$. Since all states have a failure transition, so there should be E (=2) initial modules.

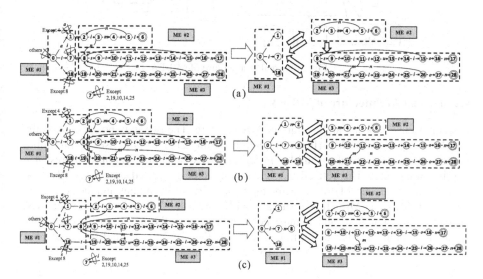

Fig. 2. (a) An example that breaks the first requirement of MB-FA. (b) and (c) meet the first requirement of MB-FA but (c) has a smaller initial module. (Modules are denoted as MEs for simplicity).

For each state, there must be one basic transition to it. Therefore, for any state in non-initial module, it is reasonable to put the next of it into the same module. Such as if state 2 is in non-initial module, state 3 should be in the same module as state 2.

Following above thought, Fig. 2 (a), (b) and (c) show three (not all possible) results of different storage scheme of BM-FA. The modules are denoted as MEs for simplicity. (a) is an incorrect scheme because ME 2 and ME 1 both have transition to ME 3, so it does not meet the first requirement of MB-FA. (b) and (c) all satisfy the first condition. However, (c) is better than (b) since it has a smaller initial module.

Before introducing the construction of MB-FA, for any state, we denote the shortest length of string that leads to the state from initial state as its *level*. When building MB-FA, we define a *threshold m*. For each pattern, we put states whose level less than *m* into the initial module, and for states with level larger than *m*, we retrieve all the existing paths in the DFA to find the module that has the most cross transitions to these states, and store them in the module.

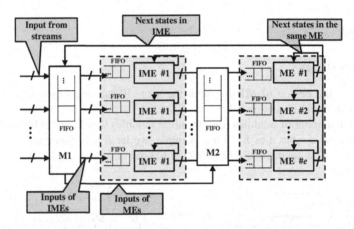

Fig. 3. Formal architecture of MB-FA

4.2 Formal Architecture of MB-FA

Fig. 3 presents a formal architecture of MB-FA here. The two gray boxes contain the matching engines. An IME (Initial module matching engine) processes as the initial module, and it is copied to build *e* instances. MEs (matching engines) represent *e* non-initial modules. Theoretically, 2*e* streams could be processed simultaneously if no access conflicts occur. M1 receives the input character from streams and the access the content in IMEs and MEs. It is essentially a FIFO register. The most recently received characters are sent first, and it must be combined with the next state of the corresponding streams. As the definition of MB-FA, there is little mutual transitions between different MEs. So the logic in MB-FA design is simple.

4.3 Compiling a New Pattern

In real pattern matching cases, new patterns are always added to the pattern set. A design of matching engine which is easy to compiling new patterns to it is a challenge to the matching algorithm design. In our approach, when add a new pattern, we only need to do the following updates: For the states whose levels are less than the given level threshold m, we allocate them in the Initial Modules. For the states whose levels are more than the given level threshold m, we should search all the DFA subtrees to find out which branch should be inserted into.

5   Evaluation

We evaluate the algorithm by the critical parameter e which is the number of IMs. IMs would be copied to store in MB-FA architecture, so the memory cost influences a lot in our whole space efficiency. In order to evaluate the effect of MB-FA, we perform experiments on rule set of Snort and ClamAV. The rule sets are extracted from the latest Snort[8] and ClamAV[9]. In Fig 4, we applied the DFA splitting algorithm on Snort and ClamAV pattern sets. It can be observed that:

1. Fig. 4(a): The memory cost (using state number to depict) of initial module is significantly reduced when the number of non-initial module increases. When
2. Fig. 4(b): The whole memory cost of MB-FA increases very little when speedup achieves 20 times (in average).

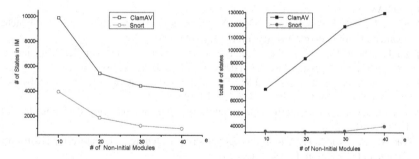

Fig. 4. (a) Number of states in IM with different e. (b)Total number of states MB-FA with different e.

6   Conclusions and Future Work

In this paper, we analyze the DFA structure of multi-string matching from a new point of view, and problem of memory access conflict in parallelism system is studied. Based on the analysis, we propose a novel DFA-based matching algorithm (called BM-FA). A complete architecture of BM-FA is further introduced. In a network processor environment, it can exploit inter-flow parallelism to its maximum, so that large acceleration can be achieved. Our architecture is easy to be implemented and supports fast pattern updating when new patterns are added. The algorithm has no conflicts with other works which means our architecture can be further optimized (on space or time) by other techniques used on DFA. There can be various directions that improve this work further. How to extend the idea of module based design to accelerate regular expression matching? How to optimize the module splitting to get a better load balance?

References

[1] Navarro, G., Raffinot, M.: Flexible PatternMatching in Strings-Practical On-Line Search Algorithms for Texts and Biological Sequences. Cambridge Univ. Press, Cambridge (2002)

[2] Coit, C.J., Staniford, S., McAlerney, J.: Towards faster string matching for intrusion detection or exceeding the speed of snort. In: Proc. DARPA Information Survivability Conf. Exposition (DISCEX II 2001), pp. 367–373 (2001)

[3] Fisk, M., Varghese, G.: Fast content-based packet handling for intrusion detection. UCSD, UCSD Tech. Rep. CS2001–0670 (2001)

[4] Anagnostakis, K.G., Markatos, E.P., Antonatos, S., Polychronakis, M.: E2XB: A domain-specific string matching algorithm for intrusion detection. In: presented at the 18th IFIP Int. Information Security Conf., Athens, Greece (2003)

[5] Liu, R.T., Huang, N.F., Chen, C.H., Kao, C.N.: A fast string-match algorithm for network processor-based network intrusion detection system. ACM Trans. Embedded Comput. Syst. 3, 614–633 (2004)

[6] Aho, A.V., Corasick, M.J.: Efficient string matching: an aid to bibliographic search. Commun. ACM 18(6), 333–340 (1975)

[7] Walter, B.C.: A string matching algorithm fast on the average. In: Maurer, H.A. (ed.) ICALP 1979. LNCS, vol. 71, pp. 118–132. Springer, Heidelberg (1979)

[8] Snort (2009), http://www.snort.org/

[9] ClamAV, http://www.clamav.net/

[10] Song, T., Zhang, W., Wang, D., Xue, Y.: A memory efficient multiple pattern matching architecture for network security. In: IEEE INFOCOM (2008)

[11] Lu, H., Zheng, K., Liu, B., Zhang, X., Liu, Y.: A memory-efficient parallel string matching architecture for high-speed intrusion detection. IEEE JSAC 24(10) (2006)

[12] Dharmapurikar, S., Lockwood, J.W.: Fast and scalable pattern matching for network intrusion detection systems. IEEE JSAC 24(10) (2006)

[13] van Lunteren, J.: High-performance pattern-matching for intrusion detection. In: IEEE INFOCOM (2006)

[14] Tan, L., Sherwood, T.: A high throughput string matching architecture for intrusion detection and prevention. In: ISCA (2005)

[15] Fang, Y., Katz, R.H., Lakshman, T.V.: Gigabit rate packet pattern matching using tcam. In: IEEE ICNP (2004)

[16] Hua, N., Song, H., Lakshman, T.V.: Variable-Stride Multi-Pattern Matching For Scalable Deep Packet Inspection. In: IEEE INFOCOM (2009)

[17] Brodie, B.C., Taylor, D.E., Cytron, R.K.: A scalable architecture for high-throughput regular-expression pattern matching. In: ISCA (2006)

Architecture of Personal Healthcare Information System in Ubiquitous Healthcare

Mangal Sain[1], Sachin Bhardwaj[2], HoonJae Lee[3], and Wan-Young Chung[4]

[1] Graduate School of Design and IT, Dongseo University, Busan, South Korea
[2] Dept. of Mathematics and Computer Science,
Technical Unviersity of Eindhoven,
The Netherlands
[3] School of Computer and Information Network Engineering,
Dongseo University, Busan, South Korea
[4] Division of Electronics, Computer and Telecom. Engg.,
Pukyong National University, Busan, South Korea
mangalsain1@gmail.com, s.bhardwaj@tue.nl, hjlee@dongseo.ac.kr,
wychung@pknu.ac.kr

Abstract. Due to recent development in Ubiquitous Healthcare now it's time to build such application which can work independently and with less interference of Physician. In this paper we are try to build the whole architecture of personal Healthcare information system for ubiquitous healthcare which also included Middleware, existing between application GUI and data source. To build this application we studied several existing application and ongoing projects and tried to build an architecture which can be appropriate to handle necessary information related to healthcare of individuals. We already succeed to design a prototype of Ubiquitous Healthcare Data Analysis and Monitoring Using Multiple Wireless Sensors for Elderly Person at home. Our proposed architecture will also provide diagnoses report to the doctors for further instructions. The diagnoses report will consist of healthcare data analysis results and history of patient. We have considered healthcare data like ECG, Accelerometer and temperature for experiment, which are important as a basic health need.

Keywords: Ubiquitous Healthcare, Information System, Data processing, Databases, J2EE, ECG, Accelerometer, middleware.

1 Introduction

The requirements to build this kind of application arises when we analyze the population aging has become one of the most significant demographic processes of modern times. The proportion of older persons that is those aged 65 years and over currently comprises around 10 per cent of the world's population, and is projected to increase to 22 percent by 2050[1]. To resolve this problem, we have developed prototype for ubiquitous healthcare system which can give early alarm to doctor's PDA [2]. As said earlier we already design a prototype of Ubiquitous Healthcare Data Analysis and Monitoring Using Multiple Wireless Sensors[3] In this paper the main concern is on

D. Ślęzak et al. (Eds.): FGCN/ACN 2009, CCIS 56, pp. 157–164, 2009.
© Springer-Verlag Berlin Heidelberg 2009

system architecture, application development, availability of tools and their utilization and creates an interface between data source and GUI. To build this architecture J2EE technology, Weblogic server, and oscilloscope (java program) used.

This system develop a robust platform for real-time monitoring of patients staying in their home and transmitting health data to doctors working at the hospital with extended ECG. Application developers mostly rely on third party middleware, tools and libraries to respond the emerging trends of their target domain. As stated earlier with GUI and database. We also build a middleware, to enhance the efficiency of application by decrease their memory uses, data processing and decision making by putting all module on application server which is independent of each application. For each healthcare application the requirement are different point to point. Due to that we analyze some different low level and high level middleware technology which were used to build different kind middleware likewise CAMUS[4], MiLAN[5], MOBIWARE[6], LIME[7] etc and try to find the best solution.

2   Background

Healthcare information system is one of the most emerged areas of research these days; there are several personal and public healthcare research group and society which are working on healthcare information system and management. OpenEHR [8], HIMSS [9], HL7 [10] are some of them which are working from many years.

In OpenEHR a person all health data is stored once in a lifetime, vendor-independent and person centered. Their main focus is on message standards such as ISO13606 and HL7 rather than exchange of data between EHR-systems. It also explains the storage, management, retrieval and exchange of health data into system. OpenEHR specification includes service and information model for EHR, demographics, archetypes, clinical workflow and are designed to be the basis of medico-legally sound, distributed versioned EHR infrastructure.

HiMSS is a Healthcare Information and Management Systems Society which represents more than 2,000 nurses and brings together 18 distinct nursing informatics. It is the premier professional member organization exclusively focused on providing leadership for the optimal use of healthcare information technology.

HL7 was formed to build hospital information system, which is now a volunteer as a non-profit organization involved in to build international healthcare standards worldwide. HL7 and its other member also provide a framework for exchange information, integration, sharing and retrieval of information.

The main problem with Healthcare system is lack of shareable and computable Information. After studying all above technologies and research work we tried to build such an application which can play an important role in Healthcare Information system. We build an application which can take both kind of data (offline and live data) and process that data into useful information like diagnosis message which are still missing all above application. To handle such data processing and information sharing we also build a middleware which exist between data source and GUI, which build with J2EE technology & Weblogic Server. System architecture is inspired by OpenEHR and HL7 and we tried to build an application which consist probably most of the quality of OpenEHR and HL7. To make advancement in our Healthcare system especially in communication and data sharing, middleware is added, which encourage and can be useful to implement more application with this system.

As we know HL7, OpenEHR, ISO and many nonprofit organizations are working on to build and universal healthcare data standard. We also try to track the same healthcare data format but we come to conclusion it still need some time to finalize this data format. Due to that, we are using MIT-BIH database and their predefined data format which we explain later in our paper in brief.

3 System Design

Our design prototype consists of several Healthcare Application deployed on multiple physical hosts and a web base application deployed on each application and server which is accessible everywhere through internet. The main web application is able to collect the whole data onto main server, process them and convert into useful information with the help of middleware and special program which is developed in C#.net. The main controller of the application is programming interface which is developed in J2EE Technology which is centralized service in our architecture.

These days all personal healthcare devices are developed with only through Industry standard and with big organization and with big project. As stated earlier there are several applications and research has been done but if we consider real time healthcare application and real data processing on this area it still need big attention.

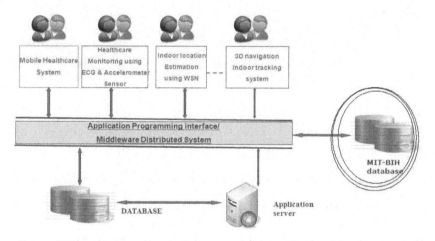

Fig. 1. System architecture of Personal Healthcare Information system

The building of the Personal Healthcare system brings the testing and integration specialized sensors for healthcare monitoring through the use of an enhanced version of the USN sensor mote developed at Ubiquitous sensor lab, with Tinyos and Personal healthcare module.

Figure 1, is the system architecture of personal healthcare system which is developed in contrast to project of Ubiquitous healthcare system in USN Lab. In this paper our focus is on one application between Ubiquitous Healthcare monitoring using ECG and accelerometer sensor. But it doesn't mean that for each other application we have to build different application. As this application is build with J2EE technology and

based on Model–view–controller (MVC) [11] so with a little modification we can
implement this application and Middleware on any other application too.

In the figure 1, there are several users in correspondence to different application.
All users are connected with the database through web application and Middleware,
which exist between data source and different healthcare application. To process and
execute all application data and information we use application server which reduce
the memory, execution time and reduce the load on web application due that it increase lot of speed and performance of each application. As we can see there is another data source which we mentioned as MIT-BIH database, hence for a start only
the MIT-BIH database is implemented. The test system should run with various other
ECG database types. The MIT-BIH database was created in a cooperation between
the Massachusetts Institute of Technology (MIT) and Beth Israel Hospital (BIH) in
order to develop and evaluate real-time ECG rhythm analysis [12]. This data type is
only meant for research and practice for some specific users and it's not a part of
system architecture.

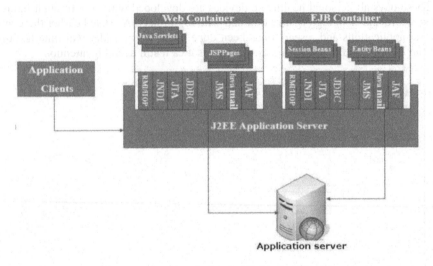

Fig. 2. J2EE Client Server Application architecture

After study various personal healthcare systems we come to conclusion, this is one
of the most unique field where we can find lot of work has already been done but still
there is long way to go. In figure 1, different user accessing Personal healthcare module with the help of different sensor embedded in USN sensor mote. We can take
measure through Oscilloscope (implement in personal healthcare module). After
measurement we can see the current health status as well as past record too (this feature already added in web application through personal healthcare database). We can
also analyze some of data and find some health status (On with personal healthcare
module and without the help of any other body like physician. Old health data is
stored in database which accessible anywhere through web application.

To build web application for a common interface between different users and data
source and various healthcare applications, J2EE technology with eclipse as IDE is

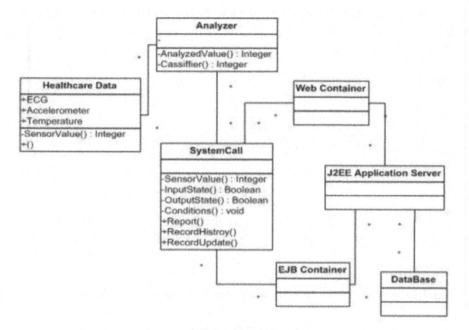

Fig. 3. Logical View of Healthcare Data Processing with J2EE Server

used. In figure 2 we can see the J2EE architecture which is most known technology to build such kind of application. As we can see how client send request to server with the help of middleware and how both use a common architecture to communicate. To build a perfect architecture Sun Microsystems' Java-based Architecture is used. After study several architecture such as CORBA(Common Object Request Broker Architecture), DCOM(Distributed Component Object Model) etc we come to conclusion that J2EE architecture is most suited to our requirement.

Whole application is developed and incorporated with Tinyos [13] which is design and develop by University of California, with joint research effort with Intel Research. In our application, the healthcare data like ECG, accelerometer or temperature will be captured from human body and transfer to the analyzer for processing it. All the results will be called by a system call for further utilization. It can send request to update data on server and can be retrieve by of client or send to the doctors PDA or cell phone. Figure3 shows one example of logical view with healthcare data analysis.

4   Simulation Work and Results

Our experimental set-up obtains the ECG and accelerometer data from the sensors placed on real human body and MIT-BIH arrhythmia database. Firstly data are transmitted from human body to base station and then to server for ECG and accelerometer analysis. Commonly most fibrillation detection algorithms are tested with the MIT-BIH database, hence for a start only the MIT-BIH database is implemented. The test system should run with various other ECG database types, which are not described here.

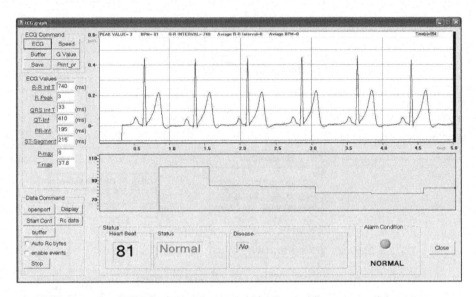

Fig. 4. Example of ECG Analysis Algorithm which is providing processed data to server

Table 1. ECG Packet Format

Head data part (5 bytes)				Payload data part(26 bytes)			
Message Address	Active message handler	Group ID	Message length	Mote ID	Count	ADC channel	data
2 bytes	1 byte	1 byte	1 byte	2 bytes	2 bytes	2 bytes	20 bytes

Table 2. Accelerometer Packet Format

Address	AM_type	Group ID	Data Length
2 byte	1 byte	1 byte	1 byte
TOS Header			
Node ID	Last Sample Number	Channel	Data
2 byte	2 byte	2 byte	20 byte

In this paper our goal was to provide a capability for real time (software) analysis of ECG signal with activity monitoring at server. After detecting an abnormality [14] then transfer that data into server and which can be use later on by some specific user like himself, nurse and physician and if user wants that data can used for other purpose like research etc. The services provided to client from server made possible by using healthcare middleware. Designing of middleware format is still in progress due to compatibility between healthcare data packet format like ECG packet format, Accelerometer packet format. We are using healthcare packet format provided in table 1 and table 2 and having experiment with middleware suitability.

5 Conclusion and Future Work

In this paper we tried to build an application which can work as an independent body and fulfill most of the requirement of latest ubiquitous healthcare system. OpenEHR, HiMSS and HL7 are the basic inspiration for whole architecture. As we know all above healthcare society are leaders in Electronic Healthcare record, information processing etc. We tried to take most of the feature in our application. We also try to concentrate on data format which can use worldwide commonly but as we know still it will take lot of time. Here we implement only one phase of whole application but still it's just base to whole unifiied Ubiquitous healthcare system which has to be developed in our USNproject.

After adding middleware between data source and web application, this application system is totally improved with much better performance than previous work. In the new application a web application interface also added which support several new features and a new GUI which can be accessible worldwide. In this way we tried to enhance the efficiency of application by decrease their memory uses, data processing and decision making by putting all these modules on application server which is independent of each application.

To deploy this web application on whole USNproject is really a big task and need lot of effort. In our future work we will try to incorporate all other applications, mobile Healthcare, indoor location estimation tool etc and try find the common healthcare data format which can implemented with all applications. It's a long way to go merge all these application with single entity. In future our concentration will also be on data format, as ISO also working on to develop common healthcare data format. As soon as it will finalize we will be able to see the real ubiquitous healthcare system which will work worldwide.

References

1. Report of an expert group meeting population aging and development: social, health and gender issues with a focus on the poor in old age, October 29-31, VALLETTA (2001)
2. Chung, W.-Y., Bhardwaj, S., Purwar, A., Lee, D.-S., Myllylae, R.: A Fusion Health Monitoring Using ECG and Accelerometer sensors for Elderly Persons at Home. In: 29th Annual International Conference of the IEEE Engineering in Medicine and Biology Society, EMBS 2007 (2007)
3. Sain, M., Lee, H., Chung, W.-Y.: Personal Healthcare Information system. In: NCM 2009: 5th International Joint Conference on INC, IMS and IDC (2009)
4. Moon, A., Kim, H., Kim, H., Lee, S.: Context-Aware Active Services in Ubiquitous Computing Environments. ETRI Journal 29(2) (April 2007)

5. Heinzelman, W.B., Murphy, A.L., Carvalho, H.S., Perillo, M.: Middleware to support sensor network applications. IEEE Network (January/February 2004)
6. Angin, O., Campbell, A.T., Kounavis, M.E., Liao, R.R.-F.: The mobiware toolkit: programmable support for adaptive mobile networking. IEEE Personal Communications (August 1998)
7. Murphy, A., Picco, G., Roman, G.-C.: LIME: A Middleware for Physical and Logical Mobility. In: Proc.21st International Conference on Distributed Computing Systems ICDCS (2001)
8. http://www.openehr.org/home.html
9. http://www.himss.org/ASP/aboutHimssHome.asp
10. http://www.hl7.org/
11. http://java.sun.com/blueprints/patterns/MVC.html
12. Moody, G.B.: WFDB Applications Guide, Harvard-MIT Division of Health Sciences and Technology (2004), http://www.physionet.org (retrieved April 25, 2004)
13. http://www.tinyos.net/
14. Pan, J., Tompkins, W.J.: A real-time QRS detection algorithm. BME-32, 230–236 (1985)
15. Wu, W., Cao, J., Zheng, Y., Zheng, Y.-P.: WAITER: A Wearable Personal Healthcare and Emergency Aid System. In: Sixth Annual IEEE International Conference on Pervasive Computing and Communications, PerCom 2008 (2008)
16. Jea, D., Balani, R., Hsu, J.-L., Cho, D.-K., Gerla, M., Srivastava, M.B.: Diagnostic quality driven physiological data collection for personal healthcare. In: 30th Annual International Conference of the IEEE Engineering in Medicine and Biology Society, EMBS 2008 (2008)

BcN Deployment Strategies in Korea

Hyongsoon Kim and Eun-Young Lee

National Information Society Agency, Seoul, Korea
Dongduk Women's University, Seoul, Korea

Abstract. UBcN (Ultra-Broadband Convergence Network) is the next generation network with high speed, on which broadband multiple play services are supported safely and seamlessly. Developing UBcN as the common infrastructure for converged services is considered to be essential for increasing the power of competition of IT industries. The Korea government is going to establish UBcN by 2013 with the speed of up to 1Gbps for 46 million fixed and wireless subscribers. They also have a multi-year plan to discover and stimulate new converged services for UBcN. In this paper, we discuss Korea's development plan of UBcN and their strategies.

Keywords: UBcN, broadband, NGN, converged service.

1 Introduction

Korea has become a leading country with the world's top class information infrastructure through continuous projects to establish the high-speed information and communications network (1.5 2Mbps), and broadband convergence Network (50Mbps or above) since 1995. As the result of preemptive policies, Korea has possesed the most advanced IT infrstructure in the world, and created a new market in the related areas. As of 2007, Korea is ranked first in the world in the digital opportunity index (DOI) and third in the national computerization index.

The need for high-speed network has been accelerated by digital convergence, that is, the convergence of broadcasting, communications and the Internet. Convergence of integrated terminals and services is expanding, through which all types of information such as voice, data, image, multi-media, etc. are converged. Convergence between industries and services is even accelerated due to the information technology development such as telematics, u-Health, u-Learning, u-City, and so on. The world is moving to the integrated digital economic system in which distinction in economic activities disappears.

We predict that the broadcasting and telecommunication services in the future will be converged and be serviced on mobile devices. MPS (Multiple Play Service) beyond TPS (Triple Play Service) or QPS (Quadruple Play Service) will be provided that combines voice call, Internet and broadcasting in various environment including the mobile environment. Also, SoTV (Service over TV) looks likely to emerge, which combines various application services such as education, healthcare, and civil services through interactive digital TV. We also

D. Ślęzak et al. (Eds.): FGCN/ACN 2009, CCIS 56, pp. 165–171, 2009.

expect the services in the future will be more intelligent, more personalized and more realistic.

Although the continuous improvement, the current IT infrastructure does not fully meet the future demand for those converged, realistic, intelligent, and personalized services. In the aspects of the speed, coverage, interoperability, quality and security, the current IT infrastructure has much to be desired. For example, one household will consume 125 - 285Mbps bandwidth on average on a fixed-line network, and one user will consume about 10Mbps on average on a wireless network for MPS which is likely to take the major portion of broadcasting and telecommunication services in the near future. A rich, high-density and realistic media service will be also available soon, which provides images 4 - 16 times clearer than those of full HDTV. In this case, one household will consume an additional 100Mbps of bandwidth (based on a fixed line).

The required bandwitdh is not quite satisfied by the current IT infrastructure. The needs mentioned above inevitably leads us to develop a faster and more robust network infrastructure with effective strategies. We call the new infrastructure UBcN (Ultra-Broadband Convergence Networks). The UBcN development strategies are needed to cope with the trend of the broadcasting and telecommunication network after BcN, future service requirements and the intensive global competition.

In Seciton 2, we discuss the outcome of Korea's continuous and successful BcN project and the current status of IT infrastructure. The major goals and plans of UBcN development will be given in Section 3. We will discuss the strategies to achieve the goals in Section 4.

2   Current Status Analysis

In the very near future, broadcasting and telecommunication services will be combined in the form of a converged service with voice, data, wired, wireless, and communications, broadcasting which is usable anytime, anywhere (ubiquitous), seamlessly, and safely [1][2].

The market in the Information and Communications Service is expected to achieve 62.4 trillion won by 2010 from 46 trillion won of 2004 with the annual average growth rate of 5.2%. Annual growth rate from 2004 to 2007 was 5.5% on average, but for the period from 2008 to 2010 about 5.2% on annual average is expected by the matured market of the information and communications service. The market of BcN Communications and Broadcasting Devices is expected to grow up to 9.7 trillion won by 2010 at annual growth rate of 7.5% on average from 6.3 trillion won in 2004.

Demand for the next generation network devices is expected to increase as the communications-broadcasting convergence environment changes and the optical subscriber network expands. At the same time, replacement demand for digital devices and broadcasting equipment is expected to steadily grow as world-wide digital television transition comes near. However, the broadcasting equipment market is prospected to record a minus growth in 2009 by the slowed market of world digital media equipment, relocation of foreign operations.

Siginificant amount of investment for BcN establishment has been made for the last 5 years. Private sector investment of around 25.2 trillion won was generated for BcN transport network, subscriber network, and control network through the leading investment of 618.4 billion won from 2004 to 2007. Additional network investment of 18.2 trillion won from the private sector is expected for the three years to come [3].

Establishment of BcN transport network (premium network) by major wired operators has begun in earnest. KT established nation-wide transport network by the end of 2007 and Hanaro Telecom and LG Dacom respectively established premium node throughout the major metropolitan cities. Upgrading the wired/wireless BcN subscriber network achieved earlier through the promoted investment by the BcN base and conditions established. The subscriber network of the wired service of 7.01 million and the wireless service of 5.63 million as of the end of December, 2007 have upgraded to BcN, and public communications benefit has increased by the provision of the broadband multi-media service to the total 12.64 million of households and subscribers.

During the previous phases, new BcN-based service models and supporting commercialization have been created and verified. Network test-bed was established and trial services were developed and provided to nation-wide households of about 2,700 through the four grand consortiums for BcN pilot businesses. Twenty five new services including IPTV, VoIP/Video phone, u-Work were created and verified [4][6]. Also commercializations of 14 services such as TV portal, interactive digital CATV (SD), WPABX (IP-based Wireless Private Automatic Branch Exchange) were supported.

BcN pilot business consortiums generated the investment which amounts to 145.9 billion won from 2004 to 2007 (government - 23.4 billion won). BcN core technologies and commercial network applications have been developed. Core technologies such as QoS provision, Network Control Platform (NCP), the optical subscriber network sector were timely developed and commercial network began to support BcN key functions such as service guarantee, broadband, IPv6, seamless service. As of 2006, 49 cases of key technology development, 80 cases of technology transfer, and 3.64 billion won of technology fee achieved. Network establishment where the end-to-end quality of the BcN service is guaranteed is promoted by preparing BcN service quality standards and establishing a measurement and evaluation system. Quality standards for the BcN VoIP/Video phone (wired) service were established [5][7].

A suite of software for quality measurement was developed and the technology has transferred to the total 12 businesses including communications operators, equipment manufacturers, and terminal manufacturers (February, 2007). As a result of BcN establishment business, production of the BcN communications and broadcasting equipment amounts to 32.9 trillion won, and accumulated exportation reached to about 10.2 billion dollars by 2007. As of 2007, the BcN related industry held 12.9% of production and 6.7% of exportation in the overall communications and broadcasting equipment industry and contributed to the economic development [8][9].

3   Major Plans of UBcN Development

Figure 1 shows the leading trend of network policies of advanced countries including Japan, the U.S. and the European Union. They all try to secure technological competitiveness and to preempt the market in the future network area. The goals of Korea's UBcN plan are to build a good infrastructure, and to provide world-class converged broadcasting and telecommunication services. Achieving these goals requires developing core technologies and it is the necessary condition to enter into overseas markets.

The goals can be categorized into 6 areas: backbone network, fixed-line subscriber network, wireless subscriber network, broadcasting network, sensor network and services.

To strengthen the backbone network, the phone network and mobile communication network will be integrated with the backbone network with supporting IP protocol. The fixed-line phone network (PSTN) will be switched into the IP by 2010, and the local call sector will be integrated with the all-IP network completely by 2015. The service control platform of the wired/wireless network based on the IMS (IP Multimedia Subsystem) will be developed. The platform will be used for providing converged, intelligent, personalized and customized services. The platform will be designed to provide uninterrupted portability among heterogeneous networks such as WiFi, HSDPA and WiBro.

To enhance the fixed-line subscriber network, the BcN subscription target area will be extended continuously. BcN coverage will be expanded to rural areas and the existing xDSL method will be switched to FTTH for single-family houses and LAN for apartments. The commercial Giga-Internet service will be provided from 2012 mainly for the metropolitan area after establishing the ultra-broadband subscriber network.

For enhancing wireless subscriber network, WiBro network will be expanded to cover up to 84 cities in 2009, and the average speed of mobile communication networks such as HSPA will be increased from 1Mbps to 2Mbps by introducing HSPA$^+$ technology. In 2013, a total of 300,000 subscribers will be accommodated by establishing a nationwide network to provide 3.9G/4G commercial services

Item	GENI	FIRE	New Generation Network
Country	U.S.	E.U.	Japan
Features	Concentrated study on alternative IP technology and combined technology such as security and sensors	concentrated study on wireless communication and context-recognition technology	Concentrated study on alternative IP technology and wireless/optical communication technology
Period	2004 - 2013	2007 - 2013	2008 - 2015
Budget	400 million dollars	40 million Euros	30 billion yen

Fig. 1. Status of Future Network Implementation of Major Countries

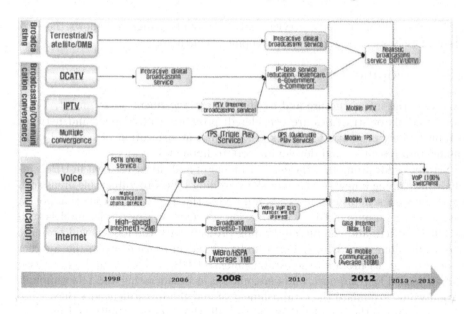

Fig. 2. New UBcN Services

with 10Mpbs-level on average. Femtocell technology will be applied to expand the WiBro coverage and to provide the HSDPA broadband service.

Broadcasting network will be improved as follows: first of all, terrestrial broadcasting will introduce the interactive service by 2010, and the digial broadcasting coverage will be expanded to 96% by 2013. The interactive service for terrestial DMB will be introduced by 2010, and the AT-DMB (Advanced T-DMB) will be commercially serviced by 2012. Digital radio broadcasting services will be experimented with comparing various methods of digiral radio broadcasting until the standard digital radio method is determined by 2010. The test broadcasting will begin by 2012.

UBcN also includes sensor networks. The sensor networks, which have been operated independently by public agencies or other entities so far, will be linked and integraged into the all-IP broadcasting and telecommunication network. The combined network will be used as a testbed and equipped with 8 hubs at major cities in Korea by 2010. The interface specification of public sensor network, such as weather, environment, disaster prevention safety and facility management, will be prepared and open to the public by 2012.

In addition to the enhancement of various networks, the converged services will be discovered and developed. Interactive TV-based service (SoTV), mobile IPTV and MPS will be provided in Korea in 2012 through the two-way information ultra-highway. Interactive services to households include education, healthcare, e-Government and e-Commerce as well as broadcasting and phone services. As the networks evolve to ultra-broadband which are 10 times faster (1G for wired, 10M for wireless) than the existing broadband network (100M for wired, 1M for wireless), more realistic services will be provided. Figure 2 shows the suggested UBcN services and their development timelines.

4   Development Strategies

To create the infrastructure and its supporting investment environment, 4 major directions of strategies are considered: promoting investment and network establishment, promoting network usage, efficient utilization of national communication resources and developing core technologies.

Strategies for promoting the estabilishment of and the investment in UBcN include developing a new service model, expanding UBcN to vulnerable areas such as rural areas, schools and libraries, improving the investment promotion policy, and preparing a map of UBcN information. Developing new service models such as killer services and conducting leading projects with the models will promote the establishment of UBcN. Legal and political improvement can be another good strategy to promote the establishment of UBcN. For example, decreased tax/increased loan support, and deregulation in broadcasting and telecommunication would stimulate the establishment of and the investment in UBcN.

To encourage the use of UBcN, first of all, the interoperability and mobility will be improved. Also the information security will be improved by fortifying quality management. The public sectors will be encouraged to use UBcN to improve the quality of civil services. More users will utilize UBcN with uninterrupted migration among various UBcN services, regardless of the user's location and terminal. The security of UBcN services can be improved by preparing the quality index/criteria of future UBcN services and by providing the information security guidelines.

The efficiency of national communication resources should be considered in the UBcN development. The method for integrating the current network infrastructure and the new one efficiently must be prepared in order not to waste the national resources.

The last, but not the least important strategy is developing core technologies of our own. Securing core technologies related with UBcN will significantly increase the power of competition in the global broadcasting and telecommunication industry. The core technologies are related to the implementation of future network technologies and services, the integrated infrastructure, 4G mobile communication, and realistic and personalized interactice services. As well as developing new techologies, the testing and verification environment of new technologies should be supported. The establishment of open field testbed environment can be one of good solutions. At the same time, standardization of the newly developed technologies must be considered. Without standardization, the new technologies cannot survive the global market where a lot of technologies emerge and disappear very fast. Therefore, developing and propagating a standard must be done in line with providing new services. The status and the trends related with UBcN should be surveyed and analyzed comprehensively and intensively, and the international standardization activities should be conducted according to the survey and analysis.

5   Conclusion

UBcN is the next generation network with high speed, on which broadband multiple play services are supported safely and seamlessly. UBcN is considered as the best infrastructure for the new growth engines of the IT industries, and the Korean government has deployed the multi-year plan for establishing UBcN as an infrastructure network of Korea.

In this paper, we analysed the current status of high-speed, broadband network in Korea. Then, we discussed the Korea's development plan of UBcN and their strategies. The main goal of the UBcN development is to establish the information and communications environment where anybody can use converged network services anytime and anywhere with convenience. For this goal, UBcN will be upgraded to the 46 million-subscriber network with the speed of 1Gbps by 2013. We have explained six detailed plans for major agendas of UBcN, and discussed the necessary strategies.

As the one of the leading countries in the IT industry, we think the deployed development plan of Korea would help other countries make a plan for their own development strategies. We also expect that we can make a complete discussion and analysis of the plans after these multi-year plans in progress are completed.

References

1. Basic blueprint for building the Broadband convergence Network, MIC (2004)
2. Second phase plan for establishing BcN, MIC (2006)
3. Third phase plan for establishing BcN, MIC (2008)
4. Broadband convergence Network Annual Report 2007, NIA, MIC (2007)
5. A master plan for stimulating IPv6, MIC (2007)
6. IPv6 Status Report 2006, NIA (2007)
7. A Study on the Implementation of the Next Generation Internet infrastructure, NIA (2007)
8. Lee, Y., Min, K., et al.: A Business Development for the Digital Convergence Services based on BcN, NIA II-RIR-07044. NIA press (December 2007)
9. Yi, J.: A Study on the Specification for BcN Service Interworking, NIA II-RIR-07086. NIA press (December 2007)

Communication Delay Prediction of Pipelined Circuit Switching in Mesh-Based Networks*

Farshad Safaei[1,2] and Mohammad Mahdi Gilak[3]

[1] School of Computer Science, Institute for Research in Fundamental Sciences (IPM)
[2] Dept. of ECE, Shahid Beheshti Univ., Tehran, Iran
[3] Faculty of Mathematical Sciences, Shahid Beheshti Univ., Tehran, Iran
safaei@ipm.ir, f_safaei@sbu.ac.ir, mo.gilak@mail.sbu.ac.ir

Abstract. Several analytical performance models for Pipelined Circuit Switching (PCS) in k-ary n-cubes have been reported in literature over the recent years. However, the inherent asymmetry of the mesh topology renders derivation of an analytical model for this class of networks more challenging. This paper proposes the first analytical performance model for 2-D mesh networks employing PCS with virtual channels. Simulation results show that this model is able to predict message latency with a good degree of accuracy.

1 Introduction

The switching techniques specify the connection activities performed by the switching elements when a message is received at the input port. The message enters into the network from the source node and is forwarded through a series of switches towards its destination. Several well-known switching techniques notably Pipelined Circuit Switching (PCS for short), Packet Switching (PS), Wormhole Switching (WS), and Circuit Switching (CS) have been widely adopted in practice [1].

Gaughan and Yalamanchili [2] have proposed PCS that combines aspects of CS and WS. PCS sets up a path before starting data transmission as in CS. Basically, PCS differs from CS in that paths are formed by *virtual channels* instead of physical channels. As opposed to WS, in PCS, data flits do not immediately follow the header flits into the network until a complete path has been established. When the header finally reaches the destination, an *acknowledgement flit* is transmitted back to the source node. Now data flits can be pipelined over the path just as in WS. This approach is flexible in that headers can perform a backtracking search of the network, reserving and releasing virtual channels in an attempt to establish a fault-free path to the destination. Several researchers have recently proposed router architectures that incorporate PCS to efficiently support multimedia applications [3, 4].

The remainder of this paper is structured as follows. Section 2 gives some preliminaries. Our model assumptions are demonstrated in Section 3. Moreover, the performance modeling approach is presented in this section. Section 4 compares the message latencies captured by analytical model with those obtained through simulations. Finally, Section 5 summarizes our findings and concludes the paper.

---

* This research was in part supported by a grant from IPM. (No. CS1387-4-07).

D. Ślęzak et al. (Eds.): FGCN/ACN 2009, CCIS 56, pp. 172–179, 2009.

2 Preliminaries

Definition 1: *A 2-D $k \times k$ mesh with $N = k^2$ nodes has an interior node degree of 4 and a network diameter of $2(k-1)$. Each node is given by a coordinate pair (x,y), where $1 \leq x,y \leq k$. Two nodes are neighboring if they have the same horizontal coordinate and their vertical coordinates differ by exactly 1, or they have the same vertical coordinate and their horizontal coordinates differ by exactly 1.*

The mesh topology is inherently asymmetric as a result of the absence of the wrap-around connections along each dimension. As a result, nodes at the corners and edges in the network have two and three neighbors, respectively.

3 The Analytical Modeling

3.1 Assumptions

The proposed analytical model is based on the following assumptions that are widely accepted in literature [3-5].

(a) Each node generates messages independently, which follows a *Poisson process* with a mean rate of λ_{node} messages/node/cycle.

(b) The arrival process at a given communication network is approximated by an independent Poisson process.

(c) The destination of each message would be any node in the network with uniform distribution.

(d) Message length is fixed at M flits, each of which requires one cycle to cross from one node to the next.

(e) V virtual channels $(V \geq 1)$ are used per physical channel. When there is more than one virtual channel available that bring a message closer to its destination, one is chosen at random.

(f) In the event of message blocking, the message header releases the last reserved virtual channel and backtracks to the preceding node, then searches for finding an alternative virtual channel to advance towards its destination [1-4].

3.2 Derivation of the Model

The analytical model computes the *mean message latency* using the following steps. First, the mean time to establish a path is calculated. Second, the *mean network latency*, i.e., the time for a message to cross the network from source to destination, is determined. Then, the *mean waiting time* seen by a message at the source before entering the network is derived using M/G/1 queuing system [6]. Finally the mean message latency is obtained by including the effects of *virtual channel multiplexing*.

Let us first calculate the average message arrival rate on a given channel $\prec a,b \succ$ where a and b are two adjacent nodes. Many distinct paths exist between every pair of nodes in a mesh network. By selectively dividing traffic over these paths, load can be balanced across the network channels. In general, if there are n dimensions numbered 0 to $n-1$ and there are Δ_i hops from a to b in the $i-th$ dimension, then the total number of minimal routes from a to b is calculated by

$$\|\mathcal{R}\|_{\prec a,b\succ}^n = \prod_{i=0}^{n-1}\left(\frac{\sum_{j=i}^{n-1}\Delta_j}{\Delta_i}\right) = \left(\sum_{i=0}^{n-1}\Delta_i\right)! / \prod_{i=0}^{n-1}\Delta_i! \tag{1}$$

For every source-destination pair of nodes, s and d, for which channel $\prec a,b\succ$ may be used, the probability that channel $\prec a,b\succ$ is traversed can be expressed as

$$P_{(s,d),\prec a,b\succ} = \|\mathcal{R}\|_{\prec s,a\succ}^2 \times \|\mathcal{R}\|_{\prec b,d\succ}^2 / \|\mathcal{R}\|_{\prec s,d\succ}^2 \tag{2}$$

With uniform traffic pattern, messages generated at a node have an equal probability of being destined to any other node. Hence, the rate of messages produced at a specific node and destined to another node is equal to the ratio of the message generation rate, λ_{node}, to the number of nodes in the network except itself. Therefore, the rate of messages generated at a specific node, s, and destined to another node, d, that traverse the channel $\prec a,b\succ$ on its path is given by

$$\lambda_{(s,d),\prec a,b\succ} = \left(\lambda_{node} / \left(k^2 - 1\right)\right)\cdot P_{(s,d),\prec a,b\succ} \tag{3}$$

The rate of messages traversing a specific channel can be calculated as the aggregate of (3) over all source-destination pairs that have at least one path between each other that traverses channel $\prec a,b\succ$. This parameter is denoted by

$$\lambda_{\prec a,b\succ} = \sum_{(s,d)\in G_{\prec a,b\succ}} \lambda_{(s,d),\prec a,b\succ} = \left(\lambda_{node}/\left(k^2-1\right)\right)\sum_{(s,d)\in G_{\prec a,b\succ}} P_{(s,d),\prec a,b\succ} \tag{4}$$

where $G_{\prec a,b\succ}$ is the set of all pairs of source and destination nodes that have at least one path between each other that traverses channel $\prec a,b\succ$. Let $s = (s_x,s_y)$ be the source node and $d = (d_x,d_y)$ denote a destination node. We define the set $H = \{h_x,h_y\}$, where h_x and h_y signify the number of hops that the message makes along X and Y dimensions, respectively.

$$h_x = \|s_x - d_x\|, \quad h_y = \|s_y - d_y\| \tag{5}$$

where $\|x - y\|$ denotes the distance between a source x and a destination y. Furthermore, the total number of hops made by the message between source and destination nodes is given by

$$\|H\| = h_x + h_y \tag{6}$$

We define $\overline{S}_{(s,d)}$ as the network latency seen by a message crossing from source s to destination d. The network latency, $\overline{S}_{(s,d)}$, consists of two parts: One is the delay due to actual message transmission time, $\|H\| + M$, and another term accounts for the

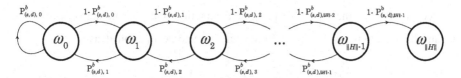

Fig. 1. The Markov chain diagram for calculating the average path setup time in PCS

average set up time, $\overline{C}_{(s,d)}$, needed to reserve a dedicated path from the source to destination. Thus, $\overline{S}_{(s,d)}$ is determined by

$$\overline{S}_{(s,d)} = \|H\| + M + \overline{C}_{(s,d)} \tag{7}$$

where M and $\|H\|$ denote the message length and mean message distance (given by (7)), respectively.

In order to calculate the quantity of $\overline{C}_{(s,d)}$, we employ a Markov chain (illustrated by Fig. 1) to model the behaviour of header in crossing through the network [3].

Each state, in Fig. 1, represents the current location of the header along its network path. States ω_0 and $\omega_{\|H\|}$ denote that the header is at the source and destination nodes, respectively. State ω_i corresponds the case where the header is at intermediate node that is i hops away from the source. Details of this figure can be found in [3].

Suppose $\overline{C}_{(s,d),i}$ is the average time interval to reach the state $\omega_{\|H\|}$ starting from state ω_i. $\overline{C}_{(s,d),i}$ is always finite [7], and $\overline{C}_{(s,d),i+1}$ denotes the header at state ω_i succeeds in acquiring a virtual channel and it can proceed to state ω_{i+1}. On the other hand, when the header encounters situation of blocking, it backtracks to the preceding node corresponding to state ω_{i-1} and the residual expected duration would be $\overline{C}_{(s,d),0}$. It is assumed that the header needs one cycle to move from one node to another. The above argument reveals that the average time, $\overline{C}_{(s,d),i}$, can be defined recursively as follows

$$\overline{C}_{(s,d),i} = \begin{cases} \left(1 - P^b_{(s,d),i}\right)\overline{C}_{(s,d),i+1} + P^b_{(s,d),i}\overline{C}_{(s,d),i-1} + 1 & 1 \le i \le \|H\| - 1 \\ \left(1 - P^b_{(s,d),i}\right)\overline{C}_{(s,d),1} + P^b_{(s,d),i}\overline{C}_{(s,d),0} & i = 0 \\ 0 & i = \|H\| \end{cases} \tag{8}$$

Once the header reaches its destination, an acknowledgment flit is transmitted back to the source via the reserved path. Therefore, the mean time to setup a path for an $\|H\|$-hop message can be written as

$$\overline{C}_{(s,d),\|H\|} = \overline{C}_{(s,d),0} + \|H\| \tag{9}$$

where the term $\|H\|$ accounts for the number of cycles that are required to send the acknowledgement flit back to the source.

Averaging over the $(k^2 - 1)$ possible destination nodes in the network gives the mean time to set up a path, $\bar{C}_{(s,d)}$, from source s and destination d as

$$\bar{C}_{(s,d)} = 1/(k^2 - 1) \sum_{d \in G - \{s\}} \bar{C}_{(s,d), \|H\|} \tag{10}$$

The probability of blocking depends on the number of output channels, and thus on the virtual channels that a message can use at its next hop. A message is blocked at its $i - th$ hop, if all the virtual channels that can be chosen for its next hop, are being busy. Let T_i be the set of possible ways that i hops can be distributed over two dimensions such that the number of hops made in dimensions X and Y be at most h_x and h_y. T_i can be expressed as

$$T_i = \{(i_x, i_y) : i_x + i_y = i \,;\, i_x \leq h_x,\, i_y \leq h_y,\, i_x,\, i_y \geq 0\} \tag{11}$$

The probability that a message has entirely crossed dimension X on its $i - th$ hop is given by

$$P^X_{(s,d),i} = \|T_i\|_{i_x = h_x} / \|T_i\| \cdot P^X_{(s,d),i,V} \tag{12}$$

where $P^X_{(s,d),i,V}$ is the probability that all virtual channels used by a message over all the possible paths from s to d in dimension X are busy; this probability can therefore be written as

$$P^X_{(s,d),i,V} = \sum_{j=1}^{\|T_i\|_{i_x = h_x}} P_{\prec a_j, b_j \succ, V} / \|T_i\|_{i_x = h_x} \tag{13}$$

On the equation above, $P_{\prec a_j, b_j \succ, V}$ is the probability that V virtual channels at a specific physical channel in path $j, \prec a_j, b_j \succ$, are busy. This probability is obtained later from (21) using a Markovian model. Similarly, the probability that a message has entirely crossed dimension Y on its $i - th$ hop is determined by following equations

$$P^Y_{(s,d),i} = \|T_i\|_{i_y = h_y} / \|T_i\| \cdot P^Y_{(s,d),i,V} \,, \quad P^Y_{(s,d),i,V} = \sum_{j=1}^{\|T_i\|_{i_y = h_y}} P_{\prec a_j, b_j \succ, V} / \|T_i\|_{i_y = h_y} \tag{14}$$

On the other hand, the probability that a message has not entirely passed dimension X on its $i - th$ hop can be expressed as

$$P^{\overline{XY}}_{(s,d),i} = \|T_i\|_{i_x < h_x, i_y < h_y} / \|T_i\| \cdot P^{\overline{XY}}_{(s,d),i,V} \,, \quad \text{where} \quad P^{\overline{XY}}_{(s,d),i,V} = \sum_{j=1}^{\|T_i\|_{i_x < h_x, i_y < h_y}} P_{\prec a_j, b_j \succ, V} / \|T_i\|_{i_x < h_x, i_y < h_y} \tag{15}$$

Finally, the blocking probability, $P^b_{(s,d),i}$, is calculated as the aggregate of the blocking probabilities at the $i - th$ hop. Therefore, the $P^b_{(s,d),i}$ can be obtained as

$$P^b_{(s,d),i} = P^X_{(s,d),i} + P^Y_{(s,d),i} + P^{\overline{XY}}_{(s,d),i} \tag{16}$$

When the header does not encounter any blocking during the path set up stage, a minimum duration to establish a path is $2\|H\|$ cycles. So, the minimum average network latency seen by the message can be written as

$$\overline{S}_{\min,(s,d)} = M + 3\|H\|, \quad \overline{S}_{\min} = 1/(k^2 - 1) \sum_{d \in G - \{s\}} \overline{S}_{\min,(s,d)} \tag{17}$$

For a given node s in the network, the average latency seen by a message originated at that node to enter the network, $\overline{S}_s$, is equal to the average of all $S_{(s,d)}$ resulting in

$$\overline{S}_s = 1/(k^2 - 1) \sum_{d \in G - \{s\}} \overline{S}_{(s,d)} \tag{18}$$

Since a message can enter the network through any of the V virtual channels, the average traffic rate on each injection virtual channel is λ_{node}/V. Using adaptive routing under the uniform traffic results in the mean service time seen by messages at all source nodes being the same, and equal to the average network latency, i.e., $\overline{S}_s$. As a result, modeling the local queue in the source node as an M/G/1 queue, with the average arrival rate of λ_{node}/V and service time $\overline{S}_s$ with an approximated variance $(\overline{S}_s - \overline{S}_{\min})$ [8] yields the average waiting time, $\overline{W}_s$, seen by a message at the source node s as

$$\overline{W}_s = (1/k^2) \sum_{d \in G - \{s\}} \left[(\lambda_{node}/V) \overline{S}_s^2 \left(1 + (\overline{S}_s - \overline{S}_{\min})^2 / \overline{S}_s^2 \right) / 2 \left(1 - (\lambda_{node}/V) \overline{S}_s \right) \right] \tag{19}$$

(18) gives the network latency seen by a message to cross from the source s to the destination d. Averaging over all the k^2 possible nodes in the network yields the mean network latency as

$$\overline{S} = (1/k^2) \sum_{s \in G} \overline{S}_s \tag{20}$$

The probability $P_{\prec a,b \succ,v}$ that $v, 0 \le v \le V$, virtual channels at a given physical channel $\prec a,b \succ$ are occupied can be determined using a Markovian model (details of the model can be found in [3-5]). In the steady state, the model yields the following probabilities [5].

$$P_{\prec a,b \succ,v} = \begin{cases} Q_{\prec a,b \succ,0} = 1 \\[2mm] Q_{\prec a,b \succ,v} = Q_{\prec a,b \succ,v-1} \lambda_{\prec a,b \succ} \overline{S} & (1 \le v \le V - 1) \\[2mm] Q_{\prec a,b \succ,v} = \dfrac{Q_{\prec a,b \succ,v-1} \lambda_{\prec a,b \succ}}{1/\overline{S} - \lambda_{\prec a,b \succ}} \\[3mm] P_{\prec a,b \succ,0} = \left(\sum_{l=0}^{V} Q_{\prec a,b \succ,l} \right)^{-1} \\[3mm] P_{\prec a,b \succ,v} = P_{\prec a,b \succ,v-1} \lambda_{\prec a,b \succ} \overline{S} & (1 \le v \le V - 1) \\[2mm] P_{\prec a,b \succ,v} = \dfrac{P_{\prec a,b \succ,v-1} \lambda_{\prec a,b \succ}}{1/\overline{S} - \lambda_{\prec a,b \succ}} \end{cases} \tag{21}$$

When multiple virtual channels are used per physical channel in dimension X or Y, they share the bandwidth in a time-multiplexed manner. The average degree of virtual channel multiplexing that takes place at a specific channel $\prec a,b \succ$, can be estimated as

$$\overline{V}_{\prec a,b \succ} = \sum_{v=1}^{V} v^2 \cdot P_{\prec a,b \succ,v} / \sum_{v=1}^{V} v \cdot P_{\prec a,b \succ,v} \tag{22}$$

Let $\overline{V}_{\max,(s,d),j}$ be the maximum $\overline{V}_{\prec a,b \succ}$ of channels traversed by the path j, between source s and destination d. This quantity can be calculated as

$$\overline{V}_{\max,(s,d),j} = (1/\|H\|)\sum_{i=1}^{\|H\|} \overline{V}_{\prec a_i,b_i \succ,j} \qquad (23)$$

where j is a specific path between s and d, and $\|H\|$ is the distance (in terms of the number of hops made by the message) between the source and destination nodes. The parameter $\overline{V}_{<a_i,b_i>,j}$ is the average multiplexing degree of channel $\prec a_i,b_i \succ$, which is the channel traversed by the $i-th$ hop of path j.

Let there be $\mathcal{L}$ different paths of minimal length from s to d. We then calculate the average degree of virtual channel multiplexing from s to d along path $j, 1 \le j \le \mathcal{L}$, as

$$\overline{V}_{(s,d)} = (1/\mathcal{L})\sum_{j=1}^{\mathcal{L}} \overline{V}_{\max,(s,d),j} \qquad (24)$$

Averaging over all possible source-destination pairs, results in the overall virtual channels multiplexing degree as follows

$$\overline{V} = \left(1/k^2\right)\sum_{s \in G} 1/\left(k^2 - 1\right)\sum_{d \in G - \{s\}} \overline{V}_{(s,d)} \qquad (25)$$

Scaling the mean network latency and waiting time at the injection channel by a factor $\overline{V}$ to model the effects of virtual channel multiplexing yields the mean message latency as [3, 4]

$$Mean\ Message\ Latency = (\overline{S} + \overline{W}_s)\overline{V} \qquad (26)$$

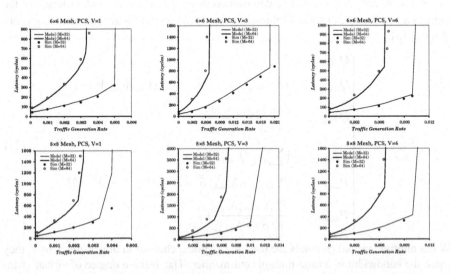

Fig. 2. The mean message latency predicted by the model vs. simulation results for the 6×6, and 8×8 mesh networks using PCS under Poisson traffic, V=1, 3, and 6 virtual channels per physical channel, with message lengths M =32, 64 flits

Examining the above equations of the analytical model reveals that many parameters that can affect the network's behavior have been considered and some of these parameters are dependent on each other and vise versa. Given that closed-form solutions for such models are very difficult to determine; therefore, the equations of the proposed analytical model are solved iteratively [6].

4 Model Validation

The proposed analytical models have been validated by means of a discrete-event simulator that mimics the behavior of PCS in 2-D mesh at the flit level. The results of simulation and analysis for the 6×6, and 8×8 networks with message length M =32 and 64 flits, V =1, 3, and 6 virtual channels per physical channel are depicted in Fig. 2. The figure reveals that the analytical model predicts the mean latency with a good degree of accuracy in all regions.

5 Conclusions

This paper described the first analytical model to predict the message latency in 2-D mesh networks with PCS when fully adaptive routing and virtual channels flow control are used. Simulation experiments have revealed that the latency results predicted by the proposed analytical model are in good agreement with those obtained through simulation. Another interesting line of research for future work may be the extent of the modeling approach described here to consider the behavior of PCS with other traffic patterns, e.g. hotspot traffic, and in the vicinity of failures in mesh networks.

References

1. Duato, J., Yalamanchili, S., Ni, L.M.: Interconnection networks: An engineering approach. Morgan Kaufmann Publishers, San Francisco (2003)
2. Gaughan, P.T., Yalamanchili, S.: A family of fault-tolerant routing protocols for direct multiprocessor networks. IEEE Transactions on Parallel and Distributed Systems 6(5), 482–497 (1995)
3. Min, G.: Performance modelling and analysis of multicomputer interconnection networks, Ph.D. Thesis, Computing Science Department, Glasgow University (2003)
4. Min, G., Ould-Khaoua, M.: A comparative study of switching methods in multicomputer networks. The Journal of Supercomputing 21(3), 227–238 (2002)
5. Dally, W.J.: Virtual channel flow control. IEEE Transactions on Parallel and Distributed Systems 3(2), 194–205 (1992)
6. Kleinrock, L.: Queueing Systems, vol. (1). John Wiley & Sons, New York (1975)
7. Feller, W.: An introduction to probability theory and its applications, vol. (1). John Wiley & Sons, New York (1967)
8. Draper, J.T., Ghosh, J.: A comprehensive analytical model for wormhole routing in multicomputers systems. Journal of Parallel and Distributed Computing 23(2), 202–214 (1994)

The Distance-Power Consumption Tradeoff for Cooperative Wireless Sensor Networks*

Inwhee Joe and Sungmoon Chung

Division of Computer Science and Engineering, Hanyang University
{iwjoe,dear1115}@hanyang.ac.kr

Abstract. Cooperative communication is known for its various advantages, such as robust to fading, improved diversity gains, capacity gains and increased power consumption performance. It allows for the achievement of effects of the virtual MIMO, so that diversity gain can be obtained from just merely one antenna for each node. However, conventional cooperative communication has low data rates when diversity gain increases. If we do not consider diversity gain to avoid this, we cannot achieve diversity gain. In addition, increasing the number of relays makes networks consume more power. This is one of the most important issues that increase power consumption performance in terms of WSN. Therefore, we propose an appropriate scenario which would increase the number of relays for optimal power consumption in a Wireless Sensor Network in consideration of the data rate, studying the tradeoff between distance (from Source to Destination) and power consumption to determine the optimal power consumption for a network.

Keywords: cooperative communication, diversity, power consumption, tradeoff, wireless sensor networks.

1 Introduction

WSN systems typically consist of resource-constrained micro sensor nodes that self-organize into a multi-hop wireless network. This sensor network monitors the environment, collects sensed data and relays the data back to a collection point typically residing on the Internet [1]. Cooperative communication allows for the achievement of effects of a virtual MIMO by sharing nodes' antennas among more than one node. Fading, in particular, is frequently generated in WSN. However, this phenomenon can be overcome by acquiring diversity gain. In addition, the acquisitions of diversity gains allows for communication increases in terms of reliability and improved power consumption by reducing retransmissions. Conventional cooperative communication has low data rates when diversity gain increases; therefore, if diversity gain is not consider, it is impossible to achieving diversity gain. In addition, increasing the number of relays will increase the network's power consumption. Power consumption is the one of the most important

---

* This work was supported by the ITRC Support Program (IITA-2009-C1090-0902-0047) and the IITA R&D Support Program of the MKE.

D. Ślęzak et al. (Eds.): FGCN/ACN 2009, CCIS 56, pp. 180–187, 2009.

issue in WSN. Because it is impossible that change the battery when the sensor node is used [2]. There have been many protocols proposed to overcome this tradeoff; however, a wire-less sensor node cannot have more than one antenna due to hardware complexity. Because of that, it is necessary to design an appropriate scenario for optimal power consumption in which the number of relays is increased, so that we can study the tradeoff between the number of relays and distance. Therefore, in this paper, we propose an appropriate scenario which increases the number of relays for optimal power consumption in Wireless Sensor Networks in light of the data rate, studying the tradeoff between distance (from Source to Destination) and power consumption for the power consumption of an optimal network. The rest of the paper is organized as follows. In Section 2 we outline previous studies that attempted to increase performance in terms of power consumption. This is followed by a description of our system model in Section 3. We present the optimal power consumption, after analyzing system performances in Section 4 and Section 5 concludes with our observations.

2   Related Work

Cooperative communication is one of the methods to improve communication performance by overhearing a sender's signal through the wireless channel. Cooperative communication is called cooperative MIMO, because the antennas created using mutual cooperation to make a virtual MIMO system [3]. Generally, it is impossible to make a MIMO system using the node's limited power and size due to the antenna interval in terms of WSN.

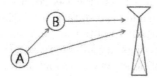

Fig. 1. Basic concept behind cooperative communication

Figure 1 describes the basic concept behind cooperation communication. It shows two senders communicating with one receiver. If each sender transmits its independent data to the receiver, it is impossible to achieve diversity gain; however, if node B receives data from node A and then retransmits this data to the receiver, node B can then transmit data with diverse overhead information to the receiver. In this case, it is possible to achieve diversity gain, because each path is an independent path. Generally, the transmission power model in a WSN is as follows [4]: to transmit a k bit message over a distance d, the node consumes power:

$$E_{TX}(k, d) = E_{elec} * k + \epsilon_{amp} * k * d^2 \tag{1}$$

Where E_{elec} is the 50nJ/bit needed to run the transmitter circuitry and ϵ_{amp} is 100pJ/bit/ necessary for the transmit amplifier to achieve an acceptable signal-to-noise ratio. Based on Equation (1) there has been a study done which found

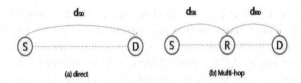

Fig. 2. Direct Network & Multi-hop Network

the optimal power consumption in a Multi-hop WSN, which is similar to a co-operative WSN.

Figure 2 shows that there is a power consumption gain when the power consumption of the Multi-hop network is less than that of the Direct network. This is due to the fact that a Multi-hop network can decrease the transmit amplifier power in order to achieve an acceptable signal-to-noise ratio. The power consumption gain of the Multi-hop network can be represented in Equation (2) [5].

$$4E_{elec} + \epsilon_{amp} * d_{SR}^2 + \epsilon_{amp} * d_{RD}^2 < 2E_{elec}$$
$$+\epsilon_{amp} * d_{SD}^2 \tag{2}$$

or

$$2E_{elec}/\epsilon_{amp} < d_{SD}^2 - d_{SR}^2 - d_{RD}^2$$

Where d_{SR} is the distance between S and R, d_{RD} is the distance between R and D, and d_{SD} is the distance between S and D. However, Equation (2) does not consider diversity gains, because it was released for use with a multi-hop network. In addition, it does not consider the data rate or the network increasing the number of relays. It is important to note that, in a cooperative WSN, the signal to noise ratio decreases when diversity gain increases. In wireless communication, Shannon's theory (3), which determines the maximum data rate, is as follows:

$$C = B \, \log_2(1 + S/N) \tag{3}$$

where C is the maximum data rate, B is the bandwidth, and S/N is the signal to noise ratio. When diversity is increased so as to achieve more diversity gain, the time must be increased in order to receive the data. Thus, we find that data rates and diversity are inversely proportional to each other. Their relationship in a cooperative WSN is shown in Table 1.

In an MIMO system, if a receiver has multiple antennas and can receive independent copied signals simultaneously, the data rate will not decrease as shown in Table 1. In a WSN, however, each node must have a single antenna, which creates more relays and diversity gain and a lower signal to noise ratio. There is a cooperative protocol known as NAF (none- orthogonal amplify and forward) [6][7] used to obtain diversity without decreasing the data rate. In NAF, the sender receives independent data during the second time slot at the same time that the relay sends the data received from the sender during the first time slot as shown in Table 2. This system, unfortunately, cannot be applied to a WSN,

Table 1. Diversity gain & Data rate & S/N

Diversity gain	Data rate	S/N
1	R	$2^{\frac{R}{B}}$
2	R/2	$2^{\frac{R}{2B}}$
3	R/3	$2^{\frac{R}{3B}}$
⋮	⋮	⋮
N	R/N	$2^{\frac{R}{NB}}$

Table 2. The transfer process of the protocol

Timeslot	Conventinal Cooperative	NAF
1st timeslot	S → R,D	S → R,D
2nd timeslot	R → D	S,R → D

because it is impossible for a receiver to receive independent copied signals simultaneously. There was a proposal [8], which advocated dividing one time slot into two smaller time slots so as to receive signals at the same time without decreasing the data rate;however, this was not applicable in our study, as it does in fact cause a decreased amount of data.

Therefore, we propose a scenario which would increase the number of relays for optimal power consumption, subsequently studying the tradeoff between distance (from S to D) and power consumption in a cooperative WSN in light of the data rate.

3 System Model

In our cooperative system, each node had a single antenna and used the same frequency. We assumed that all of the senders had knowledge of the distance. All of the terminals were assumed to operate in half-duplex mode. There are many possible models for these wireless sensor networks. In this work, we consider wireless networks where:

- All the sensor nodes are fixed .
- All nodes in the network are homogeneous and energy constrained.
- Channel status between nodes are all the same.
- Relay node only has a role that forward the information which is received from the source or previous relay node.
- The network is a simple linear network.

Figure 3 shows the radio model of our cooperative system. Relay node foward the information which is received from the source or previous relay node.

To study the tradeoff between distance and power consumption, we increased the number of relays as shown in Figure 4 and the diversity gain was always set to 2, regardless of the number of relays. Figure 4 shows the system model that

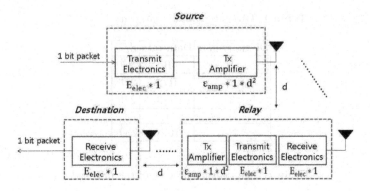

Fig. 3. Radio model of cooperative system

achieved two diversity gain from the nearest node and the second nearest node from D.

In conventional cooperative communication, a direct path from S to D must always be considered. In our proposed scenario, the node's interval was shortened when the number of relays increases. Therefore, the diversity gain as always set to two, as calculated from Equation (1) to reflect the data rate and data received from the nearest and the second nearest nodes to D in terms of the optimal power consumption. The distance unit was set to 10m, as a practical measurement, for the study of optimal power consumption. Each relay interval was to set to be the same amount, as calculated by Equation (1); thus, the relay interval was d/(N+1), when with N number of relays. The MRC [9] which is the most commonly used combining technique for an MIMO system, has only a single antenna at each node; therefore, it was necessary to use another combining technique in order to combine the received data sequentially. The combining technique used in this research increased the signal to ratio. But the Combining gain is not considered here. Because each of the gains of the signal to ratio was the same as the diversity gain, the diversity gain was always set to two, regardless the number of relays.

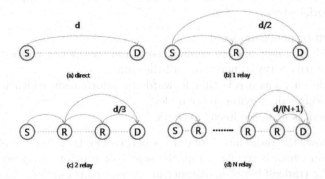

Fig. 4. Increasing relay scenario for the cooperative WSN

4 Performance Analysis

We calculated consumed power when each node sends a 1-bit for performance analysis in our proposed scenario. So Equations (4) and (5) were used in our proposed scenario when 1-bit data was transmitted:

$$E_{TXRX}(1,d) = 2(N+1)E_{elec} +$$
$$\epsilon_{amp} * (\frac{d}{N+1})^2 * N + \epsilon_{amp} * (\frac{2d}{N+1})^2 \qquad (4)$$

where N is the number of relays. If we applied $E_{elec} = 50nJ/bit$ and $\epsilon_{amp}=100pJ/bit/$, as calculated in Equation (1) to Equation (4), Equation (4) can then be described as follows:

$$E_{TXRX}(1,d)[nJ] = 2(N+1) * 100 +$$
$$0.1 * (\frac{d}{N+1})^2 * (N+4) \qquad (5)$$

As mentioned in the previous section, Equation (5) represents the system which acquired diversity gain 2 from the nearest and second nearest nodes to D. From Equation (5), the analysis results can be calculated as shown in Figure 5.

Figure 5 shows that the number of relays necessary for optimal power consumption differs according to distance (from S to D). This is caused by decreasing power consumption due to the tradeoff, which requires that the node interval shortens as the number of relay increases. However, power consumption increases after this tradeoff, due to the fact that the nodes' power consumption exceeds the nodes' power consumption gain per interval as shown in Table 3.

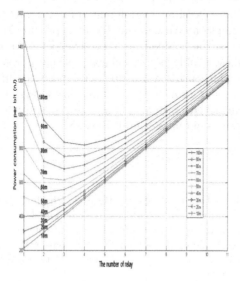

Fig. 5. Tradeoff between the number of relay and power consumption

Table 3. The optimal number of points in terms of power consumption

Distance	The number of relay	Power consumption(nJ)
100m	4	820
90m	3	754
80m	3	680
70m	3	614
60m	2	540
50m	2	466
40m	1	400
30m	1	312
20m	1	250
10m	1	212

The optimal power consumption uses 4 relays with a distance of 100m. And this point is a 3 relays when the distance is from 90m to 70m, 2 relays when the distance is from 60m to 50m, 1 relay when the distance is from 40m to 10m.

The optimal number of relay is increased when the distance between S and D become more distant. Because ϵ_{amp} gain is much more than consumed E_{elec}. Also the optmal number of relay is 1 when the distance is less than 40m. Because ϵ_{amp} gain is much less than consumed E_{elec}.

5 Conclusions

Diversity gain is an essential factor in cooperative communication. However, there exists a problem with this, as a wireless sensor node cannot have more than one antenna. This necessitates a different approach to the issue of achieving optimal power consumption. We were unable to apply previous WSN scenarios in this research, due to the tradeoff between diversity gain and data rates. In order to overcome these problems and achieve optimal power consumption, we proposed a scenario which utilized a cooperative WSN, requiring two diversity gains from the two nodes nearest to D, and considering the data rate. In a practical sense, we achieved optimal power consumption when we applied the optimal number of relays in our cooperative WSN.

References

1. Bhatti, S., Carlson, J., Dai, H., Deng, J., Rose, J., Sheth, A., Shucker, B., Gruen-wald, C., Torgerson, A., Han, R.: Mantis os: An embedded multithreaded operating system for wireless micro sensor platforms. In: ACM/Kluwer Mobile Networks and Applications (MONET), Special Issue on Wireless Sensor Networks (2005)
2. Wireless Sensors and Integrated Wireless Sensor Networks (Technical Insights), Frost and Sullivan (2002)
3. Yuan, Y., He, Z., Chen, M.: Virtual MIMO based cross-layer design for wireless sensor networks. IEEE Transactions on Vehicular Technology 53(3) (2006)

4. Heinzelman, W.R., Chandrakasan, A., Balakrishnan, H.: Energy-Efficient Communication Protocol for Wireless Microsensor Networks. In: Proc. Hawaii International Conference on System Sciences (2000)
5. Chen, C., Aksoy, D., Demir, T.: Processed Data Collection using Opportunistic Routing in Location Aware Wireless Sensor Networks. In: Proceedings of the 7th International Conference on Mobile Data Management (2006)
6. Nabar, R.U., Kneubuhler, F.W., Bolcskei, H.: Performance limits of amplify-and-forward based fading relay channels. In: Proc. IEEE Int. Conf. Acoustics, Speech and Signal Processing, May 2004, vol. 4, pp. 565–568 (2004)
7. Azarian, K., Gamal, H.E., Schniter, P.: On the achievable diversity- vs-multiplexing tradeoff in cooperative channels. IEEE Trans. Inf. Theory 51, 4152–4172 (2005)
8. Kim, G.S., Kong, H.Y.: System Optimization, Full Data Rate and Transmission Power of Decode-and-Forward Cooperative Communication in WSN. Korea Information Processing Society Paper C 14C(7), 597–602 (2007)
9. Zhang, Q.T.: Maximal-ratio combining over Nakagami fading channels with an arbitrary branch covariance matrix. IEEE Trans. Veh. Technol. 48, 1141–1150 (1999)

Research on Rule-Based AR System for Users' Situation Awareness

Jae-gu Song, Sungmo Jung, and Seoksoo Kim

Department of Multimedia Engineering, Hannam University, Daejeon, South Korea
bhas9@paran.com, sungmoj@gmail.com, sskim@hnu.ac.kr

Abstract. Recently, more researches have been done on a new interface which induces reactions based on user behavior patterns through augmented reality (AR) agent design to which context-aware technology is applied. Most researches are still in an early stage and insufficient for recognizing/utilizing information of context between reality and virtual reality. This study, therefore, analyzes profiles and behavior patterns of users by developing a health management-based scenario and combines it with an AR system. At the same time, a user is allowed to induce interaction with an AR system in order to prevent unnecessary exposure of information and provide additional data. To that end, this research analyzes context-aware patterns and marker information-aware patterns, which examine user behavior patterns, so as to activate AR information with the data provided as the result of the analysis. The system suggested in this research can be applied to educational contents. Learned context information and AR analysis are expected to make data delivery and communications with customers more effective.

Keywords: AR, Context-aware, Rule-Base system.

1 Introduction

As the interest in AR technology is of growing interest, more researches have been done on various education systems using the technology. In particular, most researches are focused on applying AR technology to printed teaching materials and field training for schools [1, 2]. However, the previous research has shown behavior patterns solely based on an AR agent application scenario, not sufficient for meaningful selection of behaviors or planning to solve complex problems. Thus, there is an attempt to use context-aware technology to provide contents with dynamic selection of behaviors and planning according to changing situations [3, 4]. In line with such efforts, this research aims to provide AR contents by taking into account user profiles and context information, offering user-oriented service by means of user-identified data produced within a limited marker. At the same time, the system is designed to prevent unnecessary exposure of data, provided that a user is already aware of the data. Related research is presented in Chapter 2, the structure of an interactive system introduced in Chapter 3, what is realized by the system explained in Chapter 4, and the conclusion is provided in Chapter 5.

D. Ślęzak et al. (Eds.): FGCN/ACN 2009, CCIS 56, pp. 188–192, 2009.

2 Background

Most researches on AR provide visual data produced by applying user behaviors to virtual reality. Particularly, AR has more value in education systems. M. White has conducted a research project that articles of a museum are reproduced in three-dimensional figures which are provided through the Web. The research aims to provide articles augmented by a computer using the context information of the exhibits in a museum [5]. The HIT Lab NZ (New Zealand) has developed a story book that a learner can use AR. If the user opens the book, characters of each page are animated [6]. Such case shows potentialities of an AR agent, utilizing interactive data between a user and AR systems.

3 System Design

3.1 System Workflow

AR is also referred to as mixed reality continuum. This is because various types of AR could be produced according to the degree of mixture of virtual reality and reality. In view of this, the system suggested in this research includes a user and context information-aware stage based on a sensor and user profiles, a data selection stage based on the information collected a contents exposure stage that delivers data to display devices of a user, and a received data-aware stage. The entire structure of the system is as follows.

① In the User and Context Data-Aware stage, the system reads user data such as his/her gender or ages and the information provides the basis for selecting proper AR contents.

② Video Input is the basic step for AR system application in which data are received through a camera.

③ In the Data Extract stage, target images are extracted by removing backgrounds from received images.

④ Marker Detection refers to the stage in which the system locates a marker matching with a corresponding image defined as a binary code.

⑤ Extract Rectangle is the stage that the system recognizes the scope of a marker.

⑥ Template Matching is the stage that corresponding contents are put into a marker.

⑦ Profile & CA Analysis verifies if the content input in the Template Matching stage are suitable for a user based on his/her profiles and context information, which was initially provided, in order to modify or complement the contents. The system exposes proper contents to a user after taking into account the ages, gender, and frequency of learning. To do this, contents defined as a corresponding marker are developed and saved in an AR system while standards are established in order to utilize such data. In addition, time and frequency of contents exposure are calculated, which is required to process a decision function with pattern sorting standards.

⑧ AR Content Matching is the final stage that analyzed data are exposed to a user through an AR system.

The overall structure of the module is as follows.

Fig. 1. System Workflow

3.2 Context information Analysis Based on User Profiles

The key part of the system suggested in this research is the application of context information based on user profiles to an AR system through established standards. In order to apply the system standards, a rule engine is used in extracting accurate systems. The purpose of the rule engine is to produce consistent behavior patterns, minimizing ambiguity of context-awareness. That is, implicit data are received from the manager that collects existing data, from which standards are established for pattern definition. Also, data are analyzed to find out relations. In this way, tag data, which describe patterns of context data, are produced and used to search for defined rules. Lastly, extracted tags become key factors in securing explicit data and conducting AR Content Matching in the system.

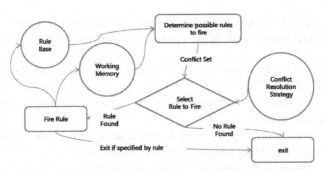

Fig. 2. Rule Engine Workflow

In the last stage of AR Content Matching, a marker is read in order to verify the awareness rate between a user and an AR system. Awareness and interest in learning is estimated taking into account time and frequency of contents exposure. That is, such situated learning is recognized as apprenticeship of context while frequency and exposure higher than certain standards provide basis for evaluating to what degree the system is familiar with service.

The data between a user and a marker shall be controlled through a history, which is considered standards for selecting ever-exposed AR contents. The history information is also managed by the profile-processing module. The data managed by the history are used for providing users of the similar profile patterns with corresponding contents.

4 System Realization

The system was realized using a desktop, Visual Studio 2008, and C#. NyARToolkit [7] was used for tracking and simple drawings such as a circle or a square for the contents. As a physical device a web cam (KMC-90) was employed. Gender, age, and observation time were three patterns defined. The following is the classification standards.

    RULEsex = {Female, Male}
    RULEage = {teens, twenties, thirties}
    RULEtime = { short, normal, long}

These standards were applied to rules as follows.

    (default Check-state
    (insert device(camera_para#? exist)
    (insert device(marker_data #? exist)
    (time?t)
    (content?"")(start-time?stime)(end-time?etime)
    (sex ?sex(not(and(>=?Female True))))
    (age ?time((>= ?time 1000)(<= ?time 500)))
    age&(not(and(>= ?age 10)(<= ?age 30))))
    => (insert(user(content?#)(make a drawing))))

Various contents were expected to be shown according to the results of rule engines recognizing user profiles and context information.

The scenario was designed to maximize education effects by showing AR contents to a user according to his/her education level. That is, if different users read the same book (made up of markers), his/her age, gender, the period that he/she has read the book are taken into account so as to provide effective contents. The contents are selected by rules defined in the system.

Figure 3 depicts how AR contents may vary according to different users. This shows how the prototype system was realized, where the rules were applied to NyARToolkit (used for tracking) and thus proper 3D contents were exposed to users. The triangle in the right was exposed to a man in 20's while the square in the left to a woman in 20's. In the future, more sophisticated designs or characters shall be developed for educational contents.

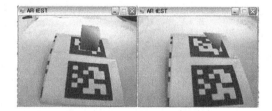

Fig. 3. AR contents change according to different users

5 Conclusion

The suggested AR system, which considers situations of a user, produces contents based on basic profiles and AR usage time. Particularly, the rule engine is designed to deal with situations more flexibly. There is a lack of research on active recognition of user information. This calls for further research efforts on more active AR system that can recognize not only user profiles but also learning behavior patterns so as to develop a more efficient AR system.

References

1. Shelton, B.E., Hedley, N.: Using Augmented Reality for Teaching Earth-Sun Relationships to Undergraduate Geography Students. Program for Educational Transformation Through Technology (2002),
   http://depts.washington.edu/pettt/papers/
   shelton-hedley-art02.pdf
2. Shelton, B.E.: Augmented Reality and Education: Current Projects and the Potential for Classroom Learning, New Horizons for Learning,
   http://www.newhorizons.org/strategies/technology/shelton.htm
3. Barakonyi, I., Weilguny, M., Psik, T., Schmalstieg, D.: MonkeyBridge: autonomous agents in augmented reality games. In: Advances in Computer Entertainment Technology, pp. 172–175 (2005)
4. Shin, H., Woontack, W.: Behavior Generaton System of Context-aware Augmented Reality Agent for Realistic Activation of Agent's behavior. In: HCI 2009, pp. 579–582 (2009)
5. White, M., Liarokapis, F., Mourkoussis, N., Basu, A., Darcy, J., Petridis, P., Lister, P.F.: A lightweight XML driven architecture for the presentation of virtual cultural exhibitions (ARCOLite). In: ADIS International Conference of Applied Computing, pp. 205–212 (2005)
6. Woods, E., Binder, G., Stangl, M., Billinghurst, M.:
   http://www.hitlabnz.org/wiki/Black_Magic_Book
7. PukiWiki Developers Team, http://nyatla.jp/nyartoolkit/wiki/
   index.php?NyARToolkitCS%2FUma2Desktop

Automatic Web Service Detection in Oil and Gas

Kari Anne Haaland Thorsen, Odd Frode Torbjørnse, and Chunming Rong

Department of electrical engineering and computer science, University of Stavanger,
4036 Stavanger, Norway
kari.a.thorsen@uis.no

Abstract. Semantic described web services are proposed to leverage automatic web service discovery. The proposed framework is suggested for use within the oil and gas domain to simplify data flow between collaborating partners, but could easily be adapted to other similar business domains. Instead of having a direct, hardcoded mapping between each and every systems it is suggested to provide information throughout web services which partners easily can connect to. The Web services are semantically described using the unified oil and gas ontology, which constitutes on ISO 15926. Smart agents' reason upon web service descriptions and find web services based on the processes the web services offer.

Keywords: Semantic Web Service, Integrated Operations, Smart Agents.

1 Introduction

Web services add a new level of functionality to the Web, an environment of distributed applications. The SOAP protocol and the Web Service Description Language (WSDL) enable systems to communicate over the internet. But the XML-description of web services still demands human interpretation in order to set up the workflows needed to exchange data between services offered. Given the nature of an autonomic distributed environment, this means that the industry needs to face the challenges of resolving a large degree of automation in searching for available and adequate web services and integrating them without the need of human interactions. Capabilities to discover, extract, and model knowledge, as well as enhance information with semantic metadata are needed to do automatic reasoning.

The Web Service Description Language (WSDL) specifies a way to describe the functionalities of web services and how and where to invoke them. However, the WSDL W3C Recommendation dose not include semantic in the description of Web services. Thus, two services can have similar description but different meaning, or they can have different descriptions but similar meaning. Resolving these ambiguities in Web service descriptions is an important step toward automating the discovery and composition of web services. Being able to discover and compose new web services, based on existing web services, will give a more dynamic web of data, which would be an improvement to the current web of documents.

Semantic tools provide capabilities for automatic discovery of topics and concepts. These tools may also extract the meaning of the information provided, categorize,

D. Ślęzak et al. (Eds.): FGCN/ACN 2009, CCIS 56, pp. 193–200, 2009.
© Springer-Verlag Berlin Heidelberg 2009

correlate, and map information from different sources. By using ontologies and semantic technologies it is possible to automatically discover and deploy semantic annotated web services and make use of their functionalities. By using semantic, computers may discover and even combine services to create new services, and in this sense enable the web services to grow together with the data on to the web. The sequence of web service requests may be orchestrated, and the responses may be reasoned upon and put together into composites that deliver a more comprehensive view of the data.

The Norwegian Oil Industry Association, OLF, claims that only one-fourth of the estimated oil and gas resources on the Norwegian Continental Shelf has been produced, and strongly believes that getting hold of more real-time data will provide a basis for better decision making, which again will lead to increased production [1]. In the last few years the industry has managed to increase the real-time data stream significantly. But, instead of achieving better decision support, the industry now experiences an information overload that results in reduced decision quality [2]. Operators do not have enough resources nor the ability to interpret this ever increasing flow of data. There is an expressed need to integrate web services based on the widely accepted WSDL protocol WITSML [3] used by the Oil and Gas upstream industry and the OPC-UA [4] used by the Oil and Gas processing industry. This could easily be conducted by using traditional point-to-point integration methodology, but this would require a new mapping every time we want to connect to a new service. By elaborating semantic annotated web services and annotating different WSDL domains to a common ontology, we could (at least in theory) automatically discover and integrate any given WSDL protocol that is annotated to the same ontology.

This paper demonstrates how semantic description of web services and a semantic search engine may facilitate the discovery process.

2 Related Work

In the resent years there have been several proposals to semantically describe web services, like OWL-S (former DAML-S), SWSO and WSMO [5-7]. In general they provide a way to describe (1) the functionalities of the web service; what the web service does, (2) how these functionalities are achieved and (3) how to access the web service; how to interact with it. The functionally description includes description of expected/required inputs, produced outputs, pre-conditions, and effects (IOPEs), and is used to support automated web service discovery. This description may also hold other basic information not directly related to the functionality, like: name of author, name of service provider, version number, textual description, and notation of quality (e.g. reliability).

The description on how to achieve the described functionalities (referred to as the Process Model in OWL-S and SWSO and web service interface in WSMO) states how the functionalities are carried out; how to use the service. It gives details like: the condition under which particular outcomes will occur and the step by step processes leading to these outcomes. E.g. a web service can be constructed by a set of other more primitive web services. The functionality description details how these other web services are used, e.g. the sequencing of the services and the IOPEs of the different services.

The description of functionalities is an abstract description, it dose not provide any information on how to actually interact with the web service. This information is specified in a grounding description. The grounding gives details on how to map from an abstract to a concrete specification, e.g. how to actually access the service. It contains information about transport protocol, message format, network address, port number etc. The WSDL already provides a well developed and industry adopted means of specifying details on how to interact with the service. To leverage one the significant body of work in this area and its industry adoption, the different web service description frameworks have choosen to make use of the WSDL in crafting an initial grounding mechanism. Abstract service descriptions are grounded by defining mapping from ontologically described concepts to WSDL constructs that describes the concrete realization of these concepts. The concept of grounding is in general consistent with WSDL's concept of binding.

Based on the grounding specification different engines for mapping existing WSDL-descriptions to semantic web service descriptions have been proposed (e.g. WSDL2OWL-S[1], ASSAM[2] and OWL-S Editor[3]). To our knowledge, these solutions generate a separate ontology for each web service, which subsequently needs to be mapped onto other existing ontologies to be utilized. This mapping can either be carried out by a one-to-one mapping between all the different ontologies, or with the use of an intermediary e.g. the oil and gas ontology. Both solutions provide semantic described web services, which enable reasoning, intelligent search and queries, but the first solution demands for a new mapping every time we want to integrate with a new service. The second solution conquers this challenge as the web service ontologies will only need to be mapped towards the common oil and gas ontology. But, the idea of ontologies is to have a common ontology for all parts in a domain.

SAWSDL (Semantic Annotations for WSDL and XML Schema) [8] defines a set of extension attributes for the Web Service Description Language and XML Schema definition language. This enables description of semantic in the WSDL. The specification defines how semantic annotation is accomplished by the use of references to semantic models. It is not a language for representing semantic models, but provides mechanisms by which concepts from a semantic model, defined in an ontology or in a Resource Description Format, RDF, can be referenced from within WSDL and XML Schema components using annotations. When expressed in a formal language these semantics can help disambiguate the description of Web services during automatic discovery and composition of Web services [8].

With this recommendation, WSDL-elements can be linked to a common ontology directly, instead of first constructing a web service specific ontology and map this onto the common ontology. Other industries that have done similar evaluation of SAWSDL are within life sciences, like glycoproteomics. Glycoproteomics is a branch of proteomics that identifies, catalogues, and characterizes proteins containing carbohydrates as a post-translation modification [9]. In [10], a description on how to

---

[1] http://projects.semwebcentral.org/projects/wsdl2owl-s/
[2] http://www.andreas-hess.info/projects/annotator/index.html
[3] http://staff.um.edu.mt/cabe2/supervising/undergraduate/owlseditFYP/OwlSEdit.html

ground WSMO descriptions with the use of WSDL is given, but this is based on linking to a ontology which is only applicable for this one web service description. In addition a lot of tools like Radient and WSMO are supporting this way of annotating web services. But to out knowledge there has not been done any similar evaluation within the Oil and Gas industry earlier.

POSC Caesar Association (PCA) has, in closed collaboration with the industry developed a unified reference data library (RDL) constituted on the ISO 15926. ISO 15926 has 9 separately published parts. It defines, inter alia, an upper abstract ontology (Part 2), a core library containing abstract classes used by all domains (Part4), and an implementation architecture based on the W3C Recommendation of the Semantic Web is described (Part 7). Part 4 is the "core library", of the RDL. An RDL is like a class library where the classes define types of things. The ambition of ISO 15926 is to provide a standardized data model for all kind of facilities, thus enabling the industry to harmonize their internal proprietary data models. By harmonizing data models two or more models, usually within a domain of interest, is compared, with the goal of reducing data redundancy and inconsistencies, and improving the quality and format of data. This is usually done to perform data mapping, data normalization, or data integration. RDL provides interoperability to the industry, which means that data may be compared and exchanged.

3 Semantic Described Web Services

The aim is to automatically discover and connect to web services in the oil and gas domain. A client should be able to do semantic search for web services, and upon discovery automatically connect to the selected web service(s).

In [11] we demonstrated that it is possible to integrate WITSML and OPC-UA by using the ontology defined in ISO 15926. SAWSDL was used to annotate WSDL-descriptions with concepts defined in the RDL. A small subset of Daily Drilling Report (DDR) and a simplified proprietary dataset in OPC-UA were used for demonstration. The purpose of the prototype was to receive a Survey Station as defined in the DDR. A Survey Station is a point in the drilling process where a measurement of the inclination and azimuth of the borehole is performed. The DDR survey station is defined by a WITSML complex element, and consists of the following five fields: Data/time for survey operation (dTim), measured depth (md), true vertical depth (tvd), hole inclination (incl), and hole azimuth (azi). The Survey Station (the measured point) is used to calculate the trajectory of the well.

Process data can be accessed through a web service (henceforward referred to as the OPC-UA web service), and are presented according to the OPC-UA structure. The above mention readings; measure depth, true vertical depth, hole inclination, and hole azimuthe, can all be acquired from the OPC-UA web service. Thus, all the readings required for a WITSML survey station element can be acquired from this web service.

The OPC UA web service takes as input an element containing a list of all the items the requester wants a value of, and returns a list of all the requested values. Thus, the requester can choose only to get one or some of the values or all of them in once. This is specified in the input message to the server. The expected input is zero or more of the following items: MDEPTH, TVDEPT, INCL_V_DEG and AZMH_TN_DEG. The expected output is the value of the given items and depends on items given in the input. The service is semantically described by using OWL-S. All the different concepts that the web service might consume and produce need to be described in a common vocabulary. This is done throughout the oil and gas reference data library (RDL)[4]. All local definitions are mapped onto their equivalent RDL definitions.

In addition, all the processes that can be performed by a service need to be described. Processes should be categorized on the basis of what they do. E.g. all processes for finding a location can be categorised in a findLocation class. The granularity of the classification depends on the scale of the web services. E.g. if it is expected to be many services providing "find gps coordinates based on place name" then there should be a separate class classifying these web services. It would then be possible to sett restriction on what type of input and output these processes can have. If, on the other side, it is expected only to be a couple of services providing a findLocation functionality it would be more appropriate to classify all these in a findLocation class, and let them define their own input and output parameters.

Service profiles, which are used in the find process, are categories according to their functionalities. A class, GetSurveyStation, and two subclasses, GetSurveyStationByOperator and GetSurveyStationByWell were constructed. The first expects an Operator and the second a well as input, and they will both have survey station as output.

4 Semantic Search Engine and Smart Agents

To enable efficient Web service discovery the services need to be registered somewhere, it is not enough to publish the description on the service providers' home page. Several solutions for web service registry and discovery exist, like the Universal Description, Discovery, and Integration specification (UDDI) [12]. These are primarily key word based, and human interpretation is needed to discover and connect to Web Services. Use of a semantic search engine describing web service functionalities is proposed. Service providers can register their services at the search engine by adding the semantic description of the services, and clients can thereafter search for web services. The description of web services is functional based, giving a semantic description of operations and expected IOPEs. E.g. a client can search for a web service which provides the operations of adding to numbers.

To fulfil the tasks designed in [11] a matching engine is needed. This engine must provide discovery, negotiation, filtering, choreography, orchestration and reasoning. It was populated with description of the different services; which services performs which operations, what are the expected IOPE's (input, output, preconditions, and effects) [7].Three essentials types of knowledge about a web service needed to be provided: (1) what the service does/provide; (2) how it is used/works; and (3) how to interact with it [7].

The OWL-S descriptions where collected in a search engine which enabled semantic search for operations and proper web services to perform the desired operations.

---

[4] Due to the fact that the RDL and the OGO is still under construction, it was not used directly. Instead, a smaller ontology that may be regarded as a snapshot of the RDL was designed and used instead.

The semantic description enabled queries for web services based on their expected input and/or output. E.g. a query could ask for all web services with true vertical depth as output and list the expected input for those service, or: find all web services that take wellName as input and give the true vertical depth as output. All the concepts in the queries are related to the ISO 15925 definitions, and thus independent of local naming.

Based on the web service descriptions, smart agents can reason over the descriptions and orchestra new services. These functionalities can either be provided by the same unit as the search engine, or by separate units. Different parties can construct their own smart agent with reasoning abilities as desired.

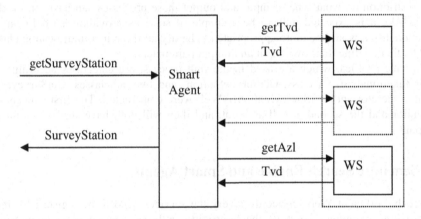

Fig. 1. Smart Agent - collection, organising, and compose new information

By example, the semantic description of the OPC-UA web service defines the different outputs the service can produce and the required inputs for each of the outputs. A smart agent might reason over the information acquired in a survey station, search for web services that might provide this information, combine the information and return it to the end user, as illustrated in Figure 1. The end user quires for a Survey station, the smart agent interpret the survey station element and appreciate that it consist of several measurement that can be acquired from one or several web services. It requests the data, collects and gathers it, and responds to the user with a survey station element.

5 Discussion and Future Work

Utilizing ISO 15926 enables organizations to meet their asset information requirements. The costs associated with defining, collecting, transforming, deploying and sustaining this information over the lifecycle of assets and facilities are reduced as the task is reduced to linking the appropriate reference in RDL. However, the number of instances and triples indicate that the RDL repository is very large, which may imply search performance issues and cumbersome mapping. E.g. a search for true vertical dept in the RDL returns about 50-60 different definitions, where three of them relate to the survey point. Thus, care need to be taken to assure correct mapping between local namings and the unified definitions.

As there will be little or no control once the mapping is done, special care needs to be taken in the mapping process when going from manual, human based mapping to automatic mapping. One can only assure and control the mapping to and from once own domain and ISO 15926. The mapping from other systems to ISO 15926 is not possible to control, and one just have to trust the mapping process of others.

Focus in this paper has been on web service discovery. Upon discovery, the search engine should maintain information needed for the client to automatically connect to the web service and map web service output format to the client's input format. The serviceGrounding specifies a communication protocol, message format, port number etc. For each semantic type of input and output specified in the serviceModel the serviceGrounding must specify an unambiguous way of exchanging data elements for that type. All the different communication protocols supported by the service provider need to be described, and a mapping-functionality, mapping to and from the unified data structure to the service specific structure, should be provided.

6   Conclusion

Most large organizations suffer from having many different systems that need to share information. In addition the industry is experiencing a higher demand to adapt to new collaboration partners as fast as possible, and the oil and gas industry is no exception. Due to these changes in requirements for information sharing the semantic approach seems to be promising as it makes information more adaptable and offer better support services.

Applications built using semantic technologies are much more flexible then traditional applications because semantic technologies are able to integrate data, content, applications and processes by the means of a shared ontology. No software needs to be modified. This has potential for minimizing development and maintenance costs drastically. Developers can spend less time on coding applications and more time to make better models of the problem domain. Minimizing the need to do changes in the source code will eventually make the programs more robust, and modifications to the model can be done in runtime.

In this paper, semantic descriptions of web services are propose to facilitate the discovery of web services. Web services can then be discovered based on what services they provide, expected input, output, precondition and effects. The description is based on a unified reference data library to assure consistency in terms and definitions. An OPC-UA web service was semantically described using the OWL-S and concepts and definitions defined in the RDL. In addition, process descriptions were needed to classify the different processes and services provided. The proposed framework is suggested for internal use within the oil and gas domain to simplify dataflow between collaborating domains and partners, but should be suitable for other similar business domains. Instead of having a direct mapping between different units that need to share information it is suggested to provide information throughout web services, which partners can easily connect to. A complete categorisation of web service operations for the oil and gas domain needs to be developed.

References

1. Integrerte operasjoner, http://www.olf.no/io/ [cited September 10, 2007]
2. Landre, E.: IT Architecture for Integrated Operations. In: Semantic Days, Stavanger, Norway (2008),
   https://www.posccaesar.org/svn/pub/SemanticDays/2008/
   EinarLandre-ArchitectureforIntegratedOperations.pdf
3. Wellsite Information Transfer Standard Markup Language, http://www.witsml.org/ [cited September 2, 2007]
4. OPC Unified Architecture,
   http://www.opcfoundation.org/Default.aspx/01_about/UA.asp?MI
   D=AboutOPC [cited (2008)]
5. Battle, S., et al.: Semantic Web Services Ontology (2005)
6. Feier, C., Domingue, J.: WSMO Primer (2005),
   http://www.wsmo.org/TR/d3/d3.1/v0.1/ [cited Oktober 2008]
7. Martin, D., et al.: OWL-S: Semantic Markup for Web Services. W3C Member Submission (2004), http://www.w3.org/Submission/OWL-S/ [cited 2006]
8. Farrel, J., Lausen, H., et al.: Semantic Annotations for WSDL and XML Schema - W3C Recommendation (2007),
   http://www.w3.org/TR/2007/REC-sawsdl-20070828/ [cited 2008]
9. Baker, C.J.O., Cheung, K.H.: Semantic Web: Revolutionizing the knowledge discovery in the life sciences. Springer, Boston (2005)
10. Kopecky, J., Schütz, A.: WSMO grounding in SAWSDL (2008)
11. Torbjørnsen, O.F.: SAWSDL in Oil & Gas. In: Department of Electrical Engineering and Computer Science, University of Stavanger, Stavanger (2008)
12. Papazoglou, M.P.: WEB services: principles and technology, vol. XXXII, p. 752. Person Prentice Hall, Harlow (2008)

Eperfi: Design and Implementation of End-to-End Network Performance Measurement and Diagnosis System for High-Speed Networks

Young-Ju Han[1], Min-Woo Park[1], Jong-Myoung Kim[2], Yoonjoo Kwon[3], and Tai-Myoung Chung[1]

[1] Internet Management Technology Laboratory,
Department of Electrical and Computer Engineering, Sungkyunkwan University,
300 Cheoncheon-dong, Jangan-gu, Suwon-si, Gyeonggi-do, 440-746, Republic of Korea
Tel.: +82-31-290-7222; Fax: +82-31-299-6673
{yjhan,mwpark}@imtl.skku.ac.kr, tmchung@ece.skku.ac.kr
[2] Incidents Analysis Team, Korea Internet Security Agency(KISA),
Republic of Korea
jmkim@kisa.or.kr
[3] HPcN Project Div, HPcN Development Team,
Korea Institute of Science and Technology Information (KISTI), Republic of Korea
yulli@kisti.re.kr

Abstract. This paper presents the design and implementation result of Eperfi (the end-to-end network performance measurement and diagnosis system) in high-speed networks. Eperfi offers 1)the measuring and diagnosing mechanism to find out the cause of the low data transmission rate from link layer to application layer for all nodes on an end-to-end path, 2)the measuring and diagnosing mechanism to inspect whether a bulk data transfer tool such as SCP, SFTP and RSYNC is the cause of low throughput, 3) the graphical view representing real-time network traffic flow and information based on Weathermap, MRTG and Iperf. By using Eperfi, end-users can not only adjust their system to achieve more fast data transmission but also choose a more efficient data transfer tool to fine-tune their system into high-speed networks. Additionally, a network manager can offer an enhanced network service to an end-user by adjusting efficiently their managed network.

1 Introduction

Recently, the speed of network has been tremendously increased as the need for a bulk data transmission such as GRID computing or super-computing is increased. Although the network infrastructure has grown greatly in bandwidth, an end user cannot use the full advantage of the improved network. Indeed, the data transmission speed is limited, despite of the fact that the underlying network can support higher data transfer rate. This problem is resulted from the inadequate configuration of the host system and its application adapted into the low speed network.

Many researches have been done for dealing with this problem. NDT(Network Diagnostic Tool)[1] and NPAD(Network Path and Application Diagnosis)[2] are the

D. Ślęzak et al. (Eds.): FGCN/ACN 2009, CCIS 56, pp. 201–215, 2009.
© Springer-Verlag Berlin Heidelberg 2009

representative projects among them. The purpose of these projects is the development of the network performance diagnosis tool to diagnose the network performance problems and to provide some solutions for an efficient data transmission. To achieve a high transmission throughput, they provide a method for diagnosing problems in the network and end-systems which are known for common causes of all severe performance degradation over an E2E(end-to-end) path. By using these tools, end users can test their host and find the cause of a low data transfer rate. The scope of diagnosis includes the fault TCP setting, the wrong MTU size, the duplex-mismatch, the cable fault and so on. However, they only diagnose the problems under the transport layer of TCP/IP layer model so they cannot detect the problem that a data transmission tool may have. For example, SCP uses an internal window mechanism just like TCP to control the overall data transmission and the window size of SCP is limited up to $64Kbyte$[10]. If the BDP(Bandwidth Delay Product) of the data transmission connection is larger than $64Kbyte$, SCP usually acts as a bottleneck but general end users cannot know this fact. Experts have to advise them to use another efficient data transfer tool. Another problem of existing E2E network diagnosing tools are that a user cannot select the path where to test because the testing path using these tools is always from the end-host where their web page is running to their web server.

In this paper, we propose Eperfi(End-to-End Network Performance Measurement and Diagnosis System). EPerfi is a web-based client/server system for measuring and diagnosing both the E2E network performance and the bulk data transfer tool performance in high speed networks. Eperfi makes an end user or an administrator test network performance for the specific E2E path selected by themselves and supports the performance test for a data transfer tool using user unlike NDT and NPAD.

The main contribution of the E2E performance test of Eperfi is to offer the overall diagnosis results from link layer to application layer for all nodes(end-hosts or routers) on E2E path to a testing user. In addition, the testing user can understand easily and intuitively about the measurement and diagnosis results through the web-based graphical views which shows real-time traffic flow while testing. For the tool test, the end user can easily test their own transfer tool and may find out how their tool works efficiently by accessing simply the Eperfi web page. Finally, Eperfi will help the end users fine-tune their system and choose another efficient data transfer tool for achieving a high data transmission throughput.

This paper is organized as follows. Section 2 reviews the cause of the low performance over E2E communication in high-speed networks and the motivation of our research. Section 3 describes the design, the measurement and diagnosis metrics and the procedures of EPerfi in details. Section 4 describes implementation result of EPerfi. In section 5 we explore related works and compare the EPerfi with them. At last, Section 6 summarizes our work and discusses future works.

2   Backgrounds

In this Section, we discuss the cause of a low data transmission throughput in the high-speed network that was reflected on the design of our proposed system, Eperfi. We then describe the goals of EPerfi.

2.1 The Cause of the Low Data Transmission Throughput on E2E Connection in High-Speed Networks

The utilization of a network path refers to how much of the capacity is being consumed by traffic. Available bandwidth describes what portion of the path is currently unused by other competing traffic [14]. More precisely, available bandwidth is determined by subtracting the utilization from the capacity of the network path. Data transmission performance of a specific application on E2E connection depends on achievable bandwidth. Achievable bandwidth is the throupput which the application can actually obtain over the path, that is, the maximum amount of data per time unit that the network path can provide to the application, given the utilization of the network path (that is, available bandwidth), the transmission protocol and operating system used, and the end-node load and setting and so on[14].

A node adapted into a low-speed networking environment can make achievable bandwidth degrade, even though available bandwidth is greatly improved by deploying a high-speed networking technology. To find out the cause of the low data transmission throughput into the high-speed network, we need to know the effective factors in achievable bandwidth. For doing so, we categorize the factors into layer and node type as we can see in Table 1.

Table 1. The effective factor in achievable bandwidth on E2E connection per layer by node type

Layer\Node Type	End-Node	Intermediate Node
Network and Link layers	Link capacity, MTU, Duplex mode	Link capacity, MTU, Duplex mode, The amount of cross traffic
Transport Layer	A window size	N/A
Application Layer	Internal window size control CPU and Memory load	N/A

Network and Link Layers. Since these layers perform real data transmission at each link on E2E path, available bandwidth of each link on E2E path must be considered for the diagnosis of E2E network performance. The factors which affect basically in link available bandwidth are the link capacity, the amount of cross-traffic, the path MTU and the duplex mode[6].

Transport Layer. A window size is the most important factor which influences on achievable bandwidth. We can get the theoretical optimum window size from BDP[11]. BDP is calculated as $BDP = total\ available\ bandwidth(bits/sec) \times RTT(sec)$. The result, an amount of data measured in bits, is equivalent to the maximum amount of data on the network at any given time [14]. As the link capacity of the high-speed network has been increased greatly, BDP also has been increased. As the result, larger window size must be required on the high-speed network and the window size adapted into a low-speed networking environment must be fine-tuned. The others which affect on control of the window size are TCP window scaling and TCP buffer auto-tuning

Table 2. Measuring and Diagnosing Metrics

Test	Node Type	Layer	Diagnosis Metrics	Measurement Metrics (Static[S] or Dynamic[D])
Tool	End Node	Application	Internal Bottleneck	• [D]Internal window Size information - X_RcvBuf and X_SndBuf from web100 • [D]Achievable Bandwidth - Iperf[7] Result
E2E	End Node	Application	Low Throughput	• [D] Achievable Bandwidth - Iperf Result
			Resource Problem	• [S]CPU Usage - idle_stat, sys_stat, user_stat by top • [S]Memory Usage - used_mem, free_mem by top
		Transport	Invalid window size	• [S]Window Size information from proc o /proc/sys/net/core/rmem_default - Default receive buffer size o /proc/sys/net/core/rmem_max - Maximum receive buffer size o /proc/sys/net/core/wmem_default - Default send buffer size o /proc/sys/net/core/wmem_max - Maximum send buffer size o /proc/sys/net/ipv4/tcp_rmem - Min, Default, Max value of receive window size o /proc/sys/net/ipv4/tcp_wmem - Min, Default, Max value of send window size
			Window size Mis-control	• [S]Window Scaling information - 7ipv4/tcp_window_scaling • [S]TCP Socket Buffer auto-tuning information - 7ipv4/tcp_moderate_rcvbuf
		Network & Link	Link-Speed Mismatch	• [S]Link Capacity Info. • [S]Link Type(Full or Half Duplex) Info. • [S]Port Type(Fiber, Twisted Pair etc.) Info. - from kernel using SIOCETHTOOL ioctl
			MTU Mismatch	• [S]MTU Info. by ifconfig
E2E	Int-erm-edi-ate Node	Network & Link	Link-Speed Mismatch	• [S]Link Capacity Information - SNMP OID ifHighSpeed
			MTU Mismatch	• [S]Link MTU Information - SNMP OID ifMtu
			Bottleneck Problem	• [D]Link Available Bandwidth - Link Capacity − MRTG Cross-traffic

and so on. we need to know whether TCP window scaling and TCP buffer auto-tuning option are enabled.

Application Layer. In general, a bulk data transfer tool such as FTP, SCP, SFTP and RSYNC are sensitively influenced by network performance. Some tools using SSH among them can make some problem with high-speed transfer, even if all nodes on the E2E path already have been fine-tuned to improve network performance and there is no bottleneck link on the path. SSH uses a flow control mechanism just like the TCP window mechanism and the maximum internal window size is very small(up to $64Kbyte$)[5]. Usually, the window size to support the high-speed network upward of 1G must support at least more than about $1Mbytes$[5]. The bulk data transfer tool cannot achieve the maximum throughput because the maximum window size which can be used by an application is limited by the internal window size of the application, even though the window size of the transport layer is enough large[10]. We refer performance degradation resulted from not enough the internal window size of a bulk data transfer tool as *Internal Bottleneck*. More detailed information about *internal bottleneck* of application can be referred in our previous work [12].

2.2   The Goals of Eperfi

For the point of view of an end user, whenever the end user feels that the transfer rate of the network is very low, it is difficult to complain to a network manager or find out a problem by themselves through test tools such as Iperf, NDT and Pathload which support the limited functions. Besides, from the point of view of the network service provider which offers the high-speed network like GLORIAD[13], it is difficult or impossible for the network manager to run repetitive tests to every end-hosts or network elements on the managed site whenever the end user complains about inadequate network performance. The major objectives of Eperfi for solving this problem are to:

1. show what is going on an E2E path through the real-time graphic views.
2. give the end user one-shot information for how we can improve network performance of the E2E connection.
3. provide a simple tool for end users to test their bulk data transfer tools and to diagnose the problems of their tools by themselves
4. make end users choose other efficient bulk data transfer tools if their tools are inadequate in the high speed network.

3   The Design of EPerfi

EPerfi is a web-based client/server system for measuring and diagnosing performance of both E2E network and a bulk data transfer tool in high speed networks. Eperfi makes an end user or a network manager measure network performance on the E2E path selected by themselves and supports performance measurement of any bulk data transfer tool using user unlike NDT and NPAD. For users, Eperfi provides a view of the backbone networks which can allow to track easily whether a problem is located in the backbone. From now, we call the performance test of E2E network as **E2E Test** and the performance test of a bulk data transfer tool as **Tool Test**.

In this section, measuring and diagnosing metrics on which Eperfi adopts are introduced. And then the architecture of Eperfi, the measuring and diagnosing procedure are described.

3.1   Measuring and Diagnosing Metrics

Table 2 shows measurement and diagnosis metrics per layer by node type on the basis of the test type introduced in Section 2.1. A measurement metrics divide into a static metric and a dynamic metric. A static metric like TCP setting information cannot be changed during test and a dynamic metric such as achievable and cross-traffic bandwidth can be changed while testing.

For E2E Test, Eperfi collects the static measurement metrics from all nodes on E2E path where to test. The static measurement metrics for an end-node is based on LINUX system. The measured method of dynamic metrics will be addressed in Section 3.3.

We define the new metrics, x_RcvBuf and x_SndBuf which are the web100 variables [3], for measuring the internal bottleneck of a bulk data transfer tool introduced in Section 2.1[12]. X_SndBuf and x_RcvBuf maintain the sender and receiver internal window sizes referred by an application running on a specific TCP connection [8]. So, we can find out how much data the application sends and receives by monitoring these variables while tool testing. That is, we can figure out whether the application achieves maximum performance by comparing achievable bandwidth calculated by the values of these variables with path available bandwidth. Refer our previous work [12], if you want to know more detailed information about Tool Test using these variables.

3.2   The Architecture of EPerfi

As you can see in Fig. 1, Eperfi consists of *EperfiWebClient*, *EperfiManager* and *EperfiClient*. Each component works as described below.

EperfiWebClient. It is a web client that an end user or a network manager can perform E2E Test and Tool Test. The end user or the network manager can select the end-hosts what they want to test and can see the real-time traffic flow per time-line through *EperfiWebClient*. It has two views: a user-view and a admin-view. The user-view contains the E2E Test Page for diagnosing performance of E2E network, the Tool Test Page for diagnosing performance of a bulk data tool and the Download Page to let you download the *EperfiClient* program. Especially, tester can see what is going while testing through a real-time graphical view, because E2E and Tool Test Page are the views based java applet which shows performance measuring and diagnosing process. This visualization makes a tester understand current situation of network easily and intuitively. The admin-view has all of the user-view as well as the Statistic View Page, the Log View Page and some Configuration Page to manage Eperfi system.

EperfiManager. It performs E2E Test or Tool Test according to a tester's request through *EperfiWebClient*. When *EperfiWebClient* requests the E2E Test from H_a

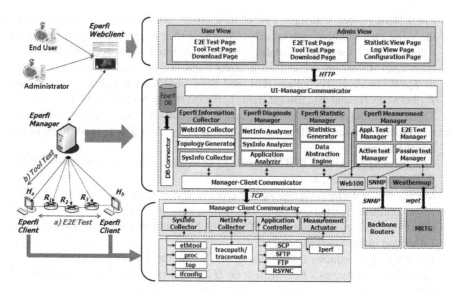

Fig. 1. The Architecture of Eperfi

to H_b in Fig. 1, *EperfiManager* performs the collecting process from all node(H_a, H_b, R_1, R_2 and R_3) on E2E path, the measuring process between H_a and H_b and the diagnosis process in turn. If *EperfiWebClient* requests the Tool Test for a specific tool on H_a in Fig. 1, *EperfiClient* on H_a acts as the sender for the tool and *EperfiManager* acts as the receiver for the tool. So, measuring the dynamic metrics(X_RcvBuf and X_SndBuf) of the Tool Test from web100 is performed by *EperfiManager*.

The one of a main role of Eperfi is to provide a real-time graphic view for a tester. For doing so, according to a test type, it collects the values of the dynamic metrics related with traffic information per 1 minutes and sends them to *Eperfi-WebClient*. In addition, it has charge of managing a log, statistic data and user information.

EperfiClient. It works on an end-host. It acts as E2E Test mode or Tool Test mode under *EperfiManager*'s request. It collects the values of static measurement metrics of End-Node in Table 2 or measures the dynamic metrics of End-Node in Table 2.

3.3 Measurement and Diagnosis Procedure of E2E Test

The measurement and diagnosis procedures of E2E Test are divided into the collecting, measuring and diagnosing sub-procedure. In Fig. 2(a), each circle of A, B and C presents the collecting, measuring and diagnosing sub-procedure. Let us explain these procedures based on the example of E2E Test in Fig. 1.

1. A end user requests *EperfiManager* to E2E Test through the *EperfiWebClient*. IP of H_a, IP of H_b and Test Duration are also transferred to *EperfiManager*.

2. *EperfiManager* requests each *EperfiClient* on H_a and H_a to report the values of the static measurement metrics. *EperfiManager* then requests the *EperfiClients* to collect the RTT for BDP calculation and route information between H_a and H_b.
3. Each *EperfiClient* on H_a and H_b collects requested information and sends them to *EperfiManager*. To collect RTT and route information (IP of R_1, R_2 and R_3)between H_a and H_b, *EperfiClients* performs traceroute each other.
4. The *EperfiManager* requests R_1, R_2 and R_3 to send MTU and link capacity.
5. Each router measures MTU and link capacity. And then it sends them to the *EperfiManager*.
6. *EperfiManager* requests MRTG server to send the amount of cross-traffic of the E2E path between H_a and H_b.
7. MRTG server collects the amount of cross-traffic of each link. And then MRTG server sends the least cross-traffic information among them.
8. *EperfiManager* visualizes cross-traffic of the E2E path by using the Weathermap embedded in the *EperfiWebClient*.
9. *EperfiManager* requests *EperfiClient* on H_b to run Iperf in a server mode.
10. *EperfiManager* requests *EperfiClient* on H_a to run Iperf in a client mode for Iperf test.
11. *EperfiClient* on H_a reports to *EperfiManager* about achievable bandwidth per second.
12. *EperfiManager* visualizes achievable bandwidth by using the line chart embedded in the *EperfiWebClient*.
13. The *EperfiManager* performs the diagnosis process in Fig. 3(a) based on the monitored achievable bandwidth through the Iperf and the collected data from H_a,H_b and routers.
14. The *EperfiManager* reports the diagnosis results to the user. If the tested end-to-end path has a problem, some solutions are introduced.

3.4   Measurement and Diagnosis Procedure of Tool Test

Figure 2(b) describes the operation of measuring and diagnosing performance of a bulk data transfer tool. The description of each step in Fig. 2(b) is as following.

1. A end user requests *EperfiManager* to diagnosis a specific data transfer tool α(SCP, SFTP or RSYNC) of the host H_a through *EperfiWebClient*. The port number that will be used for diagnosis is also transferred to *EperfiManager*.
2. *EperfiManager* measures the RTT and the path MTU between itself and H_a and calculates the BDP. If the BDP is smaller than the maximum window size which is defined in tcp_wmem and tcp_rmem, the *EperfiManager* increases the BDP by delaying the packets with NETEM[9].
3. *EperfiManager* requests H_a to send the data to a specific port and starts to monitor the X_Rcvbuf.
4. *EperfiClient* on H_a starts the Iperf test.
5. *EperfiClient* starts the data transmission by using the tool α.
6. *EperfiManager* stops the X_Rcvbuf monitoring and requests the data transmission to pass the firewall which may exist at H_a.

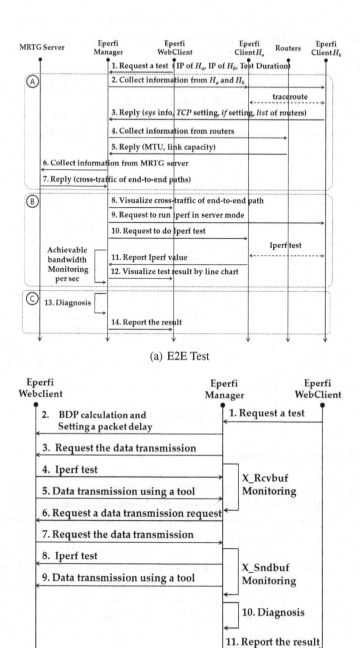

(a) E2E Test

(b) Tool Test

Fig. 2. The Collecting and Measuring Procedure

7. *EperfiManager* requests *EperfiClient* to start the data transmission. Once *Eperfi-Manager* receives this request, it starts to monitor the X_Sndbuf.
8. *EperfiManager* starts the lperf test.
9. *EperfiManager* starts the data transmission by using the tool α.
10. The *EperfiManager* performs the diagnosis process in Fig. 3(b) based on the monitored web100 variables through the tool α and the lperf.
11. The *EperfiManager* reports the diagnosis results to the user. If the tested tool has a bottleneck problem, some preferred data transfer tools are introduced.

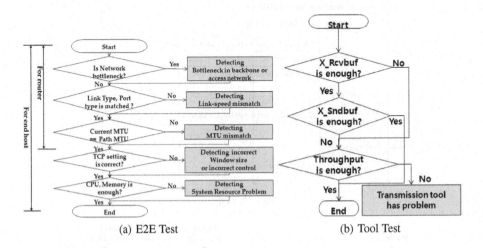

(a) E2E Test   (b) Tool Test

Fig. 3. The Diagnosis Procedure

4   Implementation Result

In this Section, we discuss the result of the Eperfi implementation. We tested our Eperfi in GLORIAD(Global Ring Network for Advanced Application Development) [13] which is a high-speed computer network used to connect scientific organizations in Russia, China, United States, the Netherlands, Korea and Canada. We firstly tested E2E Test from the host on Jeju to the host on Daejeon using 1G GLORIAD networks. The RTT from Jeju to Daejeon is about 41.8ms. Table 3 show our test environment.

Figure 4(a) shows the screen shot of the collecting and measuring process of E2E Test view in *EperfiWebClient*. E2E test view has three parts: ① the user input and command request view, ② the real-time traffic view, and ③ the geographical view as you can see Fig. 4(a). If you want to test, you must input source ip, destination ip and test

Table 3. Window Size of EperfiClient on Jeju, byte

Type	Min	Default	Max(for E2E Test)	Max(For Tool Test)
tcp_wmem	4096	87380	476160	4194304
tcp_rmem	4096	16384	476160	4194304

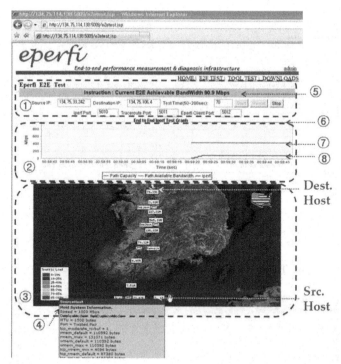

(a) The screen-shot captured during the collecting and measuring process

(b) The diagnosis result

Fig. 4. The screen-shot of E2E Test

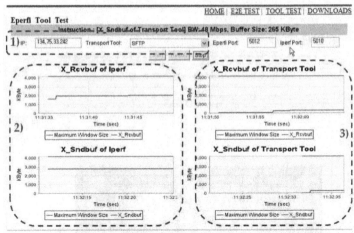

(a) The screen-shot captured during measuring process

(b) The diagnosis result

Fig. 5. The screen-shot of Tool Test

time through ①. Since this screen shot was captured during test, Eperfi collected already the route information from Jeju to Daejeon and configuration information of each node on E2E path. In ③ part in Fig. 4(a), the route from Jeju(134.75.33.242) to Daejeoun(134.75.106.4) was represented graphically. If you click a specific node on the path, you can see the detailed information of the clicked node like ④. Part ② represents ⑥ path link capacity, ⑦ path available bandwidth, and ⑦ achievable bandwidth from Jeju to Daejeon during test by using the line chart and you can also see numerical achievable bandwidth through ⑤.

Figure 4(b) shows the diagnosis result. Measured achievable bandwidth(about $90mbps$) is very low, even though available bandwidth(about $400mbps$) is enough as you can see in Fig. 4(a). So, we can conclude that there is no bottleneck link on the E2E path and any node on the E2E path may have a problem. As the result by ⑧ and ⑨, we can see that Jeju has the problem of the invalid window size. The BDP from Jeju to Daejeon is about $2Mbytes$. Since the maximum window size of Jeju is about $475Kbytes$, maximum achievable bandwidth achieved by Jeju host is limited by about $91mbps$. Our Eperfi diagnoses exactly the problem of the sender host.

Figure 5 shows the screen-shot of the measuring process of Tool Test view in *Eperfi-WebClient*. Tool Test view has three parts: 1) the user input and command request view, 2) the monitoring view of X_RcvBuf and X_SndBuf of Iperf, and 3) the monitoring view of X_RcvBuf and X_SndBuf of Transport Tool as you can see Fig. 5(a). If you want to test, you must input ip of running tool which want to test, a tool type through 1) in Fig. 5(a).

This test was for testing SFTP on Jeju. The RTT between Jeju to *EperfiManager* is about $45ms$. So, iperf and SFTP can transfer the data without limitation of the TCP window size because the BDP is about $2.3Mbytes$ which is smaller than the maximum window size($4Mbytes$). As you can see in 2) and 3) of Fig. 5(a), X_RcvBuf and X_SndBuf of SFTP are very smaller than them of Iperf. Finally, we can get the diagnosis screen-shot in Fig. 5(b) which shows the values of the measured metrics and the diagnosis result. According to the diagnosis result in Fig. 5(b), the upload and download throughput of SFTP are only 6.9% and 14.5% of the Iperf throughput and we can find out that SFTP uses a internal window control mechanism and has the internal bottleneck problem.

5   Related Works and Comparison

Network Diagnostic Tool(NDT)[1] is one of the Internet2 projects to enhance the network performance. It is a server/client program that performs the E2E network performance measurement and diagnosis based on the web100. The client is a java applet program and an end user can easily download the client program by accessing the NDT web page. By using NDT, the end users can find out what is wrong with their data transmission. NDT tries to detect the cause of low data transfer at the end host or on the network. Currently, NDT only can perform the bottleneck detection and duplex mismatch detection[6].

Network Path and Application Diagnosis(NPAD)[2] is a joint project of the PSC(Pittsburgh Supercomputing Center) [4] and NCAR(National Center for Atmospheric Research). Similar to NDT, NPAD is a server/client program based on a java

Table 4. Comparison Eperfi with NDT and NPAD

	E2E Test	Real-time Graphical View	Test on specific E2E path	Tool Test
Eperfi	○	○	○	○
NDT	○	×	×	×
NPAD	○	×	×	×

applet. This project addresses the set of problems associated with end-hosts and their connections to a high speed backbones network. NPAD performs diagnosis about TCP tuning problem, duplex mismatch, cable fault, packet loss, and so on.

Table 4 shows comparison Eperfi with NDT and NPAD. Both NDT and NPAD can diagnose the problem only under the transport layer of TCP/IP model. If the data transfer tool acts as a bottleneck point, NDT and NPAD cannot find out the cause of performance degradation. They even report a wrong diagnosis result to an end user who does not have enough knowledge. The wrong report may make the end user waste their time and labor. Additionally, Since these tool perform performance measurement only between the user and the server, even if a network manager wants to test between any point to any point within the managed network, he or she cannot easily test it.

6   Conclusion

In this paper, we presented Eperfi that provides both E2E Test and Tool Test. By using Eperfi, an end user or an administrator can test E2E network performance for the E2E path selected by themselves and a performance test for any bulk data transfer tool. The end user can fine-tune its system according to the diagnosis result of E2E Test and can choose an efficient data transfer tool through Tool Test. Tool Test of Eperfi can be also applied to the work for developing a high speed data transfer tool. A further direction of Eperfi will adopt a data-mining method to diagnose more accurately for E2E Test and study performance measurement of another data transfer tool.

References

1. http://e2epi.internet2.edu/ndt/
2. http://www.ucar.edu/npad/
3. http://www.web100.org/
4. http://www.psc.edu/networking/pro-jects/applight/
5. Rapier, C., Bennett, B.: High speed bulk data transfer using the SSH protocol. In: Proceedings of the 15th ACM Mardi Gras conference (2008)
6. Technical Paper, Network Diagnostic Tool (NDT): An Internet2 Cookbook, Internet2
7. http://dast.nlanr.net/Projects/iperf/
8. Mathis, M., Heffner, J., Reddy, R.: Web100: Extended TCP Instrumentation for Research, Education and Diagnosis. ACM Computer Communications Review (July 2003)
9. http://www.linux-foundation.org/en/Net:Netem
10. Rapier, C., Stevens, M.: Application Layer Network Window Management in the SSH Protocol. In: Presented at Supercomputing Conference (2004)

11. Mahdavi, J.: TCP Performance Tuning. In: High Performance Data Networking Conference at Northwestern University (April 1997)
12. Kim, J.-M., Han, Y.-J., Lee, G., Seok, W., Chung, T.-M.: DTPD: Data transfer tool performance diagnosis system in high speed networks. In: Ma, Y., Choi, D., Ata, S. (eds.) AP-NOMS 2008. LNCS, vol. 5297, pp. 266–275. Springer, Heidelberg (2008)
13. http://www.gloriad.org/gloriad/index.html
14. Lowekamp, B., Tierney, B., Cottrell, L., Hughes-Jones, R., Kielmann, T., Swany, M.: A Hierarchy of Network Measurements for Grid Applications and Services Document (draft) Global Grid Forum NMWG Febuary 17 (2003)

FIST: A Framework for Flexible and Low-Cost Wireless Testbed for Sensor Networks

Cheng Guo, R. Venkatesha Prasad, JiangJie He, and Martin Jacobsson

Faculty of Electrical Engineering, Mathematics and Computer Science
Delft University of Technology, Mekelweg 4, 2600 GA Delft, The Netherlands
{c.guo, r.r.venkateshaprasad,j-he2, m.e.jakobsson}@tudelft.nl

Abstract. Setting up a wireless sensor network for an experiment is both time and effort intensive. Sometimes, the time required to set up the experimental framework is even more than that of the experiment itself. Many existing fixed testbeds manage nodes using gateways and require a lot of support and maintenance. Changing the deployment place – especially if it is a crowded area – is difficult. We propose a framework for implementing a Flexible and low-cost wIreless for Sensor network Testbed (FIST). Downloading the experimental code, reprogramming, testbed control, logging and collecting experimental results and synchronization are all carried out by the sensor motes wirelessly. Thus the testbed can be easily and quickly deployed anywhere. We present our framework and also a case study using FIST.

Keywords: Testbed, Wireless Sensor Networks, Experiment, Flexibility, Low-cost.

1 Introduction

In wireless research, the simulation and analytical work outnumber real-world experiments. At the same time this is absolutely crucial for understanding the characteristics and issues regarding Wireless Sensor Networks (WSNs) in real environments. In fact at some point the algorithms and ideas need to be verified practically. It is important to enable researchers to conduct the experiments while developing the ideas. The main reason for the lack of experimental research is the difficulty in conducting experiments. Setting up an experimental platform and conducting an experiment are cumbersome and time consuming. To fill this gap and making it easier to do more real wireless network experiments instead of solely relying on simulations, we developed a testbed. While designing the testbed, we developed a framework that makes the testbed flexible and easy to deploy. This paper is an account of our understanding, experiences and accomplishments of designing a framework for a sensor network testbed.

We first list all the requirements: a testbed should support implementation of protocols, algorithms, easy and changeable deployment and testing. It should have interfaces for researchers and developers to conveniently develop their code, load and test. Later they can deploy the network in an environment inline with

D. Ślęzak et al. (Eds.): FGCN/ACN 2009, CCIS 56, pp. 216–225, 2009.

the application scenarios of the protocol. The users should be provided the functions to freely start, stop or reset the experiment. Further the experimental results should be collected so that an analysis can be performed. Frequently, a user also has to update the experimental code due to bugs, errors or simple enhancements to the already available code. On a WSN, all these requirements will indeed make it difficult for the experimentalists to run their code and get the results. In summary, a testbed should provide functions such as experimental program (denoted as *exp-program* in the rest of the paper for convenience) dissemination, reprogramming, command dissemination, data logging and data collection. Sometimes, a user may also require the experimental network to be synchronized and nodes can discover and report their neighboring information. Therefore services like time synchronization and neighbor discovery are also in demand.

Existing testbeds [1, 2, 3] normally require a fixed support system to control individual nodes/devices, here sensor motes, through gateways. These gateways have interfaces such as USB or Ethernet through which they are wired into a network. A user issues new experimental code or commands to sensor motes by first sending them to the gateways which then relay them to the sensor motes. Similarly, data is collected by server. In such a testbed, sensor motes only take care of experiments. The control and management are all carried out by the backbone consisting of wired servers and gateways. Although this can reliably carry out experiments, they are not flexible since their physical topology can not be easily changed. Moving these testbeds from one place to another, especially to the places which are crowded, is difficult and time consuming. Moreover, additional supporting devices increase cost of a testbed.

In this paper, we propose a new Flexible and low-cost wIreless Sensor network Testbed (FIST), which removes the wired backbone but uses wireless connection itself to perform testbed management and control. It means that all the functions and services are all carried out by sensor motes and through wireless links between them. Since wires are removed, it can be quickly deployed at any place and does not cause obstacles to people. However, the removal of wires and gateways requires the testbed control and maintenance traffic not to interfere with the experimental traffic since they share the same medium. Furthermore, a smart software should be designed and implemented in sensor motes so that it can realize all the functions with a reasonable amount of resources. We show that our testbed framework can meet these requirements by well designed software and hardware architecture and fine-tuned implementation. We give the users the freedom to choose functions that are required in their specific experimental environments and load only necessary modules. Therefore memory – which is one of the limited resources in motes – can be saved for loading the experimental code. FIST can fulfill most of the requirements of usual sensor network experiments unless an experiment generates a large amount of results, or desperately requires two separate medium for experimental traffic and control traffic, such as results have to be collected during an experiment or experiments have to run under user's instructions. The design requirement and both hardware and software architectures of FIST are presented in the next section.

2 Requirements and Architectures of FIST

2.1 Requirements of a WSN Testbed

Before we describe our design of FIST, we first list all the requirements to aid us in ahead. We have to review the process of doing a WSN experiment since the ultimate use of FIST framework is for doing WSN experiments. Usually, for any WSN we start with programming the nodes then deploy them in the field. Once deployed, neighbor discovery needs to be done then the command to start an experiment is issued or implicitly assumed. During the experimentation, usually one will find some bugs. Then the experiment has to be stopped. After collecting the error codes, the exp-program needs to be debugged. Later motes have to be reprogrammed with newer exp-program; then test procedures starts again. If no bug is found, then the necessary data has to be stored somewhere or transmitted back to a data server. In case that data is stored locally, we have to collect it from each node in the network. We list here the functions to be incorporated in a testbed: (a) We need to have a mechanism by which we can disseminate commands to a particular or any number of nodes. (b) To guarantee a successful dissemination we have to build routes between the control station and each node in the testbed. The route must be reliable. (c) We have to disseminate exp-program and reprogram to the motes. (d) The experimental results have to be logged and reported to the user. (e) Some services such as time synchronization and neighbor discovery should also be provided.

We also have some non-functional requirements of the proposed testbed. The testbed has to be: (1) flexible to deploy and re-deploy in any environment; (2) reliable; (3) convenient, simple and user friendly; and (4) low cost.

2.2 Hardware Architecture of FIST

As introduced in Section 1, we want to get rid of the wired backbone from the testbed and take advantage of wireless connections to manage and control experiments. Thus we propose a simple hardware architecture for FIST. An example of such architecture is as shown in Fig. 1. A root mote is connected to a root server by USB and other motes are connected wirelessly to the root mote. We have a tree topology in the network since it is easy to configure, control and maintain yet proven to be relatively reliable network topology and widely used in many existing networks. We can see that the motes act as both experimental devices and experiment management devices. Any PC or handhold equipments which have Linux OS and Java Runtime Environment can be used as the root server of our testbed.

We can see that there are no extra devices required in FIST and more importantly we do not have wires. This feature allows us to deploy this testbed quickly

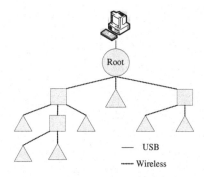

Fig. 1. Hardware Architecture

at any place especially in the environments where wires can be a hassle, such as canteen, crowded markets or museums. The deployment neither requires any specialized personnel to drill or mount the motes on ceilings nor needs dedicated place. Moreover, when we want to add more sensor nodes into our testbed, we can easily power up the motes and allocate them anywhere within the radio coverage of our testbed. Thus the architecture meets the non-functional requirement of flexibility.

Currently we choose Tmote Sky motes as our wireless sensor motes for its rich on-board modules, reliable quality and acceptable price. The transceiver of the mote complies with IEEE802.15.4 standard. It provides USB interface through which a mote can be programmed. The mote equips an 8MHz Texas Instruments MSP430 micro-controller with 10KB RAM and 48KB Programming Flash. Besides, it also has a 1 MB flash memory. A user can choose to have integrated temperature, humidity and light sensors on board. The transceiver has a data rate of 250kbps at 2.4GHz and the transmission range of about 50m indoor and 125m outdoor.

2.3 Software Architecture of FIST

Fig. 2 shows the software architecture of FIST. We divided the whole software into two spaces. One is the Testbed Program Space (TPS) and the other is the User Experimental Program Space (UEPS). Code developed for realizing the functions of FIST is isolated from users' exp-program so that a user does not have to consider the testbed program when develops exp-program. A few interfaces are provided to link the two spaces so that the testbed program can control the exp-program, such as start, stop or reboot. Services, such as time synchronization and neighbor discovery, are shared between the two spaces. A user control the functions in TPS by either console commands or a GUI interface so that the non-functional requirement of being user-friendly can be fulfilled. The testbed program uses the standard 802.15.4 MAC and physical layer. Inside the user's space, one can implement and test protocols from MAC to application layer or services.

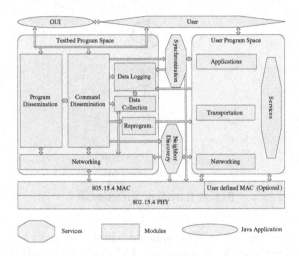

Fig. 2. Modules

There are several necessary modules in the TPS, *viz*, networking, program dissemination, data logging, data collection and reprogram. Among them the command dissemination module is directly controlled by user. The rest of the modules are controlled indirectly via the command dissemination module. We introduce these modules in the next section.

3   Modules and Services in FIST

3.1   Networking

We start the introduction of modules and services from the network module since others depend on it. The networking module in the TPS is designed to construct and maintain the routes between the root node and all the nodes in the testbed. As shown in Fig. 1, we organize the nodes in the testbed in a tree topology. The routing strategy is straightforward in this module. Messages are disseminated from the root (basestation) to branches and then to their leaves. So first of all every node in the network must know its parent and its leaves if there are any.

Every node maintains a node list shown in Fig. 3(b) which keeps the information about its upstream and downstream nodes. The variable "count" in a *node_list* structure keeps track the number of downstream nodes. The structure named *node_state* is made up of a unique id and a linkstate variable as shown in Fig. 3(a). Since we may have to reprogram the motes from time to time during an experiment, the connectivity configuration of each mote are saved in its permanent flash.

3.2   Command Dissemination

The format of command and ACK packets is shown in Fig. 4. For different types of commands and ACKs, we define two sets of constants. All the commands have

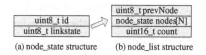

(a) node_state structure   (b) node_list structure

Fig. 3. Data structure for configuring tree topology

the prefix *CMD_* and the ACK have the prefix *ACK_*, e.g., *CMD_COLLECT* is the command to start data collection while *ACK_COLLECTION* is to acknowledge the command. There are five fields in this format. "cmd" is the type of commands or ACK. "data" stores parameters associated with commands or ACK. "error" is a 32-bit variable used with ACK. The flag is a global variable of our software framework that each bit stands for one kind of error, so it is possible to report 32 kinds of errors. Last two fields "src" and "des" keep the source and the destination id of a message and des = 0xff for broadcast. Commands are broadcasted to downstream nodes in the *node_list*. Before sending out commands to nodes in the list, the "linkstate" of each node in the list are set to "NOT_RESPONDED" with an ACK state is set as "ACKed". If the destination node/nodes specified in the command message is set as ACKed, the node has finished the command dissemination and sends an ACK to its upstream node. Nodes rebroadcast the message until the maximum retrial count, i.e. 10. Then the ID of the non-ACKed node is reported to the upstream node until the root node and in turn the user knows which node is out of order to support reliability. In general, there are four kinds of ACKs. (a) *For command dissemination*: the ACK confirms that commands are received by destination(s). (b) *For data collection*: the ACK confirms the start of collection. (c) *For reporting errors*: the ACK reports different kinds of errors to the user for diagnosis. (d) *For confirmation of received program*: the ACK reports which of the nodes have received the new program.

3.3   Program Dissemination

Program dissemination is also carried out through the network set up by the networking module. Since an program can be up to 48KB large, which is the size of the program memory in the Tmote Sky, we have to split a program into several pieces. Here we take the split mechanism as it is in the well-known Deluge [4] implementation. Dissemination of program is same as the one of command dissemination except that the receiver only acknowledges the receiving of an entire program instead of page by page to avoid interference with the

nx_uint16_t	cmd
nx_uint16_t	data
nx_uint16_t	error
nx_uint16_t	src
nx_uint16_t	des

Fig. 4. Format of command packets

experiment. Compared to the dissemination method used in Deluge [4], our method provides users the information whether and when a node has received a new program. In our method, adding a node has to be done by manually configuring the upstream and downstream node id in the networking module then a program dissemination process has to be carried out.

3.4 Data Logging

Since experimental results are valuable for analyzing the performance of a test program later, data logging is a necessary function in a WSN testbed. The wireless transceivers in FIST are shared by users and testbed program, thus during the execution of a user's exp-program, the wireless transceiver should be fully occupied by user's program to avoid interference. Consequently, experimental results have to be saved in the flash memory of nodes, that will be collected after the completion of the experiment. Normally, we should have up to 900 kB space. A user can define the structure of the results he wants to store. The *user_data_t* structure contains a 16 bits integer for temperature value, a 32-bit integer for a timestamp and another 16-bit integer as a packet sequence number.

3.5 Data Collection

The data collection module also takes advantage of the networking module. The packet format in the data collection module is shown in Fig. 5. The packet contains a 16-bit sequence number, a source and a destination id and logged experimental result introduced in the last subsection. The size of the structure varies with the *user_data_t* structure. The sequence number is used to distinguish redundant packets. Two commands and two ACKs are dedicated for controlling this module, namely, *CMD_COLLECT*, *CMD_ERASE*, *ACK_COLLECTION* and *ACK_CLDONE*. *CMD_ERASE* is used to erase all the data in the flash of a sensor mote. When a node receives a command *CMD_COLLECT*, it will first return an *ACK_COLLECTION* feedback of which the "data" field is the size of *user_data_t* in bytes. When PC has received this feedback, it will initialize a message instance with the size and register a new listener for this type of messages. During data collection, the node will read out a logged result and send it via the ACK route introduced in Subsection 3.2. The procedure continues until the entire log data have been read out and the node sends an ACK_CLDONE to the PC.

nx_uint16_t uid
nx_uint32_t source
nx_uint32_t dest
user_data_t content

Fig. 5. An example of experimental result message

3.6   Reprogramming

The reprogramming event can be triggered in two ways as indicated in Fig. 2. A user can ask a node to reprogram via the command dissemination module or the event can be triggered using a timer. Using the first method, we can reprogram the node with a new program received from the program dissemination module. The second, we provide a timer in the testbed by which a user can set a node to reprogram from exp-program to TPS program after the timer expires. The expiration of the timer will trigger the reprogramming no matter the state of the experiment. Thus the user is supposed to carefully set the timer.

3.7   Time Synchronization and Neighbor Discovery Services

Many time synchronization protocols are proposed recently. We chose FTSP [5] for our current implementation of FIST. The protocol relies on periodically exchanging synchronization messages between nodes to ensure the network wide synchronization. We added a few commands to control this service, namely, *CMD_STOPSYNC* and *CMD_STARTSYNC*. Both of them have corresponding ACK messages. In the neighbor discovery service, the root node sends ten flooding messages into FIST testbed. Each is identified with a unique id. Once a node receives a new flooding message, it will retransmit it once. Thus every node in the network retransmits a unique message once. With these GUI tools, a user need not have to remember and type different commands to control the testbed, and does not have to look up our instruction document to know the meanings of different feedbacks. It saves much time for the user and fulfill the requirement of convenience and user-friendliness.

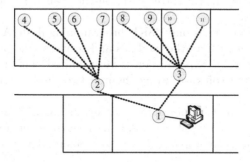

Fig. 6. Deployment of nodes in the case study

4   A Case Study

Due to the flexibility of our testbed we need not to deploy it in a fixed fashion and place. We intended to measure the room temperature of four offices in our university building. The deployment of the testbed is shown in Fig. 6. Nodes are packaged in small boxes which can be easily posted on the walls. Each node is

Table 1. Two program images

Image	Modules and Service	Functions
Reprogram Image	Program Dissemination Command Dissemination Reprogramming	Disseminate program and reprogramming
Control Image	Command Dissemination Data logging Data Collection Reprogramming Synchronization	Run and control the experiment

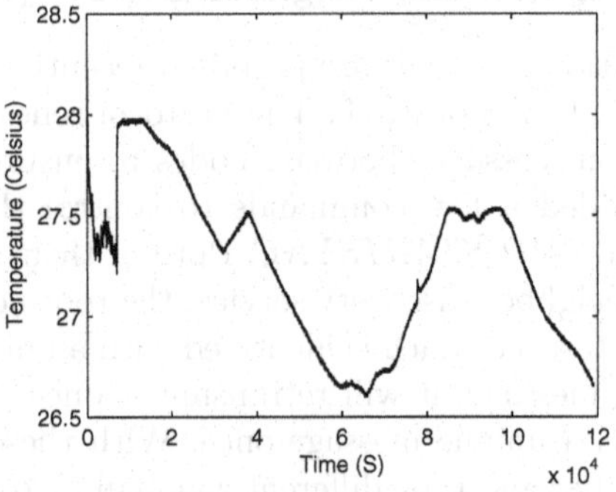

Fig. 7. Temperature measured from environment

programmed with an unique id as shown in the figure. Motes can be powered by batteries or mains. In the latter case, off-the-shelf USB hubs can replenish power from sockets.

The Tmote Sky mote has only 48KB programming flash. A complete version of the TPS program with all the modules and services takes as much as 40KB. The remaining space for exp-program is very limited. Thanks to the modular design of the testbed software, we configured two program images, which are listed in Table 1.

We let the experiment run for approximately one and half days. The temperature is collected every five seconds. All the measurement are tagged with an id and a timestamp then stored in the flash memory. The results are shown in Fig. 7.

5   Conclusions

When more and more applications are to be supported, the sensor networks need to be studied and programs need to be developed on the testbed. We designed a testbed framework called FIST and an account of our baby steps in planning, designing and implementing FIST is given. The main advantage is that it is flexible and transparent to deployment scenarios, location and the topology. Moreover, it fits our requirements of a testbed yet keeps a low-cost. We plan to reduce the time taken for the code dissemination and data collection on FIST. We are also planning a thorough comparisons with some of the available testbeds.

References

1. Girod, L., Ramanathan, N., Elson, J., Stathopoulos, T., Lukac, M., Estrin, D.: Emstar: A software environment for developing and deploying heterogeneous sensor-actuator networks. ACM Trans. Sen. Netw. 3(3), 13 (2007)
2. Sheu, J.-P., Chang, C.-J., Sun, C.-Y., Hu, W.-K.: Wsntb: A testbed for heterogeneous wireless sensor networks. In: First IEEE International Conference on Ubi-Media Computing, Lanzhou, China, July 31- August 1, pp. 338–343 (2008)
3. Handziski, V., Köpke, A., Willig, A., Wolisz, A.: Twist: a scalable and reconfigurable testbed for wireless indoor experiments with sensor networks. In: REALMAN 2006: Proceedings of the 2nd international workshop on Multi-hop ad hoc networks: from theory to reality, pp. 63–70. ACM Press, New York (2006)
4. Hui, J.W., Culler, D.: The dynamic behavior of a data dissemination protocol for network programming at scale. In: SenSys 2004: Proceedings of the 2nd international conference on Embedded networked sensor systems, pp. 81–94. ACM Press, New York (2004)
5. Maróti, M., Kusy, B., Simon, G., Lédeczi, A.: The fooding time synchroniza- tion protocol. In: SenSys 2004: Proceedings of the 2nd international conference on Embedded networked sensor systems, pp. 39–49. ACM Press, New York (2004)

A Novel Energy Optimization Approach for Wireless Sensor Networks

Lianhe Luo[1], Yuebin Bai[2], and Wei Wu[1]

[1] Communication Telemetry & Telecontrol Research Institute
China Electronics Technology Group Corporation, Shijiazhuang 050081, China
[2] School of Computer Science, Beihang University, Beijing 100191, China
byb@buaa.edu.cn

Abstract. Energy efficiency is one of the determining factors for survivability and lifetime of wireless sensor networks (WSNs). In this paper, an energy optimization approach based on cross-layer for wireless sensor networks is proposed, which consider the joint optimal design of the physical, medium access control, and routing layer. The approach focuses on the computation of optimal transmission power, routing, and duty-cycle schedule that optimize the WSNs energy-efficiency. The approach is validated on a CROSSBOW's MicaZ mote platform, and evaluated using the TOSSIM simulator, the simulation results show that it is an energy-efficient approach and able to achieve significant performance improvement as well.

Keywords: wireless sensor networks, energy optimization, cross-layer.

1 Introduction

Recent years have seen the applications of wireless sensor networks (WSNs) in a variety of applications. In most applications, WSNs are required to be operating in order to months to years but constituent sensor nodes have limited battery power. Therefore survivability is one of the critical issues and the most important research topics in the fields of wireless sensor networks (WSNs). Energy efficiency is one of the determining factors for survivability and lifetime of WSNs. Thus it is not surprising that developing approach to optimize the energy efficiency of WSNs has been a major research topic.

Major source of energy waste are idle listening, retransmission resulting from collision, unnecessarily high transmission power and sub-optimal utilization of the available resource. Corresponding to these problems, there is a significant body of approaches to addressing different aspects of energy waste. To mitigate this energy consumption of idle listening, duty cycling mechanisms have been introduces in sensor network MAC protocol. For example, S-MAC, SCP-MAC and so on. Some approaches control the transmission power aiming to reduce the unnecessary transmission energy consumption and decrease the interference among nodes while maintaining network connectivity. Power aware routing protocols save significant energy

D. Ślęzak et al. (Eds.): FGCN/ACN 2009, CCIS 56, pp. 226–233, 2009.

by choosing the appropriate route according to the available energy of nodes or energy demand of transmission paths. Clearly, a WSN needs to reduce the energy consumed in all states (i.e., transmission, reception, idle) in order to minimize its energy consumption. This requires a WSN to effectively apply all the above approaches. In this paper, we propose a cross-layer energy optimization approach, which minimizes the aggregate energy consumption in all power states. In sharp contrast to above these approaches that optimized some aspect of energy waste. It provides a cross-layer approach that integrates these approaches as a joint optimization problem.

The rest of this paper is organized as follow: Section 2 reviews existing cross-layer scheme. The approach is described in Section 3.In section 4, the validation and performance evaluation of the approach is presented; Finally, section 5 concludes the paper.

2 Related Works

Some cross-layer approaches have been proposed for WSNs. They can be roughly divided into three categories in terms of interaction or modularity among physical (PHY), medium access control (MAC), routing, and transport layers.

MAC+PHY: The energy consumption for physical and MAC layer is analyzed in [1], the analysis is based on a linear networks, so the conclusion may not be practical in realistic scenarios. In [2], a cross-layer solution among MAC layer, physical phenomenon, and the application layer for WSNs is proposed.

MAC+Routing: In many work, the receiver-based routing is exploited for MAC and routing cross-layer modularity. Receiver-based routing has been independently proposed in [6] [7]. The performance evaluations of all these propositions present the advantages of cross-layer approach at the routing and MAC layer.

PHY+MAC+Routing: In addition to the proposed methods that focus on pairwise cross-layer interaction, more general cross-layer approaches among three protocol layers exist. In [8], the optimization of transmission power, transmission rate, and link schedule for TDMA-based WSNs is proposed. In [9], joint routing, MAC, and PHY layer optimization is proposed. A variable-length TDMA scheme and MQAM modulation are adopted.

These above works either provide analytical results without any communication protocol design, or perform pairwise cross-layer design within limited scope, e.g., only routing and MAC layer, which do not consider all of the networking layers involving in the communication in WSN, such as routing, medium access and physical layers.

3 Approach Description

Cross-layer approach mentioned in this paper considers the interaction between corresponding protocol layers, and preserves the traditional layered structure. Each layer is informed about the conditions of other layers, while the mechanisms of each layer still stay intact. Guided by above cross-layer principle, we design our cross-layer optimization approach named as EOA. Fig.1 shows the frame of EOA. In the physical layer, EOA controls transmission power dynamically and obtains the proper transmission power level between two nodes. In the meanwhile, each node maintains a neighbor table to record this proper transmission power level. Then each node in the network layer constructs its routing table by utilizing the neighbor table of the physical layer. Finally, EOA uses the cross-layer routing information to determine the duty-cycle of each node, and meanwhile EOA also pays attentions to collision and overhearing problem in the MAC layer.

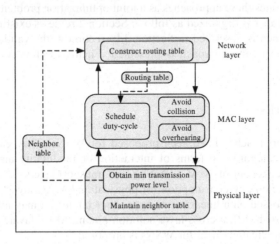

Fig. 1. Frame of the approach

A.   *Transmission Power Control*

The transmission power between two nodes is affected by spatial and temporal factors. The spatial factors include the surrounding environment, such as terrain and the distance between the transmitter and the receiver. Temporal factors include surrounding environmental changes in general, such as weather conditions. This phenomenon indicates the previous topology control solutions, which use static transmission power, lead to worse link quality and unnecessarily high energy consumption. As a result, the transmission power of each node needs to be set the right level dynamically with spatial and temporal change. ATPC [3] reveals that radio CC1000 [4] and CC2420 [5] offers a Received Signal Strength Indicator (RSSI) to specify the transmission power level during runtime, such that system design is able to dynamically control the transmission power. Therefore, we present a dynamic transmission power control algorithm based on RSSI, which contains two phases, the initialization phase and the running tuning phase. At the initialization phase, the objective of this algorithm is to make every node in a WSN find the minimum transmission power level that can communication with its neighboring nodes successfully. At the same time, the neighbor table is maintained at each node. The neighbor table contains the proper transmission power level and the number of neighbor node. At the runtime tuning phase, it could adjust the proper transmission power dynamically to adapt environmental change.

B. Method of Routing Table Construction

In this section, we discuss the construction of route using the neighbor table mentioned in previous section. At the route construction step, each sensor node needs to figure out a better way to select its next-hop node. An efficient route for WSN is expected to be able to 1) minimize the end-to-end delivery time, i.e. the sensing data could be timely delivered to the sink such that the decision maker can take immediate action to deal with that emergency event, and 2) save more energy consumption via the better routing decision. Therefore, source nodes must find the energy-efficient routing path to the sink node.

We construct the nodes' routing table based on the ISTH algorithm and the nodes' neighbor table. Each node calculates the power consumption with neighbor nodes , and finds an energy-efficient routing path to the sink by ISTH algorithm. During this process, each node sets the neighbor node with the minimum energy consumption to the sink as its next-hop node and constructs a table to record its routing information.

Each node in WSN maintains a routing table that contains the routing entries and status of neighbors. Specifically, an entry in the routing table of node u includes following fields: < *next_hop, cost, power_level, destination*>where *next_hop* is the neighbor node with the minimum cost to the sink, *cost* is the cost of node u to the sink through *next_hop*, *power_level* is the power level between node u and *next_hop*. *destination* is the routing path's destination node.

C. Duty-cycle Scheduling of Nodes

Duty cycle mechanisms have been used in sensor networks to improve energy efficiency. For example S-MAC, each sensor node follows a periodic synchronized listen/sleep schedule. However, S-MAC introduces nonessential idle-listening, since node must be waken up when its sleep period expires, even when the node is not transmitting or receiving a data packet. This nonessential idle-listening is very inefficient and wasted significant energy. In the meanwhile, the duty-cycle mechanisms have other limitations. Most importantly, end-to-end delivery latency may be increased substantially; for example, with S-MAC, in each operational cycle, a data packet can be forwarded over a single hop only, since an intermediate relaying node has to wait for its next-hop node to wake up to receive the packet. Motivated by the above problem, we exploit cross-layer routing information to design the duty-cycle scheduling scheme for each sensor node. In this scheme, we exploit the routing information to form the nodes' duty-cycle schedule. This process contains two stages: synchronization stage and packets' transmitting stage.

1) Synchronization Stage

In the synchronization stage, nodes in the same routing path own the same duty-cycle schedule in order to reduce end-to-end delivery latency, So that data packets would be forwarded to sink node rapidly. Firstly, sink node computes duty-cycle schedules according to known routing information. Then, sink node disseminates computed duty-cycle schedules to every node through the routing paths. Each node exchanges duty-cycle schedules with all 1-hop neighbors, so that nodes in the same path wake up and sleep at the same time. Specially, if a node belongs with multiple paths, it follows the duty-cycle schedule of source node which has early wake-up schedule. If a node doesn't belong to any routing paths, its duty-cycle schedule is set to infinity. Fig.2 shows a simple network topology, node E, node F and node A belong to path-1; node A, node B, node C and node D belong to path-2.node E and node F own the same duty-cycle schedule; node B, node C and node D also own the same duty-cycle. And node A not only belongs to the path-1, but also belongs to the path-1, so its schedule depends on source node F and D. If node F's schedule is earlier than node D's, node A follow the schedule of node F, or it follow the node D. Node G don't any routing paths, then its schedule is set to infinity.

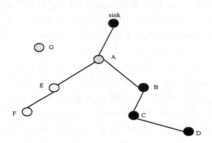

Fig. 2. A network topology

To record each node's schedule, routing tables is modified by introducing a new field. So an entry in the routing table of node *u* becomes following fields: < *next_hop, cost, power_level, destination, schedule* >.

In the S-MAC protocol, nodes exchange and coordinate on their sleep schedules by periodically broadcasting SYNC frame to all immediate neighbors. We also employ SYNC frame to exchange all nodes' duty-cycle schedule. After sink node computed duty-cycle for each path, sink node send SYNC frame to disseminate schedule information, node that receives this SYNC frame record his duty-cycle.

2) Transmission Stage

Packet transmitting stage contains wake-up stage and transmission stage. When a node has data to send, the node firstly checks whether intermediate nodes are active period in the wake-up stage. In Fig 3, source node A has data to send to final destination sink node. Node A first picks a random period from the contention window and waits for the medium to be quiet for that period and an additional (DIFS) period before sending a wake-up frame to B. If node B is active state, and receives the wake-up frame from node A, then it sends a CTS frame back to node A. After B receives a wake-up frame, unless B is the final destination of this routing path, B gets the next-hop address for this destination from its own routing table. B then waits a SIFS period before transmitting its own wake-up frame. As in IEEE 802.11, SIFS is long enough for a node to switch its transmitting/receive mode and to do necessary data processing. Upon receiving B's wake-up frame, C performs the same steps as A. This process of receiving a CTS and immediately transmitting another wake-up frame continues

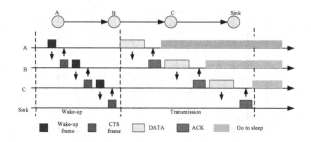

Fig. 3. Duty-cycle scheduling scheme

until either the final destination has received the wake-up frame or the end of the current node's active period is reached.

All data packets are transmitted in the transmission stage. In the example in Fig 3, when the first node A receives the CTS frame, it waits until the start of the transmission stage to transmit the data packets. Node B keeps awake to receive the data packet at the start of the transmission stage, and after node B receives the data packet, it sends and ACK frame to S. After receiving the ACK, node A goes to sleep mode. This data packets relaying process continues at each hop until the final destination is reached or the data frame reaches some node that did not receive a CTS from it next hop, in which case the node just hold data frame until the wake-up period of the next operational cycle. This entire process is repeated until the final destination is reached.

4 Validation and Performance Evaluation

To evaluate our approach, we firstly use a real MicaZ mote platform to implement EOA. The real experimental platform enables us to study the applicability and some performance. Second, we use simulation to compare EOA with other energy-saving approach.

A. Validation on MicaZ mote

We implemented our approach using the low power MicaZ platform. MicaZ mote represents the latest generation of Berkeley motes, and is commercialized by Crossbow. We placed 8 MicaZ motes in a lab environment We compare EOA with against MicaZ mote's default MAC protocol which is similar to B-MAC, but has the Low Power Listening functionality. Besides, this MAC protocol associates with a routing protocol named as DSDV which has been implemented in TinyOS. A 72-hour experiment is conducted to demonstrate the advantage of EOA.

Fig.4 shows the number of living nodes over time. From the Fig.4, we can observe that: the defective nodes increases with the runtime increasing, but the number of living nodes of EOA is more than default MAC of MicaZ mote. The reason is that EOA lets nodes sleep when they don't take part in actually transmission activity, so that nodes is impossible to waste the idle-listening energy, the lifetime of nodes' battery is extended. However, in default MAC of MicaZ mote, nodes are set in receiving

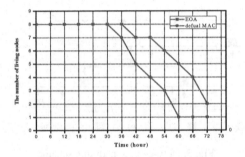

Fig. 4. The Number of Living Nodes over Time

mode whenever they don't transmit data packets, and prepare to receive data sent by other nodes at any time. This so-called idle listening leads to nodes always keep active state, even if they hasn't any communication activity. Thus, when the runtime increases, the energy consumption of nodes significantly increases, and lifetime of nodes reduces. When the number of the living nodes drops to a certain extent, the entire WSN becomes failure.

B. Simulation Results

We conduct computer simulation to evaluate the performance of the proposed approaches. For the performance comparison, we consider four different schemes: 1) non-transmission power control and routing and duty-cycle scheduling (namely, NTPC-EOA), 2) non-duty-cycle scheduling and transmission power control and routing (namely NDCY-EOA),3) non-transmission power control and DSDV and S-MAC (namely NTPC-S-MAC), 4) transmission and routing and duty-cycle scheduling (namely EOA). In the case of non-transmission power control, we take the following arrangement: the static transmission power is used in the approaches, which is set to the average value between the maximal value and minimal value. The CSMA mechanism is used in the process of non duty-cycle, where nodes keep idle listening without transmitting data.

The experiments are done through the simulation implemented in TOSSIM, which is the simulator of TinyOS by UC Berkeley.

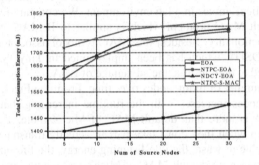

Fig. 5. Total energy consumption according to the number of source nodes

The most important metric of our performance evaluation is energy consumption. For each approach, we measure the total energy consumption that all source nodes successfully send data packets to sink. Fig.5 shows EOA is the most energy-efficient solution.

5 Conclusion

In this paper, an energy optimization approach for wireless sensor networks is presented, which exploits the cross-layer principle that takes into the physical layer (i.e. the transmission power), MAC layer (i.e. the duty-cycle scheduling), and network layer (i.e. the routing protocol) account. The approach is able to use the physical layer's transmission power as metric to choose the routing path with optimal energy consumption, and use the network layer's routing information to determine the MAC layer's duty-cycle. The results of analytical simulation experiment and real platform shows that the approach conserves more energy and leads to the better system performance.

Acknowledgment

This work is supported in part by the National Science Foundation of China under grants 90612004, the National High Technology Development 863 Program of China under Grant No. 2007AA01Z118.

References

1. Haapola, J., Shelby, Z., Pomalaza-Raez, C., Mahonen, P.: Cross-layer energy analysis of multi-hop wireless sensor network. In: EWSN 2005, pp. 33–44 (2005)
2. Vuran, M.C., AKyildiz, I.F.: Spatial correlation-based collaboration medium access control in wireless sensor network. IEEE/ACM Transaction on Networking 14(2) (June 2006)
3. Lin, S., Zhang, J., Zhou, G., Gu, L., He, T., Stankovic, J.A.: Atpc:adaptive transmission power control for Wireless Sensor Networks. In: SenSys 2006 (2006)
4. CC1000 A unique UHF RF Transceiver, http://www.chipcon.com
5. CC2420 2.4 GHz IEEE 802.15.4 / ZigBee-ready RF Transceiver, http://www.chipcon.com
6. Skraba, P., Aghajan, H., Bahai, A.: Cross-layer optimization for high density sensor networks: Distributed passive routing Decision. In: Nikolaidis, I., Barbeau, M., Kranakis, E. (eds.) ADHOC-NOW 2004, vol. 3158, pp. 266–279. Springer, Heidelberg (2004)
7. Zorzi, M., Rao, R.: Geographic random forwarding (GeRaF) for ad hoc and sensor networks: multihop performance. IEEE Trans. Mobile Computing 2(4), 337–348
8. Madan, R., Cui, S., Lall, S., Goldsmith, A.: Cross-layer design for lifetime maximization in interference-limited wireless sensor networks. In: Proc. IEEE INFOCOM 2005 (2005)
9. Cui, S., Madan, R., Goldsmith, A., Lall, S.: Joint routing, MAC, and link layer optimization in sensor networks with energy constraints. In: Proc. IEEE ICC 2005 (2005)

Intrusion Detection Systems for Wireless Sensor Networks: A Survey

Ashfaq Hussain Farooqi and Farrukh Aslam Khan

FAST National University of Computer and Emerging Sciences,
A. K. Brohi Road, H-11/4, Islamabad, Pakistan
{ashfaq.farooqi,farrukh.aslam}@nu.edu.pk

Abstract. Wireless sensor networks (WSNs) are vulnerable to different types of security threats that can degrade the performance of the whole network; that might result in fatal problems like denial of service (DoS) attacks, routing attacks, Sybil attack etc. Key management protocols, authentication protocols and secure routing cannot provide security to WSNs for these types of attacks. Intrusion detection system (IDS) is a solution to this problem. It analyzes the network by collecting sufficient amount of data and detects abnormal behavior of sensor node(s). IDS based security mechanisms proposed for other network paradigms such as ad hoc networks, cannot directly be used in WSNs. Researchers have proposed various intrusion detection systems for wireless sensor networks during the last few years. We classify these approaches into three categories i.e. purely distributed, purely centralized and distributed-centralized. In this paper, we present a survey of these mechanisms. These schemes are further differentiated in the way they perform intrusion detection.

Keywords: Wireless Sensor Networks (WSNs), Intrusion Detection System (IDS), IDS agent installation.

1 Introduction

Wireless sensor networks (WSNs) are distributed, infrastructure-less, fault tolerant, scalable and dynamic in nature [1]. WSNs are vulnerable to several types of security threats that can degrade the overall performance of these networks. Key management, authentication protocols and secure routing protocols provide secure transmission while lacking reliable delivery of messages. In other words, these mechanisms can protect the network from outside attacks but show failure against inside attacks. They aim to provide data confidentiality, data authentication and data integrity. In an outside attack, when an intruder tries to get access to the data, these approaches hide secret information. In an inside attack, sensor node that is a part of the sensor network starts performing maliciously without trying to get access to the information present in the received messages. Roosta et al. [2] explain various possible attacks on wireless sensor networks i.e. denial of service, routing attacks, Sybil attack etc.

Intrusion detection system (IDS) is a security mechanism used to detect the abnormal behavior in the network. It is thought that intrusion detection systems are "not fit" for securing WSNs. This is true to some extent because IDS approaches are

D. Ślęzak et al. (Eds.): FGCN/ACN 2009, CCIS 56, pp. 234–241, 2009.

usually computationally expensive. But if we consider a WSN that works for tracking the movement of the enemy, this network can provide very useful information for making a strategy to beat the enemy in that area. Moreover, there is a rapid change in technology and keeping in mind the future perspectives; the capabilities of a sensor node will increase in near future. Sensor nodes will have more memory and survival time i.e. they might be used for transmitting multimedia information as well as for underwater applications. Due to the recent advancement in sensor technology, these networks will become visible and would be used by us in our daily life. Hence, there is a requirement of a secure WSN that ensures secure transmission and reliable delivery of packets in the network. IDS based mechanisms can be very effective to detect abnormal behavior of sensor nodes whether they cause DoS attacks, act as Sybil nodes or perform any other malicious activity.

In IDS, the unit that analyzes the network and detects abnormal behavior of node(s) is called an IDS agent. IDS agent collects network data for some time 't', applies detection policy to detect abnormal activity and takes appropriate actions. Rajasegarar et al. [3] analyze several anomaly detection mechanisms in their work. Since 2005, researchers have proposed a number of IDS based security mechanisms that analyze the working of sensor node(s) and efficiently detect abnormal activities. They mostly target routing protocol attacks to explain their proposed methodology. Their work differ from each other in two ways i.e., installation of IDS agent, and the detection policy. There are three possibilities of installing an IDS agent; purely centralized, purely distributed and hybrid. In the first approach, it is installed at sink or BS only while in the second approach, IDS agent is present in every sensor node. In the third approach, monitor nodes are used for intrusion detection.

The rest of the paper is organized as follows: Section 2 contains a brief introduction of an IDS. We classify IDS based security mechanisms in Section 3 and explain each methodology. Finally, Section 4 concludes the paper.

2 Intrusion Detection System

Intrusion detection system (IDS) is a system that checks the network behavior and finds the nodes that are not working normally. It is an additional unit installed at the clients or server or both. This unit is called IDS agent. IDS agent works in three phases and each phase has a unit. *Collection unit* collects network data. *Detection unit* performs detection policy accordingly to find intrusions. *Response unit* generates alerts in case of abnormal activities.

2.1 IDS Agent Installation

IDS agent performs an important task for securing network from intrusive attacks. Researchers use three different ways of installing IDS agent in WSNs. These are; purely centralized, purely distributed and distributed-centralized.

Purely Distributed IDS Agent Installation Mechanism. In purely distributed IDS approach, IDS agent is installed in every node. It checks abnormal behavior of neighboring nodes locally. It analyzes the data that it receives from its radio range. There are further two ways for declaring a node as compromised or not. In *individualized decision making*, node that detects the anomalous behavior of another node sends that information to the sink or BS. In *cooperative decision making*, node that detects the anomalous behavior of any node communicates with other nodes and finally that node is declared compromised after voting.

Purely Centralized IDS Agent Installation Mechanism. In WSNs, sensor nodes sense the environment and transmit processed information to the sink or base station (BS). In purely centralized IDS approach, IDS agent is installed in the sink or BS. It requires an additional special routing protocol that gathers or collects information from nodes to analyze the behavior of sensor nodes collectively.

Distributed-Centralized IDS Agent Installation Mechanism. Cluster-head approach lowers the power consumption and efficiently reduces control overhead. The concept of monitor node is derived from this philosophy. In distributed-centralized approach, IDS agent is installed in monitor nodes only. This node performs two types of functions simultaneously. First, it performs activities like normal nodes and secondly, it checks for intrusion detection. The logic behind that approach is to minimize the detection overhead faced by purely distributed approach.

2.2 Detection Policy

In an intrusion detection system, detection of intrusion is the major phase. There are three different policies of detection; misuse detection, anomaly-based detection and specification-based detection.

Misuse Detection System. There are various attacks that follow same sequence of steps to launch its effect. In misuse detection system, these sequences of steps are used in order to detect these attacks. This detection mechanism is also called signature-based detection. It is like pattern matching. It works better for known attacks only but cannot cater unknown attacks.

Anomaly Detection System. Signature-based approach cannot detect attacks for which signature (known pattern) is not present. There are a number of attacks that change the signatures frequently. These attacks are hard to detect. Anomaly-based systems provide a security environment in which anything that deviates from the normal behaviour are declared anomalous or malicious.

Specification-based Detection System. Specification-based detection system works by defining rules for attacks. Sensor node's behaviour is checked against each rule sequentially. There is a failure bit associated with each node. If the sensor node violates any rule, failure bit is incremented. If number of failures of a particular node increases than a threshold after a time interval t; an alert about that node is generated.

3   IDS Based Security Mechanisms for Wireless Sensor Networks

Since recently, various intrusion detection systems have been proposed for detecting compromised node(s) in WSNs. We categorize these methodologies into three major classes depending upon the way they install IDS agent in the network.

3.1 Purely Distributed Approach

In purely distributed mechanisms, IDS agent is installed in each sensor node to analyze the working of other node(s).

Spontaneous Watchdog Approach. Roman et al. [4] introduce neighbor monitoring technique known as spontaneous watchdog. IDS agent also has two detection bodies; local agent and global agent. Local agent audits data that comes from those nodes that lie inside its radio range or are its neighbors. It generates alert if any node works abnormally, like flooding or if it receives message from a node that is not present in the neighbor list. On the other hand, node activates its global agent if it senses any communication in promiscuous mode. Here, global agent acts like a spontaneous watchdog. It checks whether nodes rebroadcast received message (s) or not.

Cooperative Local Auditing. Krontiris et al. [5] propose a specification based cooperative local auditing mechanism for detection of selective forwarding and black-hole attacks. They further extend their work for sink-hole attack in [6]. According to their approach, IDS agent is composed of five main components; local packet monitoring, local detection engine, cooperative detection engine, communication, and local response. The local packet monitoring component gathers packet from the radio frequency range of the node and transmits to the local detection engine. Specification-based detection mechanism is applied to find intrusions. In [5] and [6], they have mentioned four rules for detecting black-hole, selective forwarding and sink-hole attacks. Local detection engine performs this task. It checks whether packets of a particular node obey the rules or not. If it violates the specifications then an alert is sent to cooperative detection engine. This component then communicates with other nodes to check the status of that node among these nodes. If majority of the nodes validate the maliciousness of that node then an alert is passed to the local response about that node. There may be different types of responses to secure the network from that compromised node depending upon the configuration.

Fixed Width Clustering Algorithm. Another distributed anomaly detection mechanism is proposed by Loo et al. [7]. In this approach, twelve various features like number of packets received or sent or broadcast, route request sent or forwarded or received etc. are loaded. They are used to determine mean or standard deviation for each neighboring node in normal messaging. These values are normalized to get a single value. This value is utilized to form fixed width clusters. If it is close to any cluster central value, it is placed in that cluster. Otherwise, it forms another cluster and becomes a central value of that cluster. A range is also calculated for it. These values are also calculated by simulating various attack scenarios and are placed in the cluster. After analyzing these clusters, compromised nodes are detected. It is assumed that those clusters that have fewer points indicate the abnormal activity.

Artificial Immune System. Drozda et al. [8] propose an AIS based detection mechanism for wireless sensor networks because it is computationally less expensive and provides better detection performance. In this mechanism, system maintains a list of self-strings (normal behavior) and non-self strings (misbehavior). System learns normal behavior by maintaining strings called self-strings from the header of each received message. After that *random generate and test process* is introduced to form detector set. Self strings are compared with randomly generated strings. If newly produced string matches the self string, it is rejected; else, it is stored in the detector set. After that new strings are again randomly produced. This time, they are compared with detector set entities. If match appears, it confirms a non-self string and it is stored in the list of non-self string. This process is called negative selection because it determines those behaviors (strings) that are used for determining abnormal activity. When this process completes, attacks are launched to analyze the false positive rate.

Intrusion-aware Validation Algorithm. It enhances those distributed cooperative IDS systems that lack confirmation about the source of the alert because compromised nodes can generate false alarms about normal node(s) [9]. It works in two phases. In *consensus phase,* node checks after receiving any alert about occurrence of malicious activity that whether it is any declared (available in list) abnormal node or not. If the information is not available then it checks the anomaly type and the threat level. It randomly selects n number of neighbors, according to the threat level, for consensus and sends confirmation request packet(s). When any node receives confirmation request packet, d*ecision phase* activates. Neighbor node replies with three types of responses: 1 agrees with claim, 0 don't know and -1 does not agree with claim. Sensor node takes decision on the basis of the responses received from the randomly selected nodes. There are three possible decisions; validate (node is abnormal), no consensus (not identified) and invalidate (node that sends the alert is compromised).

Pair-based Abnormal Node Detection. Ahmed et al. [10] propose a novel distributed abnormal node detection technique. It uses both signature and anomaly based techniques to identify compromise node. In this technique, sensor network is divided into pairs that further lead to form groups. These groups communicate with each other in hierarchical way. They are controlled by central pairs or cluster-heads. Every sensor node analyzes behavior of its pairing node. It has a local detection engine and a local knowledge base while there are two central containers; central knowledge base and central signature key management engine. *Central signature key management engine* is responsible for secure transmission of messages between the pairs and groups. Data is collected based on some predefined features by the local knowledge base about pairing node and is used by the local detection engine to detect the anomaly. *Central knowledge base* collects and stores information about all the nodes present in the group or outside the group. The information updates frequently and it shares the relevant information about the nodes with individual node. Node performs anomaly detection to generate alert about the pairing node, if it is found abnormal. This updates the central knowledge base too.

3.2 Purely Centralized Approach

In this approach, the sink or the base station collects some specific information from sensor nodes using any special routing protocol and analyzes it to detect intrusions.

ANDES. Gupta et al. [11] present a centralized anomaly detection mechanism for detecting fail-stop failures and several routing protocol attacks. It works in two main phases i.e. collection of information and detection. ANDES gathers information from the sensor network using two sources; data plane (normal or regular collection of data in the sensor network) and management plane (specific information from sensor nodes using a specialized routing protocol). Sink or BS collects sufficient information before applying anomaly detection. ANDES consist of three main components. *Collection of application data* collects regular data. *Collection of Management information* uses an additional management routing protocol to collect address, parent, hops, send_cnt, receive_cnt, fwd_cnt, etc from each node after an interval of time. *Detection policy* works in three phases; analysis of application data, analysis of management data and cross checking to determine the root cause of the attack.

Application Independent Framework. Zhang et al. [12] present simple graph theory based approach that efficiently detects compromised beacon nodes. Beacon nodes provide location information to the sensor nodes. It is assumed that IDS agent is installed at beacon nodes. It produces alerts about the maliciousness of sensor nodes. A compromised beacon node transmits false information about other nodes and degrades the performance of the routing protocol. It is not a pure centralized IDS methodology. It is centralized-distributed because beacon nodes generate alerts about the malicious activity. Sink or BS receives these alerts by any secure transmission protocol. Once efficient amount of data is gathered, it applies the proposed graph theory based detection mechanism to find whether information is received from reliable source or not.

3.3 Distributed-Centralized Approach

IDS agent is installed in some nodes called monitor nodes. Monitor node listens in two modes i.e. normal and promiscuous. In normal listening, monitor node interprets and forwards after processing (application dependent) those messages that are destined to it. In promiscuous listening, monitor node interprets all messages whether they are destined to it or not. They avoid the complexity of using an additional specialized routing protocol (purely centralized) and limit the overall energy consumption of sensor nodes (purely distributed).

Decentralized Intrusion Detection Model. Da Silva et al. [13] present a specification based distributed centralized IDS mechanism. IDS agent is installed in monitor node. It works in three phases. In *Data Acquisition*, monitor node listens in promiscuous mode and maintains an array data structure for each node. This contains information about those nodes that lie in the neighborhood. In *rules application*, monitor node checks whether any node violates any rule or not, after collecting sufficient amount of data in the first phase. Several rules or specifications are discussed i.e. retransmission rule for selective forwarding or black-hole attack, repetition rule for flooding etc. There is a failure counter for each node. If a node's data structure violates any rule, its respective counter is incremented. In *intrusion detection*, monitor node evaluates failure history table of each node. If counter value exceeds from certain threshold 'th' in time interval t, an alert is generated.

Cumulative Summation. Phuong et al. [14] propose an anomaly-based distributed centralized detection mechanism to analyze the behavior of nodes. It secures wireless sensor network from three categories of attacks. These are 1) Compromised nodes attract the attention of other nodes i.e. black-hole, sink-hole or worm-hole attack 2) Affects message like collision 3) Flooding to exhaust resources. Cumulative Summation (CUSUM) works in two phases. In *data acquisition*, monitor node maintains a table containing total number of incoming packets and outgoing packets that relate to neighbor n (1, 2, 3... N). In *anomaly detection*, CUSUM works on the collected data to detect three changes; amount of messages received or collision occurrence with the packets or number of packets emerging from a particular node. If these values are above certain threshold, an alert is generated.

Table 1. IDS based security mechanisms

Proposed Approach	Detection Policy	Decision	Attacks
Spontaneous Watchdog [4]	Any	Individual	Novel
Cooperative local audit [5]	Specification-based	Cooperative	Routing
Fixed-width clustering [7]	Anomaly-based	Individual	Routing
Artificial Immune System [8]	Anomaly-based	Individual	MAC/Routing
Intrusion-aware validation [9]	Anomaly-based	Cooperative	-------
Pair-based approach [10]	Both	Pairing node	Novel
ANDES [11]	Anomaly-based	Sink or BS	Phy./Routing
App. Independent Framework [12]	Anomaly-based	Sink or BS	-------
Decentralized IDS [13]	Specification-based	Monitor node	Trans./Routing
Cumulative Summation [14]	Anomaly-based	Monitor node	Trans./Routing

4 Conclusion

In this paper, a detailed discussion and analysis of the existing Intrusion Detection Systems (IDS) for Wireless Sensor Networks is presented. IDS is an essential part of security for every network. Energy-efficient intrusion detection systems are suitable for wireless sensor networks. Purely centralized IDS approaches are power efficient because the most powerful part of the network (sink or BS) detects intrusion. But, these techniques are complex and require some specialized routing protocol that gathers data from each sensor node to BS or sink for anomaly detection. On the other hand, purely distributed IDS techniques are not energy-efficient because IDS agent is installed in every node. It increases extra computation or power consumption at node level. Distributed-centralized IDS approach suits WSNs in accordance with energy consumption and complexity; but it has its own constraints. Wireless sensor networks are vulnerable to a number of inside attacks that affect the overall performance of the network. These attacks results in wrong interpretation of the sensor field. There is a requirement of an energy-efficient intrusion detection system that works in distributed manner and cooperates with other nodes to identify the abnormal behavior of nodes.

References

1. Akyildiz, I.F., Su, W., Sankarsubramaniam, Y., Cayirci, E.: A Survey on Sensor Networks. IEEE Communication Magazine, 102–114 (2002)
2. Roosta, T., Shieh, S.P., Sastry, S.: Taxonomy of Security Attacks in Sensor Networks and Countermeasures. In: Proc. of 1st IEEE Int. Conf. on System Integration and Reliability Improvements (2006)
3. Rajasegarar, S., Leckie, C., Palaniswami, M.: Anomaly Detection in WSNs. In: IEEE Wireless Comm., Security in Ad hoc and Sensor Networks, pp. 34–40 (2008)
4. Roman, R., Zhou, J., Lopez, J.: Applying Intrusion Detection Systems to WSNs. In: IEEE Consumer Communications and Networking Conference, vol. 1, pp. 640–644 (2006)
5. Krontiris, I., Dimitriou, T.: Towards Intrusion Detection in Wireless Sensor Networks. In: Proc. of 13th European Wireless Conference, Paris, France (2007)
6. Krontiris, I., Dimitriou, T., Giannetsos, T., Mpasoukos, M.: Intrusion Detection of Sinkhole Attacks in Wireless Sensor Networks. In: Kutyłowski, M., Cichoń, J., Kubiak, P. (eds.) ALGOSENSORS 2007. LNCS, vol. 4837, pp. 150–161. Springer, Heidelberg (2007)
7. Loo, C.E., Ng, M.Y., Leckie, C., Palaniswami, M.: Intrusion Detection for Routing Attacks in Sensor Networks. International Journal of Distributed Sensor Networks 2(4), 313–332 (2006)
8. Drozda, M., Schaust, S., Szczerbicka, H.: Is AIS Based Misbehavior Detection Suitable for Wireless Sensor Networks? In: Proc. of IEEE Wireless Communications and Networking Conference, Hong Kong, pp. 3130–3135 (2007)
9. Shaikh, R.A., Jameel, H., Auriol, B.J., Lee, S., Song, Y.J.: Trusting Anomaly and Intrusion Claims for Cooperative Distributed Intrusion Detection Schemes of WSNs. In: Proc. of International Symposium on Trust Computing, China, pp. 2038–2043 (2008)
10. Ahmed, K.R., Ahmed, K., Munir, S., Asad, A.: Abnormal Node Detection in WSN by Pair Based Approach using IDS Secure Routing Methodology. International Journal of Computer Science and Network Security 8(12), 339–342 (2008)
11. Gupta, S., Zheng, R., Cheng, A.M.K.: An Anomaly Detection System for Wireless Sensor Networks. In: Proc. of IEEE International Conference on Mobile Ad hoc and Sensor Systems, pp. 1–9 (2007)
12. Zhang, Q., Yu, T., Ning, P.: A Framework for Identifying Compromised Nodes in WSNs. ACM Transaction Information System Security 11(12) (2008)
13. Da Silva, A.P.R., Martins, M.H.T., Rocha, B.P.S., Loureiro, A.A.F., Ruiz, L.B., Wong, H.C.: Decentralized Intrusion Detection in WSNs. In: Proc. of the 1st ACM Int. workshop on Quality of service & security in wireless networks, Canada, pp. 16–23 (2005)
14. Phuong, T.V., Hung, L.X., Cho, S.J., Lee, Y.K., Lee, S.: An Anomaly Detection Algorithm for Detecting Attacks in WSNs. In: Mehrotra, S., Zeng, D.D., Chen, H., Thuraisingham, B., Wang, F.-Y. (eds.) ISI 2006. LNCS, vol. 3975, pp. 735–736. Springer, Heidelberg (2006)

A New Routing Protocol Based on Fuzzy Combination Model for Predicting Link Stability of Wireless Ad Hoc Networks

Yi Sha, Xing-zi Wei, Yan Yang, Li Huang, and Guang-xing Wang

Department of Communication and Information System
Northeastern University
Shenyang, P.R. China
shayineu@163.com, alenweixingzi@163.com, yan_yang123@163.com,
alenhuangli@163.com, alenguangxingwang@yahoo.com

Abstract. In this article, we proposed a new routing protocol based on fuzzy combination model for link stability prediction-FCMSP. In this protocol, the fuzzy combination model was introduced to predict the move path of nodes and calculate the distance between nodes at next moment which was a measure of link stability. The geographical position of nodes was gotten by GPS. In addition, through predicting the link is to be unstable at next moment, we could do early start routing beforehand repair mechanisms before link failure in order to avoid link frequent fracture. Simulation was done on a NS2-based platform for comparing the properties of the new protocol presented and conventional AODV protocol. The simulation results showed that the packet delivery ratio, the average end-to-end delay and the normalized routing overhead have all improved better.

Keywords: ad hoc networks; routing protocol; fuzzy combination model; link stability prediction.

1 Introduction

Ad Hoc network [1] is an autonomous system temporarily composed by a series of dynamic nodes with wireless transmitters, which doesn't rely on the default infrastructure. Due to wireless communications in Ad Hoc networks, each node can move fast independently, and the network topology structure is changing constantly, so the link can be down frequently. When any link is down, another available link or a new route should be found to restore the connections, which can cost limited network resources and node's energy greatly in Ad Hoc networks. Also, routing maintenance starts up only after link failure is detected; this not only leads to great delay but also increases packet loss probability. Especially when the topology change frequently, the quality of network application service is greatly influenced, this can reduce the operation performance of the network. Consequently, it is valuable to propose a stable routing protocol with prediction function.

D. Ślęzak et al. (Eds.): FGCN/ACN 2009, CCIS 56, pp. 242–249, 2009.
© Springer-Verlag Berlin Heidelberg 2009

Recently, various stable routing schemes for Ad Hoc networks have been proposed in [2-9]. References [2] proposed Associatively Based Routing (ABR), which chose the most stable link rather than those temporarily links. A prediction-based link availability estimation to quantify the link reliability was presented in [3]. A prediction of the link stability between nodes by the change of the signal strength was presented in [5]. But these prediction methods use the past or present state to measure the future state, which can not track the change of topology dynamically, that is, the stable link at current time may become unusable in the future due to the node mobility. References [7, 8] proposed a link usability prediction algorithm which measured the link usability of the future by the available lifetime of the link.

A stable routing protocol based on the fuzzy combination model prediction is proposed in this paper. The proposed protocol predicts nodes' trajectory by the fuzzy combination model according to nodes' positions acquired by the global positioning system (GPS). And then the future link stability is calculated according to the future distance between two nodes. Then performs routing pre-restoration before the link is down, which can avoid link failure and improve network performance. Simulation results prove the feasibility of the proposed protocol.

2 Trajectory Prediction Model

Combination prediction method [10] is a comprehensive combination prediction model composed by kinds of prediction methods with different weights.

2.1 The Mathematical Model and the Solution of the Parameters of Fuzzy Combination Prediction

Let $f_{it}(i = 1, 2, \cdots, k; t = 1, 2, \cdots, n)$ denote the predictive value of the $i-th$ prediction method at time t , so the value of the prediction for the k kinds of combination prediction method is:

$$\hat{f}_t = \sum_{i=1}^{k} A_i f_{it}, (t = 1, 2, \cdots, n), \text{ and } \sum_{i=1}^{k} A_i = 1 \tag{1}$$

By the fuzzy set theory, the prediction value of $\hat{f}_t = \sum_{i=1}^{k} A_i f_{it}$ is also a fuzzy number and the membership function of $\hat{f}_t$ is:

$$\mu_{\hat{f}_t}(x) = \begin{cases} 1 - \dfrac{|x-a|}{c}, & a-c \leq x \leq a+c; \\ 0, & \text{otherwise.} \end{cases} \tag{2}$$

where $a = \sum_{i=1}^{k} a_i f_{it}, c = \sum_{i=1}^{k} c_i f_{it}$.

For the prediction accuracy of the fuzzy combination model is higher, the fuzzy interval $[a-c, a+c]$ must be the lest. The size of the fuzzy interval of every fuzzy number A_i is very important to the prediction accuracy.

At a certain level value λ $(0 < \lambda < 1)$, the value of membership functions satisfies:

$$\mu_{\tilde{f}_t}(x) = 1 - \frac{\left| x - \sum\limits_{i=1}^{k} a_i f_{it} \right|}{\sum\limits_{i=1}^{k} c_i f_{it}} \geq \lambda \tag{3}$$

According to the above conditions, the sanction a_i of the fuzzy number A_i and the span C_i must satisfy the following inequality:

$$\sum_{i=1}^{k} a_i f_{it} + (1-\lambda)\sum_{i=1}^{k} c_i f_{it} \geq f_t \tag{4}$$

$$\sum_{i=1}^{k} a_i f_{it} - (1-\lambda)\sum_{i=1}^{k} c_i f_{it} \leq f_t \tag{5}$$

The combination prediction model can reach the highest accuracy at n moments and the linear programming model can be structured as follows:

$$\min \quad s = c_1 + c_2 + \cdots + c_k$$

$$\begin{aligned}
s.t. \quad & \sum_{i=1}^{k} a_i f_{it} + (1-\lambda)\sum_{i=1}^{k} c_i f_{it} \geq f_t \\
& \sum_{i=1}^{k} a_i f_{it} - (1-\lambda)\sum_{i=1}^{k} c_i f_{it} \leq f_t \\
& t = 1, 2, \cdots, n \\
& a_i, c_i \geq 0, (i = 1, 2, \cdots, k)
\end{aligned} \tag{6}$$

This is an optimization problem, and we solve a_i by simplex method [11] in this paper.

2.2 Trajectory Prediction

Assume that the positions f_i at time t and n moments before t are given. According to the statistical test and goodness-of-fit, four kinds of curve model as follows are chosen to predict the future position of the node, respectively. Then we predict the parameters by the fuzzy combination model. Four kinds of curve model are as follows:

(1) Linear model: $f_{1i} = \beta_{10} + \beta_{11} t_i$
(2) Logarithm function model: $f_{2i} = \beta_{20} + \beta_{21} \ln t_i$
(3) Exponential model: $f_{3i} = \beta_{30} e^{\beta_{31} t_i}$
(4) The power function: $f_{4i} = \beta_{40} t_i^{\beta_{41}}$

The parameters of the above functions are determined by least-square method. According to function (6), $a_i (i = 1, 2, \cdots, k)$ of the combination model can be obtained. The future position of the nodes can be calculated as follows.

$$\begin{aligned}
\hat{f}_{t+1} = {}& a_1 \times (\beta_{10} + \beta_{11}(t+1)) \\
& + a_2 \times (\beta_{20} + \beta_{21} \ln(t+1)) \\
& + a_3 \times \beta_{30} e^{\beta_{31}(t+1)} + a_4 \times \beta_{40}(t+1)^{\beta_{41}}
\end{aligned} \tag{7}$$

3 Link Stability Prediction

Let i, j denote any two nodes in the network. D_{ij} is the actual distance of the nodes in the network, which can be calculated by the positions of the two nodes acquired by the global positioning system (GPS). Assuming that each node is of the same type with the same transmitted power, thus the effective communication distance (D_0) is determined. Assume that s_{ij} is the link stability between nodes. s_{ij} is defined as follows:

$$s_{ij} = \begin{cases} 0 & , \quad D_{ij} \geq D_0; \\ 1 - \dfrac{D_{ij}}{D_0} & , \quad 0 \leq D_{ij} < D_0. \end{cases}$$

(8)

Let $(x_i(t), y_i(t))$ and $(x_j(t), y_j(t))$ denote the position of nodes i and j at time t. The stability $s_{ij}(t)$ of link between nodes i and j at time t can be calculated as follows:

$$s_{ij}(t) = \begin{cases} 0 & , \quad D \geq D_0; \\ 1 - \dfrac{\sqrt{(x_i(t) - x_j(t))^2 + (y_i(t) - y_j(t))^2}}{D_0} & , \quad 0 \leq D \leq D_0. \end{cases}$$

(9)

By the fuzzy combination model, the future position of the nodes can be predicted. Assume that the positions of time t and $n-1$ moments before t are given. According to (7), the future position $(\hat{x}_i(t+1), \hat{y}_i(t+1))$ and $(\hat{x}_j(t+1), \hat{y}_j(t+1))$ of nodes i and j at time $t+1$ can be obtained. Thus the prediction of stability between nodes i and j at time $t+1$ is as follows:

$$\hat{s}_{ij}(t+1) = \begin{cases} 0 & , \quad D \geq D_0; \\ 1 - \dfrac{\sqrt{(\hat{x}_i(t+1) - \hat{x}_j(t+1))^2 + (\hat{y}_i(t+1) - \hat{y}_j(t+1))^2}}{D_0} & , \quad 0 \leq D \leq D_0; \end{cases}$$

(10)

4 FCMSP

The proposed protocol has added new link-choosing mechanism and new prediction parameters processing function base on the source code of AODV class. For the general AODV routing, it may be in one of three kinds of states which are the connection mode, repair mode and interruption mode.

To achieve a new routing prediction function, we increase the new state – pre-restoration. In the process of routing maintenance, it monitors the link stability in the used route. When any link trend unstable (the link stability is less than the reliable threshold), the node will send a warning single and start to look for a new route. The data will forward from the original neighbor node before the route really fails. After establish the new route it will update the route table to forward the data from the new route, which will avoid the routing interrupt caused by nodes' movement and the change of path.

4.1 The Structure of the Data Table in the Protocol and the Calculation of the Stability Threshold

(1) The structure of the historical data table

To store historical data, we add a new form of historical data. Each node gets their geographic information with interval (equal to GPS). The historical data table of the node records x, y and extracting time. The length of the table is set to n so the table can store the geographic information of n moments.

(2) The threshold of stability s_0 in the routing establishment stage

Considering the worst case: The hops of the two procedures are the number of nodes (N) or the diameter of the network ($NETWORK\_DIAMETER$).According to AODV, the value of $NETWORK\_DIAMETER$ is 30. The time of one hop T_{hop} is 30 ms, then

$$T = \begin{cases} 2 \times N \times T_{hop}, & N < 30 \\ 2 \times 30 \times T_{hop}, & N \geq 30 \end{cases} \tag{11}$$

Fig. 1 shows that node B is in the effective communication range of node A. D_N is the distance between them. Node B removes from A with maximum speed $2v_{max}$. After a period of time T node B moves out of the effective communication range of node A. Then D_N corresponding stability s_0 is the reliable communication threshold of stability. The effective communication distance is D_0 in Ad Hoc network, so

$$D_N = D_0 - 2v_{max}T \tag{12}$$

$$s_0 = 1 - \frac{D_N}{D_0} = 1 - \frac{D_0 - 2v_{max}T}{D_0} = \frac{2v_{max}T}{D_0} \tag{13}$$

Fig. 1. The stability threshold solving schemes

(3) The threshold of stability s_0' in the routing establishment stage

Assume that after increasing the stability prediction and the pre-restoration, the necessary time to get a new routing is T'.Considering the worst case: the hops of warning signal is 1, the other two procedures is the same to the above, then

$$T' = \begin{cases} 2 \times N \times T_{hop} + T_{hop}, & N < 30 \\ 2 \times 30 \times T_{hop} + T_{hop}, & N \geq 30 \end{cases} \tag{14}$$

where s_0' is the threshold of stability, D_N' is the corresponding distance and $2v_{max}$ is the maximum speed between nodes in the network. The effective communication distance is D_0, so

$$D_N' = D_0 - 2v_{max}T' \tag{15}$$

$$s_0' = 1 - \frac{D_N'}{D_0} = 1 - \frac{D_0 - 2v_{max}T'}{D_0} = \frac{2v_{max}T'}{D_0} \tag{16}$$

4.2 Routing Mechanism

(1) Route discovery stage

In the route discovery stage, the proposed protocol chooses the link whose stability is less than s_0 to be the middle link to route, ensuring the initial route setup on stable link.

Base on AODV routing mechanism, we consider the stability factor, so we add node location information to the route request packet. By expanding RREQ, we add node location information and calculate the stability of every link, and then choose the link whose stability is less than s_0 to establish the stable route.

(2) Routing maintenance stage

In the route maintenance stage, the node sends a warning signal to its precursor node when the stability prediction is less than s_0', and then starts the pre-restoration process. When the precursor node establishes a new route, it should change the link to choose the more stable link in the circumstance that doesn't interrupt data transmission. The specific discovery process is as follows:

In AODV routing maintenance stage, we consider the future stability factor, so we add new header(*newhdr*) to the data packet to real-time transmit node's predicted location information.

Warning signal (WARN): in the case that the node has predicted the link that would be unstable in the future we add a control warning signal to inform the precursor node that the link will be not stable. The destination of control warning signal is the precursor node.

Source node initializes the *newhdr* packet. When intermediate nodes receive data packets, $\hat{x}$ and $\hat{y}$ of the next moment will be calculated according to the history information table and (7), and $\hat{s}$ of the stability between itself and its precursor node will be calculated according to (10). WARN signal is send to the precursor node through the reverse routing. After received the WARN signal, the node will determine whether to update the state of the route to advanced repair. Then start the pre-restoration process, send RREQ to the choose route.

5 Simulation and Performance Analysis

The simulation environment is NS2. FCMSP, LSRP and AODV are simulated in NS2. There are 50 nodes evenly distributed in the rectangular area which is $1000m \times 1000m$. Each node has the same wireless transceiver equipment and single gain omni-directional antennas. The wireless transmission radius is 250m and channel capacity is 2Mbit/s.

To comprehensively analyze the performances of AODV, LSRP and FCMSP, the following three performances including packet delivery rate, the number of the breaking links and the normalized routing overhead have been analyzed.

Fig. 2 shows the relationship between the packet delivery rate and the maximum speed of the nodes. With the maximum speed of node changing from 1m/s to 20m/s, the packet deliveries of the three protocols are both decreasing, however, they are both above 85%. The packet delivery of FCMSP is higher than AODV by 2%-10% and is higher than LSRP by 1%-6%. When the maximum speed of node is 20m/s, the packet deliveries of FCMSP is above 95%, and with the speed of node is increasing, the increasing degree of the packet deliveries of FCMSP is more obvious.

Fig.3 shows the relationship between the number of the breaking link and the maximum speed of the nodes. The number of the breaking link in FCMSP is lest, which is less than AODV by 84% and is less than LSRP by 80%.

Fig. 4 shows the relationship between the normalized routing overhead and the maximum speed of the nodes. With the maximum speed of node increasing, the change of topology becomes severer, the number of rerouting and the number of switch between new and old route is increasing which leads to routing overhead

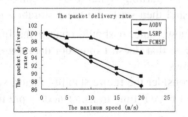

Fig. 2. The packet delivery rate-The maximum speed

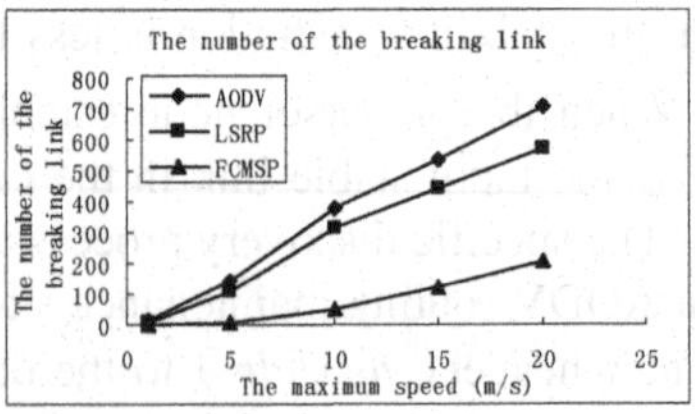

Fig. 3. The number of the breaking link-The maximum speed

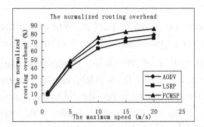

Fig. 4. The maximum speed-The normalized routing overhead

increasing. To complete the pre-restoration process, routing warning signal is added to FCMSP, which can increase the overhead in a certain extent. As shown in figure 4, when the speed of node is 20m/s, the overhead of FCM-SRPP is higher than AODV by approximately 6% and is higher than LSRP by 10%, but it is acceptable for applications relating to the improve degree of the packet delivery rate and the number of link break.

6   Conclusion

A stable routing protocol based on the fuzzy combination model prediction was proposed in this paper. The protocol predicts link stability by fuzzy combination model, and then according to the future predicted result it performs routing pre-restoration before the link is down to establish the stable route. Simulation results show that the number of breaking link in FCMSP is smaller than in AODV and LSRP. When the speed of the node is 20m/s, the number of the breaking link in FCMSP is smaller than AODV by 501 and is smaller than LSRP by 362. As the result the packet delivery rate in FCMSP is higher than AODV by 10% and is higher than LSRP by 6% obviously. And the advantage of the performance in FCMSP is more obvious when the nodes move with high speed.

References

1. Perkins, C.E.: Ad Hoc Networking. Addison-Wesley, Reading (2001)
2. Toh, C.K.: Associativity-based routing for Ad-hoc networks. Wireless Personal Communications Journal 4(2), 103–139 (1997)
3. Jiang, S.M., He, D.J., Rao, J.Q.: A Prediction-Based Link Availability Estimation for Routing Metrics in MANETs. IEEE/ACM Transactions on Networking 13(6), 1302–1312 (2005)
4. Brust, M.R., Ribeiro, C.H.C., Rothkugel, S.: Heuristics on Link Stability in Ad Hoc Networks. In: Network Operations and Management Symposium, pp. 738–741 (2008)
5. Yang, K.J., Tsai, Y.R.: Link Stability Prediction for Mobile Ad Hoc Networks in Shadowed Environments. In: Global Telecommunications Conference, November 27, pp. 1–5 (2006)
6. Tamg, J.H., Chuang, B.W., Wu, F.J.: A Radio-Link Stability-based Routing Protocol for Mobile Ad Hoc Networks. In: IEEE International Conference on Systems, Man, and Cybernetics, October 2006, vol. 5, pp. 3697–3701 (2006)
7. Jiang, S.M.: An enhanced prediction-based link availability estimation for MANET. IEEE Transactions on Communications 52(2), 183–186 (2004)
8. Jiang, S.M., He, D.J., Rao, J.Q.: A prediction-based link availability estimation for routing metrics in MANET. IEEE/ACM Transactions on Networking 13(6), 1302–1311 (2005)
9. Meng, L.M., Wu, W.X.: Dynamic Source Routing Protocol Based on Link Stability Arithmetic. In: International Symposium on Information Science and Engieering, December 2008, vol. 2, pp. 730–733 (2008)
10. Bates, J.M., Granger, C.W.J.: The combination of forecasts. Operations Research Quarterly 20(4), 451–468 (1969)
11. Zhang, W.: The optimization method, pp. 95–112. Northeast University Press (2004)

Experiments on an Election Algorithm for Decision Element Failures in 4D Future Internet Architecture

Songqing Yue[1], Yang Xiao[1,*], and Geoffrey G. Xie[2]

[1] Dept. of Computer Science, University of Alabama, Tuscaloosa, AL 35487 USA
[2] Naval Postgraduate School, Monterey, CA 93943, USA
syue@cs.ua.edu, yangxiao@ieee.org, xie@nps.edu

Abstract. A novel 4D architecture has been presented in [1], [3] for the future Internet, advocating a decomposition of network control functions into three distinct planes: decision, dissemination, and discovery, along with a streamlined data plane, to achieve more predictable network performance. An underlying concern with the 4D architecture is that the decision making is centralized at a single entity called Decision Element (DE), whose failure may disrupt the whole network [2]. A simple approach has been proposed to increase the reliability of the system by attaching a few hot stand-by DEs to the network. These hot stand-by DEs collect information from other network elements and perform computation in the same manner as the master DE. In this work, we have created a set of experiments to verify the performance of the election algorithm based on the prototype of the 4D architecture, and experimentally evaluate the re-convergence time required for the election algorithm after a failure of the master DE.

Keywords: Future Internet, 4D architecture, Election algorithm.

1 Introduction

Functions that control a current IP network can be divided into three major planes: a data plane that deals with data packets, a control plane that coordinates the distributed routing protocols, and a management plane that controls the whole network together with protocols in the control plane and mechanisms of the data plane [2]. Today's IP networks provide ever more complicated services required by different applications and various environments. The control plane of IP networks, however, was devised to run some simple distributed protocols. To ensure the robustness of IP networks, a group of researchers have proposed totally refactoring the functions of network control and management [1]. Their proposal, termed the 4D architecture, was designed based on the following three principles: network-level objectives, network-wide views, and direct control [2]. To begin with, goals for reliability and performance should not be formulated on low-level network elements like switches and routers because those objectives may be compromised because of semantic mistakes when trying to translate network-level goals into device specific mechanisms

---

* Corresponding author. Phone: 205-348-4038; Fax: 205-348-0219.

D. Ślęzak et al. (Eds.): FGCN/ACN 2009, CCIS 56, pp. 250–258, 2009.
© Springer-Verlag Berlin Heidelberg 2009

and protocols [2]. Furthermore, it is crucial in running a reliable network to have timely and precise global views of the network events, traffic, and topology [2]. However, in today's networks, the control plane often does not have the up-to-date network-wide view, which renders a great deal of guesswork and suboptimal decisions [1]. The third principle involves the direct control over the whole network. It is much easier to satisfy network-level objectives through directly configuring the data plane. To achieve the direct control over the network, the decision-making logic cannot be embedded in protocols which are distributed among routers and switches. On the contrary, only the output of the decision-making logic should be used to control other elements in networks. In contrast, today's management plane only has indirect influence over the network, so it must reproduce the state from the control plane then carry on a complex and often manual inversion process to infer possible configuration parameters from a set of network objectives.

In the 4D architecture, all decision-making logic (such as routing) is drawn out of the routers to make a decision plane that is centralized logically at an entity called Decision Element (DE). Then network-level views and objectives can be specified and implemented by directly configuring states on particular network elements [2]. A major concern with the 4D architecture is that a failure of the DE may disrupt the operation of the whole network [2]. A recent paper [3] has proposed a simple solution to the problem, by attaching a few hot stand-by DEs to the network. At any one instant these hot stand-by DEs collect information from other network elements and perform computation in the same manner as the master DE. However, only the master DE is responsible for operating the network by sending out configuration updates to routers and switches. When the master DE fails, a new master DE will be chosen from one of the stand-by DEs by performing an election algorithm. In this work, we have created a set of experiments to verify the performance of the election algorithm based on the prototype of the 4D architecture, and conduct experiments to evaluate the re-convergence time required by the new election algorithm after a failure of the master DE.

2 Introduction of the 4D Architecture

This section provides a tutorial for the 4D architecture based on what is presented in papers [1] and [3]. Let's first introduce the concepts of the 4D architecture. The 4D architecture presents an idea of decomposing the control and management plane in today's IP networks into four elements: decision, dissemination, discovery, and data planes [3], as follows:

The data plane is implemented among network routers and switches. It offers services like IP and Ethernet packet forwarding [3]. The actions of the data plane are controlled by the states in the routers or switches which are created only by the decision plane [3]. The states in switches include the packet filters, forwarding information base (FIB), tunnels and network address translation mappings, etc [3].

The discovery plane is designed to discover physical elements that compose the network, the hardware capabilities of each switch, and the connectivity to its neighbors [3]. A border switch that connects to a neighboring network takes responsibility for discovering the logical route towards remote switches that can be reached through that neighboring network [3]. The dissemination plane maintains logical connections through which the discovered information is transmitted to the decision plane [3]. The information is exploited to form the network-level views used by the decision plane.

The main function of the dissemination plane is to maintain the connectivity that allows control information to be transmitted smoothly between the network switches and the DE [3]. In order to make the dissemination plane operate without previous configuring and setting up of physical links, the dissemination paths are designed to be separately maintained from the data routes, even though control messages may go through over the same set of physical paths as the data packets in the data plane [3]. On the contrary, in today's IP networks, the data paths need to be established before sending control and management information, and this procedure may cause a dependency circle.

The decision plane is responsible for making all decisions based on the information collected by the discovery plane. The decision-making logic is centralized to a DE that makes all decisions (including access control, load balancing, reachability, and security) controlling the operation of the whole network [3]. The DE uses this information to create controlling messages which are collected by the discovery plane, and these controlling messages are transmitted as commands to switches through the dissemination plane [3]. The network switches provide the node configuration service interface that allows the DE to command the switches. To tolerate the single point of failure, multiple hot stand-by DEs are used in practice [3].

Next we introduce how Des and routers communicate. The 4D architecture centralizes the decision-making logic that controls the whole network by drawing it out of the routers [2]. The DE communicates with the routers through the channel maintained by the dissemination plane.

There are several underlying problems. On the one hand, the dissemination paths should not depend on the successful establishment of a connecting channel beforehand. The ideal case is that the dissemination plane requires no prior configuration on routers. On the other hand, myriad information is going to be sent through the dissemination paths. The information can be Link State Advertisements (LSAs) that need to be transmitted to different places. It can also be controlling messages computed and generated by a DE and sent to routers. Those controlling messages are so indispensible that they cannot be missed silently. According to those characteristics, the dissemination plane can be designed with great freedom. Also since the main function of the dissemination plane is to transmit instruction and data, many existing standard distributed algorithms can be utilized.

Next we introduce the prototype to implement the 4D Architecture. Fig. 1a shows the software organization of the applications that constitute the prototype and are implemented on Linux [1]. The two applications are the DE and the Switch. The DE and the switch work cooperatively to implement the dissemination plane. A distributed algorithm maintains reliable logical connectivity between the switches and DEs in order to realize the dissemination service.

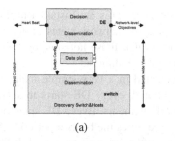
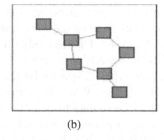

(a)   (b)

Fig. 1. (a) The overview of the prototype [1] (2) The topology created with a NS file

The discovery plane contains two major modules. One module functions to discover end hosts which are linked directly to the switch, the other to discover other neighboring switches [3]. To discover neighbors, Hello messages are exchanged. The LSAs are created based on the discovered information, are composed of the switch's interfaces status and the IDs of the switches that are directly linked to the interfaces [3]. Then the LSAs are transmitted to the DEs through the communication channels maintained by the dissemination plane. Existing filtering elements and packet forwarding protocols are used to implement the data plane. DEs and Switches communicate via the interface of configuration service. This interface is fulfilled by drivers in data plane that translates general configuration commands issued from DEs into individual configurations for those filtering elements and packet forwarding protocols [3].

The discovery, dissemination, and decision planes are implemented on DEs. Based on the information reported by the discovery plane and the specific decision algorithm, the decision plane creates a logical network-level model and calculates configuration commands for all the switches [3]. Those calculated configuration commands are transmitted to switches through the dissemination plane [3].

3   Evaluation of the Election Algorithm

3.1   Algorithm Description

In 4D architecture, an extreme design point has been taken to place all decision making logic on a DE. The prototype implements this by letting a single DE make all decisions for the whole network. A problem emerges if the DE fails or the network is partitioned so that some subnets are cut off from the current DE.

In reality, the failure of a router occurs most often because of the dysfunction of a fiber bundle or the corruption of shared resources. However, the simultaneous failure of many pieces of distributed devices is a rare occurrence. This feature of the networks and the failure models can be taken advantage of to solve the problem concerning a single failure of the DE. To be more specific, even though all DEs fail, the network can still operate based on the last states generated by DEs. All that is lost is the ability to respond to later network changes.

The prototype utilizes a hot standby DE model to solve the DE failure problem. At each instant, a master DE is responsible for creating all network states and configuring the data plane on the routers. However, many other DEs are installed in the network that gathers data from the network and compute the network states in the exact same way with the master DE. The only difference is that those hot-standby DEs keep the result of their computations to themselves without sending out.

In the prototype, the master DE can be elected in a very simple manner with the help of DE beacons. When the network is booted, every DE starts to send periodic beacons and receive data from all the network elements. Every DE spies on beacons from others for a waiting period of at least three times the beacon period (1.5s). A DE can only safely be sure it should be the master after this waiting period. It then begins to send out computation results if the DE knows it has the highest priority among all DEs from which beacons have been heard. Whenever the master DE gets a beacon from another DE whose priority is higher than its own, the master DE will immediately become a hot standby DE and stop sending data out to the network.

Based on the election algorithm described above, we can easily understand two implications. The first is that, if the master DE fails, it may take 1.5s for another DE to become the new master. The second is that, if a DE with a higher priority than the current master DE is plugged into the network and run, the current master DE will cease sending data out to routers, which will cause a 1.5 s window, during which no DE is sending commands out because the newly selected master DE is still not certain whether it will ultimately become the new master.

3.2 Evaluation Procedure

The research groups in the 4D have implemented the prototype named Tesseract in the Emulab [4] environment using Linux-based PCs as IPv4 routers [2]. Emulab is a testbed rather than a simulator [5]. It offers a framework to run user's codes on a large number of PCs that can be connected together to form a desired topology based on users' specifications.

All PCs run the standard Emulab Linux v2.4 kernel in the experiments performed during the evaluation [2]. Each PC, including those for compute-intensive DEs, has clock speed from 600 to 850 MHz and has four 100 Mbps Ethernet interfaces which can be utilized to combine PCs together to make a user-specific network topology [2].

There is a fifth control interface that is not visible to the user and is used only for experiment control (like starting or ceasing an experiment) [2]. In order to correctly relate events with the log files generated on different PCs for post experiment analysis, clocks on all PCs are synchronized by exploiting the Network Time Protocol over individual control interfaces. It has also been verified that each PC's clock is synchronized to have at most 2 ms difference from the other PCs [2]. The 4D prototype being evaluated has its own mechanism to deal with those synchronization issues, so it does not use the synchronized clocks that are used only for data analysis after experiments.

After we were accepted to the research group in Emulab, we were able to access all of the original code of the Tesseract. The study and evaluation are based entirely on the prototype code. Now we are going to specify the procedure of running the code on the Emulab and how to evaluate the election algorithm.

The prototype Tesseract can take on any of the following three roles: 1) DE: The DE is the central controller for a Tesseract network. More than one DE can be presented in the same network. At any time only one DE directly controls the network. All other DEs are hot standbys. 2) IP router: Linux kernel is the data-plane forwarding mechanism. 3) Ethernet switch: User-level click is the data-plane forwarding mechanism.

All switches (IP router/Ethernet switch) and DEs in the network must agree on whether to be IP or Ethernet. When the source is compiled, two binaries are generated, and are called 'de' and 'switch' by default. Each binary has both IP and Ethernet functionality built in. By default, the 'switch' acts as an IP router.

Below are the steps for setting up a simple 4D experiment on Emulab: 1). the first step is to download the code. Add whatever codes you would like to implement and compile it. Download the Tesseract code onto a Linux system (running RHL-9 or greater) that has gcc (v3 or v4) and perl installed. 2). untar the Tesseract code into a temporary directory on the system. This will be the 'root' directory for the code on that machine. 3). do a 'make' in the root directory to compile the Tesseract code. This generates three binaries which are called de', 'switch' and 'logdecoder' by default. The binaries are located in de/, switch/, and logdecoder/ directories respectively. 3.1). the 'de' binary is the DE and should ideally be run on a dedicated system. The 'de' takes the nodeID as input from the command line. If the nodeID is not provided, a unique nodeID is generated automatically. 3.2). the 'switch' binary is the generic Switch and should be run on all other systems that are part of the Tesseract network. The 'switch' also takes the nodeID as input from the command line. If nodeIDs are *not* supplied, unique IDs are generated automatically for each switch. 3.3). the 'logdecoder' binary can be used for parsing the logs generated by Tesseract into a format that is readable for humans. 4). An NS file is used to create a new Emulab experiment. To swap the NS file will set up physical connectivity between the several Emulab machines. The NS file should be modified so that the Emulab nodes contain the same version of the operating system as that of the machine on which Tesseract was compiled in earlier steps. For example, in our local host, in which a Linux version Ubuntu is running, the lines in the ns file are changed as follows:

```
#generated by Netbuild 1.03
set ns [new Simulator]
source tb_compat.tcl
set de1 [$ns node]
tb-set-hardware $de1 pc2000
set switch1 [$ns node]
set switch2 [$ns node]
set switch3 [$ns node]
set switch4 [$ns node]
set switch5 [$ns node]
set de2 [$ns node]
tb-set-hardware $de1 pc2000
tb-set-node-os de1 UBUNTU70-STD
tb-set-node-os switch1 UBUNTU70-STD
tb-set-node-os switch2 UBUNTU70-STD
tb-set-node-os switch3 UBUNTU70-STD
tb-set-node-os switch4 UBUNTU70-STD
tb-set-node-os switch5 UBUNTU70-STD
tb-set-node-os de2 UBUNTU70-STD

set link0 [$ns duplex-link $de1 $switch1 100Mb
0ms DropTail]
set link1 [$ns duplex-link $switch1 $switch2
100Mb 0ms DropTail]
set link2 [$ns duplex-link $switch2 $switch3
100Mb 0ms DropTail]
set link3 [$ns duplex-link $switch3 $switch4
100Mb 0ms DropTail]
set link4 [$ns duplex-link $switch4 $switch5
100Mb 0ms DropTail]
set link5 [$ns duplex-link $switch1 $switch5
100Mb 0ms DropTail]
set link6 [$ns duplex-link $de2 $switch4 100Mb
0ms DropTail]

$ns rtproto Static
$ns run
#netbuild-generated ns file ends.
```

5). upload the 'switch' binaries into the Emulab machines switch1,...,switchN. Upload the 'de' binaries into the Emulab machines de1,...deM. 6). SSH into each of the machines starting with de1 and run the respective binary: a) de1: sudo ./de -n 1000; b) de2: sudo ./de -n 1001; c) switch1: sudo ./switch -n 1; d) switch2:   sudo ./switch -n 2. 7). the above step sets up IP connectivity between switches and also to the DE, as in Fig. 1b. The DE sets up a data-plane of the switches by populating their forwarding tables. In this topology, there exist two DEs and 5 switches. We can manually terminate the master DE to measure the time taken by another DE to make the new master. Tesseract is now fully operational. We can get information from the running DE and switch,

4 Experiments Results

It is not harmful if some hot stand-by DEs fail to function as long as the master DE works well. We did several experiments to evaluate the influence caused by a master DE that fails to perform its duty. Fig. 2a displays the time consumed for a new selected master DE to be in charge of the network after the former master DE crashes. The time can be divided into three steps. The first period of time is necessary for other DEs to learn the failure of the former master DE. After all of the DEs have noticed the failure, the situation is same with the re-convergence scenario. Once the new master knows it wins the election, it will compute states for each router and send out the configuring command to each router.

With no surprises, the major part of the time consumption lies in the time consumed by the election. The election scheme has specified that every DE listens for beacons from others for 3 times the beacon period of 500ms. Therefore, it takes around 1-1.5s for a new master DE to take over all of the responsibility of controlling the whole network.

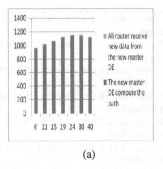
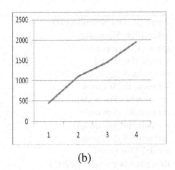

(a)   (b)

Fig. 2. (a) Time for a DE to become a new master DE after the old master fails. The X-axis shows the number of nodes in an experimental topology, and the Y-axis the re-convergence time in milliseconds. (b) Relationship between the least waiting period (x-axis) and mean propagation delay (y-axis) between the master DE and the nearest standby DE in milliseconds.

Table 1. The shortest waiting period (T) required by a new DE to learn the failure of the master DE

The least waiting period(T)	2	2	2	3	4	3	2
Topology Scale	6	11	15	19	24	30	40

Evaluation has also been made using different values for the least waiting period (T) in different topologies. The combinations tested are listed in Table 1. Further investigation shows that the shortest waiting period (T) has no direct relation to the scale of the whole topology. Rather, it relates closely to the delay between the master DE and the nearest standby DE. Fig. 2b shows that the mean propagation delay (y-axis) between the master DE and the nearest standby DE increases linearly with the least waiting period (T), i.e., the least number of a beacon period. This indicates that the system is scalable.

5 Conclusion

This work introduced the idea and concepts of the 4D architecture, according to which a prototype has been implemented. Via experiments, based on the prototype, we have evaluated certain parameters related to the election algorithm that is used to choose a new master DE whenever the old master DE fails. The evaluation result shows the viability of the 4D architecture by applying the Hot Standby DEs and the influence of different parameters on the election algorithm.

Acknowledgement

The work was supported in parts by Naval Postgraduate School, via ONR and Fleet Industrial Supply Center-San Diego (FISCSD), under the grant number N00244-08-1-0020. We appreciate the help from Yan Hong of Carnegie Mellon University who has offered the source code of 4D Prototype and also thank those who helped us to access the emulab.

References

1. Greenberg, A., Hjalmtysson, G., Maltz, D.A., Myers, A., Rexford, J., Xie, G., Yan, H., Zhan, J., Zhang, H.: A clean slate 4D approach to network control and management. ACM Computer Communication Review (October 2005)
2. Greenberg, A., Hjalmtysson, G., Maltz, D.A., Myers, A., Rexford, J., Xie, G., Yan, H., Zhan, J., Zhang, H.: Refactoring Network Control and Management: A Case for the 4D Architecture, CMU CS Technical Report CMU-CS-05-117 (September 2005)
3. Yan, H., Maltz, D.A., Ng, T.S.E., Gogineni, H., Zhang, H., Cai., Z.: Tesseract: A 4D Network Control Plane. In: Proc. of NSDI 2007 (2007)

4. White, B., Lepreau, J., Stoller, L., Ricci, R., Guruprasad, S., Newbold, M., Hibler, M., Barb, C., Joglekar, A.: An integrated experimental environment for distributed systems and networks. In: Proc. Operating Systems Design and Implementation, December 2002, pp. 255–270 (2002)
5. http://www.emulab.net/
6. Myers, A., Ng, E., Zhang, H.: Rethinking the service model: Scaling Ethernet to a million nodes. In: Proc. ACM SIGCOMM Workshop on Hot Topics in Networking (November 2004)
7. Maltz, D., Xie, G., Zhan, J., Zhang, H., Hjalmtysson, G., Greenberg, A.: Routing design in operational networks: A look from the inside. In: Proc. ACM SIGCOMM (August 2004)

A Study on Broadcasting Video Quality by Routing Protocols in the IPTV Network

Mi-Jin Kim and Jong-Wook Jang

Department of Computer Engineering, Dong-Eui University, Busan, Republic of Korea
agicap@nate.com, jwjang@deu.ac.kr

Abstract. As multimedia contents rapidly spread and high-speed broadband IP network technologies develop, development of wire and wireless technologies, multimedia and image process technologies through IP network enables various types of service such as IPTV and VoIP. Individual service of communication companies and broadcasters coexist and evolve into a convergence service. Typical broadcast/communication convergence service, IPTV is the strongest application model in this service. As IPTV-like services increase, high-definition data processing through Internet protocol emerges as the main issue of the communication industries that should implement various Internet services.

This paper provides network build-up methods for the effective IPTV services by implementing the standard routing protocol RIP used in small-sized area and the link state routing protocol OSPF used in large autonomic network, implementing the present network IPv4 and next generation internet protocol IPv6 in each routing protocol, measuring the PSNR of real-time broadcasting picture quality and measuring and evaluating the performance of IPv4 and IPv6 based on the values.

Keywords: IPTV, Routing Protocol, Next-generation Internet Protocol, IPv6, IP Network, PSNR, RIP, OSPF.

1 Introduction

As today Internet communication is widely used in home and companies, various types of service are being developed based on the IP network. The best-effort method of existing IP network is limited to provide VoIP, VPN and other various multimedia services that require the service quality. So, in order to overcome this limitation, the future communication network is expected to evolve from circuit-based PSTN into IP-based NGN (Next Generation Network). [1, 2]

Especially, the most typical application of broadcasting / communication convergence service, IPTV (Internet Protocol Television) is on the rise as a new paradigm to lead the future broadband convergence services. As IPTV-like services increase, the high-definition data processing through the internet protocol becomes the main issue in communication industries in order to process the increased data and implement various internet services.

This research used the dynamic routing protocol which improves the network performance by using the most suitable routing path of assigned protocols. On the most

D. Ślęzak et al. (Eds.): FGCN/ACN 2009, CCIS 56, pp. 259–266, 2009.

typical dynamic routing RIP and OSPF, we investigated the traffic effect by routing protocol. We will find the most suitable routing protocol for network bandwidth by measuring and analyzing the broadcasting images with PSNR.

This paper is organized as follows; Chapter 2 explains IPTV, Routing Protocol and PSNR. Chapter 3 explains that implementing network environment and measuring, analyzing and assessing its performances. Finally, Chapter 4 is for the results.

2 Paper Preparation

2.1 IP Network

Information communication technology is preparing a big and innovative change. Core of the change is to unite various elements of communication including communication and distributed computing, voice and data, electrical communication and data communication and control and management. And also, it is to attain the convergence of various networks and services to provide multi services by adding various media such as voice, data and image to a single network with sophisticated performance and capability. That is materialized by NGN of open architecture.

NGN is packet-based network, which unites telephone system, ATM, frame relay, network for personal use and wireless network. ITU (International Telecommunication Union) defines that NGN is packet-based network and IP-based network. ETSI (European Telecommunications Standardization Institute) defines that NGN is packet-based network which can provide the new services in phases using open interface. [1, 2]

The main characteristic of NGN is convergence and packet-based. It can provide various additional services such as internet telephone and multimedia messaging efficiently while receiving voices, data and images simultaneously. In addition, because it can simultaneously process several traffics by packet unit on single communication network, the circuit efficiency largely improves and voice telecom services can be provided at much lower cost than existing method. In Korea, BcN (Broadband convergence Network) is being developed. It is the next-generation convergence network, which makes quality-guaranteed broadband multimedia services that combine communication, broadcasting and internet available wherever, whenever and with no interrupt. [3]

2.2 IPTV

The notion of IPTV [4] is varied based on the service types and users. The IPTV standardization organization, ITU-T Focus Group defines that "it is multimedia services like television, video, audio, documents, graphics and data services through quality-guaranteed, secure and reliable IP network."

In IPTV service concept of Fig. 1, various visual media are provided to the streaming server and it is delivered to the subscribers through IP network on user requests.

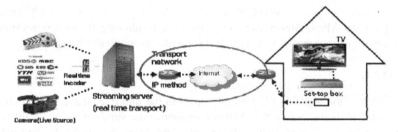

Fig. 1. IPTV service architecture

ITU-T IPTV Focus Group was organized within ITU-T (International Telecommu-nication Union-Telecommunication Standardization Sector) in July 2006 in order to revitalize the IPTV services, develop the technologies and secure the interrelation. The standardization works for IPTV structure and requirements, QoS, security, network control, middleware terminals and interpretability are on the progress in connection with various standard organizations including IETF (Internet Engineering Task Force), ATIS (Alliance for Telecommunications Industry Solution), DVB (Digi-tal Video Broadcasting) and ATSC(Advanced Television Systems Committee).

2.3 Routing Protocol

2.3.1 RIP (Routing Information Protocol)
RIP [5] is a distance vector protocol to calculate the path by hop count and it is IGP (Interior Gateway Protocol) used for routing within AS (Autonomous System). RIP chooses the path with the smallest number of passing-through router of various paths to receipt point regardless of bandwidth or latency. The number of passing-through router is hop count and RIP is calculated by only hop count. If the hop count is over 16, RIP can't deliver the packet to the receipt point and it exchanges the routing information by delivering the routing information to adjacent router in every 30 sec-onds. In exchanging the routing information, the full update method which delivers not only the changed network information but also all network information to the adjacent router periodically is used.

Hop count is not suitable for large network though it can be simply built and oper-ated. And, because only hop count can be used to choose the path, it is not possible to choose the optimal path. It is slow to change the link status because of distance vector algorithm and it can't process the subnet information.

2.3.2 OSPF (Open Shortest Path First)
OSPF [6, 7] is a routing protocol with typical link state algorithm that is used in large autonomic network. Each router organizes whole network topology and calculates routing tables by exchanging the topology and state of local link to other routers. The most suitable path is set with link state algorithm. The cost to calculate the path is based on the bandwidth.

Because OSPF transmits not the state information periodically but the only changed state information, the collecting time is faster than RIP. Also, it prevents router per-formance lowering due to exchange of much routing information and saves the band by organizing the layered structure of network by area. It supports VLSM (Variable Length Subnet Mask) and Route Summarization to allocate IP addresses efficiently and supports various network subnet masks in order to subdivide the network.

2.4 PSNR

Loss compression algorithm is generally used in the multimedia application area that requires the high compression rate. It can recognize the similarity visually though the compressed image is not equal to the original one. In order to quantify the proximity to the original data, it needs some types of distortion measurement.

Distortion measurement is to measure the proximity to the original copy with some distortion standard and it is divided into cognitive distortion and mathematical distortion. The cognitive distortion regards the visual system and visibility about the image distortion characteristic, whereas the mathematical distortion considers the quantity difference and use mainly MSE, SNR and PSNR.

Though you may think that the image quality assessment is subjective, there is an objective standard. That is the value PSNR (Peak Signal To Noise Rate) [8] also used in the international standard organizations. It is technological term to represent the rate between peek signal and noise that interrupts it. With this, the quality of compressed images are compared and measured to the original images.

$$PSNR = 10 \cdot \log_{10}\left(\frac{(2^n - 1)^2}{MSE}\right) = 20 \cdot \log_{10}\left(\frac{2^n - 1}{\sqrt{MSE}}\right)$$

Literally, PSNR is the maximum value (peak signal) to noise rate. It is measured by log unit, and it is determined by (Square of the number of maximum samples in image. Here, 'n' denotes the number of bit of image sample.), the rate between original image and lost image or by MSE (Mean Squared Error) between video frames.

$$MSE = \frac{1}{mn} \sum_{i=0}^{m-1} \sum_{j=0}^{n-1} \| A(i,j) - K(i,j) \|^2$$

MSE (Mean Squared Error) is the mean squared error between two images with same size. The less MSE is, the more equal the image size is. That is, if the decibel is high, the noise is low and the image quality is high. And, the higher PSNR is, the higher the image quality is and vice versa.

3 Implementation of Network Environment and Performance Measurement

3.1 Implementation of Network Environment

The implementation of RIP and OSPF network environment is like Fig. 2 and the Area is organized by Area0 and Area1 to present the large network system of OSPF.

Switches and routers of Cisco are used for investigation of real-time broadcasting image quality. Because present ISPs use Catalyst 6500 series of switch in connection to servers, router 3700 series in middle network and Catalyst 4500 series of switch in

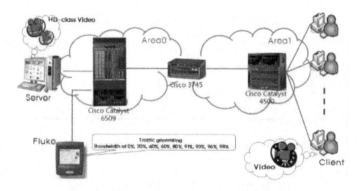

Fig. 2. Network environment of Routing Protocol

connection to the subscribers, we organized like these. Fluke is a traffic generator to make network environment by forecasting the data increase on network by users increase. We measured PSNR of real-time broadcasting image quality by increasing the packet generating rate by 0%, 20%, 40%, 60%, 80%, 91%, 93%, 96% and 98% of bandwidth.

Cisco Catalyst 6509 is suitable for the application that requires large bandwidth and provides multi-layered switching. Cisco 3745 is Multiservice Access Router and provides various capabilities such as network restoration, scalability, QoS and security. Cisco Catalyst 4500 is Multilayer Switch and provides the optimized business services and user accessibility. IOS environment of each switch is ver. 12.2 and IOS environment of router is ver. 12.4. Fluke Optiview^{TM} Series III provides communication path check, real-time usage check, error analysis, protocol analysis and present traffic check with Trace Switch Route.

3.2 Performance Measurement of RIP and OSPF

As mentioned in Implementation of Network Environment, we measured performance of RIP and OSPF by transmitting the HD images by streaming service from server and comparing PSNR of images that clients received to original images of server.

Fig. 3 shows the server monitor of RIP and OSPF in IPv4 network, and x-axis is time and y-axis is datagram per second. The transmission stream is more running in OSPF than RIP.

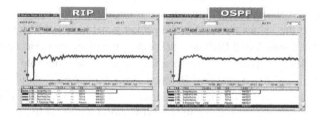

Fig. 3. Server monitor of RIP/OSPF in IPv4 Network

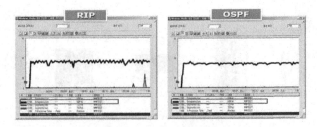

Fig. 4. Server monitor of RIP/OSPF in IPv6 Network

Fig. 5. Video comparison by PSNR value

Table 1. PSNR value of OSPF/RIP in IPv4 Network

IPv4	0%	20%	40%	60%	80%	91%	93%	96%	98%
OSPF	49.8	49.9	49.8	48.2	49.9	48.1	42.3	45.5	9.6
RIP	49.3	44.1	47	46.9	43	44.1	19.9	14.4	8.2

In Fig. 4, the transmission run in IPv6 network shows smoother running in OSPF than RIP.

When we measured PSNR of server images and client images by transmitting real-time images, we found that the image quality would be different based on PSNR. When PSNR is over 40dB, it is same as original images by naked eyes. When PSNR is 30dB and less, it shows thermal images and frame distortion.

We measured the values by varying the packet generating rates by OSPF and RIP protocol in IPv4 network and IPv6 network and summarized in Table 1 and 2. ('%' in the table is packet generating rate.) When the packet generating rate is between 0% and 91%, there is no image quality difference. From 93%, OSPF shows better quality than RIP. In Table 2, when the packet generating rate is between 0% and 93%, there is no image quality difference. From 96%, OSPF shows better quality than RIP.

Table 2. PSNR value of OSPF/RIP in IPv6 Network

IPv6	0%	20%	40%	60%	80%	91%	93%	96%	98%
OSPF	49.2	49.6	50.2	49.7	47.9	46.4	43.4	41.1	13.3
RIP	44.2	48.5	45.5	42.9	43.6	45.3	42.2	30.9	13.1

3.3 Performance Analysis

In Fig. 6, when the packet generating rate is between 0% and 91%, there is no image quality difference between RIP and OSPF in IPv4 network. From 93%, OSPF shows better quality than RIP. There is no image quality difference in 0~93% of packet generating rate in IPv6 network. From 96%, OSPF shows better quality than RIP. Therefore, when 0~93% of packet generating rate in IPv4 and IPv6 network, RIP routing protocol is more efficient than OSPF routing protocol with complex network design. In order to confirm the validity of the proposed method, it has been first applied to the simulation experiment. In this simulation experiment, the random noise is generated by use of Gaussian random numbers.

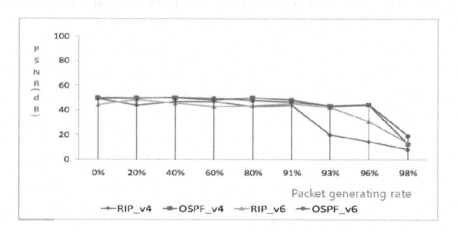

Fig. 6. Video comparison by PSNR value graph

4 Conclusion

This research investigated the real-time image quality based on the routing protocols in IPTV network with mathematical distortion measurement. Of two protocols, the performance of OSPF routing protocol is more stable and better than RIP. But in 0~91% of packet generating rate in IPv4 network and 0~93% in IPv6 network, the RIP routing protocol performance is also good. That's why small-sized ISP should use the RIP routing protocol not OSPF routing protocol with complex network design. The method to use and manage the network performance efficiently satisfying the QoS requirements at the same time is needed.

Acknowledgments. This paper was supported in part by MKE (Ministry of Knowledge Economy) & IITA (Institute for Information Technology Advancement). (08-Infrastructure-13, Convergence of IT Devices Institute Busan) and Joint Technology Development Supporting Business among Industry Academy and research institute.

References

1. Next Generation Network Development in OECD. In: OECD (June 2004)
2. NGN (2006), http://www.ngncon.com
3. Bcn Standard model. In: KICS (March 2005)
4. Choerakgwon: IPTV Service Technology and scenarios. OSIA Standard & Technology 2007 #1 Article 27(65) (March 2007)
5. Hedrick, C.: Routing Information Protocol. In: RFC 1058 (June 1988)
6. won, C.J., Yigwanghui: Implementation of performance analysis tools for network design and expansion. KICS KNOM Review 6(1), 52–58 (2003)
7. won, C.J., et al.: Simulation System Design for Network analysis. In: KICS Summer General Academic Conference 2002, Muju, Korea, July 11-13, vol. 25 (2002)
8. VQEG Draft Version 1.11 Multimedia Group TEST PLAN, VQEG Multimedia working group(MM), February 14 (2006)

A Study on Effective RS Deployment in Mobile WiMAX MMR

M.H. Bae[1], B. Otgonbayar[2], Ghishigjargal[3], and J.W. Jang[4,*]

[1] MIU
[2] MUST
[3] ETRI
[4] DEU

baemhss@hanmail.net, b_otgonbayar2002@yahoo.com,
ghishigjargal@yahoo.com, jwjang@deu.ac.kr

Abstract. IEEE 802.16j aims to enhance the coverage, per user throughput and system capacity of IEEE 802.16e. Compared with base station (BS), RS does not need a wire-line backhaul and has much lower hardware complexity. Using RSs can significantly reduce the deployment cost of the system. In this paper, the optimal relay station (RS) location and the bandwidth allocation for RS in fixed RS based radio cooperation system are investigated to maximize the data rate when the RS adopts amplify -forward (AF) scheme. For maximum achievable data rate, the MS selectively accesses BS or RS and the optimal RS location is obtained to maximize the system capacity for relaying system with three sectors within which there is one fixed RS. And then the optimal bandwidth allocation for the RS is gotten by calculating the percentage of MS which accesses RS and SNReff(the composite of SNRsr + SNRrd) and SNRsd. Simulation is implemented to find the optimal RS location and bandwidth allocation for RS in IEEE 802.16j based relay system.

Keywords: IEEE 802.16j, Mobile WiMAX, MMR, Optimal relay station, SNReff.

1 Introduction

Improved data transmission rate is the common purpose of next generation mobile communication system such as 3G LTE, IEEE 802.16 and 802.20 which are running standardizing.

In order to realize this new, technologies such as OFDM, MIMO, and smart antenna are expected to be introduced. Because High frequency of 2~6GHz than 2GHz used in current mobile communication system is inevitable to use, shadowing zone of city seems to increase [1][2].

For Coverage extension through settlement of shadowing zone and data throughput enhancement, it is easy to increase number of base station.[3][4][5]

Base station coverage is 2~5km in current mobile communication system but will be several hundred meters in next generation mobile communication system. So it is

---

* Corresponding author.

D. Ślęzak et al. (Eds.): FGCN/ACN 2009, CCIS 56, pp. 267–274, 2009.
© Springer-Verlag Berlin Heidelberg 2009

necessary to increase many base stations. Of course if a number of user increase according to base station increase, increase of base station is effective, but the number of user is saturated already in advanced nations.

So a relation station is one method in order to solve this problem. Mobile Multi-hop Relay concept is introduced in order to improve transfer rate of user and extension of service area of conventional mobile communication system or portable internet system and made representatively standard regular applied to Mobile WiMax (WiBro) in IEEE 802.16j and activity in order to adopt IMT-Advanced WiMAX in future is being performed in IEEE 802.16m.

Network (WMAN) technology by way of IEEE 802.16 has been well recognized to serve as the backhaul of broadband wireless access in the emerging fourth-generation telecommunication system.

2   System Models

To improve the performance in a relay network, some cooperative schemes have been developed recently [7][8]. Besides classic amplify-forward (AF), decode-forward (DF) and compress-forward (CF) schemes, several distributed turbo coded (DTC) schemes are developed for a two-hop relay network in, namely the hard information relaying (HIR) DTC scheme, soft information relaying (SIR) DTC scheme and decode-amplify-forward (DAF) scheme [9][10][11].

Amplify-forward is characterized by the fact that the relay rescales the power level of the analog signal waveform received from the source node without additional processing. AF requires lower implementation complexity in digital signal processing at the relay node and is operable at all channel conditions including when the inter-user channel is at outage.

From the coding perspective, amplify-forward can be viewed as a way of forwarding the signal in its soft reliability form.

Consider the basic relay system in Figure 1 that comprises a source node, a relay node and a destination node.

We consider half-duplex transmit modes, where user cooperation is operated in two stages: the broadcasting stage, where the source broadcasts a packet of data to both the destination and the relay, and the relaying stage, where the relay processes and forwards part or all of the observations to the destination.

The destination then combines the signals received from both stages to make a best estimation of the original data. Throughout the paper, we will use subscripts S, R, D and SR, SD, RD to denote the quantities pertaining to the source, relay, and destination

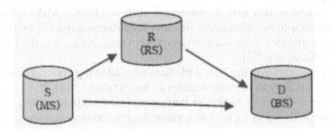

Fig. 1. Block diagram of a two-hop relay system

nodes, and those pertaining to the source-relay, source-destination and relay-destination channels, respectively [12].

For simplification, AWGN and block Rayleigh fading channel are assumed.

The signal received in relay and destination are described as

$$y_{SR}(t) = \alpha_{SR}x_s(t) + n_{SR}(t) \tag{1}$$

$$y_{SD}(t) = \alpha_{SD}x_s(t) + n_{SD}(t) \tag{2}$$

$$y_{RD}(t) = \alpha_{RD}x_R(t) + n_{RD}(t) \tag{3}$$

Where, x is the transmitted signal, y is the received signal and α is the channel state information. In the case of AWGN, α is a constant of 1.

In the case of block fading, α follows a Rayleigh distribution with variance of 1 remains fixed over a block of fixed size, and changes independently between successive blocks.

The addictive white Gaussian noises, n_{SR}, n_{SD} and n_{RD} have zero mean and variances δ_{SR}^2, δ_{SD}^2 and δ_{RD}^2 respectively.

For ease of analysis, we constrain each node to normalize the average transmit power per channel bit to unit before transmission, where the average is taken over the entire packet.

The SNR of a channel, γ, is defined as

$$\gamma \triangleq \frac{1}{N_0} = \frac{1}{2\delta^2} \tag{4}$$

We consider spatially independent channels among the source, the relay and the destination. We further assume that the instantaneous channel condition is known to the receivers (but not to the transmitter), so that the decoder can exploit efficient soft decoding algorithms.

Based on the AF, DF and DAF schemes from [9] and the Gaussian approximation method, we investigate how to locate RS location effectively [13] and bandwidth division to achieve the maximum system capacity for IEEE 802.16j-based relaying system.

The transmission mode of the IEEE 802.16j-based uplink system is depicted in Fig. 2, where MS, RS and BS are respectively the S, R and D in Fig. 1. The uplink subframe is divided into access zone and relay zone, and the MS can only access RS or BS.

For simplification, the time resource is equivalently divided between access zone and relay zone, but the bandwidth occupied by RS is to be determined. The system structure consists of three sectors as shown in Fig. 3, and within each sector there is one fixed RS locating at the angular bisector [7][14].

RS is d_{RD} apart from BS, while MS location is decided by the parameter pair (d_{SD}, θ), where $0 < d_{SD} \leq 1$ and $0 \leq \theta \leq \frac{1}{6}\pi$ due to the structure symmetry of the sector.

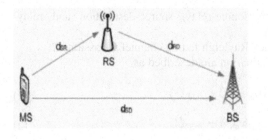
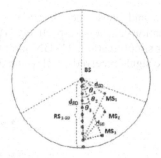

Fig. 2. Transmission mode of the IEEE 802. 16j-based relaying system(uplink)(left)   **Fig. 3.** IEEE 802.16j system structure (right)

The SNR one hop link, γ , is

$$\gamma_{SD} = 10log_{10}\frac{P_{r(sd)}}{N_0} \tag{5}$$

$$\gamma_{SR} = 10log_{10}\frac{P_{r(sr)}}{N_0} \tag{6}$$

$$\gamma_{RD} = 10log_{10}\frac{P_{r(rd)}}{N_0} \tag{7}$$

Where $P_{r(sd,sr,rd)}$ is the receive power, N_0 is the noise covariance. In this study, we denoted d_{SD}, d_{SR} and d_{RD},

d_{SD}= 50m - 1000m, d_{RD} = 100m - 1000m.

$$d_{SR} = d_{SD}^2 + d_{RD}^2 \ 12d_{SD}d_{RD}cos\theta \tag{8}$$

The effective SNR of the composite S-R-D link is

$$\gamma_{SRD} = \frac{2\gamma_{SR}\gamma_{RD}}{1 + 2\gamma_{SR} + 2\gamma_{RD}} \tag{9}$$

According to the Shannon's capacity definition, the upper-bound of per-hop rate through a binary-input AWGN(Additive White Gaussian Noise) channel with SNR γ in terms of bit/symbol/Hz is given by [8]

$$C = \frac{1}{2}log_2(1 + \gamma) \tag{10}$$

Using the equations (5)-(10), the link capacity of the S-D and S-R-D link can be calculated, and consequently the access point for the concerned MS can be determined.

The MSs are assumed to be uniformly distributed in the cell, and the upper bound of the throughput for the ith MS is

$$C_i(d_{RD}) = max\{C_{SD}, C_{SRD}\} \tag{11}$$

Which is the function of the location of RS,, and the location of the ith MS, d_{SD} and θ .

3 Simulation Condition

We described the optimal RS location and percentage bandwidth for RS in the IEEE802.16j based relaying system using MATLAB GUI. The algorithm for simulation is as shown in fig. 4 using equations 1 to 11.

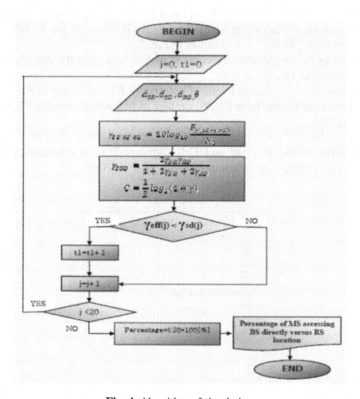

Fig. 4. Algorithm of simulation

Table 1. Basic simulation parameters

Parameter	Value	Parameter	Value
Carrier frequency	2.5GHz	RS receive antenna gain	7dBi
Cell radius	1000m	MS receive antenna gain	0dBi
Sector angle	120^0	Noise power	-69dBm
BS transmit power	40dBm	Channel model	AWGN
RS transmit antenna power	37dBm	Path loss model	20log(d)+ 39.66dB
MS transmit antenna power	24dBm	Number of RSs	10
BS receive antenna gain	17dBi	Number of MSs	20
		θ angles	$\pi/3, \pi/9$

Also Basic simulation parameters are listed in Table 1. We changed angle between RS and MS.

4 Simulation Results

Finally We make user interface of the optimal RS location and bandwidth allocation in order to calculate Percentage of MS accessing BS directly.for Mobile WiMAX MMR system in MATLAB GUI as shown in Fig. 5.

Based on Fig. 5, we calculate Percentage of MS accessing BS directly versus RS location as shown in Fig. 6.

From Fig. 6, MSs will access to one of both(BS or RS) according to RS location. When RS locates at 1000m from BS, Percentage of MS which accesses BS directly is from 60% to 65%.

And in order to get optimal RS location from Fig. 7(a) by MATLAB, SNReff(effective SNR) is γ srd and Cell Capacity 7(b) is calculated from Here, $c = \frac{1}{2} log_2(1 + \gamma)$ SNReff is the composite of SNRsr + SNRrd.

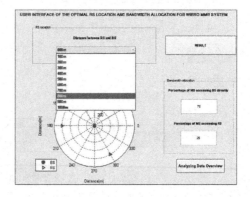

Fig. 5. Graphic User Interface (GUI) of the Optimal RS location model

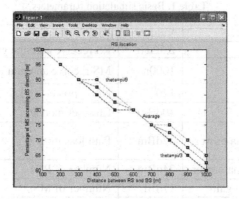

Fig. 6. Percentage of MS accessing BS directly versus RS location using AF scheme

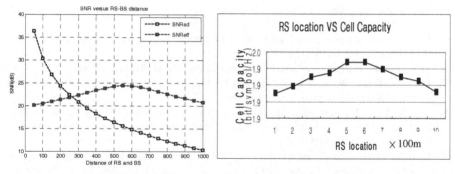

(a) SNR vs. distance of RS and BS.   (b) Cell capacity vs. distance of RS and BS

Fig. 7. (a) SNR VS Distance of RS and BS.   (b) Cell capacity VS Distance of RS and BS.

On the Fig. 7(a), SNReff competes with SNRsd and MS will select higher SNR. MS will select RS from 250m instead of BS. But Optimal RS location is 550m. In other word if RS will be installed, it needs to install RS which is at 550m from BS in order to maximize data rate. And band allocation can be 17~20% in case of 550m of distance RS-BS.

5   Conclusion

We simulate how to locate RS effectively using Matlab in Mobile WiMAX MMR. We conclude a relation between RS location and Percentage of MS accessing BS directly.

We also analyze the performances according to pi/9 and pi/3 angles. From the results of simulation , The percentage of MS accessing BS directly varies with the RS location. When RS locates at 1000m from BS, Percentage of MS which accesses BS directly is from 60% to 65%. And angle doesn't affect on Percentage of MS accessing BS directly much.

SNReff competes with SNRsd on the Figure 7 and MS will select higher SNR. MS will select RS from 250m instead of BS. But Optimal RS location is 550m. In other word if RS will be installed, it needs to install RS which is at 550m from BS in order to maximize data rate. And band allocation can be 17~20% in case of distance RS-BS.

References

1. IEEE Std 802.16-2004, IEEE Standard for Local and Metropolitan Area Networks, Part 16: Air Interface for Fixed Broadband Wireless Access Systems (October 2004)
2. Kim, Y.I., Shin, J.C., Ahn, J.H.: Trend of IEEE 802.16 Mobile Multi-hop Relay. Electronic trend analysis (June 2006)
3. Pabst, R., Walke, B.H., Schultz, D.C., Herhold, P., Yanikomeroglu, H., Mukherjee, S., Viswanathan, H., Lott, M., Zirwas, W., Dohler, M., Aghvami, H., Falconer, D.D., Fettweis, G.P.: Relay-based deployment concepts for wireless and mobile broadband radio. IEEE Commun. Magazine, 80–89 (September 2004)

4. Sendonaris, A., Erkip, E., Aazhang, B.: User cooperation diversity-Part I: system description. IEEE Trans. Commun. 51(11), 1927–1938 (2003)
5. User cooperation diversity- Part II: implementation aspects and performance analysis. IEEE Trans. Commun. 51(11), 1939–1948 (2003)
6. Sydir, J. (ed.): Harmonized Contribution on 802.16j (Mobile Multihop Relay)
7. Peng, Y., Wang, W., Kim Il, Y.: Optimal RS location and bandwidth allocation for relay system with decode-amplify-forward scheme
8. Bao, X., Li, J.: Efficient message relaying for wireless user cooperation: Decode-Amplify-Forward (DAF) and hybrid DAF and coded cooperation. IEEE Trans. Wireless Comm. 6(11), 3975–3984 (2007)
9. Bao, X., Li, J.: Decode-amplify-forward (DAF): A new class of forwarding strategy in wireless relay channel. In: Proc. IEEE Workshop on Signal Processing Advances in Wireless Commun. (SPAWC) (June 2005)
10. Bao, X., Li, J. (Tiffany): Decode-Amplify-Forward (DAF): A New Class of Forwarding Strategy for Wireless Relay Channels, Department of Electrical and Computer Engineering Lehigh University, Bethlehem, PA 18015
11. Yu, M., Li, J. (Triffani): Amplify-Forward and Decode-Forward: The Impact of Location and Capacity Contour, Lehigh University, Bethlehem, PA 18015.
12. Yu, Y., Murphy, S., Murphy, L.: Planning Base Station and Relay Station Locations in IEEE 802.16j Multi-hop Relay Networks. In: Informatics University College, Dublin, Ireland
13. 盧曉珍, 詹竣安, 陳建維, Deployment Concepts for the IEEE 802.16j networks Team 39: r95942045

Architecting Adaptable Security Infrastructures for Pervasive Networks through Components

Marc Lacoste

Orange Labs, France
marc.lacoste@orange-ftgroup.com

Abstract. Security management for pervasive networks should be fundamentally flexible. The dynamic and heterogeneous character of these environments requires a security infrastructure which can be tailored to different operating conditions, at variable levels of granularity, during phases of design, deployment, and execution. This is possible with a component-based security architecture. We illustrate the benefits of this approach by presenting AMISEC, an integrated authentication and authorization middleware. Through the component paradigm, AMISEC supports different network topologies of TTPs, cryptographic algorithms, protocols, or trust management strategies, resulting in a fully *à la carte* security infrastructure.

1 Introduction

The promise of pervasive computing to be "*optimally connected, anywhere, anytime*" implies an "optimal" management of security. What does this mean in practice? The large number and heterogeneity of devices, platforms, and networks, their complex, rich, and dynamic relationships – including a high degree of distribution and mobility – the absence of boundaries for systems which have not real inside nor outside amount from the security viewpoint to a collection of shifting, contradictory requirements. Protecting such systems thus becomes a real nightmare. This puzzle may only be tackled with a highly flexible security infrastructure, adaptable to changing conditions, to guarantee the most appropriate level of security. Three main issues remain unsolved: identity, privacy, and trust management [21].

Identity management has become a cornerstone of pervasive network security. Services are now accessed under a growing number of partial digital identities. They describe a subset of properties associated with a user, valid in a given context (e.g., car, home, office, etc.), and often linked with "real" identifying information. Many solutions have been proposed to federate identities across multiple domains [38], but are usually not well integrated with mechanisms for effective enforcement of privileges [36].

Privacy should also be addressed, since it is a key element to user acceptance of these new technologies. Several degrees of communications anonymity and unlinkability of interactions are desirable, depending on the service accessed. Yet, privacy-preserving infrastructures are still in their infancy [23], few frameworks being really available [27].

D. Ślęzak et al. (Eds.): FGCN/ACN 2009, CCIS 56, pp. 275–292, 2009.

A realistic model of trust for an open environment is needed as well. This notion remains largely not understood, with little agreement on trust models, and mostly closed platforms for managing trust [8]. For all those dimensions, an integrated and flexible security solution is clearly missing to support several security objectives, policies, mechanisms, and protocols. For instance, to capture different network topologies for the Trusted Third Parties (TTPs) involved in the infrastructure.

This objective is within reach by choosing a component-based security architecture. The component paradigm allows to reason in terms of system approach for the design of the infrastructure, with several sub-frameworks dealing with authentication, authorization, privacy, and trust management. This choice makes the infrastructure highly customizable at different levels of granularity depending on how the components are connected and deployed. The infrastructure is also reconfigurable by simple replacement of components.

We illustrate the benefits of this design approach by presenting AMISEC (AMbient Intelligence SECurity), a lightweight *Authentication and Authorization Infrastructure (AAI)*. Thanks to its component-based security architecture, AMISEC provides full flexibility for managing authentication and authorization using certificates, allowing different deployment topologies of TTPs, use of several types of certificates, cryptographic algorithms, security protocols, or strategies for privacy and trust management. We validated our design by prototyping in Java a proof-of-concept implementation on embedded devices. We also evaluated the infrastructure on sample scenarios for the home environment such as seamless authentication, both in connected and disconnected modes. We finally assessed the feasibility of realizing an extension of AMISEC for privacy.

The paper is organized as follows. Sections 2 and 3 first review related work, and give some key requirements for a security architecture for pervasive networks. Section 4 then provides some background on component-based design, and introduces the security model chosen for authentication and authorization. Section 5 describes the design and implementation of AMISEC. Finally, Section 6 presents some evaluation results on the flexibility of the infrastructure.

2   Related Work

To guarantee security of pervasive networks, many building blocks have been available for a long-time but in separate contexts. A great number of infrastructures have been proposed for authentication or privilege management, but with no real integration effort. These solutions generally present heterogeneity and scalability issues, with little possibilities for adaptation. The scheme which perhaps most reflects this situation is identity-based entity authentication through exchange of certificates managed by a PKI [29]. Many types of certificates [25,30,48] have been proposed, but infrastructure interoperability remains difficult. PKI architectures are usually quite expensive to deploy and manage. They are thus perceived as too monolithic for pervasive networks. For instance, they generally do not support both hierarchical and P2P topologies of TTPs, where devices may be both clients and certification authorities. Similarly, entity authentication is restricted to verification of identity, but not of other attributes. Some solutions to federate identities have been proposed [1,2,38], but with little support for authorization or privacy. Some integration efforts [36,37] have been undertaken such as the application of PKIs to authorization through attribute certificates [26], and the development of Privilege Management Infrastructures (PMI) [18,39], but adaptation capabilities remain limited. The agent-based PKI proposed in [28] allows different deployment topologies for TTPs, certificate formats, and protocols, and is similar to our approach, but does not address privacy.

These solutions are generally not functional in disconnected mode. They assume a TTP such as a security server to be available on-line. Many new trust models have been proposed [8] to handle disconnected modes situations, such as reputation-based trust management systems [6,7]. Yet, there is no real agreement on an adequate and realistic model of trust. Furthermore, those systems do not really allow tuning the authentication method depending on the connectivity to a TTP.

Privacy-preserving security infrastructures so far received very little attention [15]. Research mostly focused on languages such as [46] to negotiate a level of privacy, and on advanced cryptography such as anonymous credentials [17,19,15] and new types of signatures [20,33,43,45]. Pseudonymous certificates have also been investigated in the context of PKI/PMIs [12,13,22]. By and large, anonymity techniques for Internet [23,24] do not apply well to pervasive environments due to limited resources. A balance between transparent (profile management on a server) and user-controlled (user-driven release of attributes) solutions still remains to be found [27].

Existing solutions thus lack adaptation capabilities in terms of deployment, security services, and protocols. They also require too many resources to be directly usable on limited devices. A more flexible approach to security is therefore required.

3   Architectural Requirements

A distinguishing feature of pervasive environments is the dynamic interweaving of a great diversity of networks and devices. The resulting multiplicity of shifting protection requirements calls for a highly flexible security infrastructure, addressing several major challenges:

(1) **Integrated authentication and authorization.** Identity and privilege management are usually handled separately. Instead, a single *Authentication and Authorization Infrastructure (AAI)* [36] is needed to avoid theft of identities and forgery of credentials. Viewing authentication as the verification of a single identity clearly is insufficient. Federation of multiple partial identities should be considered, to establish authenticity of *attributes* such as location, from which can be derived authorizations.

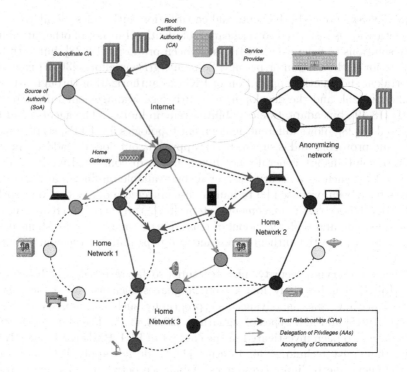

Fig. 1. Security Authorities in a Home Network

(2) **Flexible topologies of authorities.** Attributes are certified by a set of *authorities* which may be organized in a combination of widely different topologies, leading to architectures ranging from centralized to completely decentralized. This complexity is due to the great number and heterogeneity of network nodes, which are also mobile, and scattered across traditional frontiers.

Relationships between authorities are usually based on *certification*: one authority extends trust or delegates its powers to another. This leads to trust or delegation chains, typically organized in hierarchies as in traditional PKIs, where the root authority has control over its subordinates. Two hierarchies may be connected by a *bridge authority*, or by authorities cross-certifying one another. P2P links between authorities may also established and revoked, leading to more dynamic and decentralized organizations.

A combination of these approaches where authorities cooperate is also possible. The functionalities of the authority can be distributed among a set of nodes [47]. Another option is to partition the network into clusters, with a single predefined authority node responsible for managing security inside each cluster [10]. For home networks, a hierarchy of device communities which may be split or merged yields a more dynamic structure [5]. In a community, the powers of the authority may be delegated, temporarily or permanently, to another node in case of failure or migration of a device away from home. The active authority may also be randomly shifted among nodes in the cluster for very short time spans [44]. Finally, backup authorities and alternative certification paths [35] make the system more resistant to DoS attacks, without the heavy protection requirements of a PKI root CA.

To make the problem harder, the topologies of authorities are usually not the same for different security dimensions such as trust management, delegation of privileges, and anonymization of communications. The result is a set of independent overlay networks for each dimension, where nodes in each network are organized into the structures described previously: hierarchical, meshed, P2P, etc. Figure 1 shows a typical pervasive network configuration with three different overlays for authorities.

The infrastructure must thus provide enough flexibility to support these deployment topologies and dynamic relationships between authorities, depending on security requirements. Additional tuning may be necessary to further control delegation, such as introducing path length constraints, or name space restrictions – for instance, to limit delegation to a subgroup of authorities based on their attribute values.

(3) **Multiple certificate types and protocols.** The security infrastructure should be open to meet variable security objectives. For instance, it should handle several cryptographic protocols and formats of certificates. Flexibility is needed as well in management protocols [3,40,42] to tailor the security infrastructure to application requirements. This may mean customizing certificate life-cycle management such as enrollment procedures, finding the right trade-off between off-line [29] and on-line validation [40], adapting the security protocols to device and network capabilities, or interoperating with other security infrastructures. Finally, reconfiguration capabilities should also be available to match dynamic conditions of execution, e.g., to add new security mechanisms, download system patches, or personalize security settings.

(4) **Multiple trust management strategies.** Pervasive network nodes are usually highly decentralized, and follow P2P communication patterns. Those networks lack stable backbones, which results in intermittent connectivity. Therefore, centralized TTP-based trust management solutions may not be adequate. A realistic trust model is therefore required to handle disconnected mode situations. The infrastructure should enable choosing the right strategy for trust management depending on the availability on-line of a TTP, such as certificates validated by a chain of authorities in connected mode, and a reputation management system in disconnected mode.

(5) **Tunable privacy.** Flexibility in privacy management is also a major enabler of pervasive computing, often at odds with trust management: the user should control disclosure of his personal information, and yet let the infrastructure communicate transparently with TTPs to assess the validity of presented credentials. A minimal disclosure of information is also needed to establish trust relationships between entities. Customizable degrees of anonymity are thus required to

select the right trade-offs, the willingness of the user to disclose personal data also depending on its perception of the service accessed.

(6) **Embedded constraints.** Last, but not least, the security infrastructure should comply with limited computation and communication resources, with lightweight protocols, and minimal footprint on devices. Only the key security services should be included in the infrastructure.

To meet those requirements, we propose to adopt a component-based architecture for the security infrastructure. This approach allows the infrastructure to be adaptable to several types of execution environments, and to be reconfigured according to security objectives, policies, and mechanisms – either at a fine-grained level (e.g., certificate formats), or at a macroscopic level (e.g., topologies for authorities), depending on how the components are connected and deployed. This architecture naturally leads to a framework-oriented design, specific sub-frameworks dealing with each adaptability dimension (e.g., authentication and authorization, trust, and privacy management), making the infrastructure highly customizable.

In what follows, we recall the main elements of component-based design, and review the PKIX security model we use as basis to illustrate how component-based architectures meet the previous requirements.

4   Background

4.1   Component-Based Design

Components are usually defined as entities encapsulating code and data which appear in software systems as units of execution, configuration, deployment, or administration. Building a system according to a component model allows to master the complexity of implementation of a software infrastructure, since components can be composed to form higher-level units of code. The resulting infrastructure is thus very modular. Component-based architectures also offer flexibility of configuration, since functionalities can be adapted or introduced by addition or replacement of components in the system, both in the large and in the small (see Figure 2). This approach is thus well adapted to the dynamic needs of pervasive networks.

We specify the architecture of the security infrastructure with Fractal [16], a generic component model capturing reconfiguration by flexible composition of components with a minimal number of concepts : a *component* is a run-time entity built from a *controller*, which supervises execution of a *content* possibly including other components (*sub-components*). A *composite component* offers a white-box perspective of its content by revealing its organization, while a *primitive component* is a black-box encapsulating legacy code. A component only interacts with its environment through well-defined access points called *interfaces*. A Fractal component provides and may require interfaces. Interaction between components is performed by establishment of *bindings* between their interfaces.

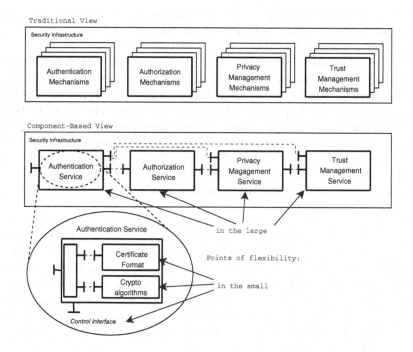

Fig. 2. AMISEC Approach to Security Flexibility

Fractal manages reconfiguration independently from component functionality by separating control interfaces from functional interfaces. The main control interfaces of the component framework cover: containment relationships and bindings between components (`BindingController`); introspection, e.g., to discover the structure of a component or configure its properties (`AttributeController`); dynamic reconfiguration, e.g., to add or remove sub-components (`ContentController`); and life-cycle management, e.g., to suspend or resume the execution of a component (`LifeCycleController`). A reference implementation of Fractal called Julia is provided to program applications according to the component model [41].

4.2   PKIX-Compliant AAIs

The PKIX working group [29,30] proposed a unified reference model for the organization of a certificate-based AAI. Two sub-infrastructures are distinguished: the *PKI (Public Key Infrastructure)* for authentication, and the *PMI (Privilege Management Infrastructure)* for authorization and attribute management. The AAI manages trust and enforces privileges through the exchange of certificates digitally signed by authorities. *Public key (or identity) certificates (PKC)* signed by *Certification Authorities (CAs)* – the root CA being the trust anchor – guarantee the link between an identity and a public key. *Attribute certificates (ACs)* signed by *Attribute Authorities (AAs)* – the root AA also being called the *Source of Authority (SoA)* – establish the relationship between the identity and a number of attributes. Authorities may delegate issuance of certificates to subordinate or peer authorities.

The main elements of the PKI model are the following. *PKI clients* initiate *Certificate Signing Requests (CSRs)* to ask for a new certificate, check the validity of certificates, or request their revocation, for instance when a public key has been compromised. A *Registration Authority (RA)* is responsible for certificate enrollment and approves CSRs which are transmitted to a CA. It may also trigger revocation of PKCs. One or more CAs verify CSRs, and issue, sign, verify, or revoke certificates. Finally, the *Certificate Repository*, usually implemented by one or more databases, allows storing and retrieving PKCs and *Certificate Revocation Lists (CRLs)*. Additional primitives may be included for certificate renewal, loss or compromise.

The elements of the PMI model are quite similar. The AAs generate, sign, and revoke attribute certificates. They also publish these certificates, and the corresponding revocation lists (ACRLs) in certificate repositories. The AAs are organized in the same structures as the CAs. The AA acts on behalf of the SoA to deliver and manage attribute certificates. *PMI clients* ask for new attribute certificates, or request their verification or their revocation. A *Privilege Verifier* is responsible for verifying the validity of an AC, or revoking the corresponding privileges. Finally, one or more Certificate Repositories allows storing and retrieving ACs and ACRLs.

5   The AMISEC Infrastructure

5.1   From High-Level Security Services...

As already shown, in an AAI security authorities (CAs and AAs) may be organized in different network topologies. Moreover, infrastructure services are the result composing several functional components (CAs, certificate repository, AAI clients...), well-described by the PKIX model. Finally, for each security service such as certificate validation, interactions between functional components can be specified with several protocols. As a result, the AAI design space is very large.

We now describe AMISEC, a PKIX-compliant AAI supporting these different types of design. The entirely component-based architecture of AMISEC provides full control over the deployment of functional components, their relationship with security services, and the interaction protocols between components.

The main security services provided by AMISEC are shown in Figure 3. Due to lack of space, we only present the PKI services. The PMI ones are similar, covering generation, distribution, validation, and revocation of attribute certificates. These services, independent from the type of design, can be mapped to the main functional PKIX components to reach a description of the services supported by each component, and of the expected interactions between these components. One then obtains a set of technical components which can be arranged very flexibly to realize several types of PKI/PMI architectures (see Figure 4). The

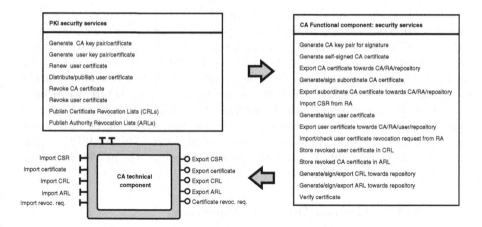

Fig. 3. From Security Services to Technical Components

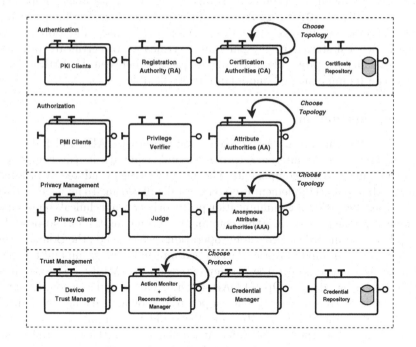

Fig. 4. AMISEC Technical Components

interfaces of these components can be specified with an ADL (Architecture Description Language) such as the Fractal ADL [41]. The CA technical component is shown in Figure 3, the other components being similar.

Using the control interfaces provided by Fractal to manage component bindings and containment relationships, the AMISEC technical components may be distributed on the network nodes according to a specific topology for authorities. The topology may be reconfigured according to the context, e.g., by creating a new CA, closer to clients, to optimize communications. Ssecurity services can also easily be customized to the execution environment (security objectives, available resources), by adding/removing specific security components in the architecture. This design approach leads to a lightweight infrastructure, where only the minimal required set of security services are included. Finally, new interaction protocols (e.g., for more efficient certificate validation) can be introduced by implementing specific bindings between components. The AMISEC design thus provides adaptability in the deployment architecture, the provided security services, and the supporting security protocols.

5.2   ...To Fine-Grained Tuning of Protection

The AMISEC technical components are composite components: they share a number of finer-grained components which allow to tune several AMISEC functionalities. For instance: cryptographic algorithms (`Cryptography` component); format of certificates (`CertificateFormat` component); initialization procedures of entities; certificate life-cycle (creation, signing, publishing, validation, renewal, revocation); local storage of key pairs and certificates; or certificate validation protocols. Thus, the protocols governing interactions between the AMISEC components can be implemented and adapted very flexibly.

5.3   Implementation

The AMISEC architecture was specified using the Fractal ADL which describes for each component its interfaces (provided, and required), its sub-components and its bindings to other components. The design was then validated by prototyping a distributed Java implementation on the Julia platform. To manage distribution, we used Java RMI as communication protocol between technical components. Exchanged certificates are X.509v3 compliant, ACs having the format described in [26]. For all standard cryptographic operations, we relied on the BouncyCastle Java library. Additional librairies developped internally for group and fair-blind signatures were also used in the privacy extension of AMISEC. The certificate repository was based on an Open LDAP server, encapsulated as a component.

A supervision console was also developed to deploy and manage dynamically each element of the PKIX architecture. We could test simply several configurations of the infrastructure for different topologies of authorities, and control certificate management procedures. The Fractal model was quite helpful to capture dynamic aspects of communication: components could be bound/unbound very easily between entities joining/leaving the network, without needing to know them in advance.

The AMISEC infrastructure is also currently being ported on an OSGi platform, using Apache Felix running on Nokia Internet tablets N800 and N810. We plan to evaluate how the infrastructure can evolve from a purely component-based towards a *Service-Oriented Architecture (SOA)* where each device may dynamically register and lookup the security services it provides and requires respectively. The objective is study possible integration of this middleware with other SOA architectures for the home environment such as [14].

6   Evaluation

6.1   Extension for Privacy

The flexibility of the AMISEC security architecture was validated by specifying and implementing a privacy-enhancing extension to support tunable degrees of anonymity of communications. This feature is highly desirable for user acceptance of digital home networking technologies to prevent observable behaviors from being linkable to user identities, and to selectively control disclosure of user attributes, which may be variably bound with personal identifying information.

Many cryptographic primitives such as anonymous credentials [17,15], fairblind signatures [45], group signatures [20], traceable signatures [33], or ring signatures [43] have been proposed to build privacy-preserving mechanisms – e.g., see [11] for a comparison of their anonymity guarantees.

A trade-off must be found between full disclosure of attributes and uncontrolled anonymity, which may lead to abuse by malicious users. We focus on pseudonymity mechanisms which guarantee privacy while preserving accountability. The degree of anonymity can be tuned depending on the type of cryptographic mechanism chosen. The component-based security architecture allows to implement simply this extension in the infrastructure, transparently to the cryptographic mechanism.

An elegant solution to enhance the PMI with anonymity services is proposed in [12]. X.509 ACs are extended into *anonymous attribute certificates (AAC)*, the link between identities and attributes being based on pseudonyms. A TTP guarantees the secrecy of the link between real identities and pseudonyms, but may disclose the identity of the certificate holder under some particular conditions. The scheme described in [12] is based on fair-blind signatures. AACs may also be based on other types of signature schemes [11] such as group signatures [13].

A special type of AA, an *Anonymous Attribute Authority (AAA)*, is introduced to issue AACs. Once users have applied for an AAC to the AAA, the AAC can be used to enforce their privileges in the same manner as a regular AC, except that the process is performed anonymously. This approach thus makes anonymity completely transparent to the authorization process. The AAA may rely on a regular AA for all primitives which are not related to anonymity in the management of certificates.

A simple manner to implement AAAs in the AMISEC architecture is to introduce a new component containing as sub-component a regular AA, as well as other sub-components specific to the chosen anonymity scheme, e.g., a group manager for group signatures-based AACs, a pseudonym manager for fair-blind signature-based AACs, implementations of the anonymity protocols, etc. TTPs may also need to be added in the infrastructure, for instance, to manage the disclosure of identities of the anonymous users.

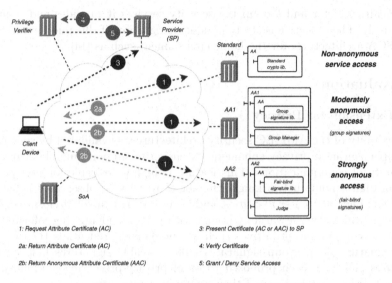

Fig. 5. Tunable Anonymity in AMISEC

A richer cryptographic interface is also needed. To support anonymity, the AMISEC `Cryptography` component interface was extended with new methods implementing advanced signature schemes, such as primitives for blinding messages, and generating group signatures. Other primitives such as commitments and zero-knowledge proofs could also be added, for instance following the cryptographic framework [9] which describes the primitives needed to implement privacy-enhancing mechanisms for certificate management infrastructures. The `CertificateFormat` component was also extended to take into account the format of AACs, including fields such as pseudonyms, TTP identities, and special conditions under which the TTP and the AA may collude to reveal user identities.

This design facilitates the support of different anonymity policies. For example, as shown in Figure 5, a user may ask several AACs to different AAs: either to a regular AA configured with the standard cryptographic sub-component if he chooses to fully disclose his identity; or to an AA issuing AACs based on group signatures (AA_1) to be moderately anonymous; or again to an AA issuing AACs based on fair-blind signatures (AA_2) to be strongly anonymous – assuming in this example that the chosen group signature scheme provides weaker anonymity than the fair-blind signature scheme. AA_1 and AA_2 both contain the standard AA as a sub-component, but configured respectively with the cryptographic component for group and fair-blind signatures. The client device then may access transparenly the service by presenting the correct AC, depending on the degree of anonymity desired.

6.2   Flexible Trust Management

We also explored the ability of AMISEC to support several strategies for trust management. Indeed, the method of authentication may be adapted depending on the connectivity status to a TTP. We thus consider two modes of operation. In *connected mode*, a TTP is available on-line to validate credentials. A traditional certificate management infrastructure such as a PKI is therefore applicable. In *disconnected mode*, due to missing information, validation cannot be performed so simply. A reputation-based system might then be preferred to manage trust between devices without central servers. These alternatives may be unified into a single abstract authentication component on each device, the interface of which may be bound to sub-components, either of the PKI, or of the reputation system. The same approach can be followed to adapt the authorization strategy depending on connectivity, using the PMI and a trust-based access control scheme [7].

To assess the feasibility of this adaptation, we included additional Fractal components into AMISEC based on the design of the PTM reputation management system [6]. These components are shown in Figure 4. An *Action Monitor* keeps track of behaviors (normal or malicious) of other devices. A *Trust Manager* combines this information with recommendations received from other devices serve to compute the reputation of each device according to the chosen trust model. A *Recommendation Manager* implements the recommendation protocol between devices. Reputation values are then converted by the *Credential Manager* into credentials for authentication, stored in a repository.

Some of these components are shared with, or can be seen as extensions of the components of the AMISEC PKI. For instance, the Credential Repository and Manager are enhancements of the Certificate Repository and Authority components respectively to manipulate trust information. Similarly, the Recommendation Manager is a connector-type of component binding two Trust Manager components on each device, implementing a specific infrastructure management protocol.

The component-based architecture of the infrastructure also allows to fine-tune some parameters such as the strength of authentication by selecting the threshold T for trust values above which user entities are authenticated in P2P mode, with $T = 1$ for boolean authentication using the PKI. One could also change the trust model, action monitoring policy, recommendation protocol, or type of exchanged credentials by replacing the corresponding components of the reputation system.

These different adaptability dimensions of AMISEC were evaluated on device authentication scenarios in the home environment, both in connected and disconnected modes. Different trust management schemes were used for each mode, AMISEC enabling smooth transition between schemes depending on the on-line availability of a TTP. A brief overview of this evaluation is given in appendix.

6.3   Some Remaining Challenges

We showed how the AMISEC architecture offered maximum flexibility in the choice and combination of security mechanisms. Assessing the impact of this flexibility on overall security remains an unsolved issue. Other dimensions may also be involved such as performance or QoS.

The problem may be viewed as selecting the most adequate component assembly, given current security objectives. One solution is to capture security at the component-level by a set of security properties assumed to be composable – in the form of discrete, continuous values, or even predicates [31]. Overall guaranteed system security can then be derived by agregating and reasoning on properties of individual components, and compared to targetted security objectives. Properties may be advertised by component-level security contracts [32], expressing adequation of guaranteed security properties with respect to security requirements. This approach may be generalized to richer notions of properties, to express trade-offs between different security or non-security dimensions such as QoS [4], or confidence in security context information [34].

Yet, this approach is based on the (strong) assumption that security properties are composable across components, which is seldom the case. The general case remains yet an unsolved issue, well beyond the scope of this paper.

7 Conclusion

We presented the design and implementation of AMISEC, a certificate-based privacy-enhanced AAI for pervasive networks. Adopting the component paradigm for the security architecture yields a highly flexible infrastructure, which may be adapted both to changing conditions and to shifting security requirements. AMISEC offers an integrated framework for authentication, authorization, and privacy, adaptable both in the large (topologies of security authorities, management protocols, trust strategies...), and in the small (cryptographic algorithms, certificate formats...), while remaining lightweight.

In future work, we plan to formalize better the privacy and trust management frameworks. First, by supporting multiple types of anonymous credentials and defining an abstract interface for anonymity, going beyond a solution purely based on group signatures. Second, by making the trust model and trust information manipulated fully customizable. We also plan to study how a service-oriented evolution of AMISEC might serve as a basis for a reference end-to-end security infrastructure for digital home and multi-homed environments.

References

1. OpenID, http://openid.net/
2. The Liberty Alliance Project, http://www.projectliberty.org/
3. Adams, C., Farrell, S.: Internet X.509 Public Key Infrastructure Certificate Management Protocols. RFC 2510 (March 1999),
   http://www.ietf.org/rfc/rfc2510.txt
4. Alia, M., Lacoste, M.: A QoS and Security Adaptation Model for Autonomic Pervasive Systems. In: International Workshop on Security of Software Engineering, IWSSE 2008 (2008)
5. Aljnidi, M., Leneutre, J.: Towards an Autonomic Security System for Mobile Ad Hoc Networks. In: Third International Symposium on Information Assurance and Security, IAS 2007 (2007)

6. Almenárez, F., Marín, A., Campo, C., García, C.: PTM: A Pervasive Trust Management Model for Dynamic Open Environments. In: Workshop on Pervasive Security, Privacy and Trust, PSPT 2004 (2004)
7. Almenárez, F., Marín, A., Campo, C., García, C.: TrustAC: Trust-Based Access Control for Pervasive Devices. In: Clark, J.A., Paige, R.F., Polack, F.A.C., Brooke, P.J. (eds.) SPC 2006. LNCS, vol. 3934. Springer, Heidelberg (2006)
8. Artz, D., Gil, Y.: A Survey of Trust in Computer Science and the Semantic Web. Web Semantics: Science, Services and Agents on the World Wide Web 5(2), 58–71 (2007)
9. Bangerter, E., Camenisch, J., Lysyanskaya, A.: A Cryptographic Framework for the Controlled Release of Certified Data. In: Christianson, B., Crispo, B., Malcolm, J.A., Roe, M. (eds.) Security Protocols 2004. LNCS, vol. 3957, pp. 20–42. Springer, Heidelberg (2006)
10. Bechler, M., Hof, H.-J., Kraft, D., Rahlke, F., Wolf, L.: A Cluster-Based Security Architecture for Ad Hoc Networks. In: Annual Joint Conference of the IEEE Computer and Communications Societies, INFOCOM 2004 (2004)
11. Benjumea, V., Choi, S.G., Lopez, J., Yung, M.: Anonymity 2.0 - X.509 Extensions Supporting Privacy-Friendly Authentication. In: Bao, F., Ling, S., Okamoto, T., Wang, H., Xing, C. (eds.) CANS 2007. LNCS, vol. 4856, pp. 265–281. Springer, Heidelberg (2007)
12. Benjumea, V., Lopez, J., Montenegro, J., Troya, J.: A First Approach to Provide Anonymity in Attribute Certificates. In: Bao, F., Deng, R., Zhou, J. (eds.) PKC 2004, vol. 2947, pp. 402–415. Springer, Heidelberg (2004)
13. Benjumea, V., Lopez, J., Troya, J.: Anonymous Attribute Certificates based on Traceable Signatures. Internet Research 16(2), 120–139 (2006)
14. Bottaro, A., Gerodolle, A.: Home SOA - Facing Protocol Heterogeneity in Pervasive Applications. In: International Conference on Pervasive Services, ICPS (2008)
15. Brands, S.: Rethinking Public Key Infrastructures and Digital Certificates: Building in Privacy. MIT Press, Cambridge (2000)
16. Bruneton, E., Coupaye, T., Leclercq, M., Quéma, V., Stéfani, J.B.: The Fractal Component Model and its Support in Java. Software – Practice and Experience, special issue on Experiences with Auto-adaptive and Reconfigurable Systems 36(11–12), 1257–1284 (2006)
17. Camenish, J., Lysyanskaya, A.: Efficient Non-Transferable Anonymous Multi-Show Credential System with Optional Anonymity Revocation. In: Advances in Cryptology, EUROCRYPT (2001)
18. Chadwick, D., Otenko, A.: The PERMIS X.509 Role-Based Privilege Management Infrastructure. In: ACM Symposium on Access control Models and Technologies, SACMAT (2002)
19. Chaum, D.: Untraceable Electronic E-Mail, Return Addresses, and Digital Pseudonyms. Communications of the ACM 4(2), 84–88 (1981)
20. Chaum, D., van Heyst, E.: Group Signatures. In: Davies, D.W. (ed.) EUROCRYPT 1991, vol. 547, pp. 257–265. Springer, Heidelberg (1991)
21. Cook, D., Das, S.: Smart Environments: Technologies, Protocols, and Applications. Wiley, Chichester (2005)
22. Critchlow, D., Zhang, N.: Security-Enhanced Accountable Anonymous PKI Certificates for Mobile E-Commerce. Computer Networks 45(4), 483–503 (2004)
23. Danezis, G., Diaz, C.: A Survey of Anonymous Communication Channels. Technical Report MSR-TR-2008-35, Microsoft Research (2008)
24. Dingledine, R., Mathewson, N., Syverson, P.: Tor: The Second-Generation Onion Router. In: USENIX Security Symposium (2004)

25. Ellison, C., Frantz, B., Lampson, B., Rivest, R., Thomas, B., Ylonen, T.: SPKI Certificate Theory. RFC 2693 (September 1999), ftp://ftp.isi.edu/in-notes/rfc2693.txt
26. Farrell, S., Housley, R.: An Internet Attribute Certificate Profile for Authorization. RFC 3281 (April 2002), http://www.ietf.org/rfc/rfc3281.txt
27. Hansen, M., Krasemann, H.: Privacy and Identity Management for Europe. IST PRIME Project White Paper (2005)
28. He, Q., Sycara, K., Su, Z.: A Solution to Open Standard of PKI. In: Boyd, C., Dawson, E. (eds.) ACISP 1998, vol. 1438, p. 99. Springer, Heidelberg (1998)
29. Housley, R., Polk, W., Ford, W., Solo, D.: Internet X.509 Public Key Infrastructure Certificate and Certificate Revocation List (CRL) Profile. RFC 3280 (April 2002), http://www.ietf.org/rfc/rfc3280.txt
30. IETF. PKIX Working Group, http://www.ietf.org/html.charters/pkix-charter.html
31. Khan, K., Han, J.: A Security Characterisation Framework for Trustworthy Component-Based Software Systems. In: International Computer Software and Applications Conference, COMPSAC 2003 (2003)
32. Khan, K., Han, J.: Deriving Systems Level Security Properties of Component-Based Composite Systems. In: Australian Software Engineering Conference, ASWEC (2005)
33. Kiayias, A., Tsiounis, Y., Yung, M.: Traceable Signatures. In: Cachin, C., Camenisch, J.L. (eds.) EUROCRYPT 2004, vol. 3027, pp. 571–589. Springer, Heidelberg (2004)
34. Lacoste, M., Privat, G., Ramparany, F.: Evaluating Confidence in Context for Context-Aware Security. In: European Conference on Ambient Intelligence, AML (2007)
35. Lee, J., Lee, M., Gu, J., Lee, S., Park, S., Song, J.: New Adaptive Trust Models against DDoS: Back-Up CA and Mesh PKI. In: Second International Conference on Human.Society@Internet, HSI (2003)
36. Lopez, J., Oppliger, R., Pernul, G.: Authentication and Authorization Infrastructures (AAIs): A Comparative Survey. Computers & Security 23(7), 578–590 (2004)
37. Mendoza, F., Carbonell, M., Forné, J., Hinarejos, F., Lacoste, M., López, A.M., Montenegro, J.: Design of an Enhanced PKI for Ubiquitous Networks. In: International Workshop on Secure Ubiquitous Networks, SUN (2005)
38. Miyata, T., Koga, Y., Madsen, P., Adachi, S., Tsuchiya, Y., Sakamoto, Y., Takahashi, K.: A Survey on Identity Management Protocols and Standards. IEICE - Transactions on Information and Systems E89-D(1), 112–123 (2006)
39. Montenegro, J., Moya, F.: A Practical Approach of X.509 Attribute Certificate Framework as Support to Obtain Privilege Delegation. In: Katsikas, S.K., Gritzalis, S., López, J. (eds.) EuroPKI 2004, vol. 3093, pp. 160–172. Springer, Heidelberg (2004)
40. Myers, M., Ankney, R., Malpani, A., Galperin, S., Adams, C.: Internet X.509 Public Key Infrastructure: Online Certificate Status Protocol – OCSP. RFC 2560 (1999), http://www.ietf.org/rfc/rfc2560.txt
41. ObjectWeb Consortium. The Fractal Component Framework, http://fractal.objectweb.org/
42. Pinkas, D., Housley, R.: Delegated Path Validation and Delegated Path Discovery Protocol Requirements. RFC 3379 (September 2002), http://www.ietf.org/rfc/rfc3379.txt
43. Rivest, R., Shamir, A., Tauman, Y.: How to Leak a Secret. In: Boyd, C. (ed.) ASIACRYPT 2001. LNCS, vol. 2248, p. 552. Springer, Heidelberg (2001)

44. Safdar, G., McLoone, M.: Randomly Shifted Certification Authority Authentication Protocol for MANETs. Mobile and Wireless Communications Summit (2007)
45. Stadler, M., Piveteau, J., Camenisch, J.: Fair Blind Signatures. In: Guillou, L.C., Quisquater, J.-J. (eds.) EUROCRYPT 1995, vol. 921, pp. 209–219. Springer, Heidelberg (1995)
46. W3C. The Platform for Privacy Preferences (P3P) Project, http://www.w3.org/P3P/
47. Zhou, L., Haas, Z.: Securing Ad Hoc Networks. IEEE Network 13(6), 24–30 (1999)
48. Zimmermann, P.: The Official PGP User's Guide. MIT Press, Cambridge (1995)

A   Flexible Authentication in Home Area Networks

The AMISEC infrastructure was tested in the environment shown in Figure 6, where devices connected to Home Area Networks (HANs) access Internet services through a residential gateway. To determine the users to trust and protect HAN resources, device authentication is required, but difficult to achieve when a security server is not available on-line.

With AMISEC, authentication is possible both in connected and disconnected modes by using the gateway as a proxy for the CA. A proxy is installed on the gateway to cache and forward certificates when the CA is on-line. Authentication is then based on the latest cached version of the certificate. The cache is updated periodically by synchronization with the certificate repository contained in the PKI security server. Most components of AMISEC for connected mode (CA, RA, and certificate repository) are installed on the PKI security server, the client components being deployed on the devices. The proxy is a surrogate for the full PKI, and thus shares with it many interfaces (e.g., credential validation or revocation status checking). AMISEC components for disconnected mode are deployed both on the gateway and the devices.

When Alice asks the proxy for a certificate, the request is forwarded to the on-line CA. A valid certificate is returned to Alice, the proxy caching the certificate and its revocation status. When Alice's certificate is presented to Bob, he can verify her identity by querying the proxy, which in turn will ask the CA to check the validity of the certificate and return the response to Bob. When the connection to the CA is lost, the validation process is similar, but the response of the proxy is based on locally cached information – such as the certificate revocation status – dating back to the last synchronization with the PKI certificate repository.

Thus, authentication is possible both when the CA is on-line and off-line. Performance is also increased by placing the authentication data closer to the devices to authenticate, since the connection to an external security server may be costly. Authentication is also possible P2P between devices (e.g., to exchange directly multimedia content between Alice and Bob) through recommendations from other devices or from the gateway, by using the components of AMISEC for disconnected mode. The strength of authentication and type of credentials used (certificates vs. trust values) may thus be freely chosen.

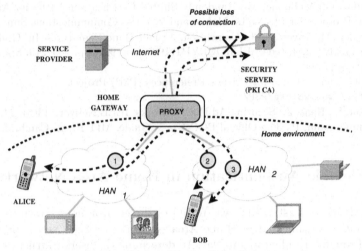

1: certificate request/reply; 2: certificate transmission; 3: certificate verification

Fig. 6. An Authentication Scenario

One can also configure parameters such as the frequency of synchronizations between the proxy and the PKI server, which directly impacts the freshness of the security data used for authentication. Thus, the degree of trust granted to the authentication process can be tuned and weighed up against the estimated risk and performance requirements.

Software Verification and Validation of Graphical Web Services in Digital 3D Worlds

Andrés Iglesias

Department of Applied Mathematics and Computational Sciences,
University of Cantabria, Avda. de los Castros,
s/n, E-39005, Santander, Spain
iglesias@unican.es
http://personales.unican.es/iglesias

Abstract. Software verification and validation (SVV) are major ingredients of current software engineering projects. Among the available methods to solve this problem, one of the most promising approaches is that based on Petri nets. This paper discusses somme issues regarding the application of Petri nets to SVV from a hybrid mathematical/computational point of view. The paper also describes a *Mathematica* package developed by the author for a class of Petri nets, which is applied to address the SVV problem in the context of graphical semantic web services based on virtual agents evolving in digital 3D worlds.

1 Introduction

Nowadays, software verification and software validation are seen as integral parts of any software engineering project. *Software verification* tries to ensure that your final software matches the original design, i.e. you built your software according to the prescribed specifications. By contrast, *software validation* concerns the problem of checking whether your software satisfies or fits the intended usage, i.e. if your software is actually doing what the user really asks for.

Many different methods can be used to accomplish the previous tasks. They can be classified as formal and syntactic methods. Formal methods are mathematical techniques for proof correctness with a high level of reliability but often very costly. Syntactic methods are aimed at looking for code failures by examining the structure of the code at its syntactic rather than its semantic level.

Among the formal methods for software verification and validation, those based on Petri nets (PN) are gaining more and more popularity during the last few years. Most of PN interest lies on their ability to represent a number of events and states in a distributed, parallel, nondeterministic or stochastic system and to simulate accurately processes such as concurrency, sequentiality or asynchronous control [9]. As a consequence, Petri nets provide the users with a very powerful formalism for describing and analyzing a broad variety of information processing systems from the graphical and the mathematical viewpoints.

In this paper we consider the use of Petri nets for software verification and validation (SVV). The paper also describes a *Mathematica* package developed by

D. Ślęzak et al. (Eds.): FGCN/ACN 2009, CCIS 56, pp. 293–300, 2009.
© Springer-Verlag Berlin Heidelberg 2009

the author for a class of Petri nets, which is subsequently applied to address the SVV issue in the context of graphical web services based on agents. In particular, we analyze a case study dealing with a recently introduced web service framework [4]. Such framework is aimed at providing the users with web services by means of virtual agents resembling human beings and evolving within a 3D virtual world. Once a web service is requested on the client side via a web browser, user is prompted into this virtual world and immediately assigned his/her own virtual agent; in other words, the user is echoed by his/her virtual counterpart. Users-system interplay is accomplished via those virtual agents, which are represented graphically in this virtual world and behave in a human-like way.

2 Basic Concepts and Definitions

A *Petri net* (PN) is a special kind of directed graph, together with an initial state called the initial marking. The graph of a PN is a bipartite graph containing *places* $\{P_1, \ldots, P_m\}$ and *transitions* $\{t_1, \ldots, t_n\}$. Figure 1 shows an example of a Petri net of three places and six transitions. In graphical representation, places are usually displayed as circles while transitions appear as rectangular boxes. The graph also contains arcs either from a place P_i to a transition t_j (*input arcs* for t_j) or from a transition to a place (*output arcs* for t_j). These arcs are labeled with their weights (positive integers), with the meaning that an arc of weight w can be understood as a set of w parallel arcs of unity weight (whose labels are usually omitted). In Fig. 1 input arcs from P_1 to t_3 and P_2 to t_4 and output arc from t_1 to P_1 have weight 2, the rest having unity weight.

A *marking* (state) assigns to each place P_i a nonnegative integer, k_i. In this case, we say that P_i *is marked with* k_i *tokens*. Graphically, this idea is represented by k_i small black circles (tokens) in place P_i. In other words, places hold tokens to represent predicates about the world state or internal state. The presence or absence of a token in a place can indicate whether a condition associated with this place is true or false, for instance. For a place representing the availability of resources, the number of tokens in this place indicates the number of available resources. At any given time instance, the distribution of tokens on places, called

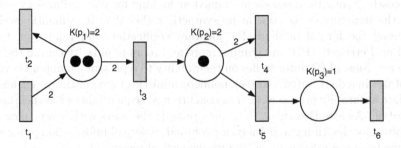

Fig. 1. Example of a Petri net comprised of three places and six transitions

Petri net marking, defines the current state of the modeled system. All markings are denoted by vectors $\mathcal{M}$ of length m (the total number of places in the net) such that the i-th component of $\mathcal{M}$ indicates the number of tokens in place P_i. From now on the initial marking will be denoted as $\mathcal{M}_0$. For instance, the initial marking (state) for the net in Figure 1 is $\{2, 1, 0\}$.

The pre- and post-sets of nodes are specified in this paper by a dot notation, where $\bullet u = \{v \in \mathbf{P} \bigcup \mathbf{T} / (v, u) \in \mathbf{A}\}$ is called the pre-set of u, and $u \bullet = \{v \in \mathbf{P} \bigcup \mathbf{T} / (u, v) \in \mathbf{A}\}$ is called the post-set of u. The pre-set of a place (transition) is the set of input transitions (places). The post-set of a place (transition) is the set of output transitions (places). The dynamical behavior of many systems can be expressed in terms of the system states of their Petri net. Such states are adequately described by the changes of markings of a PN according to a *firing rule* for the transitions: a transition t_j is said to be *enabled* in a marking $\mathcal{M}$ when all places in $\bullet t_j$ are marked. For instance, transitions t_2, t_3 and t_5 in Figure 1 are enabled, while transitions t_4 and t_6 are not. Note, for example, that transition t_4 has weight 2 while place P_2 has only 1 token, so arc from P_2 to t_4 is disabled. If transition t_j is enabled, it may or may not be fired (depending on whether or not the event represented by such a transition occurs). A firing of transition t_j removes $w_{i,j}$ tokens from each input place P_i of t_j and adds $w_{j,k}$ tokens to each output place P_k of t_j, $w_{j,k}$ being the weight of the arc from t_j to P_k. In other words, if transition t_j is fired, all places of $\bullet t_j$ have their input tokens removed and a new set of tokens is deposited in the places of $t_j \bullet$ according to the weights of the arcs connecting those places and t_j. For instance, transition t_3 removes two tokens from place P_1 and adds one token to place P_2, thus changing the previous marking of the net. The fireability property of a transition t_j is denoted by $\mathcal{M}[t_j >$ while the creation of a new marking $\mathcal{M}'$ from $\mathcal{M}$ by firing t_j is denoted by $\mathcal{M}[t_j > \mathcal{M}'$.

A marking $\bar{\mathcal{M}}$ is *reachable* from any arbitrary marking $\mathcal{M}$ *iff* there exists a sequence of transitions $\sigma = t_1 t_2 t_3 \ldots t_n$ such that

$$\mathcal{M}[t_1 > \mathcal{M}_1[t_2 > \mathcal{M}_2 \ldots \mathcal{M}_{n-1}[t_n > \bar{\mathcal{M}}.$$

For short, we denote that the marking $\bar{\mathcal{M}}$ is reachable from $\mathcal{M}$ by $\mathcal{M}[\sigma > \bar{\mathcal{M}}$, where σ is called the *firing sequence*. The set of all markings reachable from $\mathcal{M}$ for a Petri net $\mathcal{PN}$ is denoted by $\biguplus[(\mathcal{PN}, \mathcal{M}) >$. Given a Petri net $\mathcal{PN}$, an initial marking $\mathcal{M}_0$ and any other marking $\mathcal{M}$, the problem of determining whether $\mathcal{M} \in \biguplus[(\mathcal{PN}, \mathcal{M}_0) >$ is known as the *reachability problem* for Petri nets. In many practical applications it is interesting to know not only if a marking is reachable, but also what are the corresponding firing sequences leading to this marking. This can be done by using the so-called *reachability graph*, a graph consisting of the set of nodes of the original Petri net and a set of arcs connecting markings $\mathcal{M}_i$ and $\mathcal{M}_j$ iff $\exists t \in \mathbf{T} / \mathcal{M}_i[t > \mathcal{M}_j$.

A transition without any input place is called a *source transition*. Note that source transitions are always enabled. In Figure 1 there is only one source transition, namely t_1. A transition without any output place is called a *sink transition*. The reader will notice that the firing of a sink transition removes tokens but does not generate new tokens in the net. Sink transitions in Figure 1 are t_2, t_4 and t_6. A couple (P_i, t_j) is said to be a *self-loop* if $P_i \in (\bullet t_j \bigcap t_j \bullet)$ (i.e., if P_i is both an input and an output place for transition t_j). A Petri net free of self-loops is called a *pure* net. In this paper, we will restrict exclusively to pure nets.

Some PN do not put any restriction on the number of tokens each place can hold. Such nets are usually referred to as *infinite capacity net*. However, in most practical cases it is more reasonable to consider an upper limit to the number of tokens for a given place. That number is called the *capacity* of the place. If all places of a net have finite capacity, the net itself is referred to as a *finite capacity net*. All nets in this paper will belong to this later category. For instance, the net in Figure 1 is a finite capacity net, with capacities 2, 2 and 1 for places P_1, P_2 and P_3, respectively. If so, there is another condition to be fulfilled for any transition t_j to be enabled: the number of tokens at each output place of t_j must not exceed its capacity after firing t_j. For instance, transition t_1 in Figure 1 is initially disabled because place P_1 has already two tokens. If transitions t_2 and/or t_3 are applied more than once, the two tokens of place P_1 will be removed, so t_1 becomes enabled. Note also that transition t_3 cannot be fired initially more than once, as capacity of P_2 is 2.

3   Petri Nets for Software Verification and Validation

Petri nets have been widely used as a formal method for software verification and validation during the last two decades. The reason is the large amount of mathematical tools available to analyse standard Petri nets. Indeed, a PN model can be described by a set of linear algebraic equations [9], or other mathematical models reflecting the behavior of the system [1]. This allows us to perform a formal check of the properties related to the behavior of the underlying system, e.g., precedence relations amongst events, concurrent operations, appropriate synchronization, freedom from deadlock, repetitive activities, and mutual exclusion of shared resources, to mention just a few. The simulation-based validation can only produce a limited set of states of the modeled system, and thus can only show presence (but not absence) of errors in the model, and its underlying requirements specification. The ability of Petri nets to verify the model formally is especially important for realtime safety-critical systems and online operations. On the other hand, they provide a powerful formalism for axiomatic semantics, so PN are very well suited for semantic web and related fields.

Based on these considerations, some PN-based models for software verification and validation have been developed. As a general rule, we can start by creating a reduced grammar reflecting only those context-free aspects of the language under consideration controlling the modelling [2]. As a consequence, this approach can readily be applied to any given language. Then, we construct the PN components for each basis structure of the reduced grammar by following the approach described in [2]).

4 *Mathematica* **Package for Petri Nets**

In this section a *Mathematica* package (developed by the author) for dealing with Petri nets is described. For the sake of clarity, the main commands of the package will be described by means of its application to some Petri net examples. In this section we will restrict to the case of pure and finite capacity nets. We firstly load the package:

In[1]:= <<PetriNets`

A Petri net (like that in Figure 1 and denoted onwards as net1) is described as a collection of lists. In our representation, net1 consists of three elements: a list of couples {*place, capacity*}, a list of transitions and a list of arcs from places to transitions along with its weights:

In[2]:= net1={{{p1,2},{p2,2},{p3,1}},{t1,t2,t3,t4,t5,t6},
              {{p1,t1,2},{p1,t2,-1},{p1,t3,-2},{p2,t3,1},
               {p2,t4,-2},{p2,t5,-1},{p3,t5,1},{p3,t6,-1}}};

Note that arcs are represented by triplets {*place, transition, weight*}, where positive value for weights mean output arcs and negative values denote input arcs. Now, given the initial marking {2, 1, 0} and any transition, FireTransition command returns the new marking obtained by firing such a transition:

In[3]:= FireTransition[net1,{2,1,0},t2];
Out[3]:= {1,1,0}

Given a net and its initial marking, an interesting question is to determine whether or not a transition can be fired. EnabledTransitions command returns the list of all enabled transitions for the given input:

In[4]:= EnabledTransitions[net1,{2,1,0}];
Out[4]:= {t2,t3,t5}

FireTransition command allows us to compute the resulting markings obtained by applying these transitions onto the initial marking:

In[5]:= FireTransition[net1,{2,1,0},#]& /@ %;
Out[5]:= {{1,1,0},{0,2,0},{2,0,1}}

Note that, since transition $t1$ cannot be fired, an error message is returned:

In[6]:= FireTransition[net1,{2,1,0},t1];
Out[6]:= FireTransition: Disabled transition: t1 cannot be fired for the given net and the {2,1,0} marking.

From *Out[4]* and *Out[5]*, the reader can easily realize that successive applications of EnabledTransitions and FireTransition commands allows us to obtain all possible markings and all possible firings at each marking. However, this is a tedious and time-consuming task to be done by hand. Usually, such markings and firings are graphically displayed in the reachability graph. Next input returns the reachability graph for our Petri net and its initial marking[1]:

In[7]:= ReachabilityGraph[net1,{2,1,0}];
Out[7]:= See Figure 2

---

[1] For an arbitrary PN the reachability graph may be of infinite size. This is not the case in this paper, as we restrict ourselves to finite PN.

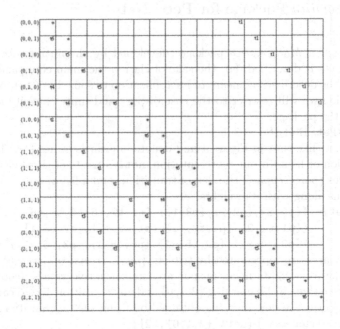

Fig. 2. The reachability graph for the Petri net **net1** and the initial marking $\{2, 1, 0\}$

outer column on the left of Fig. 2 provides the list of all possible markings for the net. Their components are sorted in increasing order from the top to the bottom, according to the standard lexicographic order. For any marking, the row in front gives the collection of its enabled transitions. Given a marking and one of its enabled transitions, we can determine the output marking of firing such transition by simply moving up/down in the transition column until reaching the star symbol: the marking in that row is the desired output.

5   Case Study: Graphical Web Services in Virtual Worlds

In a recent paper, the author described a new framework for semantic web services based on the so-called GAIVAs (Graphical Autonomous Intelligent Virtual Agents) [4]. The system was originally designed to fulfill a twofold objective: on one hand, it is a new approach to based-on-agents intelligent semantic web services: users can invoke web services interpreted by means of a sophisticated based-on-Artificial-Intelligence kernel. On the other hand, the framework incorporates a powerful GUI (Graphical User Interface) that allows the users to interact with the system in a graphical and very natural way. Once a web service is requested, user is prompted through the web into a virtual world that is actually a replica of the real environment associated with the service [5,6].

To show the performance of the proposal, we consider a simple yet illustrative example: a virtual shopping center. Different shops in this virtual environment can easily be associated with real shops. Only programmer's needs are the basic information to be provided to the DAML-S tools for semantic web services, namely, what the services do, how they work and how they are used. This information is stored into a database of services. Pointers to this database allow the user to navigate through the different services associated with the shops, compare prices and items and carry out usual tasks of a similar real environment.

The graphical tasks for the renderer system have been performed by using Open GL with GLUT (Open GL Utility Toolkit) for the higher-level functions (windowing, menus, or input) while Visual C++ v6.0 is used as the programming environment for better performance. A Prolog reasoner includes a based-on-rules expert system for making appropriate choices of items, based on the user requests and preferences [3]. The system asks the user about the services via the user interface. Some semantic tools (comprised of a DAML-S translator, a Knowledge Database and an OWL reasoner built in Prolog) are then applied to interpret user's choices and proceed accordingly. The final output is returned to the user via a Web browser [8]. Users may do shopping from their home, office or anywhere else, and get all services currently available in real shopping centers at will. The simulation framework can be implemented on a single CPU platform by creating a dynamic list of classes associated with the virtual agents. The communication between those classes and the behavioural system is achieved via DLLs to optimize the running speed.

A critical problem in this framework is the verification and validation of the underlying software. The system has been designed for multi-task, multi-user on-line operations that typically require real-time processing and instantaneous access to the virtual world and their web services. Therefore, it is crucial to ensure that no thread/process deadlocks occur and that an adequate rendezvous of those threads/processes is achieved. In order to make the problem affordable, some limitations on the number of simultaneous users and tasks are to be imposed. In the examples carried out so far up to 20 users and 100 simultaneous tasks have been considered.Under these constraints, the system is well represented by a finite pure Petri net, so the aforementioned techniques (as well as our *Mathematica* package) can be applied at full extent. Inspired by [10,11], the implementation described in this paper has been validated by interactive simulation. To this aim, we considered several hypothetical use cases for simulation and checked the corresponding results. Our evaluation results were according to our expectations,as the Web services we tested behave quite well, meaning that PN proved to be very powerful tools to achieve such goals.

6   Conclusions and Further Remarks

This paper discusses somme issues regarding the application of Petri nets to software verification and validation (SVV). It also describes a *Mathematica* package developed by the author for a class of Petri nets, which is applied to address SVV problem in the context of graphical semantic web services based on virtual agents. In our approach, interactions between end users and the system are accomplished by means of virtual agents, which exhibit a human-like physical appearance in the virtual world. Another positive feature of our work is the inclusion of autonomy for the virtual agents. In our approach, autonomy is provided by the knowledge motor via a combination of different Artificial Intelligence techniques so that the agents are able to evolve freely without human intervention (see [3,4,7] for details on the behavioral engine).

Author would like to thank FGCN'2009 conference chairs for their kind invitation to deliver a talk at that conference. This research has been supported by the Computer Science National Program of the Spanish Ministry of Education and Science, Project Ref. #TIN2006-13615.

References

1. Bourdeaud'huy, T., Hanafi, S., Yim, P.: Mathematical programming approach to the Petri nets reachability problem. European Journal of Operational Research 177, 176–197 (2007)
2. Heiner, M.: Petri Net Based Software Validation, Prospects and Limitations. Technical Report TR92-022, GMD/First at Berlin Technical University, Germany (1992)
3. Iglesias, A., Luengo, F.: New Goal Selection Scheme for Behavioral Animation of Intelligent Virtual Agents. IEICE Transactions on Information and Systems E88-D(5), 865–871 (2005)
4. Iglesias, A.: A new framework for intelligent semantic web services based on GAIVAs. Int. Journal of Information Technology and Web Engineering 3(4), 30–58 (2007)
5. Luengo, F., Iglesias, A.: A New Architecture for Simulating the Behavior of Virtual Agents. In: Sloot, P.M.A., Abramson, D., Bogdanov, A.V., Gorbachev, Y.E., Dongarra, J., Zomaya, A.Y. (eds.) ICCS 2003, vol. 2657, pp. 935–946. Springer, Heidelberg (2003)
6. Luengo, F., Iglesias, A.: Framework for Simulating the Human Behavior for Intelligent Virtual Agents. Part I: Framework Architecture. In: Bubak, M., van Albada, G.D., Sloot, P.M.A., Dongarra, J. (eds.) ICCS 2004, vol. 3039, pp. 229–236. Springer, Heidelberg (2004)
7. Luengo, F., Iglesias, A.: Framework for Simulating the Human Behavior for Intelligent Virtual Agents. Part II: Behavioral System. In: Bubak, M., van Albada, G.D., Sloot, P.M.A., Dongarra, J. (eds.) ICCS 2004, vol. 3039, pp. 237–244. Springer, Heidelberg (2004)
8. Luengo, F., Contreras, M., Leal, A., Iglesias, A.: Interactive 3D Graphics Applications Embedded in Web Pages. In: Proc. of CGIV 2007, pp. 434–440. IEEE CS Press, Los Alamitos (2007)
9. Murata, T.: Properties, analysis and applications. Proceedings of the IEEE 77(4), 541–580 (1989)
10. Narayanan, S., McIlraith, S.: Simulation, Verification and Automated Composition of Web Services. In: Proc. of the Eleventh International World Wide Web Conference-WWW 2002. ACM Press, New York (2002)
11. Narayanan, S., McIlraith, S.: Analysis and Simulation of Web Services. Computer Networks 42, 675–693 (2003)

Analysis of Priority Queue-Based Scheme to Alleviate Malicious Flows from Distributed DoS Attacks

Chu-Hsing Lin, Jung-Chun Liu, Chien-Ting Kuo, and Chi Lo

Department of Computer Science,
Tunghai University, Taichung, 40704 Taiwan
{chlin,jcliu,g96350047,g98350001}@thu.edu.tw

Abstract. In this paper, we focus on defending the DDoS attacks since they have caused many famous websites enormous losses in recent years. We propose a Priority Queue-Based scheme to analyze the interval of arrival time of the incoming packet to distinguish malicious traffic from normal traffic and to take care of malicious attacks clogging the network. We use the network simulator, NS2, to evaluate the effectiveness of the proposed scheme. The proposed Priority Queue-based scheme not only effectively decreases the flows of malicious packets from DDoS attacks with various packet rates, but also provides smooth and constant flows for packets sent by normal users. Furthermore, our priority queue-based scheme performs much better than other schemes when the number of the DDoS nodes becomes large.

Keywords: DDoS attack, network simulator, priority queue, QoS.

1 Introduction

With wide-ranging applications and services provided through the network environment, threats to the network become important issues nowadays. Numerous kinds of malicious attacks occur on the computer networks, such as SQL Injection, Worm, Trojan, and Distributed Denial-of-Service (DDoS) attacks. In this paper, we focus on defending the DDoS attacks because this type of network attacks has caused many famous websites enormous losses in recent years.

In the previous paper [1], we proposed a Priority Queue-Based scheme to analyze the interval of arrival time of the incoming packet to distinguish malicious traffic from normal traffic and to take care of malicious attacks clogging the network. But in [1], we just compared efficiency of our scheme with the Droptail queuing management algorithm. In this paper, two more experiment sets were conducted to evaluate the reliability of our priority queue-based scheme. The first experiment set compares our scheme with both Droptail and RED queuing management algorithms under various packet rates; and the second set makes comparison of those schemes by increasing the amount of malicious sources. We used the network simulator, NS2, to verify the effectiveness of our proposed scheme. Simulation results show that the Priority Queue-based scheme not only is superior to DropTail and RED queuing algorithms in detecting and defending DDoS attacks, but also is able to alleviate a great quantity of malicious flows to sustain quality of service (QoS) for normal users.

D. Ślęzak et al. (Eds.): FGCN/ACN 2009, CCIS 56, pp. 301–307, 2009.
© Springer-Verlag Berlin Heidelberg 2009

2   Related Study

Many network attackers use a number of zombie computers to achieve the objective of bandwidth consumption attacks and resource starvation attacks. These two kinds of attacks belong to DDoS attacks and are very effective.

In the bandwidth consumption attacks, bandwidth of the victim server will be filled with a large number of malicious packets flows created by the zombie computers. The normal users are prevented from connecting with the victim server. The QoS of normal users is lost momentarily since they can not obtain services from the victim server. The bandwidth consumption attack often happens on e-commerce websites. One example of this type of attacks is the ICMP flooding attack.

In the resource starvation attacks, the hardware resources such as memory of the victim server are wasted by the malicious request packets. By exploiting the characteristic of the three-way handshake of TCP protocol, the malicious request packets may ask the victim server for some network service continuously, but the malicious attacker will not respond to the ACK packet from the victim server. By this way the three-way handshake of TCP protocol will be kept in unfinished states, and the resource of the victim server is kept idle. One example of this type of attacks is the SYN flooding attack.

To prevent network attacks, one may adopt methods such as firewalls [2] or intrusion detection system (IDS), which are effective for known attacks or known IP addresses. Other methods include packet filtering [3-5], packet marking, the reverse proxy detection method [6], and ICMP and Traceback [7~12] messages, which are effective for identifying sources of attacks and implementing protection measures.

In this paper, we focus on the bandwidth consumption attacks and aim to categorize packets into "normal traffic" and "malicious traffic" packets. We analyze the packets interval time and use the harmonic mean to identify the malicious traffic. The malicious traffic will be pushed into the low priority queue and get low priority services from the server. By this mechanism, the normal user will be able to acquire better QoS from the server.

3   Structure of the Priority Queue-Based Scheme

In network environments, throughput is often used to assess quality of the network bandwidth. From analysis of throughputs of normal and DDoS nodes, a Value of Harmonic Mean (VHM) is assigned to distinguish the normal packets from the malicious ones. Harmonic mean has been used in calculation of average of flows in statistics [13]. The flowchart of our scheme is shown in Fig. 1. The records in the Database consist of:

1. Packet address
2. Packet arrival time
3. Average arriving time of the previous packet
4. Average arriving time of the current packet
5. Difference of harmonic means of incoming packets

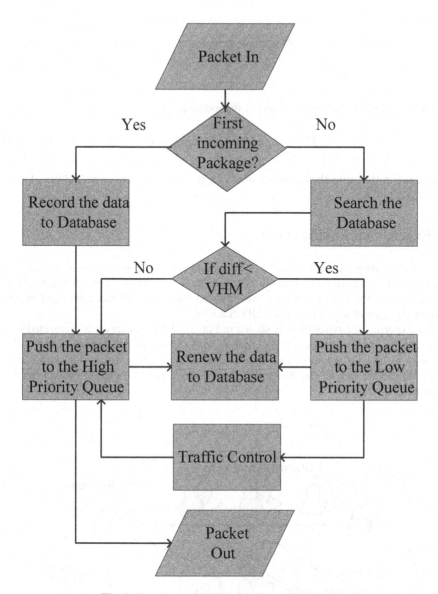

Fig. 1. Flowchart of the Priority Queue-based scheme

Each time new incoming data entering the database, formula (1), and (2) are used to calculate the harmonic mean of the arrival time of incoming packets:

$$H_{t12}(t) = \frac{2}{\sum_{i=1}^{2} \frac{1}{t_i}} \qquad (1)$$

$$H_{t23}(t) = \frac{2}{\sum\limits_{i=2}^{3} \frac{1}{t_i}}$$

(2)

The difference of harmonic means of the incoming packets is:

$$H_{avg\_diff} = H_{t23}(t) - H_{t12}(t)$$

(3)

Where suffix tij means the harmonic mean for packets from the same address of arrival times t_i and t_j.

4   Experiment Environment

We used the network simulator, NS2, to evaluate the effectiveness of the proposed scheme. We compared our scheme with Droptail and RED queuing management algorithms. In the first experiment we adjusted the DDoS packet rates, and in the second experiment we increased the DDoS nodes.

The experiment environment is shown in Fig. 2. The target server is connected to a router, which is connected to the external network consisting of four legal users and a group of zombie computers. The zombie computers on the same group simultaneously launch DoS attacks to the target server and perform the DDoS attack in the simulator environment.

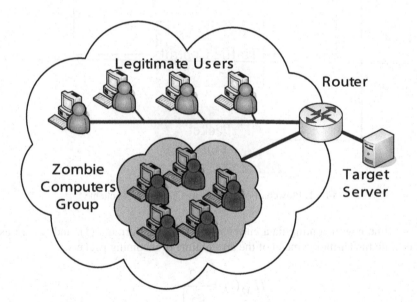

Fig. 2. A network under DDoS attacks

Every link in the simulation is set up with 1Mbps bandwidth. The limit of the queue of the priority queue-based scheme in the router is 20 Mbps. The total simulation interval is 50 seconds. The legitimate user at normal nodes start sending packets at 0 second of simulation, with the time interval of packets randomly set by a random number generator to emulate a realistic network environment. The malicious DDoS nodes start sending packets at 20 second of simulation. The average packet rate at each normal node is 100kbps and the average packet rate in the first experiment on each DDoS node is changed from 0kbps to 1000kbps. In the second experiment, numbers of the malicious node are increased. As in [1], we set VHM as 0.07 in simulations.

5 Experiment Results

Fig. 3 shows average throughputs of normal nodes and Fig. 4 shows average throughputs of DDoS nodes under DDoS attacks by using DropTail, RED, and Priority Queue-based schemes as DDoS defending schemes. From Fig. 3, we observe that when the DDoS packet rate was increased, our priority-queue based scheme has better average throughput of normal nodes than the other two schemes. From Fig. 4, we observe that when the DDoS packet rates are increased, our priority-queue based scheme allows less average throughput of malicious nodes than the other two schemes. We conclude that our priority-based scheme can effectively enhance QoS of normal users and reduce traffic of malicious users.

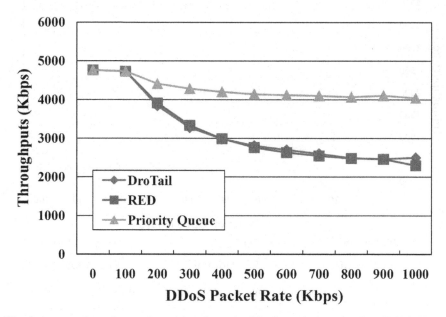

Fig. 3. Average throughputs of normal nodes under DDoS attacks by using DropTail, RED, and Priority Queue-based schemes

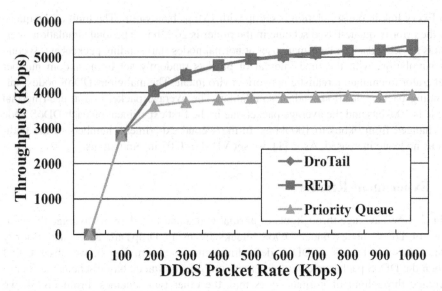

Fig. 4. Average throughputs of DDoS nodes under DDoS attacks by using DropTail, RED, and Priority Queue-based schemes

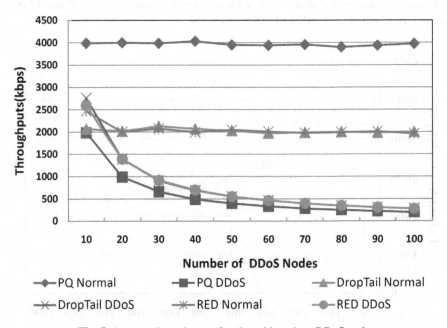

Fig. 5. Average throughputs of nodes with various DDoS nodes

Fig. 5 shows the experimental results when number of DDoS nodes was adjusted. It shows that our priority queue-based scheme performs much better than DropTail and RED queuing management algorithms when number of the DDoS nodes becomes large.

6 Discussion

Simulations by the NS2 network simulator show that the DropTail or RED queuing schemes are not very effective in alleviating flows of malicious packets under DDoS attacks. To solve this problem, we propose a Priority Queue-based scheme for defense of DDoS attacks. The proposed Priority Queue-based scheme shows that it not only effectively decreases the flows of malicious packets from DDoS attack, but also provides smooth and constant flows for packets sent by normal users.

Acknowledgement

This work was supported in part by National Science Council under grants NSC 98-2221-E-029-028, NSC 98-2221-E-029-021.

References

1. Lin, C.-H., Liu, J.-C., Kuo, C.-T.: An Effective Priority Queue-based Scheme to Alleviate Malicious Packet Flows from Distributed DoS attacks. In: The 4th International Conference on Intelligent Information Hiding and Multimedia Signal Processing (IIHMSP-2008), pp. 1371–1374. IEEE Press, Harbin (2008)
2. Lin, C.-H., Liu, J.-C., Kuo, C.-T., Chou, M.-C., Yang, T.-C.: Safeguard Intranet Using Embedded and Distributed Firewall System. In: 2008 Second International Conference on Future Generation Communication and Networking (FGCN 2008), pp. 489–492. IEEE Press, Los Alamitos (2008)
3. Lin, C.-H., Jiang, F.-C., Lai, W.-S., Lee, W.-Y., Hsu, W.-C.: Counteract SYN Flooding Using Second Chance Packet Filtering. In: Third International Conference on Ubiquitous Information Management and Communication (ICUIMC 2009). ACM Press, Korea (2009)
4. Goldstein, M., Lampert, C., Reif, M., Stahl., A., Breuel, T.: Bayes Optimal DDoS Mitigation by Adaptive History-Based IP Filtering. In: Seventh International Conference on Networking, pp. 174–179 (2008)
5. Malliga, S., Tamilarasi, A., Janani, M.: Filtering spoofed traffic at source end for defending against DoS / DDoS attacks. In: 2008 International Conference on Computing Communication and Networking, pp. 1–5 (2008)
6. Lin, C.-H., Liu, J.-C., Lien, C.-C.: Detection Method Based on Reverse Proxy Against Web Flooding Attacks. In: 8th International Conference on Intelligent Systems Design and Applications (ISDA-2008), Kaohsiung City, Taiwan, pp. 281–284 (2008)
7. Wang, B.-T., Schulzrinne, H.: An IP traceback mechanism for reflective DoS attacks. In: Proc. of IEEE Electrical and Computer Engineering 2004 (May 2004)
8. Song, M., Xu, J.: IP Traceback-Based Intelligent Packet Filtering: A Novel Technique for Defending against Internet DoS Attacks. In: Proc. of 10th IEEE Int'l Conf. Network Protocols (ICNP 2002) (November 2002)
9. Park, K., Lee, H.: On the Effectiveness of Probabilistic Packet Marking for IP Traceback under Denial of Service Attacks. In: Proc. of IEEE INFOCOM 2001 (March 2001)
10. Su, W.-T., Lin, T.-C., Wu, C.-Y., Hsu, J.-P., Kuo, Y.-H.: An On-line DDoS Attack Traceback and Mitigation System Based on Network Performance Monitoring. In: 10th International Conference on Advanced Communication Technology, vol. 2, pp. 1467–1472 (2008)
11. Qu, Z.-Y., Huang, C.-F., Liu, N.-N.: A Novel Two-Step Traceback Scheme for DDoS Attacks. In: Second International Symposium on Intelligent Information Technology Application, vol. 1, pp. 879–883 (2008)

A Heuristic Network Bandwidth Measurement with Domain-Based Model on Grids*

Chao-Tung Yang[**], Chih-Hao Lin, and Shih-Chi Yu

Department of Computer Science, Tunghai University, Taichung, 40704, Taiwan ROC
ctyang@thu.edu.tw

Abstract. Recently, Grid computing is more and more widespread. Therefore, there exists a common issue, i.e., how to manage and monitor numerous resources of grid computing environments. In most cases, we use Ganglia and NWS to monitor Grid nodes' status and network-related information, respectively. Due to users' diverse requirements, the information provided by these services is not sufficient in some scenarios. Therefore, we propose a heuristic QoS measurement constructed with domain-based information model that could provide more effective information to meet users' requirements. We hope users could manage and monitor numerous resources of grid environments more effectively and efficiently.

Keywords: Grid Computing, Heuristic, QoS, Network Information Model.

1 Introduction

It is well known that the grid computing is increasingly used by organizations to achieve high performance computing and heterogeneous resources sharing. All tasks executed in grid environments will be influenced by network status due to complicated and numerous communications between computing resources. While we design algorithms for specific usages or assign tasks into grid environments, we will evaluate the influence of network bandwidth related information, and then adjust algorithms to match up the real-time state of network [1, 2, 3, 4, 5, 6, 7, 8].

In our previous work, we found that the service provided by NWS would be affected if grid environment changed and then we had to frequently re-deploy NWS service manually. "Manual" is equivalent to "inefficiency" in network management. A typical example is illustrated in Fig. 1. If we have registered a NWS clique into for grid nodes A1, A2, A3 and A4, the header node A1 has stored network measurements among these nodes. Due to users' diverse requirements, the information provided by these services is not sufficient in some scenarios. Therefore, we propose a heuristic QoS measurement constructed with domain-based information model that could provide more effective information to meet users' requirements [9, 10, 11, 12, 13, 14].

---

[*] This paper is supported in part by National Science Council, Taiwan R.O.C., under grants no. NSC 96-2221-E-029-019-MY3 and NSC 97-3114-E-007-001.

[**] Corresponding author.

D. Ślęzak et al. (Eds.): FGCN/ACN 2009, CCIS 56, pp. 308–315, 2009.

A1(Header)

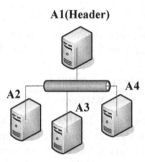

Fig. 1. This is a typical NWS clique deployment in grid environment. If A1 has registered a NWS and failed, we have to restart the service provided by NWS manually. Unfortunately, we will not be notified while service has terminated.

We hope users could manage and monitor numerous resources of grid environments more effectively and efficiently.

2   Heuristic QoS Measurement

In our previous project, we have built n integrated grid environments including a web portal composed of Ganglia and NWS service. Afterward, we start another project about PACS (Picture Archive and Communication System) [10] and most experiments were done in the same platform. The primary mission in this project is to exchange medical images efficiently with specific application developed by our team. The application, named "Cyber [9]", has successfully integrated eight algorithms.

2.1   Domain-Based Network Information Model

In this paper, we adopt Domain-based Network Information Model [2], [5], [7] for NWS services deployment. The Domain-based Network Information Model is designed for solving a complete point-to-point bandwidth measurement problem. After investigated by experiments in physical environments, we can sure that a Domain-based Network Information Model is helpful for reducing network measurements.

Take a Grid with n nodes for example. Each node measures the links between itself and all other nodes every T seconds (e.g., T=1~3 sec) for a total of NMN (n) network measurements.

$$NMN(n) = n \times (n-1) .\qquad(1)$$

Our previous work [7] used the domain-based network information model in Fig. 2 shows four sites, each containing four nodes. Each site have a head node. For sites, A1, B1, C1 and D1, the head nodes of sites are A, B, C and D, respectively. Each head node in this model periodically measures the links between itself and the other three head nodes. Each head node also periodically measures the links between itself and all other nodes in its site. Hence, using the domain-based network information model, the measurement number will be dramatically reduced to

$$NMS(n,[n_i]) = NMN(n) + \sum NMN(n_i),\qquad(2)$$

Where ni is the total number of nodes in site i. In our test-bed, the numbers of network measurements will be reduced to NMS(5, [9,4,4,3]) =102. The reduction rate R is defined as:

$$R = \frac{NMN(n) - NMS(n,[n_i])}{NMN(n)}.\qquad(3)$$

Compared to NMN (20), the Rs are 73.16%, which shows the obvious efficiency of the model. Even though this model can eliminate huge amounts of measurement effort and bandwidth use, it lacks network information between pairs of nodes belonging to different sites (unless both are borders). For example, the link (target) between nodes A2 and B1 shown in Fig. 2 is not measured. We further enhance the static model by improving the switching mechanism in the dynamic domain-based network information model. Fig. 3 shows an example. The principal improvement is to switch the site head node wth the next free node. For example, when node A1 is busy, the next free node, node A2, becomes the head node of site A, and measures the bandwidth between itself and nodes B3, C2, and D4, if they are the respective free nodes in sites B, C, and D. The purpose is to avoid having a busy node still acting as a border, which would decrease system performance.

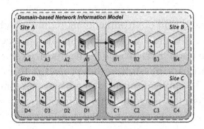
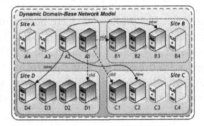

Fig. 2. The design of domain-based network information model

Fig. 3. The design of domain-based network information model

2.2 NWS Deployment and Flowchart

While deploying NWS services, we have paid a lot of attention to get rid of intruding existed services on grid nodes. In most cases, we deploy only one nameserver and multiple sensors on each computing resources. Besides, arbitrary "Persistence State" may be set up in different locations. In this paper, we simply designate one nameserver, one memory server, and one clique for a group of grid nodes.

2.3 Heuristic Approach

Statistics is helpful in many fields, especially for prediction. Some researchers have used statistical method to monitor and predict bandwidth for QoS sensitive task [11]. In this paper, we collected historical network information of grid environments and found an approach to evaluate QoS. All network relative information was periodically categorized to most used statistics. We have designed a simple model for integration

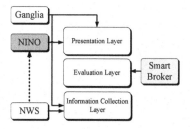

Fig. 4. A simple model that integrates Ganglia, NWS, NINO, and Smart Broker

of Ganglia, NWS, and NINO (as shown in Fig. 4).. Ganglia and NINO provide UI for users to manage and monitor grid environments. NWS and Ganglia collect related information from hosts and network regularly. And "Smart Broker" provides parameters to applications like Cyber.

Smart Broker is the key component for us to evaluate QoS. Our previous work [9], [10] has provided users with an interface for tuning up parameters which are shown as Fig. 5 below. But most parameters used by this application, Cyber, must be set manually and it's very inconvenient. We developed "Smart Broker" to help us achieve automation of parameters self-optimization in diverse scenarios. Smart Broker works as an evaluation layer between applications and information collection layer. We have pre-defined 4 task types that perform QoS measurement in various ways.

- Download
- Upload
- Computational
- Hybrid

Fig. 5. Strategy selection – UI provided by Cyber for parameters input

Cyber is a typical application of "Download" type. Fig. 6 shows the scenario used in Cyber , and Fig. 7 shows the QoS evaluation model used in this paper. And this evaluation model could be tuned at any time to approach higher accuracy in different grid environments.

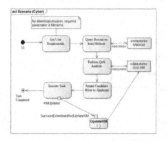

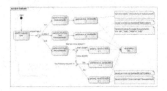

Fig. 6. The scenario used for evaluating QoS in this paper

Fig. 7. The QoS evaluation model used in this paper

3   Experimental Environment and Results

In order to verify the architect we proposed in this paper, we have performed a couple of experiments. Our test-bed has 20 grid nodes and all these hosts are divided into 4 groups. Physical deployment is shown in Fig. 8, and NWS services and database deployment are shown in Fig. 9. We have adopted a pull-based model to collect network information measured by NWS services as shown in Fig. 10.

In this paper, we have chosen 4 grid nodes as "Header", which is called "border" in domain-based network information model, to register specific NWS service – clique for gathering inter-domain network performance. Except these headers, we also registered a NWS clique named "cross-domain" to measure network performance between these headers. The information collected by NWS services is our basis to evaluate QoS. Hence, we have to ensure that the NWS services deployment we performed is applicable.

As shown in Fig.11, we could easily found that the measurements of NWS clique may be uneven. For example, eta4-delta2 has minimum measurements, 325, while zeta1-beta2 has maximum measurements, 1436. Uneven measurements may influence accuracy of our model while evaluating QoS with statistical approaches.

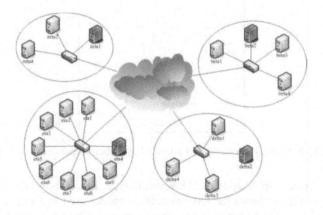

Fig. 8. Physical deployment of grid nodes that we used for test-bed

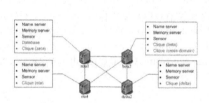
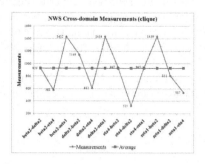
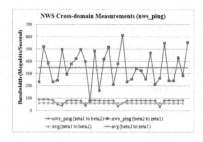

Fig. 9. NWS services and database deployment   **Fig. 10.** A pull-based model to collect network information measured by NWS services

Fig. 11. The measurements of cross-domain NWS clique   **Fig. 12.** NWS services collision test

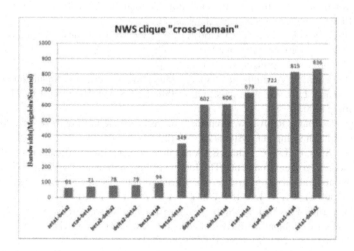

Fig. 13. NWS measurements for QoS evaluation

The NWS services have the ability to avoid collision which may cause inaccuracy of measurement, and this advantage is restricted in the same nameserver. In our test-bed, we found that the collision influences accuracy frequently. Fig. 12 is our collision test for NWS services. We could find that network performance has a great variation due to collision of NWS measurement.

Fig. 13 has shown NWS measurements of our test-bed. Although QoS evaluation model adopted in this paper could not absolutely predict real performance for real-time tasks execution. We still could pick out best selection of resources by means of QoS evaluation model. To verify usability of this QoS evaluation approach, we have also performed a simple experiment of file transmission. And the result is identical to our predication using QoS evaluation model.

4 Conclusions and Future Work

In this paper, we use Domain-based Network Information Model for experiments, but it's not a proper model for dynamic grid environments. If any grid node has hardware failure or just has been reassigned to another IP, we have to manually reconstruct NWS cliques. This has already mentioned as drawback of NWS [8]. In large scale grid environments, it's a complicated task to manage these cliques and hosts' relations. Our future work will adopt Dynamic Domain-based Network Information Model for next deployment so to reduce overheads coming from complicated management tasks.

References

1. Yang, C., Chen, T., Tung, H.: A Dynamic Domain-Based Network Information Model for Computational Grids. In: Future Generation Communication and Networking, pp. 575–578. IEEE Computer Society, Los Alamitos (2007)
2. Yang, C., Chen, S., Chen, T.: A Grid Resource Broker with Network Bandwidth-Aware Job Scheduling for Computational Grids. In: Cérin, C., Li, K.-C. (eds.) GPC 2007. LNCS, vol. 4459, pp. 1–12. Springer, Heidelberg (2007)
3. Yang, C., Chen, S.: A Multi-site Resource Allocation Strategy in Computational Grids. In: Wu, S., Yang, L.T., Xu, T.L. (eds.) GPC 2008. LNCS, vol. 5036, pp. 199–210. Springer, Heidelberg (2008)
4. Chung, W., Chang, R.: A new mechanism for resource monitoring in Grid computing. Future Generation Computer Systems 25, 1–7 (2009)
5. Yang, C., Shih, P., Lin, C., Chen, S.: A resource broker with an efficient network information model on grid environments. The Journal of Supercomputing 40, 249–267 (2007)
6. A taxonomy and survey of grid resource management systems for distributed computing. Softw. Pract. Exper. 32, 135–164 (2002)
7. Yang, C., Shih, P., Chen, S., Shih, W.: An Efficient Network Information Model Using NWS for Grid Computing Environments. In: Zhuge, H., Fox, G.C. (eds.) GCC 2005, vol. 3795, pp. 287–299. Springer, Heidelberg (2005)
8. Legrand, A., Quinson, M.: Automatic deployment of the Network Weather Service using the Effective Network View. In: Proceedings of 18th International Parallel and Distributed Processing Symposium (2004)
9. Yang, C., Yang, M., Chiang, W.: Implementation of a Cyber Transformer for Parallel Download in Co-Allocation Data Grid Environments. In: Proceedings of the 2008 Seventh International Conference on Grid and Cooperative Computing, pp. 242–253. IEEE Computer Society, Los Alamitos (2008)

10. Yang, C.T., Chen, C.H., Yang, M.F., Chiang, W.C.: MIFAS: Medical Image File Accessing System in Co-allocation Data Grids. In: IEEE Asia-Pacific Services Computing Conference, 2008. APSCC 2008, pp. 769–774 (2008)
11. Yu, Y., Cheng, I., Basu, A.: Optimal adaptive bandwidth monitoring for QoS based retrieval. IEEE Transactions on Multimedia 5, 466–472 (2003)
12. Stephen, A., Daniel, P., Helene, N., Junwei, C., Subhash, S., Graham, R.: Performance prediction and its use in parallel and distributed computing systems. Future Generation Computer Systems 22, 745–754 (2006)
13. Vazhkudai, S., Schopf, J., Foster, I.: Predicting the performance of wide area data transfers. In: Proceedings International Parallel and Distributed Processing Symposium IPDPS 2002, Abstracts and CD-ROM, 2002., pp. 34–43 (2002)
14. Krefting, D., Vossberg, M., Tolxdorff, T.: Simplified Grid Implementation of Medical Image Processing Algorithms using a Workflow Managment System, New York (2008)

Analyzing VoIP Capacity with Delay Guarantee for Integrated HSPA Networks

Shin-Hua Yang, Shun-Ren Yang, and Chien-Chi Kao

Dept. of CS & Inst. of COM, NTHU, Hsinchu, Taiwan, R.O.C.
{kim@wmnet,sryang@,mickey@wmnet.}cs.nthu.edu.tw

Abstract. Voice over IP (VoIP) is a key driver in the evolution of voice communications, and the high transmission rate property of High Speed Packet Access (HSPA) is expected to satisfy the strict delay requirements of VoIP. Therefore, the aim of this paper is to evaluate the performance of VoIP service in HSPA network. This paper presents a mathematical model for VoIP capacity in HSPA under the constraints of delay threshold and voice quality requirements. This study also analyzes the impact of scheduling schemes, the user's channel quality, and variations in packet bundle size on VoIP performance. These results are derived from simulation results, which also validate the correctness of the proposed analysis model and show that VoIP performance is limited by uplink transmission technology. Based on the E-model, this study concentrates on each VoIP connection's quality in HSUPA network.

Keywords: Delay, E-model, HSPA, VoIP capacity.

1 Introduction

Voice over IP (VoIP) is becoming a key driver in the evolution of voice communications. Compared to traditional Circuit Switched (CS) voice networks, the main advantages of VoIP are reduced operating costs and improved user flexibility. However, due to the restrictions of spectral efficiency and delay requirements, VoIP cannot exceed CS voice performance. Hence, 3GPP Release 5 and Release 6 introduced High Speed Downlink Packet Access (HSDPA) and High Speed Uplink Packet Access (HSUPA), respectively, to provide a higher transmission rate and improve system capacity. High Speed Packet Access (HSPA) is a collection of two mobile telephony protocols HSDPA and HSUPA. The evolution of HSPA was originally designed to increase data transmission rates and achieve higher capacities for high-performance applications based on innovative techniques such as shortened Transmission Time Interval (TTI) and fast packet scheduling controlled by Node B. HSPA increases the uplink and downlink peak transmission rate up to 5.76 Mbit/s and 14.4 Mbit/s, respectively. For VoIP, the end-to-end delay is the most important factor determining connection quality. The high transmission rate of HSPA should satisfy the strict delay requirements of VoIP. The maximum number of VoIP connections that HSPA systems can support is a critical performance indicator of significant interest to mobile network operators.

D. Ślęzak et al. (Eds.): FGCN/ACN 2009, CCIS 56, pp. 316–323, 2009.

The evolution of VoIP has resulted in numerous capacity analysis models for wireless networks. To maximize the resource utilization, researches in [2], [3], and [8] presented capacity analysis models that concentrate on resource allocation for each VoIP connection. Optimal resource utilization leads to the greatest VoIP performance. Nevertheless, this type of capacity analysis model is not able to predict the maximum number of supported VoIP connections because it cannot guarantee voice quality or delay. Considering voice quality, [1], [4], and [6] present VoIP capacity analysis models for HSPA. These analytical studies provide a suitable approximation for VoIP capacity, and ensure satisfactory connection quality for each user. However, this analytical model type does not discuss the effects of delay threshold on VoIP performance. Taking delay restrictions and the voice quality certification into account, this study builds a mathematical model for analyzing VoIP capacity for both HSDPA and HSUPA. This approach employs a queueing model to approximate the VoIP capacity under delay threshold which includes the packet waiting time and the packet transmission time between UE and Node B. For uplink transmission, the interference caused by other UEs affects the voice quality heavily. Hence, we take the connection quality into account when deriving the maximum number of VoIP connections. Thus, the proposed analysis model defines VoIP capacity with the guarantee of transmission time and voice quality. Results show the improved VoIP performance in an HSPA system and then the bottleneck of VoIP capacity will be HSUPA.

2   Capacity Analysis

The high transmission rate property of HSPA is expected to satisfy strict delay requirements of real time services. In this section, we build a mathematical model for analyzing the VoIP capacity when both HSDPA and HSUPA are developed. The end-to-end packet transmission delay, T_{end}, from a sending UE in BTS$_1$ to its receiving UE in BTS$_2$ consists of three parts: T_{up}, T_{cn}, and T_{down}. T_{cn} is the packet transmission time between BTS$_1$ and BTS$_2$ via the core network. Compared with the wireless HSPA transmissions of lower bit rate and higher error rate, the core network provides relatively sufficient and stable bandwidth support. In this case, T_{cn} is more steady than T_{up} and T_{down}. Therefore, we neglect the effects of T_{cn} on T_{end} and simply concentrate on T_{up} and T_{down} to derive the maximum number of VoIP connections. Let N_c be the VoIP capacity of the HSPA systems, i.e., the maximum number of supported VoIP sessions under the constraint that the average end-to-end delay of voice packets comply with the QoS requirements. Under the aforementioned assumptions, we first calculate T_{up} and T_{down}. Based on the obtained T_{up} and T_{down} values, we next derive the maximum number of VoIP connections N_{up} and N_{down} in HSUPA and HSDPA, respectively. Because of the symmetry property of voice connections, the maximum number of voice connections N_c in HSPA system is expressed as

$$N_c = Min\{N_{down}, N_{up}\}. \tag{1}$$

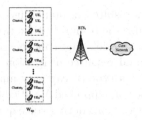

Fig. 1. Packet transmission process in the HSUPA system

2.1   Calculation of T_{up}

Every HSUPA TTI, BTS_1 schedules UEs and the scheduled UEs can transmit voice packets buffered in their corresponding queues to BTS_1. We derive the uplink transmission delay, T_{up} as follows. T_{up} is composed of two parts: the time period W_{up} during which a voice packet waits to be served in its corresponding UE queue and the transmission time T_{utx} of this uplink packet, when scheduled, from its UE to BTS_1. To simplify our analysis, Round Robin (RR) scheduling scheme is applied for HSUPA in BTS_1. Fig. 1 depicts the detailed packet transmission process at BTS_1 with the $N^{(u)}$ number of VoIP connections. In HSUPA, several UEs can transmit packets simultaneously during the same TTI. Accordingly, our model assumes that UEs under BTS_1 are grouped into X clusters, where each cluster can maximum consist of K in-service VoIP UEs. The voice packet generation process of a VoIP connection within each cluster is assumed to follow a Poisson process with arrival rate λ, whose value depends on the adopted voice codec. In this analysis, we model the BTS_1 HSUPA transmission process as a polling queueing system [5] with certain modifications. To apply the result of the polling queueing model, we assume that in the HSUPA transmission process, the UE queues within one cluster are virtually merged as a single queue. The incoming packets of each UE in $Cluster_1$ are placed in the virtual queue and transmitted to BTS_1 sequentially. We also assume that in our polling model, only one packet instead of a bundled packet in the virtual queue can be served upon every polling visit. However, the mean service time of our polling model should be modified. Let $\bar{N}_{pdu}^{(u)}$ represent the mean number of served bundled packets during a TTI for the original HSUPA transmission process. That is, the total number of transmitted packets during one TTI is $\bar{N}_{pdu}^{(u)} * N_b$. Then, under the constraint that $E[T_{up}]$ should be less than a pre-defined transmission delay budget during T_{delay} for a transmission between a UE and BTS_1, the maximum number of voice connections N_{up} in HSUPA can be derived by the following equation:

$$N_{up} = Max\{N^{(u)} : \frac{TTI^{(u)}}{\bar{N}_{pdu}^{(u)} * N_b} + \frac{N^{(u)} \lambda E[T_{utx}^2]}{2(1 - \rho^{(u)})} < T_{delay}\}. \tag{2}$$

2.2   Calculation of T_{down}

On receiving a packet, BTS_2 distributes this packet to its corresponding waiting queue. Within every TTI, BTS_2 schedules and transmits packets in the waiting queues to multiple receiving UEs using HSDPA technology. We next derive the transmission delay, T_{down}. T_{down} is also composed of two parts. The first part is W_{down}, the time period during which a voice packet waits to be served in BTS_2. The second part is T_{dtx}, the transmission time of a scheduled downlink packet from BTS_2 to the destined UE. For the tractability of our analysis model, the RR scheduling policy is adopted for HSDPA in BTS_2 as well. We assume that the packet arrivals of each VoIP connection to BTS_2 follow a Poisson process with rate, λ. Similarly, our we analysis models the BTS_2 HSDPA transmission process as a polling queueing system. Then, under the constraint that $E[T_{down}]$ should be less than a pre-defined transmission delay budget during T_{delay} for a transmission between a UE and BTS_2, the maximum number of voice connections N_{down} in HSDPA can be derived by the following equation:

$$N_{down} = Max\{N^{(d)} : \frac{TTI^{(d)}}{\bar{N}_{pdu}^{(d)}} + \frac{N^{(d)}\lambda E[T_{dtx}^2]}{2(1 - \rho^{(d)})} < T_{delay}\}. \tag{3}$$

Due to the space limitation, the details of the calculations are provided in our technical report [7].

3   Performance Evaluation

3.1   Simulation Validation

The analytical models have been validated by the simulation assumptions. Based on the system model for HSDPA and the simulation parameters shown in Table 1, Table 2 shows the analytical and simulation results. For VoIP over HSDPA, the simulations yield capabilities of 41 and 51 simultaneous connections for delay budgets 80 and 150 ms, respectively. Clearly, the simulation results match the analytical results well. For HSUPA, we take packet bundling into consideration. By applying the detailed simulation settings shown in Table 1 into our event-driven simulation model, we validate the correctness of our uplink analysis model. Table 3 compares the simulation results with those of our HSUPA polling model

Table 1. Simulation Parameters For HSDPA/HSUPA System

Parameter for HSDPA	Value	Parameter for HSUPA	Value
TTI size	2ms	TTI size	10ms
Downlink data rate	3.6Mbps	Uplink data rate	5.76Mbps
VoIP codes type	GSM6.10	VoIP codes type	GSM6.10
UE profile	Pedestrian A	UE Maximum Transmit power	21dBm
UE speed	3kmph	$(\beta_{ec}/\beta_c)^2$	3dB
UE receiver structure	Single-antenna Rake	$(\beta_{ed}/\beta_c)^2$	8dB

Table 2. Comparison Between The Analytical And Simulation Results On HSDPA

	T_{delay}=80 ms	T_{delay}=150 ms
N_{down}(Analytical)	39	49
N_{down}(Simulation)	41	51

Table 3. Comparison Between The Analytical And Simulation Results On HSUPA

$T_{delay} = 80ms$	N_b=1	N_b=2	N_b=3	$T_{delay} = 150ms$	N_b=1	N_b=2	N_b=3
N_{up}(Analytical)	63	80	53	N_{up}(Analytical)	103	127	94
N_{up}(Simulation)	62	77	51	N_{up}(Simulation)	99	123	90

under different delay budgets 80 ms and 150 ms and different packet bundle sizes. It is clear that the analytical analysis is consistent with the simulation results.

3.2 Simulation Results and Analysis

Based on the HSDPA and HSUPA simulation models validated against the analytic analysis, we design different simulation scenarios to study and compare the VoIP performance over HSDPA and HSUPA technologies. First, we concentrate on HSDPA. For HSDPA, we have provided the analytical and simulation VoIP capacity results based on RR scheduling in the last subsection. When other factors such as channel quality and throughput are taken into account for scheduling, the VoIP capacity may be influenced by the adopted scheduling algorithms. Fig. 2 shows the VoIP capacity performance over HSDPA. Fig. 2(a) represents the VoIP capacities when applying RR, Max C/I, FCDS and PF scheduling schemes under the delay budgets 80 and 150 ms. The specific relative capacity gains from each scheduling scheme compared to PF are shown in Fig. 2(b). PF provides better VoIP capacity performance than RR because it is on average able to schedule users at better channel conditions. Compared to Max C/I, PF is more fair because of taking UE's average throughput into consideration. The results verify that packet scheduling plays a key role in achieving good

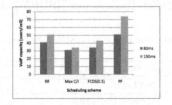 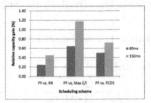

(a) VoIP cell capacities with different scheduler.   (b) Relative capacity gain of PF over the other algorithms.

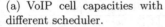

Fig. 2. VoIP capacities (a) different scheduling schemes (b) relative capacity gain

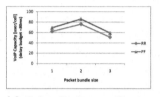
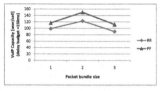

(a) Delay Budget = 80 ms   (b) Delay Budget = 150 ms

Fig. 3. Number of Supported VoIP Connections on (a) Delay Budget = 80 ms, (b) Delay Budget = 150 ms

VoIP capacity in HSDPA. From Fig. 2(a), we also note that the delay budget is another factor that affects the VoIP capacity. The longer the delay budget, the more the number of supported voice connections.

After discussing the VoIP capacity performance over HSDPA, we study the VoIP capacity over HSUPA. Considering RR, we have already provided the analytical and simulation VoIP capacity results over HSUPA. We also take the PF scheduling algorithm into account for observing the HSUPA VoIP performance. Fig. 3 shows the VoIP capacity applying the RR and PF scheduling algorithms with different packet bundle sizes under 80 and 150 ms delay budgets. From Fig. 3(a) and Fig. 3(b), PF scheduling provides better VoIP capacity than RR scheduling regardless of the delay budget or the packet bundle size. Moreover, the packet bundle size is the other factor that influences VoIP performance. Packet bundle size two provides the better capacity performance than that without packet bundling. The phenomenon is explained as follows. The bundled packet simply contains one header and then the header overhead will be shared among the two packets. Hence, packet bundling decreases the header overhead and provides better bandwidth efficiency. We also observe that applying packet bundling should waste time on waiting enough packets to be bundled and transmitted. However, when increasing the bundle size from two to three, the VoIP capacity decreases. This is because the more the packet bundle size, the longer the waiting time for bundling packets. Hence, the VoIP capacity will decrease when the packet bundling delay is intolerable. From Fig. 3, we know that there is a trade-off between the packet bundle size and the improvement of VoIP capacity. As a result, bundling two packets into one packet is the best option to enhance the VoIP performance over HSUPA in our simulation parameter settings.

After discussing the VoIP capacity over HSDPA and HSUPA, we know that the VoIP performance is influenced by the adopted scheduling scheme, the delay budget, and the packet bundle size. In the above experiments, we obtain the capacity based on the delay budget, one of the QoS requirements. From our simulation results, under the 80 ms delay budget, we obtain that the optimal capacity achieved with PF scheduling over HSDPA is 51 users. Due to the restrictions on the UE downlink data reception transmission rate, the peak data rate in our NS2 simulation scenarios is 3.6 Mbit/s while the ideal transmission rate defined in UMTS Release 5 is 14.4 Mbit/s. If the downlink transmission rate can be

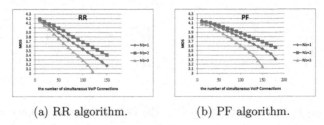

(a) RR algorithm.   (b) PF algorithm.

Fig. 4. The number of simultaneous VoIP connections under the different packet bundle sizes and the corresponding MOS values when applying (a) RR (b) PF

increased up to 14.4 Mbit/s, fourfold number of voice packets can be transmitted during each TTI. Hence, the VoIP capacity over HSDPA may be improved at least two or three times and then the maximum supported number of VoIP connections may be 102 or 153. Similarly, under the 80 ms delay budget and applying the PF scheduling, the optimal capacity achieved with packet bundling size two under HSUPA is 86 users. Thus, when both uplink and downlink packets can be transmitted with the ideal peak date rate, the VoIP performance is bounded by the uplink transmission performance. In the following, we focus on the VoIP performance under HSUPA and obtain the VoIP capacity according to E-model. Fig. 4 shows the number of simultaneous VoIP connections under the different packet bundle sizes and the corresponding MOS values. Clearly, the more restricted the demanding connection quality, the less the number of supported VoIP connections. Compared to the three curves in Fig. 4(a), those in Fig. 4(b) degrade less sharply. This means when applying PF scheduling, the increase in the number of simultaneous VoIP connections leads to less decrease in connection quality. Hence, PF scheduling algorithm provides better VoIP performance than RR scheduling algorithm. Based on E-model, we know that the connection quality of our analytical VoIP capacity is above 3.6 MOS value regardless of the adopted scheduling scheme and packet bundle size. This means that our analysis model approximates the VoIP capacity with guaranteed connection quality with which most of the users satisfy.

4   Conclusion

This paper focused on the VoIP performance in HSPA networks and builded a mathematical VoIP capacity analysis model to obtain the maximum number of supported VoIP connections that still meet transmission delay and voice quality requirements. Using simulation results, this study also validated the correctness of the proposed analytical method and discussed other factors affecting VoIP performance. Experimental results indicated that PF is the most appropriate algorithm for VoIP service, even in a mixed traffic environment or when the UE has poor channel quality. For packet bundling, there is a tradeoff between the packet bundle size and the bundle delay. In the simulated scenario in this study, a packet bundle size of two causes less bundle delay and decreases packet overhead.

Hence, bundling two packets together improves VoIP capacity tremendously. Our precise analytical model showed that VoIP performance is bounded by uplink VoIP performance. Following to the E-model, this study also examined the effects of other QoS requirements on uplink VoIP capacity and verified that our analysis model approximates the VoIP capacity with guaranteed connection quality with which most of the users satisfy.

Acknowledgment

We would like to thank Chunghwa Telecom. This work was accomplished under close discussions with the researchers of Chunghwa Telecom. This work was supported in part by the National Science Council (NSC) of Taiwan under Contracts 96-2752-E-007-003-PAE, 96-2221-E-007-025-, 96-2221-E-007-027-, 96-2219-E-007-012- and 96-2219-E-007-011-, and Chunghwa Telecom.

References

1. Chen, T., Kuusela, M., Malkamaki, E.: Uplink capacity of voip on hsupa. In: IEEE 63rd Vehicular Technology Conference, 2006. VTC 2006-Spring, May 2006, vol. 1, pp. 451–455 (2006)
2. Lee, H., Kwon, T., Cho, D.-H.: An efficient uplink scheduling algorithm for voip services. IEEE 802.16 bwa systems 5 (September 2004)
3. Lee, H., Kwon, T., Cho, D.-H.: Extended-rtps algorithm for voip services. IEEE 802.16 systems 5, 2060–2065 (2006)
4. Qualcomm White paper. Air interface cell capacity of wcdma systems (May 2007)
5. Takagi, H.: Queuing analysis of polling models. ACM Comput. Surv. (1988)
6. Wanstedt, S., Ericson, M., Hevizi, L., Pettersson, J., Barta, J.: The effect of f-dpch on voip over hsdpa capacity. In: IEEE 63rd Vehicular Technology Conference, 2006. VTC 2006-Spring, May 2006, vol. 1, pp. 410–414 (2006)
7. Yang, S.-R., Yang, S.-H.: Analyzing voip capacity with delay guarantee for integrated hspa networks. Technical Report, Natl. Tsing Hua Univ. (2009)
8. Zhao, D., Shen, X.: Performance of packet voice transmission using IEEE 802.16 protocol. IEEE Wireless Communications 14(1), 44–51 (2007)

Cross-Layering between Physical Layer and Routing in Wireless Ad-Hoc Networks

Jean Michel Dricot[1], Gianluigi Ferrari[2], and Philippe De Doncker[1]

[1] Université Libre de Bruxelles, OPERA Department
Wireless Communications Group
1050 Bruxelles, Belgium
{jdricot,pdedonck}@ulb.ac.be
[2] University of Parma, Department of Information Engineering
Wireless Ad-hoc and Sensor Networks (WASN) Lab
43124 Parma, Italy
gianluigi.ferrari@unipr.it

Abstract. Routing is a key issue in wireless ad-hoc networks. The goal of an efficient routing strategy is to set up routes so that the overall quality of communications will be the best possible. While the Open Systems Interconnection (OSI) reference model advocates for a clear separation of routing, access, and physical layers, in this paper we show that in scenarios with faded communications, cross-layer interactions have to be carefully considered. More precisely, we compare the performance of the Ad-hoc On-demand Distance Vector (AODV) routing algorithm with that of one of its physical layer-oriented variants, denoted as AODVφ . It will be clearly shown that no single routing strategy is always optimal and that an intelligent adaptation should be performed.

Keywords: Wireless networks, sensor networks, cross-layer, channel modeling, performance evaluation, fading.

1 Introduction

A wireless ad-hoc network consists of a large number of autonomous mobile nodes connected to each other directly and without the need for pre-existing configuration parameters or centralized infrastructures [1, 2]. From an architectural point of view, a Mobile Ad-Hoc Network (MANET) is formed as a *multi-hop* architecture due to the limited transmission range of wireless transceivers and node mobility. Therefore, routing plays an important role in the operation of such networks: each node has to act as both router and host.

While the Open Systems Interconnection (OSI) reference model advocates for a clear separation of the routing, access, and physical layers, this distinction is seldom guaranteed in several future generation wireless network architectures [3]. In fact, the physical layer is very variable and its characteristics profoundly influences the performance of MANETs. Therefore, its interaction with the upper layers often leads to unexpected and undesirable effects. This paper analyzes the existing cross-layer interactions between the physical layer and the routing strategy.

D. Ślęzak et al. (Eds.): FGCN/ACN 2009, CCIS 56, pp. 324–333, 2009.
© Springer-Verlag Berlin Heidelberg 2009

The goal of a routing algorithm is to find the best route according to a proper cost function. For instance, possible strategies include shortest-path routing [4], energy-aware routing [5, 6, 7], highest stability routing [8], or least-congested route selection [8]. Meanwhile, these approaches typically do not take into account the cross-layer interactions suggested in [9, 10, 3], which clearly highlight the impact that physical layer has on routing efficiency. In particular, the bit error rate (BER) at the end of a multi-hop route may, under certain conditions, represent a good indicator of the physical layer status [11, 12]. Also, it has been recently shown that the expected transmission (ETX) count of a path, defined as the expected total number of packet transmissions (including retransmissions) required to successfully deliver a packet along that path, is a good indicator of the routing quality [13]. The impact of the cross-layer interactions has received a significant attention in the last years. The interaction between the physical and the application layers (and, more precisely, VoIP and video throughput) has been quantified in [14]. The impact of the interference on throughput [15] and connectivity [16] has also been highlighted.

In the following, we consider a *regular* network topology, in the sense that every receiver has the same number of nearest neighbors and the same distance to any of these nearest neighbors. In reality, the distances will more likely be non-homogeneous and distributed around an average value. The impact of the topology is out of the scope of this paper and can be found in [17]. Also, we consider a simple slotted asynchronous random access scheme, such that, in each timeslot, every node transmits with a given probability q (obviously proportional to the traffic load). The assumption of a simple Bernoulli transmission model, which is supported by the analyses presented in [18] and [19, p. 278] can be considered simpler than other channelization schemes (such as time/frequency division multiple access) but it will allow to derive a lower bound on the performance of communication networks with more sophisticated MAC protocols under use.

2   The Log-Normal Fading Link Model

We assume a narrowband log-normal block fading (i.e., shadowing or slow fading) channel [20]. This model is implemented in the NS-2 simulator and will be used later for a simulation-based investigation of cross-layer interactions. In the log-normal fading model, the ratio of transmit-to-receive power $X \triangleq P_t/P_0$ is assumed to have the following log-normal distribution:

$$f_X(x) = \frac{1}{x\sqrt{2\pi\sigma^2}} \exp\left[-\frac{(\ln x - \mu)^2}{2\sigma^2}\right] U(x).$$

where μ is the path loss attenuation (dimension: [dB]) that can be based on an analytical model or empirical measurements and σ is the standard deviation of X (dimension: [dB]). Most empirical studies support a standard deviation $\sigma = 4 - 16$ dB. Alternatively (and in the model implemented by the NS-2), the path loss can be treated separately from the slow fading by letting $\mu = 0$ and setting

$$P_0 = P_t \, d^{-n} X \tag{1}$$

where P_0 is the received power (dimension: [W]), P_t is the transmit power (dimension: [W]), n is the path loss exponent (adimensional). A transmission on the considered link is successful if and only if the signal-to-noise and interference ratio (SINR) at the receiver, denoted as SINR, is above a pre-defined threshold Θ. This threshold value depends, among other factors, on the receiver characteristics, the modulation and coding scheme, etc. [21]. The SINR can then be written as SINR $\triangleq P_0/N + P_{\text{int}}$ where N is the background noise power and P_{int} is the total interference power at the receiver, given by the sum of the received powers from all the undesired transmitters. In large and/or dense networks, the transmission is only limited by the interference and it can be assumed that $N \ll P_{\text{int}}$. The total interference in a scenario with j interfering neighbors is $P_{\text{int}} \triangleq \sum_{i=1}^{j} P_i = \sum_{i=1}^{j} P_c d^{-n} X_i$ where $\{X_i\}_{i=1...j}$ are log-normally distributed and represent the independent fading processes associated with the links originating at the interfering nodes. The probability of successful link transmission in the presence of j interferers is

$$\mathcal{P}_s^{(j)} \triangleq \mathbb{P}\left\{\text{SINR} > \Theta \mid j \text{ interferers}\right\} = \mathbb{P}\left\{ \frac{P_0 d_0^{-n} X}{\sum_{i=1}^{j} P_c d^{-n} X_i} > \Theta \right\}.$$

By introducing the new r.v. $Y^{(j)} \triangleq \sum_{i=1}^{j} X_i$, and $\xi \triangleq \Theta \dfrac{P_c}{P_0} \left(\dfrac{d_0}{d} \right)^n$ it follows:

$$\mathcal{P}_s^{(j)} = 1 - \mathbb{P}\left\{ X \leq \xi Y^{(j)} \right\} = 1 - \iint_{x \leq \xi y} f_{XY^{(j)}}(x, y) \mathrm{d}x \mathrm{d}y$$

where $f_{XY^{(j)}}(x, y)$ is the joint probability density function of X and $Y^{(j)}$. Since X and $Y^{(j)}$ are independent, i.e., $f_{XY^{(j)}}(x, y) = f_X(x) f_{Y^{(j)}}(y)$. In the case of the log-normal fading, $Y^{(j)}$ corresponds to the sum of log-normal random variables with the same parameters. Following the approach proposed in [22,23], $Y^{(j)}$ can be approximated as a log-normal random variable with parameters $\sigma_j^2 = \ln\left(\frac{e^{\sigma^2}-1}{j} + 1 \right)$, $\mu_j = \ln j + \frac{\sigma^2 - \sigma_j^2}{2}$. Finally, the probability of successful link transmission becomes

$$\mathcal{P}_s^{(j)} = \frac{1}{2} - \frac{1}{2} \int_0^\infty \frac{\exp\left[-\frac{(\ln y - \mu_j)^2}{2\sigma_j^2} \right]}{y \sigma_j \sqrt{2\pi}} \, \text{erf}\left(\frac{\ln \xi y}{\sigma \sqrt{2}} \right) \mathrm{d}y. \tag{2}$$

A closed-form expression of $\mathcal{P}_s^{(j)}$ cannot be derived and its integral expression must be numerically evaluated. In Fig. 1, $\mathcal{P}_s^{(j)}$ is shown, as a function of the log-normal fading power σ, for various values of the number of interferers j. In all cases, $\xi = 10$ dB, and this corresponds to keeping the SINR threshold fixed. The figure suggests that the presence of lognormal shadowing *improves*

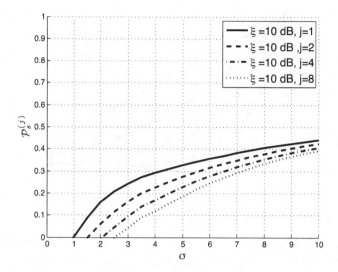

Fig. 1. Probability of link success $\mathrm{Pr}_{\mathrm{s}}^{(j)}$ as a function of σ and for a fixed value of ξ. Various values of the number of active interferers j are considered.

the connectivity properties of the network, as predicted by the results in [24,25]. Furthermore, the link probability of success is monotonically increasing in the lognormal spread σ so that it can be concluded that, even though the presence of a deep fades impacts the received power on the link, it has globally a beneficial impact on the link SINR.

Let us now considerer a link surrounded by N *possible* interfering neighbors, each of them having a probability q of transmitting a packet at a given time. In that case, the total interference is: $P_{\mathrm{int}} \triangleq \sum_{i=1}^{N} P_i \Lambda_i$ where $\{\Lambda_i\}_{i=1...N}$ is a sequence of stochastically independent Bernoulli distributed random variables with $\mathbb{P}\{\Lambda_i = 1\} = q$ and $\mathbb{P}\{\Lambda_i = 0\} = 1-q$. The probability that j nodes among the N nodes interfere at the same moment is thus a binomial r.v. with parameters q and N: $\mathbb{P}\{j \text{ interferers}|q, N\} = \binom{N}{j}q^j(1-q)^{N-j}$ and the total probability of link success in the presence of N neighbors is

$$\mathcal{P}_{\mathrm{s}} \triangleq \mathbb{P}\{\mathrm{SINR} > \Theta\} = \sum_{j=0}^{N} \underbrace{\mathbb{P}\{\mathrm{SINR} > \Theta|\ j \text{ interferers}\}}_{\mathcal{P}_{\mathrm{s}}^{(j)}} \cdot \underbrace{\mathbb{P}\{j \text{ interferers}\}}_{\binom{N}{j}q^j(1-q)^{N-j}}$$

$$= \sum_{j=0}^{N} \binom{N}{j}\ \mathcal{P}_{\mathrm{s}}^{(j)} q^j(1-q)^{N-j}.$$

where $\mathcal{P}_{\mathrm{s}}^{(j)}$ is given by (2). In Fig. 2, the link probability of success is presented as a function of the amount of active interfering nodes N and the probability of transmission q. The variable ξ is set to 10 dB. It can be observed that, even if the amount of interferers increases, the link probability of success decreases to a

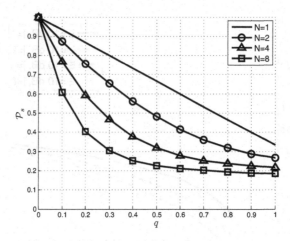

Fig. 2. Link probability success on a single link as a function of the probability of transmission q and the amount of neighbors N. The value of $\xi = 10$ dB and $\sigma = 10$ dB.

non-zero value. This is unlike in the fast fading (i.e., Rayleigh fading) scenario where the link probability of success rapidly decreases to $\mathcal{P}_s = 0$ as q increases [17].

3   Simulation-Based Analysis

Section 4 will present the key results of a simulation-based analysis of the cross-layer interactions between the physical layer and the routing. In order to perform this analysis, we compaired the Ad-hoc On-demand Distance Vector (AODV) routing algorithm and on one of its possible physical layer-oriented variants, denoted as AODVφ .

The AODV routing protocol belongs to the class of *on-demand* routing strategies [26,27]: a route is created at the time a source needs to reach a destination. In order to locate the destination node, the source broadcasts a route request (RREQ) message all over the network. Each time an intermediate node is solicited, it adds an entry in its routing tables and builds a reverse path to the source. This flooding operation stops when the messages reach the destination or when a node has already the destination in its routing table. A unicast route reply (RREP) message is sent along the reverse path leading to the source. At that moment, the route is formed and kept in cache. When a link breaks, due to mobility or bad propagation conditions, a new route discovery is triggered [28]. Finally, for each destination the route lengths are regularly computed and only the shortest route is kept, i.e., the one with smallest hop count.

The AODVφ routing algorithm is a variant of the AODV routing protocol. It implements the relaying strategy by selecting the closest possible neighbour as the next hop when constructing the routes. Only the RREQ messages of AODV are suitably modified and the remaining of the AODV protocol is kept as-is.

Table 1. Reference values for the parameters used in the simulations

Number of nodes N	50
Area A [m×m]	1500×300
Node spatial density ρ_S [m^{-2}]	1.1×10^{-4}
Active source nodes N_a	10
MAC Protocol	DCF (IEEE 802.11)
Attenuation model	Shadowing
Bit rate R_b [Mb/s]	2
Carrier frequency f_c [MHz]	914
Max. transmit power P_t^{max} [W]	0.282
Initial node energy [J]	30
Send buffer [pck]	64
Interface queue [pck]	64
Source type	Constant Bit Rate (CBR)
Probability of transmission q	0.1
Correct receive threshold [W]	3.652×10^{-10}
Threshold to avoid collisions [W]	1.559×10^{-11}
Collision Threshold Θ [dB]	10
Simulation time [s]	6000
Pause time [s]	600
Node speed v [m/s]	1

Finally, two performance metrics have been chosen in order to evaluate the performance of the routing protocols of interest: (i) the *route throughput* (also referred to as *packet delivery fraction*) that is is defined as the ratio between the packets that successfully reach their destinations and the total number of generated packets, and (ii) the *normalized routing load* that is the ratio between the number of routing messages and the number of correctly delivered packets. The other reference values for the simulation parameters are presented in Table 1.

4   Interaction between Physical Layer and Routing Protocol

4.1   Route Throughput

In Fig. 3 the throughput is shown as a function of the fading spread σ, for two possible values of n and considering both the AODV and AODVφ protocols. It can be observed that, when the fading power increases, the performance of the AODV protocol, in terms of route throughput, decreases significantly. This is an undesirable side effect of the longest hop routing strategy: in fact, when the hops are as long as the maximum transmission distance, the received power is the lowest possible. Therefore, in the presence of strong fading, it is more likely that the link SINR will fall under the minimum threshold value and an outage will occur. On the other hand, by combining expressions (1) and the definition

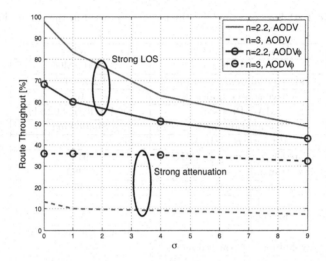

Fig. 3. Route throughput as a function of the fading spread, considering various values of the pathloss exponent n and the two routing strategies of interest

of the SINR, one can see that since the AODVφ protocol chooses shorter hop lengths than the AODV protocol, the corresponding SINR will be significantly higher and the outage event will occur less likely. From the results in Fig. 3, it can also be observed that, when the path loss exponent is high, the fading power (represented by the spread σ) plays little or no role.

It is interesting to note that an alternative analysis of the impact of the fading is carried out in [17] in the case of small-scale block fading (or Rayleigh fading). The authors find that the expression of the probability of successful link transmission depends only on (i) the path loss coefficient, (ii) the transmit power, and (iii) the network topology. Therefore, one can conclude that cross-layering between physical layer and routing protocol is limited to scenarios with *large-scale* fading (and not in scenarios with Rayleigh fading only).

4.2   Normalized Routing Load

In Fig. 4, the normalized routing load is shown as a function of the fading spread, considering the two routing strategies of interest and two possible values for the pathloss exponent n. It can be seen that, in the case of a limited attenuation (strong line-of-sight), the normalized routing load required by the AODVφ protocol is high since the routes contain a significant number of relaying nodes and this requires a substantial amount of control messages to create and maintain them. When the attenuation increases, the normalized routing load required by the AODV protocol increases significantly and exceeds the load observed with AODVφ protocol. This is due to the extended amount of route repairs triggered by the fragile long hops selected by the AODV protocol and the increasing lengths of the routes. Note that a positive feature of the AODVφ protocol

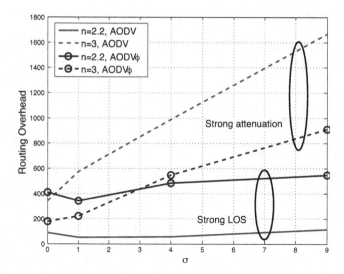

Fig. 4. Normalized routing load as a function of the fading spread, considering various values of the pathloss exponent n and the two routing strategies of interest

consists of the fact that the number of control messages observed in presence of attenuation does not extensively diverge from the strong line-of-sight situation.

Node mobility has also a clear impact of the performance of the two routing protocols (note that, according to the simulation parameters shown in Table 1, the pause time is one tenth of the simulation time). Indeed, when the attenuation is high (i.e., when the transmission distance is low) the probability that a nodes leaves the coverage zone of an emitter is important, which explains the poor performance of AODV in presence of strong attenuation. On the other hand, in the initial phase of the AODVφ protocol, the closest neighbours is picked up as the next hop. Therefore, it remains longer in the connectivity zone. The rate at which route reconstructions is triggered remains low.

5 Conclusions

In this paper, we have investigated the possible cross-layer interactions between the physical layer, medium access control, and the routing strategy. First, we have shown that for a noiseless wireless ad-hoc network, it is reasonable to adapt the routing strategy with respect to the propagation conditions. More precisely, a shortest-hops strategy is preferred when the attenuation raises above a certain level. This strategy has shown to be less sensitive to the intensity of the fading. On the opposite, classical approaches (i.e., the AODV protocol) give better results when the attenuation is limited. Recent work has shown that a reasonable estimation for the value of the attenuation factor can be easily measured by the nodes [29]. Therefore, the routing strategy should be selected according to the detected value of the attenuation factor.

Acknowledgment

This work is supported in part by the Belgian National Fund for Scientific Research (FRS-FNRS).

References

1. Boukerche, A.: Algorithms and Protocols for Wireless, Mobile Ad Hoc Networks. Wiley-IEEE Press (2008)
2. Ramanathan, R.: Challenges: a radically new architecture for next generation mobile ad hoc networks. In: Proc. of the 11th annual international conference on Mobile computing and networking (MobiCom 2005), Cologne, Germany, September 2005, pp. 132–139 (2005)
3. Choi, J., Park, K., Kim, C.-k.: Analysis of cross-layer interaction in multirate 802.11 wlans. IEEE Transactions on Mobile Computing 8(5), 682–693 (2009)
4. Tan, K., Zhang, Q., Zhu, W.: Shortest path routing in partially connected ad hoc networks. In: Proc. of the IEEE Global Telecommunications Conference (GLOBE-COM 2003), San Francisco, CA, USA, December 2003, vol. 2, pp. 1038–1042 (2003)
5. Dietrich, I., Dressler, F.: On the lifetime of wireless sensor networks. ACM Trans. Sen. Netw. 5(1), 1–39 (2009)
6. Park, G., Lee, S.: A routing protocol for extend network lifetime through the residual battery and link stability in manet. In: ACC 2008: Proceedings of the WSEAS International Conference on Applied Computing Conference, pp. 199–204. World Scientific and Engineering Academy and Society (WSEAS), Wisconsin (2008)
7. Mohanoor, A.B., Radhakrishnan, S., Sarangan, V.: Online energy aware routing in wireless networks. Ad Hoc Netw. 7(5), 918–931 (2009)
8. Meng, L., Wu, W.: Dynamic source routing protocol based on link stability arithmetic. In: ISISE 2008: Proceedings of the 2008 International Symposium on Information Science and Engieering, pp. 730–733. IEEE Computer Society, Washington (2008)
9. Akyildiz, I.F., Wang, X.: Cross layer design in wireless mesh networks. IEEE Transactions on Vehicular Technology 57(2) (2008)
10. Dricot, J.-M., De Doncker, P., Zimányi, E.: Multivariate analysis of the cross-layer interaction in wireless network similulations. In: Proc. of the Int. Workshop on Wireless Ad-hoc Networks (IWWAN 2005), London, United Kingdom (May 2005)
11. Ferrari, G., Malvassori, S.A., Tonguz, O.K.: On physical layer-oriented routing with power control in ad-hoc wireless networks. IET Communications 2(2), 306–319 (2008)
12. Tonguz, O.K., Ferrari, G.: Ad Hoc Wireless Networks: A Communication-Theoretic Perspective. John Wiley and Sons, Chichester (2006)
13. De Couto, D.S.J.: High-throughput routing for multi-hop wireless networks. Ph.D. dissertation, supervisor-Morris, Robert T (2004)
14. Tobagi, F.A., Vyas, A.K., Ha, S., Awoniyi, O.: Interactions between the physical layer and upper layers in wireless networks. Ad Hoc Networks, 1208–1219 (2007)
15. Vyas, A., Tobagi, F.: Impact of interference on the throughput of a multihop path in a wireless network. In: Proceeding of the IEEE third International Conference on Broadband Communications, Networks and Systems, BROADNETS (2006)

16. Dousse, O., Baccelli, F., Thiran, P.: Impact of interferences on connectivity in ad hoc networks. IEEE/ACM Trans. Netw. 13(2), 425–436 (2005)
17. Liu, X., Haenggi, M.: Throughput Analysis of Random and Regular Networks. EURASIP Journal on Wireless Communications and Networking 4, 554–564 (2005)
18. Tobagi, F.: Analysis of a two-hop centralized packet radio network—part i: slotted aloha. IEEE Trans. Commun. 28(2), 196–207 (1980)
19. Bertsekas, D., Gallager, R.: Data networks, 2nd edn., p. 278. Prentice-Hall, Inc., Upper Saddle River (1992)
20. Catedra, M.F., Perez, J.: Cell Planning for Wireless Communications. Artech House, Inc., Norwood (1999)
21. Rappaport, T.S.: Wireless Communications: Principles and Practice. IEEE Press, Piscataway (1996)
22. Felton, L.F.: The sum of log-normal probability distributions in scatter transmission systems. IRE Trans. on Communications Systems, 57–67 (March 1960)
23. Schwartz, S.C., Yeh, Y.S.: On the distribution function and moments of power sums with log-normal components, vol. 61, pp. 1441–1462 (September 1982)
24. Hekmat, R., Van Mieghem, P.: Connectivity in wireless ad-hoc networks with a log-normal radio model. Mob. Netw. Appl. 11(3), 351–360 (2006)
25. Miorandi, D., Altman, E., Alfano, G.: The impact of channel randomness on coverage and connectivity of ad hoc and sensor networks. IEEE Trans. Wireless Comms. (2007)
26. Perkins, C.: Ad-hoc on-demand distance vector routing (1997)
27. Belding-Royer, E.: Routing approaches in mobile ad hoc networks. In: Ad Hoc Networking. IEEE Press, Los Alamitos (2003)
28. Perkins, C.E., Royer, E.M.: Ad-hoc on-demand distance vector routing. In: Proc. of the Second IEEE Workshop on Mobile Computer Systems and Applications (WMCSA 1999), New Orleans, Louisiana, USA, February 1999, pp. 90–100 (1999)
29. Srinivasa, S., Haenggi, M.: Modeling interference in finite uniformly random networks. In: International Workshop on Information Theory for Sensor Networks, WITS 2007 (2007)

Matlab-Based KETpic Add-On for Generating and Rendering IFS Fractals

Akemi Gálvez[1], Andrés Iglesias[1], and Setsuo Takato[2]

[1] Department of Applied Mathematics and Computational Sciences
University of Cantabria, Avda. de los Castros, s/n, E-39005, Santander, Spain
{galveza,iglesias}@unican.es
[2] Department of Mathematics, Faculty of Pharmaceutical Sciences
Toho University, Miyama 2-2-1, Funabashi 274-8510, Japan
takato@phar.toho-u.ac.jp

Abstract. Fractals are among the most exciting and intriguing mathematical objects ever discovered. Although there is a wealth of programs and tools to generate fractals by computer, none of them is able to yield high-quality graphical output to be readily embedded into standard LATEX source code in a text-like form. This paper introduces a new and freely available KETpic add-on, developed in *Matlab*, to generate LATEX-readable code so that image files are no longer invoked nor required. The resulting files are astonishingly small when compared with their image file counterparts, thus leading to higher compression ratios than other conventional formats such as JPEG, GIF, PNG, EPS and the like. This paper describes our program and gives some examples to illustrate the excellent performance of our approach.

1 Introduction

Computer tools for mathematical editing and publishing are ubiquitous in today's technological era. Among them, LATEX has become the standard "de facto" for high-quality typesetting of scientific documents. But although graphical output is supported, LATEX is still very limited for graphics. Due to this reason, a research group from the "Kisarazu National College of Technology" at Kisarazu (Japan) released a new software in 2006 for high-quality mathematical drawing in LATEX [19]. The program, called KETpic (*K*isarazu *E*ducational *Tpic*), is a library of functions developed on various computer algebra systems (CAS) to generate LATEX source codes for high-quality scientific artwork. As a result, accurate graphical figures can be obtained either on a PC display or on printed matter. The corresponding libraries and some interesting examples and documentation are freely downloadable at the URL: http://www.ketpic.com. See also [6, 17, 20, 21] for examples and further information about this software.

Although smooth curves and surfaces are the most usual graphical objects displayed in scientific documents, it is also interesting to represent graphically irregular mathematical objects, such as fractals. Among them, the *Iterated Function Systems* (IFS) models, popularized by Barnsley in the 1980s, are particularly

D. Ślęzak et al. (Eds.): FGCN/ACN 2009, CCIS 56, pp. 334–341, 2009.
© Springer-Verlag Berlin Heidelberg 2009

interesting due to their appealing combination of conceptual simplicity, computational efficiency and great ability to reproduce natural formations and complex phenomena [1]. For instance, the attractors of nonlinear chaotic systems exhibit a fractal structure [3–5, 8, 9, 13–16, 18]. In the two-dimensional space IFS fractals are made up of the union of several copies of themselves, where each copy is transformed by a 2D affine transformation, so the IFS is defined by a finite number of affine transformations, and therefore represented by a relatively small set of input data [10–12]. This fact has been advantageously used in the field of fractal image compression, an efficient image compression method that uses IFS fractals to store the compressed image as a collection of IFS codes [2].

In this paper we introduce a new, freely available KETpic add-on for generating and rendering IFS fractal objects. Our program, developed in the popular scientific program *Matlab*, generates LATEX-readable code so that image files are no longer invoked nor required. The resulting text files are astonishingly small when compared with their image file counterparts, such as JPEG, GIF or EPS.

2   Iterated Function Systems

An IFS is a finite set of contractive maps $w_i : X \longrightarrow X$, $i = 1, \ldots, n$ defined on a complete metric space (X, d). We refer to the IFS as $\mathcal{W} = \{X; w_1, \ldots, w_n\}$. In the two-dimensional case, the metric space (X, d) is typically $\mathbb{R}^2$ with the Euclidean distance d_2, so the affine transformations w_i are of the form:

$$\begin{bmatrix} x^* \\ y^* \end{bmatrix} = w_i \begin{bmatrix} x \\ y \end{bmatrix} = \begin{bmatrix} a_i & b_i \\ c_i & d_i \end{bmatrix} \cdot \begin{bmatrix} x \\ y \end{bmatrix} + \begin{bmatrix} e_i \\ f_i \end{bmatrix} \iff \mathbf{w}_i(\mathbf{x}) = \mathbf{A}_i.\mathbf{x} + \mathbf{b}_i \quad (1)$$

where $\mathbf{b}_i$ is a translation vector and $\mathbf{A}_i$ is a 2×2 matrix with eigenvalues λ_1, λ_2 such that $|\lambda_i| < 1$. In fact, $|det(\mathbf{A}_i)| < 1$ meaning that w_i shrinks distances between points. Let us now define a transformation, T, in the compact subsets of X, $\mathcal{H}(X)$, by

$$T(A) = \bigcup_{i=1}^{n} w_i(A). \quad (2)$$

If all the w_i are contractions, T is also a contraction in $\mathcal{H}(X)$ with the induced Hausdorff metric [1]. Then, T has a unique fixed point, $|\mathcal{W}|$, called the *attractor of the IFS*. Let us now consider a set of probabilities $\mathcal{P} = \{p_1, \ldots, p_n\}$, with $\sum_{i=1}^{n} p_i = 1$. We refer to $\{\mathcal{W}, \mathcal{P}\} = \{X; w_1, \ldots, w_N; p_1, \ldots, p_n\}$ as an *IFS with Probabilities* (IFSP). Given $\mathcal{P}$, there exists a unique Borel regular measure $\nu \in \mathcal{M}(X)$, called the *invariant measure of the IFSP*, such that $\nu(S) = \sum_{i=1}^{n} p_i \nu(w_i^{-1}(S))$, $S \in \mathcal{B}(X)$, where $\mathcal{B}(X)$ denotes the Borel subsets of X. Using the Hutchinson metric on $\mathcal{M}(X)$, it is possible to show that M is a contraction with a unique fixed point, $\nu \in \mathcal{M}(X)$. Furthermore, $support(\nu) = |\mathcal{W}|$. Thus, given an arbitrary initial measure $\nu_0 \in \mathcal{M}(X)$ the sequence $\{\nu_k\}_{k=0,1,2,\ldots}$ constructed as $\nu_{k+1} = M(\nu_k)$ converges to the invariant measure of the

IFSP. Also, a similar iterative deterministic scheme can be derived from (2) to obtain $|\mathcal{W}|$.

However, there exists a more efficient method, known as *probabilistic algorithm*, for the generation of the attractor of an IFS. This algorithm follows from the result $\overline{\{x_k\}}_{k>0} = |\mathcal{W}|$ provided that $x_0 \in |\mathcal{W}|$, where: $x_k = w_i(x_{k-1})$ with probability $p_i > 0$. Picking an initial point, one of the mappings in the set $\{w_1, \ldots, w_n\}$ is chosen at random using the weigths $\{p_1, \ldots, p_n\}$. The selected map is then applied to generate a new point, and the same process is repeated again with the new point, thus obtaining a sequence of points that converges to the fractal as the number of points increases. This algorithm is known as probabilistic algorithm or *chaos game* [1] and generates a sequence of points that are randomly distributed over the fractal, according to the chosen set of probabilities. Thus, the larger the number of iterations (a parameter we can freely set up), the better the resolution of the resulting fractal image.

3   The Program

In this section the main components of the system and some implementation issues are given; then, a typical session workflow is briefly described.

3.1   System Components

Before getting started two basic components need to be installed:

1. the *scientific program Matlab* (version 5 or later), which supports many different platforms, such as PCs (with Windows 9x, 2000, NT, Me, XP and Vista) and UNIX workstations. A version for Apple Macintosh with Mac OS X system is also available under X11 (the implementation of the X Window System that makes it possible to run X11-based applications in Mac OS X).
2. a *TEX editor and compiler*. You can use the text editor of your choice to generate your LaTeX documents. However, some specialized text editors are usually preferred because they provide some interesting features such as syntax highlighting, shortcuts for some usual commands and procedures, menus with frequently used LaTeX macros and styles, etc. Regarding the compiler, there are several LaTeX compilers (most of them freeware) available for Windows, Mac, UNIX and Linux.

Once these programs are properly installed and configured, the only task you have to do is to copy our KETpic files into your workspace folder.

3.2   Session Workflow

This section describes a typical KETpic session workflow by means of a simple yet illustrative example. KETpic processing pipeline starts up by opening Matlab for a new session. Then, we load the add-on:

```
>> Ketinit
```

so that all new KETpic commands are automatically available from the very beginning. The main command, `Plotifs`, returns the graphical data associated with the IFS fractal. Its syntax is: `Plotifs`($sys, init, np, tr, opt_1, opt_2, \ldots, opt_n$) where sys is the system of iterated functions representing the fractal, expressed as its IFS code, formatted according to Eq. (1), $init$ is the initial point, x_0, for the iterated sequence, np is total number of iterations, tr is the trasient (the number of initial iterations that are not displayed in order to skip points that do not really belong to the attractor and might otherwise be displayed before convergence), $opts$ is optional parameters; they account for options that either are not strictly required or have a default value. Next input generates the classical *Barnsley's fern*, represented by variable `fern`:

```
>> G1=Plotifs(fern,[1,1],7000,10,'Method','Random');
```

This fractal is displayed in a new *Matlab* graphical window. The final semicolon precludes graphical data to be printed in the command window. It is however stored in variable `G1` for further use. KETpic command `Setwindow` sets up canvas dimension for LaTeX drawing: the fractal will be plotted on the prescribed area $[0, 1] \times [0, 1]$:

```
>> Setwindow([0,1],[0,1]);
```

In order to make this output data available in LaTeX, it must be converted into a LaTeX-readable format (*Tpic* in our case) and then stored into a file. Table 1 (left) summarizes this process. Line 1 opens a TeXfile called `Fern.tex` in the folder indicated in the namepath. Second line defines the units of length for the final picture (with default value 1 centimeter when empty). Command `Beginpicture` is also used to create the `\begin{picture}...\end{picture}` environment in LaTeX. Command `Generateifs` in line 3 converts 2D data points into a sequence of *Tpic* commands to be inserted into the `picture` environment created in line 2 for standard compilation. Command `Endpicture()` performs two different actions: on one hand, it closes the `picture` environment in the TeX file. On the other hand, it allows us to set up the display of cartesian axes, according to its value: 1 (empty value is also feasible) if axes are to be displayed and 0 otherwise. Finally, Line 5 closes the file.

The final output of this process is a file called `Fern.tex` in our workspace folder containing a description of the graphical objects created in *Matlab* in terms of LaTeX and *Tpic* commands. The file can be embedded into a standard LaTeX file for compilation. Code in Table 1(right) will yield a printout of Barnsley's fern fractal. It is the typical LaTeX code with a `documentclass` declaration and the `document` environment. The only difference are three lines in the preamble (lines in-between the start of the file and the `\begin{document}` command) that specify new directives for the length units, and the `\input` command in the main body of source code that causes the indicated file to be read and processed, exactly as if its contents had been inserted in the current file at that point. Compilation of the code above generates Figure 1(left) as a DVI file.

Table 1. (left) Generation of a *Tpic* file; (right) LATEX code of Figure 1

```
1    Openfile('Fern.tex');
2    Beginpicture('3cm');

3    Generateifs(G1);
4    Endpicture(1);
5    Closefile();
```

```
\documentclass[11pt]{article}
\newlength{\Width}
\newlength{\Height}
\newlength{\Depth}
\begin{document}
\input{Fern}
\end{document}
```

Fig. 1. Different schemes for the determination of probabilities for Barnsley's fern: (left) random algorithm; (middle) Barnsley algorithm; (right) optimal algorithm

4   Illustrative Examples

The efficiency of fractal rendering is related to the choice of probabilities. `Plotifs` command allows us to specify the method used to determine such probabilities. Figure 1 shows, from left to right, three standard choices for Barnsley's fern (all with 7000 points) selected by setting the option 'Method' to 'Random', 'Barnsley' and 'Optimal', respectively (see [7] for details). From this figure, it becomes clear that efficiency improves dramatically in the later cases. `Plotifs` command also allows users to enter their own choice of probabilities, by setting the option 'Method' to 'User'. In this case, a new option, 'Probabilities', is activated and the user can input his/her chosen probabilities. Fig. 2 shows three different choices of probabilities for Sierpinsky's gasket, whose input is given by:

```
>> lprob=[0.8,0.1,0.1; 0.3,0.5,0.2;0.2,0.1,0.7];
>> for i=1:size(lprob,1)
     S(:,:,i)=Plotifs(sierpinsky,[1,1],5000,10,'Method','User',...
                      'Probabilities',lprob(i,:));
   end
```

The corresponding output of previous code, depicted in Fig. 2, shows the enormous visual difference among the fractal images associated with three different sets of probabilities for the same number of iterations in all cases (5000 iterations

Fig. 2. Applying the chaos game algorithm to Sierpinsky's gasket with different probability sets: (left) (0.8,0.1,0.1); (middle) (0.3,0.5,0.2); (right) (0.2,0.1,0.7)

Fig. 3. IFS fractal images obtained by iterating different LaTeX symbols and operators

in this example). For example, with first choice of probabilities $p_1 = 0.8$, $p_2 = 0.1$, $p_3 = 0.1$ (left image in Figure 2) we are overestimating the rate of points associated with the left-most mapping. As a consequence, the points are not uniformly distributed in the resulting fractal image. Similar effects can be seen in the other two examples of this figure, where the right-most and bottom-most mappings are overestimated, respectively.

`Generateifs` command provides us with some other interesting options, such as 'Symbol', which admits all feasible LATEX commands for symbols and operators. Furthermore, such symbols are written in standard LATEX syntax, thus minimizing the time required to get accustomed to such input. Figure 3 shows four examples of IFS fractal images obtained by iterating different LATEX symbols and operators (l-r,t-b): the \star operator for the *crystal* fractal, \sharp symbol for the *blocks* fractal, \heartsuit symbol for the *spiral* fractal and \diamon operator for the *curve of Koch*. Default value for 'Symbol' is 'Point', which admits at its turn some additional options. For instance, we can set up the size of the point displayed on the screen (option 'Pointsize', with default value 0.001), the filling of the point (option 'Filled', with default value 'On') and many other options not described here to keep the paper at reasonable length.

5   Conclusions and Future Work

In this paper a new *Matlab*-based KETpic add-on for generating and rendering IFS fractal objects has been introduced. The program allows us to display any two-dimensional IFS fractal in LATEX by using a number of options that are explained throughout the paper. The reported add-on is very easy to work with; no proficiency on the software is actually required as all KETpic commands are virtually transparent to end-user. As a result, anyone with a minimal knowledge about *Matlab* can generate sophisticated LATEX-readable IFS graphical output in a very short span with reasonable effort. Further, the resulting files are amazingly small and, since no compression algorithms are applied, they preserve the highest level of quality, thus providing the best size-quality ratio. For instance, total size for all source files of this paper is less than 1 MB. Besides, this software is freely available and easy to install, with extremely low demands in terms of computer memory and data storage capacity. All these pleasant features make it a highly advisable choice for graphical printout of IFS fractals at professional level. This research has been supported by the Computer Science National Program of the Spanish Ministry of Education and Science, Project Ref. #TIN2006-13615, the University of Cantabria, the Japanese Society for Promotion of Science, Project Ref. KAKENHI #20500818 and Toho University.

References

1. Barnsley, M.F.: Fractals Everywhere, 2nd edn. Academic Press, London (1993)
2. Barnsley, M.F., Hurd, L.P.: Fractal Image Compression. AK Peters, Wellesley (1993)
3. Gálvez, A.: Numerical-symbolic Matlab program for the analysis of three-dimensional chaotic systems. In: Shi, Y., van Albada, G.D., Dongarra, J., Sloot, P.M.A. (eds.) ICCS 2007. LNCS, vol. 4488, pp. 211–218. Springer, Heidelberg (2007)
4. Gálvez, A., Iglesias, A.: Symbolic/numeric analysis of chaotic synchronization with a CAS. Future Generation Computer Systems 25(5), 727–733 (2007)
5. Gálvez, A.: Matlab Toolbox and GUI for Analyzing One-dimensional Chaotic Maps. In: Proc. of ICCSA 2008, pp. 321–330. IEEE Computer Society Press, Los Alamitos (2008)

6. Gálvez, A., Iglesias, A.: Takato: New Matlab-Based KETpic Plug-In for High-Quality Drawing of Curves. In: Proc. of ICCSA 2009, pp. 123–131. IEEE Computer Society Press, Los Alamitos (2009)
7. Gálvez, A.: IFS Matlab Generator: A Computer Tool for Displaying IFS Fractals. In: Proc. of ICCSA 2009, pp. 132–142. IEEE Computer Society Press, Los Alamitos (2009)
8. Gutiérrez, J.M., Iglesias, A., Rodríguez, M.A.: Logistic Map Driven by Correlated Noise. In: Garrido, P.L., Marro, J. (eds.) Second Granada Lectures in Computational Physics, pp. 358–364. World Scientific, Singapore (1993)
9. Gutiérrez, J.M., Iglesias, A., Rodríguez, M.A.: Logistic Map Driven by Dichotomous Noise. Physical Review E 48(4), 2507–2513 (1993)
10. Gutiérrez, J.M., Iglesias, A., Rodríguez, M.A., Rodríguez, V.J.: Fractal Image Generation with Iterated Function Systems. In: Proc. of First International Symposium of Mathematica, pp. 175–182. Computational Mechanics Publications (1995)
11. Gutiérrez, J.M., Iglesias, A., Rodríguez, M.A.: A Multifractal Analysis of IFSP Invariant Measures with Application to Fractal Image Generation. Fractals 4(1), 17–27 (1996)
12. Gutiérrez, J.M., Iglesias, A., Rodríguez, M.A., Rodríguez, V.J.: Efficient Rendering in Fractal Images. The Mathematica Journal 7(1), 7–14 (1997)
13. Gutiérrez, J.M., Iglesias, A.: A Mathematica package for the analysis and control of chaos in nonlinear systems. Computers in Physics 12(6), 608–619 (1998)
14. Iglesias, A., Gálvez, A.: Analyzing the synchronization of chaotic dynamical systems with Mathematica: Part I. In: Gervasi, O., Gavrilova, M.L., Kumar, V., Laganá, A., Lee, H.P., Mun, Y., Taniar, D., Tan, C.J.K. (eds.) ICCSA 2005. LNCS, vol. 3482, pp. 472–481. Springer, Heidelberg (2005)
15. Iglesias, A., Gálvez, A.: Analyzing the synchronization of chaotic dynamical systems with Mathematica: Part II. In: Gervasi, O., Gavrilova, M.L., Kumar, V., Laganá, A., Lee, H.P., Mun, Y., Taniar, D., Tan, C.J.K. (eds.) ICCSA 2005. LNCS, vol. 3482, pp. 482–491. Springer, Heidelberg (2005)
16. Iglesias, A., Gálvez, A.: Revisiting some control schemes for chaotic synchronization with Mathematica. In: Sunderam, V.S., van Albada, G.D., Sloot, P.M.A., Dongarra, J. (eds.) ICCS 2005. LNCS, vol. 3516, pp. 651–658. Springer, Heidelberg (2005)
17. Kaneko, M., Izumi, H., Kitahara, K., Abe, T., Fukazawa, K., Sekiguchi, M., Tadokoro, Y., Yamashita, S., Takato, S.: A Simple Method of the TEX Surface Drawing Suitable for Teaching Materials with the aid of CAS. In: Bubak, M., van Albada, G.D., Dongarra, J., Sloot, P.M.A. (eds.) ICCS 2008, Part II. LNCS, vol. 5102, pp. 35–45. Springer, Heidelberg (2008)
18. Peitgen, H.O., Jurgens, H., Saupe, D.: Chaos and Fractals. New Frontiers of Science. Springer, Heidelberg (1993)
19. Sekiguchi, M., Yamashita, S., Takato, S.: Development of a Maple Macro Package Suitable for Drawing Fine TEX-Pictures. In: Iglesias, A., Takayama, N. (eds.) ICMS 2006. LNCS, vol. 4151, pp. 24–34. Springer, Heidelberg (2006)
20. Sekiguchi, M., Kaneko, M., Tadokoro, Y., Yamashita, S., Takato, S.: A New Application of CAS to LATEX Plottings. In: Shi, Y., van Albada, G.D., Dongarra, J., Sloot, P.M.A. (eds.) ICCS 2007. LNCS, vol. 4488, pp. 178–185. Springer, Heidelberg (2007)
21. Takato, S., Iglesias, A., Gálvez, A.: Use of ImplicitPlot in Drawing Surfaces Embedded into Latex Documents. In: Proc. of ICCSA 2009, pp. 115–122. IEEE Computer Society Press, Los Alamitos (2009)

Clustering in Mobile Ad Hoc Networks Using Comprehensive Learning Particle Swarm Optimization (CLPSO)

Waseem Shahzad, Farrukh Aslam Khan[*], and Abdul Basit Siddiqui

Department of Computer Science, FAST National
University of Computer and Emerging Sciences, Islamabad, Pakistan
{waseem.shahzad,farrukh.aslam,basit.siddiqui}@nu.edu.pk

Abstract. In this work, we propose a Comprehensive Learning Particle Swarm Optimization (CLPSO) based weighted clustering algorithm for mobile ad hoc networks. It finds the optimal number of clusters to efficiently manage the resources of the network. The proposed CLPSO based clustering algorithm takes into consideration the ideal degree, transmission power, mobility, and battery power of the mobile nodes. A weight is assigned to each of these parameters of the network. Each particle contains information about the cluster-heads and the members of each cluster. The simulation results are compared with two other well-known clustering algorithms. Results show that the proposed technique works better than the other techniques especially in dense networks.

Keywords: Clustering, ad hoc networks, comprehensive learning particle swarm optimization.

1 Introduction

A wireless ad hoc network consists of dynamic nodes that freely move and communicate with each other using wireless links. They have limited ability to collect and process information in terms of battery power and processing speed. Ad hoc networks do not use centralized devices for routing as in case of 802.11 WLANs. Routing is achieved by the cooperation of multiple nodes in a distributed manner.

Ad hoc networks consist of small computing devices that can support highly dynamic mobile nodes. Due to the size and battery power limitations, these devices typically have limited storage capacity, limited energy resources, as well as limited network bandwidth. Data produced by nodes in the network propagates through the network via wireless links. The features of MANETs such as dynamic topology and non-existence of central base station brings many new problems and challenges.

Clustering is just like a graph partitioning problem. Partitioning the graph optimally with respect to certain parameters is an NP-hard problem. The neighborhood of a cluster-head is the set of nodes that lie within its transmission range. The set S is called

---

[*] Corresponding author.

D. Ślęzak et al. (Eds.): FGCN/ACN 2009, CCIS 56, pp. 342–349, 2009.

a dominating set in which every vertex of G belongs to S or has a neighbor in S. The set of cluster-heads is the dominating set of the graph. Due to mobility, the nodes can go outside the transmission range of their cluster-head thus changing its neighborhood. However, this does not result in a change of the dominant set at all.

Clustering of nodes is one of the biggest challenges of MANETs. Hence, finding the optimal number of clusters that cover the entire network becomes essential and an active area of research. An optimal selection of cluster-heads is an NP-hard problem. Though, several authors have proposed different heuristics to find the optimal number of clusters, none of them addresses all the parameters of a mobile ad hoc network. Clustering has several advantages. The system performance can be improved by allowing the reuse of resources due to clustering. Secondly, clustering optimally manages the network topology by dividing this task among specified nodes called cluster-heads, which is very useful for routing and network management [3]. The clustering algorithm must be distributed, since every node in the network only has local knowledge. The algorithm should be robust as the network size increases or decreases, hence, it should adapt to all the changes. The created clusters should be reasonably efficient i.e. the selected cluster-heads should cover a large number of nodes.

In this work, we propose a Comprehensive Learning Particle Swarm Optimization (CLPSO) based clustering algorithm for mobile ad hoc networks to find the optimal number of clusters. Particle swarm optimization is a stochastic search technique. It has simple parameters that need to be tuned during the execution of algorithms. It is an efficient and effective technique to solve optimization problems. Each particle encodes the IDs of all mobile nodes of the network. The algorithm takes a set of parameters of MANETs into consideration such as, transmission power, mobility of nodes, battery power and moving speed. Each of these parameters is assigned a weight such that the sum of all the weights is equal to one.

The rest of the paper is organized as follows: Section 2 gives an overview of the existing algorithms for mobile ad hoc network clustering. Section 3 describes the comprehensive learning particle swarm optimization algorithm. Section 4 describes our proposed CLPSO clustering algorithm. Section 5 shows the simulations results comparing the proposed algorithm with two other well-known clustering algorithms. Finally, section 6 concludes the paper.

2   Related Work

The highest connectivity clustering algorithm was proposed by Gerla et al. [5]. The algorithm is based on the degree of nodes, which is the number of neighbors of a given node. In election procedure, the nodes broadcast their identifiers. Each node computes its degree and the node having the maximum degree becomes the cluster-head. The lowest-ID, known as identifier-based clustering algorithm, was originally proposed by Baker and Ephremides [6]. It assigns a unique ID to each node and chooses the node with the lowest ID as a cluster-head. It means that whenever a new node with a lowest ID appears, it will become the cluster-head.

Weighted Clustering Algorithm (WCA) was proposed by Chatterjee et al. [3]. They proposed a weight-based clustering algorithm which elects cluster-head according to its weight. It is computed by combining a set of parameters such as battery power, mobility and transmission range. Another algorithm was proposed by Turgut et al. in [4]. In this paper, genetic algorithm is used to optimize the number of clusters in an ad hoc network. It is also a weight based algorithm. Another clustering algorithm based on d-hops has been proposed in [7].

The basic problem with all heuristic-based algorithms is that none of them include all the basic parameters. WCA algorithm does include maximum number of parameters but it does not find optimal number of clusters in the network. Genetic algorithm performs crossover and mutation process which require extra processing at each node. Since wireless nodes have limited battery and processing capabilities, genetic algorithm is not much suitable for finding optimal clusters in an ad hoc network.

3   Comprehensive Learning Particle Swarm Optimization

Particle swarm optimization (PSO) is a population-based stochastic optimization technique developed by Eberhart and Kennedy in 1995, inspired by the social behavior of bird flocking or fish schooling. In PSO, each single solution is a "bird" in the search space which we call as a "particle". All particles have fitness values which are evaluated by the fitness function to be optimized, and have velocities which direct the flying of the particles [1].

It requires only primitive mathematical operators, and is computationally inexpensive in terms of both memory requirements and speed. This feature suggests that PSO is a potential algorithm to optimize clustering in a mobile ad hoc network. In the beginning, particle positions and velocities are generated randomly. The algorithm then proceeds iteratively, updating all velocities and then all particle positions as follows:

$$v_i^d \; = \; w \, v_i^d + c1 \, r1 \, (p_i^d - x_i^d) + c2 \, r2 \, (p_g^d - x_i^d) \tag{1}$$

$$x_i^d \; = x_i^d + v_i^d \tag{2}$$

Where d= 1,2,...,D, i= 1,2,...,N, and N is the size of the population. w is the inertia weight, c1 and c2 are two positive constants, and r1 and r2 are two random values in the range [0,1].

The first equation calculates the new velocity of ith particle by taking into consideration three terms, the particle's previous velocity, the distance between the particle's previous best position and current position, and finally the distance between the best particle of the swarm. The second equation is used to fly the particle to new position. The inertia weight is used to control the impact of the previous history of velocities on the current velocity.

The basic problem with original PSO is that it restricts the social learning aspect only to the gbest. If the gbest is far away from the global optimum, particles can go to the gbest region and get trapped in a local optimum. Comprehensive learning PSO can move the particles in larger potential space to fly. CLPSO uses the information in swarm more effectively to generate better solution. In the CLPSO approach, a particle can update its pbest position by using pbest positions of all the particles in a swarm. This will ensure the diversity of the swarm and discourages the swarm to premature convergence.

The comprehensive learning technique uses the following equation for updating velocity of a particle:

$$Vi^d = w * v_i^d + c * rand_i^d * (pbest^d_{fi(d)} - x_i^d) \tag{3}$$

Where $f_i = [f_i(1), f_i(2), \ldots, f_i(d)]$ describes which particles' pbests the particle i will use. $pbest_{fi(d)}$ is the dimension of any particle's pbest including its own pbest. The algorithm employs tournament selection procedure for updating the particle's dimension. First, it chooses two particles randomly from the population excluding the particle whose velocity is updated. Then it compares the fitness values of these two particles' pbests and selecting the dimension of the better one to update its velocity. The main difference between CLPSO and the original PSO is that instead of using particle's own pbest and gbest, all particles' pbest can be used to guide the particle's flying direction. These operations increase the diversity of a swarm when solving complex multi-dimensional problems. In this strategy, the particles can fly in other directions by learning from other particles' pbest when the particle's pbest and other pbests fall into the same local optimum region. Therefore, this strategy has the ability to jump out of the local optimum by using the cooperative behavior of the whole swarm [1].

4   CLPSO Based Clustering in Mobile Ad Hoc Networks

The proposed algorithm utilizes the CLPSO technique for finding the optimum number of clusters in a mobile ad hoc network for efficient routing. It is a weighted clustering algorithm that selects the cluster-heads based on the weight of each node W_v of each node v [2]. W_v is defined as:

$$W_v = w_1 D_v + w_2 S_v + w_3 M_v + w_4 P_v \tag{4}$$

Where D_v is the degree difference, S_v is the sum of distances of the members of the cluster-head, M_v is the average speed of the nodes and P_v is the accumulative time of a node being a cluster-head. The weighting factors are such that $\sum w_i = 1$. The node v with the minimum W_v is chosen to be the cluster-head. Once a node becomes cluster-head, neither that node nor its members can participate in the cluster-election procedure further. The cluster-head algorithm will terminate once all the nodes either become cluster-heads or members of a cluster-head.

Each particle contains the IDs of all the nodes. Each node in the search space should have a unique ID. These unique IDs are used to encode each particle. The proposed algorithm works as follows:

Proposed Algorithm

---

1) Initial population of particles is generated randomly. Initialize the general parameters of CLPSO algorithm.
2) Calculate the fitness value of each particle. The individuals are sorted according to the objective function, which is the sum of the all W_v values of cluster-heads in a particle.
3) Select particle neighbors for updating of its velocity.
4) Update the position of gbests and pbests.
   If Fitness(X_i) > Fitness (pbesti) then pbesti= X_i and
   If Fitness(X_i) > Fitness (gbesti) then gbesti= X_i.
5) Update velocity and position of each particle according to equations (1) and (2)
6) Check stopping criteria.
7) Report best particle as the solution of the problem.

The algorithm goes through each node in the list and checks three conditions to decide whether a node can become a cluster-head. The conditions are:

- If the node is not already a cluster-head.

- It is not a member of any cluster.

- Number of neighbors of a node is less than the predefined maximum allowed number of neighbors a node can have.

If a node satisfies the above three conditions, it is chosen as a cluster-head. After the cluster-heads are chosen, the already calculated value of W_v of each node is used to find out the fitness of each particle by taking the summation of all W_v values of all cluster-heads in this particle.

5   Simulation Results

Simulations are performed of M different nodes on a 100x100 and 500x500 grids. All the nodes can move in all possible directions with displacement varying uniformly between 0 to maximum value (max_disp). The transmission power of each node is set to 30. In our experiments, M is varied between 20 and 80. The maximum number of nodes that a cluster can handle is 10. This restriction will ensure uniform distribution of nodes in each cluster and efficient medium access control (MAC) functioning for an ad hoc network.

The parameters of CLPSO are initialized as follows: The population size is set to the number of nodes. The maximum generations are set to 1000. The inertia weight w is set to 0.694. The learning factors c1 and c2 are 2. The results of the proposed algorithm are compared with two other well-known algorithms for mobile ad hoc networks i.e. Weighted Clustering Algorithm (WCA) and Divided Range Particle Swarm Optimization (DRPSO). The same values of different parameters are used for all these three algorithms. The results are obtained after performing fifty simulations

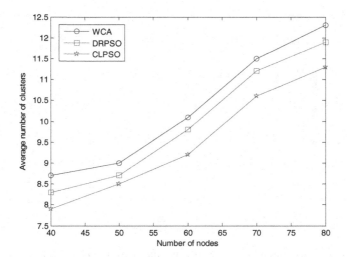

Fig. 1. Average number of clusters for WCA, DRPSO and CLPSO on 100x100 m² area with transmission range equal to 35

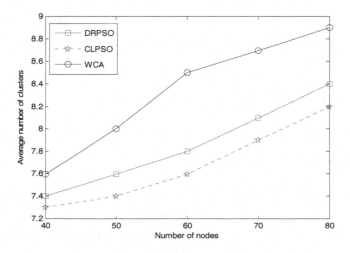

Fig. 2. Average number of clusters for WCA, DRPSO and CLPSO on 500x500 m² area with transmission range equal to 35

of each algorithm and then taking the average of fifty simulations. The simulations are performed by varying two different parameters i.e., the number of nodes in the network and the transmission range of the mobile nodes. It can be seen in Fig. 1 that our proposed algorithm based on CLPSO finds less number of clusters than WCA and DRPSO in the same environment i.e., 100x100 m² area with transmission range of 35. Moreover, the proposed algorithm converges quickly than DRPSO.

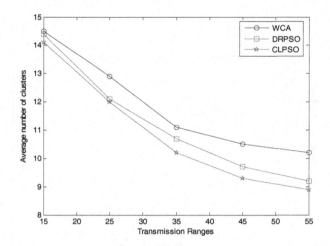

Fig. 3. Average number of clusters for WCA, DRPSO and CLPSO for 80 nodes on a 100x100 m² area

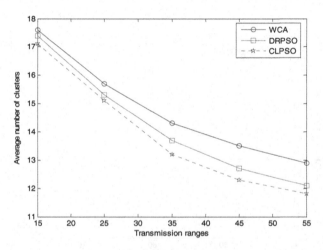

Fig. 4. Average number of clusters for WCA, DRPSO and CLPSO for 80 nodes on a 500x500 m² area

Fig. 2 also shows similar results in a 500x500 m² area with transmission range of 35. The average number of clusters is less in case of CLPSO as compared to WCA and DRPSO. The algorithms are also tested by keeping the nodes constant and increasing the transmission range of mobile nodes for both 100x100 m² and 500x500 m² area. Fig. 3 and 4 clearly show that the proposed algorithm works better than the other two algorithms in terms of producing the average number of clusters.

The simulation results show that the proposed technique covers all nodes with minimum number of clusters that can reduce the routing cost of the network. This will help minimize the number of hops and the delays associated with packet routing in a cluster-based routing environment. Number of clusters is large when the transmission range is small. From the figures, it is very clear that the proposed algorithm performs better than other two algorithms in a mobile ad hoc environment.

6 Conclusion

In the literature, we find different techniques to effectively determine the cluster-head of a group of mobile nodes in an ad hoc network. These cluster-heads are then responsible for the transmission of data between the nodes of different clusters in a cluster-based routing environment. In this paper, we have proposed a clustering algorithm called Comprehensive Learning Particle Swarm Optimization (CLPSO) based clustering for mobile ad hoc networks that assigns the responsibility of transferring packets to the cluster-heads. The algorithm attempts to minimize the average number of clusters so that the routing can be performed in an efficient manner by using minimum number of nodes that can forward packets to other nodes. It uses a set of parameters for the election of a cluster-head hence that node is elected as the cluster-head which is more powerful than the other nodes. The simulation results show that it is an effective and robust technique for clustering in mobile ad hoc networks. It reduces the routing cost by minimizing the number of clusters in order to cover the entire network. Moreover, the medium access control layer is efficient because it restricts the maximum number of nodes that a cluster can handle.

References

1. Liang, J.J., Qin, A.K., Suganthan, P.N., Baskar, S.: Comprehensive Learning Particle Swarm Optimizer for Global Optimization of Multimodal Functions. IEEE Trans. Evol. Comput. 10(3), 281–295 (2006)
2. Ji, C., Zhang, Y., Gao, S., Yuan, P., Li, Z.: Particle Swarm Optimization for Mobile Ad Hoc Networks Clustering. In: Proceedings of the 2004 IEEE International Conference on Networking, Sensing & Control, Taipei. Taiwan, March 21-23 (2004)
3. Chatterjee, M., Das, S.K., Turgut, D.: WCA: A Weighted Clustering Algorithm for Mobile Ad Hoc Networks. Cluster Computing 5, 193–204 (2002)
4. Turgut, D., Das, S.K., Elmasri, R., Turgut, B.: Optimizing Clustering Algorithm in Mobile Ad hoc Networks Using Genetic Algorithmic Approach. In: Proceedings of GLOBECOM 2002, Taipei, Taiwan, pp. 62–66 (2002)
5. Gerla, M., Tsai, J.T.C.: Multicluster, Mobile, Multimedia Radio Network. Wireless Networks 1(3), 255–265 (1995)
6. Baker, D.J., Ephremides, A.: The Architectural Organization of a Mobile Radio Network via a Distributed Algorithm. IEEE Transactions on Communications, 1694–1701 (1981)
7. Er, I.I., Seah, W.K.G.: Mobility-based D-hop Clustering Algorithm for Mobile Ad hoc Networks. In: IEEE WCNC, Atlanta, USA (2004)

On Multipath Balancing and Expanding for Wireless Multimedia Sensor Networks

Min Chen[1], Victor C.M. Leung[2], Lei Shu[3], and Han-Chieh Chao[4]

[1] School of Comp. Sci. & Eng., Seoul National Univ., Korea
minchen@snu.ac.kr
[2] Dept. of Elect & Comp Eng, University of British Columbia, V6T 1Z4, Canada
vleung@ece.ubc.ca
[3] Digital Enterprise Research Institute, Ireland
lei.shu@ieee.org
[4] Institute & Dept. of Electronic Engineering, National Ilan University, Taiwan
hcc@niu.edu.tw

Abstract. Multiple disjointed paths have been demonstrated to be effective in delivering multimedia traffic in wireless sensor networks, and improving the network performance in terms of bandwidth aggregation, reliability and network lifetime. In this paper, we investigate the use of directional geographical routing for multipath construction for multimedia data dissemination, and identify the challenging issue of achieving multipath balancing in proximity to the source/sink. While our previous work addresses the multipath expanding problem efficiently, this paper presents a novel scheme to achieve the paths balancing distribution to alleviate the contention between the paths when close to the sink. The path construction is divided into expanding phase, parallel phase and converging phase in the proposed scheme, which includes two key algorithms, i.e., the detection algorithm for path construction phase and the deviation angle adjustment algorithm. Simulation results that verify the effectiveness of the proposed scheme are presented.

1 Introduction

Wireless sensor networks (WSNs) have attracted remarkable attention in the research community recently, driven by a wealth of theoretical and practical challenges and increasing number of practical civilian applications.

Recently, with emerging advances in sensor nodes which are capable of in-node image-processing [1], there is a growing interest in the design and development of multimedia sensor systems for applications in future wireless multimedia sensor networks (WMSNs) [2], such as advanced surveillance, security monitoring, emergency response, and environmental tracking, etc. However, it remains a challenging problem to deliver multimedia streaming data with the required QoS over WSNs [3] [4], due to the bandwidth limitation in such networks. Especially for video over WSNs, the compressed video bit stream is extremely sensitive to network dynamics. Our previous works [5] [6] address this issue by exploiting

D. Ślęzak et al. (Eds.): FGCN/ACN 2009, CCIS 56, pp. 350–359, 2009.
© Springer-Verlag Berlin Heidelberg 2009

multiple disjoint paths to transmit multiple multimedia streams in parallel. In order to guarantee the requirements of aggregate bandwidth and fast packet delivery for multimedia traffic, we focus on multipath balancing and expanding at the source node. For example, the construction of multiple joint paths is divided into two phases in DGR [5]:

- *Multipath expanding*: The multiple paths are originated from a source node. In order to expand multiple paths evenly in a spatial distribution at the proximity of the source node, a series of initial deviation angles are specified for each individual path's construction. While a path is expanding in the specified direction, the initial deviation angle will be shrunk hop-by-hop to avoid the excessive expanding. Several heuristic based functions are suggested for deviation angle adjusting in [5].
- *Pointing back to the sink*: Typically, the deviation angle will be decreased to 0 after the path has been extended for a number of hops. Then, the path points back to the sink quickly through shortest path routing.

On the other hand, in a sensor network with a single sink at the center of the network, sensors around the sink need to relay every packet heading towards the sink. These sensors will quickly exhaust their energy in relaying traffic, which makes the network stop functioning as data packets cannot reach the sink. Since these sensors around the sink will be the network lifetime bottleneck, load-balancing is more important for the sensors at the proximity of the sink.

Though DGR achieves multipath expanding around a source node efficiently, the problem of multipath balancing around the sink node remains unsolved yet. Typically, the symmetric paths will form a heart-like shape, as shown in Fig. 1. The multiple disjointed paths will converge to a close proximity to each other when approaching to the sink node. Thus, there is still a lot of contention between the paths when close to the sink.

The main contribution of this paper is to enhance the original DGR algorithm, and the enhanced scheme is called E-DGR, which efficiently achieves the paths

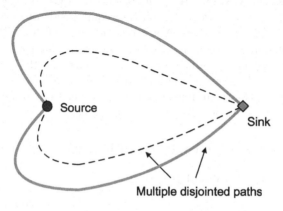

Fig. 1. Illustration of DGR's multipath construction

balancing distribution to alleviate the contention between the paths when close to the sink. Simulation shows that E-DGR exhibits better performance than the original DGR. It is expected that the higher performance improvement will be achieved when the application-specific path number is set to a large value.

The rest of this paper is organized as follows. Section 2 presents the related work. Section 3 describes the proposed algorithm for E-DGR. Simulation model and experimental results are presented in Section 4. Section 5 concludes this paper.

2   Related Works

In [2–4], three surveys on multimedia communication in WSNs have been well conducted. The authors analyzed and discussed the existing research works from both mobile multimedia and WSNs fields. These surveys showed that current existing protocols from the mobile multimedia and WSNs fields did not consider the characteristics of multimedia streaming data and natural constrains of WSNs at the same time. These papers also concluded that there exists a clear need for a great deal of research effort to focus on developing new efficient communication protocols and algorithms.

Many multipath routing protocols have been studied in the field of wireless ad hoc & sensor networks [9] [10]. However, most of the multipath routing protocols focus on energy efficiency, load balance, or fault tolerance in WSNs, and they are the extended versions of DSR [11] and AODV [12]. Only a few studies addressing time sensitive traffic transmissions over WMSNs. Due to the limited transmission capacity of sensor nodes, a single path often cannot meet the requirement of video transmissions. Consequently, multipath transmissions are needed. Chen *et al.* proposed DGR [5] to explore the application-specific number of node-disjoint routing paths to enlarge the aggregate bandwidth for the QoS provisioning in WMSNs. DGR is an algorithm designed specially for video sensor networks, and can greatly improve the performance in terms of lifetime and delay. It chooses the maximum number of paths from all found node-disjoint routing paths for maximizing multimedia streaming data transmission and guaranteeing the end-to-end transmission delay in WMSNs. Shu *et al.* proposed TPGF [6] [8] for geographical forwarding by taking into account both the requirements of real time multimedia transmission and the realistic characteristics of WMSNs. TPGF focuses on exploring the maximum number of optimal node-disjoint routing paths in the network layer in terms of minimizing the path length and the end-to-end transmission delay as well as taking the limited energy of WSNs into consideration. The TPGF routing algorithm finds one path per execution and can be executed repeatedly to find more node-disjoint routing paths.

3   Enhanced Directed Geographical Routing (E-DGR)

3.1   Directed Geographical Routing

DGR aims to compute multiple paths for a unicast video session. Fig. 2 illustrates an example of the construction of multiple disjointed paths by DGR [5]. In order

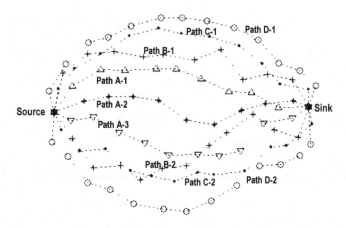

Fig. 2. Multiple paths constructed by DGR

to set up an application-specific number of paths with different initial deviation angles, the source node can transmit a series of control packets each specifying a different deviation angle. To establish a direction-aware path, a probe message is broadcasted initially by the source node for route discovery. A selected next hop will continue to broadcast probe message to find its next hop, and so forth. A node receiving a probe message will calculate its mapping coordinates based on α and the positions of the node itself, the upstream node and the sink. Then, DGR will select as the next hop node the neighbor whose mapping coordinates is closest to the *strategic mapping location*, instead of the neighbor closest to the sink as in traditional geographical routing protocols [5]. As an example, In Fig. 2 the source node changes the absolute value of the deviation angle (i.e., α) from 0° to 90° in steps of 18°, and sends a different PROB message with each deviation angle. Thus, in total 11 paths are established with α equal to -90°, -67.5°, -45°, -22.5°, 0°, 22.5°, 45°, 67.5° and 90°, respectively.

3.2 The Detection Algorithm for Three-Phases Based Path Construction

The original DGR uses the following function in adjusting α_k at the kth hop along the path: $\alpha_k = f(k) \cdot \alpha$, where α is the reference deviation angle set by the source node. Since $f(k)$ is a decreasing function with k, α_k will be decreased at each hop and become close to 0 after some hops, as shown in Fig. 3. In order to decrease the contention between the paths and achieve path balancing at the proximity of the sink, E-DGR divides the path construction into three phases (i.e., expanding phase, parallel phase, converging phase).

In the following, we propose a novel detection algorithm for these three phases. First, we introduce a reference angle, which is denoted by θ. We define θ as the deviation angle from the line connecting the current node (h or p in Fig. 3) and the sink (t in Fig. 3) to the line connecting the source (s in Fig. 3) to t (i.e., the center line).

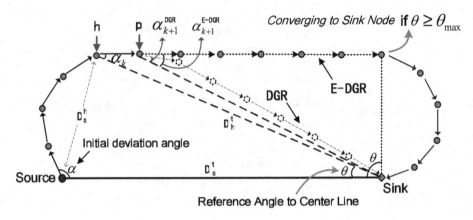

Fig. 3. The illustration of E-DGR

Fixed Fields:	SourceID	SinkID	SeqNum	DeviationAngle	SourcePOS	SinkPOS

Variable Fields:	PreviousHop	HopCount	MyPOS	Previous α	Previous θ

Fig. 4. Probe packet format in E-DGR

Let D_h^t denote the distance between current node h and sink node t; D_s^h be the distance between the source node and current node; D_s^t be the distance between source and the sink. As illustrated in Fig. 3, when node h receives a probe packet from its upstream node, D_h^t, D_s^h and D_s^t can be calculated according to the positions of itself (x_h, y_h), the source node s (x_s, y_s) and the sink t (x_t, y_t) which are piggybacked in the packet. Then, θ can be calculated by node h as: $\theta = \arccos(\frac{(D_h^t)^2 + (D_s^t)^2 - (D_s^h)^2}{2D_h^t \cdot D_s^t})$. Next, we can define the three path construction phases according to θ_k and α_k. Note that θ_k is the θ value of the kth hop node (i.e., h), while we denote θ_{k+1} as the θ value of the $k + 1$th hop node (i.e., p in Fig. 3).

- *Expanding Phase*: The expanding phase starts from the source node. Assume node h is still within this phase. Before broadcasting the probe packet to its next hop [1], h will update α_k and θ_k in the packet. Compared to DGR, the packet format used in E-DGR includes two additional variable packet fields: Previous α (i.e., α_k), and Previous θ (i.e., θ_k), as shown in Fig. 4.
  When node p receives the probe from its upstream node h, it compares α_k to θ_k. If α_k is larger than θ_k, p will mark the path construction phase unchanged, as path expanding.
- *Parallel Phase*: In the expanding phase, α_k is a decreasing function of the hop count while θ_k is increased from 0. In a certain node, α_k will become

---

[1] The detailed receiver-oriented routing algorithm is referred to [7].

very close to or smaller than θ_k. From such a node, the path construction will enter the parallel phase. Given the example of Fig. 3, p is the node where path construction changes to the parallel mode.

- *Converging Phase*: In the parallel phase, θ_k will be continuously increased. If θ_k is larger than some threshold (denoted by θ_{max}), the path construction will enter the converging phase.

3.3   The Deviation Angle Adjustment Algorithm for E-DGR

On the top of the detection algorithm for three-phases based path construction, this section presents the deviation angle adjustment algorithm corresponding to each phase:

- *Expanding Phase*:
  Let H_s^t denote the hop count from the source to the sink; let $H(k)$ denote the hop count at the kth hop (i.e., the hop count from the source to node h in Fig. 3). Then, the deviation angle adjusting factor at hop k is calculated by:

$$f(k) = (\frac{max[0, H_s^t - H(k)]}{H_s^t})^3. \tag{1}$$

  The deviation angle at hop k can be calculated as,

$$\alpha_k = f(k) \cdot \alpha. \tag{2}$$

- *Parallel Phase*:
  In the parallel mode, the path will keep approximately parallel with the center line. Thus, the deviation angle is adjusted to:

$$\alpha_k = \theta_k. \tag{3}$$

- *Converging Phase*:
  Let cp denote the node changing from parallel mode to converging mode; let H_s^{cp} denote the estimated hop count from the source node to cp; let H_{cp}^t denote the estimated hop count from cp to the sink node; For the kth hop node in converging mode, the deviation angle adjusting factor is calculated by:

$$f(k)' = (\frac{max[0, H_{cp}^t - (H(k) - H_s^{cp})]}{H_{cp}^t})^3. \tag{4}$$

Then, in converging mode, the deviation angle at hop k can be calculated as,

$$\alpha_k = f(k)' \cdot \theta_{cp}. \tag{5}$$

Table 1. Pseudo-code for E-DGR algorithm

```
f_parallel ← 0;
f_converging ← 0;
begin
01 if (f_converging = 0) then
02    if θ_{k-1} ≥ α_{k-1} then
03       f_parallel ← 1;
04    endif
05    if θ ≥ θ_max then
07       f_parallel ← 0;
08       f_converging ← 1;
09    endif
10 endif
11 if (f_parallel = 1) then
12    α_k ← θ_k;
13 else if (f_converging = 1) then
14    α_k ← f(k)' · θ_cp;
15 else
16    α_k ← f(k) · α;
17 endif
end
```

$f_{parallel}$ and $f_{converging}$: flags of parallel
        phase and converging phase, respectively;
"←" denotes an assignment operation;

Table 1 shows the pseudo-code of the joint phase detection and deviation angle adjustment algorithm.

4   Simulation Results

In order to demonstrate the performance of DGR and E-DGR, we implement our protocols and perform simulations using OPNET Modeler. The sensor nodes are uniformly random deployed over a 500m × 500m field. The source node is deployed at the left side of the field and one sink is located on the right side. The sensor application module consists of a constant-bit-rate source, which generates 1024 bits every 100ms. We use IEEE 802.11 Distributed Coordinate Function as the underlying medium access control (MAC), and the radio transmission range (R) is set to 50m. The data rate of the wireless channel is 1 Mb/s. All messages are 64 bits in length. We assume that both the sink and sensor nodes are stationary. The path number N_{path} is set to 3. The deviation angles of the three paths are set to -75°, 0° and 75°, respectively.

In order to make a visual comparison of all the algorithms, we plot the multipath constructed by DGR and E-DGR for the case of three paths, in Fig. 5 and Fig. 6. Since the main concern of this paper is multipath balancing at the proximity of the sink node, E-DGR has higher performance than DGR at this aspect. As shown in Fig. 6, the three paths are spatially distributed more evenly. Thus, in applying E-DGR, non-interfering paths are more likely to be established, alleviating the route coupling problem [13] caused by interference between packets transmitted over different paths between the same source-destination pair.

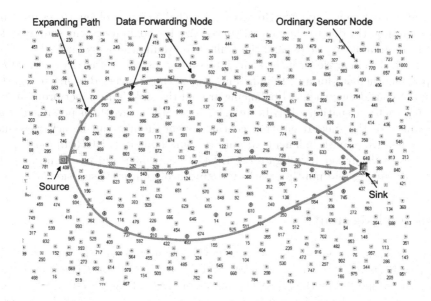

Fig. 5. Visualization of the multipath construction result computed by DGR

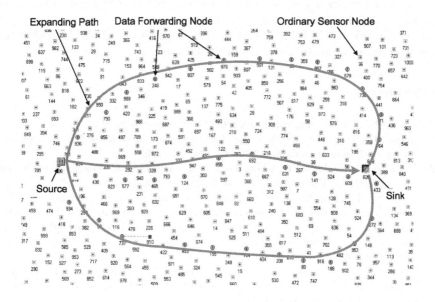

Fig. 6. Visualization of the multipath construction result computed by E-DGR

5 Conclusion

In order to support multimedia transmissions over ubiquitous wireless sensor networks in the future, multiple disjointed paths are likely required due to the specific requirements on QoS. However, it's a challenging problem to set up non-interfering paths due to the limited spatial size in proximity to the source/sink. In the original DGR, we expand the multipath around the source node by designating deviation angle with the same interval around the source. However, after expanding the path for a certain distance, the path is converted to shortest path, without considering the load-balancing around the sink. This paper proposes E-DGR to achieve spatially distributing multiple paths as evenly as possible in the proximity of the sink. It is expected that longer lifetime can be achieved due to the feature of path balancing around the sink node in E-DGR. In our future work, we will further investigate the E-DGR performance in the scenario with multiple sources and multiple paths for multimedia data transmission.

Acknowledgment

This work was supported in part by the Canadian Natural Sciences and Engineering Research Council under grant STPGP 322208-05. M. Chen's work was partially supported by the IT R&D program of MKE/IITA [2007-F-038-03, Fundamental Technologies for the Future Internet] and grant number IITA-2009-C1090-0902-0006. L. Shu's research was supported by Lion project supported by Science Foundation Ireland under grant No.: SFI/08/CE/I1380 (Lion-2). H. Chao's research has been supported in part by Cross-Layer Design for Cognitive and Cooperative 4G-IMS Wireless Networks, project No. 97-2219-E-197-001- and is sponsored by National Science Council, Taiwan.

References

1. http://blog.xbow.com/xblog/2007/06/behaviorscope_u.html
2. Gurses, E., Akan, O.B.: Multimedia Communication in Wireless Sensor Networks. Annals of Telecommunications 60(7-8), 799–827 (2005)
3. Akyildiz, I.F., Melodia, T., Chowdhury, K.R.: A Survery on Wireless Multimedia Sensor Networks. Computer Networks 51(4), 921–960 (2007)
4. Misra, S., Reisslein, M., Xue, G.: A Survey of Multimedia Streaming in Wireless Sensor Networks. IEEE Communications Surveys and Tutorials 10(4), 18–39 (2008)
5. Chen, M., Leung, V., Mao, S., Yuan, Y.: Directional Geographical Routing for Real-Time Video Communications in Wireless Sensor Networks. Computer Communications 30(17), 3368–3383 (2007)
6. Shu, L., Zhang, Y., Yang, L.T., Wang, Y., Hauswirth, M., Xiong, N.: TPGF: Geographic Routing in Wireless Multimedia Sensor Networks. Journal of Telecommunication System (to appear, 2009)
7. Chen, M., Leung, V., Mao, S., Kwon, T.: Receiver-oriented Load-balancing and Reliable Routing in Wireless Sensor Networks. Wireless Communications and Mobile Computing Journal 9(3), 405–416 (2009)
8. Shu, L., Zhang, Y., Zhou, Z., Hauswirth, M., Yu, Z., Hynes, G.: Transmitting and Gathering Streaming Data in Wireless Multimedia Sensor Networks within Expected Network Lifetime. ACM/Springer Mobile Networks and Applications 13(3-4), 305–322 (2008)

9. Tsai, J., Moors, T.: A Review of Multipath Routing Protocols: From Wireless Ad Hoc to Mesh Networks. In: Proceedings of ACoRN Early Career Researcher Workshop on Wireless Multihop Networking, Sydney, July 17-18 (2006)
10. http://snac.eas.asu.edu/snac/multipath/multipath.html
11. Johnson, D.B., Maltz, D.A.: Dynamic Source Routing in Ad Hoc Wireless Networks. In: Imielinski, Korth (eds.) Mobile Computing. Kluwer Academic Publishers, Dordrecht (1996)
12. Perkins, C.: Ad Hoc On-Demand Distance Vector (AODV) Routing. RFC 3561 (2003)
13. Pearlman, M.R., Haas, Z.J., Sholander, P., Tabrizi, S.S.: On the impact of alternate path routing for load balancing in mobile ad hoc networks. In: ACM international symposium on mobile ad hoc networking and computing, MobiHOC (2003)

Reeling in Cognitive Radio: The Issues of Regulations and Policies Affecting Spectrum Management*

Tae (Tom) Oh[1], Young B. Choi[2], Michael Guthrie[3], Kristi Harold[3], Daniel Copeland[3], and Tai-hoon Kim[4]

[1] Department of Networking, Security and Systems Administration
B. Thomas Golisano College of Computing and Information Sciences
Rochester Institute of Technology, 152 Lomb Memorial Drive
Rochester, NY 14623, U.S.A.
Tom.Oh@rit.edu
[2] Dept. of Management Information Systems and Computer Information Systems
College of Business, Bloomsburg University of Pennsylvania
Bloomsburg, PA 17815, U.S.A.
ybchoi@bloomu.edu
[3] Computer Information Systems and Management Science
James Madison University
Harrisonburg, VA 22807-0001, U.S.A.
{guthrimc,harlo95,copeladj}@jmu.edu
[4] Department of Multimedia
Hannam University, 133 Ojeong-dong, Daedeok-gu
Daejeon, Korea
taihoonn@hnu.kr

Abstract. One of today's most important developing wireless technologies is Cognitive Radio (CR). In our current fixed-assignment spectrum management policy, much of the available frequencies go unused. CR aims to make use of this unutilized space to provide wireless broadband services. This paper aims to give a background to CR and describe the key players in standardization and allocation of the unused spectrum. Furthermore, it discusses the policies and policy makers that are guiding the future of CR.

Keywords: Cognitive Radio, Regulations, Policies, standardization and Spectrum Management.

1 Introduction

1.1 Origins of Cognitive Radio

Cognitive Radio (CR) has its origins in the Defense Advance Research Products Agency (DARPA). An employee of DARPA, Dr. Joseph Mitola, co-authored the

---

* This work was supported by the Security Engineering Research Center, granted by the Korea Ministry of Knowledge Economy.

D. Ślęzak et al. (Eds.): FGCN/ACN 2009, CCIS 56, pp. 360–369, 2009.
© Springer-Verlag Berlin Heidelberg 2009

Fig. 1. Digital Modular Radio (DMR)

paper *Cognitive Radio: Making Software Radios More Personal* with Gerald Q. Maguire, Jr., which played a huge role in the concept of CR. CR is built on Software Defined Radio (SDR) technology, and is on the cutting edge in the software defined radio community. This type of technology is on the forefront and used primarily in military applications. The U.S. Navy is the largest consumer of Software Defined Radio (SDR). The Navy replaced a whole room of radios with a single rack of Digital Modular Radio (DMR). The DMR (Figure 1) is four radios in one and currently operating on submarines and surface ships [9].

For the U.S. Navy, the software-based Digital Modular Radio (DMR) is replacing room of radios with a single rack of DMR's. The unit is four-channel full duplex system that is essentially four radios in one. Currently operating on submarines and surface ships around the world, the DMR (AN/USC-61) illustrates the viability of Software Defined Radios on active duty.

Although these types of radios are only being used by the military the need for smart radios in everyday transmissions is dire and can mean the difference between life and death in some cases. The need for Cognitive Radio arises from the increasing amount of interference on different frequencies. All of this interference has caused a transmission bottleneck. To solve this problem CR has the ability to detect when other transmitters interfere with your reception. When the interference is detected, it can respond by switching you to another frequency with less traffic. The changeover would be transparent to the user and allow the transmission to continue as if nothing had happened [1].

1.2 Description of Cognitive Radio

On the basic level, CR is an advanced form wireless communication that uses radio waves on various frequencies to send information from one point to another. It is considered to be an extension of SDR implementing spectrum sharing to avoid licensed and unlicensed users from clashing. It has several main functions: spectrum

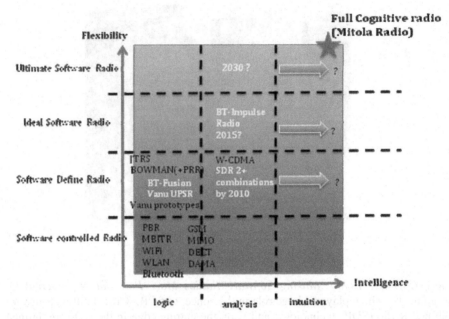

Fig. 2. Matrix of Flexibility of Hardware and Intelligence to Control (or Configure) the Hardware [13]

sensing, spectrum management, spectrum mobility, and spectrum sharing [2]. Spectrum sensing describes how CR detects unused segments of the spectrum and assigns them without interfering with any other users. Because some users have different spectrum requirements, CR employs spectrum management techniques to meet various service quality requirements. In addition to finding unused frequencies, cognitive radio can dynamically switch users to find the optimum frequency during run time by utilizing its spectrum mobility and sharing techniques [2].

The matrix shown in Figure 2 describes the potential of full CR with respect to Flexibility (shown on the Y-axis) and Intelligent Signal Processing (shown on the X-axis). It is obvious to see full CR's potential vastly outmatches its competitive mediums like WiFi, WLAN, and Bluetooth.

The progression of CR is heavily influenced by two driving forces: market demands and physical constraints. Market forces demand CR be a reliable medium to send data, because developers of competing mediums (wired, microwaves, WiFi) are striving to do the same. As with any wireless medium, reliability is a prominent concern. The physical constraint comes from the nature of the electromagnetic spectrum. The spectrum is finite in size, and although it can be divided into a larger number of frequencies, it is still a finite (and therefore scarce) resource. As with any finite resource, a sought after method is one that utilizes the resource efficiently. The developers of CR have done this by procuring a radio that is able to detect its surroundings and find unused signals. This significantly decreases unused/wasted frequencies, maximizes the usage of the electromagnetic radio spectrum, and improves cognitive radio's overall marketability.

Since its inception in 1999 CR has grown around two primary goals: reliability and efficiency. Cognitive radio developers are striving to make CR reliable and efficient [10]. To be marketable to the public and grow as a significant telecommunications medium, CR must meet these two goals.

2 Spectrum Management and Protecting License Holders

In order to become successful, there are several main operational issues CR must overcome, the first being the issue of spectrum management. The main advantage of CR over traditional wireless network technology is its ability to make dynamic use of unused spectrum space. This means that CR can make use of parts of the spectrum reserved for other purposes, such as TV broadcasts. Because the spectrum is divided up in a fixed-spectrum assignment policy, even if the space is unused, it is still assigned to the license holder by the Federal Communications Commission (FCC), or the National Telecommunications and Information Administration (NTIA). If a CR wishes to make use of an unused portion of the spectrum, the original spectrum holder's rights must be protected. As the primary user, the license holder must be protected from interference that could be caused by CR's use of a hole in the spectrum. This presents a unique problem, as CR and the organizations that regulate the spectrum must find a way to allow CR to reach its full potential, while still respecting the rights of the primary users of spectrum space. There are some techniques available that allow CR to safely make use of spectrum space without interfering with the services offered by licensed holders. These key factors effectively implement CR a viable technology, and are working to convince the regulatory bodies that CR should be allowed to make use of this spectrum space.

Currently, the FCC (Federal Communication Commission) has spectrum space set aside for unlicensed use. CR is ideal for making use of this space in the 5 GHz band. At the Federal Communication Commission's 2003 World Radio communication Conference (WRC-03), the regulatory community agreed on a method for 5 GHz spectrum sharing of radar and wireless access systems [8]. The basis for the sharing was an agreement on the use of Dynamic Frequency Selection in 5230- 5350 MHz and 5470-5725 MHz range [8]. The FCC regulations concerning this unlicensed space follow.

"(ii) Channel Availability Check Time. A U-NII (Unlicensed National Information Infrastructure) shall check if there is a radar system already operating on the channel before it can initiate a transmission on a channel and when it has to move to a new channel. The U-NII device may start using the channel if no radar signal with a power level greater than the interference threshold values listed in paragraph (h)(2) of this part is detected within 60 seconds.

(iii) Channel Move Time. After a radar's presence is detected, all transmissions shall cease on the operating channel within 10 seconds. Transmissions during this period shall consist of normal traffic for a maximum of 200 ms after detection of the radar signal. In addition intermittent management and control signals can be sent during the remaining time to facilitate vacating the operating channel.

(iv) Non- occupancy period. A channel that has been flagged as containing a radar system, either by a channel availability check or in service monitoring, is subject to a non-occupancy period of at least 30 minutes. The nonoccupancy period starts at the time when the radar system is detected [8]."

These licensing regulations express how future regulations could be passed that respects both the rights of the license holders and CR. Currently, unlicensed space is available on a first-come, first-serve basis, and as time goes by, unlicensed space becomes increasingly congested. In the unlicensed spectrum there are no safeguards to prevent a user from occupying a large amount of available space indefinitely. This could cause future problems with other users competing for that unlicensed space. For CR to reach its full potential, it must also be able to access unused licensed spectrum space.

One of the first steps CR must take to find unused spectrum space is to obtain an estimate of the Power Spectral Density (PSD) of the radio spectrum. This requires extremely sensitive radios that can measure signals at their cell edge [12]. If the radio is sensitive enough it will detect unused space. CR monitors the constantly changing spectrum, and if necessary, switches bands. If the radio detects unused space that is actually in use, the signal used by CR will interfere with the signal already being used, causing interference with the primary user. This is referred to as "the hidden node problem" [7].

Another aspect of this problem occurs when the primary user tries to access part of the spectrum currently in use by a CR. If the primary user attempts this, their signal and the CR signal will create interference. The CR must be able to detect this situation, and respond accordingly. In addition to being able to detect whether spectrum space is being used or not, CR will need to be able to detect the transmission power level. Doing so will allow the device to operate without raising the noise floor of the primary user's device beyond a specified amount [12]. The CR must be able to make use of the bandwidth without generating a signal that could raise the noise floor. This requires the CR to know two things: an estimate of the signal bandwidth used by the primary user, and the distance between the CR and the victim device [11]. This is tricky because each bands has a different values that must be calculated. Also the propagation path from the CR transmitter to the primary user's receiver could be very complex. The signal bandwidth can be used to determine the amount of noise the primary user's device can tolerate without interference, and the distance between the CR and signal device can be used to determine the signal strength of the primary user's device [7]. CR will never succeed unless both of these issues are adequately addressed. If primary users of spectrum space face any danger of interference with their services, it is very likely that they will deny any use of their spectrum space.

The FCC controls commercial and state and local government wireless users, while the NTIA regulates federal government users. These regulations cover operating frequency, effective radiated power limits, antenna height, emission type, and bandwidth limitation [12]. CR is subject to regulations from both these organizations, which can have different regional scopes and operating conditions. Since CR seeks to make use of different bands of the spectrum, it must be aware of regulations that differ per frequency band, service type, and spectrum management model [11]. If CR is not fully aware of these regulations, it runs the risk of causing interference to the primary user of that spectrum space. In order to make this possible, regulations should be made available so CR can access them in a machine-readable format [7]. This information would need to contain both allocations and spectrum sharing technical parameters [12]. Also included would be frequencies which are never to be accessed, even if unused. Such frequencies would include distress and safety channels, Radionavigation, and also Fixed Satellite bands [11].

From an economic standpoint, for CR to be effective it must make use of spectrum used by the television and phone industries. These companies will be pioneering CR and encouraging its development. In many cases, the services offered by these companies over CR could be in direct competition with the services offered by the companies that are the original license holders of the spectrum. For example, CR could open up the possibility of high speed wireless broadband video, and directly affect the earnings of television companies. Because of this, the owners of the spectrum might be unwilling, or even opposed to the sharing of their spectrum, even if it means possibly crippling CR.

3 Policy and Policy Makers

Due to the large demand for intelligent radios and the increasing numbers of wireless services crowding frequencies, CR has become a necessity, but so has spectrum management. This has caused various organizations to take notice and provide some standardization to spectrum allocation. As we have discussed, CR can sense its surroundings and learn from past experiences to utilize the unused spectrum. This unused spectrum has to be allocated properly without interfering with the transmission of other users. Therefore it must intelligently detect whether or not a segment of the spectrum is currently being used.

In order for licensees, regulators, and the general public to have comprehensive use of the spectrum, certain policies and procedures have to be in place. Organizations such as the Federal Communications Commission (FCC), Institute of Electrical and Electronic Engineers (IEEE), SDR Forum, and industry partners such as General Dynamics, Rockwell Collins, Vanu are involved in the standardization, protocols, and proper allocation of the spectrum [9].

The FCC is an independent government agency reporting to the Congress. They are responsible for the regulation of interstate and international communication by radio, satellite, television, wire, and cable. It is comprised of many different bureaus, but the bureau of wireless telecommunications is the control point for radio spectrum management. Therefore, the FCC has regulatory considerations for a functional solution to this growing problem. It has conducted Cognitive Radio Workshops, a taskforce charged with the tasks of gathering, analyzing and reviewing spectrum allocation [9].

UNITED

STATES

FREQUENCY

ALLOCATIONS

THE RADIO SPECTRUM

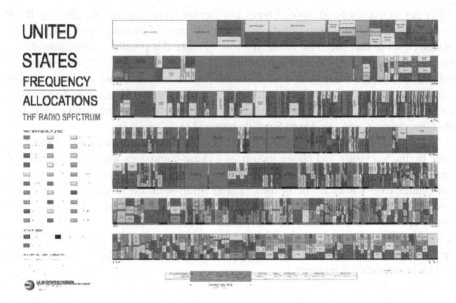

Regulatory considerations at the CSS level are a key part of the software radio story. The FCC even offers a number of CR workshops where industry and FCC regulators work to gather, analyze, and review spectrum allocations, use and licensing issues for the future. (Image courtesy of the U.S. Department of Commerce, National Telecommunications and Information Administration, Office of Spectrum Management, October 2003.) [16]

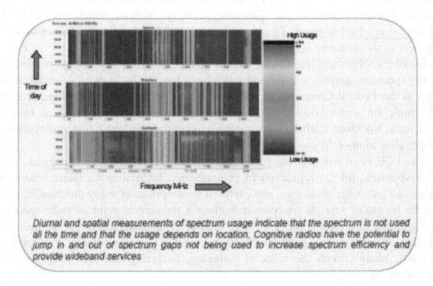

Diurnal and spatial measurements of spectrum usage indicate that the spectrum is not used all the time and that the usage depends on location. Cognitive radios have the potential to jump in and out of spectrum gaps not being used to increase spectrum efficiency and provide wideband services

Fig. 3. Not All the Spectrum is Used in Space (Geographic Location) or Time [13]

The FCC works to approve certain devices like SDRs that protect the confidentiality of software that controls the security measures regarding software defined radios. They continue to push for greater spectrum sharing in any band where licensed users agree to share the radio spectrum. The FCC also has industry partners that it is working with to resolve spectrum issues. In 2005, Vanu, Inc., a partner of the FCC, used the first Global System for Mobile Communications (GSM) base station with an RF converter. This converter makes the radio signal processable using a high-performance laptop [1]. The FCC has researched the spectrum and found that 70 percent of the allocated spectrum may be sitting idle at certain times of the day, even though it may be spoken for.

One solution for efficiently sharing the spectrum comes from a professor at the University of California. He suggested that the FCC gets priority, as the owner of the spectrum, while other devices divide the unused spectrum among themselves [15].

The Institute for Electrical Engineering (IEEE) is a leader in developing industry standards and its focus is the advancement of technology. They have begun to consider standards concerning cognitive radio. The IEEE sets many of the technical standards that drive the Internet revolution. IEEE-1900-B Working Group has been working on a protocol that can be transmitted to CRs. This protocol will enable networks to optimize behaviors and co-exist with other radio systems. The standard is intended to protect and certify the authenticity of the data and data privacy among other things.

4 Future of Cognitive Radio

The goal of regulatory bodies like the FCC when regulating natural resources, like the electromagnetic spectrum, is to promote its usage that is beneficial to the public at large. Intent aside, their regulations are certain to have an impact on the development of CR. The FCC and the Spectrum Policy Task Force (SPTF) are responsible for large and small paradigm shifts in the world of spectrum management. The SPTF is active in all aspects of the development of CR from operations to etiquette and protocol, and their actions significantly affect the progression and development of CR [10].

Regulations imposed by the FCC and SPTF are in the heart of the modern CR debate. There are extremists who believe in the complete liberalization of licenses, and there are those pushing for more regulations to strengthen the positions of the license holders. Although they differ on the means, both extremes are for the growth and development of CR.

Under the heavily regulated school of thought, it is believed strict standardizations and protocols are necessary for a multitude of radios to co-operate and function as a network. Standards set forth by the IEEE are deemed necessary to establish a regulatory framework that will encourage research and development rather than stifle it [13]. Ultimately, the regulations will provide a roadmap for the developers of CR, and promote growth that would not have happened were the regulations not in place.

On the other hand, many claim the liberalization of regulations will free bandwidth in the spectrum and allow for greater research. Government agencies have already allotted frequencies to license holders, and even those that call for extreme liberalization agree a certain level of licensing restrictions are necessary to maintain a healthy degree of standardization [13].

A study released in 2007 by Ofcom, the regulatory communications body of the United Kingdom, agreed with the FCC's and Irish Commission for Communications Regulation's (ComReg) assessment of the benefits of regulations on the growth of CR. They determined economic incentives to licensees coupled with standardizing policies would be the best combination motive and assist developers. Most agencies agree a compromise is crucial to the evolution of CR. Regulatory bodies are moving to reach middle-ground to direct CR into mainstream wireless communications. With enough collaboration, experts agree intelligent and auto-reconfigurable CRs will emerge in the next five years [13]. This would not be possible without the standardization of licenses and framework established by regulatory bodies such as the FCC and IEEE.

5 Conclusion

As discussed CR has the ability to learn from past behaviors and adapt itself to its surroundings. As this technology grows and develops, it will efficiently and intelligently make use of the spectrum while protecting license holders. While regulations offer a framework for CR developers, excessive regulation can hinder its development. Therefore, the fate of CR is in the policy makers' hands, and if they want to see the technology grow and develop, they must strive for regulations that respect the rights of both parties.

References

1. Ashley, S.: Cognitive Radio. Scientific American 294(3), 66–74 (2006)
2. Akyildiz, I., Lee, W., Vuran, M., Mohanty, S.: Next generation/dynamic spectrum access/cognitive radio wireless networks: A survey. Computer Networks 50(13), 2127–2159 (2006)
3. Brandao, A., Sydor, J., Brett, W.: 5 GHz RLAN Interference on Active Meteorlogical Radars. In: IEEE 61st Vehicular Technology Conference, vol. 2, pp. 1328–1332 (2005)
4. Calabrese, M.: Spectrum Reform an Urgent U.S. Priority. New America Foundation, http://www.newamerica.net/publications/articles/2004/spectrum_reform_an_urgent_us_priority
5. Campbell, A.: FFID Securty. Syngress, http://proquest.safaribooksonline.com/1597490474
6. Cognitive Radio Seen as Essential Enabler of Key Wireless Trends in Commercial, Public Safety and Military Markets. Wireless News, from ABI/INFORM Trade & Industry database (Document ID: 1341448651) (Retrieved October 14, 2007)
7. Cohen, D., Stewart, D.: Spectrum Regulations for Ad Hoc Wireless Cognitive Radios, http://www.alionscience.com/
8. FCC: Spectrum Policy Task Force Report," ET Docket No. 02-135, pp. 35-53 (2002)
9. Fette, B.: Cognitive Radio Show Great Promise. COTS Journal (2007)
10. Haykin, S.: Cognitive Radio: Brain-Empowered Wireless Communications. IEEE Journal on Selected Areas in Communications 23(2) (2005)

11. Ianculescu, C., Mudra, A.: Cognitive Radio and Dynamic Spectrum Sharing. In: SDR 2005 Technical Conference and Product Exposition, CA (2005)
12. Krenik, A., Batra, A.: Cognitive radio techniques for wide area networks. In: Annual ACM IEEE Design Automation Conference, Anaheim, CA, pp. 409–412 (2005)
13. QinetiQ Ltd.: Cognitive Radio Technology: A Study for Ofcom, http://www.macltd.com
14. Savage, N.: Cognitive Radio. Technology Review (2006), http://www.technologyreview.com
15. Vining, J.: RFID Alone Can't Resolve Cargo Container Security Issues, Gartner (2005)
16. National Telecommunications and Information Administration, Office of Spectrum Management, http://www.ntia.doc.gov/osmhome/allochrt.pdf

Privacy Issues for Vehicular Ad-Hoc Network*

Hang Dok[1], Ruben Echevarria[2], and Huirong Fu[1]

[1] Oakland University, Rochester, Michigan 48309
[2] University Chicago of Illinois, Illinois 60607
fu@oakland.edu

Abstract. Vehicular Ad-Hoc Networks are networks of communication between vehicles and roadside units. These networks have the potential to increase safety and provide many services to drivers, but they also present risks to privacy. Researching mechanisms to protect privacy requires two key ingredients: 1. a precise definition of privacy that reflects citizens' concerns and perceptions, and 2. an understanding of the type of attacks in VANETs. In this research, we formulate a workable definition of privacy, and focus on tracking attacks, which we found to be lacking. Although considerable research has been performed in tracking none of the published solutions ensures full protection. We propose to combine a set of published solutions, namely: Mix Zones, Silent Periods, and Group Signatures in order to improve the privacy of drivers. Vehicles enter a region where, vehicles change their pseudonyms (Mix Zone) as well as network addresses; next enter the silent period, and then use one group key for communication. It could help make tracking more difficult and increase the safety and confidence of drivers using VANETs.

Keywords: Privacy, VANET, Security, Mix Zones, Silent Periods and Group Signature.

1 Introduction

The Vehicular Ad-Hoc Network, better known as VANET, is a network devoted to communication between vehicles and roadside units. With such technology, vehicle owners could increase safety and provide many services to drivers [1]. One of the safety increasing features includes warning messages of oncoming accident sites in real time. One of the simplifying features includes messages with traffic updates to warn about possible traffic congestions on a desired route [2]. To better understand the relationship, one could look at the relationship between computers and the internet and connect it to the relationship between vehicles and VANET. Privacy is an important aspect for VANET to be successful and accepted by the majority in this paper.

* This work was partly supported by the U.S. National Science Foundation under Grants No. 0823868, No. 0716527, and No. 0552707, and Oakland University Faculty Research Fellowship (FRF). Any opinions, findings, and conclusions or recommendations expressed in this material are those of the authors and do not necessarily reflect the views of the National Science Foundation.

D. Ślęzak et al. (Eds.): FGCN/ACN 2009, CCIS 56, pp. 370–383, 2009.
© Springer-Verlag Berlin Heidelberg 2009

We proposed a combination of existed solutions to provide security in the vehicular network. This solution consists of Mix Zones, Silent Periods, and Group Navigation. In our theoretical analysis, we measured silent period's anonymity and entropy of the identifying vehicles within the proposed solution. We then found that the numbers were high in anonymity so that it would make it difficult for trackers to identify any one vehicle.

The remainder of this paper is organized as follows. In Section 2, we discuss about privacy for VANETs. Then, we present our solution in Section 3. Next, we evaluate our solution through theoretical analysis in Section 4. After the evaluation, simulation is displayed in Section 5. Finally, we conclude in Section 6 by discussing the advantages of our solution over some of the known researched solutions and our future works.

2   Privacy

Globally there is no set definition for privacy, causing some difficulties to study what should be kept private. According to the Leading Surveillance Societies in EU (European Union) and the World 2007 proves that the United States has little privacy and is under secure surveillance [3]. There are laws to protect human rights, but nothing of the sort to define privacy.

The definition of privacy used for this research is from Dr. Standler. He defined privacy as "the expectation that confidential personal information disclosed in a private place will not be disclosed to third parties, when that disclosure would cause either embarrassment or emotional distress to a person of reasonable sensitivities [4]." With an addition, from the US Code Collection from Cornell University Law School, personal information that can be used as identification should be kept private as well [5].

With a working definition of privacy, we will discuss what should be kept private relating to VANET. The privacy information is categorized into two groups: motor vehicle records and personal information. Motor vehicle records are defined as any record that pertains to a motor vehicle operator's permit [5]. A few examples of motor vehicles records include, but not limited to: motor vehicle title, motor vehicle registration, and identification card issued by a department of motor vehicles. Personal information is defined as information used as identification. A few examples of personal information include, but not limited to: photograph, full name, routine routes and time of travel, bills, and private keys.

Some may think to have VANET with anonymity, but in reality the network would fail if anonymity was introduced to the whole network for every vehicle all the time. First, it would compromise the entire idea of a secure network. False messages could be sent, such as "some pranksters might send bogus warning messages to other cars, pretending that there are dangerous road conditions ahead. This might lead to cars slowing down or breaking, resulting in traffic jams or even accidents [6]." VANET would only be a success if users feel it can be trusted and utilized it for what is was made for. Second anonymity, would not allow law enforcement to track vehicles. The law enforcement may need to track vehicles using VANET as an aid in an investigation of a stolen car or hit-and-run accidents [7].

Therefore, VANET must have a way to validate transmissions and keep security while retaining privacy, ruling out anonymity. Some researched ways to help keep privacy are pseudonyms and keys. Pseudonyms are fictitious names given to vehicles to prevent tracking. There is research to have a "vehicle generate its own pseudonyms, in order to eliminate the need of pre-loading, storing and refilling pseudonyms... [8]."

Keys are types of pseudonyms that secure the communication between the sender and receiver. There are two ways to encrypt and decrypt messages. First is the Asymmetric key consisting of a private and public pair of keys that correlate with one another. Public keys can represent mailbox addresses that everyone in the network can see. Private keys are like a key that can open the mailbox mentioned above. This key can open any messages that are encrypted with the corresponding public key. To encrypt a message, one needs the public key of the person that is being sent the message. To decrypt the message, the private key is used to decrypt and corresponds to the public key. The advantage of public and private keys is the ability to authenticate messages. The disadvantages are: high security overhead [9] [10] [11] and computationally costly storing large number of key pairs and keys must be changed frequently [12]. Another type of key is the Symmetric key that consists of a key to encrypt and decrypt messages. This key can only be seen by certain individuals with some sort of mutual agreement. The advantages to asymmetric keys are: more efficiency over asymmetric keys, less computational effort, and less vulnerable cryptanalytic advance [10] [11] [13]. The disadvantage is the key distribution process is currently unknown.

3   Proposed Solution

VANETs are vulnerable to attacks such as tracking via linking pseudonyms [14] [15] [16]. Prior to the proposal we first assume that we are dealing with attacks consists of listening to transmissions. In addition, we propose that users within the network are reliable and have no bad intention. During vehicle registration, private keys are distributed to valid members of the network. In order to avoid or minimize tracking attacks such as listening to beacons and stealing information by hacking into third party applications, we consider the combination of earlier proposed solutions from above. This solution contains of a combination of Mix Zones [19] [20] [21], Silent Period [17] [18], and Group Signature [11] [12] [17] [18]. Many proposals rely on road intersection as a way to lower chances of tracking. In this proposal we considered road intersection as the basis of the solution to privacy.

3.1   Entering Mix Zone

In this scenario we will have two types of protocols of traveling vehicles, group key and pseudonyms. Each vehicle will be assigned a new pseudonym (mix zone) before entering intersection region. In Figure 1, we see that there are groups key 13, 41, and 12 entering the region changing their pseudonym. In this process the identifiers changes for each vehicle. For example one of the cars in group key 13 may have pseudonym with 1234 but changed to 2345. This current pseudonym allows for communication among other vehicle in case of accident within the silent period region.

3.2 Entering Silent Period

After exiting the mix zone, vehicles will enter a region where transmission is disabled and enter the intersection. In Figure 2, group key 13 and 41 enters the silent period, therefore their group key or pseudonym is not revealed. This will lower chances of identifying vehicles directions due to high traffic.

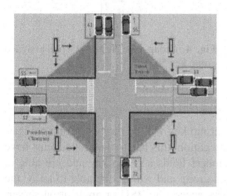 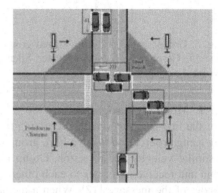

Fig. 1. Group key 13, 12, 72, 41 enter Mix Zone   **Fig. 2.** Group key 13, 12 enter Silent Period

3.3 Group Keys

When vehicles leave the silent period region, users are forced to change pseudonyms address once again. By using the same example in entering mix zone, a vehicle in group key 13 will change pseudonym from 2345 to 5678. At the same time the vehicle will be assigned to a group key 55, Figure 3. Vehicles will be assigned to encrypted group key distributed by RSU. Group key is obtained; vehicles may or may not form group navigating depending on the surrounding environment. After leaving the Mix Zone, general public are advised to become group members, while authority vehicles are group mangers. Algorithms for group navigation should be able to switch from independent traveling to group members to group managers. Group keys should change frequently after some time interval - key mixes. All group keys allow communication with a different group key. Group keys should not have any connection with identifier.

Group navigation allows member to remain anonymous among other members and possible attackers. There will be many groups navigating using the same group key depending on the road intersection traveled through. Therefore different groups can communicate with a group key. A fixed location compromises the solutions intent to protect against privacy attacks. Therefore the areas of Mix Zones and Silent Periods need to be randomly generated with an algorithm to place the combination of zones at the highest traffic intersections, preferably traffic in commercial and highway.

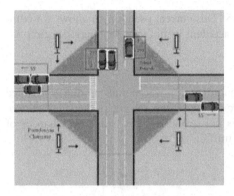 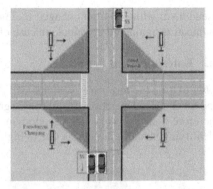

Fig. 3. Group key 13, 12 are assigned group key 55. Group key 72 and 41 enter Silent Period.

Fig. 4. Group key 72 and 41 are assigned group key 55

3.3.1 Members Navigating

For the first batch of vehicles receiving the group key will be the first group navigating using group key ####. To have group navigation, this batch of vehicles must have a similar velocity and direction. Group members holds a group key and are able to send and receive messages to each other as a group and will not be able to know the sender of the message [12]. When a members access the RSU or application server, attacks may be hack into these application but cannot distinguish vehicles because the usage of the group key. Group key therefore cannot have any connection to unique pseudonym of the member. Since there are many users of this group key, no one attack will be able to identify one person in the group.

3.3.2 Members Diverging Paths

However, if vehicles diverge different path or velocity then if will travel by sending its pseudonym address. These users will be able to listen to all the activities surrounding them but will not be able to reply to any of the messages; transmission is cut off until a group is detected nearby. Group key given during key mixes will be allowed to join other available groups as long there are a similar velocity.

3.3.3 Manager and Members

Authorities vehicle are group managers provided that there are not corrupted. Manager maintains authenticity of group members and allows member to access applications servers and RSU. The duties of the manager consist of recording all the data and pseudonym of each member. Therefore managers can look up the identities of its members to ensure authenticity in any give case. Managers should beacon out public key letting members know it is a group manager. Only group manager can communicate beyond the group, like servers and applications. Messages received by the manager from the application servers are beaconed among the members. This algorithm holds authenticity of messages and keeps private information from being exposed.

4 Theoretical Analysis

The paper is based on mix zones, silent periods, and group concept. The purpose of this section is to measure the level of privacy for each vehicle within this region. In doing so, we theoretically analyze the silent period and ignore other purposed solution due to its analytical perplexity.

We will be analyzing the silent period that contains an intersection with a heavy flow-rate. Vehicles are to send beacons every millisecond however within the silent period no vehicles are to send or receive messages due to the failure of the transmission in this region. After exiting, vehicles automatically continue sending beacons. The measurement of the privacy levels is crucial in determining the question of usage. We use two performance metrics: anonymity set and entropy level.

An anonymity set is the number of possibilities for an attacker to track a vehicle. The higher the anonymity set, the lower the probability for tracking of a vehicle. In the proposed solution, the number of vehicles exiting the combination of zones between a reasonable minimum and maximum time for one vehicle to exit is the anonymity set. There are numbers of parameter that are affected by the anonymity set as a vehicle enters the combination of zones: 1. Number of lanes for vehicle to exit assuming that there is no U turns 2.

After determining the parameter, the function that will define the anonymity set is

$$S_A = \sum_{i=1}^{N} RL_i * t \cdot \tag{1}$$

Entropy is a measure of the content of a message evaluated with respect to its probability of occurrence, or uncertainty of occurrences. In this case we are measuring the solution we proposed to see whether high anonymity set is probable. Given that the attacks are unknown, the probabilities for all the anonymity sets are equal. If the entropy is high then privacy is high as well.

$$E = -\sum_{i=1}^{SA} P_i (\log_2 P_i) \cdot \tag{2}$$

P_i Stands for probability for anonymity set $P_i = \dfrac{1}{S_A}$

Now that we know the definition of each metrics we can illustrate a traffic scenario, with the assumption of these properties from Table I. Next consider these parameters: size of Silent Periods which affects the duration of vehicles within the region given the average speed of vehicles in the scenario, flow-rate and the number of lanes for each scenario.

For each scenario, flow-rate increase over time and number of vehicles exit increases as well, known as the anonymity set. Results may affect the average speed at which vehicles are moving and due to the assumption's size of the scenario. Varying numbers are adjusted to improve the anonymity set by increasing number of lanes, time duration or flow-rate. Figure 5, illustrates that 3-lane local and 2-lane downtown has a greater anonymity set due to average time measures respectively at 5.70 s and

Table 1. Define each scenario through various speed and number of lanes

	Speed (mph)	Lanes
Downtown	25-30	1, 2
Local	35-45	2, 3
Highway	60-70	3, 4

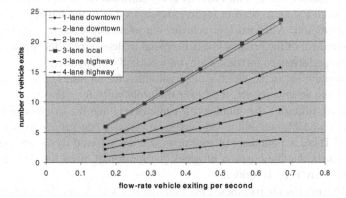

Fig. 5. Illustrate flow-rate is dependent on the anonymity set for each scenario. Assume that downtown areas should be one lane or two lanes and traveling around 27.5 mph; local area should be two or three lanes and traveling around 40mph; and highway areas should be three or four lanes and traveling around 72.5mph.

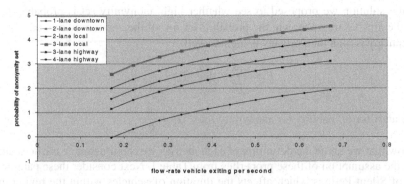

Fig. 6. Measure probability of the anonymity set in Fig. 5. 3-Lane local traffic scenario measures time duration at 3.92 seconds traveling velocity at 40mph while 2-lane downtown measures time duration at 5.70 seconds traveling velocity at 27.5mph. 3-lane and 2-lane of local and downtown, respectively have the highest probability.

3.92 s. However, increasing the time duration to 10-20seconds, highway scenario obviously has higher anonymity set. Therefore it takes vehicles longer to travel within this scenario due to higher velocity and size of the region. For the next measurement, entropy set uses figure 5 to determine the probability. Figure 6 illustrates that 3-lane

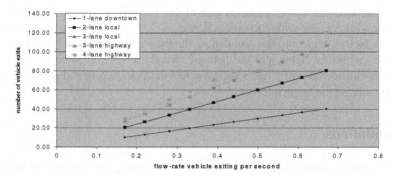

Fig. 7. Measure the time duration for max of 20 seconds. 3-lane local and 4-lane highway has the greatest anonymity set.

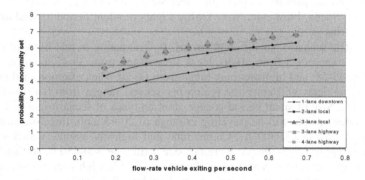

Fig. 8. Measures the entropy of the anonymity set from Fig. 7 for each scenario

Table 2. Define each multiple scenario by an average speed and number of lane

	Speed (mph)	Lanes
Downtown	27.5	1
Local	27.5	2
Local	40	3
Highway	72.5	3
Highway	65	4

local and 2-lane downtown has the preeminent results compared to other four scenarios due to particular traffic scenarios.

By determining better results, we took the measurements at higher time duration of 20 seconds. However we questioned why highway traffic scenario had the least anonymity set so we then compared to another anonymity set for a longer time duration, which resulted in highest anonymity set compared to other 4 traffic scenario. As a result, concluded that traffic scenarios with higher velocity must travel in a larger size region for a longer time within the silent period.

If more factors came into this simulation, the theoretical part would be more realistic. However, traffic lights and the path of directions vehicles were ignored. Next section we considered traffic lights and vehicle's destination path and prove that flowrate will increase the anonymity set.

5 Simulations

Matlab is used to simulate the process of vehicles moving into and out of the silent period, in order to imitate, exponentially random times in seconds were produced. Next we ordered the random times in ascending order and summed the time before and current time to give us the exact times of each vehicle entering the region. Finally we had to find the parameters that will affect the timing of vehicles inside the region: Destination, Speed, Flow-rate, Size, Traffic Lights of silent period depending on different scenarios.

Each traffic scenario has different speeds. By comparing to real life traffic (mph): downtown areas range from 20-30, local areas range from 35-45, commercial area range from 45-55, and highway may range from 60-70. The definition of flow-rate is how many vehicles will enter the region per second ranges from 0-1.0 vehicle per second (vps). Size of silent period is dependent on types of scenarios, downtown and local assumes vehicle will be traveling in range of 20-45 mph; therefore size should be 60.96-91.44m (~200-300 ft). Commercial and highway assume vehicles will be traveling in range of 45-70mph; therefore size should be 300-450 ft, so that vehicles have some decent time to traveling in the region. Traffic Lights are considered since we are dealing with busy road intersections, how long it will take to change from red and green lights, we used 10 seconds since the time we are measuring is only 20-30 seconds. Destination is for vehicles to take; either straight, right, or left. Timing will be different whether going straight (3s), right (2s), and left (4s).

Next we calculated the time it takes for each vehicle to exit the silent period. During the simulation, queries of the silent period were made to see whether it would be effective enough for privacy solution in VANET. Therefore we measure the anonymity set for each vehicle at a time, which is a set of other vehicles exiting within same range of time, depending on how long it will take that one vehicle to exit. Basically anonymity set illustrates how vehicles are able to be anonymous within the region, due to other vehicles exiting at similar ranges of time so it will be hard for some tracker to identify a particular vehicle from a mass of other vehicles.

We then took the average of the anonymity set per direction: north, south, east, west roads and also the average for the entire silent period. Then graph different parameters that will affect the privacy of the users.

Fig.9 measures the anonymity set due to varying flow-rates, where vehicles are in different scenarios (downtown, local, commercial, and highway). As you can see the local traffic scenario have a greater anonymity over the varying flow-rates set compared to the rest of the scenarios, which seem to be caused by the medium range of the velocity. Similar to previous, Fig.10 measures the anonymity set verse flow-rate depended on silent period size of 102.108 meter. As the size of the silent period increase, the anonymity set increased a bit, this does not seem to affect the anonymity set too much. However the local traffic scenario seems to have a greater anonymity set in both figures. Now let's look at the sizes of the silent period verses anonymity set. Fig.11 and 12 each shows this but since 2 regions are similar are group together. In Fig.11 we see that local region have a better anonymity set since it has a higher flow-rate than downtown. Similarly in fig. 12, shows the silent period ranges from 85-110 meters where the highway has greater anonymity set compared to commercial regions. This may tell us that flow-rates ranging from 0-40mph has a greater and stable anonymity set compared to higher ranges.

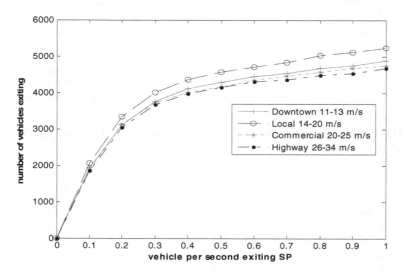

Fig. 9. Anonymity set vs. Flow-rate graph sets size of region to 76.2 meters. Measure the number of vehicles with the given protocol over the variation of flow rate of vehicles within the Silent Period.

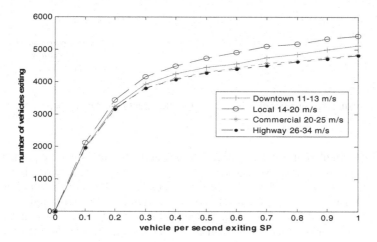

Fig. 10. Anonymity set vs. Flow-rate graph sets size of region to 102.108 meters

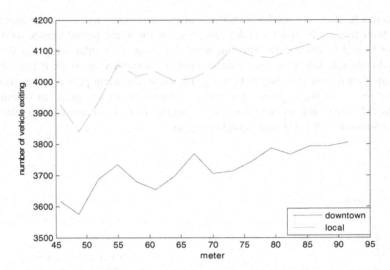

Fig. 11. Measures the number of vehicles entering the silent period depended on the varying sizes of the silent period

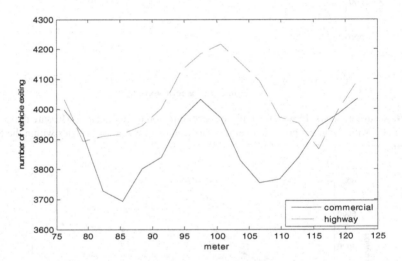

Fig. 12. Measures the number of vehicles entering the silent period being depended on the size of the silent period

After the simulation, we can expect that the parameters do affect the privacy levels of the silent period; if we were to increase the flow-rate or the size of the silent period. As one can see that different scenarios does better than others, which does not affect the silent period since our results for the anonymity set is fairly high.

One of the major issues for silent periods is that what if there was an accident inside the silent period. Since there will be others vehicles inside the region at same time, vehicles must be alert due to its surroundings and save the data of the accident onto the on-board-unit and execute message to authority, server, or other vehicles once out of the region. In doing this will increase the safety of the users in VANET.

In that situation, safety appears to be more important than privacy. Vehicles not inside the region automatically sends warnings and alerts constantly, so that some base unit nearby will disable the silent period. Some nearby authority will be able receive the message and to go the scene of the accident.

Since our protocol is not based on only one silent period but several around the region, it should randomly generate another silent period /group navigation and by replacing into another intersection. Therefore one disable mix zone and silent period would not affect the privacy of other vehicles within the region.

6 Conclusion and Future Work

This solution has many benefits for preserving privacy. The solution prevents attackers from linking transmission to a particular vehicle after an intersection. When vehicles enter the region, vehicles change their pseudonym address, and then enter the silent period, where vehicles can travel in different paths; as a result the attacker would have no choice, but to guess which path to continue following. Once in a group, vehicles are able to become anonymous, because every vehicle shares only one key to communicate. Since group keys are not related to pseudonyms, identities should not be linkable. By using one group key, security overhead is reduced opposed to asymmetric keys. Group keys reduce the number of key maintenance [12], and are more efficient. Messages encrypted with the group key can only be opened by the group key. Only group members and leaders know the group key, which was distributed by the Mix Zone. Having the Mix Zone in certain regions, congested road intersection, reduces the amount of pseudonyms that could possibly cause a delay from the RSUs. Opposed to Mix Contexts, which change pseudonyms frequently before and after places have been visited, but cause pseudonyms to be wasted [16]. For those reasons, forming groups helps vehicles retain privacy because an attacker would be challenged with the pseudonym change, network address change, Silent Periods and group navigation.

In conclusion, VANET could only be successful if vehicle owners trust the network to secure their privacy. With our proposed solution to combine a set of published solutions, namely: Mix Zones, Silent Periods, and Group Signatures to improve the protection of privacy of drivers. The more drivers using VANET, the more people will benefit from the network. The more people benefit, the more useful the information shared. Along with our proposed solution to retaining privacy, VANET could be a more trusted and therefore accepted network for vehicle owners. With such technology, vehicle owners could increase safety and provide many services to drivers.

Our solution has been tested analytically and theoretically. In future work, we intend to have our solution simulated to test efficiency, anonymity set, and entropy against other known solutions. We would also like to create the algorithm to randomly generate the areas of Mix Zones and Silent Periods for our solution.

References

1. Mahaian, A., Potris, N., Gopalan, K., Wang, A., Brothers, L.: Modeling VANET Deployment in Urban Settings. In: MSWIM 2007, Chania, Crete Island, Greece, October 22-26 (2007)
2. Moustafa, W.E.-D.M.: Privacy of location Information in Vehicular Ad Hoc Networks, http://www.cs.umd.edu/class/spring2007/cmsc818z/present.ppt
3. Privacy International Clerkenwell, London (1990), http://www.privacyinternational.org/indexs.html
4. Standler, R.B.: Privacy Laws in the US. Massachusetts (1997), http://www.rbs2.com/privacy.html
5. Bruce, T.R., Martin, E.P.: US Code Collection. Legal Information Institute, Cornell Law School, Myron Taylor Hall, Ithaca, NY (1992)
6. Kargl, F., Ma, Z., Elmer Schoch Ulm University: Institute of Media Informatics, Security Engineering for VANETs, http://medien.informatik.uni-ulm.de/forschung/publikationen/escar2006.pdf
7. Hubaux, J.-P., Capkun, S., Luo, J.: The Security and Privacy of Smart Vehicles. IEEE Security and Privacy 4(3), 49–55 (2004)
8. Calandriello, G., Papadimitratos, P., Lioy, J.-P.H.A.: Efficient and Robust Pseudonymous Authentication in VANET. In: VANET 2007, Montreal Quebec, Canada, September 10 (2007)
9. Raya, M., Papadimitratos, P., Hubaux, J.-P.: Securing Vehicular Networks. In: The 25th Conference on Computer Communications IEEE InFOCOM 2006, Barcelona, Catalunya, Spain, April 23-29 (2006)
10. Sha, K., Shi, W., Schwiebert, L., Zhang, T.: Enforcing Privacy Using Symmetric Random Key-Set in Vehicular Networks. In: ISADS Proceedings of the Eighth International Symposium on Autonomous Decentralized Systems (2007)
11. Raya, M., Hubaux, J.-P.: Securing Vehicular ad hoc networks. Journal of Computer Security 15, 39–68 (2007)
12. Guo, J., Baugh, P., Wang, S.: A Group Signature Based Secure and Privacy Preserving Vehicular Communication Framework. Mobile Networking for Vehicular Environments 11(11), 103–108 (2007)
13. Choi, J., Jakobsson, M., Wetzel, S.: Balancing Auditability and Privacy in Vehicular Networks. Q2SWinet, Montreal, Quebec, Canada, October 13 (2005)
14. tracking.WordNet® 3.0. Princeton University (July 15, 2008), Dictionary.com, http://dictionary.reference.com/browse/tracking
15. Werner, J.: Details of the vii initiative's work in progress provided at public meeting, http://www.ntoctalks.com/icdn/viipubmtgv1.php
16. Gerlach, M.: Assessing and Improving Privacy in VANETs. Published In Proceedings of Fourth Workshop on Embedded Security in Cars (ESCAR), Hamburg, Germany (November 2006)
17. Sampigethaya, K., Li, M., Huang, L., Poovendran, R.: AMOEBA: Robust Location Privacy Scheme for VANET. IEEE Journal on Selected Areas in Communications, JSAC (2007); Special issue on Vehicular Networks
18. Li, M., Sampigethaya, K., Huang, L., Poovendran, R.: Caravan: Providing Location Privacy in VANET. In: Workshops On Privacy in the Electronic Society, Proceedings of the 5th ACM workshop on Privacy in electronic society, Alexandria, VA, October 30 (2005)

19. Dotzer, F.: Privacy issues in vehicular ad hoc networks. In: Proceedings of the Workshop on Privacy Enhancing Technologies (2005)
20. Freudiger, J., Raya, M., Felegyhazi, M., Papadimitratos, P., Hubaux, J.P.: Mix-Zones for Location Privacy in Vehicular Networks. In: ACM Workshop on Wireless Networking for Intelligent Transportation Systems (WiN-ITS), Vancouver (2007)
21. Beresford, A.R., Stajano, F.: Location Privacy in Pervasive Computing. Pervasive Computing, IEEE 2(1), 46–55 (2003)

Load-Similar Node Distribution for Prolonging Network Lifetime in PMRC-Based Wireless Sensor Networks

Qiaoqin Li[1,2], Mei Yang[1], Yan Jin[1], Jun Zheng[3], Yingtao Jiang[1], and Jiazhi Zeng[2]

[1] Dept. of Electrical and Computer Engineering, Univ. of Nevada,
Las Vegas, NV, 89154, USA
meiyang@egr.unlv.edu,jinyanhit@gmail.com,
yingtao@egr.unlv.edu
[2] College of Computer Science and Technology,
Univ. of Electronic Science and Technology, Chengdu, 610054, P.R. China
helenli803@uestc.edu.cn, jzzeng@uestc.edu.cn
[3] Dept. of Computer Science and Engineering,
New Mexico Institute of Mining and Technology, Socorro, NM 87801, USA
zheng@cs.nmt.edu

Abstract. In this paper, the energy hole problem in Progressive Multi-hop Rotational Clustered (PMRC)-based wireless sensor networks (WSNs) is studied. We first analyze the traffic load distribution in PMRC-based WSNs. Based on the analysis, we propose a novel load-similar node distribution strategy combined with the Minimum Overlapping Layers (MOL) scheme to solve the energy hole problem in PMRC-based WSNs. Simulation results demonstrate that the load-similar node distribution strategy significantly prolongs network lifetime than uniform node distribution and an existing nonuniform node distribution strategies. The analysis model and the proposed load-similar node distribution strategy have the potential to be applied to other multi-hop WSN structures.

Keywords: Wireless sensor networks, energy hole problem, load-similar node distribution.

1 Introduction

Due to the benefits of low cost, rapid deployment, self-organization capability and cooperative data processing, wireless sensor networks (WSNs) have been proposed as a practical solution for a wide range of applications [1], such as military surveillance and habitat monitoring, etc. A typical WSN is formed by a large number of sensor nodes responsible for sensing data and a sink node responsible for collecting and processing data. Since the energy supply for each sensor node is usually extremely limited, energy efficiency is the primary challenge of WSNs. Previous research works show that clustered structure [2] and multi-hop routing [3] achieve better energy efficiency for large scale WSNs.

In WSNs, the data traffic follows a many-to-one communication pattern. Nodes closer to the sink tend to carry heavier traffic load, which will deplete their energy

D. Ślęzak et al. (Eds.): FGCN/ACN 2009, CCIS 56, pp. 384–393, 2009.
© Springer-Verlag Berlin Heidelberg 2009

faster. Authors in [4] argue that by the time nodes closest to the sink deplete their energy, nodes farther away to the sink may still hold up to 93% of their initial energy assuming all nodes have the same fixed transmission range and nodes are uniformly distributed in the network. In the literature, this problem is referred as the *energy hole* problem and a number of research related to this problem have been conducted.

Olariu and Stojmenović investigate the theoretical aspects of uneven energy depletion problem in sink-based WSNs [5]. Li and Mohapatra develop a mathematical model to analyze the energy hole problem in many-to-one networks [6]. Perillo *et al.* propose a general model to study the optimal transmission range distribution to maximize the network lifetime [7]. In [8], a nonuniform node distribution strategy is proposed to avoid the energy hole problem in multi-layered sensor networks with fixed layer boundary.

In our previous work [9], a highly scalable network architecture, named as Progressive Multi-hop Rotational Clustered (PMRC) structure, is proposed for the construction of large scale WSNs. In PMRC-based network, nodes are partitioned into layers according to their distance to the sink. A cluster is composed of sensor nodes in the same layer and a cluster head in the upstream layer. Fig. 1 shows the structure of a PMRC-based network with 3 layers. The operation of a PMRC-based network is divided into rounds. Each round begins with a network formation phase when clusters are formed, followed by a data gathering phase.

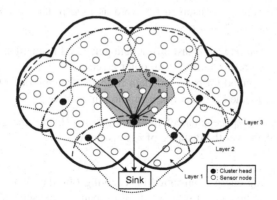

Fig. 1. Structure of a PMRC-based WSN

Like other multi-hop structures, PMRC also suffers from the energy hole problem. To attack this problem, the Overlapping Layers (OL) scheme is proposed to balance the relay load at the cluster heads for all layers by overlapping the neighbor layers following a desired overlap range [10]. However, due to the fixed layer boundary and overlap range in the OL scheme, the network lifetime is still limited by some nodes with only one candidate cluster head. To overcome this limit, the Minimum Overlapping Layers (MOL) scheme [11] is proposed to gradually increase the required minimum overlap between neighbor layers during network lifetime. As the traffic follows a many-to-one pattern, the network lifetime of MOL-enabled PMRC-based WSNs is still limited by the number of sensor nodes in the initial first layer.

As addressed in [8], node distribution strategy is rather important in balancing energy consumption in multi-hop static sensor networks with single sink node. In this paper, we propose a load-similar node distribution strategy to solve the energy hole problem for the PMRC-based WSNs. First, the load analysis in the continuous space of the network is performed, which reflects the gradual change of the layer boundary in the MOL scheme. Then based on the analysis, the load-similar node distribution strategy is proposed. Simulation results confirm the superiority of the proposed load-similar node distribution over the nonuniform node distribution [8] and uniform node distribution strategies for MOL-enabled PMRC-based WSNs.

The rest of this paper is organized as follows. In Section 2, the traffic load in PMRC-based WSNs is analyzed. The load-similar node distribution strategy is described in Section 3. Simulation results are presented in Section 4 and the paper is concluded in Section 5.

2 Analysis of Load

2.1 Energy Model

In our model, each sensor node is assumed to have the same initial energy, whereas the energy of the sink is much higher. Assume that any sensor node may be elected as a cluster head. The energy consumed (referred as *load* in later text) by each sensor node majorly consists of three parts:

- E_t: the energy consumed for transmitting data generated from all sensor nodes in its cluster and the data relayed through all outer layers;
- E_r: the energy consumed for receiving data collected from all outer layers;
- E_c: the energy consumed for network formation in each round.

Following the free space channel model used in [2], the energy consumed for transmitting l-bit data over the distance of r is given by

$$l(E_{elec} + \varepsilon r^2), \tag{1}$$

and the corresponding energy consumed in receiving l-bit data is lE_{elec}. According to [2], the system parameters used in in this paper are set as, $E_{elec}=50nJ/bit$, $\varepsilon=10pJ/bit/m^2$.

The energy consumed in network formation phase is majorly composed of the energy consumed for receiving control packets, including Control Packets (CP), Header Selection Packets (HP), Broadcast Packet (BP), and Cluster Control Packets (CCP) [9]. Here the energy consumed in sending these packets is neglected due to the small volume of such packets. The energy consumed during each network formation at layer i, E_{ci}, can be calculated as:

$$E_{c1} = (2 * cs + hs * hn)E_{elec}, \tag{2}$$

$$E_{ci} = (cs * (i+1) + bs * bn + hs * hn + ccs * ccn)E_{elec}, \quad i > 1, \tag{3}$$

where cs, hs, bs and ccs represent the packet length of a CP, HP, BP and CCP, respectively, while hn, bn and ccn represent the respective average number of HPs, BPs and CCPs received by each node during each network formation.

2.2 Analysis of Load

Assume static sensor nodes are uniformly distributed with node density ρ within a $2R \times 2R$ square area, and the sink is located at the center of the area. Assume all sensor nodes are active in transmission and a portion of these nodes (referred as source nodes in the later text) are active in sensing data. Each source node generates and sends λ bits of data per unit time. The ratio of the number of source nodes to the total number of sensor nodes is μ.

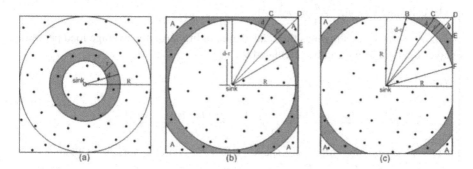

Fig. 2. Geometry relationship of layer i, $d \leq R$ (a), $R < d \leq R + r$ (b), $R + r < d \leq \sqrt{2} R$ (c)

Fig. 2 illustrates the geometry relationship of layer i (with radius r which is equal to the transmission range) within the $2R \times 2R$ square area. Assume the distance from the sink to the outer boundary of layer i is d. First, we deduce the average load per node in layers within the range of $r < d \leq R$, as shown in Fig. 2(a). According to the energy model, the total energy consumed for data receiving and transmission in a unit time by all the sensor nodes in layer i ($i>1$), E_{ri} and E_{ti}, are given by:

$$E_{ri} = E_{elec} \lambda \rho \mu (4R^2 - \pi d^2), \quad i>1, \quad r < d \leq R, \tag{4}$$

$$E_{ti} = (E_{elec} + \varepsilon r^2) \lambda \rho \mu (4R^2 - \pi (d-r)^2), \quad i>1, \quad r < d \leq R. \tag{5}$$

Assume N_i is the number of sensor nodes in layer i, which can be calculated by $\rho \pi (d^2 - (d-r)^2)$. Then the average load per node in layer i (for $i>1$ and $r < d \leq R$) in a unit time is given by:

$$L_i = \frac{E_{ri} + E_{ti}}{N_i} + \frac{E_{ci}}{T_r} = \frac{E_{elec} \lambda \rho \mu (4R^2 - \pi d^2)}{\rho \pi (d^2 - (d-r)^2)} + \frac{(E_{elec} + \varepsilon r^2) \lambda \rho \mu (4R^2 - \pi (d-r)^2)}{\rho \pi (d^2 - (d-r)^2)} +$$
$$\frac{(cs * cn + bs * bn + hs * hn + ccs * ccn) E_{elec}}{T_r}, \tag{6.1}$$

where T_r is the average lifetime per round, and $\frac{1}{T_r}$ gives the number of network formations performed in a unit time.

For $R < d \leq R + r$, shown as the shaded area in Fig. 2(b), the average load per node in layer i in a unit time can be calculated as:

$$L_i = \frac{E_{ri} + E_{ti}}{N_i} + \frac{E_{ci}}{T_r}$$

$$= \frac{4\lambda\mu E_{elec}A}{S_1} + \frac{\lambda\mu(E_{elec} + \varepsilon r^2)(4A + S_1)}{S_1} + \frac{(cs * cn + bs * bn + hs * hn + ccs * ccn)E_{elec}}{T_r},$$

(6.2)

where A gives the area of each corner outside the shaded area, which can be calculated by $(R - \sqrt{d^2 - R^2})R - (\frac{\pi}{4} - a\cos(\frac{R}{d}))d^2$, and S_1 is the area of the shaded layer which can be calculated by $4(R^2 - \frac{\pi}{4}(d - r)^2 - A)$.

For $R + r < d < \sqrt{2}R$, shown as the shaded area in Fig. 2(c), the average load per node in layer i in a unit time can be calculated as:

$$L_i = \frac{E_{ri} + E_{ti}}{N_i} + \frac{E_{ci}}{T_r}$$

$$= \frac{\lambda\mu E_{elec}A}{A' - A} + \frac{\lambda\mu(E_{elec} + \varepsilon r^2)A'}{A' - A} + \frac{(cs * cn + bs * bn + hs * hn + ccs * ccn)E_{elec}}{T_r},$$

(6.3)

where A' gives the area of shape $BCDEF$, which can be calculated as $(R - \sqrt{(d - r)^2 - R^2})R - (\frac{\pi}{4} - a\cos(\frac{R}{d - r}))(d - r)^2$, and the calculation of the area of each corner A follows that in (6-2).

For $d = \sqrt{2}R$, i.e., at the outermost layer, the average load per node in layer i in a unit time can be calculated as:

$$L_i = \frac{E_{ti}}{N_i} + \frac{E_{ci}}{T_r} = \mu\lambda(E_{elec} + \varepsilon r^2) + \frac{(cs * cn + bs * bn + ccs * ccn)E_{elec}}{T_r}.$$

(6.4)

For sensor nodes at layer 1, they will receive and forward the data coming from outside layer 1 and also send the data generated from layer 1. Then we have:

$$E_{r1} = E_{elec}\lambda\rho\mu(4R^2 - \pi r^2),$$

(7)

$$E_{t1} = (E_{elec} + \varepsilon r^2)\lambda\rho\mu 4R^2.$$

(8)

Here, L_1 is obtained as:

$$L_1 = \frac{E_{r1} + E_{t1}}{N_1} + \frac{E_{c1}}{T_r} = \frac{E_{elec}\mu\lambda(8R^2 - \pi r^2)}{\pi r^2} + \frac{\varepsilon\mu\lambda 4R^2}{\pi} + \frac{E_{elec}(2 * cs + hs * hn)}{T_r}.$$

(9)

Fig. 3 depicts the average load vs. d normalized in units of r=40m with μ=20% and λ=1600bps. The values of cs (145bits), hs (169bits), bs (205bits), and ccs (259bits) are set same as in the simulations. Other parameters, hn=3.4, bn=6.79, ccn=3.4, and T_r=25s, are estimated based on the analysis of the simulation result with uniformly distributed sensor nodes for r=40m and ρ=0.0064, and these values need to be adjusted for different r and ρ values. As shown in the figure, the average load per sensor node shows a sharp decrease with respect to the increase of the distance between the sensor node and the sink.

Consistent with our intuition, sensor nodes at layer 1 experience the heaviest load as they have to forward all the data traffic outside layer 1. When the sensor nodes

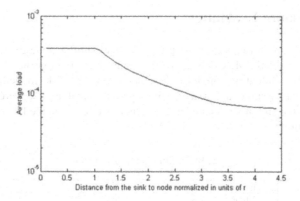

Fig. 3. Load distribution in MOL-enabled PMRC-based WSNs

close to the sink node deplete their energy, a ring-like "hole" surrounding the sink node is created, and the sensor nodes outside the "hole" area are actually separated from the sink. As such, the network lifetime is upper-bounded by the total energy of the sensor nodes within layer 1 for the MOL-enabled PMRC-based WSN.

3 Load-Similar Node Distribution

Based on the above analysis, to solve the energy hole problem in the MOL-enabled PMRC-based WSN, we propose to use a novel load-similar node distribution strategy. The underlying principle is that if the sensor nodes are deployed in the area according to the load distribution (that is, more nodes will be deployed in the range where the average load is higher), then the load among different layers in the sensor network tends to be balanced.

During the deployment of the network, the location of a node will be determined as follows. The distance from this node to the sink is randomly generated and a random load value is also generated. If the distance is less than or equal to the transmission range (i.e., the node is within the first layer), the node is deployed. Otherwise, if the generated load value is less or equal to the load calculated based on the distance, the node is deployed, or discarded otherwise. This process repeats until all the sensor nodes in the network are deployed.

Compared with the node distribution strategy proposed in [8], the node deployment in our strategy is very straightforward. The network formation and routing is simply based on the PMRC structure with the MOL scheme. Hence, there is no need to deploy the forwarding nodes deliberately. In addition, using the cluster structure, each node simply sends its data to its cluster head. This is a sharp contrast to the q-Switch routing [8], where each node needs to select one relay node with the most residual energy out of up to q possible forwarding nodes each time before it actually sends out its data. This puts extra requirement that the forwarding nodes periodically broadcast their residual energy.

4 Performance Evaluation

To evaluate the performance of the proposed load-similar node distribution strategy for the MOL-enabled PMRC-based WSN, extensive simulations have been conducted on the WSN simulation module developed on OPNET modeler [12]. In all simulations, we assume a 250m x 250m geographical area covered by a sensor network with the sink node located at the center. Table 1 lists the key parameters used in the simulations.

Table 1. Simulation parameters

Parameter	Value
Number of nodes	400
Radio transmission range	$\{40, 60, 80, 100\}m$
Initial energy per node	0.5 J
Packet generation rate	1 pkt/s
Packet length	200 Bytes
Simulation time	Until network partition

The following performance metrics are collected.

Time to first node death: in our simulation, we consider only the node death due to drained energy. Generally, this metric reflects the worst lifetime.

Network lifetime: it is defined as the time when the network is no longer connected or all source nodes drain out their energy.

Number of network formations: it is defined as the number of network formations.

Average residual energy: it is defined as the average residual energy of all sensor nodes in their initial layer when the network lifetime ends.

In the following, we present the simulation results of the aforementioned performance metrics for three different node distribution strategies: 1) *load-similar node distribution*, where sensor nodes are deployed following the load distribution analysis in Section 2; 2) *nonuniform node distribution* [8], where the number of nodes distributed in adjacent coronas C_i and C_{i+1} is initially regulated as $N_i/N_{i+1}=q$ with a common ratio of $q=2$; and 3) *uniform node distribution*, where sensor nodes are uniformly distributed in the area. The location of each node in these three distributions is generated using Matlab. In each simulation, a portion of sensor nodes (20% in our simulations) are selected as source nodes to generate and send data. Without loss of generality, these source nodes are randomly distributed in the square area. The results shown are the averaged results of 5 sets of source nodes.

Fig. 4 shows the time to first node death vs. transmission range r. In general, the time to first node death for all distributions shows an increasing trend with the increase of r. The first node death typically happens in the first layer. With the increase of r, the load carried by the nodes in layer 1 decreases because they will consume less energy in receiving packets as there are less nodes distributed outside layer 1 though they will consume more energy in transmitting packets. Among the three distributions, load-similar distribution has the longest time to first node death for $r\leq 80m$. The inconsistent trend at $r=100m$ is attributed to the fact that the initial network topology also has a significant impact to the time to first node death.

Fig. 5 shows the network lifetime for all distributions increases monotically with the increase of r. With the increase of r, the number of candidate cluster heads for each layer increases, which helps prolonging the network lifetime. Under the same transmission range, load-similar distribution achieves longer network lifetime than

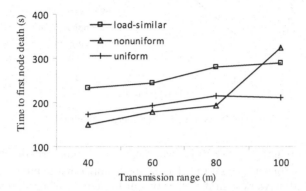

Fig. 4. Time to first node death vs. transmission range

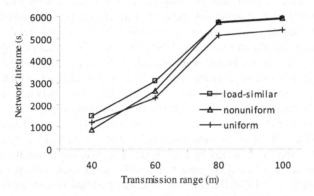

Fig. 5. Network lifetime vs. transmission range

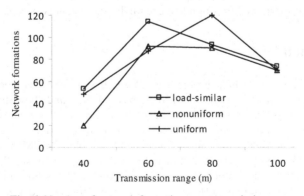

Fig. 6. Number of network formations vs. transmission range

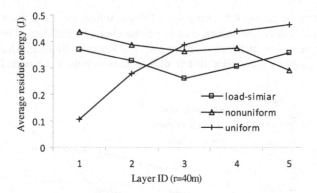

Fig. 7. Average residue energy at $r=40m$

uniform distribution (by up to 32%) for all ranges and nonuniform distribution (by up to 73%) when $r<80m$. This confirms that the load-similar distribution is more suitable for PMRC-based network than the other two distributions. When $r\geq80m$, there is no significant difference between the network lifetime for load-similar and nonuniform distributsions as the network lifetime ends when all source nodes are exhausted.

Fig. 6 presents the number of network formations vs. transmission range r. Generally, the number of network formations shows an increasing trend followed by a decreasing trend with the increase of r. When the transmission range is getting larger, more candidate cluster heads are available, which leads to more number of network formations. For $r\geq80m$, the average load at layer 1 is decreased, which leads to the longer average time per round (i.e., the average time between two network formations). As a result, the number of network formations drops.

Fig. 7 shows the average residual energy vs. layer ID when $r=40m$. Layers with larger layer ID are the ones far from the sink. The residual energy at each node is directly related to the load carried by each node. The average residual energy of uniform distribution shows an increasing trend with the increase of layer ID, which is consistent with the load distribution analysis. The residual energy of both the load-similar distribution and nonuniform distribution is better balanced than uniform distribution in most layers. However, the lifetime of nonuniform distribution is shorter than that of load-similar distribution and eventually more energy is wasted.

5 Conclusion

In this paper, the energy hole problem in PMRC-based WSNs is studied. We first analyze the traffic load distribution in PMRC-based WSNs and show that the average load per sensor node increases with the decrease of distance from the sink. Based on the analysis, we propose a novel load-similar node distribution strategy combined with the MOL scheme to alleviate the energy hole problem in PMRC-based WSNs. Extensive simulations have been conducted to validate the analysis. The simulation results confirm that the proposed load-similar node distribution strategy achieves good energy balance among different layers in the network and prolongs network lifetime than uniform node distribution and an existing nonuniform node distribution strategies. The superiority of the load-similar node distribution strategy is more evident when there are more number of layers in the network.

Acknowledgements

We would like to thank OPNET Tech. Inc. for providing license of OPNET Modeler with wireless module.

References

1. Akyildiz, I.F., Su, W., Sankarasubramaniam, Y., Cayirci, E.: A survey on sensor networks. IEEE Commu. Mag. 147, 102–114 (2002)
2. Heinzalmen, W., Chandrakasan, A., Balakrishnan, H.: An application-specific protocol architecture for wireless microsensor networks. IEEE Trans. Wireless Communications 1(4), 660–670 (2002)
3. Ding, J., Sivalingam, K., Kashyaoa, R., Chuan, L.J.: A multi-layered architecture and protocols for large-scale wireless sensor networks. In: 58th SVTC, Piscataway, N.J, pp. 1443–1447 (2003)
4. Wadaa, A., Olariu, S., Wilson, L., Eltoweissy, M., Jones, K.: Training a wireless sensor network. Mobile Networks and Applications, 51–168 (2005)
5. Olariu, S., Stojmenovic, I.: Design guidelines for maximizing lifetime and avoid energy holes in sensor networks with uniform distribution and uniform reporting. In: 25th INFOCOM, NewYork, pp. 1–12 (2006)
6. Li, J., Monhapatra, P.: Analytical modeling and mitigation techniques for the energy hole problem in sensor networks. Pervasive and Mobile Computing 3(8), 233–254 (2007)
7. Perillo, M., Cheng, Z., Henzelman, W.: On the problem of unbalanced load distribution in wireless sensor networks. In: IEEE GLOBECOM, pp. 74–79 (2004)
8. Wu, X., Chen, G., Das, S.K.: Avoiding energy holes in wireless sensor networks with non-uniform node distribution. IEEE Trans. Parallel and Distributed System 9(5), 710–720 (2008)
9. Yang, M., Wang, S., Abdelal, A., Jiang, Y., Kim, Y.: An improved multi-layered architecture and its rotational scheme for large-scale wireless sensor networks. In: 4th IEEE CCNC, pp. 855–859 (2007)
10. Wang, H., Yang, M., Jiang, Y., Wang, S., Gewali, L.: Overlapped layers for prolonging network lifetime in multi-hop wireless sensor networks. In: 5th ITNG, pp. 755–760. IEEE Computer Society, Los Alamitos (2008)
11. Li, Q., Yang, M., Wang, H., Jiang, Y., Zeng, J.: Minimum overlapping layers and its variant for prolonging network lifetime in PMRC-based wireless sensor networks. In: 5th IEEE CCNC, pp. 1–5 (2008)
12. OPNET Modeler, OPNET Tech. Inc., http://www.opnet.com

Density-Aware Route Design for Ferry-Based DTNs Using Partitive Clustering Algorithms

Behrouz Jedari and Rouhollah Goudarzi

Electronic & Computer & IT Engineering Department, Islamic Azad
University of Qazvin, Iran
{behrouz.jedari, goudarzi.ru}@gmail.com

Abstract. The *Delay Tolerant Networks* (DTNs) generally contain relatively sparse nodes that are frequently disconnected. *Message Ferrying (MF)* is a mobility-assisted approach which utilizes a set of mobile elements to provide communication services in ferry-based DTNs. In this paper, we propose a *Density-Aware Route Design* (DARD) algorithm using partitive clustering algorithms along a validity index for identifying the suitable node clusters and assigning ferries to these clusters. In the proposed algorithm, unlike using multiple ferries in a single route (SIRA algorithm) or dividing the deployment area into grid as static (NRA and FRA algorithms), the manner of node's distribution and their density are regarded as clustering metric. Evaluation results for comparing our scheme demonstrate that DARD either minimizes message delivery delay or by preserving message delay, it reduces resource requirements in both ferries and nodes resulting in increasing ferries efficiency.

Keywords: Delay Tolerant Networks, Message Ferrying, Partitive Clustering.

1 Introduction

Delay tolerant networks (DTNs) [1] in situations such as relatively sparse nodes and energy constraints are characterized by the possible non-existence of end-to-end paths. For instance, preserving end-to-end connectivity is not always possible in MANETs, especially in the presence of factors such as node mobility and physical obstacles. Such factors cause networks to partition, either temporarily or permanently. To overcome this issue, node mobility is exploited to physically carry messages between disconnected parts of the network. These schemes are referred to as *mobility-assisted routing* [2] that employs the *Store-Carry-and-Forward* (SCF) model.

In general, mobility-assisted approaches can be classified as *reactive* and *proactive* schemes. In reactive schemes such as epidemic routing [3], applications rely on movement that is inherent in the devices themselves to help deliver messages. When disconnected, nodes passively wait for their own mobility to allow them to reconnect. Since encounters between nodes can be unpredictable and rare, these approaches suffer potentially low data delivery rates and large delays. In proactive approaches, nodes modify their trajectories proactively for communication purposes. *Message Ferrying* (MF) scheme is proposed in [4], is a proactive approach which

D. Ślęzak et al. (Eds.): FGCN/ACN 2009, CCIS 56, pp. 394–404, 2009.

utilizes a set of special mobile nodes called *ferries* to provide communication services for nodes in the network. MF can be used in a variety of applications including wide area sensing, non-interactive Internet access and anonymous communication.

In this paper, identifying well qualified node clusters as well as assigning ferries to them have been studied. Utilizing multiple ferries in a single route or dividing the deployment area into grid and assigning ferries for each cell as static are considered the available methods shortcomings. In this paper, a *density-aware route design* (DARD) algorithm for node clustering has been proposed. Also, in order to determine optimal clusters, we have used a validity index.

This paper is organized as follows. Section 2 reviews the related work in ferry-based DTNs. In Section 3, route design principles in DTNs with multiple ferries are presented. In section 4, overviews of the partitive clustering algorithms are introduced. We propose our route design scheme in Section 5. Section 6 presents the performance evaluation with simulation results. This paper concludes in Section 7.

2 Related Work

Mobility-assisted communication is an active research area in sparse DTNs, ad-hoc networks, sensor networks and robotics community. In the DakNet project [5], vehicles are used to transport data between remote areas such as villages and cities to provide store-and-forward Internet access.

Li and Rus [6] consider proactive movement of nodes to deliver messages in a disconnected environment and present an algorithm to compute optimal node trajectories. In [4], Zhao et al. introduce the message ferry scheme. In [7], Tariq et al. consider the route design problem for a single ferry in sparse ad-hoc networks. Viswanathan et al. in [8] have studied the delivery quality of service (QoS) for certain urgent messages in the constrained and the relaxed constrained MF systems.

Authors in [9] study the route design problem for multiple ferries. Basically there are two extremes of route design for multiple ferries. At one end, we can have all ferries serve the whole network and follow a single route that passes through all nodes (SRT algorithm). At the other end, each ferry can serve a different portion of nodes and follow a different route (MRT algorithm). Finally, they conclude that all the MRT algorithms are scalable and achieve similar results. In [10], an analytically tractable model to a quantitative one in a multi-ferry scheme is proposed. Also, in [11], a Zone Based Message Ferrying (ZBMF) is introduced.

3 Network Model

As shown in Fig. 1, ferries follow pre-designed routes by which they can regularly visit places where stationary nodes. The network is sparsely deployed so the radio range of a node is smaller than the distance between any pair of nodes; otherwise a cluster of connected nodes can communicate with each other through traditional ad-hoc routing mechanisms, leaving ferries carrying data among gateway nodes that are located in isolated clusters. We suppose there are M ferries, f_i $(1 \leq i \leq M)$, and

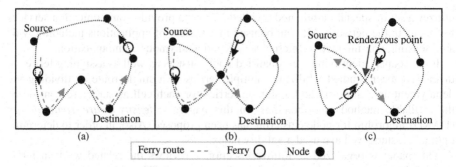

Fig. 1. MF schemes: (a) Single route with 2 ferries, (b) Multiple routes with a relaying node, (c) Multiple routes with one ferry

N nodes, n_i $(1 \leq i \leq N)$ where N is large than M. Any route design scheme for multiple ferries can be represented by an allocation of nodes to ferries $R = \{R_i\}$, where $R_i = \{n_j\}$ is a subset of nodes assigned to f_i. Note that a given node can be assigned to more than one ferry. Two ferries are regarded as connected if they share common nodes in their allocation sets. In order to make the network connected, we require that:

- $\bigcup_{i=1}^{M} R_i = \{n_i, ..., n_N\}$. Means each node must be served by at least one ferry.
- $\forall R_i, R_j, \exists$ a sequence of $R_{i0}...R_{ih}$, such that $R_{i0} = R_i$ and $R_{ih} = R_j$ and $R_{ik} \cap R_{ik+1} \neq \phi (0 \leq k < h)$. This means that any node is reachable from any other node by a ferry or a series of ferry relays.

3.1   Route Design in Ferry-Based DTNs

The ferry route problem consists of finding an optimal route T such that the bandwidth requirements for all nodes are met and the average delay is minimized. Zhao and Ammar in [4] break it into two sub-problems: Delay-minimization problem and bandwidth-requirement problem. Let d_i denote the average message delivery delay between a pair of nodes assigned to f_i. T_{ij} is the normalized traffic from nodes in R_i to nodes in R_j. In particular, T_{ii} represents the normalized traffic originated from and destined to the nodes in R_i. According to our model, the message delivery delay in MF scheme is [10]:

$$d = \sum_{i=1}^{M} T_{ii} d_i + \sum_{i \neq j} T_{ij} \left(\sum_{f_k \in path(f_i, f_j)} d_k \right) \tag{1}$$

Where $path$ (f_i, f_j) is an ordered set of ferries along the path from f_i to f_j. Now we consider how to extend the ferry route to meet the bandwidth requirements of the nodes. For any given route, the achieved data rate of a node is λW where λ is the fraction of time the node communicates with ferries. We need to extend the amount of time ferries spend in the vicinity of those nodes that do not otherwise have enough time to transmit or receive their data. This problem is formulated using *linear programming* (LP) as follows. Let x_i be the length of detour in the vicinity of node i. We assume ferries move to the location of each node, thus the total length of the ferry route that is within the radio range of node i is x_i+2r. Let S_i be the total data rate for node i which is the sum of data rates in both transmission and reception. By distributing traffic load equally to ferries, each ferry is responsible for supporting a data rate of S_i / M. Thus we have:

$$\frac{(x_i + 2r)W}{L + \sum_{j=1}^{N} x_j} \geq \frac{S_i}{M} \tag{2}$$

Where L is the length of the ferry route before extension. After transformation, we get the following optimization problem:

$$Minimize \quad \sum_{i=1}^{N} x_i, \tag{3}$$

$$Subject\ to \quad MWx_i - S_i \sum_{j=1}^{N} x_j \geq S_i L - 2MrW, \quad x_i \geq 0 \text{ and } 1 \leq i \leq N.$$

The above problem can be solved efficiently using methods like Simplex [12].

4 Partitive Clustering

Partitive clustering divide a data set into a number of clusters, typically by trying to minimize some criterion or error function. If the number of clusters is unknown, the partitive algorithm can be repeated for a set of different number, typically from two to $\sqrt{N}$, where N is the number of samples in the data set. Let $X = \{X_1,..., X_N\}$ be a set of N objects. Object $X_i = \{X_{i,1},..., X_{i,c}\}$ is characterized by a set of c variables. The k-means type algorithms [13] search for a partition of X into k clusters that minimizes the objective function P with unknown variables U and Z as follows:

$$P(U,Z) = \sum_{l=1}^{k} \sum_{i=1}^{n} \sum_{j=1}^{m} u_{i,l} d(x_{i,j}, z_{l,j}) \tag{4}$$

$$Subject\ to \sum u_{i,l} = 1, \quad 1 \leq i \leq n$$

Where:

- U is an $n \times k$ partition matrix, $u_{i,l}$ is a binary variable, and $u_{i,j}$ indicates that object i is allocated to cluster l;
- $Z = \{Z_1,..., Z_K\}$ is a set of k vectors representing the centroids of the k clusters;
- $d(x_{i,j}, z_{l,j})$ is a distance or dissimilarity measure between object i and the centroid of cluster l on the j_{th} variable. If the variable is numeric, then

$$d(x_{i,j}, z_{l,j}) = (x_{i,j} - z_{l,j})^2 \tag{5}$$

This algorithm has some inherent shortcoming such as unknown number of k, centroid initialization and sensitivity to outliers. Hence, for covering the algorithms shortcoming, the hybrid of k-means clustering with *self-organized maps* (SOMs) as a two-level method is used to find optimal clusters of nodes. The SOMs Proposed by Kohonen [14] is an unsupervised neural-network approach that provides a similarity graph of input data. The success of the SOM algorithm lies in its simplicity that makes it easy to understand, simulate and be used in many applications. The basic

SOM consists of a set of neurons usually arranged in a two-dimensional structure such that there are neighborhood relations among the neurons.

5 Density-Aware Route Design Algorithm

In this section, we have studied the manner of using clustering methods for route design in ferry-based DTNs. In the following, the term *cluster* means a group of nodes belong to a common centroid, and distance between nodes is done through a similarity function as Euclidean distance. In the rest of this paper, two partitive clustering algorithms are presented that perform Node clustering and allocate ferries to each cluster. Our proposed algorithm performs nodes clustering and ferry route designing between the nodes in two steps as follows: At first step, two clustering algorithms for network clustering are utilized, called DARD-I and DARD-II. In the next step, by choosing gateway nodes between adjacent clusters, a linear programming approach is used for establishing communication between nodes. Regarding the fact that the proposed methods make use of nodes for message relay, the comparison of these methods is also done with NRA and SIRA algorithms.

5.1 Node Assignment in DARD-I

In the DARD-I algorithm, using the k-means clustering algorithm, k points are initialized as clusters centroid. Determining the initial values for k and evaluating the quality of acquired clusters are of those issues that affect clustering quality as well as optimizing ferries traveling route. On the other hand, by reducing the length of traveling route inside each cluster and using acceptable ferries in network, message delivery and buffers consumption in ferries and nodes would be also decreased.

Identifying the number of final clusters and allocating primary values to the cluster centroid are the most important problems that k-means algorithm and generally, most of partitive methods suffer from them. Considering the fact that in k-means algorithm initially values for k are selected randomly, and these values influence the quality of final clusters, hence, in the evaluation, we have repeated clustering operation for sets of different numbers of clusters with different centroids several times and finally, clusters with high quality are selected as final clusters. Regarding the experimental results, we have considered the maximum number of clusters as $\sqrt{N}$, typically from two to $\sqrt{N}$, where N is the number of nodes in the network. At last, clusters with minimum validity index are chosen as final clusters.

Due to spherical shape of clusters in k-means algorithm, it increases the efficiency of the designed routes for message ferries. Unlike available methods such as NRA algorithm, finding the spherical-shaped clusters with low clustering error reduce the length of ferry route within clusters, which finally leads to a rapid message delivery.

5.2 Node Assignment in DARD-II

In the second method so called DARD-II algorithm, for achieving optimal clusters and designing the efficient routes through networks, a hybrid clustering method is utilized as Fig. 2. The given proposed method minimizes clustering error remarkably;

this condition leads to reducing the length of ferries traveling routes. Partitioning the network into very small area or and assigning central coordinates of each area as the centroid are the first steps in the proposed algorithm. At the first stage, distributed nodes are allocated to the nearest cluster, that in assigning nodes to the given clusters, SOMs are used. In this algorithm, each of mapping units are recognized as a cluster that their numbers experimentally are selected the same value as $5\sqrt{N}$ and are much more than the number of given final clusters.

In the second stage, instead of clustering the nodes, central values of the mapping units are grouped to reach a group of nodes. In clustering the mapping units, k-means algorithm is used. The most eye-catching characteristics of the two-level method is minimizing clustering components from N node to $5\sqrt{N}$ of the mapping units that the more optimized clusters of node are gained by preserving nodes settlement focus.

To select the best one among different partitioning, each of these results can be evaluated using some kind of validity index. In our simulations, we used the Davies–Bouldin index [15]. According to Davies–Bouldin validity index, the best clustering minimizes following equation:

$$\frac{1}{C}\sum_{m=1}^{C}\max_{l\neq m}\left\{\frac{S_c(Q_m)+S_c(Q_l)}{d_{ce}(Q_m,Q_l)}\right\} \tag{6}$$

In this equation, C is the number of clusters, m and l are representative of 2 different clusters. $S_c(Q_l)$ is intra-cluster distance and d_{ce} is inter-cluster distance. The Davies–Bouldin index is suitable for evaluation of k-means type algorithms because it gives low values, indicating good clustering results for spherical clusters.

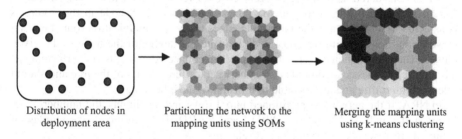

| Distribution of nodes in deployment area | Partitioning the network to the mapping units using SOMs | Merging the mapping units using k-means clustering |

Fig. 2. Node clustering using hybrid k-means method and SOMs in DARD-II algorithm

5.3 Connectivity between Clusters Using Relaying Nodes

After clustering the nodes by one of the proposed algorithms, DARD-I or DARD-II, in this section, the policy of gateway nodes assignment for establishing communication between clusters and message transfer through the network is presented. The generated messages by the nodes are divided into 2 groups: local and non-local messages. The active ferry (or ferries) in each cluster is responsible for the local message delivery at inter-cluster. Also, for carrying and delivering the non-local messages from one node to node in another cluster, the message should pass multiple relaying nodes as well as active ferries inside the clusters.

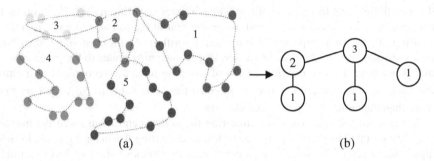

Fig. 3. (a): Communication between clusters with node relaying in DARD algorithms, (b): Each node shows a cluster with an adjacent value

Looking at the issue of message delivery to non-local targets and assuming that every cluster in the network is considered as a node of one graph, it is possible to perform the manner of clusters connectivity to each other based on graph-based approaches or to do routing and message delivery between nodes by establishing *minimum spanning tree* (MST) between clusters. Considering that full-connected graph formation between clusters increases the length of ferries traveling route, in this section, by finding MST between nodes, we have used message relaying by gateway nodes for message communication.

For identifying gateway nodes, first nodes coordinate average is calculated in every cluster. Then the established points to the number of clusters are regarded as a node of one graph that Euclidean distance average between clusters is shown by an edge which is considered as message delivery cost between clusters. In the current paper, *Dijkstra's algorithm* is used to find MST between nodes. Each node in this figure is considered as a cluster and the inter-node edges shows communication route between clusters, and numbers inside every node indicate the degree of the node in the given cluster. The nodes labeled as 4, for example, are connected to 4 clusters performing as a bottleneck in message communication between different parts of the tree and should tolerate high traffic and also be able to transmit to the other area.

In NRA, if the network is partitioned into 3 rows and 3 columns, the number of relaying nodes will be 12, but in DARD-I and DARD-II algorithms, if the number of acquired clusters is d, so the number of relaying nodes will be $d-1$.

After identifying MST between the clusters, we will discuss the manner of establishing communication between clusters. The communication edges between clusters connect the neighbor clusters by means of the nearest nodes. Also, the ferry of the neighboring cluster by establishing communication with gateway node also receivers the non-local messages from the gateway node and thus, message communication between nodes is created.

Fig 3 shows an example of applied policy in identifying relaying nodes between clusters. As you notice, the cluster 2 is a three-degree cluster that is connected to the neighboring cluster 1, 3 and 5 having 1, 2 and 1 degree respectively. Regarding high degree of the cluster 2, that tolerant high flow traffic, developing route for communicating this cluster with other neighboring clusters isn't done from this cluster and the active ferries in the neighboring clusters extend routes for visit relaying nodes.

6 Simulation Results

In this section, we evaluate the performance of the proposed schemes using simulation. We model from 50 to 300 nodes distributed in a rectangular area 4000m × 4000m. All ferries are deployed which moves at a speed of 20 m/s. We allow messages to generate until a simulation time of 4000 seconds and run the algorithms until 6000 seconds. In our simulation, we choose IEEE 802.11 as the MAC layer protocol. The antenna is omni-directional and the radio transmission range in ferries and nodes is 100m. The wireless network interface transmits data at a rate of 1Mbits/sec. Messages with size of 1 Kbytes are generated as a Poisson process. For each setting, the result is averaged over 10 runs with different random seeds.

The objective of our algorithms is to either minimize message delivery delay or by preserving message delay, it reduces resource requirements in both ferries and nodes resulting in increasing ferries efficiency. Therefore, we use the following metrics in our evaluation of the algorithm:

Message delivery delay: Average delay between the time a message is generated and the time the message is received at the destination.
Buffer consumption: Number of stored messages in ferries and nodes buffers.
Energy consumption: Number of sent and received messages for nodes and ferries.

6.1 Comparison of Algorithms

In this section, we compare the performance of the proposed algorithms in previous sections. Unlike the previous methods, DARD algorithm determines the number of optimal ferries according to the node distribution, thus for each network setting those results having the same number of ferries are evaluated.

Fig. 4 shows the delivery delay for routes computed using the four algorithms. We make the following observations. First, these algorithms achieve similar delay when the number of ferries is small. Second, DARD-I and DARD-II achieve the lowest delay when the number of ferries is large. In contrast, SIRA performs worst due to the fact that the ferries must visit all nodes which significantly increase the length of each route. Third, as a result, by increasing the number of nodes and ferries, delivery delay in both DARD algorithms are considerably reduced as compared with FRA and NRA.

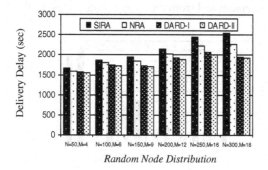

Random Node Distribution

Fig. 4. Message delivery delay under different numbers of nodes (N) and ferries (M)

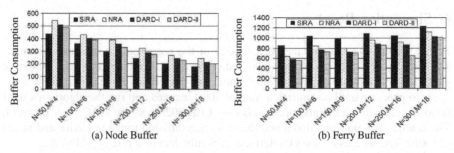

(a) Node Buffer   (b) Ferry Buffer

Fig. 5. Buffer requirement with different numbers of nodes (N) and ferries (M)

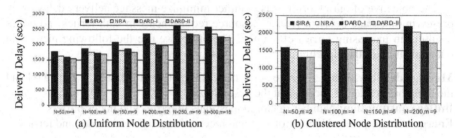

(a) Uniform Node Distribution   (b) Clustered Node Distribution

Fig. 6. Message delivery delay under uniform and clustered (C=0.8) node distribution

Fig 5 depicts the buffer requirement in the nodes and ferries. Because of the fact that SIRA doesn't use relaying nodes, it requires less buffering in nodes as compared to NRA and DARD.

Impact of Node Distribution. Fig 6(a) and Fig 6(b) show the delay for ad hoc traffic in Uniform and clustered node distribution, respectively. For Uniform node distribution, we can see that the delay increases with the throughput per node.

Impacts of Traffic load. According to the Fig 7, the DARD in normal traffic (upper to 3 messages per second) includes less delay. Also, DARD by creating MST between the clusters designs just one route between the nodes and it losses its efficiency in high traffic as compared to NRA, where there is multiple route between the nodes.

Fig. 8 shows the buffer consumption under different traffic models. In fact, the increase in buffer requirement and from the longer routes when traffic load is high. This

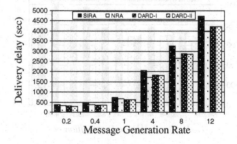

Fig. 7. Message delivery delay under different traffic loads, N=150, M=12

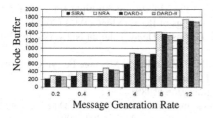 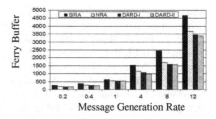

Fig. 8. Buffer consumption under different traffic load, N = 150, M = 12

is because the ferries need to spend more time communicating with nodes. When ferry routes become longer, waiting delay for data in nodes is larger. So the node buffer requirements increase. In addition, ferries need to receive more data from nodes in each visit when traffic load is high, requiring more buffers to hold the data.

7 Conclusions

In this paper, we consider the route design problem for multiple ferries in DTNs. Two designs are proposed, and they represent same trade-off points in the route design space for multiple ferries. According to simulation results, SRT has low buffer requirement in nodes, but it suffers from high delivery delay. Also, in normal traffic, the proposed scheme reduces the delivery delay and by decreasing buffer consumption in nodes, it minimizes energy consumption in nodes as well and resulting in increasing ferries efficiency. But, NRA by choosing more relaying nodes increases the delivery delay and it also requires more buffer space in ferries and nodes. Also, NRA in high traffic decreases message delay than other algorithms.

References

1. Fall, K.: A delay-tolerant network architecture for challenged internets. In: ACM SIG-COMM 2003, Karlsruhe, Germany, pp. 27–34 (2003)
2. Bai, F., Helmy, N.: Impact of Mobility on Mobility-Assisted Information Diffusion (MAID) Protocols in Ad hoc Networks. In: IEEE INFOCOM (2005)
3. Vahdat, A., Becker, D.: Epidemic routing for partially connected ad hoc networks. Technical Report CS-200006, Duke University (2000)
4. Zhao, W., Ammar, M.: Message Ferrying: Proactive Routing in Highly-Partitioned Wireless Ad Hoc Networks. In: Proc. IEEE Workshop on Future Trends in Distributed Computing Systems, Puerto Rico (2003)
5. Haqson, A.A., Fletcher, R., Pzntland, A.: DakNet: A road to universal broadband connectivity. In: wireless Inremet UN ICT Conference Case Study (2003)
6. Li, Q., Rus, D.: Sending messages to mobile users in disconnected ad-hoc wireless networks. In: MOBICOM (2000)
7. Tariq, M.M.B., Ammar, M., Zegura, E.: Message ferry route design for sparse ad hoc networks with mobile nodes. In: ACM MobiHoc (2006)
8. Viswanathan, R., Li, J., Chuah, M.: Message ferrying for constrained scenarios. In: Proceedings of the IEEE WoWMoM 2005 (2005)

9. Zhao, W., Ammar, M., Zegura, E.: Controlling the Mobility of Multiple Data Transport Ferries in a Delay-Tolerant Network. In: Proceedings of IEEE INFOCOMM (2005)
10. Zhang, Z., Fei, Z.: Route Design for Multiple Ferries in Delay Tolerant Networks. In: Proceedings of IEEE INFOCOMM (2005)
11. Polat, B.K., Khan, M., Tuli, N., Kailay, P.: ZBMF: Zone Based Message Ferrying for Disruption Tolerant Networks. In: Proceedings of ChinacomBiz, pp. 48–59 (2009)
12. Nemhauser, G., Rinnooy, k., Todd, M.J.: Optimization (1989)
13. Huang, Z.: Extensions to the k-Means Algorithms for Clustering Large Data Sets with Categorical Values. Data Mining and Knowledge Discovery 2, 283–304 (1998)
14. Kohonen, T.: Self-Organizing Maps. Springer, Berlin (1997)
15. Davies, D.L., Bouldin, D.W.: A cluster separation measure. IEEE Trans. Patt. Anal. Machine Intell. PAMI-1, 224–227 (1979)

A Distributed Deterministic and Resilient Replication Attack Detection Protocol in Wireless Sensor Networks

Chano Kim, Chanil Park, Junbeom Hur, Hanjin Lee, and Hyunsoo Yoon

Dept. of Electrical Engineering and Computer Science, KAIST, Republic of Korea
{cokim,chanil,jbhur,hjlee,hyoon}@nslab.kaist.ac.kr

Abstract. To detect replica nodes in a wireless sensor network, we propose a distributed, deterministic and resilient (DDR) replica detection protocol developed from a witness node based strategy. In DDR, while a location claim message of each node is sent towards the designated verification location in the network, the consistency of the messages is verified at intermediate nodes en route to its final destination. Compared with previous replication attack detection protocols, DDR achieves better computation and communication performance due to the use of symmetric key cryptography only and early replica detection.

Keywords: Wireless sensor network, Replication attack.

1 Introduction

To interact with sensitive data through the wireless sensor network (WSN), it is imperative that various security issues are addressed. One of the most cost-effective ways of disturbing the goal of WSN, a node replication attack has begun to be paid attention [1]. In this attack, an adversary who has captured at least one sensor node makes millions of clones out of them, and surreptitiously redeploys them into the network. Since these cloned nodes have the same security information as the original node, if undetected, they can be used to launch insidious inner attacks: making authentication mechanisms useless, mis-routing packets, subverting data aggregation protocols, or revoking the legitimate nodes [2]. For detecting the replication attack in a distributed fashion, some methods based on finding witness nodes have been proposed [3]-[5]. Unfortunately, they are not appropriate for underlying sensor network technology since they are designed on the assumption that each sensor is able to perform the expensive public key cryptographic operations. Moreover, as the fraction of failed nodes increases, the replica detection rate evidently decreases.

We develop the witness node based strategy and propose a distributed, deterministic and resilient replica detection scheme (DDR), which is based on using of symmetric key cryptography and deterministically assigning a specific verification location to each node. Compared with the previous schemes, the performance of DDR in terms of communication and computation overhead is improved significantly.

D. Ślęzak et al. (Eds.): FGCN/ACN 2009, CCIS 56, pp. 405–412, 2009.

The rest of this paper is organized as follows: Section 2 gives a brief description on main related works; Section 3 presents the network and adversary model; Section 4 describes our DDR protocol in details. Performance analysis will be given in Section 5; We will evaluate the performance of our protocol in Section 6, and Section 7 concludes the paper.

2   Related Works

Parno et al. [3] proposed two distributed probabilistic algorithms using the public key cryptography, called RM (Randomize Multicast) and LSM (Line Selected Multicast), respectively. In RM, a location claim message which was signed by each node's private key, is sent to a set of witness nodes randomly chosen. In order to ensure a high detection rate ($\geq 95\%$), each location claim message should be sent to $O(\sqrt{N})$ witness nodes, where N is the total number of nodes. In another approach, LSM is based on the fact that there exists high probability intersection for randomly drawn lines in the plane. Every intermediate node which is responsible for forwarding messages to witness nodes verifies the signature using the sender's public key. .

Zhu et al. [5] proposed LM (Localized Multicast), which deterministically maps node id to one or more groups of nodes (referred to as cell) that are deployed in the same region. After a digitally signed location claim message successfully reaches the predetermined cell, it is broadcast within the cell.

Conti et al. [4] proposed RED (Randomized, Efficient, and Distributed Protocol) that assumes all sensors have the same random value at any given time through periodic beacon messages from the base station (BS). When a replication round is started, each node determines a random witness point (referred to as wp) to be destination of the location claim message using the pseudo-random function, which takes in the id of itself and the current random value. After the closest node to wp receiving a signed location claim message, verifies the authenticity and consistency of the contents of the received location claim messages using the public key of the sender node.

3   Network and Adversary Model

We consider a network with N randomly distributed homogeneous sensors in a WSN. Once sensors are deployed, their locations are fixed. For routing of data through the network, any of geographic routing protocols (e.g. GPSR [8]) can be used. Moreover, each sensor has a unique key shared with the BS and a pairwise key with all its neighbors to support secure communications through any of existing key establishment protocols [7]. We also assume that all nodes participate in the replica detection protocol to pretend to be legitimate ones.

For the adversary threat model, an adversary has capability of capturing and compromising a limited number of nodes, and fully controls them. Moreover, he can further produce the replicated nodes and redeploy them at any place. He also tries to compromise nodes in a portion of network through physical or Denial of Service (DoS) attacks to prevent cloned nodes from being detected.

4   DDR: Our Proposed Protocol

4.1   Initialization

Before deployment, the BS associates a particular location coordinate (hereafter referred to as a verification point, vp) with each node's id using geographic hash function F. The vp is the destination point where each node's location claim message should be forwarded. For example, if area-fairness is considered to share the burden of replica detection overheads evenly among all nodes, every geographic coordinate in the sensing field has the equal potential to be chosen as vp.

Let the sensing field be a $q \times q$ square area, where q is an integer. If h_x : $\{0,1\}^* \to Z_q$ and $h_y : \{0,1\}^* \to Z_q$ are two uniformly distributed hash functions, F can be defined as follows:

$F : S \to A$ such that $F(S_i) = (h_x(S_i), h_y(S_i))$, where S_i is an arbitrarily chosen node id. As a result, vp_i can be mapped to $(h_x(S_i), h_y(S_i))$.

If there are some shadow areas, where the radio communication is difficult, these areas should be avoided to be chosen as vp. After sensors are randomly deployed, each node obtains its geographic location through GPS [9], and then estimates its priority weight ω_u. The malicious nodes in the sparsely populated network can be more harmful than those in a densely populated network because their failure or compromise may lead to a disconnected network [2]. Based on this fact, we only consider the number of neighboring nodes to determine ω_u, then it is defined as follows:

$$\omega_u = 2^{\frac{N(S_u)-1}{1-d}}, \tag{1}$$

where d is the expected average degree of neighbors of the network and $N(S_u)$ is the actual number of neighboring nodes of S_u. In Eq.(1), if $N(S_u)$ is equal to d, then the default value of ω_u is 0.5.

4.2   Replica Detection

Fig. 1 depicts a simple scenario, where two replicas $S_u{}'$ and $S_u{}''$ exist in different locations respectively, after an original node S_u was captured and removed.

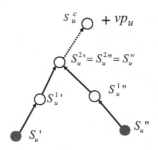

Fig. 1. A conceptual scenario of the replica detection process of DDR

When the detection process for S_u is started, S_u' calculates an average single hop distance d_u',

$$d_u' = \frac{\sum_{n=1}^{N(S_u)} dist(l_u', l_n)}{N(S_u')}. \tag{2}$$

where l_u is the location coordinate of S_u and $dist(l_u, vp_u)$ is the Euclidean distance between l_u and vp_u. Then, S_u' estimates the expected hop count to vp_u

$$E([h_u']) = \frac{dist(l_u', vp_u)}{d_u'}. \tag{3}$$

After that, S_u' generates a location claim message L_u' whose format is as follows:

$$L_u' = \langle S_u, l_u', E([h_u']), \omega_u, vp_u, MAC_{k(u,u_1)}(S_u, l_u', vp_u) \rangle$$

Here, $S_u^{1'}$ is a randomly chosen node among the neighboring nodes of S_u' and MAC means "Message Authentication Code". Similarly, L_u'' is generated by S_u'' and then forwarded to the same vp_u.

If successfully done, $S_u^{1'}$ decreases $E([h_u'])$ by 1 and generates a random value between 0 and 1 . If it is less than ω_u, $S_u^{1'}$ stores $\langle S_u, l_u' \rangle$ entry in its buffer and verifies whether it received another location claim message from S_u. Otherwise, $S_u^{1'}$ just forwards toward vp_u without storing or verifying $\langle S_u, l_u' \rangle$. On forwarding the location message, if $E([h_u'])$ is zero, the next intermediate node stores $\langle S_u, l_u' \rangle$ entry without generating a random value. This is because the location claim message gets closer to vp_u, and thus the probability of intersection of two paths becomes higher.

Also, even though $E([h_u'])$ is greater than 0 when S_u' reaches S_u^c, $\langle S_u, l_u' \rangle$ entry of the L_u' is stored at the S_u^c. Similarly, S_u'' sends the location claim message L_u'' including l_u''. As a result, although a collision does not occur at any intermediate node, it might happen at S_u^c in the end. If collision is detected, it stops transmitting the location claim message, and that node becomes the witness node S_u^w of S_u.

4.3   Replica Revocation

S_u^w, after detecting that the collision has occurred, generates a revocation request message L_{rev} and delivers it directly to the BS. L_{rev} is defined as follows:

$$L_{rev} = \langle S_u^w, l_w, S_u, l_u', l_u'', MAC_{k(w,BS)}(S_u^w, l_w) \rangle$$

Once the BS receives the revocation request message, it first checks the plausibility and forgery of L_{rev} using a shared key with S_u^w. If it is correct, the BS floods the replica list including S_u through the network. Otherwise, the BS adds S_u^w to the replica node list since an attacker sent the forgery of the replica revocation message.

5   Analysis of Communication Overheads

The radio communication is the most energy-consuming operation, and the replica detection process needs additional communication overhead. So, we should carefully design it to reduce the number of communications. Intuitively, DDR can detect replicas earlier than RED, and the closer the distance of replicas, the higher is the chance of an early collision. We can consider two possible cases depending on where the vp is located. Namely, the vp locates in the compromised area whose the radius is less than or greater than that of the communication range of the sensor R. In Fig. 2, the boundary of the compromised area is shadowed to be dark. In Fig. 2-(a), the shape of the compromised areas is circular arc-shaped, which means that attack is started from the outer of the network or some shadow areas exist around the boundary of the network. When greedy forwarding of location claim messages fails at any intermediate node, the messages are routed along the marginal nodes in the network. However, in Fig. 2-(b), the location claim messages are traveling nodes along the outer perimeter of the compromised areas. Since wp is randomly selected through the network during each detection round in RED, there has a high probability that location claim messages encounter the shadow areas, obstacles, or compromised areas. Therefore, finding the closest node to wp incurs significant communication overhead in RED. In Fig. 2-(b), the witness nodes are selected among nodes in areas of ring of $R(2 \cdot R_c + R)$, where R_c is the radius of the compromised area. As the compromised area increases in the Fig. 2-(b), the routing path for determining the candidate node is extended linearly. However, since the witness nodes are selected in the limited areas along the boundary of the compromised areas, the communication costs in DDR may be significantly decreased.

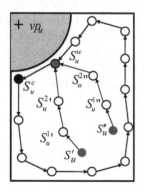

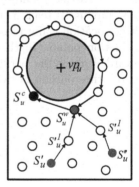

(a) Circular arc-shaped   (b) Circle shaped

Fig. 2. Replica detection scenarios in two compromised areas in the network

6   Simulation

We evaluate performance of our DDR by using extensive simulations and compare its performance with two existing schemes of RED and LM.

6.1 Environments

We have simulated our algorithm in a large scale sensor network with a variety of topologies. For this, we consider network space of 500×500, and network size of $2,674$ nodes ($d = 20$) that are randomly deployed. After we removed an original node whose vp is a randomly chosen location in the plane, we insert two replicas of it at different locations within the network. Specifically, we place the first replica at $(30, 30)$ and the other replica at various positions according to simulation requirements. Our simulation ends when at least one collision takes place, and each simulation results are obtained from average of 10 independent runs. For maintaining the consistency in simulation, as depicted by the authors of LM, after we divided the network into 10 cells of equal angular areas, we set the number of nodes within a cell s uniformly distributed and the fraction of witness nodes w to 10%.

6.2 Results

We first compared the detection rate of DDR with those of LM and RED when an attacker compromises some network areas. We assumed that the nodes in the compromised areas are disabled and do not participate in the replica detection rounds. After we put the second replica into $(100, 30)$, we compromise areas with a gradually expanding radius from the destination point in RED and DDR. For LM, we also assumed the attacker knows the destination cell of each node. According to our simulation result, DDR shows the same detection rate as that in RED and it guarantees the successful detection unless the network is separated into multiple sub-networks and each replica is located in different parts.

The next experiment was carried out to measure the performance of the network when areas around the destination are compromised. That means the shape of compromised area is a circle in the network. Fig. 3 shows the number of transmitted location claim messages as the compromised area is expanded from the destination points. In this experiment, since the location claim messages are forwarded along the perimeter out of the compromised areas in the same direction, the collision of two location claim messages in DDR could be detected

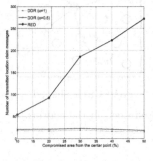   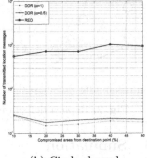

(a) Circular acr-shaped   (b) Circle shaped

Fig. 3. Average number of location claim messages ($d = 20$)

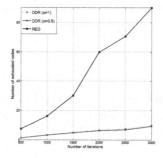

Fig. 4. The valid nodes while increasing the detection iterations

earlier than RED. As shown in Fig. 3-(a), the communication cost in RED increases almost linearly as compromised areas increase. On the contrary, as the perimeter routing is started earlier along the outer of the compromised area, the communication cost is slowly decreased.

Next, after we set the destination point as around the boundary of the network and expand the compromised areas including the destination point, we measured the number of transmitted location claim messages. Fig. 3-(b) shows the results. Note that in Fig. 3, the vertical axis is log-scaled. As shown in this figure, RED protocol has significant communication overheads as the compromised areas are expanded. However, our DDR provides a fast detection and requires significantly less communication cost than RED. In particular, in the case of known threats by environmental, the location claim messages are prevented from delivering to in-hostile areas by assigning the proper vp. The last experiment was carried out to measure the total energy consumption with enough iterations. Fig. 4 shows the results by increasing the number of rounds with varying the deployments of the second replica in the same topology. For measuring the energy consumption, we use an energy model with the same message length of 32bytes [6]. As shown in this figure, when the number of iterations is $3,000$, the percentage of the active nodes is below 9.1% for RED, while 90.3% for DDR-$\omega = 0.5$ and 90.0% for DDR-$\omega = 1$. We can see that DDR performs significantly better than RED as the number of iterations increases. This is because DDR does not use an expensive digital signature and reduces the number of communications.

7   Conclusion

In this paper, we proposed DDR to detect hostile replicated nodes in the wireless sensor network. By introducing an early replica detection and using the symmetric key cryptography, we can minimize energy consumption in terms of communication and computation at low storage cost. Moreover, our simulation results show that our proposed scheme can achieve high replica detection rates even in the case that some sensor nodes are faulty without incurring excessive resource consumptions. As a future work, we will extend our protocol to the wireless mobile sensor network, where every sensor node can move freely in the sensing field.

Acknowledgement

This research was supported by Basic Science Research Program through the National Research Foundation of Korea(NRF) funded by the Ministry of Education, Science and Technology (No. 2009-008364).

References

1. Kim, C., Shin, S., Park, C., Yoon, H.: A Resilient and Efficient Replication Attack Detection Scheme for Wireless Sensor Networks. IEICE Trans. on Letter, E92-D 7, 1479–1483 (2009)
2. Becher, A., Benenson, Z.: Maximillian Dornseif: Tampering with Motes: Real-World Physical Attacks on Wireless Sensor Networks. Security in Pervasive Computing, 104–118 (2006)
3. Parno, B., Perrig, A., Gligor, V.: Distributed detection of node replication attacks in sensor networks. In: Proc. of the 2005 IEEE Symposium on Security and Privacy (S&P 2005), pp. 49–63 (2005)
4. Conti, M., Pietro, R.D., Mancini, L.V.: A Randomized, Efficient, and Distributed protocol for the Detection of Node Replication Attacks in Wireless Sensor Networks. In: Proc. of the 8th ACM international symposium on Mobile ad hoc networking and computing (MobiHoc 2007), pp. 80–89 (2007)
5. Zhu, B., Addada., V.G.K., Setia., S., Jajodia., S., Roy., S.: Efficient Distributed Detection of Node Replication Attacks in Sensor Networks. In: Computer Security Applications Conference (ACSAC 2007), pp. 257–267 (2007)
6. Wander, A.S., Gura, N., Eberle, H., Gupta, V., Shantz, S.C.: Energy analysis of public key cryptography for wireless sensor networks. In: Proc. of the Third IEEE International Conference on Pervasive Computing and Communications (PERCOM 2005), pp. 324–328 (2005)
7. Zhu, S., Setia, S., Jajodia, S.: LEAP: Efficient Security Mechanisms for Large-Scale Distributed Sensor Networks. In: Proc. of the 10th ACM Conference on Computer and Communication Security (CCS 2003), pp. 62–72 (2003)
8. Karp, B., Kung, H.T.: GPSR: Greedy Perimeter Stateless Routing for Wireless Networks. In: Proc. of the 6th ACM International Conference on Mobile Computing and Networking (MobiCom 2000), pp. 243–254 (2000)
9. Kaplan, E.D.: Understanidng GPS: Principles and Applications. Artech House, Boston, MA (1996)

Adaptive Quality-Aware Replication in Wireless Sensor Networks

Jana Neumann, Christoph Reinke, Nils Hoeller, and Volker Linnemann

Institute of Information Systems, University of Luebeck, Ratzeburger Allee 160,
Luebeck, Germany
lastname@ifis.uni-luebeck.de

Abstract. Typical sensor network deployments are usually built for
long-term usage. Additionally, the sensor nodes are often exposed to
harsh environmental influences. Due to these constraints, it is mandatory
for applications to be able to compensate the failure of nodes. Providing a persistent storage even in the presence of failing nodes demands
for replication within the sensor network. However, recent work in the
field of replication in sensor networks often does not consider the suitability of the sensor nodes to store replicas in terms of e.g. available
storage, energy or connectivity. In this paper, we envision an adaptive
quality-aware replication scheme which enables the storage of replicas
based on a scoring system reflecting the suitability of a replica node.
Furthermore, we propose an adaptable data migration strategy using a
weighting function to achieve an adequate placement for the replicas.
A resilient storage strategy enables the survival of replicas after migration despite unpredictable node failures. We expect that our replication
scheme highly increases the availability of sensor network data despite
of node failures and network partitioning requiring only a small number
of replicas within the network.

1 Introduction

Wireless Sensor Networks (WSNs) consist of a large number of resource-
constraint sensor nodes equipped with microcontrollers, memory, wireless communication and sensors. These sensor nodes collaborate in order to perform tasks
like monitoring their environment.

Whereas in former times sampled data was sent to data sinks and stored outside the sensor network for further processing, in recent years sensor networks
are becoming more and more autonomous. Due to relocation of data processing
from external devices into the sensor network dependencies on data sinks and
gateways dissolve. Henceforth, generated data is directly preprocessed or even
evaluated and stored within the sensor network. In this manner results have to be
extracted on demand only. Permanently improving algorithms for efficient memory usage accompanied by recent technical progress in memory capacities makes
in-network storage increasingly profitable for future sensor network applications
[4]. Using internal storage schemes instead of the external scheme reduces the

D. Ślęzak et al. (Eds.): FGCN/ACN 2009, CCIS 56, pp. 413–420, 2009.
© Springer-Verlag Berlin Heidelberg 2009

number of transmitted messages drastically. As an example, imagine a network application which samples some environmental variables like light and humidity for different times of day. Imagine moreover, the sampled network data has to be further processed after a couple of weeks, e.g. computing the average or the maximum for every daytime. Storing the data and computing the average of the measurements within the network could avoid useless transmission of messages caused by external storage. The computed average values may be then extracted from the network after the expiration of this term.

However, the network has to ensure that the data is available anytime. Due to node failures and fluctuations of the radio channel, the temporary or even complete outage of nodes is very likely. Furthermore, due to network partition parts of the network data may not be accessible anymore. Therefore, the data collected in the WSN has to be stored redundantly.

Within WSNs the nodes differ in their characteristics e.g. available storage, remaining energy and connectivity depending on their tasks and locations within the WSN. Thus, the nodes are not equally suitable to store replicas resulting in differences concerning the availability and failure probability of the sensor nodes. One way to compensate loss of data anyway is to hold a high number of replicas within the sensor network. However, the number of replicas is limited by the memory restrictions of the sensor nodes. In order to enhance the availability of stored data items within WSNs, we propose an adaptive quality-aware replication scheme which requires only few replicas. The scheme achieves quality-awareness by using an availability metric for the sensor nodes. It enables the storage of replicas based on a scoring system concerning the availability and reflecting the suitability of a replica node. The user can adapt the replication scheme to his special application demands and network characteristics, e.g. by selecting the number of replicas per data item and the migration distances. Furthermore, requiring only a few additional replicas we guarantee the survival of the dispersed replicas during migration and after the storage on the replica nodes. Thus, the network data can be accessed despite network partition and network failures even after a long period of time with high probability.

The rest of the paper is organized as follows. In Section 2 and 3, we present our solutions for the scoring based data migration and the following preservation of dispersed replicas. In Section 4, we show in experiments that our replication scheme guarantees a high availability of sensor network data within the network despite message loss, node failures and network partition. Section 5 outlines related work in the field of redundant storage and replication in WSNs. We conclude the paper in Section 6 and give an outlook for further optimizations and future work.

2 Scoring

Our main idea is to enhance the availability of sensor network data by placing replicas on nodes which meet predefined demands. Furthermore, reacting on decreasing energy resources and changes in the neighborhood, data may change the replica node after placement if the demands can not be met by the current replica node anymore. In order to estimate the suitability of a sensor node, we define a scoring function which is influenced by the following characteristics.

Since the remaining energy of a node is the most significant characteristic to predict an impending node failure, our scoring function is based at first on the energy resources of the nodes. However, accessing a node by messages will always affect the energy resources of at least one neighbor node. After the consumption of the energy resources of all neighbor nodes a node will be no longer accessible, even if the node itself still has remaining energy resources. Additionally, if a node has only few neighbors it is more likely that the node may be isolated. Therefore, we propose to consider the number of neighbors as well as the energy resources of the neighbors. Furthermore, the replicas are expected to consume storage capacities. Thereby, the available memory resources of the nodes limit the amount of prospective stored data items.

The concurrence of the described characteristics determine a so called availability category ($avail$), which will determine the scoring and therewith the suitability of a sensor node for storing replicas. However, to avoid the simultaneous migration of concurrent replicas in only one direction, we use a few anchor nodes to define different directions within the WSN. Every replica of a data item will be assigned to one anchor node and achieves to migrate in the respective direction. We therefore define a scoring of a node (S) as a tuple consisting of the availability category ($avail$) and the distances to the k anchor nodes ($d_1, .., d_k$):

$$S = \{avail, \{d_1, .., d_k\}\}.$$

3 Data Migration and Resilience

The migration process executes as follows: Firstly, a predefined number of replicas is dispersed by the orginal node each intended to move in a certain direction. Using the availability of its neighbor nodes and their distances to the respective anchor nodes the original node is enabled to decide which nodes within his direct neighborhood are the best for one replica and direction. After receiving a replica, the nodes decide whether there are more suitable nodes in their direct neighborhood and whether it would be profitable to continue the migration process. If no further suitable node is found, the current node becomes the replica node for the received replica and will not accommodate further replicas of the specific data item, anymore.

To achieve an adequate migration distance between the original node and the replica nodes the migration radius h_{max} has to be determined by the user. High distances provide good protection in case of network partition, but their major drawback is the increase of message transmissions for the migration process itself and for possible data updates. Therefore, the user has to weigh the benefits and drawbacks depending on his application and network characteristics like network density and size. Furthermore, in order to avoid the endless migration of the replicas, the migration radius also defines how many nodes the data is allowed to visit in one migration cycle. Whereas the migration radius h_{max} limits the distance between original node and replica node, we also have to avoid that the replicas will always be stored in the direct neighborhood of the original node. Therefore, we introduce h_{best}, which is the distance between the original node and the migration range h_{max} with most gravity. This means, that the replica should further migrate towards this distance, even if there are equally suitable nodes closer to the original nodes. After passing the distance h_{best} the further migration should be hindered, allowing a further migration only if there is a much more suitable node. To achieve the mentioned migration towards h_{best}, we propose a weighting function which influences the migration decision. The function delivers weights which increase towards h_{best}, reaching the value 1, and decrease towards h_{max}.

In order to avoid data loss during migration we propose a reliable data forwarding strategy. This strategy is based on delayed removal of received replicas. A node which forwards data towards a neighbor node furthermore stores the data until it has received a predefined number of acknowledge messages. If a suitable replica node is found, the migration process ends. Since the network and the node characteristics change continuously over time, the node has to check whether it still meets the replication demands. If its availability is too low, the node has to initiate the migration process again in order to find a more suitable replica node.

After placing the replicas on selected replica nodes, there is still the problem of avoiding data loss caused by unpredictable node failures. For that reason, the last subproblem focuses on achieving resilience of the distributed replicas. In order to achieve and preserve a demanded reliability of a data item within the network accompanied with a high storage efficiency, a replication technique needs to control the number of replicas and replica nodes respectively. This means to deal with the following three tasks: the initial distribution of the required number of secondary replicas, the subsequent preservation of the number of replicas in case of secondary replica node failures and the data recovery in case of failed first replica nodes.

However, this part of the replication scheme is still in progress. We will focus on the recovery strategy in our future work. In this paper, we also do not consider the querying of stored data in detail. In general, in our work queries are injected into the network via a gateway that can be located anywhere in the entire WSN. Like previous approaches [10] the queries are then routed to each sensor node. This can be done by using a fixed topology, like described in [10], or by using full broadcast communication and hence avoiding communication bottlenecks.

4   Evaluation

In this section, we evaluate our proposed replication algorithm. First, we are interested in evaluating whether the nodes are able to find replica nodes with the demanded availability. Furthermore, we study the costs of the subproblems per migration cycle and the costs per data item compared with the external storage scheme.

We implemented our replication technique for the sensor node simulator Shawn [7]. We evaluated the replication technique for 100 sensor nodes randomly distributed within an area of the size 400 x 400 m. The sensor nodes had a transmission range of 70 m resulting in a neighborhood size between 1 to 19. The remaining energy resources of the nodes were between 25 and 100. For our simulations, we use availabilities between 0 and 5 and a connectivity threshold of 3.

The migration decision in our replication scheme is based on local information about scorings within the one hop neighborhood. Due to this restriction for the migration decision, we assume that the nodes will not find the best suitable node within the migration range in every case. Therefore, we evaluate first, whether the nodes are able to find replica nodes with high availabilities without having the complete scoring information of all nodes within the migration radius - the global scoring view. The comparision of resulting availabilities is shown in Figure 1. It shows the average error concerning the achieved availabilities in each case for the migration decision for migration radii (h_{max}) of 1, 3 and 5. The distances of most gravity (h_{best}) were approximately in the middle of the selected maximum distances. The number of distributed replicas was set to 4.

If the migration radius is 1, the global scoring view suits the local view of the original node. The error of approximately 0.2 can be explained by the simultaneous distribution of 4 replicas. If a node already stores a replica of a specific data item, the node has to find another replica node which possibly has a lower availability. For the migration distances 3 and 5 the error increases. An error of 1 means e.g. that the average best availability which was found is 4 instead of 5. The nodes may not find the best availability within the migration radius, but they achieve to find high availabilities using the local migration rules. In order to evaluate the communication costs of our replication scheme, we furthermore studied the transmitted bytes per participating node for every subproblem: the computation of scorings, the migration process itself, the acknowledge messages avoiding data loss during migration and the final dispersal of backup replicas. We evaluated different migration radii (h_{max}) between 1 and 5. Figure 2 shows the transmitted bytes per participating node for every migration radius. Note that the participating nodes are not the same for every subproblem. During the scoring computation, every node within the migration radius is a participant.

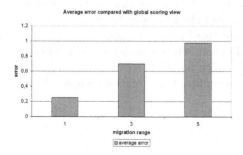

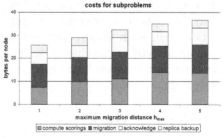

Fig. 1. Average error caused by local migration decision

Fig. 2. Costs per node for the different subproblems

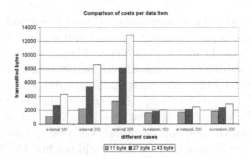

Fig. 3. Comparison of external storage and in-network storage with replication

During migration only the nodes which are situated on the migration path are involved and during the backup of replicas, a predefined number of direct neighbors take part. The major message costs were caused by the computation and the request of the scorings and the migration process itself. Acknowledge messages and the replica backup require only a small amount of transmitted bytes per node. The costs increase slightly with increasing migration range, but they are still acceptable.

Besides the evaluation of the overall costs for every participating node, we also compared our in-network approach to the external storage scheme for the example scenario in the introduction of this paper. We examined the transmission costs per processed data item for networks with 100, 200 and 300 nodes and different data packets. One data packet consists of the data item itself using 8 bytes, 24 bytes or 40 bytes and additional 3 bytes for the node id and data id. We evaluated the processing and extraction of the average of 10 sampled values of one node for each storage scheme. Afterwards, we determined the costs per sampled value and illustrated the results in Figure 3. In the external storage scheme the data item is sent to the gateway after sampling. We assume that the location of the gateway is not known, so that the data item has to be routed over every node of the network. For our replication scheme, we assume that after sampling, the data item is processed and replicated using a migration range of 5. After the sampling and processing of 9 further data items, the resulting data is sent to the gateway like described for the external storage. Since using the external scheme, the processed data has to be sent every time to the gateway, the costs per data item are many times higher than for in-network storage. The costs for replication are profitable especially for large networks.

Our evaluation shows, that our replication scheme requires an acceptable amount of bytes to find highly available replica nodes. It enables the survival of data within the network and is therefore a profitable alternative compared with the external scheme.

5   Related Work

In this section, we briefly review related work on data replication and placement in sensor networks.

Many publications in the domain of data storage in WSNs focus on data-centric storage like described in [13]. Some distinguished storage nodes, determined e.g. by a hash function, are responsible for collecting a certain type of data. Redundancy is achieved by storing replicas on neighbor nodes or by using a hierarchical decomposition of the key space of the hash function. In GEM [11] redundancy is reached by suitable splitting and distributing of data within a tree and using XOR conjunction in direction of the root of the tree in order to recover unavailable subtrees. In contrast to the described replication techniques, our approach does not rely on GPS or special topologies like trees. In addition, the mentioned approaches do not take the suitability of replica nodes into account.

Further related work on data replication has focused on the usage of specific codes to increase the persistence of information transmitted to a base station. Examples are Growth Codes [6], Decentralized Fountain Codes [2] and Priority Random Linear Codes [9]. These techniques can be used to increase the amount of sensed data that arrives at a sink (external storage), but are hardly suitable for in-network storage as well as heterogeneous applications.

In the field of data placement different approaches propose solutions either to minimize the total energy costs for querying the sensor network data (e.g. Scoop [5]) or to avoid query hotspots on storage nodes (e.g. [1,8]). However, Scoop uses a storage policy which does not focus on maximizing lifetime of data within the network, but minimizing message transmission for queries. Latter approaches aim to even energy consumption within the network, but do not intend to compensate node failures and therewith to enhance data availability within the WSN. In [3] a novel metric called accessibility is introduced to compute the capability of a node to make its data available to the rest of the network. Since the authors assume that the nodes know their locations, this metric is not feasible for networks without localization capabilities. Another adaptive replication approach which aims to increase the availability of network data is proposed in [12]. The distribution of replicas, especially the number of replicas, is defined by the policies for every data variable. However, the replica nodes are randomly selected in order to provide an equal distribution of replicas.

6   Conclusion and Future Work

Improvements in the field of memory usage and capacities of the sensor nodes make in-network storage increasingly profitable for future sensor network applications, reducing the number of transmitted messages drastically. In order to ensure data availability within WSNs anytime, the data collected in the WSN has to be stored redundantly.

In this paper, we described our adaptive quality-aware replication scheme. Based on a scoring system replicas are stored on suitable replica nodes enabling high data availability. We proposed a strategy which ensures the reliable migration of replicas. Our experiments show that our algorithm requires only limited storage and few messages in order to achieve high data availability despite node failures and network partition.

As a next step, we plan to realize the discussed recovery of replicas. Furthermore, we intend to extend the replication scheme with simple rules in order to enable self-organizing adaptations to network characteristics. Additionally, the extension of our replication scheme with adequate query mechanisms would be meaningful.

References

1. Aly, M., Chrysanthis, P.K., Pruhs, K.: Decomposing data-centric storage query hot-spots in sensor networks. In: Annual International Conference on Mobile and Ubiquitous Systems, pp. 1–9 (2006)
2. Aly, S.A., Kong, Z., Soljanin, E.: Fountain codes based distributed storage algorithms for large-scale wireless sensor networks. In: IPSN, pp.171–182 (2008)
3. Apaydin, T., Vural, S., Sinha, P.: On improving data accessibility in storage based sensor networks. IEEE International Conference on Mobile Adhoc and Sensor Systems Conference, 1–9 (2007)
4. Diao, Y., Ganesan, D., Mathur, G., Shenoy, P.J.: Rethinking data management for storage-centric sensor networks. In: CIDR, pp. 22–31 (2007), http://www.crdrdb.org
5. Gil, T.M., Madden, S.: Scoop: An adaptive indexing scheme for stored data in sensor networks. In: International Conference on Data Engineering, pp. 1345–1349 (2007)
6. Kamra, A., Misra, V., Feldman, J., Rubenstein, D.: Growth codes: maximizing sensor network data persistence, pp. 255–266 (2006)
7. Kroeller, A., Pfisterer, D., Buschmann, C., Fekete, S., Fischer, S.: Shawn: A new approach to simulating wireless sensor networks. In: Design, Analysis, and Simulation of Distributed Systems, Part of the SpringSim (2005)
8. Li, R.G.X., Bian, F., Hong, W.: Rebalancing distributed data storage in sensor networks. Techincal Report USC-CS-05-852 (2005)
9. Lin, Y., Li, B., Liang, B.: Differentiated data persistence with priority random linear codes, p. 47 (2007)
10. Madden, S.R., Franklin, M.J., Hellerstein, J.M., Hong, W.: Tinydb: an acquisitional query processing system for sensor networks. ACM Trans. Database Syst. 30(1), 122–173 (2005)
11. Newsome, J., Song, D.: Gem: Graph embedding for routing and data-centric storage in sensor networks without geographic information. In: SenSys 2003: Proceedings of the 1st international conference on Embedded networked sensor systems, pp. 76–88. ACM Press, New York (2003)
12. Piotrowski, K., Langendoerfer, P., Peter, S.: tinydsm: A highly reliable cooperative data storage for wireless sensor networks. In: International Symposium on Collaborative Technologies and Systems, pp. 225–232 (2009)
13. Ratnasamy, S., Karp, B., Yin, L., Yu, F., Estrin, D., Govindan, R., Shenker, S.: Ght: a geographic hash table for data-centric storage. In: WSNA 2002: Proceedings of the 1st ACM international workshop on Wireless sensor networks and applications, pp. 78–87. ACM, New York (2002)

Weaknesses and Improvements of Kuo-Lee's One-Time Password Authentication Scheme*

Mijin Kim, Byunghee Lee, Seungjoo Kim, and Dongho Won**

School of Information and Communication Engineering,
Sungkyunkwan University, Suwon 440-746, Republic of Korea
{mjkim,bhlee,skim,dhwon}@security.re.kr

Abstract. Authentication of communicating entities and confidentiality of transmitted data are fundamental procedures to establish secure communications over public insecure networks. Recently, many researchers proposed a variety of authentication schemes to confirm legitimate users. Among the authentication schemes, a one-time password authentication scheme requires less computation and considers the limitations of mobile devices. The purpose of a one-time password authentication is to make it more difficult to gain unauthorized access to restricted resources. This paper discusses the security of Kuo-Lee's one-time password authentication scheme. Kuo-Lee proposed to solve the security problem based on Tsuji-Shimizu's one-time password authentication scheme. It was claimed that their proposed scheme could withstand a replay attack, a theft attack and a modification attack. Therefore, the attacker cannot successfully impersonate the user to log into the system. However, contrary to the claim, Kuo-Lee's scheme does not achieve its main security goal to authenticate communicating entities. We show that Kuo-Lee's scheme is still insecure under a modification attack, a replay attack and an impersonation attack, in which any attacker can violate the authentication goal of the scheme without intercepting any transmitted message. We also propose a scheme that resolves the security flaws found in Kuo-Lee's scheme.

Keywords: One-time password, authentication scheme, impersonation attack.

1 Introduction

Mobile devices are designed to help users access the servers of service providers. They process tasks such as, stock trading, product purchases, product information collection, and banking. Once the services are available to the users,

---

* This work was supported by the Ministry of Knowledge Economy, Korea, under the ITRC(Information Technology Research Center) support program supervised by the IITA(Institute of Information Technology Advancement) (IITA-2009-(C1090-0902-0016)) and the Defense Acquisition Program Administration and Agency for Defense Development under the contract UD070054AD.
** Corresponding author.

D. Ślęzak et al. (Eds.): FGCN/ACN 2009, CCIS 56, pp. 421–430, 2009.
© Springer-Verlag Berlin Heidelberg 2009

authentication is applied to verify the identities of users. However, most current authentication methods used in M-commerce are designed for wired networks and require high computation costs, making them unsuited to wireless environments. A one-time password authentication scheme uses less computation and considers the limitations of mobile devices. The purpose of a one-time password is to make it more difficult to gain unauthorized access to restricted resources. Traditionally static passwords can be more easily accessed by an unauthorized intruder given sufficient attempts and time. This risk can be greatly reduced by constantly altering the password. There are basically three types of one-time passwords. The first uses a mathematical algorithm to generate a new password based on the previous password. The second is based on time-synchronization between the authentication server and the user providing the password. The third uses a mathematical algorithm, but the new password is based on a challenge and a counter. A one-time password system generates a series of passwords that are used to log on to a specific system. Once one of the passwords is used, it cannot be used again. The login system will always expect a new one-time password at the next login.

Lamport [1] introduced the first one-time password authentication scheme. This initial work has been followed by a number of subsequent improvements [2–9]. Of theses schemes, SAS-2 [7] suffers from a stolen-verifier attack; an attacker who has stolen user verifiers from the server can impersonate legitimate users. ROSI [8] suffers from a theft attack; an attacker who has stolen the server's secret can impersonate legitimate users. In 2004, Tsuji-Shimizu proposed 2GR [9] to eliminate a stolen-verifier attack on SAS-2 and a theft attack on ROSI. Although Tsuji-Shimizu claimed that under 2GR an attacker who has stolen the verifiers from the server cannot impersonate a legitimate user, Lin-Hung showed that the 2GR scheme is vulnerable to an impersonation attack, in which any attacker can masquerade as a legitimate user, without stealing the verifiers [10]. Kuo-Lee pointed out that the 2GR is insecure under a modification attack and proposed an improved scheme to enhance the security of the one-time password authentication scheme in 2007 [11]. However, we found in this paper Kuo-Lee's scheme is vulnerable to modification, replay and impersonation attacks.

The remainder of this paper is organized as follows: In Section 2, we review Kuo-Lee's one-time password authentication scheme. We present security weaknesses of Kuo-Lee's scheme in Section 3. In Section 4, we propose an enhanced scheme, and analyze the security in Section 5. Finally, we conclude this work in Section 6.

2 Review of Kuo-Lee's Scheme

The following notation is listed below with the descriptions to facilitate future reference.

- U: a legitimate user
- S: a server

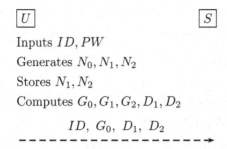

Fig. 1. Registration Phase of Kuo-Lee's Scheme

- A: an attacker
- ID: U's identity
- PW: U's password
- h: a one-way hash function
- N: a random number
- $\oplus$: an exclusive-or operation
- $U \to S$: transmitting U to S over an unauthenticated channel

Kuo-Lee's scheme consists of two phases: the registration phase and the authentication phase. The registration phase is performed only once, when a new user registers with the server; while the authentication phase is executed every time a user wants to gain access to the server. We describe these two phases as follows.

2.1 Registration Phase

Figure 1 shows the initial registration phase of the Kuo-Lee's scheme where a dashed line indicates an authenticated channel and more detailed description follows:

R1. A user U inputs $\langle ID, PW \rangle$ and generates three random numbers $\langle N_0, N_1, N_2 \rangle$. Then U stores $\langle N_1, N_2 \rangle$ and calculates $\langle G_0, G_1, G_2, D_1, D_2 \rangle$ by using the following equations:

$$G_0 = h(ID, PW, N_0),$$
$$G_1 = h(ID, PW, N_1),$$
$$G_2 = h(ID, PW, N_2),$$
$$D_1 = h(G_0, G_1),$$
$$D_2 = h(G_1, G_2).$$

R2. U sends $\langle ID, G_0, D_1, D_2 \rangle$ to S.
R3. S stores the received message $\langle ID, G_0, D_1, D_2 \rangle$.

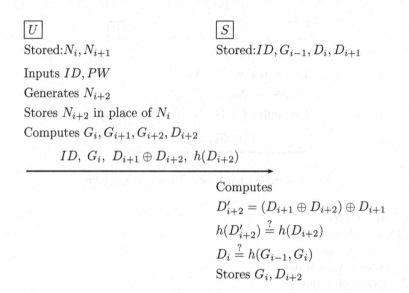

$$U$$
Stored: N_i, N_{i+1}

Inputs ID, PW

Generates N_{i+2}

Stores N_{i+2} in place of N_i

Computes $G_i, G_{i+1}, G_{i+2}, D_{i+2}$

$$ID, \ G_i, \ D_{i+1} \oplus D_{i+2}, \ h(D_{i+2})$$

$$S$$
Stored: $ID, G_{i-1}, D_i, D_{i+1}$

Computes

$$D'_{i+2} = (D_{i+1} \oplus D_{i+2}) \oplus D_{i+1}$$

$$h(D'_{i+2}) \stackrel{?}{=} h(D_{i+2})$$

$$D_i \stackrel{?}{=} h(G_{i-1}, G_i)$$

Stores G_i, D_{i+2}

Fig. 2. Authentication Phase of Kuo-Lee's Scheme

2.2   Authentication Phase

In order to log into the system, U executes the ith authentication session of Kuo-Lee's scheme. When U finishes the $(i-1)$th login session of the scheme, $\langle N_i, N_{i+1} \rangle$ is stored in U and $\langle ID, G_{i-1}, D_i, D_{i+1} \rangle$ is stored in S. Figure 2 shows the ith authentication phase of Kuo-Lee's scheme. The detailed description of the ith authentication phase is as follows:

A1. U first inputs $\langle ID, PW \rangle$. Next he generates a new random number N_{i+2} and computes $\langle G_i, G_{i+1}, G_{i+2}, D_{i+2} \rangle$ where

$$G_i = h(ID, PW, N_i),$$
$$G_{i+1} = h(ID, PW, N_{i+1}),$$
$$G_{i+2} = h(ID, PW, N_{i+2}),$$
$$D_{i+2} = h(G_{i+1}, G_{i+2}).$$

Then U stores $\langle N_{i+1}, N_{i+2} \rangle$ instead of $\langle N_i, N_{i+1} \rangle$.

A2. U sends $\langle ID, G_i, D_{i+1} \oplus D_{i+2}, h(D_{i+2}) \rangle$ to S.

A3. S first computes $D'_{i+2} = (D_{i+1} \oplus D_{i+2}) \oplus D_{i+1}$ and checks if $h(D'_{i+2})$ is equal to $h(D_{i+2})$ when he received the message $\langle ID, G_i, D_{i+1} \oplus D_{i+2}, h(D_{i+2}) \rangle$. If $h(D'_{i+2}) = h(D_{i+2})$ then S computes $D'_i = h(G_{i-1}, G_i)$ using the stored G_{i-1} and the received G_i, and checks if D'_i is equal to the stored D_i. If they match, U is authenticated, and then S stores $\langle ID, G_i, D_{i+1}, D_{i+2} \rangle$ in place of $\langle ID, G_{i-1}, D_i, D_{i+1} \rangle$. Otherwise, S rejects U's login.

3   Attacks on Kuo-Lee's Scheme

In 2006, Lin-Hung pointed out the vulnerability of the 2GR scheme to an impersonation attack [10]. Lin-Hung's approach can be directly applied to Kuo-Lee's
scheme that provides unilateral authentication. Thus the attacker can apply
server spoofing on Kuo-Lee's scheme. Kuo-Lee argued that their proposed scheme
can withstand replay, theft and modification attacks. Therefore, the attacker cannot impersonate user U to log into the system. However, under our investigation,
Kuo-Lee's scheme cannot work successfully.

We deduce the security weakness of Kuo-Lee's scheme, in which a situation
could arise whereby the original message could have been suppressed and thus
did not arrive at its destination; only the replay message arrives. We show this
by mounting three attacks, a modification attack, a replay attack and an impersonation attack, on Kuo-Lee's scheme. The scenarios of our attacks on Kuo-Lee's
scheme are as follows.

3.1   Modification Attack and Replay Attack

1. $U \to A \; \langle ID, G_i, D_{i+1} \oplus D_{i+2}, h(D_{i+2}) \rangle$
   (a) In the ith authentication session, the user U sends $\langle ID, G_i, D_{i+1} \oplus D_{i+2}, h(D_{i+2}) \rangle$ to the server.
   (b) Since the user does not authenticate the server in Kuo-Lee's scheme, we assume that using server spoofing, an attacker masquerades as the server to receive the transmitted message from the user, and accepts this login connection.
   (c) The attacker cannot provide subsequent service to the user, from user U's viewpoint, the ith authentication is accomplished but the service is interrupted.
   (d) Now the user is with $\langle N_{i+1}, N_{i+2} \rangle$ while the server is still with $\langle ID, G_{i-1}, D_i, D_{i+1} \rangle$.
2. $U \to A \; \langle ID, G_{i+1}, D_{i+2} \oplus D_{i+3}, h(D_{i+3}) \rangle$
   (a) In the $(i+1)$th authentication session, when the user U sends $\langle ID, G_{i+1}, D_{i+2} \oplus D_{i+3}, h(D_{i+3}) \rangle$ to the server, the attacker intercepts the transmitted message.
   (b) The attacker records G_{i+1}.
3. $A \to S \; \langle ID, G_i, D_{i+1} \oplus D'_{i+2}, h(D'_{i+2}) \rangle$
   (a) A forwards the server $\langle ID, G_i, D_{i+1} \oplus D'_{i+2}, h(D'_{i+2}) \rangle$ in which the attacker chooses a random number G'_{i+2} and calculates $D'_{i+2} = h(G_{i+1}, G'_{i+2})$.
   (b) After receiving the data from the attacker, server S calculates $D''_{i+2} = (D_{i+1} \oplus D'_{i+2}) \oplus D_{i+1}$, using the received $D_{i+1} \oplus D'_{i+2}$ and stored D_{i+1}.
   (c) Then S compares $h(D''_{i+2})$ with received $h(D'_{i+2})$.
   (d) If they are equal, then the server will pass the authentication check and update user's verifier as $\langle ID, G_i, D_{i+1}, D'_{i+2} \rangle$. From user U's viewpoint, the $(i+1)$th authentication is accomplished and service is supplied.

Therefore, if an attacker intercepted the transmitted message at the ith login and replayed it to gain an access, the attack can work. Kuo-Lee claimed that their proposed scheme can withstand modification and replay attacks. However, this turns out to be untrue.

3.2　Impersonation Attack

After the modification attack and replay attack, attacker A is able to impersonate U to log into the system. The attack proceeds as follows:

1. $A \rightarrow S \; \langle ID, G_{i+1}, D'_{i+2} \oplus D'_{i+3}, h(D'_{i+3}) \rangle$
   - (a) In the $(i+2)$th authentication session, A chooses a random number G'_{i+3} and calculates $D'_{i+3} = h(G'_{i+2}, G'_{i+3})$.
   - (b) A sends $\langle ID, G_{i+1}, D'_{i+2} \oplus D'_{i+3}, h(D'_{i+3}) \rangle$ to S, in which the G_{i+1} is recorded at step 3.1 2(b).
   - (c) After receiving the message from A, S calculates $D''_{i+3} = (D'_{i+2} \oplus D'_{i+3}) \oplus D'_{i+2}$, using the received $D'_{i+2} \oplus D'_{i+3}$ and stored D'_{i+2}.
   - (d) If $h(D''_{i+3})$ is equal to the received $h(D'_{i+3})$, S calculates $D'_{i+1} = h(G_i, G_{i+1})$ using the stored G_i and received G_{i+1}.
   - (e) S compares D'_{i+1} with the stored D_{i+1}. If they are equal, S will pass the authentication check.
   - (f) S updates U's verifier as $\langle ID, G_{i+1}, D'_{i+2}, D'_{i+3} \rangle$.
2. $A \rightarrow S \; \langle ID, G'_{i+2}, D'_{i+3} \oplus D'_{i+4}, h(D'_{i+4}) \rangle$
   - (a) In the $(i+2)$th authentication session, A chooses a random number G'_{i+4} and calculates $D'_{i+4} = h(G'_{i+3}, G'_{i+4})$.
   - (b) A sends $\langle ID, G'_{i+2}, D'_{i+3} \oplus D'_{i+4}, h(D'_{i+4}) \rangle$ to S.
   - (c) After receiving the message from the attacker, S calculates $D''_{i+4} = (D'_{i+3} \oplus D'_{i+4}) \oplus D'_{i+3}$, using the received $D'_{i+3} \oplus D'_{i+4}$ and stored D'_{i+3}.
   - (d) If $h(D''_{i+4})$ is equal to the received $h(D'_{i+4})$, S calculates $D''_{i+2} = h(G_{i+1}, G'_{i+2})$, using the stored G_{i+1} and received G'_{i+2}.
   - (e) S compares D''_{i+2} with the stored D'_{i+2}. If they are equal, S will pass the authentication check.
   - (f) S updates U's verifier as $\langle ID, G'_{i+2}, D'_{i+3}, D'_{i+4} \rangle$.

In this authentication phase, the attacker chooses all the numbers $\langle G'_{i+2}, D'_{i+3}, D'_{i+4} \rangle$. Therefore, from now on A can impersonate the U without intercepting any transmitted message. Hence, the attacker can successfully impersonate the user to log into the system.

4　Proposed Scheme

We propose an enhanced scheme to achieve security against the presented attacks. The scheme allows the communicating entities to protect their communications in the authentication phase. Only U and S have a shared key K in order to secure the scheme. The proposed scheme has two phases: registration phase and authentication phase.

4.1   Registration Phase

The registration phase is performed only once, when a new user registers with the server.

R1. U inputs $\langle ID, PW \rangle$
    1. U generates three random numbers $\langle N_0, N_1, N_2 \rangle$.
    2. U stores $\langle N_1, N_2 \rangle$.
    3. U computes $\langle G_0, G_1, G_2, D_1, D_2 \rangle$ using the following equations:

$$G_0 = h(ID, PW, N_0),$$
$$G_1 = h(ID, PW, N_1),$$
$$G_2 = h(ID, PW, N_2),$$
$$D_1 = h(G_0, G_1),$$
$$D_2 = h(G_1, G_2).$$

R2. $U \to S \ \langle ID, G_0, G_1, D_1, D_2 \rangle$
R3. S receives $\langle ID, G_0, G_1, D_1, D_2 \rangle$
    S stores the received message $\langle ID, G_0, G_1, D_1, D_2 \rangle$.

4.2   Authentication Phase

In the authentication phase, the user is requesting the ith service. When U finishes the $(i-1)$th authentication session of the scheme, $\langle N_i, N_{i+1} \rangle$ is stored in U and $\langle ID, G_{i-1}, G_i, D_i, D_{i+1} \rangle$ is stored in S. The detailed description of the ith enhanced authentication phase is as follows:

A1. $U \to S$ login request
    1. U inputs $\langle ID, PW \rangle$.
    2. U send a login request to S.
A2. $S \to U \ E_K(ID \oplus T_S \oplus i)$
    1. S computes $\langle ID \oplus T_S \oplus i \rangle$, where T_S is S's current timestamp and i is the current session number.
    2. S encrypts $\langle ID \oplus T_S \oplus i \rangle$, using the shared key K.
    3. S sends $E_K(ID \oplus T_S \oplus i)$ to U
A3. $U \to S \ \langle E_K(ID \oplus T_U \oplus i), G_{i-1} \oplus G_i \oplus G_{i+1}, D_{i+1} \oplus D_{i+2}, h(D_{i+2}) \rangle$
    1. U decrypts $E_K(ID \oplus T_S \oplus i)$.
    2. U checks $(T_U - T_S) \geq \Delta T$. If $(T_U - T_S) \geq \Delta T$, U quits the login request, where ΔT is the expected valid time interval.
    3. Otherwise, U generates a new random number N_{i+2}.
    4. U computes $\langle G_i, G_{i+1}, G_{i+2}, D_{i+2} \rangle$, where

$$G_i = h(ID, PW, N_i),$$
$$G_{i+1} = h(ID, PW, N_{i+1}),$$
$$G_{i+2} = h(ID, PW, N_{i+2}),$$
$$D_{i+2} = h(G_{i+1}, G_{i+2}).$$

Table 1. Security Comparisons of Related Authentication Schemes

	2GR	Kuo-Lee's Scheme	Proposed Scheme
Modification Attack	X	X	O
Replay Attack	O	X	O
Impersonation Attack	O	X	O

O means the scheme is not vulnerable to the attack. X means the scheme is vulnerable to the attack.

5. U stores $\langle N_{i+1}, N_{i+2} \rangle$ instead of $\langle N_i, N_{i+1} \rangle$.
6. U computes $\langle ID \oplus T_U \oplus i \rangle$, where T_U is U's current timestamp and i is the current session number.
7. U encrypts $\langle ID \oplus T_U \oplus i \rangle$ using the shared key K.
8. U sends $\langle E_K(ID \oplus T_U \oplus i), G_{i-1} \oplus G_i \oplus G_{i+1}, D_{i+1} \oplus D_{i+2}, h(D_{i+2}) \rangle$ to S.

A4. S receives $\langle E_K(ID \oplus T_U \oplus i), G_{i-1} \oplus G_i \oplus G_{i+1}, D_{i+1} \oplus D_{i+2}, h(D_{i+2}) \rangle$
1. S decrypts $E_K(ID \oplus T_U \oplus i)$.
2. S checks $(T_U - T_S) \geq \Delta T$. If $(T_U - T_S) \geq \Delta T$, S rejects the login request, where ΔT is the expected valid time interval.
3. Otherwise, S computes $D'_{i+2} = (D_{i+1} \oplus D_{i+2}) \oplus D_{i+1}$.
4. S checks if $h(D'_{i+2})$ is equal to $h(D_{i+2})$.
5. If $h(D'_{i+2}) = h(D_{i+2})$, then S obtains $G_{i+1} = (G_{i-1} \oplus G_i \oplus G_{i+1}) \oplus G_{i-1} \oplus G_i$.
6. S computes $D'_{i+1} = h(G_i, G_{i+1})$, using the stored G_i and the obtained G_{i+1}.
7. S checks if D'_{i+1} is equal to the stored D_{i+1}.
8. If they are equal, U is authenticated, and then S stores $\langle ID, G_i, G_{i+1}, D_{i+1}, D_{i+2} \rangle$ in place of $\langle ID, G_{i-1}, G_i, D_i, D_{i+1} \rangle$.
9. Otherwise, S rejects U's login.

5   Security Analysis

In this section, we briefly demonstrates that our proposed scheme is secure against a modification attack, a replay attack and an impersonation attack. In Table 1, we summarize the security comparisons of our proposed scheme and the related authentication schemes.

5.1   Resistance to Modification Attack

In the ith authentication session, when the user sends $\langle E_K(ID \oplus T_U \oplus i), G_{i-1} \oplus G_i \oplus G_{i+1}, D_{i+1} \oplus D_{i+2}, h(D_{i+2}) \rangle$ to the server, we assume that the attacker intercepts the transmitted message and tries to modify the message. In our proposed scheme, the attacker is unable to modify the message $\langle E_K(ID \oplus T_U \oplus i), G_{i-1} \oplus G_i \oplus G_{i+1}, D_{i+1} \oplus D_{i+2}, h(D_{i+2}) \rangle$, since the attacker cannot compute

$\langle D_{i+1} = h(G_i, G_{i+1})\rangle$ or $\langle D_{i+2} = h(G_{i+1}, G_{i+2})\rangle$ even if A eavesdropped on previous messages. Therefore, our modification attack is no longer valid against our enhanced scheme.

5.2   Resistance to Replay Attack and Impersonation Attack

We assume that an attacker eavesdrops on U's message $\langle E_K(ID \oplus T_U \oplus i), G_{i-1} \oplus G_i \oplus G_{i+1}, D_{i+1} \oplus D_{i+2}, h(D_{i+2})\rangle$ in the ith authentication session, and sends the message to S for the $(i+1)$th authentication session. Obviously, S rejects the message, because U's timestamp and session number are always updated in every authentication session and S checks the valid time interval of ΔT and the session number. Therefore, our scheme protects U and S from replay attack. Due to the failure of the modification and replay attacks, our impersonation attack is no longer valid against our enhanced scheme.

6   Conclusion

We presented the security weakness of Kuo-Lee's one-time password authentication scheme [11]. Kuo-Lee claimed that their proposed scheme could withstand a replay attack, a theft attack and a modification attack; therefore, the attacker could not successfully impersonate the user to log into the system. However, contrary to the claim, our security investigation showed that Kuo-Lee's scheme does not achieve its main security goal to authenticate communicating entities. The failure of Kuo-Lee's scheme to achieve authentication was clear using three attacks: modification, replay and impersonation attacks, on the scheme. We proposed an enhancement to the original scheme to secure the scheme, remedying these problems.

References

1. Lamport, L.: Password authentication with insecure communication. Commun. ACM 24(11), 770–772 (1981)
2. Shimizu, A.: A dynamic password authentication method by oneway function. System and Computers in Japan 22(7), 32–40 (1991)
3. Haller, N.M.: The S/KEY (TM) one-time password system. In: Proc. Internet Society Symposium on Network and Distributed System Security, February 1994, pp. 151–158 (1994)
4. Shimizu, A., Horioka, T., Inagaki, H.: A password authentication method for contents communication on the Internet. IEICE Trans. Commun. E81-B(8), 1666–1673 (1998)
5. Sandirigama, M., Shimizu, A., Noda, M.T.: Simple and Secure password authentication protocol (SAS). IEICE Trans. Commun. E83-B(6), 1363–1365 (2000)
6. Lin, C.L., Sun, H.M., Hwang, T.: Attack and solutions on strong-password authentication. IEICE Trans. Commun. E84-B(9), 2622–2627 (2001)
7. Tsuji, T., Kamioka, T., Shimizu, A.: Simple and Secure password authentication protocol, ver.2 (SAS-2), IEICE Technical Report, OIS 2002-30 (September 2002)

8. Chien, H.Y., Jan, J.K.: Robust and simple authentication protocol. Comput. J. 46(2), 193–201 (2003)
9. Tsuji, T., Shimizu, A.: One-time password authentication protocol against theft attacks. IEICE Trans. on Commun. E87-B(3), 523–529 (2004)
10. Lin, C.L., Hung, C.P.: One-Time password authentication protocol against theft attacks. IEICE Trans. on Commun. E89-B(12), 3425–3427 (2006)
11. Kuo, W.C., Lee, Y.C.: Attack and improvement on the one-time password authentication protocol against theft attacks. In: Proc. of the Sixth International Conference on Machine Learning and Cybernetics, Hong Kong, August 2007, pp. 19–22 (2007)

News Event Tracking Using an Improved Hybrid of KNN and SVM

Zhen Lei[1], Yanjie Jiang[1], Peng Zhao[2], and Jue Wang[1]

[1] Department of Information Engineering,
Academy of Armored Force Engineering, Beijing 100072, China
leizen@tom.com, williamjohnmail@126.com
[2] Department of Control Engineering,
Academy of Armored Force Engineering, Beijing 100072, China
Pengzhao76@126.com

Abstract. News event tracking is the task of associating incoming stories with events known to the system. A tracking system's goal is to automatically assign event labels to the subsequent news stories. The paper presents an improved fusion algorithm for news event tracking based on the combination of the KNN and SVM. The improved KNN utilizes density function to select some cluster centers from negative examples and the improved SVM uses sigmoid function to map the SVM outputs into probabilities. The problem of effective density radius selection is discussed, and the performance differences between the event tracking method proposed in this paper and other methods are compared. The experimental results with the real-world data sets indicate the proposed method is feasible and advanced.

1 Introduction

Internet news plays a very important role in the huge Internet information set. According to the latest statistic report of CNNIC, 84.38% of information got from Internet by Chinese users is news. Therefore, research on Internet news is becoming a hotspot in natural language processing (NLP) field. As a new direction of research on NLP, event detection and tracking[1] aims at automatically identifying and following new or previously unidentified events in several continuous news streams.

The event tracking is defined to be the task of associating incoming stories with events known to the system. A tracking system's goal is to correctly classify all of the subsequent stories. Automated tracking of events from chronologically ordered document streams is a new challenge for statistical text classification. Existing learning techniques[2] must be adapted or improved in order to effectively handle difficult situations where the number of positive training instances per event is extremely smaller than negative instances and the majority of training documents are unlabelled. K nearest neighbor (KNN), Decision Trees and Rocchio are well-known methods suited to tracking task[3].

KNN is a very efficient event tracking method and can be easily carried out. In a statistical opinion, the error rate of a KNN classifier tends to the Bayes optimal

D. Ślęzak et al. (Eds.): FGCN/ACN 2009, CCIS 56, pp. 431–438, 2009.

when k and the size of sample set tend to infinity. SVM is also a useful supervised learning algorithm with generalization ability and has been found powerful in handling classification tasks in case of the high dimensionality and scarcity of data points, however SVM is seldom used to tracking task. The main reason, we believe, is that the positive examples are extremely sparse in the training set and SVM is not always fit for learning task of small samples. One solution to this problem is to discount the influence of negative examples by sampling a small portion and ignoring the remaining negative examples. In addition, event detection and tracking requires tracking systems offer a confidence measure, but a standard SVM produces the values that are not probabilities.

There is increasing evidence that the ensemble classifier not only increases the accuracy of the classification, but also leads to greater confidence in the result. In order to overcome the limitation of SVM and use it in our tracking implementation, we present an improved K nearest neighbor combined with support vector machine (IKNN-SVM) to track event. It first utilizes density function to select some representative samples from negative samples. Then KNN is introduced into SVM to trains the new set to track news event. Finally we map the SVM outputs into probabilities.

The structure of the paper is as follows. Section 2 and Section 3 detail the proposed event tracking method used in our system respectively. Section 4 presents experimental results. Section 5 gives conclusions.

2   Document Representation and Similarity Calculation

2.1   Document Representation

For preprocessing, we transform the documents into a representation convenient for detection algorithm, perform word segmentation, recognize and normalize abbreviations, remove stop-words, remove suffixes from the word roots, perform simple corrections, and then generate term-frequency vectors.

Our approach uses conventional vector space model to represent the documents. Each document is represented by a vector of weighted terms, which can be either words or phrases. In choosing a term weighting system, low weights should be assigned to high-frequency words that occur in many documents of a collection, while high weights to terms that are important in particular documents but unimportant in the remainder of the collection. A well-known term weighting system following that prescription assigns weight w_{ik} to term T_i in document D_k in proportion to the frequency of occurrence of the term is assigned. Such a weighting system is known as a $TF \cdot IDF$ weighting system. Many variations of $TF \cdot IDF$ formulae have been presented, several of which were compiled and tested by Salton and Buckley[5] in the context of ranked-retrieval.

2.2   Similarity Calculation

In our current implementation, a similarity value is calculated while comparing two documents. We use the cosine distance as the similarity of two documents:

$$sim(k, ET) = \frac{\sum_{j=1}^{M} weight_{j,k} * weight_{j,ET}}{\sqrt{(\sum_{j=1}^{M} weight_{j,k}^{2}) * (\sum_{j=1}^{M} weight_{j,ET}^{2})}} \tag{1}$$

where $sim(k, ET)$ is the cosine similarity value between documents k and event template ET, $weight_{j,k}$ is the weight of word j in document k, $weight_{j,ET}$ is the weight of word j in event template ET, $\sum_{j=1}^{M} weight_{jk}^{2}$ is the sum of squares of the word weights in document k, and $\sum_{j=1}^{M} weight_{j,ET}^{2}$ is the sum of squares of the word weights in event template.

3 Tracking Method Based on IKNN-SVM

A tracking system's goal is to correctly classify all of the subsequent stories when they arrive. Fig.1 presents the main idea of an event tracking system.

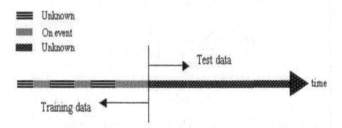

Fig. 1. Event tracking task

3.1 Support Vector Machine

SVM[6] has been shown to work in high dimensional spaces with remarkable perform-ance. It has several merits: (1) Structural risk minimization techniques minimize a risk upper bound on the VC-dimension. (2) SVM can find a unique hyper-plane that maximizes the margin of separation between the classes. (3) The power of SVM lies in using kernel function to transform data from the low dimension space to the high dimension space and construct a linear binary classifier.

3.2 Event Tracking Based on IKNN-SVM

Tracking task involves formulating a classifier from a few sample documents that contain discussion of the same topic relevant event.

In tracking, the positive examples are extremely sparse in the training set, however the negative examples are densely populated. When training sets with uneven class sizes are used, the classification result based on support vector machine is undesirably biased towards the class with more samples in the training set. That is to say, the larger the sample size, the smaller the classification error, whereas the smaller the sample size, the larger the classification error. Similarly, the populated negative examples tend to result in the wrong decision of traditional K Nearest Neighbor.

In order to compensate for the unfavorable impact caused by this bias, one can discount the influence of negative examples by sampling a small portion in the negative examples or choosing some representative examples from negative examples by clustering algorithm.

With the considerations described above, this paper utilizes density function to select some cluster centers from negative examples objectively. It can be used as the representative examples of negative examples. The error rate of a KNN classifier tends to the Bayes optimal when k and the size of sample set tend to infinity. So KNN is introduced into SVM in this paper to deal with the problem of samples in the overlapped boundary region and to improve the performance of SVM. The problem of effective density radius selection and the performance difference between this method and other methods is discussed.

The selection of initial cluster centers affects cluster results and convergence time greatly, unsuitable initial values often make results converge to an undesired minimum and affect convergence speed. In this paper, we adopt a density function[7] to initialize cluster centers. Firstly, the density function of sample x_i is defined as follows:

$$D_i^{(0)} = \sum_{k=1}^{n} \frac{1}{1 + f_d \|x_i - x_k\|^2} \tag{2}$$

Where

$$f_d = 4 / r_d^2 \tag{3}$$

Where r_d is valid density radius, it can be adopted in two forms:

$$r_f = \frac{1}{2} \min\{\max\{\|x_i - x_k\|, i = 1,...n\}, k = 1,...,n\} \tag{4}$$

or

$$r_m = \frac{1}{2} \sqrt{\frac{1}{n(n-1)} \sum_{k=1}^{n} \sum_{i=1}^{n} \|x_i - x_k\|^2} \tag{5}$$

Let $D_1^* = \max\{D_i^{(0)}, i = 1,...n\}$, corresponding x_1^* is treated as the first initial cluster center, and the density functions of latter initial cluster centers is as follows:

$$D_i^{(k)} = D_i^{(k-1)} - D_k^* \frac{1}{1 + f_d \|x_i - x_k^*\|^2}, \tag{6}$$

$$k = 1,...c - 1$$

where

$$D_k^* = \max\{D_i^{(k-1)}, i = 1,...n\} \tag{7}$$

The steps of the IKNN-SVM based event tracking method are:

Step1: Density function is utilized to get K initial cluster centers of negative samples $CenterSet\_N = \{O_1,O_2,...O_K\}$ of sample set Z ;

Step2: $TrainingSet \leftarrow CenterSet\_N \cup P^+$, let $TrainingSet$ be the final training sets of IKNN-SVM;

Step3: Compute distances of the query $TrainingSet$ and pick the nearest K neighbors, the sample is classified into the same class when its k neighbors have all the same labels, the query is labeled and exit. Otherwise, go to step4;

Step4: Apply SVM to classify the remaining unidentified samples and adapt following decision function:

$$f(e) = \text{sgn}[\sum_{i=1}^{k} y_i \alpha_i (e \cdot e_i) + b] \tag{8}$$

Step5: If $f(e) = 1$, then test document $e \in DE$, otherwise $e \notin DE$, DE is defined event.

Standard support vector machines produce an uncalibrated value that is not a probability. But constructing a classifier to produce a posterior probability is very useful, for example, posterior probabilities are required when a classifier is making a small part of an overall decision, and the classification outputs must be combined for the overall decision. In this paper, we adopted a function[4] to map the SVM outputs into probabilities. Instead of estimating the class-conditional densities $p(f \mid y)$, a parametric model is used to fit the posterior $P(y = 1 \mid f)$ directly:

$$P(y = 1 \mid f) = \frac{1}{1 + e^{-f(x)}} \tag{9}$$

Equation (4) used a logistic link function, and then proposed minimizing a negative log multinomial likelihood plus a term that penalized the norm in an RKHS:

$$-\frac{1}{m}\sum_i (\frac{y_i+1}{2})\log(p_i) + \frac{1-y_i}{2}\log(1-p_i)) + \lambda\|h\|_F^2 \tag{10}$$

Where $p_i = p(x_i)$. The output $p(x)$ of such a machine will be a posterior probability.

4 Experiment Results

We ran our system on NEM study Corpus[8]. The NEM Study Corpus comprises a set of Internet news stories, which are collected from several influential websites. Each story is represented as a stream of text. It consists of 16560 chronologically ordered news stories. There are 16 events manually identified in this corpus. Each story was assigned a label of "Yes", "No" or "Brief" with respect to each of the 16 events. Except for a small fraction of the articles, each document belongs to exactly one event.

We choose 10 events from NEM study corpus to carry out event detection and tracking experiment.

Effectiveness measures of our system were evaluated using the stories related to the 16 selected events. Our experiment is carried out in Pentium 4 2.6Ghz CPU, 512 RAM and Windows 2000 professional system. To evaluate the effectiveness of the event tracking results, six effectiveness measures including Recall, Precision, F1-measure, P_{miss}, P_{false} and $Cost_{norm}$ are used[3], they are defined as follows:

$$Miss\ Rate = P_{miss} = \frac{c}{a+c} \tag{11}$$

$$False\ Alarm\ Rate = P_{fa} = \frac{b}{b+d} \tag{12}$$

$$Cost = C_{miss} \cdot P_{miss} \cdot P_{t\,arg} + C_{fa} \cdot P_{fa} \cdot P_{nont} \tag{13}$$

$$Cost_{norm} = \frac{Cost}{min(C_{miss} \cdot P_{t\,arg\,et}, C_{fa} \cdot P_{nont})} \tag{14}$$

Table 1 shows the measure results of IKNN-SVM based tracking algorithm by using different effective density radiuses.

Table 1. Effectiveness measures of different effective density radiuses

Density radius	P_{miss}	P_{false}	$Cost_{norm}$
$R_d=R_m/8$	48.23%	3.93%	0.6749
$R_d=R_m/6$	46.65%	4.23%	0.6738
$R_d=R_m/4$	59.92%	5.12%	0.8501
$R_d=R_m/2$	65.12%	9.33%	1.1084
$R_d=R_m$	53.20%	4.89%	0.7716
$R_d=2R_m$	34.15%	2.02%	0.4405
$R_d=2.5R_m$	46.55%	6.30%	0.7742
$R_d=3R_m$	51.52%	8.66%	0.9395

We observe that an appropriate destination can be reached if we let $R_d=2R_m$, because not only $Cost_{norm}$ is smallest, but also each event follow the same rule.

Table 2 shows the result of tracking system with using IKNN-SVM and probabilistic outputs for SVM. The number of positive training examples per event in our system is 4. Table 2 indicates a minimum normalized cost of 0.4405 at a miss rate of 34.15% and a false rate of 2.02%. The optimal probabilistic output threshold is 0.45 in our experiments.

Fig.2 shows a result from comparison of four tracking methods. As it can be seen from the result, our tracking algorithm based on IKNN-SVM with probabilistic outputs showed a better performance than that of other three tracking algorithms. Though

Table 2. The result of tracking system with using IKNN-SVM and different probabilistic output thresholds

$T_{threshold}$	P_{miss}	P_{false}	$Cost_{norm}$
0.09	10.23%	19.37%	1.0514
0.18	16.65%	15.05%	0.9040
0.27	19.32%	11.79%	0.7709
0.36	27.11%	8.68%	0.6964
0.45	**34.15%**	**2.02%**	**0.4405**
0.54	41.00%	1.55%	0.4860
0.63	52.65%	0.99%	0.5750
0.72	63.64%	0.72%	0.6717
0.81	81.20%	0.28%	0.8257
0.90	92.55%	0.12%	0.9313

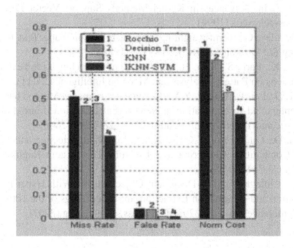

Fig. 2. Comparison of four algorithms for news event tracking (minimum normalized cost)

KNN is gaining popularity due to many attractive features and promising performance in the fields of event tracking, the performance of our algorithm is better than that of KNN in miss rate and minimum normalized cost. As far as false rate is concerned, our algorithm is close to that of KNN.

5 Conclusions

In this paper, we proposed an IKNN-SVM based algorithm to track news event. The algorithm only used a part of negative examples and all the positive examples as the training set to compensate for the unfavorable impact caused by the populated negative examples. In order to offer a confidence measure the IKNN-SVM outputs are mapped into probabilities. With real world data sets, experimental results show the algorithm's effectiveness.

In our future work we plan to concentrate on exploring the suitability of information extraction techniques[9] to event detection and tracking, and their effects on system performance.

References

1. Allan, J., Carbonell, J., Doddington, G., Yamron, J., Yang, Y.: Topic Detection and Tracking Pilot Study Final Report. In: Proceedings of the DARPA Broadcast News Transcription and Understanding Workshop, pp. 194–218. Morgan Kaufmann Publishers, Inc., San Francisco (1998)
2. Bottou, L., Vapnik, V.: Local Learning Algorithms. Neural Computation 4(6), 888–900 (1992)
3. Papka, R.: On-line New Event Detection, Clustering, and Tracking. Ph. D. Thesis, University of Massachusetts at Amherst (1999)
4. Wahba, G.: Support Vector Machines, Reproducing Kernel Hilbert Spaces and The Randomized GACV. In: Advances in Kernel Methods Support Vector Learning, pp. 69–88. MIT Press, Massachusetts (1999)
5. Salton, G., Buckley, C.: Term-weighting Approach in Automatic Text Retrieval. Information Processing & Management 24(5), 513–523 (1988)
6. Kim, K., Jung, K., Park, S., Kim, H.: Support Vector Machines for Texture Classification. IEEE Transactions on Pattern Analysis and Machine Intelligence 24(11), 1542–1550 (2002)
7. Lei, Z., Wu, L.D., Lei, L., Huang, Y.Y.: Incremental K-means Method base on Initialisation of Cluster Centers and Its application in News Event Detection. Journal of the China Society for Scientific and Technical Information 25(3), 289–295 (2006)
8. Lei, Z., Wu, L.D., Lei, L., Liu, Y.C.: A System for Event Detection and Tracking Based on Constructive-Competition Clustering and KNNFL. The System Engineering Theory and Practice 26(3), 68–74 (2006)
9. Chakrabarti, S.: Integrating The Document Object Model With Hyperlinks For Enhanced Topic Distillation and Information Extraction. In: Proceedings of the 10th ACM-WWW International Conference, pp. 211–220. ACM Press, Hong Kong (2001)

Query Based Approach Model for Mobile Commerce Applications in Manet

G. Varaprasad[*]

Department of Computer Science and Engineering,
B.M.S. College of Engineering,
Bangalore-560019, India
Ph.: 91-080-26614357; Fax: +91-080-26614357
varaprasad2001@yahoo.com

Abstract. The mobile commerce is ability to conduct commerce using mobile devices. This paper describes a detailed mobile commerce framework based on the customer query. The proposed model finds customer requirements based on query, which is made by the customer over the network. The system finds the customer product information and sends to the intended customer. The customer can choose the product, which he/she wants and based on that, the transaction has executed. Both the customer and vender will execute their transaction in a secured manner through the mobile phones.

Keywords: Mobile commerce; query, MANET, mobile agent.

1 Introduction

In mobile commerce, the applications appear in different forms. The mobile devices are used in the commerce applications. Secure data transitions, identification of the clients are more important tasks, when the transaction takes place. These goals seem to be quite simple and even though they are claimed in all applications realizing them properly is quite tricky, because there are different at application design.

Today wireless communication based on multi-hop. It has been evolving to serve a large number of applications, which rely on deployable, multi-hop and wireless infrastructure. The multi-hop mobile radio network is also called Mobile Adhoc Network(MANET). It is a self-organizing and is rapidly deployable in which, neither a wired backbone nor a centralized control exists. The mobile nodes communicate data with others in multi-hop fashion.

The MANET is highly dynamic topology. It is a new paradigm of wireless wearable devices enabling the instantaneous person-to-person, person-to-machine or machine-to-person communication immediately. The mobile commerce environment has shown in Fig.1. Here, the intelligent mobile devices are used to connect with others via wireless link. It can request the services from the local servers without any human intervention. Several interesting and difficult problems are raised to design network due to the wireless medium, transmission range, mobility and battery.

This paper presents query based model for m-commerce applications. Rest of the paper is organized as follows. Section 2 presents some of the related projects. The

---

[*] Corresponding author.

D. Ślęzak et al. (Eds.): FGCN/ACN 2009, CCIS 56, pp. 439–443, 2009.

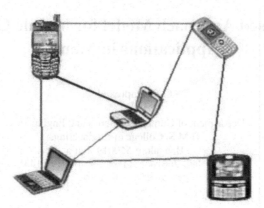

Fig. 1. Mobile commerce environment

design of proposed model is presented in section 3. Section 4 presents the simulation of proposed model. Results of proposed model are presented in section 5. Conclusions and further work are discussed in section 6.

2 Some of Related Works

This section discusses about the some of the existing projects on the commerce applications. I-mode service operated by NTT Docomo, which was the first service executed using wireless application protocol[1]. It used nearly one-fifth of the people in Japan. Shopper's Eye[2] is a system and is worked based on the customer requirements. It requires vendor to create a list that contains items to be purchased through mobile device. Swiftpass[3] allows the users to deliver the digital tickets and vouchers instantly in a secure manner through the mobile phones or handheld devices. In fact, it allows the users to interact with end-users. The system improves customer satisfactions and allows the users to take control of the ticketing and user requirements[4].

TomTom[5] is a newly invented product by Palmtop package. The users can access the travelling information by using their mobile devices. It provides the information about nearby visiting places along with the route maps. The TomTom uses GSM technology to operate Global Positioning System(GPS). Swedish YachtPosition system[6] is a GPS system., which is used for sea vehicle owners. It retrieves the information about the restaurants, fuel shops, and weather. This information is displayed on their mobile devices. WineGuide relies on the alcohol policy in Sweden[7] and supports three options such as wine list, food list and search list to the customers.

3 System Design

3.1 Service Location Protocol

Service Location Protocol(SLP) is an automatic resource discovery in Internet Protocol[8-9]. The SLP is a language independent protocol and consists of three types of the agents namely, user agent, directory agent and service agent. The user agent will acquire the services to handle the end-user applications. The service agent is responsible to advertise the services over the network. It makes the services available to the user agent. The directory agent maintains a list of advertised services in the network. The agent resides in palm pilot and keeps track of the item information. Transaction diagram of SLP is shown in Fig.2.

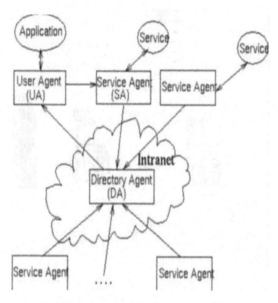

Fig. 2. Transaction diagram of SLP

Transaction diagram of proposed model is shown in Fig.3. It uses following steps:

Step1: Send customer information as well as location information to the server.
Step2: Send customer requested information to the central database.
Step3: Get information about the vendor products.
Step4: Send customer requested product information to the central database
Step5: Display a list of products, which is requested by customer.

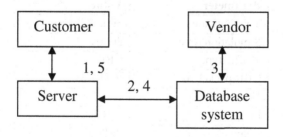

Fig. 3. Transaction diagram

A service is described by the configuration values of the attributes. For instance, a service that allows the users to download the customer information is described as in service that is a pay-per-use real-time service or a free-of-charge service. The SLP supports a simple service registration mechanism that handles the cases, where the service hardware is broken. The customer sends his/her quotation to the authorized vendor as shown in Fig.4.

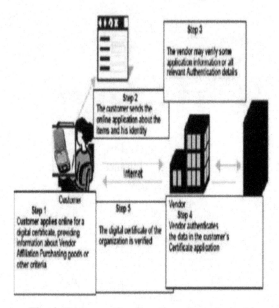

Fig. 4. Design and implantation of m-commerce

3.2 Simulation

In simulation, it considered an area 800mX800m with a list of mobile nodes selected randomly and transmission range was 150m. The simulation is carried out for different number of customers in a given topology. The simulation parameters are shown in Table 1.

Table 1. Simulation parameters

Parameter	Value
Topology area	800mX800m
Simulation time	2000s
Traffic type	CBR
CBR packet size	512bytes
Node mobility	0 to 20m/s
Frequency	2.4Ghz
Channel capacity	2Mbps
Transmission range	150m
Mobility model	Random way point

The proposed work provides a list of product formation to the intended customer and all transactions are executed in a secured manner. It also provides the services, which are easy to access the data and easy to understand. In addition to this, the proposed model is tested with different users' environments and is helped to increase the user-friendliness.

4 Conclusions

The paper has focused on query based approach for mobile commerce applications. It has described how to generate a query and finds the information about products. It would come into prominence with the advent of mobile e-commerce environment as increasing the number of people start using the mobile devices. The mobile e-commerce is obviously leading us to more refined and flexible way of accessing facilities from anywhere. The agents are one of the most important necessities in a distributed environment. The model focuses on technology rather than benefit of a service. The customer needs to be educated on benefits of the system. The pricing strategy is a key element in defining the long-term revenue.

References

1. Antonio, C., Gian, P.P., Giaovanni, V.: Designing Distributed Applications with Mobile Code Paradigms. In: Proc. of International Conference on Software Engineering, pp. 22–32 (2007)
2. Dasgupta, P., Narasimhan, N., Moser, L.E., Melliar-Smith, P.M.: MAgNET: Mobile Agents for Networked Electronic Trading. IEEE Trans.on Knowledge and Data Engineering, Special Issue on Web Applications, 120–125 (2002)
3. Alfonso, F., Gian Pietro, P., Giovanni, V.: Understanding Code Mobility. IEEE Trans. on Software Engineering 24(5), 92–98 (1998)
4. Johansen, D.: Mobile Agent Applicability. In: Rothermel, K., Hohl, F. (eds.) MA 1998. LNCS, vol. 1477, pp. 9–11. Springer, Heidelberg (1998)
5. Kotz, D., Gray, R.S.: Mobile Code: The Future of the Internet. In: Proc of Workshop on Mobile Agents in Context of Competition and Cooperation at Autonomous Agents, pp. 6–12 (2001)
6. Lange, D., Oshima, M.: Mobile Agents with Java: The Aglet API. Special Issue on Distributed World Wide Web Processing: Applications and Techniques of Web Agents, 75–83 (2003)
7. Stavros, P., George, S., Evaggelia, P.: Mobile Agents for WWW Distributed Database Access. In: Proc. of IEEE International Conference on Data Engineering, pp. 75–83 (2005)
8. Burrows, M., Abadi, M., Needham, R.: A Logic of Authentication. ACM Transactions on Computer Systems 8(1), 85–92 (2004)
9. Dolev, D., Yao, A.C.: The Security of Public Key Protocols. In: Proc of IEEE Symposium on Foundations of Computer Science, pp. 140–145 (2000)
10. Catherine, M.: Formal Methods for Cryptographic Protocol Analysis: Emerging Issues and Trends. IEEE Journal on Selected Areas in Communication 21(1), 44–54 (2003)

A Security Framework for Wireless Sensor Networks

Stuart Stent

Macquarie University, Department of Computing, Faculty of Science
NSW 2109, Australia
stuart.stent@students.mq.edu.au
www.mq.edu.au

Abstract. This paper presents an overview of the various issues and requirements of Wireless Sensor Network ('WSN') deployments, and explores the unique network architecture of WSNs and the security issues involved. It is determined that in order to provide adequate security there is a need for the integration of security services into the existing routing protocols. To this end, an extension of the 'Low-Energy Adaptive Clustering Hierarchy' ('LEACH') network routing protocol called, the 'Security Enabled - Low-Energy Adaptive Clustering Hierarchy' ('SE-LEACH') is proposed. This proposed protocol provides security services, such as data confidentiality, key management, data integrity and data freshness in the form of a flexible and extendable framework, thereby overcoming the security issues of existing WSN protocols.

1 Introduction

Recent advances in computer hardware have allowed the development of new data collection techniques utilising wirelessly networked sensor devices to sample the environment and transmit the data back to a central location for analysis. These Wireless Sensor Networks ('WSN') are becoming an invaluable tool for collecting data in dangerous or inaccessible locations such as geologically unstable or radioactive environments. As WSNs are relied on increasingly for the collection of data, the security of that data is becoming a growing concern for those considering the deployment of this technology. In order to develop a security strategy for WSN systems, it is first necessary to understand the technical requirements, architectural limitations and security issues of WSNs. These issues are discussed in Section 2. In Section 3, an extension to the LEACH protocol is proposed. This extension aims to address the security issues of WSNs, by integrating a new extendable security framework into the existing routing protocol. Finally, the findings of the paper are outlined in section 4.

2 Technical Background

2.1 Restrictions and Requirements

The unique characteristics of WSN technologies can greatly affect the ability to provide adequate security services. To this end, it is important to have an

D. Ślęzak et al. (Eds.): FGCN/ACN 2009, CCIS 56, pp. 444–454, 2009.

understanding of these characteristics and their inherent limitations when designing security solutions for WSNs.

The key issues that need to be considered when developing security services for WSNs are:

Processing and Storage. The processing power and data storage capabilities of WSN nodes are very limited and require the efficient design of computational algorithms [1, p. 3].

Power. The energy reserves available to a WSN node are generally very limited; 2-3 AAA batteries is a common configuration. Nodes are expected to run for extended periods of time (1-2 years) on this internal energy reserve [2].

Reliability. Due to the inaccessible locations in which WSNs are deployed, it is imperative that the network be reliable and not require manual intervention [1,3].

Cost. The cost of WSN deployments must not be adversely impacted by the inclusion of security services, as cost is often a major factor in selection of WSN technology over traditional methods [2].

2.2 Network Architecture

The limitations and requirements outlined in section 2.1 above preclude the use of traditional network technologies that are not energy-aware, or that require a large amount of configuration and maintenance. To meet these new requirements a range of new protocols have been proposed. These new protocols can be defined by both their data collection methodology (Continuous, Event-Driven, Data-Driven or Hybrid) [2] or by their networking paradigm (Data-Centric, Hierarchical, Location-based or QoS-aware) [3, p. 2]. Each of these models fulfils a particular usage requirement. For example, the continuous data collection or event-driven models are more suited to a security monitoring application than a query-driven model. Similarly, each network paradigm may be better suited to a particular application than another.

Some of the more prominent of these protocols are outlined below:

SPIN. The Sensor Protocols for Information via Negotiation ('SPIN') [4] protocol is a Data-Centric Event-Based protocol in which an advertisement detailing the available data is generated whenever a new piece of data becomes available. Nodes that are interested in that data request the data from the node.

Directed Diffusion. Directed Diffusion is a Data-Centric Query-Based protocol developed by Intanagonwiwat *et al.* [5]. Nodes collect data and only transmit that data when they receive an 'interest' statement from the base station node. Due to the fact that data is only transmitted when required, Directed Diffusion is more energy efficient than the earlier SPIN protocol.

LEACH. One of the first hierarchical routing protocols developed was the Low-Energy Adaptive Clustering Hierarchy ('LEACH') protocol, proposed by Heinzelman *et al.* [6]. LEACH divides the network up into smaller networks called clusters. Each cluster elects a 'cluster head' node which is responsible for aggregating all of the data from that cluster and forwarding it to the sink node. This clustering allows for much larger networks and is far more energy efficient than either SPIN or Directed Diffusion.

2.3   Security Issues

The development of new routing protocols and techniques has led to the inevitable development of new security issues and attacks. Some of the possible types of attacks are outlined below:

Denial of Service. Wood *et al.* [7] define a Denial of Service ('DoS') attack as "any event that diminishes or eliminates a network's capacity to perform its expected function". These attacks range from radio jamming to flooding the network with data [1, pp. 10-15].

Routing Protocol Attacks. These attacks misuse the routing protocol to redirect traffic to a malicious node, alter the transmitted data or selectively forward data [8].

SYBIL Attack. This attack involves a malicious node masquerading as multiple other nodes in order to disrupt routing, cluster formation or data aggregation [9].

Node Replication. This attack is similar to the SYBIL attack above; however, the malicious node only masquerades as a single already existing node.

Traffic Analysis. This attack involves the analysis of data transmission patterns to determine the location of a particular node, in order to destroy or compromise the node. This attack can be performed even if the data is encrypted [10].

Privacy. Walters *et al.* [1, pp. 13-14] highlight a concern with respect to the transmission of potentially sensitive data (such as the position of subjects and nodes) over an unattended wireless network, as well as the storage of that information on unsecured hardware.

All of the afore-mentioned attacks can be categorised as either 'information-gathering' or 'disruptive'. Techniques such as the SYBIL and Node Replication attacks, which allow one node to masquerade as another node(s), may fall into either category, while others such as the DoS attacks are explicitly disruptive.

While classical security techniques are capable of defending against these attacks, they are rarely designed with energy efficiency in mind and are therefore inappropriate for use in a WSN environment.

2.4   Security Requirements

Walters *et al.* [1, pp. 5-10] define eight requirements that are necessary to ensure a secure sensor network environment. These requirements are:

Data Confidentiality. The data being transferred should not be readable by an unauthorised party.

Data Integrity. The receiver of transmitted data should be able to verify that the data has not been tampered with or corrupted.

Data Freshness. The receiver should be able to verify that the message has not been resent. This is used to mitigate the replay attack given in section 2.3.

Authentication. The receiver should be able to verify the identity of the sender.

Availability. The implementation of security services should not adversely affect the ability of the network to function.

Self-Organisation. Due to the unmanaged nature of WSN deployments, the security services should be self-initialising once in the field and self-healing.

Time-Synchronisation. The ability to securely and accurately synchronise times between nodes is a requirement of other security services and applications.

Secure Localisation. To support applications that are based on accurate location data, it should be possible to verify that a node's location is accurate and is not being faked.

It is important to note that this list of services is neither exhaustive nor mandatory, and the security services used should be tailored to the particular requirements of a deployment. For example, an application for tracking shipping containers and their cargos is likely to require a data confidentiality service, whereas one tracking less sensitive data will not. This ability to tailor services is of the utmost importance. Each service has its own unique overheads in terms of energy and bandwidth consumption, thus reducing the operating life of the network.

3   SE-LEACH

There has been significant research into techniques to counter the attacks outlined in section 2.3; however, there has been less investigation into the integration of these services with the routing protocols outlined in section 2.2 above. This paper proposes a theoretical protocol, Security Enabled - Low-Energy Adaptive

Clustering Hierarchy ('SE-LEACH'). SE-LEACH is designed to extend the popular LEACH routing protocol by integrating several security features into the protocol using a modular framework.

The LEACH protocol is a hierarchical protocol that uses radio strength measurements to divide the network into smaller networks called 'clusters'. Each cluster elects a 'cluster head' node, which is responsible for aggregating all of the data from that cluster and transmitting it back to the sink node. In order to spread the energy consumption evenly over the network, the cluster head role is rotated around all nodes in a cluster.

3.1   Assumptions

The following assumptions have been made in the formulation of the SE-LEACH protocol:

- All devices are statically located;
- Sensor nodes all use the same hardware;
- Some pre-configuration of the nodes will be undertaken; and
- Additional pre-configuration is acceptable.

3.2   Goals

This theoretical model has been designed to meet the following set of requirements as defined in section 2.4:

- Data Confidentiality;
- Data Integrity;
- Data Freshness;
- Network Availability; and
- Self organisation.

The LEACH routing protocol was chosen as the basis for this proposal due to its hierarchical structure and energy efficient design. The proposed additions to the LEACH protocol put forward in this paper may also be applicable to LEACH-inspired, cluster-based protocols such as TEEN [11] and APTEEN [12].

Further design goals for SE-LEACH are that it should be both application and hardware agnostic, and allow for flexibility during configuration to take into account WSN hardware limitations and specific deployment requirements. This flexibility enables changes to cryptographic algorithms as well as the ability to take advantage of additional hardware features, such as a dedicated cryptographic hardware.

3.3   Design Principles

The issue of ensuring that network availability is not adversely affected by the security protocol implementation is a difficult issue to address, particularly in the case of a theoretical model. Nevertheless, in an effort to address this issue and reduce the impact of the additional security services on the performance of the WSN, the following design principles were employed:

Modular Design. The use of a modular framework allows the user to implement only the services that they require for their application, thereby maximising the operating capacity of the network.

Computation Over Transmission. The energy cost of computation as compared to radio transmission is approximately 1000 calculations to 1 bit of data transfer; however, this depends on the distance that the data must be transferred as transmission cost increases by the square of the distance. Thus, if it is possible to reduce the amount of data to be transmitted by increasing the number of calculations, then this is preferable.

Single-Way Methods. As mentioned above, the cost of data transmission is high in WSN systems. While there is an energy cost associated with each bit transmitted, there is also a cost associated with transmission overheads such as headers. It is therefore preferable to use single-way methods that require only one transmission as compared to a two or three-way method, which would require multiple transmissions. It is important to note that single-way methods are less secure than multiple transmission methods due to reduced validation and verification; however, with the focus on reducing energy consumption, this is a justifiable risk.

Integration and Re-use of Existing Mechanisms. Where there are existing mechanisms in place in the LEACH protocol it is unnecessary to re-create those mechanisms within the security protocols of SE-LEACH. For example, the proposed SE-LEACH protocol integrates key distribution functionality and the existing cluster head role, thereby making good use of the existing mechanism already present in LEACH. This existing mechanism in the LEACH protocol provides energy-use-levelling via role rotation within a cluster. This integration also allows the key management feature of SE-LEACH to take advantage of the self-organisation and self-healing features of LEACH.

3.4 Placement of Security Services

The network model used in WSNs is much simpler than the standard 4 layer TCPIP model or the more complex 7 layer OSI model. The 'WSN network model' can easily be represented as 3 layers:

Layer 1 - The Physical Link layer. This layer encompasses physical media access and serialisation of the data onto the physical medium, which may be 802.11 wireless, satellite, etc. The 'packetisation' and physical addressing of the data to be delivered is also handled at this layer. This layer is equivalent to OSI layers 1 and 2 (refer to Figure 1).

Layer 2 - The Network layer. This layer is concerned with the routing and logical addressing of data. The network routing protocol used, such as the LEACH or SPIN protocols, resides in this layer. This layer corresponds to layers 3-5 of the OSI model (refer to Figure 1).

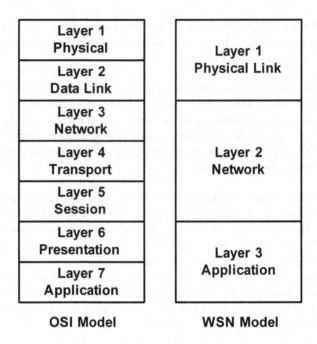

Fig. 1. A Comparison of the OSI and WSN Network Models

Layer 3 - The Application layer. This layer is concerned with general processing and generating transmission requests, and corresponds to layers 6 and 7 of the OSI model (refer to Figure 1).

Unlike the OSI or TCP/IP models found in standard network environments, there can be a great deal of interaction between the network layer and the application layer in the WSN model. This is especially so for routing protocols such as Directed Diffusion, that define interest statements and use query-based transfers. For this reason, it is necessary for the application to be written with a particular routing protocol in mind.

To protect the network from a range of attacks it is necessary to place the security services at the lowest possible position in the network stack, while maintaining the ability to port the protocol to various hardware platforms and transmission mediums. Subsequently, it is proposed that for the SE-LEACH protocol, the data confidentiality mechanism be placed between layer 1 and layer 2, with heavy interaction with layer 2 for key management etc.

3.5   Modules

The proposed SE-LEACH protocol is designed in a modular fashion to allow flexibility during deployment. Further, the security services are to be divided into the following major modules:

- Data Confidentiality;
- Key Management;

- Data Integrity; and
- Data Freshness.

Due to the interdependency between these modules, an implementation of the Key Management module is required by the Data Confidentiality, Data Integrity and Data Freshness modules.

Data Confidentiality. The integration of data confidentiality services requires two components; an encryption mechanism to obfuscate the data and a method for distributing a secret key between authorised nodes.

In order to meet the design principles outlined in section 3.3, the encryption mechanism is designed to be modular. This allows the use of any symmetric key algorithm, such as Rijndael or MISTY1, and both software and hardware implementations of these algorithms.

The encryption module relies on the key management module to provide the cryptographic key required to encrypt and decrypt messages.

Key Management. The proposed key management system for SE-LEACH uses a variation of the SEAMAN protocol put forward by Bonartz *et al.* [13], which defines a method for distributed key management within military, multi-cast, mobile, ad-hoc networks.

During the cluster formation phase of the LEACH protocol, a cluster head is elected which is responsible for aggregating all of the data for that cluster and forwarding it to the sink node. To ensure that the initialisation of the network is secure when using the SE-LEACH protocol, it is proposed that a preloaded encryption key be used. While not mandatory, its use removes a major attack vector.

It is also proposed that this cluster head node become the Key Distribution Centre ('KDC') for the cluster. The KDC/cluster head will generate a group key and forward it to all nodes in its cluster, including the sink node. In order to allow time for all nodes to switch to the new key, both the old key and new key are acceptable as decryption keys for a brief period (see Figure 2 reproduced from [13]). This key update process also allows for re-keying when a new cluster head is elected, or if a node fails. A node should only accept a new key from the current cluster head.

This module can be modified to use alternative key management strategies including the use of statically configured keys.

When a message is transmitted from one node to another, the source node will encrypt the message with the shared key. On receiving the encrypted message, the receiving node will decrypt the message with either the current key or, if the network is in a 'key update' phase, the previous key. A message transmitted from 'A' to 'B' would take the form $(Message)K_1$.

Data Integrity. Thus far, while the SE-LEACH protocol provides data confidentiality and protection from routing attacks, it provides no mechanism for data integrity. It is proposed that a Hashed Message Authentication Code ('HMAC')

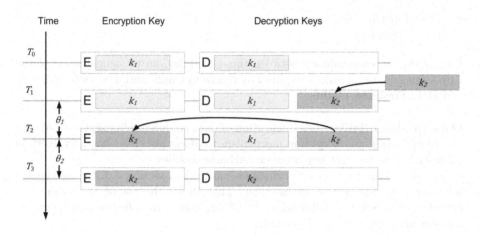

Fig. 2. Key Update Sequence

be transmitted along with the actual message so that the receiving node can validate the message. A message transmitted from 'A' to 'B' would take the form $(Message)K_1 + H(Message \oplus K_1)$. Upon receiving the transmission B would decrypt the message using K_1. B can then XOR the received message with K_1 and hash the result. If the received HMAC matches the calculated value, then the message is valid and has not been tampered with.

Data Freshness. The proposed SE-LEACH protocol can be extended to ensure data freshness. The message and HMAC could also contain a single use number or 'NONCE' to prevent message playback. This protocol uses a random number generated by the sender, which is appended to the message text. This combination is then hashed as part of the HMAC process. For example, $(Message + NONCE)K_1 + H((Message + NONCE) \oplus K_1)$. If the receiver sees two messages with the same NONCE then it determines that the message is being replayed and discards the message. To allow for matching of past NONCE values, the receiving node will need to store these values in memory. Due to variations in hardware capability and security level requirements, SE-LEACH permits the length of the NONCE and the number of past NONCE values to be configurable.

3.6   Critical Analysis

The primary purpose of the proposed SE-LEACH protocol is to highlight the ability to successfully integrate security services into an existing WSN routing protocol, in this case LEACH.

The modules defined in SE-LEACH provide a framework and a basic set of security services. The data confidentiality, key management, integrity and freshness mechanisms used in this protocol are designed to be selectable and replaceable based on the specific implementation requirements. Moreover, owing to the flexibility of the modular design, if further protection is required against advanced attacks, such as the SYBIL attack, an authentication service could easily be integrated.

4   Conclusion

This paper has presented an overview of the current state of WSN network and security technology. The research community's discourse on the possible attacks on these networks has provided a new array of malicious techniques that must be taken into account when designing a WSN security strategy. To combat these new attacks, techniques and security services have been developed; however, little there has been little investigation into the integration of these security services with the existing network protocols. An extension to the LEACH protocol, SE-LEACH, is proposed to demonstrate one method of implementing these security services, and overcome many of the security issues with current WSN protocols.

References

1. Walters, J.P., Liang, Z., Shi, W., Chaudhary, V.: 17. In: Wireless sensor network security: A survey. Auerbach Publications, CRC Press (2006)
2. Tilak, S., Abu-Ghazaleh, N.B., Heinzelman, W.: A taxonomy of wireless micro-sensor network models. SIGMOBILE Mob. Comput. Commun. Rev. 6, 28–36 (2002)
3. Akkaya, K., Younis, M.: A Survey on Routing Protocols for Wireless Sensor Networks 3, 325–349 (2005)
4. Heinzelman, W.R., Kulik, J., Balakrishnan, H.: Adaptive protocols for information dissemination in wireless sensor networks. In: MobiCom 1999: Proceedings of the 5th annual ACM/IEEE international conference on Mobile computing and networking, pp. 174–185. ACM Press, New York (1999)
5. Intanagonwiwat, C., Govindan, R., Estrin, D.: Directed diffusion: a scalable and robust communication paradigm for sensor networks. In: MobiCom 2000: Proceedings of the 6th annual international conference on Mobile computing and networking, pp. 56–67. ACM Press, New York (2000)
6. Heinzelman, W.R., Chandrakasan, A., Balakrishnan, H.: Energy-efficient communication protocol for wireless microsensor networks, pp. 3005–3014 (2000)
7. Wood, A.D., Stankovic, J.A.: Denial of service in sensor networks. Computer 35, 54–62 (2002)
8. Karlof, C., Wagner, D.: Secure routing in wireless sensor networks: attacks and countermeasures. In: IEEE International Workshop on Sensor Network Protocols and Applications, 2003, pp. 113–127 (2003)
9. Newsome, J., Shi, E., Song, D., Perrig, A.: The sybil attack in sensor networks: analysis & defenses, pp. 259–268 (2004)
10. Deng, J., Han, R., Mishra, S.: Countermeasures against traffic analysis attacks in wireless sensor networks. In: First International Conference on Security and Privacy for Emerging Areas in Communications Networks, 2005. SecureComm 2005, pp. 113–126 (2005)

11. Manjeshwar, A., Agrawal, D.P.: Teen: a routing protocol for enhanced efficiency in wireless sensor networks. In: Proceedings 15th International Parallel and Distributed Processing Symposium, pp. 2009–2015 (2001)
12. Manjeshwar, A., Agrawal, D.P.: Apteen: a hybrid protocol for efficient routing and comprehensive information retrieval in wireless sensor networks. In: Proceedings International Parallel and Distributed Processing Symposium, IPDPS 2002, Abstracts and CD-ROM, pp. 195–202 (2002)
13. Bongartz, G.T., Bachran, T., Tuset, P.: Seaman: A security-enabled anonymous manet protocol, NATO Research and Technology Organisation (2008)

Security in Tactical MANET Deployments

Stuart Stent

Macquarie University, Department of Computing, Faculty of Science
NSW 2109, Australia
stuart.stent@students.mq.edu.au
www.mq.edu.au

Abstract. Mobile Ad-hoc Networks ('MANET') are a developing technology for the transfer of data between moving groups of devices. Due to
the restrictions imposed by the operational requirements and hardware
limitations of MANETs, the implementation of data communications and
security for these networks presents several challenges, especially when
deployed as a 'tactical network'. This paper examines the unique requirements of MANETs in tactical environments, the routing protocols
proposed for use in such deployments and the possible attacks on these
networks. On examination of these requirements it was found that a
Source-Initiated On-Demand, multicast-capable, routing protocol is required in tactical deployments. Two routing protocols meeting these
requirements were examined and their security services and suitability for use in tactical MANETs were evaluated. The SEAMAN protocol was found to provide the best security implementation; however,
there are concerns about the overall performance and scalability of the
protocol. An extension to the Multicast Ad-hoc On-Demand Distance
Vector ('MAODV') protocol, called Tactical – Multicast Ad-hoc On-
Demand Distance Vector ('T-MAODV') is proposed. T-MAODV extends
MAODV through the integration of the security services necessary for
the tactical deployment of MANETs, such as forward and backward secrecy and data confidentiality, while taking into account their unique
operational requirements and hardware limitations.

Keywords: manet tactical security T-MAODV MAODV SEAMAN.

1   Introduction

The United States military's focus on leveraging advanced information dissemination techniques is driving research into the use of Mobile Ad-hoc Network
('MANET') technology to achieve its goal of Network-Centric Warfare ('NCW').
The primary goal of NCW is to have a more effective means of providing information to those who need it, when they need it, through the deployment of a
'tactical network', thereby delivering a tactical advantage. Tactical networks are
defined by Burbank *et al.* [1] as "*deployed networks supporting users and platforms within the tactical operation region*". The tactical advantages that may be
derived from the deployment of a MANET are not limited to military applications. Emergency services such as the police, search and rescue, and fire could

D. Ślęzak et al. (Eds.): FGCN/ACN 2009, CCIS 56, pp. 455–469, 2009.

all benefit from a secure information delivery system. Furthermore, while the requirements of a tactical MANET deployment differ from those of a non-tactical deployment, the techniques used may be transferable, though in a less restricted format.

2   MANET Architecture Considerations

2.1   Requirements and Limitations

A MANET is a self-configuring network made up of mobile computing devices which communicate over a broadcast medium, such as wireless or infrared transmissions. The operational context and hardware utilised in a MANET deployment can have a significant impact on the requirements and limitations placed on the network. The specific limitations of a MANET deployed in a tactical context are outlined below.

Rapid Topology Changes. The ability for nodes to change locations in a MANET deployment needs to be taken into account when developing network services. Frequent rapid changes of node location and therefore network topology, are especially evident at the 'Tactical Edge' of a network, which is defined as *"users and platforms within the tactical operation area"* [1].

Power Consumption. The power reserves of nodes within a MANET can vary dramatically from device to device. Nodes mounted on vehicles may be capable of operating at full power for an extended length of time. Nodes carried by individual personnel are likely to have very limited reserves, and therefore the management of the available power is critical to the continued availability of the network [2].

Low Bandwidth. The amount of bandwidth available within a MANET can vary based on the hardware used and the environment in which it is deployed. Ideally, protocols developed for use in MANETs should have low overheads for both network creation and maintenance [3].

Transmission Errors. The unreliable nature of wireless data transmissions requires the employment of mechanisms to ensure that data is received successfully and that the data is uncorrupted [4]. This is a major issue for tactical MANETs, as they are often deployed in environments that are not conducive to clear radio transmission, and therefore have higher transmission error rates.

Environmental. The environments in which a tactical MANET can be deployed cover every human-survivable location on earth. The wide range of possible temperatures, altitudes, terrains and particulate levels require MANET equipment to be robust and field maintainable [1].

Node Capabilities. The processing capability of MANET nodes needs to be standardised to allow any node to be a transmitter, a receiver or a router [5]. This requirement poses some interesting limitations on the hardware deployable in a MANET, as a node mounted on a vehicle can have no more processing power than a node carried by a single operative.

2.2   Routing Protocols

Several network routing protocols, designed based on various routing paradigms, have been developed for use in MANETs. Argyroudis *et al.* [6] define two broad classifications for MANET routing protocols. These two classifications are 'Table Driven' and 'Source-Initiated On-Demand'.

Table Driven. The Table-Driven or Proactive approach to network routing is ubiquitous in infrastructure-based networks, such as corporate networks or the internet. Each routing node within the network (in the case of MANETs, this is often every node) maintains a table detailing how to get to various destinations in the network. A Table-Driven network is said to be 'converged' when all links are stable and every node has an 'up-to-date' copy of the routing table. The scalability of Table-Driven protocols is limited due to the fact that each node must maintain an up-to-date table of routes to every node within the network. This can become a major issue in networks with a large number of nodes, due to increased number and frequency of updates that need to be transmitted.

Source-Initiated On-Demand. In the case of Source-Initiated On-Demand protocols, routes are only created when one node wants to send data to another node. One such method of creating a path is given in the AODV protocol [7]. The path that is created is kept alive as long as the two nodes need to communicate. This is achieved through the use of activity timeouts, whereby if no activity is sensed for a predetermined time, the path is removed from the routing tables. Some protocols use a 'keep-alive' mechanism to stop paths being marked inactive prematurely.

2.3   Tactical Network Routing Recommendations

The mobile nature of a MANET, by definition, requires network topology changes as nodes move in and out of range of each other. As noted in section 2.1, the topology changes in a tactical network can happen frequently. Moreover, the speed of mobile units can vary from 5 km/h to supersonic speeds (>1,238 km/h), requiring the ability for nodes to join and leave a network in a very short space of time [1]. The convergence time of Table-Driven protocols is likely to increase substantially as the size of the network expands (from a few seconds to minutes). Subsequently, it is not feasible to use a Table-Driven approach as the convergence time of these protocols, combined with the frequency of topology changes, would require them to be constantly converging. On the other hand, the ad-hoc route creation and low overheads of Source-Initiated On-Demand routing protocols make them ideal for a rapidly changing network environment such as a MANET. Due to the low overheads associated with the use of a Source-Initiated On-Demand protocol, the power and bandwidth requirements outlined in section 2.1 would also be met.

3   Operational and Security Requirements

The use of MANET technology in a tactical environment has several requirements and imposes various operational and security limitations.

3.1   Operational Requirements

Joining and Leaving the Network. As units divide and combine within an operational area, the secure merging and splitting of their communications channel is required [1]. Further, semi-stationary units such as 'Command and Control', as well as highly mobile support units such as 'Unmanned Aerial Vehicles', 'Close Air Support' or naval units require the ability to provide information to infantry units as they come into transmission range. The high frequency of network splits and merges found in MANETs deployed in tactical environments requires special consideration when selecting a routing protocol and security services such as key management. If a Proactive Table-Driven routing protocol is used, the routing tables of all nodes in the network would need to reconverge on every network split or merge. If, however, a Source-Initiated On-Demand protocol is used, only those paths that are severed or created as part of the network split or join are affected. Thus, due to the high frequency of these splits and merges, convergence overheads and the reconvergence time required by Table-Driven protocols, it is recommended that Source-Initiated On-Demand protocols be used in tactical MANETs.

Multicast Transmission. The hierarchical nature of military units, such as the United States Military's 'Platoon' to 'Company' relationship[1], makes the ability to transmit information to discrete groups of nodes a necessity [8]. The subscription of nodes to multicast groups allows for the transmission of data to only those nodes that require the information. This hierarchical transmission paradigm could also be extended to transmission segregation based on security clearance levels if required.

3.2   Security Requirements

Forward and Backward Secrecy. To ensure that data confidentiality is maintained, nodes that have left the network should not be able to decrypt any messages sent after they have left the network (forward secrecy). Similarly a node should not be able to decrypt any message sent before they joined the network

---

[1] A single Company is made up of 2-8 Platoons.

(backward secrecy) [9]. Providing forward and backward secrecy requires robust key management and key refresh protocols to ensure that keys are updated whenever a node joins or leaves the network, or when there is a network merge or split. Due to the high frequency of merge and split operations found in tactical MANET deployments, the task of synchronising the keys for all nodes on the network could cause a great deal of network activity.

Data Confidentiality. A malicious entity that can capture data transmitted by the nodes in the network should not be able read the contents of the transmission. This is especially important for key exchange protocols, where the secrecy of the transmitted data is paramount [9]. Due to the broadcast nature of the wireless transmissions used in MANETs, any device within the transmission range of the broadcasting node can receive a transmitted message. It is therefore imperative that all communications be encrypted with a sufficiently robust cipher. The selection of this cipher will depend on multiple factors, such as the processing power of the nodes, the bandwidth available and key management issues.

Data Integrity. Data integrity ensures that the data received is, in fact, the data that was transmitted, and that it hasn't been tampered with or corrupted [10]. A strong data integrity service is required even if a data confidentiality service is implemented, as it is theoretically possible to carry out a modification attack without any knowledge of the enciphered data.

Data Freshness. Data freshness ensures that the data received has not been received before. This is a common defence against replay attacks where a malicious entity replays an old captured message to disrupt or compromise the network [10]. This is particularly relevant in a tactical context where message content can often be repeated regularly over long periods, and variations are relied on to determine changes in situation. Examples include a 'guard post' transmitting an 'all clear' signal every hour, or, a unit's GPS co-ordinates.

Availability. The implementation of security services cannot adversely impact the lifespan or availability of the MANET in any way. This requires the management of energy reserves and the maintenance of network resilience [1].

Self-Organisation. To reduce administrative overhead and infrastructure requirements, the security protocols employed, like the routing protocols detailed above, need to be self-organising and self-healing [1].

Authentication. Authentication services provide reliable verification of the transmission source's identity. This is a vital component to various security services such as key exchange [10]. These requirements are present in many commercial and personal MANETs; however, the criticality of their implementation is several orders of magnitude higher in a tactical environment.

4   Attacks

4.1   Denial of Service

A Denial of Service ('DoS') attack, within the context of MANET routing protocols, is any attack which aims to reduce the availability of the network for legitimate users. There are multiple mechanisms that can be employed to carry out a DoS attack, including radio frequency jamming and network flooding [2].

4.2   Location Disclosure

Location disclosure attacks are the determination of a node's location via the use of signal detection equipment or traffic analysis techniques. The disclosure of a node's location while in a battlefield situation could have major tactical consequences [6]. This type of attack in itself will not adversely impact a network or its users; however, it can be used to help target weak sections of the MANET for other attacks.

4.3   Black Hole

A black hole attack refers to the injection of false replies to routing requests, which can be used to divert network traffic for the purpose of 'eavesdropping' on the data, or as part of a DoS attack by simply discarding the packets [6].

4.4   Replay

Replay attacks are the re-transmission of captured messages, which can be used by an attacker to disrupt or compromise a network [3]. This form of attack is typically a problem in systems where message contents are often repeated in a predictable manner.

4.5   Wormhole

A wormhole attack involves the tunnelling of captured data over a private link between two colluding nodes. The data can then be dropped, forwarded or modified at will by the malicious nodes [3]. This attack could be used to increase latency within the network by forcing data to take a non-optimal route, create a routing loop, or to modify or copy the data.

4.6   Blackmail

In protocols that use a 'revocation token' mechanism for the ejection of known malicious nodes, a 'blackmail' attacker could inject false tokens revoking legitimate nodes [6]. A successful blackmail attack could be used to isolate sections of the network or to take control of the network.

4.7   Route Table Poisoning

In Table-Driven protocols it is possible to advertise false routing information to other nodes. This attack can be used to segregate sections of the network or to reduce network performance by creating non-optimal routes or routing loops [6].

5   Multicast Routing Protocols

This paper has thus far determined that there are two key requirements for the selection of a routing protocol that is to be used in a tactical MANET deployment: (1) The protocol must support multicast transmissions; and (2) the protocol must provide strong security services while requiring minimal infrastructure. There are two protocols that meet the multicast and infrastructure requirements, and which have either been designed with security in mind or have secure extensions. These are the 'MAODV' and 'SEAMAN' protocols.

5.1   MAODV

A security enhanced version of the MAODV protocol has been proposed by Roy *et al.* [11], which utilises an authentication framework to provide protection against a range of attacks specific to both MAODV and multicast protocols in general.

Background and Architecture. The MAODV protocol is based on one of the most popular unicast Source-Initiated On-Demand routing protocols for use in MANETs, Ad-hoc On-Demand Distance Vector ('AODV') [7]. The AODV protocol defines a method in which a route between two hosts is only created when one host has a need to transmit data to the other. While AODV is a very lean protocol and handles route creation well, it defines no mechanism for multicast transmission; however, in a subsequent paper, Royer *et al.* [12] define an extension to AODV known as Multicast Ad-hoc On-Demand Distance Vector ('MAODV'). This extension outlines a technique for providing multicast transmission and group subscription. In order to support both unicast and multicast routing, each node within the MAODV network maintains two routing tables, one for unicast traffic and one for multicast traffic.

Unicast Routing. When node 'A' needs to communicate directly with node 'B', it broadcasts a route request ('RREQ') message, containing the address of node B. Any node with a current route to the destination node sends a route response ('RREP') back to the requesting node. Both nodes A and B, and all nodes along the path, update their routing table with information from the RREQ and RREP messages. Each route is given a lifetime for which it remains valid. If no traffic is seen matching that route within that lifetime the route is deleted.

Multicast Routing. If instead, node A wishes to communicate with a multicast group, it sends a RREQ containing the address of the multicast group. This RREQ can be sent as a unicast message to the 'group leader' if the node already has a valid route to the group leader. Alternatively the RREQ can be sent as broadcast message. In order to join the multicast group, the originating node simply sets the 'J' flag on the RREQ packet. As a joining node is likely to receive multiple routes to the group, it selects the one with the lowest hop-count and replies with a Multicast Activation ('MACT') message with the J flag set. This informs the group which route the node is going to use.

A node may revoke its status as a member of the group at any stage by sending a MACT message with the P flag set. If the node is not a leaf node it must continue to route messages for the group.

The group leader periodically broadcasts a 'group hello' message to the entire network, which contains the IP address of group, and other group information. Each node receiving this modified RREP message updates its routing table with information about the group. Member nodes also use this group hello to update their hop-count to the group leader.

If a node does not receive a group hello for a specified period, it assumes that there is a broken link and tries to find a new route to the group. If this attempt fails, the node assumes that the multicast group has been 'partitioned', and a new group leader is elected. After a partition event, if a node receives a group hello from a group leader of another partition, a repair process is initiated to rejoin the two partitions into one multicast tree.

Identified MAODV Attack Vectors. Roy *et al.* [11] identified a range of possible attacks against the MAODV protocol.

1. **False Route Attack.** On receiving a RREQ for a multicast group, a malicious node can generate a false RREP with a high sequence number, thus fooling the requesting node into selecting the false route. This type of attack can be used as part of a black hole or wormhole attack.
2. **Multiple MACT attack.** On receiving a RREP for a group a node normally selects only one route to the group to send a MACT message to. A malicious node may send MACT messages to multiple routes. This causes the group to add multiple unnecessary leaf nodes, thus causing excess resource consumption.
3. **Forced Partitioning.** An attacker may use the inbuilt maintenance mechanisms to 'partition' one segment of the multicast group. In this case, the 'prune' operation may be utilised by a malicious node that is masquerading as a legitimate tree node. The malicious node can send a MACT message with the 'P' flag set to nodes downstream of the impersonated node, thereby causing them to believe that the connection to the multicast group has been lost and effectively disrupting the network.
4. **Partition Capturing.** The forced partitioning attack above can be used as part of a two-stage attack. In stage one, a section of the multicast group is partitioned using a 'Forced Partitioning' attack. In stage two, a false RREP

message is sent (similar to the false route attack above), causing the partitioned network to initiate a repair process with the malicious node as the group leader.

5. **False Group Leader.** Another method for capturing a group is for a malicious node to generate false group hello messages. If the IP address of the malicious node is higher than the IP address of the current group leader, the malicious node will become the new leader.

6. **Dropping attacks.** A malicious node may also simply drop packets to stop partitions rejoining.

Authentication Framework. The MAODV authentication framework proposed by Roy *et al.* [11] was designed with three primary objectives in mind:

1. Only authorised nodes may participate in the network;
2. A node that is not a member of a multicast group should not be able to masquerade as a member node; and
3. A non-tree node should not be able to masquerade as a multicast tree node.

Each node in the network has both a public and private key, which are certified by the Certificate Authority ('CA'). This 'node certificate' binds the node's public key to the node's IP address. This certificate can then be used by other nodes to validate its identity. Once a node has joined a multicast group it is allocated a 'group membership certificate' which binds the node's public key and IP address to the IP address of the group. This enables other group members to verify that a node is also a group member. The allocation of certificates can be handled either offline or via out-of-band communication with the CA. The proposal by Roy *et al.* [11] assumes that each node has copy of the CA's public key and therefore certificates can be verified without the need to actually communicate with the CA. This satisfies the requirement to have no static infrastructure requirement.

Each node that makes up the multicast tree maintains a Pair-wise Shared Key ('PSK') with each of its neighbours. This PSK is used to validate all messages transmitted between nodes via the use of a Message Authentication Code ('MAC') signed with the PSK. While these mechanisms allow for secure communication between member nodes, these nodes are often separated by non-member tree nodes. A 'tree key' is disseminated to all tree nodes, which can then be used to verify that a node is a valid 'tree node'.

5.2 SEAMAN

Bongartz *et al.* [9] propose the Security-Enabled Anonymous MANET protocol ('SEAMAN') as a solution to providing security services for MANETs, which has been designed specifically for use in tactical applications. SEAMAN is based on a Proactive Table-Driven multicast routing protocol called WNet, developed by Bachran *et al.* [13]. The anonymous authentication mechanism is based on the pseudonym generation system MASK, proposed by Zhang *et al.* [14]. MASK uses a list of one-time 'pseudonyms' for every node that are pre-generated by a trusted authority. The SEAMAN key exchange protocol is based on the MIKE system developed by Aurisch *et al.* [15]. MIKE defines a completely decentralised key management system where the role of 'Key Manager' is handled by a node elected by the group, and keys are synchronised group-wide. The SEAMAN protocol differs from other MANET protocols in that it actively manages all traffic sent over the network, not only those used in the routing protocol. This allows the encryption and obfuscation of both user-generated and routing protocol traffic. Each frame that is sent over the network is encrypted and a hashed message authentication code ('HMAC') appended at the link layer. Every node along a message's path decodes the frame, increments the sequence number in the frame header and re-encrypts the frame. All frames are sent in broadcast mode which, in conjunction with the altering and re-encrypting of every frame makes it very difficult, if not impossible, to track the path of an individual message.

Detecting Foreign Nodes. The detection of foreign nodes in the SEAMAN protocol is accomplished through a series of checks when a node receives a frame. Firstly, the node checks to see if the frame is a SEAMAN frame. If the frame is a SEAMAN frame, the node tries to decrypt the message with one of the currently valid keys. If decryption is successful then the frame is either forwarded appropriately or processed if the node is the intended recipient. If the decryption fails then the frame is assumed to be from another SEAMAN network or a solo SEAMAN node and the authentication process is initiated.

Authentication. SEAMAN uses a two-stage authentication process which does not divulge the identity of the node at any stage. In Stage 1 the MASK challenge response handshake is undertaken, where the identity of both nodes is protected via the use of one-time pre-generated 'Perfect Pseudonyms' ('PP'). The outcome of a successful handshake is a key shared between the two nodes. This link can then be used to 'bridge' the two networks. In Stage 2, once a bridge is established, the foreign node transmits a 'Group Pseudonym' ('GP') which contains a copy of the group's Public Key to the challenging node. The challenging node can then verify the GP.

Key Management. The cryptographic key management system presented in SEAMAN uses a single Key Distribution Centre ('KDC') per network. The KDC is elected based on the node's ID, which is generated from the node's IP address. During the merging of networks, the node ID of each KDC is compared and the KDC with the lowest ID is elected as the KDC for the combined network. Due to the fact that key distribution in an ad-hoc network can take time, there is a period during which the current key and the previous key can both be used to decrypt messages.

5.3   Comparative Analysis: MAODV and SEAMAN

Both of the protocols detailed above have been designed with both Source-Initiated On-Demand routing and multicast transmission in mind, and therefore meet the basic networking requirements of tactical MANET deployment.

As seen in section 3.2 above, the security requirements for a tactical MANET deployment are very specific.

While the secure MAODV protocol proposed by Roy *et al.* [11] provides an authentication mechanism for routing information, there is no provision made for securing the routing protocol itself [9]. For MAODV to become viable for use in a tactical environment, a data integrity mechanism and some form of data confidentiality mechanism, providing both forward and backward secrecy, would need to be developed.

The SEAMAN protocol was designed with all of these security requirements in mind and seems to be a perfect fit for tactical MANET deployments. It does, however, use a Proactive Table-Driven routing protocol as its basis. The use of Table-Driven routing raises some concerns as to the performance characteristics of this protocol, especially when the system is expanded past the maximum of 50 nodes recommended in the protocol. This leaves the question of what happens when two platoons (approximately 50 nodes each) meet, unanswered.

6   Tactical – Multicast Ad-hoc On-Demand Distance Vector (T-MADOV)

As mentioned in section 5.1 above, while the extensions to MAODV provide some level of protection in the form of an authentication mechanism, there are still multiple security services that are not provided under this protocol, including encryption of non-routing data, forward/backward secrecy capability, data integrity checking and data freshness. In an effort to address these concerns, a set of extensions to the MAODV protocol are proposed, resulting in a new protocol, called Tactical – Multicast Ad-hoc On-Demand Distance Vector ('T-MOADV'). The security considerations and features of this proposed protocol are discussed below.

6.1   Unicast Data Confidentiality

Data transmitted over the base unicast network should only occur between nodes that have authenticated (see step 1 below) and agreed on a session key (see step 2 below).

1. **Authentication.** If node 'A' wishes to communicate with node 'B', it will send a packet containing its node certificate. Node B can then validate the certificate, and if valid, it will forward its own certificate to A.
2. **Agreement.** Once both nodes have authenticated each other, they must agree on a session key. This can be handled by a mechanism such as Diffie-Hellman or another key agreement protocol.
3. **Transmission.** After both nodes have been authenticated and a session key agreed on, the transmission of data can begin. All data should be encrypted with the session key. A message transmitted from 'A' to 'B' would take the form $(Message)K_{ab}$, where K_{ab} is the session key shared between nodes A and B.

6.2   Multicast Data Confidentiality and Key Management

The structure of multicast trees inherently provides a solid foundation on which to build ad-hoc security services. It is proposed that the multicast group leader take on the role of KDC for that multicast group. The distribution of the 'group key' is handled by the transmission of the periodic 'key update' message. This key update message should only be readable by current group members, and as such, should be encrypted with the current group key, K_g, along with the group leader's node certificate. The group key update message will take the form (Group Leader's Certificate | NewKey)K_{ab}.

Due to the propagation characteristics of these networks it is proposed that a mechanism similar to the MIKE key scheduling mechanism found in the SEA-MAN protocol be used. Therefore there should be a period where both the new key and the pervious key are valid (see Figure 1 reproduced from [9]).

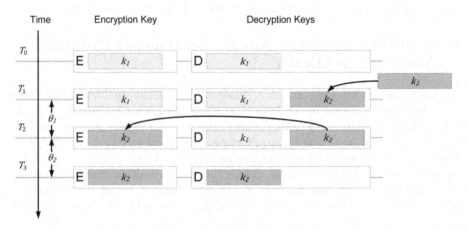

Fig. 1. Key Update Sequence

The key update process as shown in Figure 1 has 4 steps. An explanation of each step is given below.

1. **Time= T_0.** All nodes have group key K_1 for both encryption and decryption. The multicast group can be said to be in a converged state.
2. **Time= T_1.** At a predetermined interval, the group leader transmits a new key K_2 to all nodes. Each node then allows both keys K_1 and K_2 for the decryption of messages.
3. **Time= T_2.** After a predetermined time Θ_1, each node replaces their encryption key with K_2.
4. **Time= T_3.** After a predetermined time Θ_2, each node removes the decryption key K_1. At this point, all nodes will be using only K_2 for all decryption and encryption, and the network is again converged.

It order to provide both forward and backward secrecy, any multicast split, join or merge operation should require a new key update message be sent. All data sent within the multicast group should be encrypted with the multicast group key; however, to allow non-member nodes to continue forwarding data, the headers and footers should be protected by the confidentiality mechanisms of the underlying unicast protocol.

6.3   Data Integrity

To ensure end-to-end Data Integrity, all messages should contain a hashed message authentication code ('HMAC') signed with the originating node's private key. This allows the received node to validate that the message was in fact sent by the purported sender, and that the original message is intact. A unicast message transmitted from 'A' to 'B' would take the form $(Message)K_{ab} + H(Message)Priv_a$. A multicast message transmitted from node 'A' to 'Group B' would take the form $(Message)K_G + H(Message)Priv_a$.

6.4   Data Freshness

The proposed T-MAODV protocol ensures Data Freshness via the use of a single use number or 'NONCE' to prevent message playback. Each unicast message has a random number generated by the sender which is appended to the message text. This combination is then hashed as part of the HMAC process. For example $(Message + NONCE)K_{AB} + H((Message + NONCE) \oplus Pub_A)$. If the receiver sees two messages with the same NONCE from the same source, then it determines that the message is being replayed and discards the message. To allow for the matching of past NONCE values, the receiving node will need to store these values in memory. To reduce data transmission overheads, the Data Freshness mechanism is only implemented at the unicast level, and multicast messages rely upon the checking at the unicast level as well as the multicast message's sequence number.

6.5   Critical Analysis

The new proposal outlined above extends the secure MAODV protocol outlined in section 5.1 above, through the addition of data integrity, unicast data confidentiality, multicast data confidentiality and key management. There is some overlap of services between the unicast mechanisms and the multicast mechanisms; however, they provide different services to different groups. For example, while a message from node A to group B will have two HMACs and be encrypted twice, they all serve a purpose. The unicast HMAC and encryption provide data integrity from node A to B, and secrecy from any entities external to the network. The multicast HMAC and encryption provide data integrity between node A and group B, and secrecy from any entity that is not part of the multicast group.

A comparison of the various MANET protocols outlined in this paper, including the proposed T-MAODV protocol, and their ability to provide the services required by a tactical MANET deployment is shown in table 1 below.

Table 1. Summary of Requirements

Requirement	SEAMAN	MAODV	T-MAODV
On Demand Routing	N	Y	Y
Multicast transmission	Y	Y	Y
Forward Secrecy	Y	N	Y
Backward Secrecy	Y	N	Y
Authentication	Y	Y	Y
Data Confidentiality	Y	N	Y
Data Integrity	Y	N	Y
Data Freshness	Y	N	Y

7   Summary

This paper has presented an overview of the current state of MANET network-ing and security techniques. The unique operational characteristics of MANETs deployed in a tactical environment have been analysed to enable the formulation of a set of requirements. These requirements have been used to determine which network routing protocols are suitable for use in tactical MANETs. Two proto-cols that met these requirements, SEAMAN and MAODV, have been analysed.

Of the protocols examined, the SEAMAN protocol provides the most com-plete security implementation for tactical MANET deployments; however, the scalability characteristics of this Table-Driven protocol are undetermined and require further analysis.

While the MAODV protocol meets the requirements of a tactical deployment from a network architecture perspective, it fails to provide the necessary security services. In order to meet the security requirements of a tactical deployment an extension to the MAODV protocol, called Tactical – Multicast Ad-hoc On-Demand Distance Vector ('T-MAODV'), was proposed.

T-MAODV provides the security services necessary for a tactical MANET deployment, which are not currently present in MAODV, such as forward and backward secrecy, data confidentiality and data integrity. While both SEAMAN and T-MAODV provide the requisite security services, the underlying Source-Initiated On-Demand network architecture of T-MAODV makes it more suitable to tactical deployments than SEAMAN, as T-MAODV meets the full set of requirements defined for a tactical MANET.

References

1. Burbank, J.L., Chimento, P.F., Haberman, B.K., Kasch, W.T.: Key challenges of military tactical networking and the elusive promise of manet technology. IEEE Communications Magazine 44, 39–45 (2006)
2. Deng, H., Li, W., Agrawal, D.P.: Routing security in wireless ad hoc networks. IEEE Communications Magazine 40, 70–75 (2002)
3. Kannhavong, B., Nakayama, H., Nemoto, Y., Kato, N., Jamalipour, A.: A survey of routing attacks in mobile ad hoc networks. IEEE Wireless Communications 14, 85–91 (2007)

4. Kaya, T., Lin, G., Noubir, G., Yilmaz, A.: Secure multicast groups on ad hoc networks. In: SASN 2003: Proceedings of the 1st ACM workshop on Security of ad hoc and sensor networks, pp. 94–102. ACM, New York (2003)
5. Al-Hunaity, M.F., Najim, S.A., El-Emary, I.M.: A comparative study between various protocols of manet networks. American Journal of Applied Sciences 4, 663–666 (2007)
6. Argyroudis, P.G., O'Mahony, D.: Secure routing for mobile ad hoc networks. IEEE Communications Surveys & Tutorials 7, 2–21 (2005)
7. Perkins, C., Royer, E.: Ad-hoc on-demand distance vector routing, pp. 90–100 (1999)
8. Sass, P.: Communications networks for the force xxi digitized battlefield. Mob. Netw. Appl. 4, 139–155 (1999)
9. Bongartz, G.T., Bachran, T., Tuset, P.: Seaman: A security-enabled anonymous manet protocol, NATO Research and Technology Organisation (2008)
10. Papadimitratos, P., Haas, Z.J.: Secure data transmission in mobile ad hoc networks. In: WiSe 2003: Proceedings of the 2nd ACM workshop on Wireless security, pp. 41–50. ACM, New York (2003)
11. Roy, S., Addada, V.G., Setia, S., Jajodia, S.: Securing MAODV: Attacks and countermeasures. In: Proc. 2nd IEEE Int'l. Conf. SECON. IEEE, Los Alamitos (2005)
12. Royer, E.M., Perkins, C.E.: Multicast operation of the ad-hoc on-demand distance vector routing protocol. In: MobiCom 1999: Proceedings of the 5th annual ACM/IEEE international conference on Mobile computing and networking, pp. 207–218. ACM, New York (1999)
13. Bachran, T., Bongartz, H.H.-J., Tiderko, A.: A framework for multicast and quality based forwarding in manets. Communications and Computer Networks, 120–125 (2005)
14. Zhang, Y., Liu, W., Lou, W., Fang, Y.: Mask: anonymous on-demand routing in mobile ad hoc networks. IEEE Transactions on Wireless Communications 5, 2376–2385 (2006)
15. Aurisch, T.: Optimization techniques for military multicast key management. In: Military Communications Conference, 2005. MILCOM 2005, vol. 4, pp. 2570–2576. IEEE, Los Alamitos (2005)

VLSI Architecture for the Fuzzy Fingerprint Vault with Automatic Alignment Module

Sung Jin Lim[1], Seung-Hoon Chae[1], Deasung Moon[2], Yongwha Chung[3], Namil Lee[4], and Sung Bum Pan[1,5,*]

[1] Dept. of Information and Communication Engineering, Chosun Univ., 375, Seosuk-dong Dong-gu, Gwangju, 501-759, Korea
[2] Human Recognition Technology Team, ETRI, 138 Gajeongno,Yuseong-[1]gu, Daejeon, 305-700, Korea
[3] Dept. of Computer and Information Science, Korea Univ., Sejong Campus, Yeongi-gun, Chungnam, 339-700, Korea
[4] Askey Co., San 16-1, Deongmyeong-dong Yuseong-gu, Daejeon, 305-320, Korea
[5] Dept. of Control, Instrumentation, and Robot Engineering, Chosun Univ., 375, Seosuk-dong Dong-gu, Gwangju, 501-759, Korea
{gigasj83,ssuguly}@gmail.com, daesung@etri.re.kr,
ychungy@korea.ac.kr, sbpan@chosun.ac.kr

Abstract. Biometrics-based user authentication has several advantages over the traditional password-based systems for standalone authentication applications. However, security of biometric data is particularly important as the compromise of the data will be permanent. In this paper, we explain the fuzzy fingerprint vault system combining geometric hashing-based fingerprint authentication and fuzzy vault to protect fingerprint templates. Also, we propose the FPGA-based fuzzy fingerprint vault system for real-time processing. Based on the experimental results, we confirmed that the proposed system takes 0.11(0.51) second with 29 real minutiae and 100(400) chaff minutiae.

Keywords: Biometrics, Fuzzy fingerprint vault, FPGA.

1 Introduction

In current society, by developing communication medium such as Internet, we can easily approach the information anytime, anywhere. The need of the security system that can protect individual information has increased. The verified users have gained access to secure information systems, buildings, or equipment via multiple Personal Identification Numbers(PINs), passwords, smart cards, and so on. However, these security methods have critical weakness that can be lost, stolen, or forgotten. The authentication system based on biometric information offers greater security and convenience than the traditional methods of personal verification. The biometrics such as fingerprint, iris, and voice has been received considerable attentions, which refers the personal biological or behavioral characteristics used for verification or

---

* Corresponding author.

D. Ślęzak et al. (Eds.): FGCN/ACN 2009, CCIS 56, pp. 470–476, 2009.
© Springer-Verlag Berlin Heidelberg 2009

identification. Since biometrics cannot be lost or forgotten like passwords, biometrics has the potential to offer higher security and more convenience for the users.

The fingerprint is chosen as the biometrics for verification in this paper. Owing to their uniqueness and immutability, fingerprints are today the most widely used biometric features. However, some problems with fingerprint authentication systems can arise when the fingerprint information has been compromised. Thus, if the biometric data are compromised, the user may quickly run out of the biometric data to be used for authentication and cannot re-enroll[1-4]. Recently, there is an increasing trend of using the idea of the fuzzy vault to protect fingerprint templates. The fuzzy fingerprint vault protects the fingerprint information by enrolling real minutiae with a large number of chaff minutiae in the database. However, there is the problem that in applying the fuzzy vault to fingerprint, such as alignment problem about the reference point absence of fingerprint. To solve the problem given above, some results have been reported by using geometric hashing for the fuzzy fingerprint vault system[5-6]. The geometric hashing technique aligns all minutiae of fingerprint with the reference point and generates the hash table in enrollment processing. The verification processing is performed by using enrolled hash table[7-8].

This paper proposes the hardware architecture for the fuzzy fingerprint vault based on the geometric hashing. The proposed architecture consists of the software and hardware module. The hardware module consists of matching module, verification module and each memory of enrollment hash table and verification hash table. The matching module compares all transformed minutiae of enrollment hash table per one transformed minutiae of verification hash table in sequence. The verification module computes similarity on the result of matching module. As a experimental result, we confirmed that it takes 0.11 second in 100 chaff minutiae and 0.51 second in 400 chaff minutiae when real minutiae is 29.

The organization of the paper is as follows. Section 2 introduces fuzzy fingerprint vault based on the geometric hashing. Section 3 explains the hardware architecture for fuzzy fingerprint vault based on the geometric hashing, Section 4 shows the experimental results and Section 5 concludes.

2   Fuzzy Fingerprint Vault Based on the Geometric Hashing

Juels and Sudan proposed a scheme for crypto-biometric system called fuzzy vault. This is method which can protect the user's important secret key and biometric information using fuzzy concept. Clancy et al. proposed a fuzzy fingerprint vault based on the fuzzy vault of Juels and Sudan[9-10]. Using multiple minutiae location sets per finger, they first find the canonical positions of minutia, and use these as the elements of the set A. They added the maximum number of chaff minutiae to find R that locks. However, their system inherently assumes that fingerprints are pre-aligned. This is not a realistic assumption for fingerprint-based authentication schemes.

The architecture of the fuzzy fingerprint vault system of Chung et al. [5] consists of two processes: enrollment and verification processes as shown in Fig. 1. Enrollment process consists of minutiae information acquisition stage, enrollment hash table generation stage again. In minutiae information acquisition stage, minutiae information includes real minutiae of a user and chaff minutiae generated randomly. It is challenging to perform fingerprint verification with the protected template added by chaff minutiae. And then, Chung et al. applies modified geometric hashing. According to the geometric characteristics of the minutiae information, a table, called an enrollment hash table, is generated. Let $m_i = (x_i, y_i, \theta_i, t_i)$ represent a minutia and $L = \{m_i \mid 1 \leq i \leq r\}$ be a locking set including the real and chaff minutiae. In L, the real and chaff minutiae can be represented by $G = \{m_i \mid 1 \leq i \leq n\}$ and $C = \{m_i \mid n+1 \leq i \leq r\}$, respectively. Note that, the enrollment hash table is generated from L. In the enrollment hash table generation stage, an enrollment table is generated in such a way that no alignment is needed in the verification process for unlocking vault by using the geometric hashing technique. That is, alignment is pre-performed in the enrollment table generation stage.

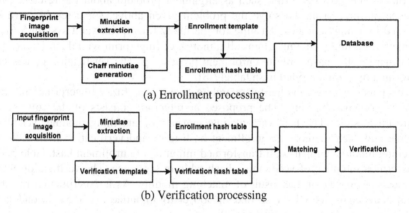

(a) Enrollment processing

(b) Verification processing

Fig. 1. Fuzzy fingerprint vault system

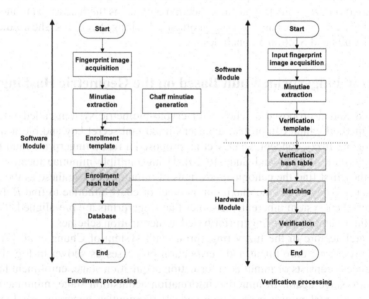

Fig. 2. Flow diagram of the fuzzy fingerprint vault system

After the enrollment process, the verification process to separate the chaff minutiae(C) from the real minutiae(G) in the enrollment minutiae table should be performed. In the verification process, minutiae information(unlocking set U) of a verification user is obtained and a table, called verification table, is generated according to the geometric characteristic of the minutiae. Then, the verification table is compared with the enrollment minutiae table, and the subset of real minutiae is finally selected. Note that, the verification table generation stage is performed in the same way as in the enrollment process. In comparing the enrollment and verification minutiae tables, the transformed minutiae pairs with the same coordinate, the same angle, and the same type are determined. The minutiae pairs having the maximum number and the same basis are selected as the subset of real minutiae(G). Also, any additional alignment process is not needed because pre-alignment with each minutia is executed in the enrollment and verification minutiae table generation stages[11-12].

3 Hardware Architecture for the Fuzzy Fingerprint Vault

To implement a fuzzy fingerprint vault system, we perform the software and hardware module of the fuzzy fingerprint vault system. Fig. 2 shows the software and hardware role assignment of the enrollment and verification processes. The enrollment processing consist of fingerprint image acquisition, minutiae extraction, enrollment template added chaff minutiae, and enrollment hash table. The Enrollment processing is handled by software. The verification processing consists of input fingerprint image acquisition, minutiae extraction, verification template, verification hash table and matching. In verification processing except for matching stage, other stages are handled by software. Note that the matching and verification stage is operated by hardware. The proposed hardware module consists of each memory of enrollment hash table and verification hash table, matching module, and verification module as shown in Fig. 3. In enrollment and verification hash table, the transformed minutiae made by software are stored. The transformed minutiae in each hash table is 32bit that coordinate(x-axis 11bit, y-axis 11bit), angle(9bit), and type(1bit) of the minutiae.

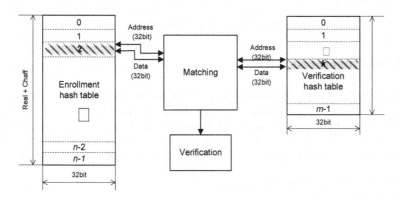

Fig. 3. The proposed hardware module architecture

Firstly, each transformed minutiae of enrollment and verification hash table are inputted in matching module. Two transformed minutiae are compared by matching signal. The similarity of the two hash tables is calculated after all transformed minutiae in enrollment hash table is inputted and compared in sequence. The next transformed minutiae of verification hash table is inputted in matching module. Above process is recursively performed. The verification module generates the candidate list on the basis of similarity calculated in matching module.

For example, when the number of transformed minutiae of enrollment hash table is n and we assume that kth transformed minutiae of verification hash table is inputted in matching module. The transformed minutiae from the 0th to the n-1th in enrollment hash table is sequentially inputted in matching module. The inputted transformed minutiae of enrollment hash table is compared kth transformed minutiae of verification hash table. After all transformed minutiae in enrollment hash table are compared, the k+1th transformed minutiae of verification hash table is inputted. The above process performed repeatedly, and the last m-1th transformed minutiae of verification hash table is compared. After the comparison of two hash table finished, the similarity is calculated by using the corresponding transformed minutiae. And then, similarity is stored in verification module.

Fig. 4 shows the architecture of matching and verification module of proposed hardware module. The enrollment hash table's data and those of verification hash table in Fig. 3, is Enroll_data and Verify_data consisted of x, y, θ, $type$, respectively.

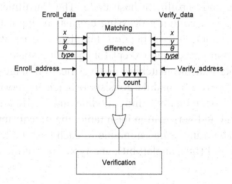

Fig. 4. The proposed architecture of matching and verification module

4   Experimental Results

In this paper, the size of fingerprint image in experiment of proposed architecture is 248 ×249. The number of the minutiae was maximum 90, minimum 16. We selected the number of the chaff minutiae as 100, 200 and 400, and they were generated by using a random number generator. The software modules were performed by using C language in Visual C++ 6.0. The PC performed the software module consisted of the following.

- Intel Core2 Duo E7300 2.67GHz
- SDRAM 2.00GB
- Windows Vista 32bit Operation System

To evaluate the execution performance of the fuzzy fingerprint vault system, we used the development board which Spartan 3E starter board. The hardware modules were design by using VHDL language. The VHDL was synthesized after functional simulation, and the synthesized results were used for validating the function blocks and evaluating the cost, complexity, and performance of the hardware. After eliminating hardware executable portions from the software-based minutiae extraction program, we added a module for hardware integration. Once the validations of each hardware and software were completed, an integrated simulation was conducted. The simulation of hardware module is performed in Modelsim XE 6.0.

Fig. 5 shows simulation result of the proposed matching module of hardware. It carried out an experiment on the fuzzy fingerprint vault system with 29 real minutiae and 200 chaff minutiae. As shown in Fig. 5, the red wave represents the Verify's x and y in Fig. 3 and blue wave also represents the Enroll's x and y.

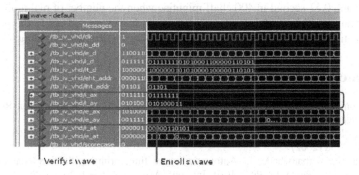

Fig. 5. The simulation result of the proposed matching module

Table 1 shows the required resources when we performed the proposed hardware module of fuzzy fingerprint vault in Spartan 3E starter board. As shown in table, this board operated at 50MHz and required the slice about 20%, and the 4 input LUTs about 19%.

Table 1. Required resources on Xilinx Spartan 3E FPGA(500K gates)

Frequency	50MHz
Number of Slices	962 out of 4,656 (20%)
Number of Slices Flip Flops	61 out of 9,312 (1%)
Total Number 4 Input LUTs	1,828 out of 9,312 (19%)

To evaluate the performance of the hardware module of the fuzzy fingerprint vault, we measured the execution time according to the number of chaff minutiae as 100, 200, and 400. When the number of real minutiae is 29, it takes 0.11 second in 100 chaff minutiae and 0.51 second in 400 chaff minutiae as shown in Table 2. It is possible to perform the fuzzy fingerprint vault system using the proposed hardware architecture in real-time.

Table 2. Required execution time(sec, Real minutiae 29)

	Chaff 100	Chaff 200	Chaff 400
Proposed hardware architecture	0.11	0.26	0.51

5 Conclusions

The user authentication based on the fingerprint provides the convenience and strong security. However serious problem can arise when fingerprint information has been compromised or leaked out. This paper proposed the hardware architecture of fuzzy fingerprint vault based on geometric hashing. Based on the experimental results, the execution time of the proposed hardware architecture takes 0.11 second in 100 chaff minutiae and 0.51 second in 400 chaff minutiae when the number of real minutiae is 29. In the future, we are studying way to perform in hardware and apply the polynomial reconstruction in the fuzzy fingerprint vault based on the geometric hashing.

References

1. Maltoni, D., Maio, D., Jain, A.K., Prabhakar, S.: Handbook of Fingerprint Recognition. Springer, Heidelberg (2003)
2. Bolle, R., Connell, J., Ratha, N.: Biometric perils and patches. Pattern Recognition 35, 2727–2738 (2002)
3. Yang, S., Verbauwhede, I.: Automatic secure fingerprint verification system based on fuzzy vault scheme. In: Proc. IEEE Int conf. Acoustics Speech, Signal Processing, vol. 5, pp. 609–612 (2005)
4. Uludag, U., Jain, A.: Securing fingerprint template: Fuzzy vault with helper data. In: Conf. on Computer Vision and Pattern Recognition Workshop, pp. 163–172 (2006)
5. Chung, Y., Moon, D., Lee, S., Jung, S., Kim, T., Ahn, D.: Automatic alignment of fingerprint features for fuzzy fingerprint vault. In: Feng, D., Lin, D., Yung, M. (eds.) CISC 2005. LNCS, vol. 3822, pp. 358–369. Springer, Heidelberg (2005)
6. Lee, S., Moon, D., Jung, S., Chung, Y.: Protecting secret keys with fuzzy fingerprint vault based on a 3D geometric hash table. In: Beliczynski, B., Dzielinski, A., Iwanowski, M., Ribeiro, B. (eds.) ICANNGA 2007. LNCS, vol. 4432, pp. 432–439. Springer, Heidelberg (2007)
7. Wolfson, H., Rigoutsos, I.: Geometric hashing: an overview. IEEE Computational Science and Engineering 4, 10–21 (1997)
8. Chung, Y., Choi, S., Prasanna, V.: Parallel object recognition on an FPGA-based configurable computing platform. In: 4th IEEE International Workshop on CAMP, pp. 143–152 (1997)
9. Juels, A., Sudan, M.: A fuzzy vault scheme. In: IEEE International Symposium on Information Theory, p. 408 (2002)
10. Clancy, T., Kiyavash, N., Lin, D.: Secure smartcard-based fingerprint authentication. In: ACM SIGMM Multim., Biom. Met. & App., pp. 45–52 (2003)
11. Uludag, U., Pankanti, S., Jain, A.K.: Fuzzy vault for fingerprints. In: Kanade, T., Jain, A., Ratha, N.K. (eds.) AVBPA 2005. LNCS, vol. 3546, pp. 310–319. Springer, Heidelberg (2005)
12. Moon, D., Chung, Y., Pan, S., Moon, K., Chung, K.: An efficient selective encryption of fingerprint images for embedded processors. ETRI Journal 28(4), 444–452 (2006)

A Study on the Korean Banknote Recognition Using RGB and UV Information

Seung-Hoon Chae[1], Jong Kwang Kim[2], and Sung Bum Pan[1,3,*]

[1] Dept. of Information and Communication Engineering, Chosun Univ., 375, Seosuk-dong, Dong-gu, Gwangju, 501-759, Korea
[2] Mechatronics R&D 1Team, LG NSYS, 253-42, Kongduk-dong, Mapo-gu, Seoul, 121-719, Korea
[3] Dept. of Control, Instrumentation, and Robot Engineering, Chosun Univ., 375, Seosuk-dong, Dong-gu, Gwangju, 501-759, Korea
ssuguly@gmail.com, kjk0329@lgnsys.com, sbpan@chosun.ac.kr

Abstract. Since the utilization of finance self-service is getting increment, bank and financial institutions has provided various services using automatic banking systems. For better efficiency of utilization of automatic banking system, banknote recognition, performing banknote classification and counterfeit detection, is getting more important. This paper used color and UV information of bankonte for banknote recognition. We have improved the accuracy of banknote classification by classify the candidate of the kind of banknote and then applying size information of the banknote. Counterfeit detection is performed to comparing UV information of reference and input image after banknote classification. Our experimental results show that the performance of banknote classification and counterfeit detection are 99.1% and 98.3%.

Keywords: Automatic banking system, Banknote recognition, Banknote classification, Counterfeit detection.

1 Introduction

Automatic banking systems that have been extensively used to have a banknote classifier that was designed to recognize and classify kinds of the banknote, a cash collection system that screens the pollution load of banknotes, a cash recognizer that was designed to recognize the kind of banknote designated and exclude other kinds, and an automatic teller machine with cash dispenser. The needs for an automatic banknote classification system encouraged many researchers to develop a robust and reliable technique. As the distribution of high-performance color copiers or color scanners have also become widespread along with technologies to counterfeit banknotes are getting more elaborate, a serious problem involving counterfeit banknotes has arisen[1-3]. Therefore, banknote classification should improve their capability to discriminate these illegally-counterfeit banknotes.

---

* Corresponding author.

D. Ślęzak et al. (Eds.): FGCN/ACN 2009, CCIS 56, pp. 477–484, 2009.
© Springer-Verlag Berlin Heidelberg 2009

The existing banknote recognition methods mainly involve image processing and neural network techniques[4]. Symmetrical masks have been used in Vila *et al.* for considering specific signs in a banknote[5]. Using the method, the summation of non-masked pixel values in each banknote is computed and fed to a neural network. In other methods, initially the edges of patterns on a banknote are recognized. In this approach, the image of a banknote is vertically divided into a number of equal small parts. Then the number of pixels associated to edges detected in each part are counted and fed to a three layer back propagation neural network for recognition[6]. Also, Zhang *et al* using the Hidden Markov Model(HMM)[7].

This paper used colors and UV information of banknotes for banknote recognition. We classified kinds of banknotes using color information of banknotes, and improved confidence using additional size information. Then, we performed counterfeit detection by comparing reference UV information and input UV information using a classified kind of bank note. As a experimental result, we confirmed that the 99.1% and 98.3% are performances of banknote classification and counterfeit detection.

The organization of the paper is as follows. Section 2 explains information of the banknote. Section 3 introduces proposed banknote recognition, Section 4 shows the experimental results and Section 5 concludes.

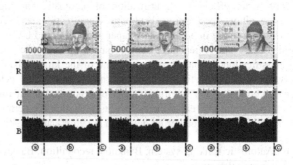

Fig. 1. The color distribution of banknotes

2   Information of Banknote

2.1   RGB and Size Information

The color is used by people for distinguishing different kinds of banknotes. However, most existing methods classified kinds of banknotes using gray information of banknotes. On the other hand, we used color information of banknotes. The colors look different according to RGB distribution. That is, banknotes have different RGB color distributions according to kinds of banknotes. However, dominant color doesn't exist in the whole area of banknote.

Fig. 1 is the result of vertical projection of RGB color for banknotes. As shown in Fig. 1, there are areas in which RGB distributions are similar in ⓐ, ⓒ ranges. Colors of the range can be noises when extracting dominant color. Consequently, we used only ⓑ ranges which differences of color distributions are more obvious. Also, for faster processing of colored images with more data than gray images, we used only part of the image.

The sizes of the banknote aren't the clear information because of tears, wears and other damage of banknotes. However, each kind of banknote has its own particular size. So the size of banknote is useful information that can supplement banknote classification using color information. Korean banknote, used in experiment, has its own size and color as shown Table 1[8].

Table 1. Size and color of Korean banknote

Kinds of banknotes	Size(mm)	Dominant color
₩10,000	148 X 68	Green
₩5,000	142 X 68	Yellow
₩1,000	136 X 68	Blue

Since the images of banknotes are received at high-speed for real-time banknote classification, the image may have low quality as shown in Fig. 2(a). There are some cases that colors of banknotes are not properly obtained. The pollutants on banknotes may cause the RGB distribution to be distorted. Therefore, we added banknote classification that used size information after banknote classification using color information. To obtain the size of banknote, the banknote area was separated from the background area in Fig. 2(b), and the length of the banknote was calculated.

(a) Color image of banknote   (b) Size image of banknote

Fig. 2. The banknote image obtained by sensor

Fig. 3 presents the mean values of brightness of RGB images using differences between R and G, R and B, and G and B. Fig. 3 presents that mean values of R, G, and B have different distributions according to kinds of banknotes. This paper differentiated the kinds of banknotes using mean values of brightness of R, G and B images.

The banknotes can be inserted in four different directions as seen in Fig. 4. However, information on mean values of brightness and size of banknotes proposed in this

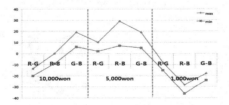

Fig. 3. RGB rate of each kind of banknotes

Fig. 4. Four different directions for inserting a banknote

paper is not affected by the direction of insertion. As it also uses sums and mean values, real-time classification is possible.

2.2 UV Information

All the banknotes that have been distributed in Korea have many counterfeit prevention systems such as minute characters, fluorescent inks, holograms and watermarks. However, as the images of banknotes that are rapidly input for real-time treatment are small and have low quality, minute characters, hologram and watermarks are difficult to apply in an automated system. However, fluorescent ink that luminance when banknotes are exposed to UV light, can be applied on a wider and more rapid basis than other counterfeit prevention systems. So, this study proposed a way to discriminate counterfeit or real banknotes by receiving reflected images of banknotes after they are exposed to UV light. Fig. 5 shows an example of the banknote exposed to UV light.

Fig. 5. The banknote image obtained by UV light

Counterfeit or real banknotes can be discriminated through the use of fluorescent ink obtained after they are exposed to UV light. As fluorescent ink is not distributed all over the note, only fluorescent areas, where technology of fluorescent ink is applied, are used for classification. Thus, when part of the note images is used, quick discrimination is possible thanks to reduced amount of calculation. The area of the notes used for this study is presented in Fig. 6(a). Fig. 6(b) presented UV information obtained through sensor as binary image. It isn't easy to obtain a clear image due to high speed of image scan. However, counterfeit banknote doesn't obtain UV information because fluorescent pattern doesn't embed in banknotes.

(a) Area of banknotes used for experiment   (b) Images obtained by UV sensor

Fig. 6. Banknote area used for experiment and image obtained by UV sensor

This paper differentiates counterfeit banknotes from real banknotes using their reflected images after the banknotes are exposed to UV light and calculates similarity between the reference and the reflected images. The reference images are ten images obtained after banknotes are exposed to UV light. Note that, for rapid counterfeit detection, this paper used only an operator of simple sum and remainder instead of a complex pattern recognition system.

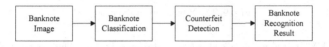

Fig. 7. The flow chart of the proposed method

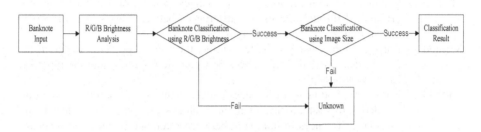

Fig. 8. Stage of banknote classification

3 Proposed Banknote Recognition

This paper used size, color and UV information of the banknote to recognition. Fig. 7 shows the flow chart of the proposed banknote recognition method. First, banknote classification is performed, and counterfeit detection is performed using the result of classification.

We differentiated the kinds of the banknote using mean values of brightness of R, G, and B, followed by additional classification using the size of banknotes to reduce errors of classification. Fig. 8 presents a flow chart of the proposed banknote classification method.

If the banknote is input, the RGB images of color areas are extracted from banknote. The mean value of brightness is calculated and then the kind of banknote is separated from different value of R and G, R and B, B and G as shown in Fig. 3. The results separated from banknote measure the image size of banknote and the banknote is finally confirmed the kind of banknote. If the differences of size of reference image and input image are more than reference range, the image isn't banknote. We called the case 'unknown'. We performed counterfeit detection using reference UV information of classified kind of banknote.

As shown in Fig. 9, the counterfeit detection method we used utilizes the UV information of reference image. The counterfeit detection is carried out, comparing the UV information both input and reference image. We tested the four methods

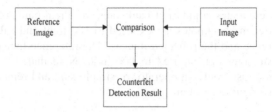

Fig. 9. The flow chart of the proposed

comparing UV information of input and reference image. The comparative methods used in the experiment are presented as follows:

Method 1.   For the method using total sum of images, counterfeit banknotes are discriminated through the use of differences between sums of entire pixels and sum of pixels of input images.

Method 2.   For the method using complete frame, the sum of pixels in different images is used after the differences between the reference and the input images are obtained.

Method 3.   For the method using differences between sums of block units, images are divided into 3×4 blocks, then three blocks are randomly selected and through differences in total sum between reference images and other images, the banknotes are discriminated.

Method 4.   For the method that uses block unit frames, images are divided into 3×4 blocks, then three blocks are randomly selected and through differences in total sum between the reference images and those discriminated, the banknotes can be discriminated.

4   Experimental Results

For the experiment of this paper, Korean banknote is used as samples. We made a banknote input machine using two image sensors and two image transmission sensors and obtained a total of 360 sample images with three denominations (10,000 won-bill, 5,000 won-bill, and 1,000 won-bill) in four different directions three times. Fig. 10 shows the banknote scanner we designed for the experiment.

When banknotes are judged as wrong as a result, they are defined as failures and when they are out of the standard brightness values of R, G and B and sizes, they are defined as defected.

Fig. 10. Implemented banknote scanner

Table 2. Banknote classification results

	10,000	5,000	1,000	Total
Success	119	118	120	357
Error	0	0	0	0
Unknown	1	2	0	3
Accuracy(%)	99.1	98.3	100.0	99.1

Table 2 presents the results of banknote classification by the proposed method. It was found that experimental results are showed about performance of 99% in every kind of banknotes.

Table 3. Counterfeit detection results

	Accuracy(%)	
	Real banknote	Counterfeit banknote
Method 1	80.7	100.0
Method 2	98.0	100.0
Method 3	98.3	100.0
Method 4	98.3	100.0

Table 3 shows that the accuracy of the proposed counterfeit detection system. As a result of the experiment, Method 2, Method 3, and Method 4 showed almost 99% of exactness (more than 98%). And when all of the four methods are used for discrimination experiment, they showed 100% exactness.

5 Conclusions

This paper proposed an algorithm for real-time banknote classification using information on colors, sizes and UV of banknotes. The proposed algorithm used only part of the banknotes for real-time classification, a simple expression and a conditional expression. We differentiated the denominations of banknote using mean values of brightness of R, G, and B, followed by additional classification using the size of banknotes to reduce errors of classification. The counterfeit detection method used images obtained from image sensors after the banknotes were exposed to UV light for detection. Note that the proposed method used an operator of addition and subtraction rather than complex pattern recognition. Common fluorescent ink shows fluorescent patterns in G image when UV light is illuminated. However, when images of banknotes are input at high-speed for real-time experiment, the images have low quality. Therefore, we haven't used complex pattern recognition and performed counterfeit detection by comparing reference UV information and input UV information. As a experimental result, the accuracy of proposed banknote classification method had 99.1%. Then, we found that they showed 100% of exactness for counterfeit banknotes and 98.3% of exactness for real banknotes.

In the future, we are going to experiment performance using banknotes with different status and conduct research on banknote classification from different countries such as USD and JPY.

References

1. Sun, B., Li, J.: The recognition of new and old banknotes based on SVM. In: Proc. Intelligent Information Technology Application, vol. 2, pp. 95–98 (2008)
2. Sun, B., Li, J.: Recognition for the banknotes grade based on CPN. In: Proc. Computer Science and Software Engineering, pp. 90–93 (2008)
3. Kong, F., Ma, J., Liu, J.: Paper currency recognition using Gaussian mixture models based on structural risk minimization. In: Proc. Machine Learning and Cybernetics, pp. 3213–3217 (2006)
4. Takeda, F., Nishikage, T.: Multiple kinds of paper currency recognition using neural network and application for Euro currency. In: Proc. International Joint Conference on Neural Networks, vol. 2, pp. 143–147 (2000)
5. Vila, A., Ferrer, N., Mantecon, J., Breton, D., Garcia, J.F.: Development of a fast and non-destructive procedure original and fake euro notes. Analytica Chimica Acta 559, 257–263 (2006)
6. Zhang, E.H., Jiang, B., Duan, J.H., Bian, Z.Z.: Research on paper currency recognition by neural networks. In: Proc. The Second International Conference Machine Learning and Cybernetics, pp. 2193–2197 (2003)
7. Hassanpour, H., Farahabadi, P.M.: Using hidden markov models for paper currency recognition. Expert Systems with Applications 36(6), 10105–10111 (2009)
8. Korea Minting & Security Printing Corporation, http://www.komsco.com/

Performance of a Forwarding Layer for Mesh Network

Woonkang Heo, Mina Lee, Chohee Kim, and Minseok Oh

Department of Electronic Engineering, Kyonggi University
San 94-6 Yiui-dong, Yeongtong-gu, Suwon-shi, Gyeonggi-do, Korea
her777@hanmail.net, mina7928@naver.com, chciel@hanmail.net,
msoh@kgu.ac.kr

Abstract. In this paper[1], we introduce our experience with implementation of an ad hoc network. The routing algorithm uses in-band traffic to distribute the routing information instead of providing a separate routing protocol. A 4 hop straight line topology ad hoc network is established for measuring the throughput in terms of hops. The experimental results show that the throughput reduces exponentially approximately by 60% for every hop increment. The delay seems to increase linearly for every hop increment. We have also compared the throughput and delay when the routing protocol is applied with those when it is not, to see how much the routing protocol affects the performance for one hop link connection. We have found that the routing protocol indeed consumes network resources such that the throughput reduces by 6.45% and the delay by 95.8%. The cause of the performance degradation for this specific routing protocol has been analyzed.

Keywords: Mobile Ad Hoc Network, Wireless Mesh Network, Routing Protocol.

1 Introduction

A mobile ad hoc network enables the nodes to communicate with others without help of a fixed infrastructure. The mobile nodes have a higher degree of freedom in participating in or leaving a wireless network than the ones in a wired network. Generally in a centralized fixed infrastructure network, the nodes are connected hierarchically and function passively, which means that the packet delivery relies on a center node. The mobile ad hoc networks have been expanding their application areas the last few years mainly thanks to flexibility of the network topology and its easiness of the fast deployment. Ad hoc networks can exist either independently of or in connection with an infrastructure which provides access to the Internet. Recently ad hoc networks interworking with an infrastructure have been studied to broaden its applications, such as a ubiquitous sensor network.

The ad hoc network is connected to the outer world through one or more gateways. The gateway performs a packet routing functions between the ad hoc network and the Internet. It is not an easy task to establish and maintain paths between nodes within a

---

[1] This paper includes an updated test result following the article published in [1].

D. Ślęzak et al. (Eds.): FGCN/ACN 2009, CCIS 56, pp. 485–492, 2009.
© Springer-Verlag Berlin Heidelberg 2009

mobile ad hoc network because the mobility and power consumption of nodes, and the link quality between nodes as well affect the decision criteria for routing. The mobility of nodes changes the topology of the network. This demands that every node broadcasts regularly its existence to update the routing information. The routing protocols used for fixed networks such as RIP (routing information protocol) [2] or OSPF (open shortest path first) [3] allow routers to exchange their routing table, which consumes too much transmission bandwidth. Moreover, they lack in adjusting the routing information fast enough for the mobile environment. These shortcomings make those protocols unsuitable for mobile environments. The IETF (Internet Engineering Task Force) have proposed several routing protocols for mobile networks.

The mobile ad hoc routing protocols can be categorized largely into three types: table-driven or proactive routing protocols, on-demand or reactive routing protocols, and hybrid routing protocols which are combinations of the two [4][5]. The table-driven routing protocols broadcast the routing information periodically or whenever the network topology changes, to maintain the up-to-date routing table in the routers. They include DSDV (Destination Sequenced Distance Vector) [6], and CGSR (Clusterhead Gateway Switching Routing) [7]. In the table-driven routing protocols, the nodes always maintain the most recent routing information so that a packet can be delivered with limited delay, but periodic broadcasting of routing information uses up too much scarce transmission bandwidth in the mobile environment.

The on-demand routing protocols reduce the excessive overhead by searching a route to the destination immediately before a packet is transmitted when it is not available. They include AODV (Ad Hoc On-demand Distance Vector) [8] and DSR (Dynamic Source Routing) [9]. Due to the delay in the initial route search process, many on-demand routing protocols have been proposed to minimize the initial route search delay.

In this experiment we have applied a publically available ad hoc network routing protocol package called FLAME (Forwarding Layer for Meshing) [10]. We present some results from the experiment. Chapter 2 briefs the operation of FLAME, Chapter 3 describes the application procedure and test results, and finally Chapter 4 concludes the paper.

2   Forwarding Layer for Meshing

Forwarding Layer for Meshing (FLAME) is a protocol layer designed for wireless networks in which the area covered by the network is larger than the coverage area of individual devices, developed by Wireless and Mobile Communications (WMC) [10]. FLAME provides an intermediate layer between the network layer (e.g., IPv4/IPv6) and the link (MAC) layer, providing L2 meshing. Both network layer and MAC layer can be used unchanged: To the network layer FLAME appears as a normal Ethernet-type MAC layer and the underlying MAC layer will see it as just another type of network layer.

FLAME runs as an intermediate layer between network and MAC layer as shown in Fig. 1, so it will intercept transmission requests from the network layer, and use the destination link address, to determine how and where to send the request over the MAC layer. This destination link address may be a unicast, multicast or broadcast address.

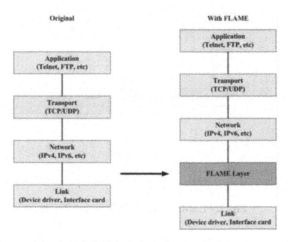

Fig. 1. FLAME in the TCP/IP protocol suite

If the destination address is unicast, FLAME will determine a next hop, and send the request to that next hop. The FLAME layer in the next hop will repeat this procedure, and the data is retransmitted until it arrives at its final destination. If the destination address is nonunicast, FLAME will broadcast the data. It has a built-in broadcast dampening mechanism ensuring that data is forwarded only once by each device.

FLAME does not have or need any knowledge of the contents of the network layer payload; its forwarding mechanism is entirely based on MAC addresses. Therefore FLAME can be used under any type of network layer that can communicate over Ethernet and WLAN devices, including IPv4 and IPv6.

FLAME uses a forwarding mechanism based on in-band information exchange: Extra data, in the form of a FLAME header is added in between Ethernet header and network layer payload. The header data is used by all FLAME layers that receive the data to build and maintain a forwarding table. This extra header costs some additional bandwidth and diminishes the maximum payload size as seen by the network layer, but also saves bandwidth because no separate communication protocol is required to exchange forwarding information.

The heart of the FLAME layer is a forwarding table that is used to find a next hop for a packet that has to be forwarded to a certain destination. This table is also used for broadcast dampening, i.e., to drop packets that have already been seen before.

Whenever a packet is received and accepted by the FLAME layer, FLAME will create/refresh the forwarding table entry for the original sender (OrigSrc) of the packet, registering the hop from which the packet was received (EthSrc) as the next hop to use for sending a packet to the original sender, as well as the sequence number (SeqNo) in the message. A forwarding entry has a limited lifetime (currently 2 minutes) if is not refreshed. If this limit is exceeded the entry is removed

When the FLAME layer receives data to transmit from the network layer, it will construct a packet with a FLAME header as shown in Fig. 2. This FLAME packet will then be given to the FLAME packet transmitter.

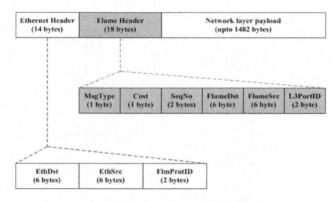

Fig. 2. FLAME in the TCP/IP protocol suite

When a FLAME packet is received from the underlying MAC layer, first a check will be done on the SeqNo, using the forwarding table: If the packet has a SeqNo that is lower than or equal to the SeqNo in an earlier received packet from OrigSrc, then the packet will be dropped.

If the packet is accepted, FLAME will register the newly received SeqNo for this OrigSrc in its forwarding table. It will also register from which hop (EthSrc) the message from OrigSrc was received, in order to use it as next hop for future transmissions to OrigSrc. Then it can increment the Cost field (hop count is used currently) in the FLAME header.

3 Implementation of Ad Hoc Network

After installing FLAME module on 4 Linux-based PCs, we modified both WLAN and Ethernet drivers for L2 frames to be delivered to the FLAME layer before reaching the network layer. The Linux kernel used is 2.6.18-1.2798.fc6, the WLAN and Ethernet device drivers are Atheros madwifi 0.9.3.3 and Realtek 8139 0.9.27, respectively.

Among 4 PCs, one functions as a MPP (mesh portal point), 2 of them serve as MPs (mesh points), and one of them serves as an MAP (mesh access point). A station (STA) is able to establish a connection only to the MAP and the MAP is connected to the MPP via MPs or directly, depending on the relative distances between mesh nodes

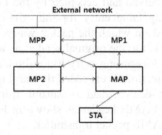

Fig. 3. Ad hoc network topology

for the station to communicate with a server outside of the network as shown Fig. 3. The channel used for the ad hoc network itself is set differently from the one between the MAP and the STA to allow a STA to connect through the MAP. To reduce the WLAN device's radio transmission range, we inserted attenuators of configuration at each mesh node. Table 1 shows the interface name, mode used, channel used, and ESSID of mesh nodes and the STA.

Table 1. Interface configuration of nodes

node	interface	configurations
MPP	ath0	ad hoc mode, ch6, essid: MeshNet
	eth1	promiscous enabled
MP1, MP2	ath0	ad hoc mode, ch6, essid: MeshNet
MAP	ath0	ad hoc mode, ch6, essid: MeshNet
	ath1	infrastructure mode, ch1 (autoconfigured) essid: Client
STA	Windows Vista	

By adjusting the relative distances, we can set up a 4-hop ad hoc network. Table 2 shows the MAC address information of each node.

Table 2. The MAC address information of each node

node	MAC address
GW	ethernet: xxxxxxxx752e
MPP	eth1: xxxxxxxxf3f5 ath0(adhoc): xxxxxxxxfac5
MP1	ath0(adhoc): xxxxxxxx011d
MP2	ath0(adhoc): xxxxxxxx028a
MAP	ath0(adhoc): xxxxxxxxa537 ath1(ap): xxxxxxxx027b
STA	wlan: xxxxxxxx2b6e

Table 3 only lists the forwarding table entries in each node necessary for forwarding the frames when a connection STA-MP2-MP1-MPP-GW is made. In the table, the destination indicates the destination node's MAC address and the next-hop indicates the next hop's MAC address to reach the destination. For example, the entries of the

Table 3. Forwarding tables of nodes

node	destination	next hop
MPP (fac5)	xxxxxxxx752e xxxxxxxx2b6e	xxxxxxxx752e xxxxxxxx028a
MP1	xxxxxxxx752e xxxxxxxx2b6e	xxxxxxxx028a xxxxxxxxa537
MP2	xxxxxxxx752e xxxxxxxx2b6e	xxxxxxxxfac5 xxxxxxxx011d
MAP (a537)	xxxxxxxx752e xxxxxxxx2b6e	xxxxxxxx011d xxxxxxxx2b6e

MAP show that when a frame is sent by the MAP to the STA, the next hop becomes the destination (xxxxxxxx2b6e) because they are one hop apart. On the other hand, when the MAP sends a frame to the GW (xxxxxxxx752e), the next hop must be MP2 (xxxxxxxx011d) as shown in Table 2.

A performance measuring tool called *iperf* has been used to measure the data rate between nodes for 1 minute with the TCP window size set to 16 kbytes.

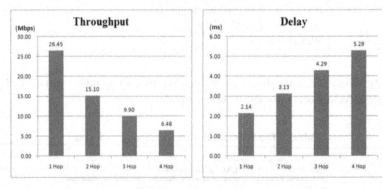

Fig. 4. Throughput and delay for various numbers of hops with FLAME applied

Fig. 4 shows that the throughput between nodes starting from 1 hop apart to 4 hops apart. It is so natural to observe that the throughput decreases as the number of hops between a source and a destination increases. The experimental results show that the throughput reduces exponentially approximately by 60% for every hop increment. The delay seems to increase linearly for every hop increment. The degradation seems to be caused by frequent routing update to maintain the forwarding table as fresh as possible.

We have also compared the throughput and delay when the routing protocol is applied with those when it is not, to see how much the routing protocol affects the performance for one hop link connection (since more than one hop connection always requires a routing protocol). We have found that the routing protocol indeed consumes network resources such that the throughput reduces by 6.45% and the delay by 95.8%.

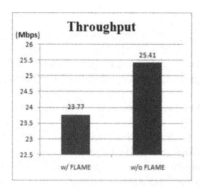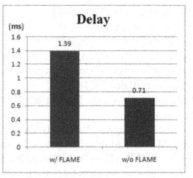

Fig. 5. Throughput and delay with FLAME and without FLAME

FLAME does not seem to degrade the throughput performance a great deal, but it has caused the delay to be almost doubled. It is speculated that the additional processes of attaching and detaching the FLAME header and looking up for the forwarding entry may cause delay, but since most of the information for routing remains unchanged (because it is a simple two-station network) during the experiment period, the transmission rate is not affected a great deal as seen in Fig. 5.

4 Conclusions

We have implemented an ad hoc network by inserting a routing protocol between layer 2 and layer 3. A 4 hop ad hoc network has been formed in a linear fashion to measure the throughput variation with respect to the hop distance. The throughput and delay deteriorate exponentially and linearly, respectively, as the number of hops increases. It can be speculated that the throughput reduces because the more hops a route has the more interference it experience, which results in a lower transmission rate. Each node en route will add more delay as frames pass through. We also formed a one-hop network (consisting of only two stations) to see how much negatively the routing protocol affects on those performance measurements. When the routing protocol is applied, the throughput has decreased slightly (only by 4.2% and, however, the delay has almost doubled. We can see from this result that the negligible throughput degradation is due to the static network topology of a simple two-node network and the delay can be explained by the same reason as the first experiment.

Acknowledgments. This work was supported by the "GRRC" Project of Gyeonggi Provincial Government.

References

1. Heo, W., Lee, M., Oh, M.: On Implementation of an Ad Hoc Network. In: Proceedings of the 8th KIIT Summer Conference (June 2009)
2. Hedrick, C.: Routing Information Protocol (RIP). IETF RFC 1058 (June 1988)

3. Open Shortest Path First (OSPF),
   http://www.cisco.com/en/US/docs/internetworking/technology/
   handbook/OSPF.html
4. Ghosh, J., Philip, S.J., Qiao, C.: Performance Analysis of Routing Protocols for Mobile Ad-hoc Networks, Technical Reports, Dept. of Computer Science and Engineering, University of Buffalo (2004)
5. Akyildiza, I.F., Wangb, X., Wangb, W.: Wireless mesh networks: a survey. Elsevier, Amsterdam (2005)
6. Perkins, C., Bhagwat, P.: Highly Dynamic Destination-Sequenced Distance-Vector Routing (DSDV) for Mobile Computers. In: ACM Sigcomm 1994 (1994)
7. Hollerung, T.D.: The Cluster-Based Routing Protocol, project group Mobile Ad-Hoc Networks Based on Wireless LAN winter semester 2003/2004
8. Perkins, C., Belding-Royer, E., Das, S.: Ad hoc On-Demand Distance Vector (AODV) Routing, IETF RFC 3561 (July 2003)
9. Johnson, D.B., Maltz, D.A., Broch, J.: DSR: The Dynamic Source Routing Protocol for Multi-Hop Wireless Ad Hoc Networks. In: Ad Hoc Networking, pp. 139–172. Addison-Wesley, Reading (2001)
10. FLAME, Forwarding Layer for Meshing (March 2006), http://www.ti-wmc.nl

Design and Performance Analysis of Automatic Wireless Routing Mechanism for the Effective Formation of IMR (Integrated Meter Reading) Network

Moonsuk Choi, Seongho Ju, Yonghun Lim, and Jong-mock Baek

KEPRI(Korea Electric Power Research Institute),
Munji-dong, Yusung-gu, Daejeon, 305-380, Republic of Korea
{cms96,shju1052,adsac,baekjmo}@kepco.co.kr

Abstract. To secure the communicaton reliability of an integrated meter reading network consisting of BPL and RF networks, the communication route may be changed between both networks automatically when the communication environment changes. This paper not only designed the automatic wireless routing mechanism to create the wireless meter reading terminal route and communicate with the BPL terminal next to it but also verified the communication performance of the developed mechanism via a verification test. Such verification test revealed a meter reading success rate that was 11% higher than the existing BPL-based integrated meter reading system which is not adopted automatic wireless routing mechanism.

Keywords: IMR (Integrated Meter Reading), BPL (Broadband over Power Line), Automatic wireless routing.

1 Introduction

Recently, automatic meter reading(AMR) technology has been studied for the remote acquisition of the meter belonging to each customer via a communication network; efforts of building the AMR system are being made by every energy supplier considering the increasing demand these days [1]. Note, however, that each energy supplier has built its own AMR system. Such has resulted in redundant investment in construction of the AMR infrastructure and further national loss in the end. Moreover, every supplier differs in terms of the system interoperability; hence the difficulty in securing interoperability between AMR systems.

In dealing with these obstacles, research on the integrated meter reading (IMR) technology for meter reading by integrating electricity, gas, and water meter reading data is the current trend. KEPCO (Korea Electric Power Corporation) developed an IMR system consisting of BPL and RF networks to collect electricity, gas, and water meter reading data remotely and subsequently established a consortium with Seoul City Gas Company and Waterworks of the Seoul Metropolitan Government in 2007 to build the test bed against 100 households in Mok-dong, Seoul and verify the IMR system operability and communication reliability [2].

D. Ślęzak et al. (Eds.): FGCN/ACN 2009, CCIS 56, pp. 493–500, 2009.
© Springer-Verlag Berlin Heidelberg 2009

The one-year operation result revealed that the meter reading success rate improved from the gas and water AMR system consisting of a wireless communication network only. Aside from the long time required and considerable costs incurred in construction of the communication network, however, the meter reading success rate also dropped in the poor wireless communication environment. Moreover, the initially constructed wireless communication route was unavailable for communication due to the change in the wire communication environments such as noise and attenuation level. Whenever this situation occurred, the operator was obliged to visit the site to check the wireless communication environment and change the RF communication route manually; thus requiring time and manpower.

This paper aimed at rendering stability to the IMR system performance regardless of any change in the wireless communication environment. For this purpose, it proposed the automatic wireless routing mechanism (AWRM) capable of automatically building an efficient network by searching the optimum communication channel to the everchanging communication environment to change the route; these are all designed to solve the aforementioned issues. The rest of this paper is organized as follows: Chapter 2 describes the IMR system architecture; Chapter 3 presents the AWRM design and implementation; Chapter 4 proposes the developed system and verification test result; Finally, Chapter 5 presents the conclusion.

2   Overview of the BPL-Based IMR System

This chapter describes the overall composition of the BPL-based IMR system and function of each equipment for better understanding of AWRM.

The most efficient and economical communication method for building the AMR communication network through low voltage grid below any pole transformer is the BPL method. To use the BPL technology via gas or water meter reading data communication, however, power line must be laid from electricity meter to the gas and water meter. The BPL technology may also cause explosion when surge current is induced at a gas meter; thus making the use of the technology more difficult. Consequently, this research used BPL for communication between the pole transformer and the electricity meter to construct the IMR communication network but utilized RF communication within the frequency band of 42 MHz for stable communication between the electricity meter and gas and water meter.

The IMR system consists of the IMR server, FEP (Front End Processor), DCU (Data Concentration Unit), HCU (Home Concentration Unit), WMU (Wireless Metering Unit), and electricity/water/gas meter. Fig. 1 illustrates the entire structure of the IMR system.

- DCU: This not only controls the small-scale BPL networks interconnected around a transformer but also collects and controls the meter reading data.
- HCU: Collects the electricity, gas, and water meter reading data, acting as a communication gateway between energy suppliers (utility) and their customers
- WMU: Collects the reading data from gas or water meter and transmits them to the HCU module
- Meter: Reads and records the sum of energy consumed for a period

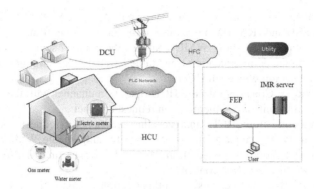

Fig. 1. IMR system diagram in KEPCO

3 Design and Implementation of AWRM

This chapter introduces the AWRM followed by the function design of the major components of the BPL-based IMR system such as WMU, HCU, and DCU together with the corresponding prototype production result.

3.1 Proposed Mechanism of the AWRM

Fig.2 illustrates the network topology of the IMR system proposed by this paper. As shown in Fig.2, WMU actively responds to the ever-changing wireless communication channel while automatically searching for the HCU that is available for the network and is routable.

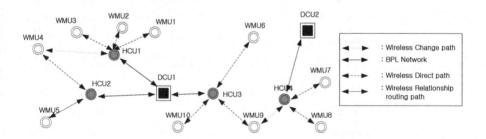

Fig. 2. Convergence network topology of the IMR system

The operation method of the AWRM used to secure the wire communication route for the smooth transmission of IMR data between communication HCU and WMU is described below in detail (refer to Fig.3).

    step 1. HCU initialization: Converts channel and keeps waiting for signal
    step 2. WMU initialization: Converts channel and keeps waiting for signal
    step 3. Channel scan: varies the operation frequency channel to start searching HCU

step 4. Channel status response: HCU transmits Receive Signal Strength Intensity (RSSI) and HCU ID in response to the channel scan frame

step 5. Route table creation: WMU analyzes the channel scan response frame to create the communication route table based on the communication channel information with each HCU

step 6. Routing: Converts into the HCU operation channel with the highest RSSI and transmits the authentication request channel

step 7. Authentication: HCU analyzes the certification request frame received from WMU, requests the IMR server to authenticate WMU, receives the authentication response frame from the server, and subsequently adds WMU in the WMU control list

step 8. Mode change: Receives the authentication response frame from HCU and subsequently converts the WMU mode from Initial Setup to metering mode

step 9. Rerouting: Executes steps 6~8 one by one in the order of priority if the set communication route is useless for normal communication

step 10. Channel re-scan: Repeats the route scan procedure from steps 3~8 if the communication route cannot be secured for all HCUs in the communication route table

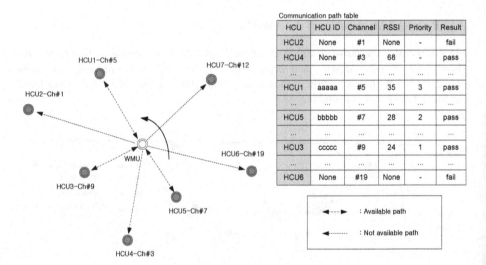

Fig. 3. Concept diagram of the auto path selection algorithm

3.2 Function Design of Communication Devices

This section describes the functions and requirements of communication terminals as necessary for realizing the AWRM.

3.2.1 Function Design of WMU
WMU has the following main functions:

- Gas and water meter reading data collection
- Periodic and real-time meter reading data transmission to HCU
- RF communication channel search and routing

WMU uses a battery as the main power source because it is unable to receive power from the outside. Thus, the power consumption of WMU must be minimized as the wireless network [3].

WMU consists of various modules such as MCU module, RF module, and serial communication interface to carry out the functions and meet the requirements above. The following are the detailed functions of each module:

a) MCU module
- Scans and selects the RF route for AWRM: The MCU module controls the RF module to subdivide the frequency band into 20 channels and collects and controls the communication channel information between HCU and RF module, varying the frequency channel in regular sequence. It also selects the optimum communication channel and requests for registration from the upstream system. Fig. 4 illustrates the flow chart of automatic wireless routing.

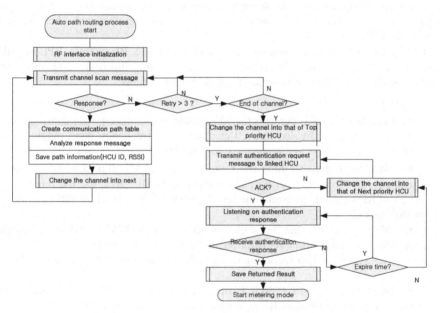

Fig. 4. Flow chart of automatic wireless routing (WMU)

- Supports Active/LPM (Low Power Mode) to minimize the current consumption of WMU (uses 12V DC power): Two methods were adopted to switch to Active mode from LPM mode. One uses external interrupt received from the RF module to activate the system, and the other uses timer interrupt for switchover.

b) RF module
- WMU uses the SPI (Serial Peripheral Interface) and interrupt input ports connected to the out port of RF module to receive the incoming data.
- The wireless communication antenna shall be of the external helical type to enhance wireless communication reliability.

3.2.2 Function Design of HCU

The following are the main functions of HCU:

- Meter reading schedule control (periodic and real-time meter reading)
- Electricity/gas/water meter reading data collection:
- Meter reading data conversion: Converts the gas and water meter reading data into the DLMS-based frame format as the meter reading standard of KEPCO
- IMR data transmission to DCU via BPL communication
- RF communication route scan assistance
- RF network control(authenticates, registers, and deletes the WMU linked below)

If separately installed, HCU may cause trouble not only with the power supply or damage the modules but also adversely affect information protection as a result of meter reading data handling. As such, this research made use of the internal space of an electricity meter to install a micromini HCU platform. The RF communication antenna was designed to be as small as possible so that it can be included in the wattmeter since installing it is also difficult; it may also be damaged when installed outside a wattmeter.

HCU consists of various modules such as MCU module, RF module, BPL module, and serial communication interface to carry out the functions and meet the requirements above. Each module has the following functions:

a) MCU module
- Like WMU, MCU controls the RF module to minimize power consumption.
- MCU will be divided into 20 channels with frequency band ranging from 424.7 to 424.95MHz for communication with WMU.
- MCU supports searching the route of every WMU linked to HCU. Fig. 5 illustrates the flow chart of wireless routing to WMU. Reading the intensity of received RF signal, it transmits the results (RSSI Value and HCU ID) in response to the transmitter.
- MCU monitors the network connection with WMU and provides the function of authentication, registration, and deletion to the server.
- MCU collects data according to the collection interval determined by HCU.
b) RF module
- HCU uses the SPI (Serial Peripheral Interface) and Interrupt Input ports connected to the out port of RF module to receive data from WMU.
- The wireless communication antenna shall be extremely small enough to be included in a wattmeter and shall be of the external helical type to improve wireless communication reliability.
c) BPL module
- HCU uses the UART (Universal Asynchronous Receiver Transmitter) port connected to the out port of BPL from the BPL module to receive data from DCU.
- The BPL module uses OFDM technology to modulate the meter reading and communication data from MCU to analog signals and demodulate BPL signals from the power line to digital ones.

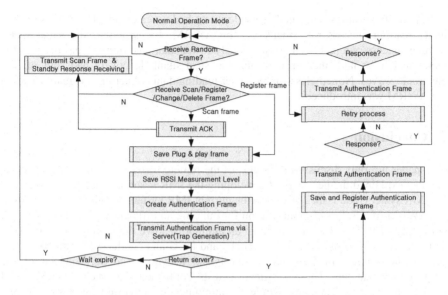

Fig. 5. Flow chart of automatic wireless routing (HCU)

4 Actual Verification Test Result

To verify the performance of the implemented AWRM, we built a test bed against 100 household in Ido-2dong, Jeju-si in January 2009, installed the required system, and measured the success rate of meter reading for a month. The wireless communication environment of the test bed in Jeju was similar to that of the Mok-dong district in Seoul -- which had been built in 2008 -- except that it adopted the AWRM.

In February 2008, the meter reading success rate of the Mok-dong test bed was 89% on the average for gas and water. Meanwhile, the rate was 99% on the average in Jeju in February 2009 for water. Fig.6 is the meter reading success rate of Jeju test bed.

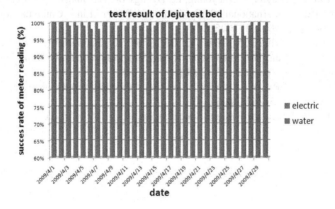

Fig. 6. Success rate of meter reading

The verification test executed at the Jeju test bed revealed an 11% increase in the meter reading success rate, thanks to the AWRM. In particular, the water meter reading success rate had been conspicuously lower than electricity or gas because the meter had been laid underground, and the steel manhole covers had shut off the electronic waves. Nonetheless, stable meter reading data collection was realized when the AWRM was introduced.

5 Conclusion

This paper not only discussed the status of the remote meter reading system in Korea but also explained the necessity of developing the IMR system, development status of the IMR system, and issues related to the current IMR system. In addition, it proposed the AWRM of wireless communication for building an efficient IMR system network consisting of BPL and RF networks in an attempt to solve the aforementioned issues and subsequently established WMU, HCU, and DCU and conducted verification tests on 100 households in Mok-dong, Jeju Island to verify the performance of the proposed mechanism. These verification tests confirmed that such AWRM could respond to the ever-changing wireless communication environment positively and facilitate the formation of more effective and stabler IMR communication network. Since the AWRM proposed by this paper can automatically search the route for building the IMR network through the installation of the IMR device (WMU), the installation process may be simplified with minimum installation period; thus eventually reducing the cost of system introduction innovatively.

As a next step, we are preparing a bigger verification test to verify the performance of the mechanism proposed by this paper and secure communication reliability. We are also planning to design the RF communication cell based on a large-scale verification test for economical integrated meter reading network formation.

References

1. Younghyun, K., Sungho, J., Taeyoung, L., Byungseok, P., Dukhwa, H.: PLC technology of KEPCO: IEEE International Symposium on Power Line Communications and Its Applications, pp. 390–393 (2005)
2. Moonsuk, C., Seongho, J., Yonghun, L.: Design of integrated meter reading system based on power-line communication: IEEE International Symposium on Power Line Communications and Its Applications, pp. 152–157 (2008)
3. Kemal, A., Mohamed, Y.: A survey on routing protocols for wireless sensor networks: Ad Hoc Networks 3, 325–349 (2005)
4. DLMS: Device Language Message Specification, http://www.dlms.com

An Improved Shock Graph-Based Edit Distance Approach Using an Adaptive Weighting Scheme

Solima Khanam[1], Seok Woo Jang[2], and Woojin Paik[1]

[1] Dept. of Computer Science, Konkuk University,
322, Danwol-Dong, Chungju-Si, Chungcheongbuk-do 380-701, Korea
{solima,wjpaik}@kku.ac.kr
[2] Dept. of Digital Media, Anyang University,
701-113, Anyang 5-dong, Manan-gu, Anyang-si, Gyeonggi-do, 430-714, Korea
swjang@anyang.ac.kr

Abstract. Matching and recognition of shape is one of the important issues in the field of image processing. In this paper, we focus on one of the skeleton based representations of shapes, called *shock based* representation. For the matching part, to find the best correspondence between two shapes, we will apply *edit cost* measure with taking into consideration the weights of the shock points of the skeleton. This reduces the number of sample points as well as the computational complexity and gives the correct match in the presence of some visual transformations. Here we consider the binary shape as a simple closed curve for unrooted graph. We will investigate the previous results of different skeleton based approaches to realize why the improvement on shock graph based approach is necessary to recognize and classify shapes efficiently.

Keywords: Medial axis, shock graph, edits distance, adaptive weight.

1 Introduction

In the content based image retrieval (CBIR), object can be matched and recognized from their shapes, colors and textures which typically provide complementary information about the respective objects. Shape is an important cue in CBIR in many application areas like hand written character recognition, prototype formation, and medical diagnosis.

In the shape based image retrieval, visual transformation of shape is an important issue for shape matching. It is desirable that small changes in the shape boundary should result in the small changes in the shape descriptor. If any large changes in the shape boundary of the object result in very slight changes in the shape descriptor, then the shape descriptor is considered not sensitive and we will get the robustness of result. The indexing of image databases by the shape of their embedded objects is complicated by the variety of visual transformations like as occlusion, articulation and viewpoint variation. So, the research related to shapes, derives the representation schemes of shape and similarity measures that are robust against the visual transformations. Another important issue is to reduce the computational complexity for matching and indexing of the shapes.

D. Ślęzak et al. (Eds.): FGCN/ACN 2009, CCIS 56, pp. 501–508, 2009.
© Springer-Verlag Berlin Heidelberg 2009

For the purpose of similarity measure, shape can be segmented relying on two approaches; one is *shape contour* and the other is *shape interiors*. The second one gives rise to the *skeleton based* approach which compares sketches directly against images [1]. Superiority of skeleton based approaches on contour based approaches [2] is that it contains useful information from the shapes; especially topological and structural information and also it shows robustness against visual transformations. *Medial axis* of a shape is one type of skeleton defined as the subset of the closure of a set of centers of maximal disks (bitangent) that fit within the shape [2], [3], [4]. *Shock graph* is an idea which arises from the concept of *medial axis* augmented with some additional dynamic properties. For those additional properties, shock graph can capture a shape that is complete and unique. It is said that shock graph is a richer descriptor than medial axis [2].

In this paper, we apply the shock graph based edit distance approach to represent and retrieve a shape uniquely. The edit distance for shape matching is robust to visual transformations like occlusion, articulation, view point variation, etc. We improve the edit cost by applying an adaptive *weighing* algorithm to reduce the sample points as well as the computational complexity. As a result, the edit distance needs not to depend on the dynamic programming to get the optimal solution. Moreover, the edit cost will take all the shock points (both end and branch) into consideration to get the correct match.

The rest of the paper is organized as follows. Section 2 contains the short description of shock based approach and then the previous works related to shock based approach. In section 3, we will discuss how a shape can be reconstructed from shock points [2, 6]. An adaptive weighing algorithm proposed for the selection of shock points to calculate edit distance for shape matching is described in section 4. Experiments are discussed in section 5. Finally, we draw conclusions in section 6.

2 Shock Graph Based Representation and Related Works

The idea of shock graph can be defined in different ways in different fields. In the field of shape retrieval, the idea of shock graph is used to represent complex objects. The *shock graph* is the locus of the centers (singularities or shocks) of maximal circles which touch [Fig. 1(a)] the boundary at least at two points, referred to as characteristic point and endowed with geometric and dynamic information [2]. The Shock locus dynamically interprets the path of a moving particle with associated direction and speed of flow [6]. According to the type of tangency and the number of touching points on the boundary, a shock point can be denoted by $A_k^n - m$, $m=1$, 2, 3, and 4 [order of shock], which represents the shock with k-fold tendency at n distinct points. For all $m=2$ and 4, i.e. for second and fourth order shock point, we get the shock nodes (both end and junction nodes).When $m=1$, we get the links and $m=3$ is a non generic case. Nodes contain the first order property; tangent and speed, where link contains the second order properties; curvature and acceleration. The loci of all the shocks in fig. 1(b) give the Blum's medial axis [4], [5], [6], and also the idea of the whole shock graph as well as the boundary information of shape [6]. This representation is unique, dynamic and ideally suited to represent a shape [1].

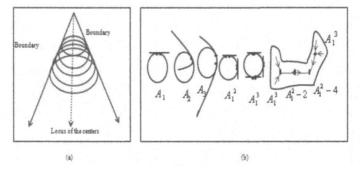

(a)   (b)

Fig. 1. (a) Locus of the center of maximal circles touching at least two boundary points (b) Different types of shock points form the locus of the shock graph and corresponding boundary

Now, we will discuss some previous works related to skeleton and shock based approaches. One of the drawbacks of shock based representation was its implicit model against the instability to get the robustness of the matching under some visual transformations. We had to face the instability problem in shape matching using *shock tree* by Siddiqi et al. [5] which is not appeared in *shock graph* based representation by Sharvit et al. [7]. The problem of instability of shock based representation was solved in a work of Sebastian et al. [2], [9] using edit distance algorithm and the accuracy is 100% using the 216 images of MPEG-7 database [11]. In this paper, the instability of the graph under the slight deformation of the boundary is defined as shock transition and an edit distance algorithm for matching of two shapes is developed. Edit distance or the optimal alignment of two curves uses the *dynamic programming (DP)* for matching which requires the computational complexity of $O\ x^2y^2$), where x and y are the number of sample points. The total time required to implement the edit distance algorithm is $O(x^3y^3)$, which makes the approach time consuming and impractical [9].

Again, a *shape tree* based approach by Felzenszwalb et al. [10] shows 87.7% accuracy using the MPEG-7 database of 1400 image of 40 classes [11]. To deal with the occlusion and missing parts, a sub curve of the model is left unmatched. Again the algorithm runs in $O(x^3y^3)$, where x and y represent the number of samples and *end* points respectively. A skeleton based approach proposed by Latecki's group [12], where the shortest paths between the end points are only considered. The instability problem occurred due to the junction points are avoided in their paper [Fig. 2(a)]. Using *Optimal Subsequences Bijection* (OSB), some endpoints are skipped considering them *dummy* nodes [7 is a dummy node in Fig. 2(a)] to get the correspondence for matching. They get the same accuracy and robustness of result as shock graph based approach [2] for the same database of 99 and 216 shapes [2] with time complexity $O(x^2y^2)$. However, their skipping of too many end points may give the erroneous result in some cases. Moreover, to reduce the time complexity, considering only the end nodes is not always accurate [14]; the method is not applicable for the shapes that have no end point.

A contradictory concept appears in the works of Zaboli et al. [13] and M. Rahmati et al. [3]. They improve the shock tree based method [5]. In their paper, the end nodes are ignored since they appear as a single point. They said that junction points or

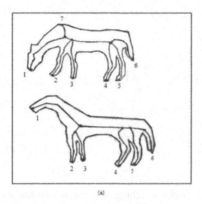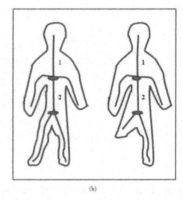

(a)   (b)

Fig. 2. (a) End points are more significant for matching than branch points and (b) Branch points are more stable than end points

branch points are more stable than the end points [Fig. 2(b)]. Their paper used the MPEG-7 database of 490 various binary shapes [11] and get the better performance than graph edit [2]. However, matching in terms of the branch points may cause erroneous match [12].Two different shapes may have the same branch point [12].

The shock graph based approach has the special characteristics to represent a shape uniquely from the intrinsic point of view. All nodes and links (interior or branch points) of a shock graph are important for shape construction and matching. To reduce the time complexity of the shock graph based edit distance approach, we can match either in terms of the end or branch nodes. Skipping of nodes or links depends and varies database to database. Here in this paper, to find the best correspondence between the database and query shape, we suggest to apply an adaptive weighing algorithm to select either of (branch or end) the shock points depending upon images. Taking those selected points into consideration, an edit cost measure is then applied based on Sebastian et al. [14].Our proposed weighing algorithm will reduce the number of sample points to compute edit cost. Furthermore, we get optimal solution for matching without using dynamic programming.

3 Shape Reconstruction

To reconstruct a shape boundary from intrinsic properties, the shock acceleration and curvature are sufficient. This concept is stated as a theorem by Giblin et al. [6], using the intrinsic properties of the shock point. According to their paper, using the velocity of shock and distance from the boundary, we get the following equation of the boundary curve of a shape:

$$B^{\pm}(s) = B(s) - \frac{r}{v}\vec{T} \pm \frac{r}{v}\sqrt{v^2 - 1}\vec{N}. \tag{1}$$

where $B^{\pm}(s), B(s), r, v, s$ represent the boundary point, the first order shock curve, corresponding radius, velocity and arc length, respectively [Fig.3]. Also, $\vec{T}$ and

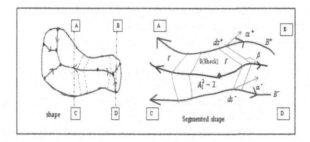

Fig. 3. The shock graph of a shape represents the corresponding boundary

$\bar{N}$ denote velocity direction and normal to the boundary curve, respectively. This equation will be used to find cost between two shock edges.

4 Matching the Shock Graphs

For the purpose of matching of shapes, we will use the edit distance and edit operation based on the works of the Sebastian et al. [2, 14]. Edit distance has the advantage of working well in the presence of visual transformation as it uses intrinsic properties of shape. To reduce the computational complexity of the traditional edit distance algorithm, we will use weighing scheme that will reduce the number of sample points. Our whole process of matching is dived into 2 steps: a *selection step* of the shock points by weighing and a *matching step* of calculating the edit distance for the selected points.

4.1 Weighing Scheme for Sample Point Selection

We apply the weighing scheme for the purpose of exploring the more important part and reducing the less important part of a shape. Our adaptive weighing scheme is able to select and skip the shock points adaptively according to the images of applied database and query. We will consider the same weight for each of the end and branch nodes of the shock points. If the weight is one for each point then the total number of end points will be the total weight for end points.

Let $G_1(B_{1,i}, E_{1,j})$, $i=1, 2, 3, ..., M_1$, $j=1, 2, 3, ..., M_2$ and $G_2(B_{2,p}, E_{2,q})$, $p=1, 2, 3, ..., N_1$, $q=1, 2, 3, ..., N_2$ are two shock graphs. Here, $B_{1,i}$, $B_{2,p}$ and $E_{1,j}$, $E_{2,q}$ are the weights of the branch and end nodes, respectively. Let $B = (B_{1,i}, B_{2,p})$ denote the total weight cost between the branch nodes of the two graphs and $E = (E_{1,j}, E_{2,q})$ denote that of end nodes of the two graphs. We will skip the branch nodes if the value of B is less than E. Conversely, end nodes will be skipped if the value of E is less than B. The following pseudo codes represent the procedure of weighing the shock points.

```
Procedure Selection of the Shock Points, SP;
  Calculate total weight cost for the end nodes (between
  query and data image),E;
```

```
Calculate total weight cost for the branch nodes,
(between query and data image),B;
      For all E and B
         If E>B
            Then select only end nodes, EP;
         Else if B>E
            Then select only branch nodes, BP;
         Else if B=E
            Then select all the shock points,(EP+BP);
   End selection;
```

The selected shock points found by the above algorithm are used to measure the edit distance for matching of two shapes.

4.2 Edit Distance for Shape Matching

When a little change in the shape boundary causes a significant change in the shock graph, then the shock graph experiences the instability which can be defined as *shock transition* [2], [8],[15]. *Shock transition* or the instability of matching can be removed by some edit operations: *deform, contract, merge, and splice*. Therefore, the total edit cost for two shapes will be the sum of the costs of those operations. So, the edit cost, D between two shock edges is as follows:

$$D(c,c') = \left| \int ds'^{\pm} - \int ds^{\pm} \right| + R \left| \int d\alpha'^{\pm} - \int d\alpha^{\pm} \right| + 2 \left| \int dr' - \int dr \right| + 2 \left| r_0' - r_0 \right| + 2R \left| \int d\beta' - \int d\beta \right| + 2R \left| \beta_0' - \beta_0 \right|. \quad (2)$$

where R is a scale constant that depends on average size of ds, c, c' are shock edges and α, β represent the orientations related to boundary and shock edges [Fig.3]. Also, r and s represent radius and arc length respectively. This cost measure does not depend on dynamic algorithm to get optimal solution.

5 Experiments

In this section, we will evaluate the performance of the proposed approach in two parts: firstly, we will select the sample points using the weight algorithm. We use 3 groups of 15 images; apple, bat, and beetle from the MPEG-7 data set [11]. The following table 1 shows that the adaptive algorithm selects all points (in table 1. image No.1to 6), when the difference between the total numbers of branch points, B (for sample and query image) and that of the end points, E are the same. For example, the branch points (BP) and end points (EP) for the query image are 5 and 7 respectively and that of a data image (e.g.apple-3), 6 and 8, are the same. So, in that case, all points (6+8=14) will be our sample points, SP. But when the difference is not the same then that point will be selected for which the difference is greater. For beetle images, the sample points consist of only the branch points. This procedure reduces the sample points; in some cases about half the sample points. But it gives the priority on both the points adaptively depending upon the images.

Table 1. Selecting the shock points for 15 images from the MPEG-7 [11] data set

Im.No.	Image	*BP*	*EP*	*B*	*E*	*SP*	Selected points
	Query image	5	7	0	0	12	All points
1	Apple-1	5	7	0	0	12	All points
2	Apple-3	6	8	1	1	14	All points
3	Appple-9	7	9	2	2	16	All points
4	Apple-14	7	9	2	2	16	All points
5	Apple-15	8	10	3	3	18	All points
6	Bat-3	25	27	20	20	52	All points
7	Bat-4	40	40	35	33	40	Branch points
8	Bat-8	160	138	155	131	160	Branch points
9	Bat-10	65	64	60	57	65	Branch points
10	Bat-20	32	35	27	28	35	End points
11	Beetle-3	154	129	149	122	154	Branch points
12	Beetle-7	80	72	75	65	80	Branch points
13	Beetle-10	94	83	89	76	94	Branch points
14	Beetle-11	127	117	122	110	127	Branch points
15	Beetle-20	148	107	143	100	148	Branch points

In the second part, after selecting the sample points (from the first part), we will determine the edit cost for matching. Since we use the shock based edit distance algorithm, the accuracy is like Sebastian et.al [2, 14]. Moreover, avoiding the dynamic programming is a significant speed up for matching. It is obvious that reducing the sample points by the weight algorithm needs less complexity than dynamic programming and gives the optimal solution for shape matching. Again, our approach takes all the shock points (both end and branch) into consideration and selects adaptively to get the correct match. The performance of shape matching on the MPEG-7 database [11] is now undergoing to compare our final result to the previous methods. We expect to show the better result in our future work.

6   Conclusions

Many researchers have worked on the improvement of the skeleton based shape retrieval approaches with reducing the time complexity for large databases. Shock based approach is also improved; but avoiding some of the shock points to reduce the time complexity. On the other hand, to represent a shape sufficiently from the intrinsic point of view, we must take all the shock points into consideration. To the best of our knowledge, the shock graph approach containing all shock points for shape retrieval using large dataset has not yet been examined with reducing the time complexity. In this paper, we have proposed our *weighing* algorithm to reduce the time complexity of previously developed edit distance algorithm for shape matching that is robust to visual transformations. Our work is processing on a complete implementation of the above algorithms on the database of MPEG-7 [11] using Matlab programming language. We will present more comprehensive results and comparison with the other approaches in our subsequent paper.

References

1. Klein, P., Tirthapura, S., Sharvit, D., Kimia, B.B.: Indexing Based on Edit Distance Matching of Shape Graphs. Multimedia storage and archiving systems III 2, 25–36 (1998)
2. Sebastian, T., Klein, P., Kimia, B.: Recognition of shapes by editing their shock graphs. Patt. Anal. Mach. Intel.IEEE Trans. 26, 550–571 (2004)
3. Zaboli, H., Rahmati, M., Mirzaei, A.: Shape Recognition by Clustering and Matching of Skeletons. Journal of Computer 3, 24–33 (2008)
4. Blum, H.: A Transformation for extracting new descriptors of Shape. In: Whaten-Dunn, W. (ed.), pp. 362–380. MIT Press, Cambridge (1967)
5. Siddiqi, K., Shokoufandeh, A., Dickinson, S., Zucker, S.: Shock Graphs and Shape Matching. Int'l J. Computer Vision 35, 13–32 (1999)
6. Giblin, P.J., Kimia, B.B.: On the Intrinsic Reconstruction of Shape from Its Symmetries. In: Proc. IEEE Conf on Computer Vision and Pattern Recognition, pp. 79–84 (1999)
7. Sharvit, D., Chan, J., Tek, H., Kimia, B.B.: Symmetry-Based Indexing of Image Databases. J. Visual Comm. and Image Representation 9, 366–380 (1998)
8. Klein, P., Tirthapura, S., Sharvit, D., Kimia, B.: A Tree-Edit Distance Algorithm for Comparing Simple, Closed Shapes. Symp. Discrete Algorithms. In: Proc. ACM-SIAM, pp. 696–704 (2000)
9. Wong, W.T., Shih, F.Y., Liu, J.: Shape-Based Image Retrieval Using Support Vector Machines, Fourier Descriptors and Self-organizing Maps. Information Sciences 177, 1878–1891 (2007)
10. Felzenszwalb, P.F., Schwartz, J.D.: Hierarchical Matching of Deformable Shapes. In: Computer Vision and Pattern Recognition, IEEE CVPR, pp. 1–8 (2007)
11. Latecki, L.J., Lakamper, R., Eckhardt, U.: Shape Descriptors for Non-rigid Shapes with a Single Closed Contour. In: IEEE Conf. on Computer Vision and Pattern Recognition, CVPR, pp. 424–429 (2000)
12. Bai, X., Latecki, L.J.: Path Similarity Skeleton Graph Matching. IEEE Transaction on Pattern Analysis and Machine Intelligence 30, 1282–1292 (2008)
13. Zaboli, H., Rahmati, M.: An Improved Shock Graph Approach for Shape Recognition and Retrieval. In: Proceedings of the First Asia International Conference on Modeling & Simulation, AMS (2007)
14. Sebastian, T.B., Klein, P.N., Kimia, B.B.: Shock-Based Indexing into Large Shape Databases. In: Proc. European Conf. Computer Vision, pp. 731–746 (2002)
15. Klein, P.N., Sebastian, T.B., Kimia, B.B.: Shape Matching Using Edit-Distance: An Implementation. In: ACM-SIAM Symp. Discrete Algorithms, pp. 781–790 (2001)

Design of an Object-Based Video Retrieval System Using SCA and Invariant Moments

Jang-Hui Kim and Dae-Seong Kang

Department of Electronic Engineering, Dong-A University
840 Hadan2-dong, Saha-gu, Busan, Korea
tortelli@dreamwiz.com, dskang@dau.ac.kr

Abstract. In recent years, it has become more important to process multimedia data efficiently. Especially, in the case of multimedia information, the user interface technique and retrieval technique are necessary. Video information takes large portion among the multimedia information. In this paper, we present a video retrieval system. For the video retrieval, we propose SCA (Single Colorizing Algorithm) and CSB (Color- and Spatial-based Binary) tree map algorithm. The SCA reduces the dimensions of the color features. The CSB tree map is a kind of clustering algorithm that increases the number of groups by binary tree structure, and determines suitable numbers of the group to extract optimized objects. In addition, we apply invariant moments to above preprocessed images. Through experiments, the proposed video retrieval system presents high performance comparing with existing retrieval methods.

Keywords: video retrieval, video segmentation, SCA (Single Colorizing Algorithm), CSB (Color- and Spatial-based Binary) tree map, invariant moments.

1 Introduction

Multimedia characterized by multi-media, multi-features, multi-representations, huge volume, and variety is rapidly spreading due to the increasing number of application domains [1]. But the existing retrieval systems are limited when users demand many functions, such as huge amounts of data, various formats, and extraction of data. Therefore, a system is needed to retrieve data promptly and accurately.

While conventional retrieval systems have focused on text, current multimedia systems have developed along the lines of content-based video retrieval due to the wide use of available digital video data.

In this paper, we present an object-based video retrieval system. For the video retrieval, video segmentation is carried out first. Video segmentation is the task of dividing videos into shots. To retrieve video effectively, detecting shots are very important. Proposed retrieval technique extracts features in images by SCA and CSB tree map. These processes reduce the binary number of the color considerably, and the queried object has become a clear image. And then, we apply invariant moments to above pre-processed images. Invariant moments describe a shape's layout, and are constant only with change in position, and no other appearance transformation [2]. By

D. Ślęzak et al. (Eds.): FGCN/ACN 2009, CCIS 56, pp. 509–516, 2009.

these steps, we can implement video retrieval system that shows higher detection rate than the existing methods about recall and precision.

The rest of the paper is organized as follows. In Section 2, the background theory of the video structure is introduced. In Section 3, feature extraction algorithms are described. The experimental process and results of the proposed method are shown in Section 4. Finally, the conclusions are given in Section 5.

2 Video Structure

The standard unit of the video is a frame. The positions where scene changes occur are called cuts. The shots are separated by a cut. Small video units consist of consecutive shots called episodes or scenes. The task of dividing videos into shots is called video segmentation. The shot is used as a standard unit of a video segmentation. Figure 1 shows a video structure that consists of frames, shots, and episodes.

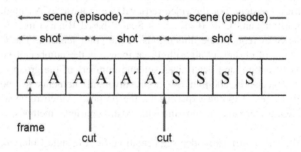

Fig. 1. Video structure

In figure 1, the first shot consists of frame A and the second shot consists of frame A'. They are separated by a cut, but they belong to the same episode because they are similar or tell the same logical story. On the other hand, the third shot, which consists of frame S, is a wholly different scene.

A video is a set of consecutive frames. In the continuous scene, the similarities between the neighboring frames are strong. On the contrary, in the region where scenes change, the similarities between neighboring frames are relatively weak. Therefore, to extract cuts, we use the differences between the frames, and calculate the continuous features. Last, we regard the discontinuous region as a cut.

3 Feature Extraction

To present a retrieval system that is suitable for a multiple query system that follows the user's demand, it is essential that the user choose and extract an interesting object. To extract an interesting object, input images that are based on the object must be divided, and to divide the images suitably, it is necessary to simplify images. This processing reduces the binary number considerably, so it can reduce the processing time during the retrieval process. In this paper, we can simplify images using a single colorizing algorithm, and extract objects using the CSB tree map algorithm.

3.1 SCA (Single Colorizing Algorithm)

As a whole, we use a single colorizing algorithm proposed by John R. Smith and Shih-Fu Chang [3]. The single colorizing algorithm reduces the dimensions of the color features. Color quantization of the HSI color model can avoid wrong color binary mapping, and improve allowable error of luminosity, brightness, and saturation, which are not efficient from a human point of view. Emphasized color and regions are clearly presented by this process.

The HSI color model reduces color distortion and loss considerably. The HSI color model can convert easily though it is non-linear [4]. In the HSI color model, hue is a represented angle that ranges from $0°$ to $360°$. Saturation corresponds to a radius that ranges from 0 to 1. Brightness corresponds to the z-axis; when it is 0, it represents black, and when 1, it represents white. Hue is expressed from $0°$ to $360°$ in the Hue region. The angle increases, and H changes into red ($0° = 360°$), yellow ($60°$), green ($120°$), and blue ($240°$). When I=0, hue does not define H. When S=0, hue represents only brightness. When we control I, hue becomes bright or dark. If we maintain S=I and control I, we can transform the density of the hue.

Quantized images still have noise. We use 5×5 color median filtering to reduce the noise. Color median filtering, which is non-linear in the HSI channel, does not generate distortion hue about all images. The large advantage is effective on boundary classification because the filtering maintains a strong edge and maintains existing edges more specifically.

3.2 CSB (Color- and Spatial-Based Binary) Tree Map

Generally, image segmentation by anisotropic diffusion and a watershed algorithm is not suitable for a still image when extracting objects. In the case of clustering, other clustering algorithms as well as a k-means algorithm determine the number of grouping data according to the initial input vectors. But when similar feature vectors are grouped in the image database, the number of groups mostly cannot be determined in advance. Therefore, according to the cases, an algorithm that determines the number of groups dynamically is needed.

In figure 2, the CSB tree map algorithm is a method that increases the number of groups by binary tree structure, and determines suitable numbers of the group to extract optimized objects. Each node has the number of pixels, representative color information, and the pixels' coordinates information as in figure 2(b). In figure 2(b), the information about each node is composed of the number of pixels, (h, s, i) color vector, and the coordinates of the cluster. V, c, and s are represented separately, and the information per each node is renewable during clustering processing.

In figure 2(a), we assume that the input image is the root node, and choose an arbitrary seed's values $s(c)_1$ and $s(c)_2$, and apply a 2-means algorithm grounded on the color vector of each node. In this time, if the cluster radius, r, of the each child node is larger than the cluster similarity, τ_c, designated by the user, we perform clustering by applying the 2-means algorithm to each child node again.

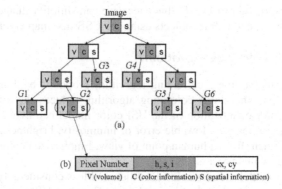

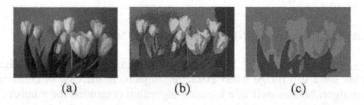

Fig. 2. (a) Clustering process of CSB tree map, (b) Class information of each node

$$r(c)_{N_i} = \max(dist_{cb}(z(c)_{N_i}, x(c)_{N_i}))$$ (1)

In equation 1, $z(c)_{N_i}$ is the center of the i th node N_i, and $x(c)_{N_i}$ is the element under i th cluster N_i. So, radius $r(c)_{N_i}$ means the Euclidean distance between the cluster center and the element far from the cluster center among the elements under the cluster in the HSI color space. Each clustering node sets the representative color and renews the cluster center.

Fig. 3. (a) Original image, (b) Processed image by single colorizing algorithm, (c) Processed image by CSB tree map algorithm

In figure 3, single-colorizing and clustering are performed on the image. As shown in figure 3, the process of using the CSB algorithm reduces the binary number of the color considerably, and the queried object has become a clear image. These processed objects require a labeling algorithm to make up a multiple queries system that meets the user's demand.

3.3 Invariant Moments

Moment invariants are calculated algebraic moment from images, and they are constant only with change in position, and no other appearance transformation. Moments describe a shape's layout (the arrangement of its pixels), a bit like combining area, compactness, irregularity and higher order descriptions together [5].

For a 2-D continuous function $f(x, y)$, the moment of order $(p+q)$ is defined as equation (2) for $p, q = 0, 1, 2, \ldots$ [6].

$$m_{pq} = \int_{-\infty}^{\infty} \int_{-\infty}^{\infty} x^p y^q f(x, y) dx dy \qquad (2)$$

For discrete images, equation (2) is usually approximated by equation (3), where ΔA is again the area of a pixel.

$$m_{pq} = \sum_x \sum_y x^p y^q f(x, y) \Delta A \qquad (3)$$

If $f(x, y)$ is piecewise continuous and has nonzero values only in a finite part of the xy-plane, moments of all orders exist, and the moment sequence m_{pq} is uniquely determined by $f(x, y)$. On the contrary, m_{pq} uniquely determines $f(x, y)$.

The central moments are defined as equation (4) for $p, q = 0, 1, 2, \ldots$, $\overline{x} = m_{10} / m_{00}$, $\overline{y} = m_{01} / m_{00}$, and are only translation invariant.

$$\mu_{pq} = \sum_{x=0}^{N-1} \sum_{y=0}^{N-1} (x - \overline{x})^p (y - \overline{y})^q f(x, y) \qquad (4)$$

The normalized central moments η_{pq} is defined as $\eta_{pq} = \mu_{pq} / \mu_{00}$ where $\gamma = (p+q)/2 + 1, \forall p + q \geq 2$. Seven invariant moments are shown below equations (5), and this set of seven moments is invariant to rotation, scale change and translation.

$$\phi_1 = \eta_{20} + \eta_{02},$$
$$\phi_2 = (\eta_{20} - \eta_{02})^2 + 4\eta_{11}^2$$
$$\phi_3 = (\eta_{30} - 3\eta_{12})^2 + (3\eta_{21} - \eta_{03})^2,$$
$$\phi_4 = (\eta_{30} + \eta_{12})^2 + (\eta_{21} + \eta_{03})^2$$
$$\phi_5 = (\eta_{30} - 3\eta_{12})(\eta_{30} + \eta_{12})[(\eta_{30} + \eta_{12})^2 - 3(\eta_{21} + \eta_{03})^2] \qquad (5)$$
$$\quad + (3\eta_{21} - \eta_{03})(\eta_{21} + \eta_{03})[3(\eta_{30} + \eta_{12})^2 - (\eta_{21} + \eta_{03})^2]$$
$$\phi_6 = (\eta_{20} - \eta_{02})[(\eta_{30} + \eta_{12})^2 - (\eta_{21} + \eta_{03})^2] + 4\eta_{11}(\eta_{30} + \eta_{12})(\eta_{21} + \eta_{03})$$
$$\phi_7 = (3\eta_{21} - \eta_{03})(\eta_{30} + \eta_{12})[(\eta_{30} + \eta_{12})^2 - 3(\eta_{21} + \eta_{03})^2]$$
$$\quad + (3\eta_{12} - \eta_{30})(\eta_{21} + \eta_{03})[3(\eta_{30} + \eta_{12})^2 - (\eta_{21} + \eta_{03})^2]$$

4 Experimental Results

Table 1 shows detailed information of the image used in the experiments. It shows the length of the movie, the number of the frames and the number of detected key frames of each video clip. The frames of each video clip were composed of pixels 352×240 in size.

Table 1. Detailed information of video clips

	video clip 1	video clip 2	video clip 3	video clip 4
length of videos	3.43′	3.25′	3.56′	4.20′
# of total frames	6687	6150	7102	7822
# of key frames	600	769	232	190

4.1 Computing Invariant Moments

The seven invariant moments of each frame of video clips have been calculated. Figure 4 shows the key-frames and consecutive frames from 4518th frame to 4535th frame of video clip 1. The first frame of each scene is selected as key-frame.

Fig. 4. Consecutive frames of video clip1

Table 2. Seven invariant moments of each frame from 4518th to 4535 of the video clip 1

IM ＼ FN	ϕ_1	ϕ_2	ϕ_3	ϕ_4	ϕ_5	ϕ_6	ϕ_7
4518	5.86	12.97	20.98	21.91	48.07	28.87	43.48
4519	5.89	13.07	21.01	22.00	45.64	29.11	43.64
4520	5.90	13.15	21.19	22.15	44.77	29.60	44.03
4521	5.90	13.15	21.23	22.22	44.67	29.86	44.24
4522	5.93	13.24	21.50	22.47	44.85	30.67	44.99
4523	5.96	13.39	21.56	22.47	44.74	31.21	45.29
4524	6.01	13.52	21.65	22.41	44.70	31.29	45.27
4525	6.05	13.62	21.79	22.40	44.86	30.59	45.09
4526	6.13	13.84	22.05	22.49	45.28	30.29	45.17
4527	6.69	15.52	24.94	27.52	54.04	35.47	54.34
4528	6.69	15.52	25.08	27.51	54.24	35.43	54.14
4529	6.67	15.48	25.17	27.37	53.82	35.40	54.59
4530	6.66	15.47	25.24	27.29	53.65	35.65	56.05
4531	6.66	15.44	25.38	27.35	53.82	35.76	56.17
4532	6.66	15.44	25.43	27.48	54.07	36.15	55.37
4533	6.66	15.44	25.38	27.78	54.58	37.07	55.19
4534	6.66	15.43	25.35	27.93	55.46	37.26	54.79
4535	6.66	15.42	25.34	27.80	56.53	36.07	54.48

IM: Invariant Moments, FN: Frame Number.

Table 2 shows the seven invariant moments of each frame mentioned figure 4. From 4518th frame to 4526th frame, they are same scene, and invariants moments are very similar. In case of ϕ_1, key-frame's moment is 5.86, and the other frame's average error is 0.13. From 4527th frame to 4535th frame, they are also same scene, and average error is much smaller than previous scene's average error. Key-frame's moment is 6.69, and the other frame's average error is 0.03. Other invariant moments, $\phi_2 \sim \phi_7$, also have small error between key-frame and the other frames.

4.2 Experimental Results

Recall and Precision is generally used to compare the efficiency of content-based image data retrieval.

$$Recall = f(x) = \frac{d}{d+m} \times 100 \qquad (6)$$

$$Precision = f(x) = \frac{d}{d+f} \times 100 \qquad (7)$$

In the equations, d (detection) means the real shot conversion and it denotes the number of detected shots. The m (mis-detection) means that the real shot conversion occurred but it was not detected. The f (fault) means that the real shot conversion did not occur but it was detected.

Table 3. Detection rate(%) for recall and precision

	IM		IM + EHD		Proposed method	
	Recall	Precision	Recall	Precision	Recall	Precision
video clip1	87.7	80.7	91.1	81.1	92.5	89.2
video clip2	84.2	74.7	91.2	81.8	92.6	85.3
video clip3	88.5	84.7	91.18	81.88	93.0	85.7
video clip4	87.1	79.9	91.7	82.4	92.8	83.7

IM: Invariant Moments, EHD: Edge Histogram Descriptor.

Table 3 shows that we performed efficiency appraisal by using Recall and Precision. The proposed detection method shows improved results with recall 5.85% and 1.43%, precision 5.975% and 4.2%, respectively.

5 Conclusions

In this paper, we present the video retrieval system using SCA, CSB tree map algorithm and invariant moments. SCA and CSB tree map algorithm reduce the binary number of the color considerably, and the queried object has become a clear image. Invariant moments are constant with translation, rotation and scale change. It can be powerful feature to retrieve the image from the image sequence. Proposed retrieval system presents improved performance for recall and precision.

Acknowledgement

This work was supported by the NEXT work (Nurturing Excellent engineers in information Technology), granted by the IITA (Institute for Information Technology Advancement).

References

1. Davies, N.J., Weeks, R., Revett, M.C.: Information agents for the World Wide Web. In: Nwana, H.S., Azarmi, N. (eds.) Software Agents and Soft Computing: Towards Enhancing Machine Intelligence. LNCS, vol. 1198, pp. 81–99. Springer, Heidelberg (1997)
2. Nixon, M., Aguado, A.: Feature Extraction & Image Processing, pp. 318–320. Academic Press, London (2008)
3. Bovik, A.: Handbook of Image and Video Processing, pp. 687–688. Academic Press, London (2000)
4. Smith, J.R., Chang, S.-F.: Tools and Techniques for Color Image Retrieval. In: IS&T/SPIE proceedings, Storage & Retrieval for Image and Video Database, vol. 2670 (1995)
5. Swain, M., Ballard, D.: Color indexing. International Journal of Computer Vision 7(1), 11–32 (1991)
6. Nixon, M., Aguado, A.: Feature Extraction & Image Processing, pp. 318–320. Academic Press, London (2008)
7. Gonzalez, R.C., Woods, R.E.: Digital Image Processing SE, pp. 672–675. Prentice-Hall, Englewood Cliffs (2002)

Configurations of Dual RAID System

Bongen Gu[1], Yun-Sik Kwak[1], Seung-Kook Cheong[2], Jung-Yeon Hwang[2],
and Kijeong Khil[1]

[1] Dept. Of Computer Engineering, Chungju National University,
Chungju-si Chungbuk, 380-702, Korea
{bggoo,yskwak}@cjnu.ac.kr, kijung84@nate.com
[2] Electronics and Telecommunications Research Institute, Daejeon, 305-700, Korea
{skjeong,jyhwang}@etri.re.kr

Abstract. The RAID system is used to get the high performance and reliability
of disk system. The many RAID system concerned the disk failure, and have
the recover policy. But the probability of the RAID system failure is not lower
than that of the disk failure. To implement the robust RAID system, the redundancy of RAID controller is also needed. In this paper, we provide three configurations of Dual RAID system. And we consider the characteristics of each
Dual RAID system.

Keywords: RAID, Dual RAID, Redundant Disk, Disk Array.

1 Introduction

The internet is very important social infra in human life. Especially the internet is
basic resource to provide the user-oriented services in the pervasive computing environment. As the bandwidth and the transmission speed of the internet connection are
higher, people want the higher level of services. To provide these services, many new
services and the business models are developed. The on-demand HDTV, IPTV, the
health case system, the internet search engine like *google*, and various portal such as
daum, *naver*, and *yahoo* are examples of theses services[3].

These services are very different but have the same feature like that all of these
services are based the big size data. To provide these new services, the storage system
is required. The storage system can store many big size data, and has to respond to the
data i/o requests seamlessly[4]. The storage system has to have three features : high
performance, high reliability, and low cost. From the 1980's late, the RAID is considered to implement the storage system with the high performance, the high reliability.
The meaning of RAID is the redundant array of independent disks[1][5].

For the high performance, the RAID uses multiple disks operable independently.
For the high reliability and the high availability, the RAID uses the redundant information. If there is a failure in a disk drive during the normal operation, the RAID
continues the disk i/o services using the redundant information. And the failure disk is
replaced with new disk, the RAID recovers the contents of the failure disk by using
the redundant information. The main objective of using the redundancy is to cover
the disk failure, and make the storage system robust[1][3].

D. Ślęzak et al. (Eds.): FGCN/ACN 2009, CCIS 56, pp. 517–521, 2009.

The magnetic disk drive consists of the electronic parts and mechanical parts. That's why the probability of occurring the fault in the disk drive is high. The technology of the disk driver continues to enhance until now, and currently the reliability of the disk drive is very high. Therefore in some case, the disk driver is more reliable than other system components such as a power system, operator, or software[1].

To maximize the performance and the reliability of the storage system, the RAID system itself has to be also redundant[2]. In this paper, we describe the dual RAID system. The dual RAID system consists of two RAID controllers, which are functionally redundant. There will exist many configurations on the dual RAID. In this paper, we provide three configurations of the dual RAID system. For each configuration of the dual RAID system, we describe the characteristics, the advantages, and the disadvantages. And we describe the focus of the further study on the dual RAID system.

We begin this paper by presenting the configurations of the dual RAID system, and follow it with descriptions of the configurations. This includes the features, the advantages, and the disadvantages. And we conclude with a summary of this paper.

2   Configurations of the Dual RAID System

The dual RAID system consists of two RAID controllers and two or more disks. We define many configurations of the dual RAID system as how to configure the connections of two RAID controllers and the host. The host is the main system, which runs many user and system processes. In this paper, we define four configurations of the dual RAID system.

2.1   RAID-Pair Configuration

The figure 1 shows the RAID-pair configuration. Each RAID Controller is directly connected to the host and all disks. The host uses two bus interfaces to connect to two RAID Controllers in this configuration. The disk has two ports or channels. Each port or channel is connected to one of RAID Controller.

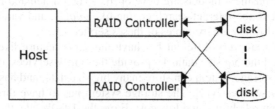

Fig. 1. The RAID-pair Configuration

In this configuration, the software executed in the host controls the operations of two RAID controllers in some operating mode. The active-active mode and active-standby mode are well known mode in the redundant system. In the active-active mode, two RAID controllers are always operating. In this mode, the control software acts as the load balancer. When the system, like the kernel, makes the disk io request, the control software inspects the state of two RAID controller, and decides that the request is where to go. In the active-standby mode, only one active RAID controller is operating. The standby controller is operating when the active controller is fault. In this mode, the control software inspects the state of the active controller, and initiates the standby controller when the active controller is fault.

2.2 Coordinator Configuration

The figure 2 shows the Coordinator configuration. All RAID controllers are directly connected to the Coordinator, which is connected to the host. In this configuration, the host uses only one bus interface for the RAID system.

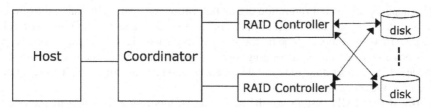

Fig. 2. Coordinator Configuration

The function of the Coordinator is the same as the software in the RAID-pair configuration. But the Coordinator is separate component. That's why the load balancing and the RAID controller failure inspection are more efficiently executed. Like the control software in the RAID-pair configuration, the Coordinator executes the different functions corresponding to the operating mode.

2.3 Master-Slave Configuration

The figure 2 shows the Master-Slave configuration. One of two RAID controllers is connected to the host. This RAID controller acts as the Master. In this configuration, the host also uses only one bus interface for the RAID system to exchange the disk i/o message with the Master.

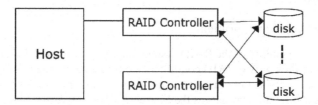

Fig. 3. Master-Slave configuration

The Master executes the function of the Coordinator described in the previous subsection. The host makes the message related to the disk i/o, and transmits it to the Master through the host bus, and then the Master decides how to treat the message from the host. In this configuration, basically the active-active mode is used. Therefore, if one of RAID controllers is fault, the alive RAID controller processes all request. To do this, one assumption is required : the bus interface functions in the Master survives although the RAID function in the Master is lost because of some failure.

3 Features of the Dual RAID System

In this section, we describe the features of the dual RAID system. Also, we describe the advantage and the disadvantage of each dual RAID configuration.

3.1 RAID-Pair Configuration

The features of this configuration are as the followings. No additional hardware cost for constructing the dual RAID system is required. Because the operation control of two RAID Controllers is done by the software layer like the kernel device driver. And it is possible to design the operating mode easily. There will be many other operating modes. If new operating mode is designed, we update the control software, and can use new operating mode.

But if the RAID system are the active-active mode, it is possible to saturate the bandwidth of the host interface with the message related to the disk i/o services. And the software periodically inspects the aliveness of RAID controllers. This operation uses the CPU computing power of the host, and needs time more or less. Therefore, the response to the RAID controller failure is delayed.

3.2 Coordinator Configuration

Because the Coordinator executes the load balancing functions and the RAID controller failure inspections in the integrated circuit level, the dual RAID system in this configuration has the highest performance. And the bandwidth saturation state of the host bus is not occurred.

But the additional cost to design and implement the Coordinator is required. The cost required is corresponding to the design level of the Coordinator. The Coordinator is implemented by using hardware design technology. That's why the reliability of the Coordinator is very high but not complete. If the Coordinator is fault, all disk i/o services are stopped.

3.3 Master-Slave Configuration

To get the high reliability of the RAID system, the assumption in 2.3 is necessary.

The architectures of two RAID controllers are the same in other configuration. But the architectures in this configuration are different because the functions of two RAID controllers are different. One acts as the Master, another acts as the Slave.

Therefore the additional cost to differently design the controllers is required. And the plural architecture requires the more maintenance efforts.

3.4 RAID Level of the Dual RAID

There are many RAID levels corresponding to how to distribute the data and how to use the redundant information. Currently, RAID level 0, 1, 5, and its variants are normally used.

If the dual RAID system described until now uses the RAID level 0, we can't construct the reliable RAID system. Because the dual RAID system covers the RAID controller failure, not the disk failure. The disk failure is covered in the RAID controller. Therefore RAID level 0 which has no redundant information is not reliable. If one disk is fault in the RAID system, all disk i/o service is stopped, and can't recover. To resolve this problem, the RAID level 1 is alternative way to get the reliability. But this level requires the high cost to duplicate the contents of the disks.

To get the high performance and the high reliability with the reasonable cost, the RAID level 5 is good choice. This RAID level makes and uses the minimum redundant information known as the parity. But the disk write operation requires at least 4 disk accesses to update the parity information. Therefore almost RAID controller except the very cheap RAID controller has the accelerating circuits to enhance the parity updating speed.

4 Conclusion

The new services based the internet requires the big data and the high quality of service. From this reason the storage system has the high performance and the high reliability in disk system.

The RAID system is used to get the high performance and reliability of disk system. The RAID system is focused on the reliability in spite of the disk failure. But all disk service is stopped when the RAID controller is fault in spite of the healthy state of disk drives.

To implement the robust RAID system the RAID controller itself has to be redundant. In this paper, we provide three configurations of Dual RAID system. And we consider the characteristics of each Dual RAID system. We remain two subjects as further study : the design of the detailed architecture, and development of the RAID level 5 acceleration method in the dual RAID system.

References

1. Chen, P.M., Lee, E.K., Gibson, F.A., Katz, R.H., Patterson, D.A.: RAID: High-Performance, Reliable Secondary Storage. ACM Computing Surveys 26, 145–185 (1994)
2. Cao, P., Lim, S.B., Venkataraman, S., Wilkers, J.: The TickerTAIP Paralle RAID Architecture. ACM Tr.on Computer System 12(3), 236–269 (1994)
3. Gu, B., Kwak, Y., Cheong, S., Ko, D.: Performance Anaylsis between Implements of RAID System. In: 2009 summer conference, KIIT (June 2009)
4. Kang, Y., Yoo, J., Cheong, S.: Performance Evaluation of the SSD based on DRAM Storage System IOPS. Journal of KIIT 7, 265–272 (2009)
5. Stallings, W.: Computer Organization and Architecture. Prentice-Hall, Englewood Cliffs (2003)

Efficient Data Transmission Scheme among Multi-devices

Sang-Bong Byun[1], Byungin Moon[2], and Yong-Hwan Lee[1]

[1] School of Electronic Engineering, Kumoh National Institute of Technology, Gumi, Korea
[2] School of Electrical Engineering & Computer Science, Kyungpook National University,
Daegu, Korea
sb5816@kumoh.ac.kr, bihmoon@knu.ac.kr, yhlee@kumoh.ac.kr

Abstract. Existing serial interface using a point to point connection, if it is used in complex system, shows decreased efficiency and increased complexity. Therefore, we will use the link switch for high speed data transmission protocol so that communication among various devices in the mobile environment can be performed by packet switching.

Keywords: MIPI, PHY, Mobile, Low power, Switch, Serial interface.

1 Introduction

Mobile device with various functions is increasing and efficient connection between devices is required. In this paper, we design switch and efficient communication between multi-devices. Fast serial interface is capable of transferring bits at nearly 800Mb/sec on each differential data pair. The protocol has been designed to allow this speed to be increased with multi-lane implementations and high speed PHYs.[1]

2 Overveiw

As is customary in the design of network protocols, fast serial interface is split into layers which are roughly structured according to the OSI reference architecture for networking. This layering strategy makes the specification more modular and allows reuse of existing best practice while allowing the protocol to focus on special protocol characteristics needed for specific requirements. Serial interface consists of three layers and one physical.

Layer of serial interface supports high compatibility each divided by function. PHY Adapter Layer[2] provides frame and slice unit for consistent data transmission irrespective of PHY and Data Link Layers. Data Link Layer classifies data by TC (Traffic Class) and enables smooth streaming data. Network Layer is provides the functional and procedural means of transferring variable length data sequences (Packets) from a source Endpoint to a destination Endpoint. Transport Layer is responsible for messages and, in particular, owns the End-of-Message bit within the packet headers.

Fig. 1 shows the examples of using the switch. If switch is used, Device A can communicate with at the same time other device communicate with Device B. All devices connected to the switch can communicate with each other.

D. Ślęzak et al. (Eds.): FGCN/ACN 2009, CCIS 56, pp. 522–527, 2009.

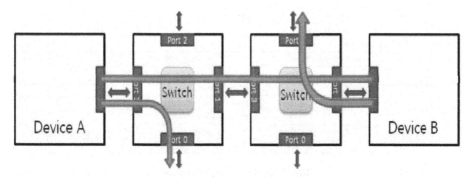

Fig. 1. Examples of using the+ switch

3 Layer Structure

3.1 PHY Adaptor Layer

PHY Adaptor Layer connects between Data link layer and PHY Layer. The PHY Adaptor layer primarily serves to hide the differences between different PHYs in order to achieve a consistent interface to upper layers. PHY Adaptor Layer can use several PHY because it can regulate band-width and support Power Management Unit for efficient power management. This layer uses 17-bit symbols that consist of one special Ctrl bit and two bytes. If Ctrl=1, the symbol is a special control symbol. For some byte-oriented PHYs these 17-bit symbols are directly shifted out onto the line by a serializing PHY. For on-chip interfaces, a symbol might be transmitted simply using 17 parallel lines. If Ctrl=0, the symbol contains normal bytes used to convey user data or protocol units

The 17 bits presented from the data link layer are directly translated to two full D-PHY symbols. The last remaining bit is transmitted in the next D-PHY symbol, together with the first seven bits of the next data link layer symbol, and so on. Visually speaking, the 17 bit data link layer symbols are concatenated, and then transmitted as 8 bits "slices".

PHY Adapter Layer has Power Management Unit[3]. Power Management Unit supports On, Sleep, Reset, Coma, Off, Auto mode.

3.2 Data Link Layer

Data link layer connects between Network layer and PHY Adaptor Layer.

The main features of the Data Link Layer

- Responsibility for link-level communication via frames.
- Flow control – avoiding buffer overflow at the link level.
- Error correction – corrupt frames are detected and retransmitted.
- Arbitrates traffic in multiple Traffic Class / Virtual Channel.
- Controls the PHY Adapter Layer (e.g. power modes)

Symbol															
Ctrl	B1 byte								B0 byte						
Ctrl	b15	b14	b13	b12	b11	b10	b9	b8	b7	b6	b5	b4	b3	b2	b1	b0
1	Ctrl_DLL(=0000001)								ID=SoF(=000)			TC		Reserved(=000)		
0	One or more symbols used by L3 header														
0	Data Payload														
0	Data Payload														
0	Data Payload														
1	Ctrl_DLL(=0000001)								ID=EoF(=001)			Frame Sequence Number				
0	CCITT CRC-16														

Fig. 2. Typical frame structures

Fig. 2 shows typical frame structures. The first symbol is called the header and indicates the start of frame ("SoF") while indicating its Traffic Class (TC). The end of frame, or the so-called L2 trailer, starts with the second-to-last symbol and contains, a code indicating that the payload has an even number of bytes ("EoF"), a sequence number needed for acknowledging frames and a 16-bit CRC. The CRC is used to determine if there are any transmission errors in the frame and allows damaged frames to be retransmitted.

Data Link Layer controls data flow using TC(Traffic Class)[4]. Data is saved to buffer in TC. Read data sequentially in control logic, saving message start address and end address to buffer.

The DL layer supports two different user traffic classes (TC0 and TC1), which are provided to DL service user with TC1 being the highest priority and TC0 being the lowest priority. For each traffic class it may provide one logical buffer for transmit path and will provide one logical buffer for receive path and are accessible by DL service user. The traffic class of a frame is identified by the value of traffic class identifier, which is encapsulated in SOF.

3.3 Network Layer

Network Layer connects between Data Link Layer and Transport Layer. Network Layer in the OSI model is L3.

The main features of the Data Link Layer.

- It is responsible for creating and interpreting *packets*.
- It is responsible for *routing* packets through the network towards their destination.

Network Layer provides services to assure the transparent transfer of user-data between service users. The way in which the supporting communication resources are utilized to achieve this transfer is transparent to the service users. The services are provided via Network Service Access Points (N-SAPs). Network Service shall utilize a system of addressing which is used by Network Service users to refer unambiguously to N-SAPs. Network Service does not restrict the content, format or coding of the user-data, nor shall it ever need to interpret its structure or meaning. Network Service does not lose any user-data within its field of responsibility.

3.4 Transport Layer

Transport Layer connects between Application Link Layer and Network Layer.
  The main functions of Transport Layer.

- Transport Layer is responsible for *messages* and, in particular, owns the End-of-Message bit within the packet headers.
- Transport Layer owns the ProtocolID field.
- Support CPort[4] for connect to Application Layer.
- For the Real-Time traffic class, Network layer provides admission control.

4 Switch

Four devices are not linked each other. But, all devices are linked to switch as shown in Fig 3. Connected devices on the switch can communicate with each other. Routing to the destination by destination address in the packet header. If Device A and Device B want to connect to Device C, Virtual Channel(VC) Arbitration and Port Arbitration are used Fig 4 shows the switch Implements Port Arbitration and VC Arbitration.[5]

- Virtual Channel Arbitration: Determines the priority of transactions being transmitted from the same port.
- Port Arbitration: Determines the priority of transactions with the same VC assignment at the output port, based on the priority of the port at which the transactions arrived.

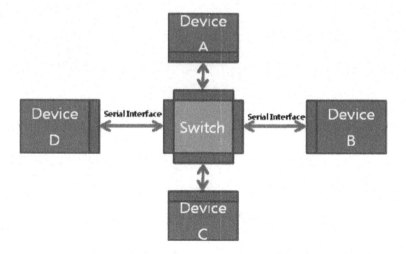

Fig. 3. Example of a Serial Interface using switch

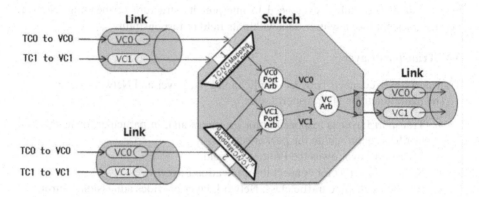

Fig. 4. Switch Implements Port Arbitration and VC Arbitration

5   Simulation Result

To validate the designed fast serial interface, simulation has been performed. In the simulation, two designs were connected to each other, as a transmitter and a receiver respectively. Fig.5 ~ 6 shows simulation waveforms of each layer.

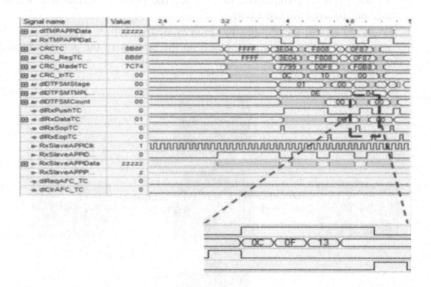

Fig. 5. Rx Data Link Layer

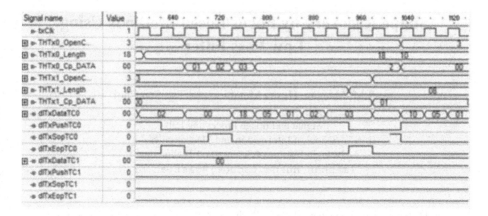

Fig. 6. Tx Network Layer

6 Conclusions

The fast serial interface was described in verilog HDL and verified with Active-HDL. Design tool uses Altera Quartus II 8.0. To validate the feasibility and operation, FPGA implementation was executed. FPGA verification used Altera Cyclone EPIC60Q240C8. The verified HDL design was synthesized to a netlist of logic gates using 0.35um CMOS technology.

References

1. Kim, Y.J., Kim, D.-H., Cho, K.-R.: Design of the Digital D-PHY for MIPI standard in Mobile Applications
2. Lee, Y.-H., Ju, H.-W.: PHY Adapter Layer Design for Low-power fast serial bus protocol. In: ITC-CSCC 2008, pp. 1505–1508 (July 2008)
3. Lee, J., Ahn, B., Lee, D.H., Lee, S.H.: A Design and Implementation of Low Power Management for Personal Multimedia Systems. IEEE Journal of Solid-state 10, 22–24 (2007)
4. Mun, Y., Lee, H.K.: Understanding Ipv6. Springer, New York
5. PCI Express System Architecture

Shape Recovery by Focus Based Methods Using Low Pass Filter

S.M. Mannan, Husna Mutahira, and Tae-Sun Choi

Signal and Image Processing Lab
School of Information and Mechatronics
Gwangju Institue of Science and Technology
{mannan,husna,tschoi}@gist.ac.kr

Abstract. Estimating the relative 3D shape of the object is an important research topic in the area of computer vision, and is being used in a wide range of applications such as robot vision, computer games, animations, broadcast, and many more. Several active and passive methods have been proposed for recovering 3-D shape of the objects from their 2-D images. Passive methods like Shape from Focus (SFF), Shape from Defocus (SFD), Shape from Shading (SFS) etc are cheap and more effective, requiring stack of images by a single camera. In this paper, we have developed a simple and fast algorithm for SFF to calculate depth. The pixel intensities in the image sequences are modified by subtracting the maximum of first or last frame in the image sequence. A low pass filter is applied on these modified values to eliminate the noise. The proposed algorithm is fast and precise, as compared to earlier SFF methods.

Keywords: Shape from Focus, Low Pass Filter, Noise Removal.

1 Introduction

Recovery of 3D shape from its 2D image can be broadly categorized into active and passive techniques. In active methods, sonar, laser range finders and many more like them are included. Whereas, passive methods include shape from shading, shape from motion (motion parallax), stereo vision, shape from defocus and shape from focus. In microcopy active methods, being expensive, are sometimes impractical to use. Whereas, passive methods are more popular because of being cheaper they are easier to implement. Particularly shape from focus (SFF) has many advantages over other passive methods such as stereo and motion parallax since these methods encounter the correspondence problem. However, accuracy of SFF methods need to be further improved for better 3D shape.

In SFF methods, a stack of images is acquired by a single camera at different focus levels. The first step is to compute the focus quality of each pixel of every frame by applying a focus measure operator, and then the depth map is computed by maximizing focus value along the optical axis. Focus measure is defined as a quantity for locally evaluating the sharpness of a pixel. In literature, many focus measures have been reported in spatial as well as in transform domains. Laplacian, modified Laplacian, sum of modified Laplacian (SML), Tenenbaum, gray level variance (GLV) and

D. Ślęzak et al. (Eds.): FGCN/ACN 2009, CCIS 56, pp. 528–538, 2009.

M_2 are the famous focus measures among them [1] [2]. The Laplacian operator, being a point and symmetric operator, is a commonly used focus measure [8][10] [11]. The focus value of an image is obtained by adding second derivatives in the x- and y-directions. In the case of textured images, the x and y components of the Laplacian operator may cancel out and subsequently yield no response [10]. Therefore Laplacian is modified by ML which can be computed by adding the squared second derivatives. Tenenbaum focus measure is based on first derivatives of and image in x and y directions. It is a gradient magnitude maximization method that measures the sum of the squared responses of the horizontal and vertical Sobel masks. For robustness, it is also summed in a local window. One of the other well known focus measure is the GLV focus measure, based on the idea that in the case of a sharp image, the variance of the intensities is higher than that for a blurred image. The M_2 focus measure is actually modified version of Tenenbaum focus measure. The effects of illumination have also been studied in SFF [4].

SFF can be implemented through a variety of techniques including traditional methods [9] [11] [12], wavelet analysis [5], neural networks[6], dynamic programming [7][8] etc, but all these techniques start with the estimation of depth map using focus measures. Hence, the techniques for the estimation of this initial depth map become quite significant, and any error that occurred in them is carried forward to next stage, too. Also, when the images for SFF are corrupted with noise, these algorithms must show robustness even in the presence of noise.

In this paper we have proposed a new Focus Measure which normalizes the pixel values along the optical axis, a Low-Pass Filter is designed to remove the noise which consists of high frequencies. Then the best focus points are found by maximizing the focus curve and the corresponding frame number is taken as depth for the particular point. The process is repeated to recover the shape of the object.

The paper is organized in the following way. In section 2 some details of related work are given from the literature. Section 3 describes the low pas filter. In section 4 the proposed algorithm has been discussed. In section 5, the noise and its affects are shown. Section 6 gives the results of shape reconstruction in the presence of noise and comparisons with other commonly used focus measures have been discussed. In the final section we have concluded the outcome of our results.

2   Shape from Focus

In SFF methods, a sequence of images are used, taken by a single camera at different focus levels, to compute the depth of the object in the scene. Then, the entire image sequence is searched to find the best focused image frame for a particular point in the image space. By setting the camera parameters for that image frame, the distance of the corresponding object point is computed by using the Lens-Formula (1). Where f is focal length, Δ_o and Δ_i, are the object and image distance from the lens, respectively. Since this method involves focusing the object for finding 3-D shape, therefore it is called shape from focus (SFF).

$$\frac{1}{f} = \frac{1}{\Delta_o} + \frac{1}{\Delta_i} \tag{1}$$

In a well-focused (gray-scale) image the values of the pixels (white and black) have relatively greater difference than that in an ill-focused (gray-scale) image. The equation for the blur radius 'R' caused by the focusing of the object surface is given by the (2).

$$R = s\frac{D}{2}(\frac{1}{f} - \frac{1}{\Delta_o} - \frac{1}{\Delta_i}) \qquad (2)$$

Where 'D' is the diameter for the lens aperture and 's' is the distance for the image sensor plane from the lens as shown in Figure 1.

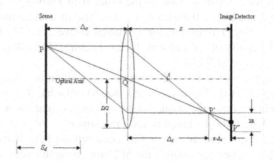

Fig. 1. Image formation in CCD Camera

Using the Thin-Lens-Model stated above, when the point 'P' on the object is best focused in the focused plane, its corresponding pixel intensity value in the image is its true value (i.e. in a gray-scale image, for white object points on the body the pixel intensity value in the image will be near to maximum and for the black object points the pixel intensity value will be near to minimum), whereas, when the point is defocused it will have the defused value (i.e. between white and black). This is explained by Figure 2.

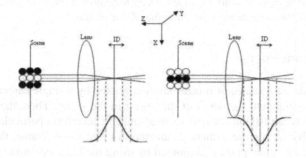

Fig. 2. Typical behavior for two different types of object points in the image sequence

3   Low-Pass Filter

A low-pass filter is a filter that passes low-frequency signals but attenuates (reduces the amplitude of) signals with frequencies higher than the cutoff frequency. The actual amount of attenuation for each frequency varies from filter to filter. It is some-times called a high-cut filter, or treble cut filter when used in audio applications. A low-pass filter is the opposite of a high-pass filter, and a band-pass filter is a combination of a low-pass and a high-pass.

The concept of a low-pass filter exists in many different forms, including electronic circuits (like a hiss filter used in audio), digital algorithms for smoothing sets of data, acoustic barriers, blurring of images, and so on. Low-pass filters play the same role in signal processing that moving averages do in some other fields, such as finance; both tools provide a smoother form of a signal which removes the short-term oscillations, leaving only the long-term trend.

One simple electrical circuit that will serve as a low-pass filter consists of a resistor in series with a load, and a capacitor in parallel with the load. The capacitor exhibits reactance, and blocks low-frequency signals, causing them to go through the load instead. At higher frequencies the reactance drops, and the capacitor effectively functions as a short circuit. The combination of resistance and capacitance gives the time constant of the filter $\tau = RC$. The break frequency, also called the turnover frequency or cutoff frequency (in hertz), is determined by the time constant:

$$f_c = \frac{1}{2\pi\tau} = \frac{1}{2\pi RC} \tag{3}$$

or equivalently (in radians per second):

$$\omega_c = \frac{1}{\tau} = \frac{1}{RC} \tag{4}$$

We can understand this circuit in a way that the idea of reactance at a particular frequency:

- Since DC cannot flow through the capacitor, DC input must "flow out" the path marked V_{out} (analogous to removing the capacitor).
- Since AC flows very well through the capacitor — almost as well as it flows through solid wire — AC input "flows out" through the capacitor, effectively short circuiting to ground (analogous to replacing the capacitor with just a wire).

The effect of a low-pass filter can be simulated on a computer by analyzing its behavior in the time domain, and then discretizing the model. From fig.4 , according to Kirchoff's Laws and the definition of capacitance

$$V_{in}(t) - V_{out}(t) = RC\frac{dV_{out}}{dt} \tag{5}$$

This equation can be discretized. For simplicity, assume that samples of the input and output are taken at evenly-spaced points in time separated by Δ_T time. Let the samples of V_{in} be represented by the sequence $(x_1, x_2, ..., x_n)$, and let V_{out} be represented by the sequence $(y_1, y_2, ..., y_n)$ which correspond to the same points in time. Making these substitutions:

$$x_i - y_i = RC\frac{y_i - y_{i-1}}{\Delta_T} \tag{6}$$

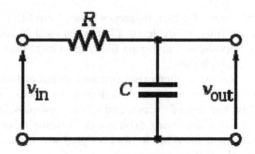

Fig. 3. A simple Low Pass RC Filter

And rearranging terms gives the recurrence relation

$$y_i = x_i \left(\frac{\Delta_T}{RC + \Delta_T} \right) + y_{i-1} \left(\frac{RC}{RC + \Delta_T} \right) \tag{7}$$

That is, this discrete-time implementation of a simple RC low-pass filter is same as the exponentially-weighted moving average.

4 Proposed Method

Using the Thin-Lens-Model (stated section 2), when the point 'P' on the object is best focused in the focused plane, its corresponding pixel intensity value in the image is its true value (i.e. in a gray scale image, for white points on the body the pixel intensity value in the image will be near to maximum and for the black points the pixel intensity value will be near to minimum), whereas, when the point is defocused it will have the defused value (i.e. between white and black). This change in pixel intensity follows a 'Generalized Gaussian' curve [3]. Figure 2 shows the typical pixel behavior for two different pixels of simulated cone in the image sequence.

In the figure, the vertical axis shows the 'pixel intensity' in gray scale image and horizontal axis shows 'image frame numbers' in the image sequence.

From these figures it is clear that the values of both 'white' and 'black' pixels in the image sequence have relatively very close values in defocused region, and only for focused regions these values vary from each other with great difference. We modified these values according to the following formula:

$$\left[{}^{(i,j)} m_k \right]_{nx1} = \left[\sum_{\Omega} \left({}^{(i+x,j+y)} p_k - \max \left\{ {}^{(i,j)} p_1, {}^{(i,j)} p_n \right\} \right)^2 \right]_{nx1} \tag{8}$$

for all $1 \leq k \leq n$

Where, ${}^{(i,j)} p_k$ is the kth value in the original pixel intensity vector ${}^{(i,j)} P$, ${}^{(i,j)} p_1$ and ${}^{(i,j)} p_n$ are $1st$ and $last$ values in pixel intensity vector, ${}^{(i,j)} m_k$ is the kth value in the modified pixel intensity vector ${}^{(i,j)} M$, i and j are the x and y position of the pixel in special domain, Ω is the summing window for the focus measure and n is the total number of images in the image sequence.

Low pass filter is then applied to the modified pixel intensity vector to remove the noise. Equation (9) yields the final focus curve of the proposed focus measure.

$$^{(i,j)}y_k = {}^{(i,j)}m_k\left(\frac{1}{\sigma_1\sigma_2+1}\right) + {}^{(i,j)}y_{k-1}\left(\frac{\sigma_1\sigma_2}{\sigma_1\sigma_2+1}\right) \tag{9}$$

Where σ_1 and σ_2 is tuned for the low pass filter. The lag in the focus curve is given by the following equation.

$$\ell = \sigma_1\sigma_2 \tag{10}$$

5   Effect of Noise

In the previous section the proposed FM was described, while in this section the effect of noise on shape reconstruction are discussed. When the images used for SFF are corrupted with noise, the computation of depth map becomes difficult. In real time applications, various type of noise (like Rayleigh, Exponential, Uniform, Shot, Speckle, Gaussian etc.) may occur. Therefore, a robust method is required to deal with noisy situations.

Many Focus Measures discussed in the literature are based on the second-derivative on the image gradient, hence, are more prone to noise. Laplacian and its variants are based on second-derivative, whereas Tenenbaum is based on single derivative technique which is again sensitive to noise (but less than second-derivative techniques). Same problems are also faced when incorporating mean and gray-level-values.

For experiments we have used the image sequences of simulated cone, real cone and real plane as shown in fig. 4.

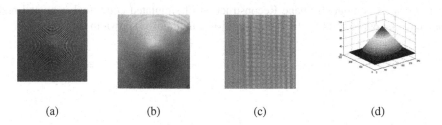

(a)   (b)   (c)   (d)

Fig. 4. Experimented objects, (a) Simulated Cone, (b) Real Cone, (c) Real Plane, (d) Original Depth Map of Simulated Cone

We have added Gaussian noise to the image sequence with zero mean ($\mu = 0$) and different variances to compare our results. The results are compared and discussed in the next section. Figure 5, shows the frame 10th of the Simulated Cone Image Sequence, degraded by the Gaussian noise with ($\mu = 0$; $\sigma = 0.05 \sim 0.00005$).

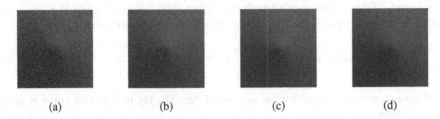

(a)   (b)   (c)   (d)

Fig. 5. Frame 10th of Simulated Cone corrupted with Gaussian Noise with $\mu=0$, (a) $\sigma=0.05$, (b) $\sigma=0.005$, (c) $\sigma=0.0005$, (d) $\sigma=0.00005$

6   Results and Discussions

Considering two object points ($^{(110,110)}P$) in the simulated cone image sequence, we computed pixel intensity vector by taking values in all the images for a fixed object point as shown in the Figure 6, along Z-axis. Figure 6 shows the pixel intensity vector for the object points ($^{(110,110)}P$) in the simulated cone image sequence. The original intensity vector object point $^{(110,110)}P$ has first and last values as 85 and 82 with maximum as 154 at 42. When equation (8) is applied to these vectors we get modified intensity vectors. The modified intensity vector $^{(110,110)}M$ have maximum at 40, shown in Figure 6. It can also be seen from Figure 6 that the proposed FM modified the two problem of finding maxima and minima (of two types of object points) into one-single problems of finding maxima, thus reducing the complexity of the whole image space. To compute final values for the depth-map, equation (9) is applied to the modified intensity vector to get the smoothened curve .The depth values was found by searching maxima of result of low pass filter and its corresponding frame number, and was found to be 40.

Once, the depth for all the object points in the image sequence is found, the initial depth map is computed. Shape Reconstruction of simulated cone, real cone and real plane by using proposed method and traditional methods is shown in fig.7.

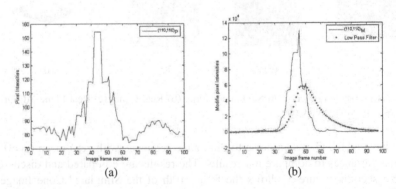

(a)   (b)

Fig. 6. Pixel behavior of object point $^{(110,110)}P$, Modified Pixel behavior of object point $^{(110,110)}P$, Low Pass Filter output

Fig.8 shows the shape reconstruction of these objects by proposed method and traditional methods with Gaussian noise (μ=0; σ=0.05).

Table 1 show the RMSE and correlation values of the simulated cone without noise computed by proposed method and traditional FMs. In Table 2 and 3 the comparison of RMSE and correlation for the simulated cone in the presence of Gaussian Noise, computed by proposed method and other traditional FMs is made. Figure 9 and 10 represent the RMSE and correlation of table 2 and 3 in graphical form. It is clear from these tables and figures that the proposed method has performed well and shows good results even in the presence of high noise.

Table 1. RMSE and Correlation of different methods compared with proposed method

Method	RMSE	Correlation
SML	12.4475	0.7389
GLV	10.9586	0.8021
M_2	10.8687	0.8081
Tenenbaum	10.8675	0.8016
Proposed	8.3706	0.9515

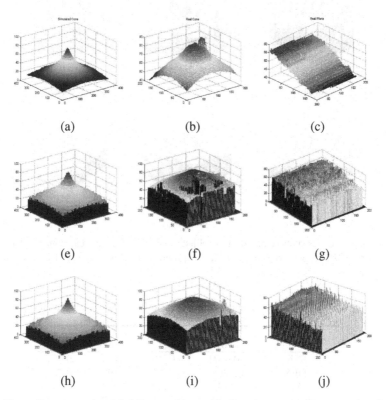

(a)   (b)   (c)

(e)   (f)   (g)

(h)   (i)   (j)

Fig. 7. Shape Reconstruction of different objects (simulated cone, real cone, and real plane) (a,b,c)by proposed method,(e, f, g) by SML; (h, i, j) by GLV

Table 2. RMSE for Gaussian Noise (σ=0) with different Variances

Method	Variances			
	0.05	0.005	0.0005	0.00005
SML	40.8012	35.0583	11.7718	11.4098
GLV	12.8301	11.1016	11.1524	11.2033
M₂	33.6564	11.3369	11.2324	11.2673
Tenenbaum	14.3892	11.0811	11.1050	11.1290
Proposed	9.7397	9.6961	9.7096	9.7428

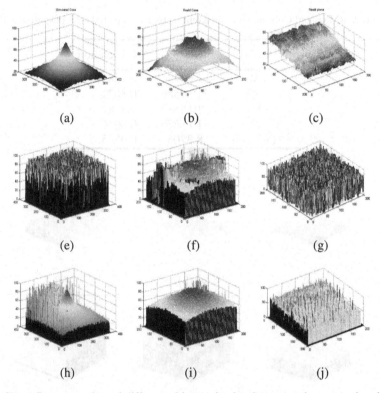

(a)   (b)   (c)

(e)   (f)   (g)

(h)   (i)   (j)

Fig. 8. Shape Reconstruction of different objects; simulated cone, real cone, and real plane, with Gaussian Noise (μ=0; σ=0.05)), (a,b,c) by proposed method; (e, f, g) by SML; (h, i, j) by GLV

Table 3. Correlation for Gaussian Noise (μ=0) with different Variances

Method	Variances			
	0.05	0.005	0.0005	0.00005
SML	-0.0671	0.0619	0.7744	0.7877
GLV	0.7305	0.8007	0.7981	0.7969
M₂	0.1139	0.7949	0.7997	0.7989
Tenenbaum	0.6653	0.8001	0.7979	0.7965
Proposed	0.9499	0.9511	0.9511	0.9507

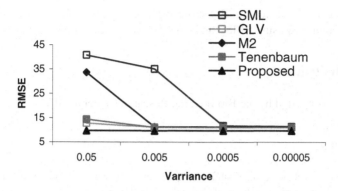

Fig. 9. Comparison of RMSE by Different Methods with Proposed Method for Simulated Cone

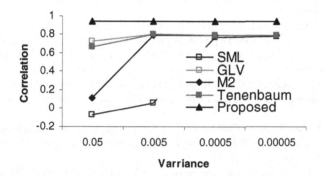

Fig. 10. Comparison of Correlation by Different Methods with Proposed Method for Simulated Cone

7 Conclusion

In this paper, we have proposed a new focus measure especially for the shape reconstruction using focus based passive method (Shape from Focus). For this purpose, we have developed a simple but robust algorithm to calculate best focus measure using the idea of a simple RC Low Pass Filter. The proposed FM has shown good results even in the presence of noise.

In Shape from Focus the images are taken by varying the focus value in different steps, and each pixel in the image is taken as a single measurement. The Thin-Lens-Model is used to estimate the change in pixel's energy. The pixel values are modified by subtracting the maximum of first and last frame along the optical axis. An analogous of a simple RC filter is used to eliminate the noise present in the modified values. The maximum value in the modified pixel intensity vector and its corresponding frame number is searched.

The proposed method is more precise as compared to previous methods and also the robustness of the method to accommodate different types of noise at different standard deviations makes the FM more vigorous against noisy measurements. The results are compared using RMSE and Correlation.

Acknowledgement

This work is supported by the Bio Imaging Research Center at GIST.

References

[1] Helmli, F.S., Scherer, S.: Adaptive Shape from Focus with and Error Estimation in Light Microscopy. In: Proceedings of the 2nd International Symposium on Image and Signal Processing and Analysis, ISAP 2001, June 2001, pp. 188–193 (2001)

[2] Subbarao, M., Choi, T., Nikzad, A.: Focusing Techniques. Optical Eng. 32(11), 2824–2836 (1993)

[3] Mannan, S.M., Saeed, A., Choi, T.S.: A Fast Algorithm for 3D Camera using Pixel-Intensities as a model for Depth Measurement. In: Proceedings of International Conference on Consumer Electronics (ICCE) 2008, Las Vegas, Nevada USA, January 11-13, pp. 4–24 (2008)

[4] Noguchi, M., Nayar, S.K.: Microscopic Shape from Focus Using Active Illumination. In: IEEE International Conference on Pattern Recognition, October 1994, pp. 147–152 (1994)

[5] Asif, M., Malik, A.S., Choi, T.S.: 3-D Shape Recovery from Image Defocus Using Wavelet Analysis. In: ICIP 2005, IEEE International Conference on Image Processing, September 2005, vol. 1 (2005)

[6] Asif, M., Choi, T.S.: Shape from Focus using Multilayer Feed-forward Neural Networks. IEEE Transactions on Image Processing 10(11) (November 2001)

[7] Ahmed, M.B., Choi, T.S.: A Heuristic Approach for Finding Best Focused Shape. IEEE Transactions on Circuit and System for Video Technology 15(4) (April 2005)

[8] Ahmed, M.B., Choi, T.S.: Fast and Accurate 3-D Shape from Focus Using Dynamic Programming Optimization Technique. In: ICASSP 2005, IEEE International Conference on Acoustics, Speech and Signal Processing, March 2005, vol. 2 (2005)

[9] Subbarao, M., Choi, T.: Accurate Recovery of Three-Dimensional Shape from Image Focus. IEEE Trans.on Pattern Analysis and Machine Intelliegence 17(3), 266–274 (1995)

[10] Nayar, S.: Shape from Focus System for Rough Surface. In: Proc. IEEE Computer Soc. Conf. Computer Vision and Pattern Recognition, Champaign, III, June 1992, pp. 302–308 (1992)

[11] Nayar, S.K., Nakagawa, Y.: Shape from Focus System. IEEE Transactions on Pattern Analysis and Machine Intelligence 16(8), 824–831 (1994)

[12] Choi, T.S., Asif, M., Yun, J.: Three-Dimensional Shape Recovery from Focused Image Surface. In: IEEE International Conference on Acoustics, Speech and Signal Processing, ICASSP 1999, March 1999, vol. 6 (1999)

An Ant Colony Optimization Approach for the Preference-Based Shortest Path Search

Seung-Ho Ok[1], Woo-Jin Seo[1], Jin-Ho Ahn[2], Sungho Kang[3], and Byungin Moon[1]

[1] School of Electrical Eng. & Computer Science, Kyungpook National University,
Daegu, Korea
{wintiger,swj82}@ee.knu.ac.kr, bihmoon@knu.ac.kr
[2] Dept. of Electronic Engineering, Hoseo University, Chungcheongnam-do, Korea
jhahn@hoseo.edu
[3] Dept. of Electrical and Electronic Engineering, Yonsei University, Seoul, Korea
shkang@yonsei.ac.kr

Abstract. In this paper, a modified ant colony system (ACS) algorithm is proposed to find a shortest path based on the preference of links. Most of the shortest path search algorithms aim at finding the distance or time shortest paths. However, these shortest paths are not surely an optimum path for the drivers who prefer choosing a less short, but more reliable or flexible path. For this reason, we propose the preference-based shortest path search algorithm which uses the properties of the links of the map. The properties of the links are specified by a set of data provided by the user of the car navigation system. The proposed algorithm was implemented in C and experiments were performed upon the map that includes 64 nodes with 118 links.

Keywords: heuristic shortest path algorithm, car navigation system, ant colony optimization algorithm, artificial intelligence.

1 Introduction

In recent years, there has been a resurgence of interest in the shortest path search problem for use in various engineering applications such as the highway systems, railroads, transportation planning systems and communication networks [1,2]. In particular, car navigation systems have exhibited explosive growth in popularity due to recent developments in Intelligent Transportation Systems [2].

A single-pair shortest path search from a source node to a destination node is one of the most important problems for the car navigation systems because there are many possible paths to the destination node. During the past years, A number of shortest path search algorithms such as A* (A-star), Dijkstra and heuristic algorithms have been proposed for use in car navigation systems [2,3,4,5].

Sara Nazari et al. suggest a modified version of dijkstra algorithm, which states that search space is restricted by the use of a rectangle or a hexagon in order to improve run time and memory usage of the algorithm [3]. Hao Yue et al. study the application of A* shortest path searching algorithm in real-time urban dynamic traffic environment [4]. M. Noto and H. Sato proposed a method for obtaining a path that is

D. Ślęzak et al. (Eds.): FGCN/ACN 2009, CCIS 56, pp. 539–546, 2009.

as close as possible to the path obtained by the Dijkstra method with decreased searching time [2]. Also, a car navigation system based on the ant algorithm is proposed in [5]. Most of these shortest path search algorithms aim at finding the shortest path whether it is distance shortest or time shortest. Compared to previous works, we propose the preference-based shortest path search algorithm which is a modified version of the ACS algorithm. Proposed algorithm uses the properties of the links of the map.

The rest of the paper is organized as follows. In Section 2, we briefly introduce the ant system (AS) and the ACS algorithm. Section 3 describes the proposed ACS algorithm for the preference-based shortest path search. In Section 4, we present the implementation of the algorithm and analyze the experiment results of the algorithm as a function of various parameters. Finally, we summarize and conclude the paper in Section 5.

2 Ant Colony Optimization Algorithm

The ant colony optimization (ACO) algorithm was proposed by Dorigo and his colleagues as a method for solving optimization problems [6]. It takes inspiration from the foraging behavior of some ant species. These ants deposit pheromone on the ground in order to mark some favorable paths that should be followed by other ants of the colony. As time goes on, the pheromone on the shorter path from their nest to the food source is reinforced sooner than that on the longer path by the ants. Thus, most of the ants can find the shortest path because the shortest path has the highest pheromone intensity.

The first ACO algorithm was developed by Dorigo, referred to as ant system (AS) [6]. And the ACS was developed by Gambardella and Dorigo to improve the performance of AS [7]. ACS differs from AS in four aspects. First, a different transition rule is used. Second, a different pheromone update rule is defined. Third, local pheromone update are introduced. Finally, candidate lists are used to favor specific nodes.

In ACS, ant k, currently located at node i, selects the next node j using the rule (1).

$$
j = \begin{cases} \arg\ \max_{u \in N_i^k(t)}\ \{\tau_{iu}(t)\eta_{iu}^{\beta}(t)\} & \text{if } r \leq r_0 \\ \text{choose } j \text{ using the probability function (2)} & \text{if } r > r_0 \end{cases} \tag{1}
$$

where r is a random variable uniformly distributed in [0, 1], r_0 is a user-specified parameter.

$$
p_{ij}^k(t) = \frac{\tau_{ij}(t)\eta_{ij}^{\beta}(t)}{\sum_{u \in N_i^k(t)} \tau_{iu}(t)\eta_{iu}^{\beta}(t)} \tag{2}
$$

where N_i^k is the set of candidate nodes connected to node i, with respect to ant k. τ_{ij} represents pheromone from node i to node j. η_{ij} is a heuristic function that is defined to the inverse of the distance between node i and j. Parameter β is a positive constant used to amplify the influence of the heuristic function.

Unlike the AS, only the ant that constructed the shortest path is allowed to reinforce the pheromone on the links of the corresponding best path using the global update rule (3).

$$\tau_{ij}(t+1) = (1 - \rho_1)\tau_{ij}(t) + \rho_1 \Delta\tau_{ij}(t) \tag{3}$$

with ρ_1 in (0, 1), and $\Delta\tau_{ij}(t)$ is the amount of pheromone deposited by the ant k of time step t on the link (i, j). In addition to the global update rule, ACS uses the local updating rule (4).

$$\tau_{ij}(t) = (1 - \rho_2)\tau_{ij}(t) + \rho_2\tau_0 \tag{4}$$

with ρ_2 also in (0, 1), and τ_0 is a small positive constant value.

3 Proposed Algorithm

In this section, we propose the modified version of the ACS algorithm to find the preference-based shortest path. The flowchart of the proposed algorithm and its differences from the conventional ACS algorithm are described in details.

The flowchart of the proposed algorithm is described in Fig. 1. At the first step, parameters of the algorithm such as the number of ant (n_k), coefficient of the heuristic function (β), balancing factor of the node selection (r_0) and maximum number of Try and $Iteration$ are initialized. After setting the cost of the iteration best ant to the infinity, unlike the conventional ACS, the pheromone of each link is initialized to the distance of each links of the map.

In this algorithm, the $Iteration$ loop is nested within the Try loop as shown in Fig. 1. Within a single Try loop iteration, if the $Iteration$ loop is finished, this algorithm outputs the path of the final iteration best ant as the best path for the current β, and the next Try loop iteration for another best path starts after increasing β. That is, as the iteration number of Try loop is increased, we can find the more biased path in favor of the user's preference, because the heuristic function represents the preference of the move from node i to node j.

In the $Iteration$ loop, all ants construct the path from the source node to the destination node using the different transition rule from the conventional ACS algorithm. The transition rule (5) uses the inverse of the multiplication of the pheromone and the heuristic function because the pheromone is initialized by the distance of the links of the map.

If $r > r_0$, an ant k, currently located at node i, selects the next node j using the transition rule (5). When the small value of r_0 is used, most of the ants explore paths more widely according to the probability p_{ij}^k. Otherwise, if $r \leq r_0$, the transition rule (6) is used. If there are no candidate nodes at the node i, the transition rule (5) is used like $r > r_0$,. Therefore, when the large value of r_0 is used, most of the ants choose

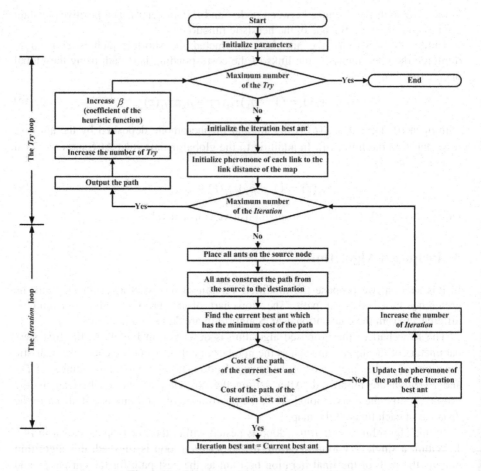

Fig. 1. The flowchart of the proposed algorithm

paths using the candidate list, which is a list of preferred nodes. For these reasons, r_0 is used to balance exploration and exploitation of the ant behavior.

$$p_{ij}^k(t) = \frac{1/\left(\tau_{ij}(t)\eta_{ij}^\beta(t)\right)}{\sum_{u \in N_i^k(t)} 1/\left(\tau_{iu}(t)\eta_{iu}^\beta(t)\right)} \tag{5}$$

where η = avoidance of the link/preference of the link

$$j = \begin{cases} \arg \min_{u \in N_i^k(t)} \{\tau_{iu}(t)\eta_{iu}^\beta(t)\} & \text{if } \exists j \in \text{candidate list} \\ \text{chosse } j \text{ using the rule (5)} & \text{if } \exists j \notin \text{candidate list} \end{cases} \tag{6}$$

After all ants construct the path from the source to the destination, the iteration best ant, which has the minimum cost of the path, is selected. At the end of each iteration, unlike the conventional ACS, only the pheromone of the path of the iteration best ant is updated by the rule (7) in order to prevent premature convergence of the algorithm.

$$\tau_{ij}(t+1) = \left(1 - \Delta\tau_{ij}(t)\right)\tau_{ij}(t) \tag{7}$$

where $\Delta\tau_{ij}(t) = 1/f(t)$, and $f(t)$ represents the cost of the paths of the current best ant.

4 Implementation and Experiments

In this section, we describe the implementation of the algorithm and analyze the experiment results as a function of various parameters.

4.1 Implementation

After the algorithm is implemented in C, experiments were performed upon the map that includes 64 nodes with 118 links.

Each link of the map has a property of the preference and avoidance. If the preference and avoidance of the link is equal, this link is treated as a common link. If the preference of the link is bigger than avoidance, this link is treated as a preferred link. Otherwise, the link is treated as a non-preferred link. The preference and avoidance values of the links are set to 1 or 2 to make the comparison of the experimental results easy. Our map includes 61 common links, 20 preferred links and 37 non-preferred links.

4.2 Parameters

Parameters of the algorithm, such as the number of ants n_k, balancing factor of the node selection r_0, coefficient of the heuristic function β and the number of *Iteration* loop iterations have a large influence on the performance of the algorithm. To measure the influences of these parameters, n_k, r_0, and β were examined individually.

The number of the *Try* loop iterations is set to 11 and the maximum number of the candidate nodes of a node is set to 3, whereas n_k, r_0, β and number of *Iteration* loop iterations vary with the experimental procedures and setup.

4.3 Experimental Results and Analysis

The first important experimental result is that the number of non-preferred and common links decreases in the final best path as β increases as shown in Figure 2. As β increases, the total distance of the path increases. This is because with the increase of β, the algorithm tends to accept longer detours which include preferred links. On the contrary, the cost, which is defined as the multiplication of the distance and the heuristic function, decreases gradually with increasing β. We can also observe that for the high values of β, the algorithm converges towards the same path (β from 1.4 to 2).

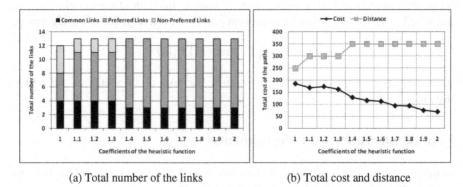

(a) Total number of the links

(b) Total cost and distance

Fig. 2. Total number of the links and total cost and distance of the selected best paths as a function of the coefficients of the heuristic function β. (*Iteration* = 50, n_k = 40, r_0 = 0.5)

The experimental results of different settings of r_0 in comparison with the previous experiments are shown in Figure 3 and 4. As can be seen in Figure 3, when the small value of r_0 (0.1) is used, various paths are selected depending on the value of β. That is because most of the ants explore paths more widely according to the probability p_{ij}^k. On the contrary, when the large value of r_0 (0.9) is used, most of the ants use the candidate lists. As a result, the algorithm tends to converge rapidly to the same path as shown in Figure 4. We can also observe that as β increases, the algorithm converges towards the same path irrespective of the value of r_0.

Figure 5 and 6 show the experimental results of different settings of n_k. As can be seen in Figure 5, when the small number of ants (n_k = 10) is used, the algorithm do not converge rapidly to the same path in comparison with the large number of ants is used (n_k = 70) as shown is Figure 6. These experimental results may indicate that the large number of ants causes the premature convergence of the algorithm.

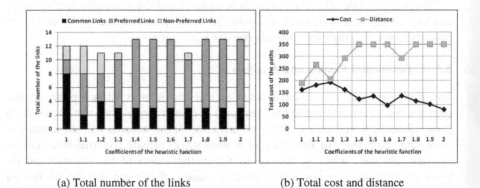

(a) Total number of the links

(b) Total cost and distance

Fig. 3. Total number of the links and total cost and distance of the selected best paths as a function of the coefficients of the heuristic function β. (*Iteration* = 50, n_k = 40, r_0 = 0.1)

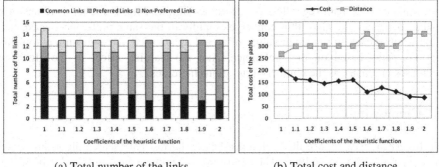

(a) Total number of the links   (b) Total cost and distance

Fig. 4. Total number of the links and total cost and distance of the selected best paths as a function of the coefficients of the heuristic function β. (*Iteration* = 50, $n_k = 40$, $r_0 = 0.9$)

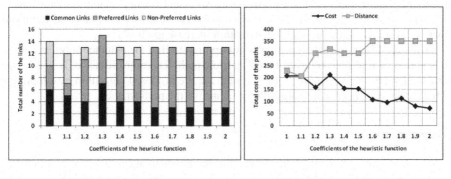

(a) Total number of the links   (b) Total cost and distance

Fig. 5. Total number of the links and total cost and distance of the selected best paths as a function of the coefficients of the heuristic function β. (*Iteration* = 50, $n_k = 10$, $r_0 = 0.5$)

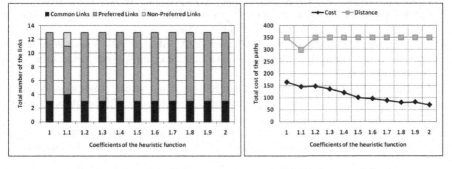

(a) Total number of the links   (b) Total cost and distance

Fig. 6. Total number of the links and total cost and distance of the selected best paths as a function of the coefficients of the heuristic function β. (*Iteration* = 50, $n_k = 70$, $r_0 = 0.5$)

Putting it all together, we observed that as β increases, the algorithm converges towards the same path regardless of the values of r_0 and n_k. If the large values of r_0 and n_k are used, the algorithm converges rapidly to the same preference-based path. On the other hand, if the small values of r_0 and n_k are used, the algorithm outputs the various paths based on the preference. And the learning effect of the algorithm increases gradually as the number of iterations increases.

5 Conclusions

In this paper, we propose the preference-based shortest path search algorithm which uses the properties of the links. The algorithm was implemented in C and experiments were performed upon the map that includes 64 nodes with 118 links as a function of various parameters.

The results show that as β increases, the final best path includes more preferred links while the number of non-preferred and common links decreases. On the other hand, the total distance of the path increases with increasing β while the total cost of the path decreases gradually. Also, we can observe that as the number of iterations increases, the learning effect of the algorithm increase gradually.

Although the proposed algorithm is not optimal to find the distance shortest path, it is suitable to find the preferred-based shortest path. Therefore it can be a viable and practical solution. Our future work will upgrade the proposed algorithm by adopting a distance shortest path search algorithm to improve the performance.

References

1. Fu, L., Sun, D., Rilett, L.R.: Heuristic shortest path algorithms for transportation applications: state of the art. Computers and Operations Research 33(11), 3324–3343 (2006)
2. Noto, M., Sato, H.: A method for the shortest path search by extended Dijkstra algorithm. In: IEEE International Conference Systems on Man, and Cybernetics, vol. 3, pp. 2316–2320 (2000)
3. Nazari, S., Meybodi, M.R., Salehigh, M.A., Taghipour, S.: An Advanced Algorithm for Finding Shortest Path in Car Navigation System. In: International Workshop on Intelligent Networks and Intelligent Systems, pp. 671–674 (2008)
4. Yue, H., Shao, C.: Study on the Application of A* Shortest Path Search Algorithm in Dynamic Urban Traffic. In: Third International Conference on Natural Computation, vol. 3, pp. 463–469 (2007)
5. Salehinejad, H., Talebi, S.: A new ant algorithm based vehicle navigation system: A wireless networking approach. In: International Symposium on Telecommunications, pp. 36–41 (2008)
6. Dorigo, M., Maniezzo, V., Colorni, A.: Ant system: optimization by a colony of cooperating agents. IEEE Transactions on Systems, Man, and Cybernetics-Part B 26(1), 29–41 (1996)
7. Gambardella, L.M., Dorigo, M.: Solving Symmetric and Asymmetric TSPs by Ant Colonies. In: Proceedings of the IEEE Conference on Evolutionary Computation, pp. 622–627 (1996)

A Study on the Composite Power Line Communication Network

Duckhwa Hyun, Younghun Lee, and Youngdeuk Moon

Principal Researcher in Smart Communication Part,
KEPRI (Korea Electric Power Research Institute), Daejeon, Korea
hyundh@kepri.re.kr, yhlee@hnu.ac.kr, ydm@pufs.ac.kr

Abstract. The existing Power Line can be used as Communication Medium by using Power Line Communication (PLC). PLC can be adopted as a main Communication Means, and other wired/wireless technologies can be adopted as second means. In order to this, the Medium Voltage PLC has to be used as a long distance Communication Network. In our study, the Routing Algorithm is also fit for PLC on the basis of Power Distribution Line. It is designed more useful in case of accidents when roundabout Routes are requested. It makes Power Distribution Network more efficient as Communication Network. In case of accidents, we suggest the Intelligent Composite Communication System for optimal roundabout routes in Communication Network, and verify its performance and reliability in the real Test Field.

Keywords: Power Line Communication, Composite Communication System, Composite Routing Algorithm.

1 Introduction

Recently, Power Line Communication (PLC) technology economically can be used for communication network technology and can be complemented before being applied to long distance communication network for Automatic Power Distribution System[1].

In this paper, PLC is adopted as a main communication means to construct economical communication network, and other wired/wireless communication technologies as second ones for reliability, extensibility, and flexibility of communication network. The result is the Composite Communication System (CCS) that helps to maintain the stability of power system, the topology of CCS, and the Routing Algorithm. We also verified the success rate of PLC signal packets on Medium Voltage Distribution Line (DL), the range of PLC, and time to recover communication network against line troubles [2].

The CCS was installed and tested in Ko-Chang Power System Test Center to verify its performance and reliability before practical usage in Real Field. It passed various communication tests, and was applied to Distribution Automation System (DAS) which is the strictest power service among many ones.

Its performance and reliability also was verified through the some accident scenarios in DAS, and we could found out it met all requirements of DAS.

D. Ślęzak et al. (Eds.): FGCN/ACN 2009, CCIS 56, pp. 547–554, 2009.

2 Analysis of Medium Voltage Power System Structure

The general model of DL structure is as shown in Fig. 1. We define the typical structure of Power Distribution System, and suggest the optimal Communication System for it.

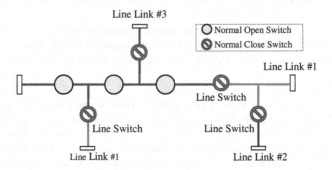

Fig. 1. Topology by Connecting of 3 DLs

The Standard Model of Medium Voltage Distribution Lines consists of at least two DLs which are linked to one another. Each DL is several kilometers in length, and many Automatic Switches as well as Feeder Remote Terminal Unit (FRTU) in each DL. The average length of DL is about 33 km, and the average length between nearby Automatic Switches is 5 km considering DL is usually divided by six parties.

We define each party as a Unit LAN (UL), and all ULs are connected with each other by Bridges or Gateways. Three (or four) ULs organize one Unit Network (UN) which is a virtual unit network to be protected or restored by using optic/satellite communication in emergency [3].

3 Analysis of Requirements from CCS

3.1 Transmission Range of PLC Signal

Medium voltage lines from substations reach transformers. The length is 10 km in downtown and 30 km in country. The average length of DL is about 33 km. Switches are installed in each one to two km; 500 m in downtown, 1.5 km in the outskirts of downtown, and 2 km in country). This environment demands that medium voltage PLC signal reaches at least 5 km without repeating function, which can cover more than 33 km in a unit communication network. The coverage may extend up to 66 km when DLs are broken and make a round to other DL.

The backbone network from a point of DLs to DAS server in control center uses optic, HFC (Hybrid Fiber Coaxial), or other wire/wireless network. This backbone network is already used commercially so that its communication range needs not to be considered; only the requirements of delay and response time would be considered below.

3.2 Transmission Rate

Table 1 shows the requirement from power automation system like DAS, AMR.

According to Table 1, the required transmission rate is less than 9,600 bps that is not strict. Therefore CCS based on PLC has only to meet this requirement. Other communication network like satellite and optic do not support high speed transmission rate, however, faster transmission of data would be guaranteed to support intelligently automatic routing algorithm in case of communication line trouble or node breakdown.

Table 1. The Required Transmission Spec. of Power Automation Devices

Service	Link Bandwidth	Transmission Duration	Max. data Length (Byte)	Max. Data Quantities (Kbyte)	Required Response Time(Sec.)
Distribution Automation	<2,400	3 sec × # of Switches	250	1	10(Wired), 30(Wireless)
Monitoring Transformer	<9,600	1 Time/Hour	250	32	10~
AMR	<9,600	4 Times/Hour	600	256	10~
Load Control	<1,200	Several Times/Year	<10	10	no Ack. (10)

4 Design of Routing Algorithm in CCS

The Message Framework is designed on the basis of the analyzed result beyond, and is shown in Fig. 2 and Fig. 3 [4].

Random route establishment function is useful when no routing available or need to be updated. The information of communication network structure can be obtained

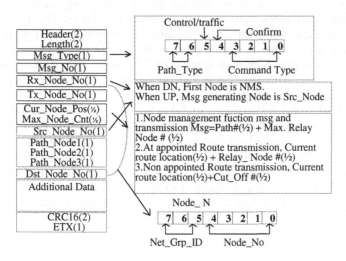

Fig. 2. Basic Message Format

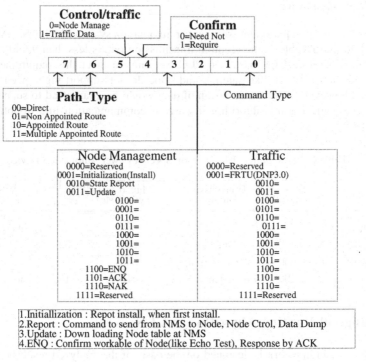

Fig. 3. Message Type

by using this function. All newly installed nodes broadcast setup information including destination address but not repeater's addresses. All repeating nodes receiving the information packet attach their own ID and retransmit the packet. The destination node can make a Routing Table with Routing Information included in the received data. This Routing Table is retransmitted in the reverse order, which makes other nodes in the route have their own Routing Table. It is the early stage of route establishment procedure. After that, flexible automatic routing function is carried out without additional setting up any route.

Route Establishment Function is useful in a viewpoint of network reliability, but brings about another problem (excess of data traffic). Therefore the function is restricted to be used in the early installation or once in a long while if necessary.

Considering PLC characteristics, unreasonable traffic from packet broadcasting can drop off in network performance, and cause a bottleneck or an obstacle in network. For those reason, PLC Network is divided by Network ID, and the excess of broadcasting Packets do not go over to other Network. It removes duplicated traffic.

5   Construction of CCS in Real Field

The existing PLC Transceiver is a simple communication device. So there is no routing function among different communication networks within it. That means it is not possible to build automatic routing network using it. Hence, intelligent CCS device is required so as to link among different networks against emergencies.

This Router is in charge of monitoring communication lines, establishing round-about ways between PLC lines or wired/wireless media, and repeating function. It is also designed to monitor operation and status of Power Switches linked in Serial Ports. CCS Router monitors network status frequently, and use a satellite path as a roundabout way when it interprets there is no wired route available [5].

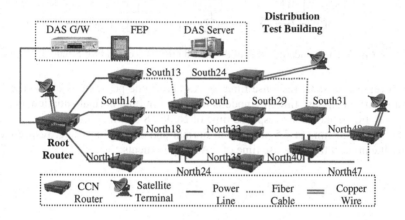

Fig. 4. DAS Field-Test System on CCS

The power distribution line (22.9 kV) is composed of two north lines and two south lines of which the beginning point is the switch-house. The distance is 8 km in total. One CCS Root Router was installed in Switch-House, and other CCS slave routers in each switch pole among fifteen CCS Routers installed in Ko-Chang.

The main communication path is on PLC Lines, and satellite path is used in an emergency. Satellite modem and antenna were installed in Switch-House, South 24, and North 44 poles. Fig. 4 shows the structure of CCS. CCS is consisted of 'south sub-network' and 'north sub-network'. Each sub-network has its own satellite path which means each sub-network has its own detour and is independent communication network. The last CCS Router in each sub-network attached to satellite modem and offers satellite communication path.

6   Field Test and Verification

The PLC routing algorithm designed above was verified by the standard model of the distribution power grid shown in Fig. 5. In Fig. 5, node 0 is directly connected to DAS Server. Node 6, 12, 18, 24 are endpoint nodes in this Network. We simulate the model using NS-2 simulation tool, low-speed PLC modem (9,600 bps).

DAS polling frequency is 3 seconds per node, and response packet frame is 250 Bytes that is the maximum size in DAS. We intentionally cause in the nodes ran-domly chosen, those are 2 times every 500 seconds, 9 times every 1,000 seconds, 12 times every 1,500 seconds and 21 times every 2,000 seconds.

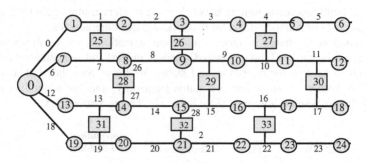

Fig. 5. The Standard Model of the Distribution Power Grid for Simulation

DAS requires a strict response time, so response time per node is checked in the simulation. The response time per node is measured in both normal situation and link failure one. Fig. 6 shows the response time of Node 18 of which the time is the longest. The measured time is 7.5 seconds in normal and link failure state, respectively. The result can meet the response time of DAS requirements.

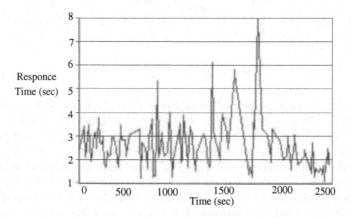

Fig. 6. Link 18 Response Time on the Link Fail

6.1 Noise and Communication Signal Test

It is reasonable to check the basic communication functions of CCS routers before evaluating the performance and reliability of CCS. The data size was fixed at 50, 100, and 200 bytes in basic communication test because DAS is the main target application of CCS and the size of data is like those in DAS.

The communication test is basic 'ping' test between arbitrary two CCS routers, and the average time delay was 640 ms at most when the data size is maximally 200 bytes.

It is assumed that it won't take more than 5 seconds between any two CCS routers regardless of the distance. In the test, other CCS routers made signal in order to consider interference phenomena that are generally happened in PLC. It helped make communication circumstance same as PLC network [6].

In Fig. 7, communication signal strength is fully high compared noise level in the Real Field, so we can confirm to successfully communicate among Routers by power line communication.

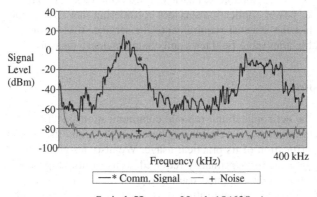

Switch House – North 18(638m)

Fig. 7. Noise and Signal Level on Distribution Line

6.2 Scenario-Based Verification of CCS

In this test, CCS was tested in terms of its performance and reliability under incidents which happened arbitrarily. CCS was assumed to detect incidents, establish an optimum detour, and guarantee successful communication even if incidents happen in any point within network. CCS was actually verified according to many reasonable scenarios, but two major scenarios are referred here. And three functions among DAS's ones were used to inspect whether CCS would apply to DAS or not - 'event measurement', ' status measurement', and 'total measurement'. The received data is 48, 36, 54 bytes, and the transmitted data is 34, 56, 212 bytes in size, respectively.

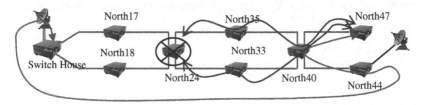

Fig. 8. Detour only through Satellite

Fig. 8 shows the case that there is no available path on wired path when an incident blocks a part of network. When the CCS router in North 24 was broken down, DAS server cannot communicate with North 47 through any wired path. Then, the CCS root router concludes there is no wired path to North 47, and establishes a detour through satellite network. The routing table is, of course, sent to all CCS routers in north sub-network. The delay time is 4~7 seconds, 2~5 seconds, and 8~10 seconds in event measurement, status measurement, and total measurement, respectively.

However, the results also guarantee that CCS can apply to DAS in spite of the strict requirements of DAS. In addition to those scenarios, CCS was verified to be most suitable for the reliable communication network of DAS by numerous experiments according to reasonable scenarios. Furthermore, CCS may be very useful system for other power application services considering that DAS is the power application which has the strictest requirements for service. It is assumed that CCS becomes invaluable after more field tests and complementary measures.

7 Conclusion

In this paper, the economical and reliable communication system is developed using the different communication technologies based on PLC, and the system is applied to DAS for the verification of its practical usage. We also design the standard model of power distribution facilities primarily required so as to utilize power line as a communication medium. Our designed routing algorithm is enough to upgrade the reliability of PLC network. The algorithm is verified through both simulation and field test. The test results show that the developed CCS can meet the requirements of other application services as well as DAS. The developed System (CCS) was tested on Ko-Chang Power System Test Center according to the variety of realistic circumstance and scenarios especially targeting DAS. Power is applied to the distributed lines and some load makes worse communication circumstance as a matter of course. The system is not complete for common use. However, it must be helpful to construct reliable, flexible, and extensible communication network for most applications.

References

1. KEPCO, Distribution Automation System, Lecture note on KEPCO education center (2006)
2. KEPCO, "DAS experts", Lecture note on KEPCO education center (2006)
3. System Architecture, Approval Testing. OPERA consortium, 06.05 (2005)
4. Bumiller, G., Lu, L., Song, Y.: Analytic performance comparison of routing protocols in master-slave PLC, ISPLC 2005 (2005)
5. Bilal, O.: Design of Broadband Coupling Circuits for Powerline Communication. In: 7th ISPLC Proceedings (2004)
6. Stallings, W.: Data and computer communications, 7th edn., p. 626. Pearson Education International

FMEA (Failure Mode Effect Analysis) for Maintenance of Mail Sorting Machine

Jeong-Hyun Park, Hoyon Kim, and Jong-Heung Park

Postal Logistics Technology Research Department,
Electronics and Telecommunications Research Institute (ETRI)
161 Kajong-Dong, Yusong-Ku, Daejeon, 305-700, Korea
{jh-park,hoyon,jpark}@etri.re.kr

Abstract. This paper describes the diagnosis item and cycle update for maintenance of mail sorting machine based on FMEA (Failure Mode Effect Analysis). We show the FMEA deployment step, result, and statistics analysis for maintenance of mail sorting machine. There is the update method of diagnosis item and cycle using RPN (Risk Priority Number) which was calculated by severity, occurrence, and detection value. There is also the maintenance status such as failure cause, failure step, and failure parts of 150 mail sorting machines on 30 mail distribution centers in nationwide, Korea. The proposed maintenance system will be adapted for safety and efficient operation and maintenance of mail sorting machine.

1 Introduction

Maintenance through the last several decades, until recently, was a relatively monolithic central function. It was usually staffed for peak activities, and often had excess capacity waiting for the breakdown to occur. With the advent of international competition in the 80's, many maintenance staffs were cut dramatically, and over several layoffs became smaller than half their original size. These cuts were often made strictly according to either financial rules (non-union companies laid-off the most senior, expensive workers) or seniority rules (union shops left seniority in place). In neither case were skills and experience the major consideration [1-2]. Simultaneous with reducing costs, companies were forced to increase quality, productivity and safety. These efforts focused on the manufacturing unit, looking to reduce variation in product, reduce production bottlenecks, and assure safe work practices. Quality theory told us to define who our customers are and get close to them. Most plants defined operations as the maintenance customer, and in increasing accountability for operating unit managers, gave them more control of the resources. The initial result was a surge in machine's operability, as operations managers directed resources towards equipment problems that had been chronic problems. The craftsmen dedicated to the units felt needed and like they were making a more direct contribution than before as part of a pool. They learned their unit's equipment intimately, and became more proficient and committed to unit performance.

There are 5 – 6 billion mails/Year, 250 million registered mails/Year, and 60 million parcels/Year without commercial home delivery parcels, in Korea. We also have about 150 different sorting machines in 30 mail distribution centers, Korea. So, it's an

D. Ślęzak et al. (Eds.): FGCN/ACN 2009, CCIS 56, pp. 555–562, 2009.

important to define the maintenance plan of heterogeneous mail sorting machines in distributed area. There are also 21 mail distribution centers, 2 logistics centers, 1 mail switching center, about 3,600 post offices with 517 delivery centers. We have 53 OVIS (OCR (Optical Character Recognition) VCS (Video Coding System) Interface System)/LSM (Letter Sorting Machine) machines for ordinary letter sorting, 22 Plat Sorting Machines for plat, 28 Packet Sorting Machines for packet, 30 Parcel Sorting Machines which has two types (slide shoe and tilt tray) for parcel, 3 Registered Mail Sorting Machines for registered mail, and 4 Delivery Sequence Sorting Machines in delivery center, in Korea. Seoul, East Seoul, Busan, and Daegu have a large sorting volume as the big size mail distribution center, Suwon, EuJeongbu, DaeJeon, An-Yang, Bucheon have a medium sorting volume, WonJu, JeonJu, KoYang have a semi-medium, others have small size mail distribution [3-5].

This paper describes the update method of diagnosis item and cycle based on FMEA (Failure Mode Effect Analysis) for maintenance of mail sorting machine. In section 2 of this paper, we show the maintenance status such as failure causes and steps of mail sorting machine in Korea. In section 3, we describe the FMEA deployment step, result, and statistics analysis for maintenance of mail sorting machine. This paper also shows the update method of diagnosis item and cycle using RPN (Risk Priority Number) which was calculated by severity, occurrence, and detection value, in section 3, and conclude with summary and further study in section 4.

2 Maintenance of Mail Sorting Machine

2.1 Maintenance Status

In this section, we show failure causes and steps of sorting machine, and find major failure cause and step via statistics analysis of failure data of sorting machine in Korea.

■ Failure Causes
The failure cause of mail sorting machine on current maintenance system, Korea has 7 cases such as Life Cycle of Part [LCP], Operation Failure of Part [OFP], Manufacturing Error of Part [MEP], Misplace of Part [MPP], Mistreat of Part [MTP], Cause from Other Part [COP], Others [O]. The figure 1 shows the statistics data from 2001 to 2007 of failure cause of mail sorting machines. The major failure cause of mail sorting machine based on figure 4 is LCP of 40% and OFP of 15%. It needs more systematic support such as standard procedure of part, the definition of priority of parts, and part list.

■ Failure Steps
The failure step of mail sorting machine on current maintenance system, Korea has 5 cases such as simple operation problem & clean of mail sorting machine [MSM] [Step1], replace of simple parts & align & tilt of MSM [Step2], replace of unit and parts & test of MSM [Step3], replace of critical unit and parts of sorting machine & test [Step4], need urgent help of sorting machine manufacture & hot line connection

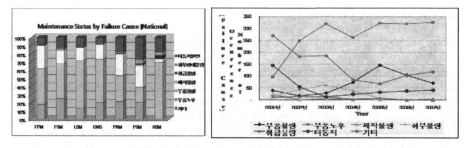

Fig. 1. Failure Causes & Statistics of Mail Sorting Machines [4]

[Step5]. The figure 2 shows the statistics data of failure step of all mail sorting machines at the end of 2007. The major failure step of mail sorting machine based on the
figure 2 is step 1 of 67% and step 2 of 23%. It shows 31.4 % failure rate of stacker
part and 22.3 % failure rate of feeder part on mail sorting machine.

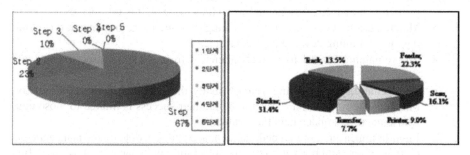

Fig. 2. Failure Steps & Statistics of Mail Sorting Machines [4]

Of course, the failure rate of sorting machine is different from sorting machine
such as OVIS, PSM, FSM, and so on. Major failure sorting machine is OVIS/LSM
which shows 66.7 % failure rate, and flat sorting machine shows 20% failure rate. The
figure 3 shows the statistics data of failure rate of all mail sorting machines from 2001
to 2007 (at the end of 2007).

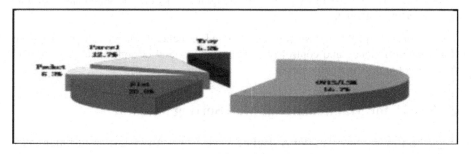

Fig. 3. Failure Rate of Mail Sorting Machines [4]

2.2 Maintenance Problem

There are no diagnosis and repair manuals of mail sorting machine. Also, there are no standard procedure and guideline of diagnosis and repair of sorting machine. Even there is no part list and replace manual of part for sorting machine. We need stock management and demand and support planning of part for sorting machine. Even if there is 5 failure steps and 7 failure causes for maintenance of mail sorting machine, it's a difficult to use and share the failure data for maintenance of mail sorting machine. Because maintenance data is not classified clearly for use of mail sorting machine, and defined by subjective judge of internal maintenance staff. So, we need standard failure steps and causes and guidelines which can use for maintenance of mail sorting machine. Otherwise, there are many barriers to overcome to be successful in improving reliability, and we won't be able to sustain the attention necessary to achieve internal change.

- There is no consistency to how units are performing maintenance.
- Planners dedicated to units do very little routine planning. Instead they are expediters, on-call supervisors, and when they do plan, it is for outages.
- Maintenance craft skills are deteriorating. No one in the organization is assuring the continuing development of craft skills
- The remaining central force feels alienated from the unit based maintenance crew.
- The Reliability Engineering Team (usually those who perform the Predictive Maintenance function) are frustrated that their success is limited to those units whose managers understand their value.
- Important measures of planned maintenance and schedule conformance are declining or very stubborn at improving. Operating units have no standard definitions of these measures, and may or may not even measure and record them.
- There is no program and education for professional of maintenance staff, and training centre.
- There is no function and system to share maintenance data which performed diagnosis and repair the sorting machine on each mail distribution centre.
- There is no practical contract for maintenance of sorting machine between operator and manufacture.
- There is no consistency policy, planning and schedule for maintenance of mail sorting machine.

For any of these problems, we consider is based, in general, on centralizing functions that create efficiency and control of in maintenance, and decentralizing functions of work effectiveness in maintenance.

3 FMEA for Maintenance of Mail Sorting Machine

In this section we describe FMEA (Failure Mode Effect Analysis) considerations such as FMEA deployment step and problem, FMEA deployment and result, statistical analysis for maintenance of mail sorting machine. We also describe the update method of diagnosis item and cycle using RPN (Risk Priority Number) which was calculated by severity, occurrence, and detection value in this section.

3.1 FMEA for Maintenance of Mail Sorting Machine

■ FMEA Deployment Step

FMEA (Failure Mode Effect Analysis) is a kind of maintenance technique for increase of usability of mail sorting machine and decrease of failure rate through decision of potential failure mode based on analysis of potential failure factor and its effect using FMEA table and sub system and unit specification [2]. FMEA has unit (part) list, its function, potential failure mode and effect, and severity, potential failure cause, occurrence, detection, RPN, and recommended action & taken.

The figure 4 shows the FMEA deployment step for maintenance of mail sorting machine. The first is to define potential failure mode and effect through maintenance data collection and analysis in step 1, the second is to calculate RPN using severity, occurrence, and detection in step 2, and update diagnosis item and cycle using RPN.

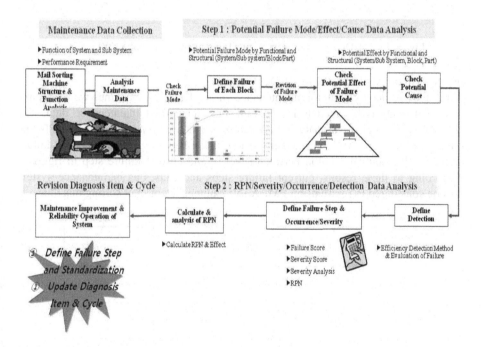

Fig. 4. FMEA Deployment Step for Maintenance of Mail Sorting Machine

■ FMEA Deployment Result

The figure 5 shows the FMEA deployment result using current maintenance data (5 failure steps and 7 failure causes) for maintenance of Toshiba OVIS machine which have run on the field since 2002. Some units which have 144 and 150 RPN value are considered to update in short of diagnosis cycle for failure protection of mail sorting machine.

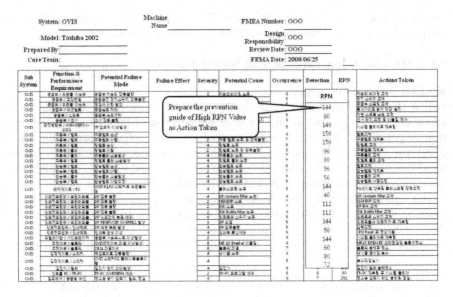

Fig. 5. FMEA Deployment Result for Maintenance of Toshiba OVIS (2002)

■ Statistical Analysis of FMEA Deployment

After FMEA deployment for maintenance of mail sorting machine, we also have statistical analysis between FMEA parameters and current maintenance data. The figure 6 shows statistical analysis between severity, occurrence, detection, RPN and current failure steps. We can see there is no relation between RPN and current failure steps, but has mutual relation between severity and current failure step in figure 6. According to these results, current failure steps and causes as maintenance system will be considered to revise using FMEA for maintenance of mail sorting machine.

Dependent Variable	Independent Variable	Significance Level(Pr<F)	Expectation(R^2)
Severity	Failure Step	< .0001	0.2311
Occurrence	Failure Step	0.2793	0.0169
Detection	Failure Step	0.7018	0.0021
RPN	Failure Step	0.0183	0.0781

Fig. 6. Statistical Analysis of FMEA Deployment of Current Failure Step

3.2 Diagnosis Item and Cycle Update Method Based on FMEA

In this subsection, we considered how to use FMEA technique for update of diagnosis item and cycle.

■   Diagnosis Item & Cycle Update using RPN Value

After FMEA deployment for maintenance of mail sorting machine, it's possible to use RPN value for update the diagnosis item and cycle of mail sorting machine. The figure 7 shows the update method of diagnosis item and cycle for maintenance of mail sorting machine. If RPN value of failure mode is high then the failure mode considers as intensive check item and short term check cycle, and if RPN value of

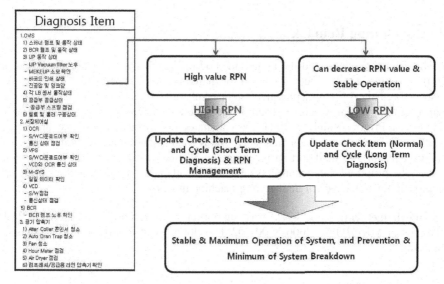

Fig. 7. Update Method of Diagnosis Item and Cycle Based on RPN Value

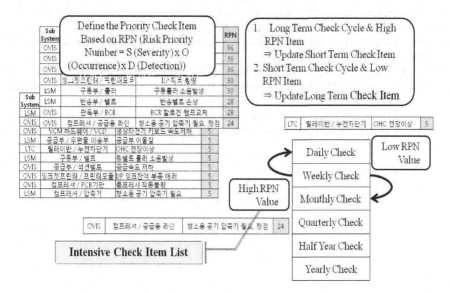

Fig. 8. Example of Diagnosis Item and Cycle Based on RPN Value

failure mode is low then the failure mode considers as normal check item and long term check cycle.

The figure 8 shows the example of diagnosis item and cycle for maintenance of OVIS mail sorting machine. We can see that in case of the RPN value is 5, the diagnosis cycle is changed to weekly check from monthly check as normal check item, and in case of the RPN value is 24, the diagnosis cycle is changed to daily check from weekly check as intensive check item in figure 8.

4 Concluding Remark

In this paper, we described the update method of diagnosis item and cycle based on FMEA (Failure Mode Effect Analysis) for maintenance of mail sorting machine. We also showed the FMEA deployment step, result, and statistics analysis for maintenance of mail sorting machine. There is the update of diagnosis item and cycle using RPN (Risk Priority Number) which was calculated by severity, occurrence, and detection value. There is also the maintenance status such as failure cause, failure step, and failure parts of 150 mail sorting machines on 30 mail distribution centers in nationwide. The proposed maintenance system will be adapted for safety and efficient operation and maintenance of mail sorting machine in Korea.

Acknowledgement. This work was supported by the Postal Technology R&D program of MKE/IITA. [2006-X-001-02, Development of Real-time Postal Logistics System].

References

1. BS EN 50126, Railway Applications – The Specification and demonstration of Reliability, Availability, Maintainability, and Safety (RAMS), British Standard (1999)
2. MIL-STD-1629A, Procedures for performing a Failure Mode, Effects, Criticality Analysis, USA (2000)
3. Post, K.: Operation and Maintenance., Korea Post Statistical Report (2008)
4. Park, J.-H., et al.: Maintenance Status and TO-BE Considerations of Mail Sorting Machines., ETRI, Korea, 12 (2008)
5. Hong, J.H., et al.: Analysis for Efficient Maintenance of Heterogeneous Mail Sorting Machine on Distributed Operation Environment., HanSeong University, Korea, 12 (2008)

Advanced Integrated Model-Driven Development Tool for USN Applications in Pervasive Computing Environment

Woo-jin Lee[1], Jang-Mook Kang[1,*], Yoon-Seok Heo[2], and Bong-Hwa Hong[3]

[1] Dept. of Information and Communication Eng., Se Jong University,
98 Gunja-Dong, Gwangjin-Gu, Seoul, 143-747, Korea
[2] Faculty of Electrical and Electronic Eng., Chung Cheong University
330 Kangnae-Myun, Chungwon-Kun, Chung-Buk, 363-792, Korea
[3] Dept. of Information and Communication, Kyung Hee Cyber University
1 Hoegi-Dong, Dongdaemun-Gu, Seoul, 130-701, Korea
{woojin,redsea}@sejong.ac.kr, hys@ok.ac.kr, bhhong@khcu.ac.kr

Abstract. In sensor networks, nodes should often operate under a demanding environment such as limited computing resources, unreliable wireless communication and power shortage. And such factors make it challenging to develop ubiquitous sensor network (USN) applications. This article presents a model-driven development tool for USN applications. USN applications are programs that are installed into nodes which consist in sensor networks. The presented tool automatically generates applications for nodes from the sensor network model. Users can develop USN applications by first developing a model for the sensor network and then designing applications by setting the values of the pre-defined attributes. The source code for applications is automatically generated from the model. The tool will help users can easily develop a large number of validated USN applications even if they do not know the details of low-level information.

Keywords: Model-Driven development tool, Sensor network application, Ubiquitous computing, Ubiquitous Sensing Network, pervasive computing.

1 Introduction

Ubiquitous sensor network (USN) [1] is a wireless network which consists of a lot of lightweight, low-powered sensor nodes. The nodes are connected to a network and sense geographical and environmental changes of the field. Through USN, things can recognize other things and sense environmental changes, so users can get the information from the things and use the information anytime, anywhere.

Currently, most sensor network operating systems provide abstraction mechanisms to help developers can construct applications without care about the limitation of USN applications. Moreover, a sensor network consists of a large number of nodes

---

* Corresponding author.

D. Ślęzak et al. (Eds.): FGCN/ACN 2009, CCIS 56, pp. 563–570, 2009.

that have various roles (i.e. data sensing, data transmitting, data collecting, data processing and acting) and a large number of various applications for those roles should be constructed.

Accordingly, a tool to help developers easily develop USN applications without learning abstraction mechanisms of operating systems and efficiently develop a large number of various applications is necessary. Advance integrated Model-driven development tool is used to automatically generate applications from a model. Therefore, model-driven development tool for efficiently developing a large number of USN applications without learning abstraction mechanisms is necessary.

2 Advance Integrated Model-Driven Development Tool for USN Applications

The proposed Advance integrated model-driven development tool for USN applications implemented as a plug-in for Eclipse [2,3] platform. Generally, application size is increased when applications are constructed using automation tools. But, the size of the automatically constructed application using the proposed tool is similar to the size of the application which is manually developed without using the tool because the tool constructs an application by composing the components which are provided by the target operating system. Therefore, USN applications which should be performed using limited resources can be appropriately developed through the proposed model-driven development tool in pervasive computing environment.

The tool consists of seven modules - *Graphical User Interface (GUI), Modeler, Configuration Information Generator, Model Validity Checker, Source Code Generator, Target Image Generator* and *Templates Storage.*

Followings are detailed descriptions of modules of the tool.

- Graphical User Interface (GUI): The GUI provides interfaces for the development of USN applications.
- Modeler: Developers write USN model diagrams and design USN applications through the Modeler. The Modeler consists of the Model Viewer and the Model Controller. The Model Viewer is a graphical representer of the USN model. The Model Controller is a manager that mediates and communicates between the model and the view. The Model Controller generates the model information using XML.
- Configuration Information Generator: The Configuration Information Generator creates the configuration information of nodes in the model using the model information.
- Model Validity Checker: The Model Validity Checker confirms whether the model of USN application is valid. It checks validity of association between the nodes, and checks validity of each node.
- Source Code Generator: The Source Code Generator creates C source files of nodes using the predefined templates and the configuration information generated by the Configuration Information Generator.
- Target Image Generator: The Target Image Generator constructs ROM image files which are installed into nodes by compiling the C source files. The ROM

image files are generated by reflecting the hardware platform of nodes in the sensor network.

- Templates Storage: The Templates Storage stores predefined templates for the generation of source codes of nodes. Modules and code templates, which are provided by target operating system, are stored in the Template Storage.

Table 1 presents the functions which are supported by the advance integrated model-driven development tool for USN applications.

Table 1. Functions of the model-driven development tool

Functions	Description	Benefits
Drawing Graphical Model Diagram	The tool provides graphical modeling notation by extending UML notation.	The developer can graphically model ubiquitous sensor network.
Setting Elements of Kernel/ Application	Through the tool, the developer sets attribute values of nodes in the model. By setting attribute values, OS kernel components are selected and application information is set up.	The developer does not need to learn any abstraction mechanisms because applications are simply designed by setting attribute values.
Model Validation	The tool checks whether USN model is designed by accepting constraints according to the role of each node and constraints of target platform.	Through model validation, defects of applications can be found in early stage of development. Accordingly, the developer can construct correct applications and therefore development cost is decreased.
Automatic Code Generation	The tool automatically generates application code from the model.	The tool supports to automatically generate application codes for all nodes in the USN model at a time. Therefore, the developer can save development effort and cost.
Program Code Editing	The developer can edit the generated application code using the tool.	The developer can modify or add application code if needed.
Automatic Generation of Target Image	To execute the application, ROM image file should be created and installed into the node. To support that, the tool automatically creates ROM image file corresponding to the target platform.	The developer can easily deploy applications by installing the generated ROM files without care about target platform.

3   USN Application Development Using the Proposed Tool

3.1   USN Application Development Process

The following is the process for developing USN applications using the advanced integrated model-driven development tool.

① Write a USN model diagram for a USN application.
② Set attribute values of nodes in the model. Through setting of attribute values, OS components for the application are selected.

③ Validate the USN model. Go to ① or ② if the model is not valid. Model validation is important because the correct USN application is not generated if the model is not valid.

④ Generate program codes to control nodes from the USN model using the predefined templates and OS modules.

Figure 1 shows the USN applications development process described in the above.

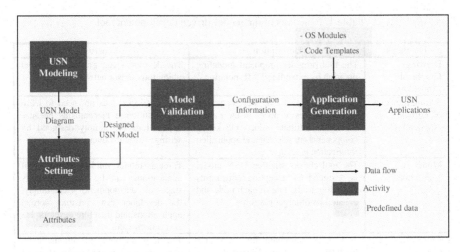

Fig. 1. USN applications development process

3.2 USN Modeling

A USN model consists of four factors: nodes, node types, links, and associations. The notations of the USN model are described in Table 2.

Table 2. The notation of the USN model

Name	Notation	Description
Node	Node name Attributes Operations	Rectangle represents a node of USN. Node name becomes a file name of C source code generated by the tool in order to control the node. Users can add attributes and operations in a node if they want.
Node Type		Ellipse represents a node type. There are four types – Sensor, Router, Sink, and Actuator.
Link	------------------	Dashed line represents a link between a node and a node type. Each node has one primary node type.
Association	⟶	Arrow represents association. Association presents the movement of packet between nodes.

There are four types of nodes in a sensor network: sensor, router, sink, and actuator. Each type of node has following features.

- SENSOR: A sensor node senses data and transmits the data to a coordinator node.
- ROUTER: A router node plays a coordinator role. It controls a sub network. A router node receives data from other nodes which belong to the sub network, an d transmits the received data to the PAN [4] coordinator node.
- SINK: A sink node plays a PAN coordinator role. It controls the whole network . A sink node collects data from other nodes which belong to the sensor networ k, and controls the nodes.
- ACTUATOR: An actuator node controls devices.

3.3 Attributes Setting

To generate applications from the designed model, the developer should configure the attributes of each node. The developer can set attribute values of each node in the model using the tool. Table 3 shows the examples of attributes for designing applications based on Nano-Qplus [5,6] operating system.

Table 3. Examples of attributes for the application based on Nano-Qplus operating system

Attribute Group	Attribute	Description
OS Functions	EEPROM_Enable	Enable EEPROM module.
	Timer_Enable	Enable Timer module.
	Zigbee RF	Select RF module.
	Sensor_Gas_Enable	Enable Gas sensor module.
	Sensor_Light_Enable	Enable Light sensor module.
	...	...
Network Configuration	nodeID	Write identification number of node.
	nodeType	Select the type of the node.
	nextHopRoutingFirstNodeID	Write identification number of the n ext node in routing path.
	...	...

3.4 Model Validation

It is necessary to validate the model before source code generation because the developer cannot develop correct applications if the model is not valid.

Followings are general requirements which should be satisfied through model validation for a USN application.

- Communication between nodes should be performed without any problems.
- Data should be transmitted to the server through the correct path which is determined by designer of the sensor network model.
- Applications should be designed by accepting constraints according to the role of each node.
- Applications should be designed by accepting constraints of target platform.

To confirm whether a USN model satisfies the general requirements, this article presents three types of model validation – commonality validation, association validation, and node validation. In commonality validation, the tool confirms common requirements of all nodes in the model in order to ensure that communication between nodes can be performed without any problems. Common requirements for communication are communication protocol compatibility and communication channel compatibility. In association validation, the tool checks whether associations between nodes are valid. Associations in the USN model present the routing path. Therefore, routing path of a sensor network is validated in association validation. Through association validation, the developer can confirm whether data is transmitted to the server through the correct path determined by him or her. In node validation, the tool checks attribute values of each node in the model whether the attributes are set to their correct values. Through node validation, the developer can confirm whether applications are designed by accepting constraints according to the role of each node and constraints of target platform.

3.5 Code Generation

The following is the process for generating source code to control each node.

Step 1 – Read model information from the designed USN model in order to get the attribute values of a node.

Step 2 – Extract selected modules from model information. Then read headers, data, function, and main codes from hash table according to the selected modules and save them to the template.

Step 3 – Combine the templates.

Figure 2 presents the process for generating source code of each node. Headers, data, and function codes are generated according to the type of the target node.

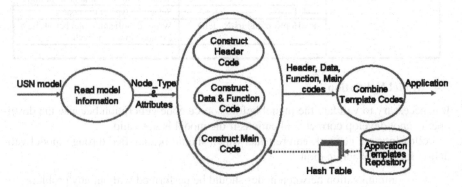

Fig. 2. Application generation process

4 Evaluation

In order to evaluate the efficacy of the proposed development tool, we also manually developed USN application and compared the results from the two approaches.

In the size of the resulting programs, there was not much difference in the two cases. In the required effort, it took only a few minutes to construct template codes of application programs for all the nodes from the USN model using the proposed tool but it took more than 10 times when we manually generated the template codes of application programs. Furthermore, the number of errors for application programs was reduced to about one fifth when using our tool, which is due to that the proposed tool performs model validation.

Through the empirical study, we could confirm that valid USN application programs are easily and rapidly constructed by using advanced integrated tool.

5 Related Works on Development Tools for USN Applications

Currently, there are development tools for USN applications such as TinyOS Plugin [7] and NanoEsto [8]. TinyOS Plugin is the model-based tool for developing USN applications based TinyOS operating system and developed as a plug-in for Eclipse platform. NanoEsto is the tool for development USN applications based on Nano-Qplus operating system and also developed as a plug-in for Eclipse platform. TinyOS Plugin supports graphical modeling, detection of program errors and automatic code generation. But the tool does not support model validation. Also, the developer should learn the nesC [9] language in order to develop applications using TinyOS Plugin because the tool supports nesC language for designing applications. NanoEsto does not provide graphical modeling and model validation. Moreover, TinyOS Plugin and NanoEsto do not support to construct several applications at a time.

There are also model-based development tools that achieve easy and rapid programming such as LabVIEW [10] and RTDS [11]. However, they are the tools for embedded application development and are not suitable for USN application development. They support embedded operating systems but embedded operating systems have the characteristics different from sensor network operating systems, which are lightweight and low-power, and capable of controlling resource-constrained hardware platform. So such tools cannot be easily adopted for developing applications for sensor network operating systems.

6 Conclusion

The existing tools for generating USN applications do not provide the model validation function which is necessary to develop qualified application and support to develop only one application at a time. To complement the existing tools, we proposed advanced integrated model-driven development tool to help developers construct valid USN applications easily, rapidly, and consistently in pervasive computing environment. The proposed tool has the following strength:

- USN modeling support: The proposed tool supports that developers graphically model ubiquitous sensor networks.
- Application design by setting attribute values: When developers construct USN applications using the tool, they do not need to learn any abstraction mechanisms because applications are simply designed by setting attribute values.

- Generation of several applications from one model: Since the proposed tool generates code from sensor network model instead of models of applications, a large number of application programs can be generated at once. This contrasts with the traditional model-based approach where only one application at a time could be developed.
- Model validation: The tool provides methods to validate USN models so that developers can check USN applications with them in terms of commonality validation, association validation, and node validation.

References

1. Chong, C.Y., Kumar, S.P.: Sensor networks: evolution, opportunities, and challenges. Proceedings of the IEEE 91(8), 1247–1256 (2003)
2. Clayberg, E., Rubel, D.: Eclipse: Building Commercial- Quality Plug-ins. Addison-Wesley, Reading (2004)
3. Moore, B., Dean, D., Gerber, A., Wagenknecht, G., Vanderheyden, P.: Eclipse Development, International Business Machines Corporation (2004)
4. Patten, K., Passerini, K.: From personal area networks to ubiquitous computing: preparing for a paradigm shift in the workplace. In: Proc. Wireless Telecommunications Symposium, pp. 225–233. IEEE CS Press, Los Alamitos (2005)
5. Lee, K., et al.: A Design of Sensor Network System based on Scalable & Reconfigurable Nano-OS Platform. In: Proc. IT SoC Conf., pp. 344–347 (2004)
6. ETRI Embedded S/W Research Division, Nano-Qplus, http://qplus.or.kr/
7. TinyOS Plugin for Eclipse, http://www.dcg.ethz.ch/~rschuler/
8. ETRI Embedded S/W Research Division, NanoEsto, http://qplus.or.kr/
9. Gay, D., Levis, P., von Behren, R., Welsh, M., Brewer, E., Culler, D.: The nesC language: A holistic approach to networked embedded systems. In: Proc. ACM SIGPLAN 2003 Conf. on Programming Language Design and Implementation (PLDI 2003), pp. 1–11. ACM Press, New York (2003)
10. LabVIEW for Embedded Development, http://www.ni.com/pdf/products/us/2005-5554-821-101-LO.pdf
11. http://www.pragmadev.com/index2.html

MSMAP: A Study on Robust Multiple Selection Scheme of Mobility Anchor Point in Hierarchical Mobile IPv6 Networks*

Randy S. Tolentino[1], Kijeong Lee[1], Minho Song[1], Yoon-Su Jeong[2], Yong-Tae Kim[3], Byungjoo Park[3,**], and Gil-Cheol Park[3]

[1] Department of Multimedia Engineering, Hannam University
133 Ojeong-dong, Daeduk-gu, Daejeon, Korea
daryn2004@yahoo.com, kijeong@hnu.kr, smh5110@nate.com
[2] Department of Computer Science, Chungbuk National University,
Cheongju, Chungbuk, Korea
bukmunro@gmail.com
[3] Department of Multimedia Engineering, Hannam University
133 Ojeong-dong, Daeduk-gu, Daejeon, Korea
{ky7762,bjpark,gcpark}@hnu.kr

Abstract. In Hierarchical Mobile IPv6 networks, how a mobile node selects an appropriate mobility anchor point (MAP) has a vital effect on the overall network performance. In this paper, we evaluate the performances of MAP selection schemes: the furthest MAP selection scheme, the nearest MAP selection scheme, the mobility-based MAP selection scheme, and the adaptive MAP selection scheme. The dynamic schemes can achieve load balancing among MAPs, where the adaptive MAP selection is better than the mobility-based MAP selection scheme. We also discussed our proposed scheme which is called the Multiple Selection of MAP in HMIPv6 (MSMAP-HMIPv6). We will show the comparison of performance analysis of HMIPv6 and our propose scheme, based on the assumptions of the new scheme, we can minimize the signaling of the mobile node and based on the pre-binding update research can minimize the handover latency.

Keywords: MSMAP- HMIPv6, HMIPv6, Movement Detection, HMIPv6 mobility management.

1 Introduction

Mobile IPv6 allows nodes to move within the Internet topology while maintaining reachability and on-going connections between mobile and correspondent nodes. To do this a mobile node sends Binding Updates (BUs) to its Home Agent (HA) and all Correspondent Nodes (CNs) it communicates with, every time it moves.

---

* This work was supported by the Security Engineering Research Center, granted by the Korea Ministry of Knowledge Economy.
** Corresponding author.

D. Ślęzak et al. (Eds.): FGCN/ACN 2009, CCIS 56, pp. 571–578, 2009.
© Springer-Verlag Berlin Heidelberg 2009

Authenticating binding updates requires approximately 1.5 round-trip times between the mobile node and each correspondent node (for the entire return routability procedure in a best case scenario, i.e., no packet loss). In addition, one round-trip time is needed to update the Home Agent; this can be done simultaneously while updating correspondent nodes. These round trip delays will disrupt active connections every time a handoff to a new AR is performed. Eliminating this additional delay element from the time-critical handover period will significantly improve the performance of Mobile IPv6. Moreover, in the case of wireless links, such a solution reduces the number of messages sent over the air interface to all correspondent nodes and the Home Agent. A local anchor point will also allow Mobile IPv6 to benefit from reduced mobility signaling with external networks.

For these reasons a new Mobile IPv6 node, called the Mobility Anchor Point, is used and can be located at any level in a hierarchical network of routers, including the Access Router (AR).

2 Related Study

Hierarchical Mobile IPv6 scheme introduces a new function, the MAP, and minor extensions to the mobile node operation. The correspondent node and Home Agent operation will not be affected.

A mobile node entering a MAP domain will receive Router Advertisements containing information on one or more local MAPs. The MN can bind its current location (on-link CoA) with an address on the MAP's subnet (RCoA). Acting as a local HA, the MAP will receive all packets on behalf of the mobile node it is serving and will encapsulate and forward them directly to the mobile node's current address. If the mobile node changes its current address within a local MAP domain (LCoA), it only needs to register the new address with the MAP. Hence, only the Regional CoA (RCoA) needs to be registered with correspondent nodes and the HA. The RCoA does not change as long as the MN moves within a MAP domain (see below for definition). This makes the mobile node's mobility transparent to the correspondent nodes it is communicating with [1].

A MAP domain's boundaries are defined by the Access Routers (ARs) advertising the MAP information to the attached Mobile Nodes. The detailed extensions to Mobile IPv6 and operations of the different nodes will be explained later in this document.

The network architecture shown in Figure 1 illustrates an example of the use of the MAP in a visited network; the MAP can help in providing seamless mobility for the Mobile node as it moves from Access Router 1 (AR1) to Access Router 2 (AR2), while communicating with the correspondent node. A multi- level hierarchy is not required for a higher handover performance.

Hence, it is sufficient to locate one or more MAPs (possibly covering the same domain) at any position in the operator's network [2].

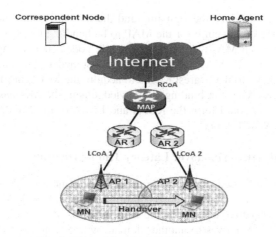

Fig. 1. Hierarchical Mobile IPv6 topology

3 Proposed Scheme

Fig. 2 shows our proposed scheme Multiple Selection of MAP in HMIPv6 (MSAMP-HIMPv6) was based on HMIPv6, in which the mobile node has two addresses, an RCoA on the MAP's subnet and an on-link CoA (LCoA).

When a mobile node moves into a new MAP domain, it need to configure the two CoAs. After forming the RCoA based on the prefix received in the MAP option, the mobile node sends a local binding update to the HA via MAP. This specifies the mobile node's RCoA in the home address option. The LCoA is used as the source address of the BU. Upon registering with the MAP, the mobile node sends will register its new RCoA with its home agent by sending a BU that specifies the binding between the RCoA and the home address.

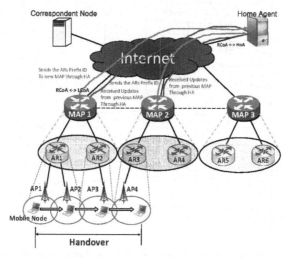

Fig. 2. Multiple Selection of MAP in Hierarchical Mobile IPv6

So, in order to minimize the signaling and the messages sent, the author assumes the new messaging architecture for the MAP to be handling the messaging: When the mobile node enters an MAP1 domain, the mobile node sends a binging update message (only once) to the MAP1. The MAP1 is assumed to be sending neighboring solicitation messages to the nearest MAPs to acquire the MAPs prefixes, and the ARs prefixes. After receiving the binding acknowledgement the MN has the neighboring MAPs prefixes, and could form the RCoA and LCoA of the MAP2 and AR3, while still being in the MAP1 domain.

3.1 MSMAP-HMIPv6 Handover Latency Timing Diagram

Fig. 3 shows our proposed scheme. The proposed scheme has the ability to store AP prefix ID from previous MAP in a certain domain into a new MAP in the other domain. The main objective of our scheme is to minimize the binding update of LCoA and RCoA if the MN moves to another domain with a different MAP and its corresponding AR and AP. Each MAP in each domain has the capability to store the AR Prefix ID. Also, one of the advantages of the proposed scheme is to provide an MN the needs to consider several factors when selecting the appropriate MAP in a foreign network. Two MAP selection schemes were recommended. The first scheme is a distance-based selection scheme, where an MN chooses the furthest MAP, in order to avoid frequent re-registrations.

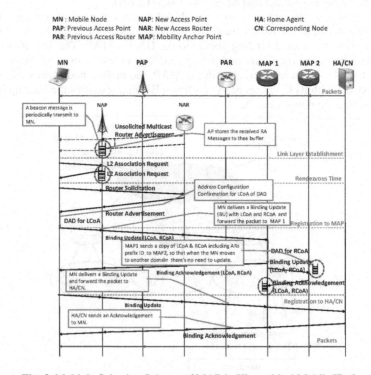

Fig. 3. Multiple Selection Scheme of MAP in Hierarchical Mobile IPv6

This scheme is particularly efficient for fast MNs performing frequent handover, because by choosing the furthest MAP, the fast MNs reduce the frequency of changing the serving MAP and informing the HA and their CNs of this change. However, since each MN has different mobility characteristics, the furthest MAP may not constitute an appropriate solution for some MNs (e.g., slow MNs). Furthermore, if all MNs select the furthest MAP as their serving MAPs, this MAP would become a single point of performance bottleneck, resulting in a higher processing latency. The alternative scheme recommended is to announce the MAP's information (e.g., traffic load on the MAP), so that an MN can choose a MAP by considering MN's mobility characteristics and MAP's current state.

In this paper, we study the MAP selection schemes: the furthest MAP selection scheme, the nearest MAP selection scheme, the mobility-based MAP selection scheme, and the adaptive MAP selection scheme. We analyze and evaluate their performances quantitatively with focus on the binding update traffic and the packet tunneling overhead. Furthermore, we discuss how MNs are distributed among MAPs (i.e., load balancing).

3.2 MSMAP-HMIPv6 Movement Detection

With each movement the MAP should send the binding message to CNs (if on the same link, only LCoA is required), and HA (to specify the binding between RCoA and the home address).
This is done, for two reasons:

1. The distance between the MAPs can be calculated, and the most suitable MAP can be chosen.
2. When the mobile node moves, the new MAP, it does not need to send the binding update. Only in the case of a new MAP (MAP2) in the prefix table, the mobile node should send the binding update to the MAP (MAP1) in order for the MAP2 to achieve the LCoA and RCoA of the mobile node, in the case of movement to MAP3 domain. In order to accelerate the handover between MAPs, the new MAP, besides sending NS message to the nearest MAP, it should the NS to the previous MAP will receive packets addressed to the mobile node's RCoA (from HA or CN). The packets will be tunneled from the previous MAP to the mobile node's LCoA.

With this messaging architecture, the handover process in advance can be easily implemented which includes neighbor AR discovery scheme, but can be performed on an MAP basis [3].

4 Performance Analysis

In this section we will show and explain and compare the performance of Multiple Selection of MAP in Hierarchical Mobile IPv6 Scheme and the standard HMIPv6. We will show the latency handover analysis of each scheme. Table 1 shows symbol, description, and value of common parameters, MSMAP-HMIPv6 and HMIPv6. Each simulation used an assumed data in order to get the latency handover analysis in MAP selection.

Each simulation used an assumed data in order to get the difference between schemes. We assigned a value for each symbol, t_a=50ms, t_b=40ms, t_c=60ms, t_d=80ms, t_e=100ms with their corresponding description.

Table 1. Parameters for performance analysis

Symbol	Description	Value
t_a	MN ↔ NAP	50ms
t_b	NAP ↔ NAR	40 ms
t_c	NAR ↔ MAP	60ms
t_d	MAP ↔ MAP	80ms
t_e	MAP ↔ HA/CN	100ms
tCoA	Form a CoA	1000ms

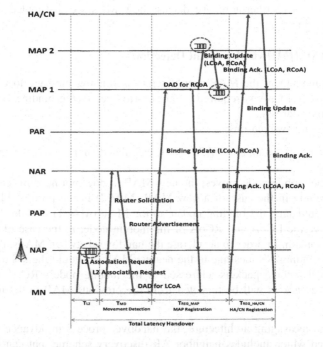

Fig. 4. MSMAP-HMIPv6 Handover Latency Timing Diagram

We measured the handover latency, the interval between the last packet in the previous access router and the first packet in the next access router and the handover of LCoA and RCoA from MAP1 to MAP2. The main purpose of this is to minimize the latency handover of MN from one domain to another domain with MAP, AR, and AP.

4.1 Formula and Results

In this section, we will show the formula of the standard HMIPv6 and our proposed scheme based on the timing diagram that we made. After analyzing the scheme and making a formula we compared the performance analysis of MSMAP-HMIPv6 in terms of handover latency. Below shows the formula of each scheme and the graph shows the comparison of total latency handover based on assumed time at time t_a, t_b, t_c, and t_d .

$$
\begin{aligned}
T_{HMIPv6} &= t_{L2} + t_{MD} + 2t_{CoA} + t_{REG\_MAP} + t_{REG\_HA/CN} \quad (1)\\
&= 2t_a + 2(t_a + t_b) + 2t_{CoA} + 2(t_a + t_b + t_c)\\
&\quad + 2(t_a + t_b + t_c + t_d)\\
&= 2(4t_a + 3t_b) + 2t_{CoA} + 2(2t_c + t_d)\\
&= 8t_a + 6t_b + 2t_{CoA} + 4t_c + 2t_d
\end{aligned}
$$

$$
\begin{aligned}
T_{MSMAP-HMIPv6} &= t_{L2} + t_{MD} + 2t_{CoA} + t_{REG\_MAP} + t_{REG\_HA/CN} \quad (2)\\
&= 2t_a + (2t_a + 2t_b) + 2t_{CoA} + (2t_a + 2t_b + 2t_c + 2t_d)\\
&\quad + (2t_a + 2t_b + 2t_c + 2t_e)\\
&= 8t_a + 6t_b + 2t_{CoA} + 4t_c + 2t_d + 2t_e\\
&= 8t_a + 6t_b + 2t_{CoA} + 4t_c + 2(t_d + t_e)
\end{aligned}
$$

Fig. 5. show the Handover Latency comparison betweeen HMIPv6 and MSMAP-HMIPv6 from MN ↔ NAP at time t_a, in which we assigned a assumed starting value of 10ms, 20ms, and 40ms.

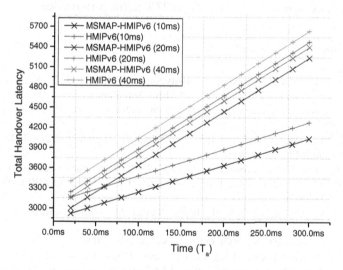

Fig. 5. Handover Latency Comparison I betweeen HMIPv6 and MSMAP-HMIPv6

We formulate the binding update (BU) and the packet deliver (PD) in a HMIPv6 network with a two Mobility Anchor Point (MAP). The network consists of two types of MAPs: MAP 1, which is a MAP in the first domain MAP 2 in the second domain. First domain covers a number of ARs and APs, whereas a second domain covers several ARs and APs. Therefore, the average residence time of the MAP 1 domain is longer than that of the LMAP. Also, the main objective of our proposed scheme is minimize the time of BU, most especially the authentication of ARs prefix ID when the MN moves to another AR in a different MAP or Domain.

5 Conclusion

The theory our proposed scheme is for the multiple selection of MAP in HMIPv6 was made, based on the assumptions of the new scheme, which can minimize the signaling of the mobile node and based on the pre-binding update research can minimize the handover latency.

In this paper, we have conducted a study for MAP selection schemes: the furthest MAP selection scheme, the nearest MAP selection scheme, the mobility-based MAP selection scheme, and the adaptive MAP selection scheme. Overall, the dynamic schemes (i.e., the mobility-based and the adaptive MAP selection schemes) achieve more desirable performances than the static schemes (i.e., the furthest and the nearest MAP selection schemes). Also, the adaptive MAP selection scheme performs better in terms of load balancing than the mobility-based MAP selection scheme. From the analytical results, MSMAP-FHMIPv6 can further reduce the handover latency, most especially when the MN moves to a different domain. Also, note that ES-FHMIP6 additionally can reduce the potential out of sequence possibility of the existing HMIPv6 scheme so that it can obtain better TCP traffic performance.

References

1. Johnson, D., Perkins, C., Arkko, J.: Mobility Support in IPv6. RFC 3775 (2004)
2. Thomson, S., Narten, T.: IPv6 Stateless Address Auto-configuration. RFC 2462 (1998)
3. Narten, T., Nordmark, E., Simpson, W.: Neighbor Discovery for IP version 6 (IPv6). RFC 2461 (1998)
4. Soliman, H., Castelluccia, C., Malki, K.E., Bellier, L.: Hierarchical Mobile IPv6 Mobility Management. RFC 4140 (2005)
5. Hsieh, R., Seneviratne, A., Soliman, H., El-Malki, K.: Performance Analysis on Hierarchical Mobile IPv6 with Fast-handover End-to-end TCP. In: IEEE GLOBECOM 2002, pp. 2488–2492 (2002)
6. Soliman, H.: Hierarchical Mobile IPv6 Mobility Management (HMIPv6). RFC 4140 (2005)
7. Jay Guo, Y.: Advances in mobile radio access networks (2004)
8. Jongpil Jeong, Min Young Chung and Hyunseung Choo.: Improved Handoff Performance Based on Pre-binding Update in HMIPv6. LNCS pp.525-529. Springer, Heidelberg (2006)
9. Tolentino, R.S., Lee, K., Park, B., Park, G.-C.: RFRB: A study on Robust Fast Handover Scheme using Reverse Binding Mechanism. In: Conference of KIIT 2009 (2009)
10. Han, Y.H.: Hierarchical Location Chacing Scheme for mobility Management. Ph.D. dissertation, Dept. of Computer Science and Engineering, Korea University (2001)

A Personalization Recommendation Service Using Service Delivery Platform in IMS Networks

Youn-Gyou Kook[1], Jae-Oh Lee[1], Jin-Mook Kim[2,*], Hwa-Young Jeong[3], Yoon-Seok Heo[4], and Bong-Hwa Hong[5]

[1] School of Information Technology, Korea University of Technology and Education
Byungcheon-myun, Cheonan, Chungnam, Korea 330-708
{ykkook,jelee}@kut.ac.kr
[2] Faculty of IT Education, Sunmoon University
100, Galsan-ri, TangJeong-myun, Asan-si, ChungNam, Korea 336-708
calf0425@sunmoon.ac.kr
[3] Faculty of General Education, Kyunghee University
1, Hoegi-dong, Dongdae-mun-gu, Seoul, Korea, 130-701
hyejeong@khu.ac.kr
[4] Faculty of Electrical and Electronic Eng., Chung Cheong University
330 Kangnae-Myun, Chungwon-Kun, Chung-Buk, Korea 363-792
hys@ok.ac.kr
[5] Dept. of Information and Communication, Kyunghee Cyber University
1, Hoegi-dong, Dongdae-mun-gu, Seoul, Korea, 130-701
bhhong@khu.ac.kr

Abstract. In this paper, we wish to propose method to provide personalization recommendation service that is optimized to user using Service Delivery Platform in IMS environment. So we studied method to create personalization recommendation service base on web service. Creation process of personalization recommendation service for user must analyze user basis information and service use pattern in IMS Environment. And we can create and offer suitable personalization recommendation service with this. I can provide integration service using SDP that is development to provide more effective personalization recommendation service in IMS environment. And we are thought to provide order style service to user according to recommendation algorithm and Guideline.

Keywords: IMS, SDP, Personal Recommendation Service.

1 Introduction

In recent, the communication environments converge into only the network based on All-IP that can be provided the digital convergence service with communications, broadcastings and internet for the customers. It was suggested that an IMS (IP Multimedia Subsystem) will be the next generation networks by 3GPP (3rd Generation

---

* Coresponding author.

D. Ślęzak et al. (Eds.): FGCN/ACN 2009, CCIS 56, pp. 579–585, 2009.
© Springer-Verlag Berlin Heidelberg 2009

Partnership Project)[1]. The IMS is the integration communication environments that made up wired and wireless networks based on IP to provide the multimedia services which included a voice, audio, video, large scale data and others for the customers [8,11]. The service providers would needed new paradigm services will be to build up that.

And they have to prepare the various services for providing through the IMS and encourage the customers in their using that. So they need to develop the new services and contents that are in any type and orchestrate the partial services which are existed service, new services, service enablers, the various contents and 3rd party services. It is difficult that the customers select a suitable service within the extended service delivery markets included the communication, broadcasting, internet and others.

It is necessary that the service providers provide the personalized recommendation service which is customized on analyzing of user profiles and usage patterns. That could be acquired from the SIP (Session Initiation Protocol) messages and HSS (Home Subscriber Server) [8,9]. And the service providers need open SDP (Service Delivery Platform) to provide the digital convergence services and the new paradigm services like a 3rd party service which is developed by the other service developers [4,7,12].

Therefore, this paper presents the implementation of IMS infrastructure and the PRS (personalized recommendation service) based on analyzing of that. This service is composed of the analyzed elements that are service type, service timestamp, used time, used devices and user's private information. The elements of that can be detailed and extended by their policy for providing the appreciated customized service to customers. And I describe about method that can use development method for Service Delivery Platform to offer effective personalization recommendation service. So this paper simulates the personalized recommendation service with the analyzed elements on our scenario in our IMS infrastructure.

The reminder of this paper is structured as follows. The next section presents the IMS and the SDP. Next personalized recommendation services in IMS are presented. Section 4 describes the implementation of our IMS infrastructure and the simulation of the personalized recommendation service on our scenario.

2   Related Works

2.1   The Personalization Recommendation Service in the IMS

In these days, the requirement of the user is transforming the passive service environments in which uses the listed services by the service provider into the interactive and conventional ones in which the user has the opportunity to request the customized services. It is necessary that these service environments can be supported to provide the digital convergence services, large scale services and individual specific services. The IMS networks is suited to be in that environments because that is made up of wired and wireless networks based on All-IP and is able to provide the various personalization services. Figure 1 shows the overview of the personalization service in the IMS networks.

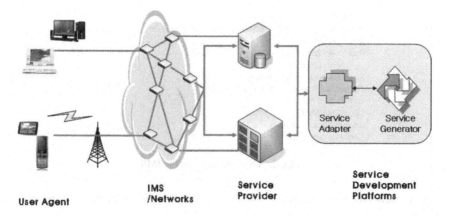

Fig. 1. The overview of PRS in the IMS

The service provider to serve the customized services based on the IMS infrastructure has to possess many services of all kinds and to develop the various service types. He must consider optimization, customization and profit problems when he develops and provide the services. And he has to extend his roles to being 'the service enablers' who can support the 3rd party services, it means that he can develop a new paradigm service, support the 3rd party services and orchestrate the partial services of an existing service, a new service and the 3rd party service.

However, the user faces complexities of selecting the appropriate services. It is difficult to select one from his interesting contents. So the service provider has to consider the customized services when he generates and orchestrates a new service. It could be solved the problem by the personalization service based on analysis of user's profiles and usage patterns.

'The Service Provider' manages the services that are composed of the existing service enablers and the new ones to guarantee the stability in the IMS environments. 'The Service Adapter' analyzes the user's profiles and usage patterns and acquires the elements of the personalization services. 'The Service Generator' generates the new services and orchestrates the partial services within the 3rd party services based on Web services.

We can analyze the customer's information that are transported by the SIP protocol and recorded the user's log on HSS in the IMS. The SIP protocol includes the used device information, status, timestamp, expiration and others. Figure 2 shows a SIP message on the IMS.

And the HSS is in charge of that: the management of user's mobility, the support of call and session, the creation of user's security information, user's authority, message integrity, message encryption, the management and store of user's information. So we analyze the user's profiles and the usage patterns including his interesting services and so on. And we acquire the elements of the personalization services. The elements can be analyzed in detail by the service provider's policy, but this

```
INVITE sip:jolee@kut.ac.kr  SIP/2.0
Via: SIP/2.0/UDP 220.68.70.190:5000 comp=sigcomp; branch=z9hg4bk9hah
Max-Forwards:70
Route:<sip:220.68.70.190:5000 comp=sigcomp>
        <sip:220.68.70.190:4000;lr>
From:Infotel <sip:Infotel@kut.ac.kr>
To:JaeOhLee<sip:jolee@kut.ac.kr>
Call-ID:23fi571ju
CSeq:8348 INVITE
Content-Type:application/sdp
Content-Length:187
```

Fig. 2. A SIP message on the IMS

paper presents the basic elements. The elements of the personalization services follow as that:

1) **Service Type:** It is a kind of service that is served by the service provider. These are voice communications, MMS, SMS, e-mail, game, web browsing, searching, notifications, advertisement service, and so on. Where U_{s_type} is the set of 'service type'.

$$U_{s\_type} = \{ Type_1, Type_2, \cdots, Type_{n-1}, Type_n \}, \ n \leq number \ of \ services .$$

2) **Service Timestamp:** It is the timestamp that the user accesses to use the services. To be the various time slots that user accesses the service, it orders the set of time-stamps on which based the length of time used or the most frequently accessed and indicated the priority timestamp. The service timestamps are composed of the time slots ranged from TS_1 to TS_{24} slot. Where $U_{s\_timestamp}$ is the set of 'service timestamp'.

$$U_{s\_timestamp} = \{ TS_1, TS_2, \cdots, TS_i \cdots,, TS_{23}, TS_{24} \}, i \ is \ a \ time \ slot \ of \ a \ day .$$

3) **Service Span:** It is the time that the user used each service. We could know user's royalty and favor of a service and define a service size of the personalization services. The service span is the average span of using each service in a day. It follows that: T_{od} means that the service span is over a day. T_d is ranged from over a few hours to under 24 hours, T_{oh} is ranged from over 1 hour to under a few hours, T_h is ranged from over a few minutes to under 1 hour, T_{om} is ranged from over 1 minute to under a few minutes, T_m is ranged from over a few seconds to under 1 minute and T_s is used for seconds. Where U_{s_span} is the set of 'service span'.

$$U_{s\_span} = \{ T_{od}, T_d, T_{oh}, T_h, T_{om}, T_m, T_s \}, an \ element \ is \ a \ time \ unit .$$

4) **Service Device:** It is a kind of device that the user accesses to use the service. We could know the user's device information from the SIP messages. Where U_{s_device} is the set of 'service device'.

$$U_{s\_device} = \{ Device_1, Device_2, \cdots, Device_{n-1}, Device_n \}, n \leq number \ of \ devices .$$

5) **Service User:** It is the user's profiles such as his age, sex, job and so on. It is used to recommend what, when and how service is fit for him. Where U_{s_user} is the set of 'service user'.

$$U_{s\_user} = \{ sex, age, job, \cdots \} \; elements \;\; are \;\; composed \;\; of \;\; user \;\; profiles \,.$$

We generate and orchestrate the personalization services based on the analyzed elements of the user's profiles and usage patterns. And we can define to serve the what, when and how of service.

We define the size of service to analyze 'service timestamp', 'service span' and 'service size'. Figure 3 shows the analysis algorithm of the personalization services for service size.

```
public String getServiceSize(S_timestamp, S_span) {

    ServiceSize = null;

    if (S_timestamp != null && S_span != null) {
        switch S_span
            case overDay:
                ServiceSize = over 2 hours;
            case Day:
                if (S_timestamp > T22 && S_timestamp < T6)
                    ServiceSize = over 2 hours;
                else if (S_timestamp > T6 && S_timestamp < T10)
                    ServiceSize = under 2 hours;
                else if (S_timestamp > T10 && S_timestamp < T18)
                    ServiceSize = under 1 hour;
                else if (S_timestamp > T18 && S_timestamp < T22)
                    ServiceSize = under 2 hours;
            case overHour:
                if (S_timestamp > T22 && S_timestamp < T6)
                    ServiceSize = over 2 hours;
                else if (S_timestamp > T6 && S_timestamp < T10)
                    ServiceSize = over 1 hour;
                else if (S_timestamp > T10 && S_timestamp < T18)
                    ServiceSize = under 1 hour;
                else if (S_timestamp > T18 && S_timestamp < T22)
                    ServiceSize = over 1 hour;
            case Hour:
                if (S_timestamp > T18 && S_timestamp < T6)
                    ServiceSize = under 1 hour;
                else if (S_timestamp > T6 && S_timestamp < T18)
                    ServiceSize = under 20 minutes;
            case OverMinute:
                ServiceSize = under 10 minute;
            case Minute:
                ServiceSize = under 1 minute;
            case Second:
                ServiceSize = under 1 minute;
    }
    return ServiceSize;
}
```

Fig. 3. The analysis algorithm of the personalization services for service size

3   Implementation of the Personalization Service

In this section, we describe the scenario and implementation of the personalization services in the IMS infrastructure. As described in Part 2, the personalization services have the structure of the meta-data that are composed of a service type, service size and service time.

The IMS infrastructure is implemented in JAIN SIP 1.2 API and Apache for Webservice. We designed to route a specified IP address and Port, and simulated the personalization services in a user's local area networks. Figure 4 shows the implemented IMS infrastructure that is P-CSCF node, I-CSCF node and S-CSCF node. P-CSCF (proxy-call/session control function) node executes the role of proxy and user agent,

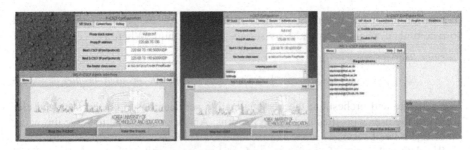

Fig. 4. The infrastructure of the IMS

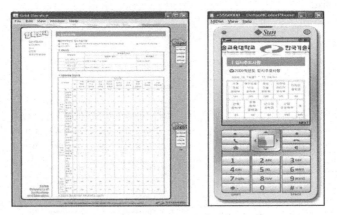

Fig. 5. The personalization service is simulated on the application and the mobile emulator

transports the SIP messages to I-CSCF node. I-CSCF (interrogating-CSCF) node acquires the address of S-CSCF from HSS and routes the received SIP messages from the other networks as like a P-CSCF through S-CSCF node. S-CSCF (serving-CSCF) node manages the customer's information at HSS, interacts with SDP.

We have implemented the application service with Java and WSDL2Java. And the mobile service has been implementing Java with the stub generator. To generate the customized service, we considered the elements of a personalization service as above presented. Figure 5 shows the application and mobile service on the mobile emulators.

4   Conclusion

The IMS is the convergence communication environments that are made up of wired and wireless networks based on IP to provide the multimedia services which include a voice, audio, video, large scale data and others for the customer. It is necessary that the service delivery platform is open to include the 3rd party service and the customer specific service. So, the service provider makes efforts to possess the many and various services and develop a new paradigm service that converge the digital contents with another service environments. However it is difficult that the user use on his fit the services because of the more and various services.

In this paper, we described the personalization service in the implemented IMS infrastructure to provide the digital convergence service. Moreover we presented the architecture of an open service delivery platform and analyzed the elements of the personalization services based on the customer's profiles and usage patterns. On generating the personalization services, we considered the extracted elements is composed of service type, service timestamp and service size. The elements of the personalization services can be analyzed in detail by the policy of the service provider. The future work includes the monitoring and security of service in the IMS.

References

1. TFC3131(3GPP2-IETF), http://www.3gpp2.org/
2. http://java.sun.com/webservices/docs/1.3/tutorial/doc/index.html
3. http://www.analysysmason.com/
4. http://www.parlay.org/en/products/
5. http://www.serviceoriented.org/web_service_orchestration.html
6. Pichot, A., Audouin, O.: Alcatel Research: Grid services over IP Multimedia Subsystem. In: BroadNet 2006, IEEE, October 2006, pp. 1–7 (2006)
7. Devoteam Group, Service Delivery Platform: The Key to Service Convergence, Devoteam white paper (October 2007)
8. Camarillo, G., Garcia-Martin, M.A.: The 3G IP Multimedia Subsystem (IMS), 2nd edn. Wiley, Chichester (2006)
9. Hurtado, J.A., Martinez, F., Caicedo, O., Ramirez, O.: Providing SIP services support on Mobile networks. In: 4th ICEEE (September 2007)
10. Kim, S., Min, J., Lee, J., Lee, H.: W3C, Mobile Web Initiative Workshop (November 2004)
11. Cho, J.-H., Lee, J.-O.: The IMS/SDP Structure and Implementation of Presence Service. In: Ma, Y., Choi, D., Ata, S. (eds.) APNOMS 2008. LNCS, vol. 5297, pp. 560–564. Springer, Heidelberg (2008)
12. Ren, L., Pei, Y.Z., Zhang, Y.B., Ying, C.: Charging Validation for Third Party Value-Added Applications in Service Delivery Platform. In: 10th IEEE/IFIP Network Operations and Management Symposium, 2006. NOMS 2006 (October 2006)
13. Maes, S.H.: Service Delivery Platforms as IT Realization of OMA Service Environment: Service Oriented Architectures for Telecommunications. In: WCNC 2007. IEEE Communications Society, pp. 2885–2890 (2007)
14. Boll, S.: Modular Content Personalization Service Architecture for E-Commerce Applications. In: WECWIS 2002, June 2002, pp. 213–220. IEEE Computer Society, Los Alamitos (2002)
15. Chou, W., Li, L., Liu, F.: Web Services for Communication over IP. IEEE Communications Magazine, 136–143 (March 2008)
16. Cheng, Y., Leon-Garcia, A., Foster, I.: Toward an Autonomic Service Management Frame work: A Holistic Vision of SOA, AON, and Automatic Computing. IEEE Communications Magazine, 138–146 (2008)

Enhanced SVD Based Watermarking
with Genetic Algorithm

Heechul Jung and Moongu Jeon

Gwangju Institute of Science and Technology,
Gwangju 500-712, Korea
{hcjeong, mgjeon}@gist.ac.kr

Abstract. In this paper, we propose an enhanced robust watermarking algorithm based on singular vector decomposition(SVD). Previous SVD based watermarking algorithms have a problem of false-positive detection. For solving this problem, our algorithm performs an extra verification job for watermark using reference images. To find optimal scaling factors in the algorithm which satisfy both robustness and high quality of the watermarked image, we employed the genetic algorithm(GA).

Keywords: Watermarking, SVD, Genetic Algorithm, Wavelet.

1 Introduction

Digital watermarking is the state-of-the-art technique for protecting ownership or authenticating images. The digital watermarking can be classified into 3 categories as robust, fragile and semi-fragile. While the robust watermarking techniques are used for protecting rightful ownership, the fragile and the semi-fragile watermarking algorithms are usually used for image authentication. It can be also classified into two categories, the spatial and the transform domains [2]. The spatial domain based watermarking techniques are simple but not robust against some signal processing attacks. On the other hand, the watermark which is embedded into the transform domain is more robust against some signal processing attacks such as low pass filtering, high pass filtering and so on.

Because SVD transform-based watermarking technique is robust against various attacks including some geometrical attacks, it is widely used for protecting the copyright of multimedia data [1, 6]. However, it has one serious problem of the false-positive detection which has been investigated by many researchers [3–6]. The algorithms proposed by Yavuz and Telatar embed a watermark into each transform domain such as wavelet and discrete cosine transform for verification of watermark [8, 12]. Hence, the robustness of algorithms is dependent on strength of each of frequency domains which are not robust against geometrical attacks. Mohammad also proposed improved SVD-based watermarking scheme [6], but it has some problems. Mohammad's first algorithm is not robust against the rotation attack. Second algorithm looks like very robust. However, it is not SVD-based algorithm but just spatial domain based watermarking algorithm,

D. Ślęzak et al. (Eds.): FGCN/ACN 2009, CCIS 56, pp. 586–593, 2009.
© Springer-Verlag Berlin Heidelberg 2009

meaning it is not robust against some signal processing attacks. Mohan's algorithm embeds the watermark into left-top and right-bottom of the host image [7]. If the attacker removes top-left and bottom-right of the watermarked image, the watermark is also removed.

In this paper, we propose a new method which solves the false-positive detection problem through verification of input watermark. The overall process of our algorithm is similar to existing DWT-SVD based watermarking algorithm [8, 9]. First, we perform wavelet transform on the host image for embedding the watermark into low frequency. Next, perform SVD on the transformed image and the embedded watermark. In extraction step, parts of the embedded watermark which is called the reference image are used for verification of input watermark.

This paper is organized as follow: SVD based watermarking is described in Section 2. Section 3 explains the proposed algorithm and optimization of scaling factors using GA. Section 4 gives the experimental results, and finally Section 5 concludes the paper.

2   SVD Based Watermarking

This section describes the conventional SVD based watermarking algorithm and its problem. First, embedding and extraction processes are stated, and then the problem of this algorithm is mentioned.

2.1   Embedding Process

In this process, we insert a watermark W into a host image I. As ouput we keep the singular value matrix (Σ) of the target image, and sets of singular vectors (U_w, V_w) of $\Sigma + \alpha W$, where α is a scaling factor.

Step 1, apply SVD to the host image $I = U \Sigma V^T$

Step 2, add the watermark W multiplied by α to the singular value matrix Σ of I, and denote it as $\Sigma_m \leftarrow \Sigma + \alpha W$

Step 3, apply SVD to the matrix Σ_m obtained from step 2, $\Sigma_m = U_w \Sigma_w V_w^T$

Step 4, reconstruction with U, V^T of I and Σ_w of Σ_m gives the watermarked image I_w which will be availble to users, $I_w \leftarrow U \Sigma_w V^T$

2.2   Extraction Process

In this process, we examine whether the target image is copyrighted or not by extracting an embedded watermark and comparing it with that we own.

Step 1, perform SVD on the target image, $I_w^* = U^* \Sigma_w^* V^{*T}$

Step 2, construct Σ_m^* using the singular value matrix obtained from the target image and sets of singular vectors from the original host image we keep, $\Sigma_m^* = U_w \Sigma_w^* V_w^T$

Step 3, extract the watermark embedded into the target image and compare it
   with the watermark embedded into the original host image,
$$W_{ext} = (\Sigma_m^* - \Sigma)/\alpha$$

2.3   False-Positive Detection Problem

The problem of false-positive detection is described in [4]. It is caused by U_w and
V_w, which have a lot of information of watermark. If we use different matrices
instead of U_w and V_w in the second step of the extraction process, then the
extracted watermark W_{ext} must be changed due to the reconstructed matrix
Σ_m^*. Since any kind of watermark can be extracted from the watermarked image
if one uses one's own singular vectors, anyone who has the watermarked image
can claim their ownership of the image.

3   Proposed Watermarking Algorithm

In this section, we describe our proposed watermarking algorithm. In addition
to SVD, we use the discrete wavelet transformation (DWT) for embedding a
watermark into low frequency band which is more robust against some attacks.
Although we use frequency domain, our algorithm can be applied to any domain.

   In the proposed algorithm, we use scaling factors α and β for controlling
robustness. The larger value of the scaling factors is more robust than smaller
value, but the quality of watermarked image is deteriorating. This is a trade-off
between the robustness and the quality of a watermarked image. To find optimal
values of scaling factors, the genetic algorithm is employed.

3.1   Embedding Process

Let's denote components of 3-level DWT of the host image I as f_3^θ, where
$\theta \in \{LL, HL, LH, HH\}$. In this process, we produce the watermarked image
to be published, and sets of singular vectors U_w, V_w of the low frequency component embedding the watermark and the high frequency component. Two sets of
singular vectors $\{U_w, V_w\}$, Σ and f_3^{HH} should be kept to varify the ownership
of image later.

Step 1, add the low frequency component f_3^{LL} of I to $\alpha \times (f_3^{HH} + W)$, and denote
   it as $f_w^{LL} \leftarrow f_3^{LL} + \alpha \times (f_3^{HH} + W)$
Step 2, perform SVD on both f_3^{LL} and W,
   $$[U\Sigma V^T] \leftarrow svd(f_3^{LL}), \quad [U_h \Sigma_h V_h^T] \leftarrow svd(W)$$
Step 3, multiply U_h and V_h^T to the left and right sides of f_w^{LL}, respectively,
   $$A_w^{LL} \leftarrow U_h f_w^{LL} V_h^T$$
Step 4, perform SVD on A_w^{LL}, $[U_w \Sigma_w V_w^T] \leftarrow svd(A_w^{LL})$
Step 5, add the singular value matrix Σ_w multiplied by a scaling factor β to Σ,
   $$\Sigma_w^* \leftarrow \Sigma + \beta \times \Sigma_w$$

Step 6, construct the modified low frequency component f_w^{LL*} using the modified singular value matrix Σ_w^* computed in *Step 5*, $f_w^{LL*} \leftarrow U\Sigma_w^* V^T$

Step 7, using f_w^{LL*}, perform inverse 3-level DWT for obtaining watermarked image I_w which will be available to users

3.2   Extraction Process

Given U_w, V_w, Σ and f_3^{HH} which were obtained in the embedding process, to test if an image I_w^* is copyrighted or not, we insert a watermark into it, extract the watermark, and compare the extracted watermark with the one inserted. For that task, we perform 3-level wavelet decomposition on it as in embedding process, and then conduct the following steps. The components of the decomposition are denoted as $f_3^{\theta*}$, where $\theta \in \{LL, HL, LH, HH\}$.

Step 1, perform SVD on f_w^{LL**} and any watermark W^*,
$$[U\Sigma_w^{**}V^T] \leftarrow svd(f_w^{LL**}), \quad [U_h^*\Sigma_h^*V_h^{*T}] \leftarrow svd(W^*)$$
Step 2, extract singular value matrix $\Sigma_w^* \leftarrow (\Sigma_w^* * -\Sigma)/\beta$
Step 3, reconstruct A_w^{LL*} using the stored singular vectors U_w and V_w,
$$A_w^{LL*} \leftarrow U_w\Sigma_w^* V_w^T$$
Step 4, for verification of input watermark, multiply U_h^{*T} and V_h^* to A_w^{LL*},
$$f_w^{LL***} \leftarrow U_h^{*T} A_w^{LL*} V_h^*$$
Step 5, extract watermark W_{ext} from the relation in Step 1 of the embedding process

$$W_{ext} = \frac{(f_w^{LL***} - f_3^{LL})}{\alpha} - f_3^{HH*}$$

Step 6, compute the normalized correlation (NC) between the input watermark W^* and the extracted watermark W_{ext},

$$NC = \frac{\sum_{i=1}^{M}\sum_{j=1}^{N} W^*(i,j)W_{ext}(i,j)}{\sum_{i=1}^{M}\sum_{j=1}^{N}\{W^*(i,j)\}^2}$$

If input watermark W^* is the same as the watermark W in the embedding process, and if NC is close to 1, then the test image I_w^* is copyrighted. Otherwise it is not. As the conventional SVD-based method, if we use only U_w and V_w for verification of input watermark, we have the similar problem of the false positive detection. To solve this problem, we use the verification with HH band as in *Step 1* of embedding process. If the f_3^{HH} of embedding process is different from f_3^{HH*} in *Step 5* of sxtraction process, then the watermark cannot be extracted.

3.3   Optimization of Scaling Factors Using GA

Since scaling factors are related with the quality of the watermarked image, the robustness of the embedded watermark against attacks, and the watermark extraction problem from fake watermarked images, it is very important to select proper values of scaling factors. We employ a genetic algorithm (GA) to find optimal scaling factors. GA is very useful especially when the objective function is complex and has several local optimal values. Some researchers have already applied GA to watermarking problems, and their results were excellent [3, 11–15].

In a basic GA, candidate solutions are encoded to bit strings which are called chromosome. Survivability of each bit string is estimated by computing its fitness value of the objective function. Selection operator chooses proper chromosomes which have higher fitness value, and crossover operator exchanges the portion of the bit strings between two chromosomes. Mutation operator flips randomly selected bits of the chromosomes according to the mutation rate to provide more diverse individuals to future generation, which is effective in escaping from local optima. Then evaluate the fitness value again. If the stopping criteria are satisfied, then the fittest among survived chromosomes is the optimal solution.

Now we adopt the basic GA to our watermarking algorithm with the minimizing following objective function,

$$F(NC, PSNR) = \frac{1}{\sum_{i=1}^{K} w_i \times NC_i} - w_{K+1} \times PSNR/C + w_{K+2} \times NC_{K+1}, \quad (1)$$

where K is the number of attacks, w_i is the ith weight value for each variable and NC_i is the $i^{th} NC$ value between the input watermark and the extracted watermark. NC_{K+1} denotes the normalized correlation between the input watermark and the extracted watermark which comes from fake watermarked image. C is a constant value and $PSNR$ is defined as

$$PSNR = 10 \times \log_{10} \frac{255^2}{\sum_{i=1}^{M} \sum_{j=1}^{N} \{I(i,j) - I_w(i,j)\}^2}, \quad (2)$$

where $I(i,j)$ is the pixel value of index (i,j) of the $M \times N$ host image, $I_w(i,j)$ is that of the corresponding watermarked image.

4   Experimental Results

We use 512×512 grayscale host images and 64×64 grayscale watermarks. 17 attacks including Gaussian blur, rotation, and so on, are applied to the watermarked image, and its experimental results are summarized in Table 1. Comparisons are made between the proposed method and other SVD-based watermarking algorithms with the discrete wavelet transform. The table shows that Ganic-Eskicioglu algorithm has the problem of false-positive detection, and Erakan-Ziya have improved Ganic-Eskicioglu's algorithm to solve the problem. However, their algorithms are fragile against some attacks. PSNR of our result is 31.35dB, α is 4.6282, β is 0.0337. and constant C is 40.

Fig. 1 shows the results of watermark detection. 500 watermark images are randomly generated, and then the 51th watermark is embedded into the host image. For watermark detection, we extract the watermark using the 51th watermark only and then check the NC between the extracted watermark and the

Table 1. Experimental Results

Attacks	Proposed Algorithm	Erakan-Ziya (Wavelet)[8]	Erakan-Ziya (DCT)[10]	Ganic-Eskicioglu[9]
No attack	0.9995	0.9995	0.9997	1
JPEG2000 50:1 (xnview)	0.9988	not given	not given	0.989
JPEG 10%(xnview)	0.9218	not given	0.8816	not given
Gaussian Blur 5x5	0.9932	0.7805	0.991	0.885
Gaussian Noise 0.01	0.8474	not given	0.8332	not given
Average Blur 3x3	0.9407	0.9384	0.9477	not given
Median Filter 3x3	0.9423	0.9879	0.9865	not given
Resizing 256-512	0.995	0.9984	0.9955	0.94
Sharpen 80 (xnview)	0.6653	0.7417	not given	0.699
Crop 25%	0.2291	not given	not given	not given
Salt-pepper 0.01	0.9047	0.8924	not given	not given
Salt-pepper 0.02	0.712	not given	not given	not given
Rotation 30	0.2633	not given	not given	not given
Rotation 20	0.2608	not given	not given	0.963
Rotation 10	0.2628	not given	not given	not given
Histogram Equalization (photoshop)	0.4391	0.8085	not given	0.823
Gaussian Noise 0.3 (xnview)	0.8999	0.8574	not given	0.865
Pixelate (mosaic) 2 (photoshop)	0.9992	0.8825	not given	1

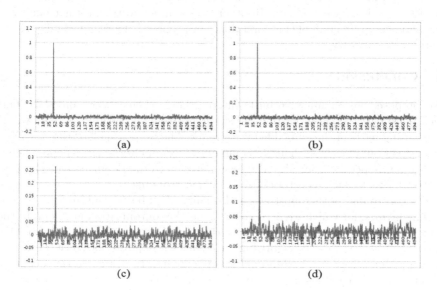

Fig. 1. X-axis is watermark number, Y-axis is the NC value. (a) No attack (b) Resizing 256-512-256 (c) Rotation 30 (d) 25% Cropping.

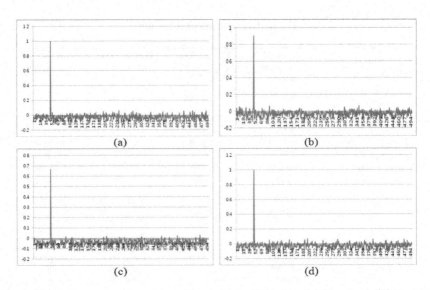

Fig. 2. X-axis is watermark number, Y-axis is the NC value. (a) No attack (b) Gaussian Noise 0.3 (c) Sharp 80 (d) Mosaic 2.

51th watermark. The figures show that the extracted watermark has the highest value. Fig. 2 is the results of the false-positive detection test. For the test, the 51th watermark is embedded into the host image and all 500 watermarks are used for watermark extraction. In other words, input watermark is changed in extraction step. In spite of this condition, our proposed algorithm can detect the watermark correctly.

5   Conclusion

We proposed an enhanced robust watermarking scheme based on SVD. Our method solves the false-positive detection problem by verifying input watermark using parts of the embedded watermark. The proposed algorithm is robust against various attacks such as Gaussian blur, median filtering, salt-pepper noise, and so on. Especially, our algorithm can detect watermark correctly under geometrical attacks such as rotation, resizing and cropping.

For controlling both robustness and quality of watermarked image, we used scaling factors, for which we need to solve a global optimization problem. In the paper, we employed GA, which is powerful global optimization algorithm. One weak point of the proposed algorithm is that since it requires both host image and reference image, we need additional storage media. To overcome the weakness of our method, We'll do more research on the SVD based blind watermarking algorithm as a future work.

Acknowledgments. This research was financially supported by the Center for Distributed Sensor Network, and the System biology infrastructure establishment grant provided by GIST.

References

1. Liu, R., Tan, T.: An SVD-Based Watermarking Scheme for Protecting Rightful Ownership. IEEE Trans. on Multimedia 4(1), 121–128 (2002)
2. Aslantas, V.: A singular-value decomposition-based image watermarking using genetic algorithm. Int. J. Electron. Commun.(AEU) 62, 386–394 (2008)
3. Xing, Y., Tan, J.: Mistakes in the paper entitled, A singular-value decomposition-based image watermarking using genetic algorithm. Int. J. Electron. Commun. (AEU) (2008) doi: 10.1016/j.aeue, 09.007
4. Zhang, X.-P., Li, K.: Comments on An SVD-Based Watermarking Scheme for Protecting Rightful Ownership. IEEE Trans. on Multimedia 7(2), 593–594 (2005)
5. Xiao, L., Wei, Z., Ye, J.: Comments on Robust embedding of visual watermarks using discrete wavelet transform and singular value decomposition. J. Electron. Imaging 17(4), 40501 (2008)
6. Mohammad, A.A., Alhaj, A., Shaltaf, S.: An improved SVD-based watermarking scheme for protecting rightful ownership. Signal Processing 88, 2158–2180 (2008)
7. Chandra Mohan, B., Srinivas Kumar, S.: A Robust Image Watermarking Scheme using Singular Value Decomposition. Journal of Multimedia 3(1) (2008)
8. Yavuz, E., Telatar, Z.: Improved SVD-DWT Based Digital Image Watermarking Against Watermark Ambiguity. In: SAM 2007, Seoul, Korea (2007)
9. Ganic, E., Eskicioglu, A.M.: Robust Embedding of Visual Watermarks Using DWT-SVD. Journal of Electronic Imaging (2005)
10. Yavuz, E., Telatar, Z.: SVD Adapted DCT Domain DC Subband Image Watermarking Against Watermark Ambiguity. In: Gunsel, B., Jain, A.K., Tekalp, A.M., Sankur, B. (eds.) MRCS 2006. LNCS, vol. 4105, pp. 66–73. Springer, Heidelberg (2006)
11. Lu, Y., Han, J., Kong, J., Yang, Y., Hou, G.: A Novel Color Image Watermarking Method Based on Genetic Algorithm and Hybrid Neural Networks. In: Greco, S., Hata, Y., Hirano, S., Inuiguchi, M., Miyamoto, S., Nguyen, H.S., Słowiński, R. (eds.) RSCTC 2006. LNCS (LNAI), vol. 4259, pp. 806–814. Springer, Heidelberg (2006)
12. Lee, D., Kim, T., Lee, S., Paik, J.: Genetic Algorithm-Based Watermarking in Discrete Wavelet Transform Domain. In: Huang, D.-S., Li, K., Irwin, G.W. (eds.) ICIC 2006. LNCS, vol. 4113, pp. 709–716. Springer, Heidelberg (2006)
13. Shih, F.Y., Wu, Y.-T.: Enhancement of image watermark retrieval based on genetic algorithms: J. Vis. Commun. Image R. 16, 115–133 (2005)
14. Chu, S.-C., Huang, H.-C., Shi, Y., Wu, S.-Y., Shieh, C.-S.: Genetic Watermarking for Zerotree-Based Applications. Circuits Syst. Signal Process 27, 171–182 (2008)
15. Shieh, C.-S., Huang, H.-C., Wang, F.-H., Pan, J.-S.: Genetic watermarking based on transform-domain techniques. Pattern Recognition 37(3), 555–565 (2004)

Analysis and Comparison of Multicast Routing Protocols for Mobile IPTV

Yu-Doo Kim and Il-Young Moon

Korea University of Technology and Education, Dept. of Information Media Engineering,
1800 Chngjeollo Byeongcheon-Myeon Cheonan Chungnam province, Korea
{kydman,iymoon}@kut.ac.kr

Abstract. Recently, Many people are using IPTV(Internet Protocol Television) services because it provide various contents when they want. And it can send a real-time request to the service provider. So we can utilize various services in IPTV such as shopping, banking, SMS(Short Message Service), education, etc. But recent IPTV services are provided in the home only because it use wired network. Therefore future IPTV will be changed mobile IPTV using mobile network technology. If the mobile IPTV is commercialized, we will enjoy the various IPTV services anytime and anywhere because it can communicate in various heterogeneous networks. But recent throughput of mobile network technology is not enough. So we need analysis the various multicast routing protocols. In this paper, we analyze existing multicast routing protocols of mobile network and compare it for mobile IPTV.

Keywords: Mobile IPTV, Multicasting, Routing Protocol, Mobile Network.

1 Introduction

A growth of network infra brought high speed Internet connections to most households. Telecommunication technology which started with telephone networks marks a quantum development forwards by a convergence with IT technology.

IPTV is a convergence technology of telecommunication combined with IT and broadcasting. Its fundamentals are broadband network, digital broadcasting and web 2.0.

To provide IPTV service properly, the current 'best effort' Internet is not enough. The network providing IPTV must support QoS(Quality of Service), security and reliability. IPTV started with duplex VOD (Video-on-demand) service on wired networks. But convergence of wired and mobile networks has been a hot research topic and the next version of IPTV will provide service on mobile networks. It is going to provide 4A (Any Service, Ant Device, Any Time, Any Where) service. Also the IPTV service will be changed from walled garden to open access. Various kinds of devices and platforms will be turned out to support open access IPTV services [1].

D. Ślęzak et al. (Eds.): FGCN/ACN 2009, CCIS 56, pp. 594–601, 2009.
© Springer-Verlag Berlin Heidelberg 2009

We anticipate that the IPTV will be a stepping stone into the ubiquitous era. In a ubiquitous environment, people can use the networks anytime and anywhere freely without being conscious of real networks or computers. Current IT environment could be an 'IT life' step characterized by a popularization of Internet and mobile communication. The next step, 'IT everywhere', will be the ubiquitous era realized through a home network; a concept of personalization of networks.

Many experts anticipate that the need to share contents and service will be increased. To support those changes, the shift of IT paradigm is required of client/server network structures to P2P(Peer to Peer), ad-hoc structures.

In this paper, we analyze the various multicast routing protocols based on mobile network. Especially, ad-hoc multicast routing protocols will use in mobile IPTV. So we compare existing multicast routing protocols.

2 Current and Future IPTV

IPTV are duplex television services using broadband network that the TV audience can select program anytime. It is different from cable TV services. And it use television instead of computer monitor. So it is different from internet TV too. Current IPTV systems are constructed TV, STB(Set-top box) and Modem by wired network.

2.1 Current IPTV

Figure 1 is show current IPTV services. It separated TV-Portal services and Multi-Channel services. TV-Portal provide various useful services such as banking, email, etc. and funny services such as game. The others it consider security. Next, we can enjoy real and near VoD(Video On-Demand) services. Finally, it provide public and charged broadcasting services.

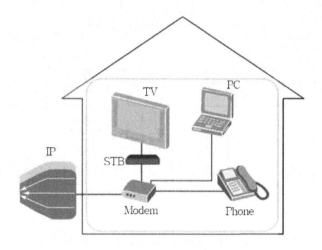

Fig. 1. Structure of current IPTV

2.2 Future IPTV

Recent IPTV has some weak points than DMB and existing broadcasting services. First, it can't find different point with existing TV services. Now, IPTV services provide a rebroadcasting and contents recording only. So many people not need recent IPTV services. Next, it can't provide mobility.

The concept of future IPTV is 4G(Any Service, Any Device, Any Time, Any Where). Also the IPTV service will be changed from walled garden to open access. Various kinds of devices and platforms will be turned out to support open access IPTV services. We anticipate that the IPTV will be a stepping stone into the future internet era. In a future internet environment, customers can use the networks anytime and anywhere freely without being conscious of real networks or computers. Current IT environment could be an IT life step characterized by a popularization of Internet and wireless communication. he next step, IT everywhere, will be the future internet era realized through a home network; a concept of personalization of networks. Then, Many experts anticipate that the IPTV will be a stepping stone towards the ubiquitous era in the aspect of home network's business models.

3 Type of Multicast Routing Protocol in Mobile Network

Through previous chapter, we know that the multicast routing protocol is very important for improve performance in mobile IPTV. Therefore we must study multicast routing protocols in mobile network. In first step, we survey exist multicast routing protocols of mobile network.

Multicast routing protocols in mobile network separated various types. Figure 2 shows type of multicast routing protocols in mobile network.

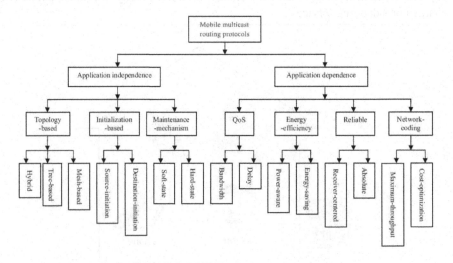

Fig. 2. Type of multicast routing protocol in mobile network

3.1 Application Independence-Based

Multicast Routing protocols based on application independence stem from the conditional multicast routing protocols in the wired environment, where there are two popular networks multicast schemes: the shortest path multicast tree and core based tree. Most multicast routing protocols based on application independence for MANETs use "hop-number" as a metric.

If there are multiple routing paths available, the path with the minimum hop number will be selected. If all wireless links in the network have the same failure probability, short routing paths are more stable than the long ones and can obviously decrease traffic overhead and reduce packet collisions. The application independence-based multicast routing protocols is to maintain the state of a link considered in the routing construction phase. And existing multicast routing approaches for MANETs can be divided into topology, initialization and maintenance-mechanism multicast routing protocols.

3.2 Application Dependence-Based

Compared with the wired network applications, some special applications in MANETs introduce some new problems in addition to the ones already present in fixed networks. Multicast routing protocols based on application dependence are designed for those special applications when needed. And application dependence-based multicast routing protocols can further divided into QoS, energy-efficiency network-coding and reliable multicast routing protocols.

4 Comparison of Multicast Routing Protocol in Mobile Network

4.1 The Enhanced on Demand Multicast Routing Protocol (EODMRP)

The Enhanced On-Demand Multicast Routing Protocol (EODMRP)[2] is an enhancement of ODMRP, which is a reactive mesh-based multicast routing protocol. It is an enhanced version of ODMRP with adaptive refresh. Adaptation is driven by receivers' reports. The second enhancement is the "unified" local recovery and receiver joining scheme. As the time between refresh episodes can be quite long, a new node or a momentarily detached node might lose some data while waiting for the routing to it to be refreshed and reconstructed. Upon joining or upon detection of broken route, a node performs an expanding ring search to proactively attach itself to forwarding mesh or to requests a global route refresh from the source. Compared to ODMRP, a slightly lower packet delivery ratio might be expected in E-ODMRP in light load since the new scheme uses packet loss as indicator of a broken link. The major advantage is reduced overhead, which translates into a better delivery rate at high loads, yet keeping the same packet delivery ratio as the original ODMRP.

4.2   The Mesh-Based Multicast Routing Protocol with Consolidated Query Packets (CQMP)

The Mesh-based multicast routing Protocol with Consolidated Query packets (CQMP) [3] is a reactive mesh-based multicast routing protocol with an idea of "query packet consolidation" to address this scalability problem. It retains all of the advantages of the ODMRP, such as high packet delivery ratio under high mobility, high throughput. Moreover, the protocol significantly reduces control overhead, one of the main weaknesses of ODMRP, under the presence of multiple sources. This feature is a crucial contributing factor to the scalability of multicast routing for MANETs. Instead of each source sending advertising packets to the network, in CQMP, each core disseminates to the network the mappings of multicast addresses to one or more core addresses. CQMP, however, assumes the availability of routing information from a uni-cast routing protocol. This uni-cast routing protocol is also required to provide correct distances to known destinations within a finite amount of time. CQMP also assumes the existence of a beaconing protocol, which may be embedded into the uni-cast routing protocol. In addition, CQMP relies on the associated routing protocol to work correctly in the presence of router failures and network partitions.

4.3   Efficient Hybrid Multicast Routing Protocol (EHMRP)

The Efficient Hybrid Multicast Routing Protocol (EHMRP) [4] is a hybrid multicast routing protocol to be suitable for high mobility applications and improve the scalability of the ODMRP. It separates out data forwarding path from join query forwarding path. EHMRP incorporates low overhead local clustering technique to classify all nodes into core and normal categories. When multicast routes to destination nodes are unavailable, join-query messages are sent to all nodes in the network and data packets are forwarded by the core nodes to the destination nodes using DDM, which is a stateless multicast approach where multicast tree information is appended with each data packet header. EHMRP does not require any underlying uni-cast protocol. There are key components of EHMRP as follows: (1) Classifying core and normal nodes; (2) Separating out data forwarding path while sending join request and sending data packets using DDM; (3) Separate handling of received data packets coming through DDM path; (4) Group membership update; (5) Normal functionality of ODMRP protocol.

4.4   The Robust Multicasting in Ad-hoc Network Using Tree (ROMANT)

The Robust Multicasting in Ad-hoc Network using Tree (ROMANT) [5] is a reactive tree-based multicast routing protocol. Instead of using a new kind of control packet, the existing control packet, the group hello is used to avoid the problem in fixing broken links faced by MAODV. ROMANT fixes the performance problems faced by MAODV (high control overhead and low packet delivery ratio in situations of high mobility, high traffic load and a large number of members). Moreover, ROMANT does not introduce new problems. The process of merging of partitions in ROMANT is much simpler than that of MAODV. ROMANT eliminates the drawbacks of

MAODV and avoids any dependency on uni-cast routing protocols without incurring any extra overhead. It also provides equal or better packet delivery ratio than ODMRP at only a fraction of the total overhead incurred by ODMRP.

4.5 The Power-Aware Multicast Routing Protocol (PMRP)

The power-aware multicast routing protocol (PMRP) [6] is a tree-based minimum energy multicast routing protocol with mobility prediction. In order to select a subset of paths that provide increased stability and reliability of routes in routing discovery, each node receives the RREQ packet and uses the power-aware metric to get in advance the power consumption of transmitted data packets. If the node has enough remaining power to transmit data packets, it uses the GPS to get the location information (i.e. position, velocity and direction) of the MNs and utilizes this information to calculate the Link Expiration Time (LET) between two connected MNs. During routing discovery, each destination node selects the routing path with the smallest LET and uses this smallest link expiration time as the Route Expiration Time (RET). The destinations nodes collect several feasible routes and then select the path with the longest RET as the primary routing path. Then the source node uses these routes between the source node and each destination node to create a multicast tree. In the multicast tree, the source node will be the root node and the destination nodes will be the leaf nodes.

4.6 The Distributed QoS Multicast Routing Protocol (DQMRP)

The Distributed QoS Multicast Routing Protocol (DQMRP) [7] is a shared-tree QoS-based multicast routing protocol. The multicast tree is formed incrementally by source node. Source node sends an explored frame, which recodes every intermediate node it passes, including source node, to every neighboring node with feasible path from itself. And the intermediate node transfers this frame received within limited time to all its neighbor nodes expect source node. If it receives over the constrained time, it discards any frame. The destination node chooses the path with minimum cost from more than on feasible paths. At the same time, destination node reverse sends a resource reservation information and acknowledge reply to source nodes and adds it into the multicast tree. Then destination node keeps all other feasible paths recorded by other explorer frame as backup paths. Acknowledge reply finds the path to the source nodes through the previous node's information kept among the intermediate nodes, meanwhile, the intermediate nodes update their previously node's information through the source of the acknowledge reply information. When resource reservation information or acknowledge reply information finally reaches source node, the destination node is added into the multicast tree successfully.

4.7 Comparison of Multicast Routing Protocol

In the table 1, the classification of the multicast routing protocols.

The table lists the multicast routing philosophies (ex. proactive, reactive, flat, hierarchical, location-awareness and power sensitiveness etc), the underlying multicast routing metrics and the primary routing selection principles of those protocols[8-16].

Table 1. Comparison of multicast routing protocols

#	Protocol/ Algorithm Acronym/ Name	E	F	H	HY	L	M	P	Q	R	S	T	Primary Multicast Routing Metric	Multicast routing selection philosophy	
														AI	AD
1	AMRIS	N	Y	N	N	N	N	Y	N	N	Y	Y	Minimum hop	Y	N
2	MAODV	N	Y	N	N	N	N	N	N	Y	Y	Y	Minimum hop	Y	N
3	AMRoute	N	Y	N	N	N	N	N	N	Y	Y	Y	Minimum hop	Y	N
4	LAM	N	Y	N	N	N	N	N	N	Y	N	Y	Link affinity	Y	N
5	ODMRP	N	Y	N	N	N	Y	Y	N	N	N	N	Minimum hop	Y	N
6	CAMP	N	Y	N	N	N	Y	Y	N	N	N	N	Link affinity	Y	N
7	LGT	N	Y	N	N	N	N	N	N	Y	N	Y	Maximum Forward Progress	Y	N
8	DDM	N	Y	N	Y	N	N	Y	N	N	N	N	Minimum hop	Y	N
9	HQMRP	N	N	Y	N	N	N	Y	N	N	Y	N	Localized reactions to topology changes	N	Y
10	SOM	N	N	Y	N	N	N	N	N	Y	Y	N	Link affinity	N	Y
11	LGF	N	Y	N	N	Y	Y	N	N	Y	N	N	Maximum Forward Progress	Y	N
12	SPBM	N	Y	N	N	Y	N	N	N	Y	N	Y	Maximum forward progress	N	Y
13	STAMP	N	Y	N	N	N	N	N	N	Y	Y	T	Max. forward progress/ Minimum hop	N	Y
14	ACMP	N	Y	N	N	N	N	N	N	Y	Y	Y	Max. forward progress/ Minimum hop	Y	N
15	CQMP	N	Y	N	N	N	Y	N	N	Y	Y	Y	Minimum hop	Y	N
16	E-ODMRP	N	Y	N	N	N	Y	N	N	Y	N	Y	Minimum hop	Y	N
17	BODS	N	Y	N	N	N	Y	N	N	Y	Y	Y	Minimum hop	Y	N
18	EHMRP	N	Y	N	Y	N	N	Y	N	N	Y	Y	Max. forward progress/ Minimum hop	Y	N
19	MWIA	Y	Y	N	N	N	N	Y	N	Y	Y	N	Minimum overall end-to-end transmission power	N	Y
20	PCHMR	Y	Y	N	N	Y	N	Y	N	N	N	Y	Minimum transmission power	N	Y
21	RAMP	N	Y	N	N	N	Y	Y	N	N	N	N	Minimum hop	N	Y
22	RORP	N	Y	N	N	N	N	Y	N	N	Y	Y	Max. forward progress/ Minimum hop	N	Y
23	ROMANT	N	Y	N	N	N	N	N	N	Y	Y	Y	Max. forward progress/ Minimum hop	N	Y
24	OPHMR	N	Y	N	Y	N	N	N	N	Y	N	N	Minimum hop	N	Y
25	MAMR	N	Y	N	N	N	N	N	N	Y	N	Y	Min. hop path on stronger stable channels	N	Y
26	MPGC	Y	Y	N	N	N	N	Y	N	N	Y	Y	Minimum overall end to-end transmission delay	N	Y
27	P-REMiT	Y	Y	N	N	N	Y	Y	N	N	Y	Y	Minimum transmission power	N	Y
28	PMRP	Y	Y	N	N	N	Y	Y	N	N	Y	N	Minimum end-to-end transmission power	N	Y
29	CCMRP	N	Y	N	N	N	Y	Y	N	Y	Y	N	Min. hop path on stronger stable channels	N	Y
30	ONCRM	N	Y	N	N	N	N	Y	N	N	Y	N	Min. hop path on stronger stable channels	N	Y
31	DQMRP	N	Y	N	N	N	N	Y	Y	N	Y	Y	Maximum forward progress	N	Y
32	HVDB	N	N	Y	Y	N	N	Y	Y	N	Y	Y	Maximum forward progress	N	Y

AI-Application Independence AD-Application Dependence E-Energy-aware F-Flat
H-Hierarchical HY-Hybrid L-Location-aware M-Mesh
P-Proactive Q-QoS-aware R-Reactive S-Stability T-Tree

5   Conclusion

In this paper, we survey and compare various multicast routing protocols in mobile network. The future IPTV will changed mobile network. So IPTV provide funny and convenience to many people. But current multicast routing protocols of mobile network not show enough performance. Therefore we must design a new multicast routing protocol basis the current multicast routing protocol of mobile network. That reason we decide the future work that study and develop multicast routing protocol for mobile IPTV. So this study will be useful our future work.

References

1. http://www.worldwidewords.org/turnsofphrase/tp-pro4.htm
2. Soon, Y.O., Park, J.-S., Gerla, M.: E-ODMRP: Enhanced ODMRP with motion adaptive refresh. In: Proc. ISWCS, pp. 130–134 (2005)
3. Dhillon, H., Ngo, H.Q.: CQMP: A mesh-based multicast routing protocol with consolidated query packets. In: Proc. IEEE WCNC 2005, vol. 4, pp. 2168–2174 (2005)
4. Biswas, J., Barai, M., Nandy, S.K.: Efficient hybrid multicast routing protocol for ad-hoc wireless networks. In: IEEE LCN, November 2004, pp. 180–187 (2004)
5. Vaishampayan, R., Garcia-Luna-Aceves, J.J.: Robust tree-based multicasting in ad-hoc networks performance. In: Proc. IEEE IPCCC, 2004, vol. 23, pp. 647–652 (2004)
6. Song, G., Leung, V., Yang, O.: A distributed minimum energy multicast algorithm in MANETs. In: Proc. WoWMoM, vol. 2006, pp. 134–140
7. Sun, B., Li, L.: Distributed QoS multicast routing protocol in adhoc networks. J. Systems Engineering Electronics 17(3), 692–698 (2006)
8. Royer, E.M., Perkins, C.E.: Multicast operation of the ad-hoc ondemand distance vector routing protocol. In: Proc. ACM MOBICOM, August 1999, pp. 207–218 (1999)
9. Xie, J., Rajesh, R., McAuley, A., et al.: AMRoute: Ad-hoc multicast routing protocol. Mobile Networks and Applications, Multipoint Communication in Wireless Mobile Networks 7(6), 429–439 (2002)
10. Garcia-Luna-Aceves, J.J., Madruga, E.L.: Core-assisted mesh protocol. IEEE J. Select. Areas Commun. 17(8), 1380–1394 (1999)
11. Ji, L., Corson, M.S.: Differential destination multicast-A MANET multicast routing protocol for small groups. In: Proc. IEEE INFOCOM, vol. 2, pp. 1192–1201 (2001)
12. Transier, M., Fussler, H., Widmer, J., et al.: A hierarchical approach to position-based multicast for mobile ad-hoc networks. Wireless Networks 13(4), 447–460 (2007)
13. Inn Inn, E.R., Seah, W.K.: Distributed steiner-like multicast path setup for mesh-based multicast routing in ad-hoc networks. IEEE TIME, 192–197
14. Biswas, J., Barai, M., Nandy, S.K.: Efficient hybrid multicast routing protocol for ad-hoc wireless networks. IEEE LCN, 180–187 (November 2004)
15. Cheng, W., Wen, C., Feng, K.: Power-controlled hybrid multicast routing protocol for mobile ad-hoc networks. In: Proc. IEEE VTC 2006, vol. 3, pp. 1087–1091 (2006)
16. Cheng, M.X., Sun, J., et al.: Energy-efficient broadcast and multicast routing in multi-hop ad-hoc wireless networks. Wireless Communications and Mobile Computing 6(2), 213–223 (2006)

Monitoring-Control System Using Multi-modal Interaction Agent in Ubiquitous Environment*,**

Sungdo Park, Jeongseok Kim, Hyokyung Chang, Bokman Jang, and Euiin Choi

Dept. of Computer Engineering, Hannam University, Daejeon, Korea
{sdpark,jskim,hkjang,bmjang}@dblab.hannam.ac.kr, eichoi@hnu.kr

Abstract. Multi-modal is a technology which can convert information to suitable format for the optimum communication between the system and the user. We should represent as modalities to contexts with the user and the environment for improved monitoring-control system in ubiquitous environment. Also, we need to context-awareness and multi-modal technologies for understanding contexts and providing suitable services. User's actions then are used as main information of context-awareness and multi-modal service. In order to constrain user's actions as basic ones and provide a good service by grasping each user's situation through context model, there needs a multi-modal interface and it makes for an agent with this to provide a multi-modal interaction service. Therefore, this paper presents a more improved monitoring-control system using a multi-modal interaction agent than existing one.

Keywords: Ubiquitous computing, Multi-modal interaction, Monitoring-control system.

1 Introduction

The purpose of ubiquitous computing is to construct an environment that helps people pursue a convenient life in daily life by supporting services at anytime at anywhere without showing devices themselves [1]. It is important for the system to aware information of what users want and is doing in the ubiquitous environment. Hence, interests and studies in multi-modal interaction in ubiquitous computing and home networking field have been getting high and doing actively to provide required services through suitable media by context awareness that correctly grasps the situation which human beings' actions are done and reasoning.

Multi-modal is a technology that looks for a variety of ways of utility, converts information into suitable formats for the system to let itself communicate optimally with user and transmits. It helps humans and computers interact by using 2 or more of input/output modality including a few of modes, aspects, and senses [2].

---

* This work was supported by the Security Engineering Research Center, granted by the Korea Ministry of Knowledge Economy.
** This research was financially supported by the Ministry of Education, Science Technology (MEST) and Korea Industrial Technology Foundation (KOTEF) through the Human Resource Training Project for Regional Innovation.

D. Ślęzak et al. (Eds.): FGCN/ACN 2009, CCIS 56, pp. 602–607, 2009.

The direction for study of multi-modal can be divided into 3 big parts; first, it has an direction to replace natural movements like speaking, gazing, and acting to the way of input of equipment operation so as to use the study as a method that heightens the measurement of input method for each; voices, steady gaze of eyes, and movements, or overlapped ones and the precision of grasp of intention. Second, it is the study of the optimum interface of output equipment. While products are combined centered space and service purpose in the ubiquitous environment, existing services provide product-centered interfaces such that audio let people hear the music through speaker and TV transmits contents with images and sound at the same time. For instance, it is the study to develop integrated media service, not TV. Third, it aims to embody a multi-modal that knows the situation rightly, confronts appropriately, provide a visual, sound or which complicated interface and how much information [3].

There are various results from the first directed study among them, however, the results from the second and third whose technologies are able to integrated to products and applied to services are not good enough yet. So, we in this paper would like to discuss the monitoring-control system that manages and controls surroundings to fit user's requirements through analysis of user's modality in the side of service offering.

It is not good enough for the existing monitoring-control products to be utilized in ubiquitous computing environment that IT field pursues today. There are a lot of inconveniences such that it has a problem of limited space, a problem that it is ok to control in certain places, and a problem of supplement of personnel because a manager or a clerk related to needs to be involved. Thus, this paper proposes a improved monitoring-control system compared to existing ones by using a multi-modal interaction agent which applies suitable multi-modal interaction services by catching user's situations through embodiment of context model.

2   Related Works

2.1 Multimodal Interface

2.1.1 Multimodal Framework
Multi-modal interface means that the user can communicate easily and conveniently with the computer using compounded modalities such as speech, visual, tactile, etc. And multi-modal interface which is different with current uni-modal based interfaces should need to synchronize between each interface. Hence, W3C(World wide web consortium) defined Multimodal Interaction Framework which is composed of inter-action manager, service session element, system environment element and application service element. The information which is inputted by the user using input interfaces such as speech, pen touch, keyboard, etc is sent to interaction manager which can generate semantic information, and then multimodal input data that is called EMMA(Extended Multimodal Annotation) is generated[4]. EMMA can represent semantic information which is described by XML as well as all characteristics of input data. Thus, EMMA data which is generated by each modalities is integrated by interaction manager. Interaction manager provide to send data to application server in back-end through compositing each input EMMA data, and the result which is converted to the specialized language for applications is sent to the user [5].

2.1.2 SCXML (State Chart XML)

SCXML is a state machine that made by combining Harel State Tables with a event based state machine, and is represented to XML[6]. Harel State Tables which is also included UML are state machine presentation model, and can represent to semantics about parallel states. Figure 1 shows SCXML which has a core role in interaction manager and multi-modal runtime which compose of languages based on XML.

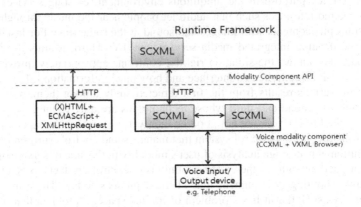

Fig. 1. Multi-modal Runtime Diagram

Graphic interface is represented by HTML and speech interface is represented by VoiceXML. In case of implementing speech interface using telephone, CCXML(Call Control XML) is optionally used for a detailed control each other. SCXML is loosely coupled with interface and has state transition based on events, so has a structure that can easily add new various modalities instead of graphic and speech.

2.2 Context-Awareness

2.2.1 Gaia Project

Gaia project is a typical case among systems applying ontology and semantic web technology in ubiquitous computing environment[7]. CORBA, traditional middle-ware, is used for a way of transmission between distributed objects in ubiquitous environment based on Gaia. Middleware based on CORBA, Java RMI and SOAP can be possible to communicate between a variety of objects, but they do not provide a method for semantic interoperability. In this project, machine study based reasoning is possible using ontology which is describe a CORBA middleware based context as a predicate. When each agent interacts with other agents in ubiquitous environment, they can share context information by applying semantic technology.

2.2.2 SOCAM

SOCAM is proposed as a middleware for easy development of context-aware service in mobile environment[8]. Ontology is used in SOCAM as a method of various context information modeling, and context information model using ontology can provide semantic representation, context reasoning, context sharing, etc. Also, service-oriented middleware has been developed for supporting acquisition, detection, interpretation of context information between context-aware systems. Through context information modeling using ontology language, the system can share the knowledge about context between other objects and can reason a high-level context from a low-level context.

3 Composition of Monitoring-Control System Using Multi-modal Interaction Agent

3.1 User Interaction

The user activity is used as core information of multi-modal and context-aware services in ubiquitous system. But, we need to grasp interaction level of the user activity which we can understand the user requirement for connecting services and activities. The user interaction of purpose and state level has a large scope of activity, so embodiment and personalization of services are difficult. However, basic activity is defined as the least unit of activity that has definite and concrete purpose among the user activities, and purpose of basic activity is possible to grasp by current technology and has proper interaction level for ubiquitous service. Hence, we have applied basic activities level to user interaction.

3.2 Context-Aware Modeling

In this paper, we used a concept model which can describe both context and context-aware. This model represent specific space, use-device, time, basic activity of the user using a pattern which compose of coordinates and the sum total of coordinates in space of three dimensions. Through this model, we have tried to draw required interaction to the user, and have studied about relation between user interaction and context-aware. This model is called context cube and Figure 2 shows context cube. Context cube is composed of environment, basic user activity, time as three axis and they are used for describing the user activities in ubiquitous space [2].

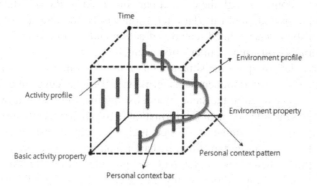

Fig. 2. Context cube

Table 1. Composition of context cube

Factors	Details
Basic Activity Property	Enumeration of basic activity
Environment Property	Enumeration location and composition factor of location
Time	Description of the time as unit of repetitive living pattern
Activity Profile	Schedule that presents user basic activities as standard
Environment Profile	Use schedule of environment property related to the user activities
Context-aware Space	Space that user context bars represented in three-dimension space through crossing activity information and environment information are formed
Personal Context Pattern	A set of context bars; forms user's own pattern for individual

This cube of context-awareness model is a unit life area of home or company and the pattern of individual is distinguished through context bar in a module. The mark of the context bar has transparency according to frequency of user interaction and includes a concept that if user's action changes, inference changes as well.

3.3 Context-Awareness/Multi-modal Interaction Agent

Context and context-awareness are explained through embodiment of each user's Context Cube and multi-modal interaction for ubiquitous service will be unfolded built on a basis of this information. Information of user's action, location, used equipment, and used time will be situations. It is also possible to know what purpose of action user is doing through the context bar composed by the schedule of the time. And it is able to provide multi-modal interaction service by inferring suitable service method by grasping other related features of action and environment. Figure 3 shows the composition of multi-modal interaction agent.

For example, let's suppose the situation that a user is sitting on a sofa in the living room at 8pm and an entertainment channel is on TV at the same time. Environment information of context bar at the same time tells you that the user follows the normal schedule by the schedule and action information is for leisure. As the user goes to the kitchen at this time, the volume of TV gets higher to help the user hear it and as the user still stays there after certain time, it searches an equipment that makes the user watch TV in the kitchen, chooses web pad, and provides an interaction service which telecasts TV broadcasting without cutting. In the case of passing information to user's device, it converts interface and provides information which is suitable for the device.

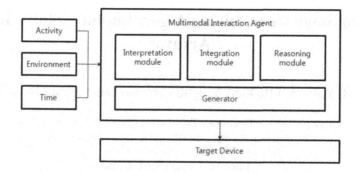

Fig. 3. Composition of Multi-modal interaction agent

4 Conclusions

We in this paper designed components of monitoring-control system which observes situations "at anytime at anywhere" using context-awareness technique and multi-modal technique and enables to offer multi-modal interaction service by inferring suitable service method. Context-awareness technique enables to judge the given monitoring-control environment or situation correctly and objectively and helps provide a service type suitable for the situation judged through context-awareness reflecting user's movements and modality of surroundings. The monitoring-control system proposed by this paper does not reflect the standards of multi-modal interaction framework and ontology, so its structure should be improved by applying these in the future. As it also should fragment each situation, draw user interaction scenarios, embody each component, the process of evaluation and verification of proposed system would be proceeded.

References

1. Coen, M.H.: Design principles for intelligent environment. In: Proc. The Fifteenth National Conference on Artificial Intelligence(AAAI 1998), Madison, Wisconsin, pp. 547–554 (1998)
2. Nigay, L., Cutaz, J.: A design space for multimodal systems:concurrent processing data fusion. In: Proc. INTERCHI 1993, p. 172. ACM Press, New York (1993)
3. Kim, H.-J., Lee, H.-J.: Ubiquitous Context-aware Modeling and Multi-Modal Interaction Design Framework. Korean Society of Design Science, 273–282 (2005)
4. EMMA(Extended Multimodal Annotation) W3C Candidate Recommendation (December 2007), http://www.w3.org/TR/emma/
5. W3C Emotion Markup Language Incubator Group, http://www.w3.org/2005/Incubator/emotion/
6. SCXML (State Chart XML) W3C Working Draft (February 2007), http://www.w3.org/TR/scxml/
7. Roman, M., Hess, C.K., Cerqueira, R., Ranganathan, A., Campbell, R., Nahrstedt, K.: Gaia: A middleware infrastructure to Enable Active Spaces. IEEE, Los Alamitos
8. Gu, T., Pung, H.K., Zhang, D.Q.: A Middleware for Building Context-Aware Mobile Services. In: Proceedings of IEEE Vehicular Technology Conference (2004)

Two Stage Demosaicing Algorithm for Color Filter Arrays*

Hyeon-Mi Yang[1], Sea-Ho Kim[1], Yang-Ki Cho[2], Joo-Shin Lee[1], and Hi-Seok Kim[1]

[1] The Department of Electronics Engineering Cheongju University, Korea
{Hyeon-Mi Yang,Sea-Ho Kim,Joo-Shin Lee,
Hi-Seok Kim}kensean@paran.com
[2] Embedded System R&D Center
renai21c@cbic.or.kr

Abstract. This paper proposes an efficient two stage demosaicing method to interpolate color filter array images. The proposed method based on the edge sensing technique improves the interpolation performance by adopting the color difference model for a green channel as well as a red/blue channel. In particular, the green channel interpolation method with a new concept includes the gradient operator, which uses the total amount of slope changes in adjacent color information, and the missing green color estimation, which uses Approximated Directional Line Averages. Comparing with various comparative experiments between the conventional results and the proposed ones, the performances of the proposed method in this paper outperform to existing algorithms in terms of visual performance both in numerical and visual aspects. Our method of demosaicing improves the standard performance by8.927dB on the average in comparison of other methods in MSE(Mean square Error).

Keywords: Color difference, Demosaicing, CFA interpolation.

1 Introduction

As digital imaging devices such as digital cameras with a single image sensor have been popular, a lot of researches to improve image quality obtained by a single image sensor have been actively performed. The single image sensor only takes the signals filtered by the color filter array (CFA). The CFA is an array pattern where three filters, each of which enables only one color of red(R), green(G), and blue(B) to be penetrated into a pixel, are combined and crossed. The Bayer's pattern is the most popular among CFA patterns [1]. The Bayer's pattern is composed of 50 percent of green color filters, 25 percent of red color filters and 25 percent of blue color filters. The images obtained through the digital image process have only one color per pixel, which is called as CFA data. The CFA images are grayscale images that have one

* This research was financially supported by the Ministry of Education, Science Technology (MEST) and Korea Industrial Technology Foundation (KOTEF) through the Human Resource Training Project for Regional.

D. Ślęzak et al. (Eds.): FGCN/ACN 2009, CCIS 56, pp. 608–620, 2009.

color per pixel. Therefore, the grayscale images must go through the CFA interpolation or the demosaicing process to be reconstructed as full color images.

A lot of studies have been performed for several years and a variety of methods have been introduced. The simplest method among them is the bilinear interpolation, which estimates missing color components by averaging the values of the adjacent color pixels with the same color as the color to be interpolated. This method is so simple to implement, but a lot of color artifacts are shown on the edge region or texture region of a restored image, which is a shortcoming of the method. The edge-sensing based method is adopted to overcome such shortcomings. This paper proposed a very efficient demosaicing method based on the edge-sensing method and the color difference model. This method provides green color estimation that uses not only correlation between local channel averages but also the gradient operator that uses the total amount of slope changes in the local region to select interpolation direction. The method proposed in this paper improves interpolation performance of green channel so that overall performance of demosaicing is improved. This paper is composed as follows. Section 1 discusses the principles and problems of the interpolation methods based on the edge-sensing or the color-difference model and describes the principles and features of the proposed method in detail. Section 2 propose TDSA(Two stage Demosaicing Algorithm) and section 3 shows a variety of performance test results. Finally, Section 4 includes the conclusion of this paper.

2 Demosaicing Methods

Most CFA interpolation methods interpolate green channels first and red/blue channels later. In addition, the edge-sensing methods determine interpolation direction by performing a gradient test at the location of the missing green color before the green color is interpolated. In the edge sensing based methods, the gradient operator is a very important factor to affect visual quality of a reconstructed image. In addition, since the green channel interpolation preceding the red/blue channel interpolation has a remarkable influence on overall performance of demosaicing as well as other channel interpolation for other colors, many demosaicing techniques are more significantly focused on improvement of the green channel interpolation performance. Suppose that S and T of the Bayer's CFA data shown in the Fig. 1 represent red (or blue) color and blue (or red) color, respectively. The AICG[4]uses the second order derivatives of red/blue information in the local region so that the capability to preserve the edge or texture region is more improved than the bilinear interpolation [5] method.

However, the interpolation direction is incorrectly estimated due to no detecting changes in green color. For this problem, it color, use the average of adjacent green colors, this method has a defect of blur image. The ACPI[4] more accurately estimates the missing green color by adding the average of adjacent green colors to the correction value of neighboring S colors in the location to be interpolated.

To compute a gradient in a direction the first order derivatives of green colors are used for AICG whereas both the second order derivatives of S colors and the first order derivatives of G colors are used for ACIP and PCI[3][4]. Such methods sometimes estimate a wrong interpolation direction because they estimate gradients of green colors to be flat and gradients of S colors to be lower than those of actual ones

$S_{i-2,j-2}$	$G_{i-2,j-1}$	$S_{i-2,j}$	$G_{i-2,j+1}$	$S_{i-2,j+2}$
$G_{i-1,j-2}$	$T_{i-1,j-1}$	$G_{i-1,j}$	$T_{i-1,j+1}$	$G_{i-1,j+2}$
$S_{i,j-2}$	$G_{i,j-1}$	$S_{i,j}$	$G_{i,j+1}$	$S_{i,j+2}$
$G_{i+1,j-2}$	$T_{i+1,j-1}$	$G_{i+1,j}$	$T_{i+1,j+1}$	$G_{i+1,j+2}$
$S_{i+2,j-2}$	$G_{i+2,j-1}$	$S_{i+2,j}$	$G_{i+2,j+1}$	$S_{i+2,j+2}$

$S : R$ (or B)
$T : B$ (or R)

Fig. 1. Bayer CFA Pattern

when S colors are in a straight line although there are great differences of gradients between green colors and S colors in a certain test direction.

3 Two Stage Demosaicing Algorithm

The types of demosaicing algorithm can be broadly categorized into two types according to the number of processing per channel. One category is known as single process interpolation technique, which outputs full-color image via one time demosaicing of each channel. The other is referred to as iterative demosaicing technique, which undergoes more than one updating process for the image resulting from a single demosaicing. The demosaicing algorithm proposed in this paper is a two-stage demosaicing algorithm, which updates in a single process the image resulting from an initial interpolation. Stage 1 interpolates G channel from CFA image and uses the interpolated G channel and uninterpolated channels R and B and interpolates channels R and B. The result of stage 1 processing of CFA image is a full-color image. Next, the initial green channel interpolation of stage 1 and the green channel updating of stage 2 in TSDA both include the process of sorting the interpolation direction. However, the former, as shown in Fig.3., estimates the gradient for 2 directions (horizontal and vertical) in the R or B second stage updates G channel using information on the full-color acquired from stage 1 and afterwards, updates channels R and B. In other words, the proposed demosaicing algorithm is made up of an initial process of interpolation and a process of updating like existing iterative demosaicing algorithm, but the difference is that the proposed algorithm processes the updating process of each channel just once.

As shown in Fig.2, TSDA(Two Stage Demosaicing Algorithm) is composed of IDP(Initial Demosaicing Process) and IUP(Image Updating Process). IDP represents as stage 1, and IUP represents as stage 2. That is, the proposed TSDA has no stage where the same process is iteratively processed like POCS[6] or DSA[1] algorithms. In the stage 1 of the proposed algorithm, IDP has outstanding performance that is comparable to existing single process demosaicing methods, but its performance has been further improved via image updating process. Single process demosaicing methods can also be classified according various forms of approach, the edge-directed method is an approach with outstanding performance for preserving an image's edge which the human visual system most sensitively assimilates. The method which proficiently maintains the correlation between each color channel is the progressive-hue-change. Hence, many demosaicing algorithms combine these two methods and implement image interpolation. The proposed algorithm also combines the edge-directed and progressive-hue-change methods and executes demosaicing. Among the progressive-hue-change methods, the proposed algorithm especially uses the color-difference rule rather than the color-ratio rule.

The initial green channel interpolation of stage 1 and the green channel updating of stage 2 in TSDA both include the process of sorting the interpolation direction. However, In Fig. 3., CDFD(Central Difference Forward Difference) estimates the gradient for 2 directions (horizontal and vertical) in the R or B pixel of CFA image, but

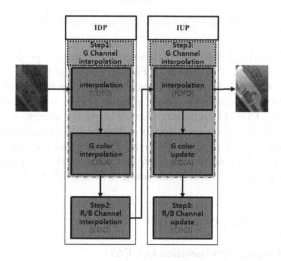

Fig. 2. Interpolation process of the proposed TSDA algorithm CFA

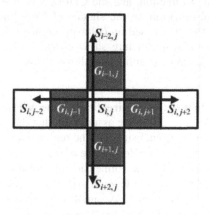

Fig. 3. Estimation directions for the CDFD

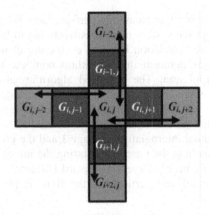

Fig. 4. Estimation directions for the FDFD

FDFD(Forward Difference Forward Difference) estimates the gradient for 4 directions (up, down, left, and right), as shown in Fig. 4. While the CDFD selects 1 direction which has the lower gradient of the 2 directions as interpolation direction, the FDFD selects 2 directions which have the lowest gradients of the 4 directions as interpolation direction. Also, the CDFD interpolates G color using the average regional correlation among the channels in interpolation direction, but the FDFD performs interpolation by averaging the hue signals (R-G or B-G) of 2 pixels that are immediately adjacent toward the two interpolation direction. In the IDP and IUP processes, the R and B channel interpolations both interpolate using CDCI(Color Difference Chrominance Interpolation).

3.1 Initial Demosaicking Process(IDP)

3.1.1 CGI (G Channel Interpolation of CFA)
This paper has proposed a new method of gradient operation to enhance the sorting capability of interpolation direction, and the CDFD, which is the proposed gradient operation, uses slope information on the signals of CFA line which lie toward the direction of gradient estimation based on color-difference rule. In Fig. 4 , the square points and circular points in the picture show G and S signals respectively of the original full-color image, and the solid line shows the line of the signals that have been sampled via CFA.

3.1.2 CDLA (Correlation between Directional Line Averages)
The color-difference rule is based on the assumption that the difference between the R (or B) channel signal and G channel signal in the regional area is uniform. We induce CDLA[2] from the perspective of color-difference rule for the purpose of evaluating G color in GCI. To explain CDLA, one dimensional color lines of each color channel - originally, an S line which is a set of R (or B) signals, G line which is a set of G signals, and CFA line which is a set of CFA samples of an image - are shown in Fig. 4. The directional line average, which is the average value of 5 components centered around $x=3$ which is a location included in each channel line, has also been represented

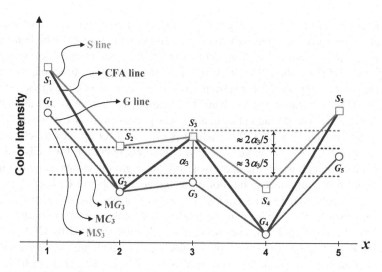

Fig. 5. One-dimensional channel lines for the explanation of the correlation between channel

in Fig. 4. The MS_3, MG_3 and MC_3 each reveals the directional line average of S line, of G line, and of CFA line at the position, $x = 3$ in Fig. 5.

$$\overline{G}_3 \cong S_3 - \frac{\alpha_3' + \alpha_3''}{2}$$

$$= S_3 - \frac{5}{4}(MS_3 - MC_3) - \frac{5}{6}(MC_3 - MG_3) \tag{1}$$

In equation (1), G_3 denotes G color signal which has been estimated at the location of pixel S_3. In general, The equation interpolates G color components of the location (i,j) using the CDLA as shown in equation (2)

$$\overline{G}_{i,j} = S_{i,j} - \frac{5}{4}(MS_{i,j} - MC_{i,j}) - \frac{5}{6}(MC_{i,j} - MG_{i,j}) \tag{2}$$

Since IDP has good performance when compared to existing single process demosaicing algorithm, it can be utilized as individual demosaicing method. However, to propose a demosaicing algorithm that is more better than existing high performance iterative demosaicing algorithms, In this paper we have proposed an image up dating process in session 2.

3.2 IUP (Image Updating Process)

3.2.1 GCU (G Channel Update)

To preserve the edge components of an image in IDP, the interpolation direction has been set and G color has been interpolated in the interpolation direction. This has used the characteristics of human visual system that are sensitive to the edge components of an image. Hence, we has placed its basis in edge-directed even for G channel updating during the process of image updating. Unlike interpolating CFA image, since the process of image updating uses the already interpolated full-color image, the gradient is computed by using only G colors and not CFA samples which are aligned to the gradient estimation direction. While the CDFD gradient operation sequentially applied the CDFD for the CFA line which is in the estimation direction, the gradient operation in GCU applies the forward difference twice for the G line in the estimation direction. This is because the G channel is interpolated where it has already been interpolated. Also, while gradient estimation was performed only for two directions at vertical and horizontal in GCI, the gradient is estimated for up, down, left, and right directions in GCU. In other words, the FDFD gradient operation for GCU is for each of the G pixels which are in the up, down, left, and right directions using the interpolation location as a reference point. For more explanation about FDFD gradient operation, we have referenced to the G channel pattern that has already been interpolated and as shown in Fig. 4. Those that are marked in bright color in Fig. 4 are G pixels which have been interpolated, and the G pixels that are sampled by CFA have been marked with dark color. If each set of G color signals which are the subject of gradient estimation for up, down, left, and right is $C^U_{i,j}$, $C^D_{i,j}$, $C^L_{i,j}$, $C^R_{i,j}$, then each set can be represented as follows.

$$C^U_{i,j} = \left\{ G_{i-2,j}, G_{i-1,j}, G_{i,j} \right\} \tag{3}$$

$$C^D_{i,j} = \left\{ G_{i-2,j}, G_{i-1,j}, G_{i,j} \right\} \tag{4}$$

$$C^L_{i,j} = \left\{ G_{i-2,j}, G_{i-1,j}, G_{i,j} \right\} \tag{5}$$

$$C^R_{i,j} = \left\{ G_{i-2,j}, G_{i-1,j}, G_{i,j} \right\} \tag{6}$$

To explain using calculation of the gradient for upper G line as shown by formula (3) as an example, $Slp^U_{i,j}$ which is a set of slopes for upper G line and $Dif^U_{i,j}$ which is a set of the difference of those slopes can be shown as equation (7), equation (8) respectively.

$$Slp^U_{i,j} = \left\{ 0, \left(G_{i-1,j} - G_{i-2,j} \right), \left(G_{i,j} - G_{i-1,j} \right), 0 \right\} \tag{7}$$

$$Dif^U_{i,j} = \left\{ \begin{matrix} \left(G_{i-1,j} - G_{i-2,j} \right) \\ , \left(G_{i,j} - G_{i-1,j} \right) - \left(G_{i-1,j} - G_{i-2,j} \right), \\ \left(G_{i,j} - G_{i-1,j} \right) \end{matrix} \right\} \tag{8}$$

If the size of the slope differences is obtained using formula (8) and those values are added, we can obtain $Grd^U_{i,j}$, which is the upper gradient, as shown in equation (9).

Similarly, if $Grd^D_{i,j}$, $Grd^L_{i,j}$ and $Grd^R_{i,j}$ are taken as the gradient for the lower, left, and right directions respectively, then each gradient formula can be represented as follows.

$$Grd_{i,j}^{U} = \left| G_{i-1,j} - G_{i-2,j} \right|$$
$$+ \left| \left(G_{i,j} - G_{i-1,j} \right) - \left(G_{i-1,j} - G_{i-2,j} \right) \right|$$
$$+ \left| G_{i,j} - G_{i-1,j} \right|$$
$$\tag{9}$$
$$= \left| G_{i-1,j} - G_{i-2,j} \right|$$
$$+ \left| 2G_{i-1,j} - G_{i,j} - G_{i-2,j} \right|$$
$$+ \left| G_{i,j} - G_{i-1,j} \right|$$

$$Grd_{i,j}^{D} = \left| G_{i+1,j} - G_{i+2,j} \right|$$
$$+ \left| 2G_{i+1,j} - G_{i,j} - G_{i+2,j} \right| \tag{10}$$
$$+ \left| G_{i,j} - G_{i+1,j} \right|$$

$$Grd_{i,j}^{L} = \left| G_{i,j-1} - G_{i,j-2} \right|$$
$$+ \left| 2G_{i,j-1} - G_{i,j} - G_{i,j-2} \right| \tag{11}$$
$$+ \left| G_{i,j} - G_{i,j-1} \right|$$

$$Grd_{i,j}^{R} = \left| G_{i,j+1} - G_{i,j+2} \right|$$
$$+ \left| 2G_{i,j+1} - G_{i,j} - G_{i,j+2} \right| \tag{12}$$
$$+ \left| G_{i,j} - G_{i,j+1} \right|$$

The above equations appear to be similar to the gradient operation of ACPI that has combined the size of secondary difference and the size of primary difference. However, the gradient of ACPI differs from FDFD in that it has combined the secondary difference of S colors that are adjacent to each other at certain distances with the primary difference of two G colors that are immediately adjacent to the central pixel S. GCU sets as interpolation direction 2 directions out of up, down, left, and right directions and implements interpolation at the applicable 2 directions. While GCI focuses only on preserving the edge in respect to 2 directions by implementing interpolation for vertical, horizontal, or both directions, GCU focuses on preserving detailed image components such as texture and not just on the edge of opposite direction. In the example of GCU, two cases where the boundary area of an object in a sample image is found on the upper left area of the estimation region are represented in Fig. 6 (a) and Fig.6(b). This sample picture has shown the object's region as G signal density (light and shade) of each pixel. Fig.6 (a) has shown the boundary of a circle object, and Fig. 6 (b) has represented the diagonal edge of an object that is sloped obliquely towards the upper right area from the lower left area. Since the density of the signals found on the upper and left area from the central pixel is similar to the density of the central pixel, the two patterns are both appropriate for interpolation of the upper and left area. If interpolation is achieved towards the horizontal or vertical direction passing the central area like in GCI, a significant color error arises because the change to the volume of color signals is large.

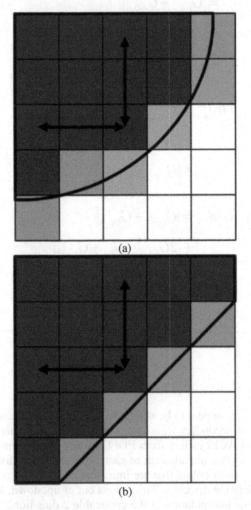

Fig. 6. (a) Boundary of an circle object, and (b) an diagonal edge

Since the GCU already uses full-color image that has already been interpolated, G color is updated utilizing information on pixels that are immediately adjacent to the pixel to be estimated from the two interpolation directions. As a result of acquiring 4 gradients for the pattern is shown in Fig. 4, let the 2 directions with the lowest gradient among them are $O_{i,j}$ and $O'_{i,j}$ respectively. Then, the G colors at the location (i,j) can be updated as shown in the equation (13). $R'_{i,j}$ as shown in equation (13) denotes the difference between G color components and S color components in the pixel immediately adjacent toward interpolation direction of $O_{i,j}$ from the interpolation location of (i,j), and it is the same for $r'_{i,j}$ of equation (14). That is, formula (15) is like adding the average value of the difference of G and S color signals at 2 pixels found in the interpolation direction among up, down, left, and right pixels immediately adjacent to interpolation pixel to the CFA sample signal of the interpolation pixel.

$$\gamma'_{i,j} = \begin{cases} G_{i-1,j} - S_{i-1,j}, & \text{if } O'_{i,j} = U \\ G_{i+1,j} - S_{i+1,j}, & \text{else if } O'_{i,j} = D \\ G_{i,j-1} - S_{i,j-1}, & \text{else if } O'_{i,j} = L \\ G_{i,j+1} - S_{i,j+1}, & \text{else if } O'_{i,j} = R \end{cases} \tag{13}$$

$$\gamma''_{i,j} = \begin{cases} G_{i-1,j} - S_{i-1,j}, & \text{if } O''_{i,j} = U \\ G_{i+1,j} - S_{i+1,j}, & \text{else if } O''_{i,j} = D \\ G_{i,j-1} - S_{i,j-1}, & \text{else if } O''_{i,j} = L \\ G_{i,j+1} - S_{i,j+1}, & \text{else if } O''_{i,j} = R \end{cases} \tag{14}$$

$$\overline{G}_{i,j} = S_{i,j} + \frac{\gamma'_{i,j} + \gamma''_{i,j}}{2} \tag{15}$$

Is, formula (1-15) is like adding the average value of the difference of G and S color signals at 2 pixels found in the interpolation direction among up, down, left, and right pixels immediately adjacent to interpolation pixel to the CFA sample signal of the interpolation pixel.

3.2.2 R/B Channel Update
As described before, R/B channel update has used the CDCI algorithm utilized in the initial R/B channel interpolation.

4 Experiment Result

This section has compared the proposed TSDA algorithm with the proposed IDP as well as with POCS and DSA which are two existing iterative demosaicking algorithms. A comparison of MSE and PSNR performance of each algorithm for the test images has been shown in Table 1,. The test images to be used for the experiment are the 24 images shown in Fig 7.

As sample images of KODAK Photo CD, the present test images are 24 bit lossless images of 512x768 resolution used in many researches on demosaicing (http://r0k.us/graphics/kodak/). Prior to the experiment, each test image was downloaded and sampled according to Bayer CFA format. Difference image was

Fig. 7. Test images

Table 1. Comparison results of TDSA

PSNR			
Image No.	POCS	DSA	IDP	TSDA
image01	7.391	6.287	5.909	5.582
image02	4.679	4.699	4.428	4.256
image03	6.696	6.561	6.418	6.31
image04	4.6	4.616	3.957	4.111
image05	4.312	4.132	4.545	3.686
image06	4.359	4.316	4.669	4.047
image07	3.64	3.485	3.88	3.225
image08	7.789	7.348	8.348	7.793
image09	4.063	4.305	5.661	3.666
image10	4.797	5.098	6.614	4.987
image11	5.695	5.644	6.673	5.155
image12	4.363	4.27	3.43	4.137
image13	10.204	9.046	18.017	10.919
image14	11.863	14.327	13.74	11.791
image15	8.829	7.811	12.789	8.142
image16	17.839	16.186	25.788	16.475
image17	7.619	8.094	10.515	7.409

Table 1. (*continued*)

image18	23.112	20.496	45.481	27.523
image19	18.305	22.301	14.66	15.243
image20	12.493	12.98	18.348	13.679
image21	6.479	6.47	8.403	5.897
image22	8.555	8.072	13.182	8.796
image23	10.691	10.243	11.326	9.88
image24	22.333	21.778	30.421	23.534
Average	9.152	9.11	11.704	8.927

PSNR (dB)				
Image No.	POCS	DSA	IDP	TSDA
image01	39.444	40.147	40.416	40.663
image02	41.429	41.411	41.668	41.84
image03	39.873	39.961	40.057	40.131
image04	41.504	41.488	42.157	41.991
image05	41.784	41.969	41.555	42.466
image06	41.737	41.78	41.439	42.06
image07	42.52	42.708	42.242	43.046
image08	39.216	39.469	38.915	39.214
image09	42.042	41.792	40.602	42.489
image10	41.322	41.057	39.926	41.152
image11	40.576	40.615	39.887	41.008
image12	41.733	41.826	42.778	41.964
image13	38.043	38.566	35.574	37.749
image14	37.389	36.569	36.751	37.415
image15	38.672	39.204	37.062	39.023
image16	35.617	36.04	34.017	35.962
image17	39.312	39.049	37.913	39.433
image18	34.492	35.014	31.552	33.734
image19	35.505	34.648	36.469	36.3
image20	37.164	36.998	35.495	36.77
image21	40.016	40.022	38.887	40.424
image22	38.808	39.061	36.931	38.688
image23	37.841	38.026	37.59	38.183
image24	34.641	34.751	33.299	34.414
Average	39.195	39.257	38.466	39.422

made for interpolated image and original image for the purpose of performance comparison based on numerical value. After obtaining the mean square error, peak signal-to-noise ratio.

The best performance values in the performance comparison of each test image have been indicated in bold. In MSE performance comparison, POCS showed most outstanding performance in image 10 and image 20, DSA for image 08, image 15, image 16, image 18, image 19, image 22, and image 24, and IDP for image 04, image 12, and image 19. TSDA was most outstanding in the remaining test images and overall average performance. In terms of PSNR comparison, POCS was outstanding in image 10 and image 20, DSA was outstanding in image 08, image 13, image 15, image 16, image 18, image 22, and image 24, and IDP was outstanding in image 04, image 12, and image 19. TSDA was outstanding in the remaining test images and overall average performance.

5   Conclusion

This paper proposes a new two stage demosaicing method for CFA images. The proposed method can reduce color errors occurring in the image updating process by adopting high performance interpolation in the first stage. Therefore, the green channel interpolation uses a total amount of the calculation becomes less complicated than existing iterative demosaicing algorithms due to the image updating process without repetition. In order to evaluate the performance algorithm, we have performed various experiments. From the experimental results, our proposed TSDA is better than existing POCS and DSA in terms of visual performance and the comparison results of MSE and PSNR.

References

1. Li, X.: Demosaicing by successive approximation. IEEE Trans. Image Process. 14(3), 370–379 (2005)
2. Cho, Y.K., Kim, H.S., Yang, H.M.: An Efficient Color Demosaicing Using Approximated Directional Line Averages. In: ISOCC 2008, November 24-25, vol. 02, pp. 125–129 (2008)
3. Hibbard, R.H.: Apparatus and method for adaptively interpolating a full color image utilizing luminance gradients, U.S. Patent 5,382,976
4. Hamilton Jr., J.F., Adams Jr., J.E.: Adaptive color plane interpolation in single sensor color electronic camera, U.S. Patent 5,629,734 (1997)
5. Pei, S.-C., Tam, I.-K.: Effective color interpolation in CCD color filter arrays using signal correlation. IEEE Trans. Circuits Syst. Video Technol. 13(6), 503–513 (2003)
6. Gunturk, B.K., Altunbasak, Y., Schafer, R.W., Mersereau, R.M.: Color plane interpolation using alternating projections. IEEE Tran. Image Processing 11(9), 997–1013 (2002)

Face Recognition Using Region-Based Nonnegative Matrix Factorization

Wonmin Byeon and Moongu Jeon

Gwangju Institute of Science and Technology,
Gwangju 500-712, Korea
{wonmin,mgjeon}@gist.ac.kr

Abstract. This paper presents a new method of the face recognition using the nonnegative matrix factorization (NMF) and division of face into several regions. The proposed method divides facial images into 6 sub-regions, and then apply NMF to each sub-region producing basis images and encoding matrices. To recognize a target face, we compare the encoding coefficients of the target image with the encoding coefficients of training images. Test results show that our method is more robust to changes of illumination and facial expression, and occlusions than other methods, and that recognition with 3 sub-regions gives the best result.

Keywords: non-negative matrix factorization, region-based face recognition, local feature.

1 Introduction

Over the past few years, face recognition has been one of the most challenging research areas in computer vision. It is also very useful in any field which requires verification of the personal identity. One of difficulties in face recognition is that the recognition rate is degraded when there are some changes in the normal face such as aging, pose, facial expression, occlusions, make-up and plastic surgery. Thus, for the face recognition system to be reliable, we need a robust algorithm to such changes.

The facial feature representation for face recognition is divided into two approaches: the holistic approach and the feature-based approach. There are several well-known holistic representation techniques such as the principal component analysis (PCA) and the linear discriminant analysis (LDA) [2, 3]. Since this approach extracts global face features, it handles whole pixel information of face images.

The feature based approach, such as the elastic bunch graph matching (EBGM) and the active appearance model (AAM), analyzes explicit local facial features and their texture information with the geometric relationships [5–7]. EBGM describes faces using the Gabor features from the Gabor coefficients of face images. Since the dimension of the feature vector in this approach is too high, the dimensionality reduction method such as PCA or LDA is applied to the Gabor feature vector [8]. However, both approaches are sensitive to even small

D. Ślęzak et al. (Eds.): FGCN/ACN 2009, CCIS 56, pp. 621–628, 2009.

changes of background, illumination, occlusion, or pose variations [9]. Moreover, features are sensitive to the geometric transformation like rotation, translation, and scaling, which are caused by misalignment of facial components [10]. To deal with the problem of recognizing faces under natural occlusion, David Guillamet introduced the non-negative matrix factorization (NMF) technique in a face classification framework. After that, Lee and Seung proposed the part representation of data, like semantic features of text or parts of faces, using NMF [11, 12].

In this paper, we try to resolve the problem of different illumination conditions, facial expression, and natural occlusions with local region feature descriptor using NMF technique. The reminder of this paper is organized as follows. In Section 2, we explain the NMF technique briefly, and in Section 3, we introduce how the local NMF feature can be applied to face recognition. After presenting our experimental results in Section 4, we conclude in Section 5.

2   Nonnegative Matrix Factorization

NMF is one of the matrix factorization techniques, and a useful tool to find part-based representation of non-negative data [12, 13]. For the face recognition problem, each m-dimensional column vector of $m \times n$ matrix V represent one image of training data. Then, NMF is expressed as $V_{mn} \approx (WH)_{mn} = \sum_{r=1}^{i} W_{mr} H_{rn}$, where W is a matrix containing the r number of vectors called basis images, and H is matrix of r-dimensional vector set called encoding. r called rank is decided within $(n + m) \cdot r < m \cdot n$. An encoding is the coefficient of each basis image. Thus, an original object image is represnted as a linear combination of the basis images with corresponding encoding coefficients. There is a very important constraint in NMF, which is non-negativeness of base images and encoding. Non-negativity constraint leads to a part-based representation because it allows only additive combination without any subtraction in the object data. This is most different from other matrix factorization algorithms like PCA or Vector Quantization (VQ). The part-based representation extracts localized and relevant features, and finds a simple description. Therefore, we can get simpler and more reliable features with less computation time.

NMF algorithm is started with random initial matrices W and H. The matrix multiplication (WH) is updated iteratively until it become closed to V through maximizaing the cost function, $F = \sum_{i=1}^{n} \sum_{\mu=1}^{m} V_{i\mu} \log(WH)_{i\mu} - (WH)_{i\mu}$. During each iteration, multiplicative update rule is applied to get the approximate W and H :

$$H_{a\mu} \leftarrow H_{a\mu} \frac{(W^T V)_{a\mu}}{(W^T W H)_{a\mu}}, \tag{1}$$

$$W_{ia} \leftarrow W_{ia} \frac{(V H^T)_{ia}}{(W H H^T)_{ia}}, \quad W_{ia} \leftarrow W_{ia} \frac{W_{ia}}{\sum_j W_{ja}} \tag{2}$$

This update rule is fast and easy to implement. Encoding H is coefficient to visualize the dependencies between original image V and basis image W.

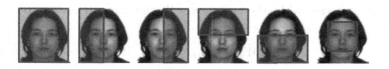

Fig. 1. Six regions of a face image

3 Face Recognition Using Local NMF Features

3.1 Local Faces

Face features from whole face are very weak for face changes like different illumination, facial expression, and occlusion. In these conditions, we need to extract more robust face feature. Tuzel et al. introduced the region covariance matrix (RCM) using inside region of an image [17]. It gave a great result in face detection and object tracking, but failed for face recognition. Later, the Gabor based region covariance matrix (GRCM) was proposed and demonstrated better performance for face recognition [4].

For local face, we present a face with six regions which are five local face regions and one whole face as illustrated in Fig. 1.

The first region is a global representation of the face and next four regions describe left, right, upper, and lower parts of the face. The last region represents the middle part of the face. By using these regions, we can consider every part of the face region, but we can deal with changing conditions more smoothly.

3.2 Region NMF Features

By the result of NMF algorithm, we get the basis image W and the encoding H from original image V as described in Fig. 2.

The NMF features are considered locally significant features and each local part has a different spatial locality like eye, nose and mouth. Each column of the basis image W represents these locality in different locations for every face. From the result, one face uses at least one W feature vector, and every face has the encoding H as the coefficient of each vector W. The idea of recognizing face is simple. To recognize an image v, we need to compute the encoding h for v with the basis image W obtained from training with NMF. Then, the input image

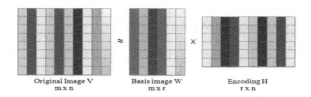

Original Image V
m x n

Basis image W
m x r

Encoding H
r x n

Fig. 2. Basic structure of NMF algorithm

v can be reconstructed by the basis image W and the estimated encoding h as following,

$$v_{mp} \approx (W_{m \times r})h_{r \times p} = \sum_{i=1}^{r}\sum_{a=1}^{m} W_{ai}h_{ip}, \qquad (3)$$

Now, the encoding h for v is compared with each encoding of H from training face V. The key point of the proposed method is that we apply NMF to local faces, which produces namaly the region NMF feature. We extract the region NMF features from each region, calculate the Euclidean distance as the similarity measure between the training encoding H and the test encoding h, and then select the one with the highest similarity measure. To deal with the natural occlusion, illumination, facial expression and other noise, we select a subset of the six regions, which have better discriminative power than the full set of six regions. From our experiments and heuristics, three regions contain the important parts of the face, and may affect the recognition significantly. Therefore, the rest of regions, which are more unreliable parts of face, can be discarded. Finally, test face is recognized to the face k from the training faces (see Fig. 3).

$$d(H_j, h) = \min_{j} \left[\sum_{i=1}^{6} dist(H_i, h_i) - dist(H_j, h_j) \right] \qquad (4)$$

$$= \sum_{i=1}^{6} dist(H_i, h_i) - \max_{j} \left[dist(H_j, h_j) \right] \qquad (5)$$

The main advantages of the region NMF features are as follow:

- It is considered more about natural conditions such as illuminations, occlusions, facial expression, and noise etc.
- It does not need preprocessing of face images. Normally, all the images for training and test are cropped based on the centers of eyes because of normalizing pixel positions in a face.
- Although it reduce the dimensionality of face features, it shows good performance compared to other algorithms such as PCA, Gabor feature etc. We only need to consider encoding H of each region for recognizing the faces. It reduces computation time substantially.

The procedure of region based NMF approach for face recognition is illustrated in Figure 4.

$$\boxed{\begin{array}{l} \text{Descending sort}(\ dist(H_j^{(k)}, h_j)\ )\,,\ j = 1, ..., 6 \\[2mm] D(V_k, v) = \arg\min_{k} \left[\sum_{i=1}^{6} dist(H_i^{(k)}, h_i) - \sum_{j=1}^{3} dist(H_j^{(k)}, h_j) \right] \end{array}}$$

Fig. 3. The similarity calculation between training encoding k and test encoding based on Equation (5)

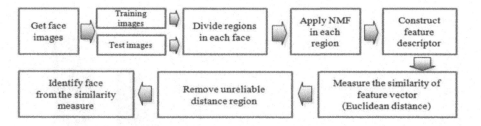

Fig. 4. The procedure of proposed algorithm

4   Experimental Results

4.1   Face Database

Our experiment was performed on AR database [1]. It contains two diferrent kinds of normal faces, facial expressions, illuminations, and four kinds of occlusions. Fig. 5 shows an example of one individual taken under these different conditions. From the database, 200 images were selected - that is twenty people with ten various images (10 males and 10 females). The Original image is 768×576 pixels but resized to 60×70 for efficiency. This process does not affect the accuracy of recognition at all. Among the 10 images per person, two normal face images (ARDB 01 shown in Fig. 5) were used for training and the remained eight for testing (ARDB 02-04 shown in Fig. 5).

The distinct characteristic of the proposed algorithm is that it produced good results without any preprocessing. In general, some preprocessing is needed for face recognition such as center of eye position normalization, background removal and pixel normalization with zero mean and unit variance.

4.2   Evaluation of the Algorithm

Fig. 6 shows recognition results with different ranks (r) when NMF is applied to each region of faces. From previous research, occlusion situations are the most

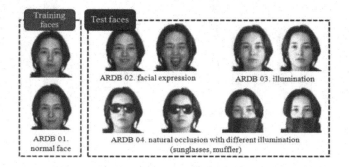

Fig. 5. An example of one individual in database

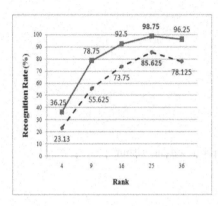

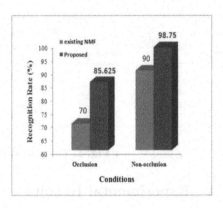

Fig. 6. (a)Recognition results according to various ranks: top red line is from non- occluded faces (ARDB 02-03 in Fig. 5); bottom blue line is from occluded faces (ARDB 02-04 in Fig. 5)

Fig. 7. Recognition accuracy comparison between existing NMF and Proposed NMF

obvious problems in face recognition. Therefore, our test performance is divided into two parts: non-occluded conditions with other various situations (ARDB 02-03 in Fig. 5), occluded conditions include non-occluded conditions (ARDB 02-04 in Fig. 5). The top red line is the recognition rate from non-occluded faces and the bottom blue line is from occluded faces. This figure represents that there are the much better result in non-occluded condition and rank 25 gives the best result using region NMF feature.

As can be seen in Fig. 7, we compared the recognition performances between existing NMF and the proposed method under non-occlusion faces and occlusion faces. By using a whole face in existing NMF, the recognition result is much lower than our approach.

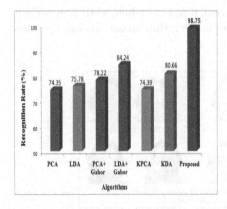

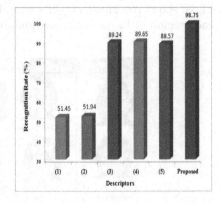

Fig. 8. Recognition accuracy comparison with non-occluded conditions

Fig. 9. Recognition accuracy comparison with region based methods

Table 1. Region based feature descriptor

Method	Descriptor
(1)	$[\,x, y, I(x, y), |I_x|, |I_y|, |I_{xx}|, |I_{yy}|\,]$
(2)	$[\,x, y, I(x, y), |I_x|, |I_y|, |I_{xx}|, |I_{yy}|, (x, y)]$
(3)	$[\,x, y, g_{00}(x, y), g_{01}(x, y), ..., g_{uv}(x, y)]$
(4)	$[\,x, y, I(x, y), g_{00}(x, y), g_{01}(x, y), ..., g_{uv}(x, y)]$
(5)	$[g_{00}(x, y), g_{01}(x, y), ..., g_{uv}(x, y)]$
Proposed	$[h_0, h_1, ... h_r]$

From Figure 8, we compare it with the various existing algorithms which are PCA (Eigenface), LDA (Fisherface), PCA+Gabor, LDA+Gabor, KPCA (Kernel Principal Component Analysis, and KDA (Kernel Discriminant Analysis) [2, 3, 14–16]. This experiment is under non-occluded conditions. The proposed algorithm is much more robust to various conditions with less dimension and computation time. Also, we got the highest performance.

Finally, region based methods are considered in Fig. 9. The detailed methods are listed in Table 1. In Table 1, x and y are pixel location and (x, y) is the edge orientation. $|Ix|$ and $|Ixx|$ are the first- and second-order derivatives, respectively. From (3) to (5), Yanwei Pang constructed new descriptor which is based on Gabor features in the regions. u and v define the orientation and scale of the Gabor kernels. The Gabor kernels are constructed by taking eight orientations ($u \in (0,..,7)$) and five different scales ($v \in (0,..,4)$). Lastly, r is defined as rank above, and we took 25 rank for best performance according to Fig. 6. As can be seen in Fig. 8-9, our proposed method experimentally shows that the region based NMF feature is a good feature for discriminating between different faces.

5   Conclusion

We have presented region based NMF technique to solve the problems of recognizing faces captured under the various conditions such as facial expression, occlusions and changes in different light conditions. NMF finds part-based compositions of data whereas it only allows the positive subspace. We applied this approach to the reliable sub-region face for high recognition rates under the partial changes of faces. Experimental results show that the region NMF feature is much more robust to recognize faces than using whole faces with other approaches. Also, it is simpler than other methods like Gabor based method or combination methods.

To apply our method in real world, face feature should be considered under the changes in time sequence and face scale changes etc. In addition, we expect to overcome the problem in occlusions for the better performance of face recognition in the near future.

Acknowledgment

This research was financially supported by the Center for Distributed Sensor Network, and the System biology infrastructure establishment grant provided by GIST.

References

1. Martinez, A.M., Benavente, R.: The AR Face Database: CVC Technical Report 24 (1998)
2. Turk, M., Pentland, A.: Eigenfaces for Recognition. J. Cognitive Neuroscience 3(1), 71–86 (1991)
3. Martinez, A.M., Kak, A.C.: PCA versus LDA. IEEE Trans. Pattern Analysis and Machine Intelligence 19(7), 711–720 (1997)
4. Pang, Y., Yuan, Y., Li, X.: Gabor-based region covariance matrices for face recognition. IEEE Trans. Circuit Systems for Video Technology 18(7) (2008)
5. Brunelli, R., Poggio, T.: Face Recognition: Feature versus Templates. IEEE Trans. Pattern Anal. and Macine Int. 15(10)(October 1993)
6. Wiskott, L., Fellous, J.M., Kruger, N., Malsburg, C.V.D.: Face Recognition by Elastic Bunch Graph Matching. IEEE Trans. Pattern Analysis and Machine Intelligence 19(7), 775–779 (1997)
7. Edwards, G., Talylor, C.J., Cootes, T.F.: Interpreting face images using active appearance models. In: Proc. IEEE Int. Conf. Automatic Face and Gesture Recognition, pp. 300–305 (1998)
8. Liu, C., Wechsler, H.: Gabor feature based classification using the enhanced fisher linear discriminant model for face recognition. IEEE Trans. Image Process. 11(4), 467–476 (2002)
9. Phillips, P.J., Flynn, P.J., Scruggs, T., Bowyer, K.W., Chang, J., Hoffman, K., Marques, J., Min, J., Worek, W.: Overview of the face recognition grand challenge. In: Proc. IEEE Comput. Vision Pattern Recog. Conf., pp. 947–954 (2005)
10. Shan, S., Cang, Y., Gao, W., Cao, B., Yang, P.: Curse of mis-alignment in face recognition: Problem and a novel mis-alignment learning solution. In: Proc. IEEE Autom. Face Gesture Recog. Conf., pp. 314–320 (2004)
11. Lee, D.D., Seung, H.S.: Algorithms for non-negative matrix factorization. In: Advances in Neural Information Processing Systems, vol. 13, p. 556. MIT Press, Cambridge (2001)
12. Lee, D.D., Seung, H.S.: Learning the parts of objects by non-negative matrix factorization. Nature 401, 788–791 (1999)
13. Paatero, P., Tapper, U.: Positive matrix factorization: A non-negative factor model with optimal utilization of error. Environmetrics (1994)
14. Baudat, G., Anouar, F.: Generalized discriminant analysis using a kernel approach. Neural Comput. 12, 2385–2404 (2000)
15. Scholkopf, B., Smola, A., Muller, K.R.: Nonlinear component analysis as a kernel eigenvalue problem. Neural Comput. 10, 1299–1319 (1998)
16. Liu, C., Wechsler, H.: Gabor feature based classification using the enhanced fisher linear discriminant model for face recognition. IEEE Trans. Image Process. 11(4), 467–476 (2002)
17. Tuzel, O., Porikli, F., Meer, P.: Region covariance: A fast descriptor for detection and classification. In: Proc. Eur. Comput. Vision Conf., vol. 2, pp. 589–600 (2006)

Analysis of On-Chip Antennas with Multi-band due to Change the Slot Size in the Silicon Substrate

DongHee Park[1], IlJun Choi[2], Baekki Kim[3], and Yoonsik Kwak[4]

[1] Dept. of Electronic Communication Engineering,
Chungju National University, Chungbuk, Korea
dhpark@cjnu.ac.kr
[2] Dept. of computer eng. Chungbuk national university
61283@cjnu.ac.kr
[3] Dept. of Information and communication. Gangnungwonju national university
bkim@gwnu.ac.kr
[4] Dept. of Computer Engineering, Chungju National University,
Chungbuk, Korea
yskwak@cjnu.ac.kr

Abstract. This paper has design and analysis on-chip antennas with multi-band in UWB (Ultra Wide Band). Also, to adjust the frequency of each bands, we made the small slots in the Si wafer substrate. Then, this paper suggests be moved each of the bands in the direction to increase the frequency as for increasing the number of slot. We have chosen HRS (High Resistivity Silicon) Si wafer in order to integrate a wireless micro-system. Also we insert SiO_2 layer between patch and substrate to increase effects of antennas.

Keywords: integrated chip antennas; on-chip antennas; multi-band antennas.

1 Introduction

We are moving towards the ubiquitous communication based on radio waves. The modern people have been using wireless communication terminals almost every day and the antenna technology that is a key element has been developing remarkably. However, considering current circumstances as wireless communication services are varied and the environment that the radio waves propagating in is getting poorer, the performance of wireless communication strongly depends on the quality of antennas. Also, recently, a variety of technical approaches of designing an antenna in RF and millimeter-wave systems have been proposed to develop excellent antennas as viable USN(ubiquitous sensor networks) service [1, 2].

In this paper, we have design and analysis multi-band on-chip antennas with UWB characteristics. The designed on-chip antennas have septet central frequency bands by making a sector of circle 4-slots which are symmetrical in the patch with inset feeding. Also, we added an addition slots to Si substrate to adjust the frequency of each bands. The slot-loaded antenna for UWB is categorized to reactive loading antenna and the frequency range can be varied in the range from 3 GHz to 12 GHz.

D. Ślęzak et al. (Eds.): FGCN/ACN 2009, CCIS 56, pp. 629–633, 2009.
© Springer-Verlag Berlin Heidelberg 2009

Therefore, the return loss characteristics for four different cases which make no slot and small rectangular slots in the substrate are depicts. As a result, a novel multi-band antenna structures for UWB applications are proposed for a septet band application; S-band, C-band and X-band.

2 Multi-band On-Chip Antenna Configuration

In this paper, the type of substrate we have investigated integrated multi-band antenna design is the high resistivity silicon (HRS). A schematic diagram of the microstrip patch antenna is indicated in Figure 1. The Si wafer have a thickness $h_1=525$ μm and $\varepsilon_r=11.9$ as a dielectric permittivity and a conductivity $\sigma=0.307$ S/m. To decrease the substrate losses when HRS is used, a thickness $h_2=300$ nm layer of thermal silicon dioxide is used. This layer has an $\varepsilon_r=4.0$ and $\tan\delta=0.05$ and is assumed as an insulator. The metallization layers were realized using a t=2 mm layer as an aluminium.

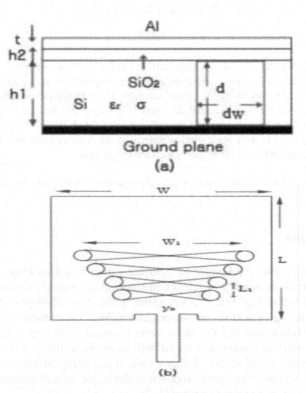

Fig. 1. Multi-band on-chip antenna for integration: a) HRS side view with slot in substrate, b) Top view of inset feed patch with slots of sector forms

The patch size is suitable for a central frequency 6 GHz to design and analysis of minimized on-chip antenna. The size of the slot in wafer is to have the depth $d=h_1$ and width dw=500 μm to adjust each of the multi-band center frequencies.

As shown in Figure 1. (b), the structure and size of the multi-band on-chip antenna have the width W=9 mm and length L=7.45 mm, the inside of patch have an array of a sector of circle shape 4-slots. Here, we designed width W_1=8 mm and distance between two slot L_1=0.5 mm.

The patch antenna is fed with a inset feeder connected to a point y_o=0.1 mm inside the patch where the input impedance is 50 Ω. Also, the width of strip line has a 0.55 mm.

3   Antenna Design and Simulated Results

The following analysis results were carried out with models built in HFSS 11. This tool was previously used for successful on-chip antenna design on HRS substrate. This paper designed with small slot in the Si substrate to adjust of septet multi-band resonant frequency. The Figure 2 depicts the return loss characteristics for two different cases which make no slot in case of data1 and a slot in substrate in case of data2.

Then, the size of the slot has a width dw=0.5 mm, length dL=2 mm and depth d=h_1. The data2 in Figure 2 is the result of return loss that the position of slot is just under the first sector. This result shows that all the bands except first and fourth shift to the right a bit. The third mode moves to the left.

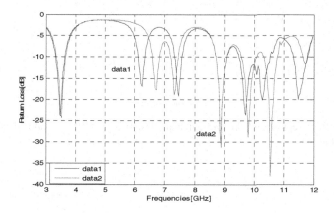

Fig. 2. RL[dB] of septet-band on-chip antennas designed on HRS Si wafer data1: no slot, data2: one slot

Also we used two slots as the interval 0.25 mm to adjust the central frequencies of multi-band. The data3 of Figure 3 shows return loss of designed septet band on-chip antenna with two slots in the substrate. This result shows that all the resonant bands except first and fourth mode shift to the right. In this case, data3 is wider than data2.

The data4 of Figure 4 presents the return loss for three slots, when all the other dimensions are kept unchanged. The central frequency of septet resonance bands is shifted to the right and adjusted possibly, as the number of slot increases.

From above results, we suggested the variations of central frequency in Figure 5 as increase of the number of slots. This results shows that the first band is not almost

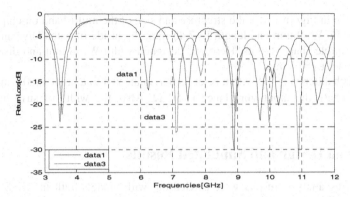

Fig. 3. RL[dB] of septet-band on-chip antennas designed on HRS Si wafer data1: no slot, data3: two slots

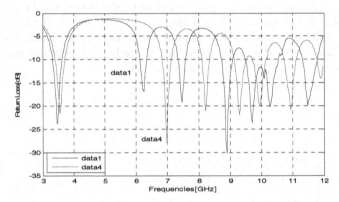

Fig. 4. RL[dB] of septet-band on-chip antennas designed on HRS Si wafer data1: no slot, data4: three slots

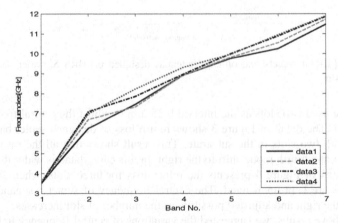

Fig. 5. The variation of central frequency in the numbers of mode, data1: no slot, data2: one slot, data3: two slots, data4: three slots

change, the forth band shifts when the slots are three. In addition, the more the number of slots is, the wider the range of all the resonant bands is.

As a result, this paper proposes enable design of septet band on-chip antenna with UWB characteristics for near RF network.

4 Conclusions

This paper has design and analysis on-chip antennas with multi-band in UWB. Also, to adjust the frequency of each bands, we made the small slots in the Si wafer substrate. Then, this paper suggests be moved each of the bands in the direction to increase the frequency as for increasing the number of slot.

The future of researches of this paper is continuously required on the design of on-chip antennas for near multi communication using multi-band and RF cognitive techniques.

References

[1] Park, D.: Design of Novel On-Chip Antennas with Multi-Band for Wireless Sensor Networks. In: LAPC 2008. Loughborough Antennas & Propagation Conference, March 17-18, pp. 101–104 (2008)
[2] Sorgel, W., Waldschmidt, C., Wiesbeck, W.: Antenna Characterization for Ultra-wideband Communications, XXVIII URSI Conv Radio Sci and FWCW Mtg, University of Oulu, Finland (2003)
[3] Sorgel, W., Waldschmidt, C., Wiesbeck, W.: Antenna Characterization for Ultra-wideband Communications, XXVIII URSI Conv Radio Sci and FWCW Mtg, University of Oulu, Finland (2003)

Closely Spaced Multipath Channel Estimation in CDMA Networks Using Divided Difference Filter

Zahid Ali, Mohamed A. Deriche, and M. Adnan Landolsi

King Fahd University of Petroleum and Minerals, Dhahran 31261, Saudi Arabia
{zalikhan,mderiche,andalusi}@kfupm.edu.sa
www.kfupm.edu.sa

Abstract. We investigate time delay and channel gain estimation for multipath fading code division multiple access (CDMA) signals using the second order divided difference filter (DDF). We consider the case of paths that are a fraction of chip apart, also knwon as closely spaced paths. Given the nonlinear dependency of the channel parameters on the received signals in multiuser/multipath scenarios, we show that the DDF achieves better performance than its linear counterparts. The DDF, which is a derivative-free Kalman filtering approach, avoids the errors associated with linearization in the conventional extended Kalman filter (EKF). The numerical results also show that the proposed DDF is simpler to implement, and more resilient to near-far interference in CDMA networks and is able to track closly spaced paths.

Keywords: CDMA Channel Estimation, Non-linear filtering, Kalman filters, closely spaced multipaths, multiple access Interference.

1 Introduction

Research in time delay estimation has attracted a lot of attraction in the past few years. Time delay estimation techniques are used in numerous applications such a radiolocation, radar, sonar, seismology, geophysics, ultrasonic, to mention a few. In most applications, the estimated parameters are fed into subsequent processing blocks of communication systems to detect, identify, and locate radiating sources.

Direct-sequence code-division multiple-access technology includes higher bandwidth efficiency which translates into capacity increases, speech privacy, immunity to multipath fading and interference, and universal frequency reuse [1,2], over existing and other proposed technologies make it a popular choice. As with all cellular systems, CDMA suffers from multiple-access interference (MAI). In CDMA, however, the effects of the MAI are more considerable since the frequency band is being shared by all the users who are separated by the use of the distinct pseudonoise (PN) spreading codes. These PN codes of the different users are non-orthogonal giving rise to the interference, which is considered to be the main factor limiting the capacity in DS-CDMA systems.

D. Ślęzak et al. (Eds.): FGCN/ACN 2009, CCIS 56, pp. 634–644, 2009.
© Springer-Verlag Berlin Heidelberg 2009

Accurate channel parameter estimation for CDMA signals impaired by multipath fading and multiple access interference (MAI) is an active research field that continues to draw attention in the CDMA literature. In particular, the joint estimation of the arriving multi-path time delays and corresponding channel tap gains for closely-spaced (within a chip interval) delay profiles is quite challenging, and has led the development of several joint multiuser parameter estimators, e.g., [3,4]. These have been extended to the case of multipath channels with constant channel taps and constant or slowly varying time delays [7]. An attempt at extending subspace methods to tracking time delays was given in [6], On the other hand, time delay trackers based on the Delay Lock Loop (DLL) combined with interference cancellation techniques have also been developed for multiuser cases [10]. Near-far resistant time delay estimators are not only critical for accurate multi-user data detection, but also as a supporting technology for time-of-arrival based radiolocation applications in CDMA cellular networks [5,8-10]. The maximum-likelihood-based technique has been employed in [11], and [12] for single-user channel and/or multiuser channel estimation with training symbols or pilots.

The Kalman filter framework based methods were considered in [10, 13-16], where EKF and unscented Kalman filter (UKF) has been applied to parameter estimations. Many of the algorithms presented in previous work have focused on single-user and/or single-path propagation models. However, in practice, the arriving signal typically consists of several epochs from different users, and it becomes therefore necessary to consider multi-user/multi-path channel models. In this paper, we present a joint estimation algorithm for channel coefficients and time delays in a multipath CDMA environment using a non-linear filtering approach based on the second order DDF with a particular emphasis on closely spaced paths in a multipath fading channel.

The rest of the article is organized as follows. In Section 2, the signal and channel models are presented. Section 3 provides a description of the nonlinear filtering method used for multiuser parameter estimation that utilizes Divided Difference Filter. Section 4 describes computer simulation and performance discussion followed by the conclusion.

2   Channel and Signal Model

We consider a typical asynchronous CDMA system model where K users transmit over an M-path fading channel. The received baseband signal sampled at $t = lT_s$ is given by

$$r(l) = \sum_{k=1}^{K} \sum_{i=1}^{M} c_{k,i}(l) d_{k,m_l} a_k(l - m_l T_b - \tau_{k,i}(l)) + n(l) \qquad (1)$$

where $c_{k,i}(l)$ represents the complex channel coefficients, d_{k,m_l} is the mth symbol transmitted by the kth user, $m_l = \lfloor [(l - \tau_k(l)/T_b] \rfloor$, T_b is the symbol interval, $a_k(l)$ is the spreading waveform used by the kth user, $\tau_{k,i}(l)$ is the time delay associated with the ith path of the kth user, and $n(l)$ represents Additive

White Gaussian Noise (AWGN) assumed to have a zero mean and variance $\sigma^2 = E[|n(l)|^2] = N_0/T_s$ where T_s is the sampling time.

As in [13], in order to use a Kalman filtering approach, we adopt a state-space model representation where the unknown channel parameters (path delays and gains) to be estimated are given by the following $2KM \times 1$ vector,

$$x = [c; \tau] \tag{2}$$

with $c = [c_{11}, c_{12}, ..., c_{1M}, c_{21}, ..., c_{2M}, ..., c_{K1}, ..., c_{KM}]^T$
and $\tau = [\tau_{11}, \tau_{12}, ..., \tau_{1M}, \tau_{21}, ..., \tau_{2M}, ..., \tau_{K1}, ..., \tau_{KM}]^T$

The complex-valued channel amplitudes and real-valued time delays of the K users are assumed to obey a Gauss- Markov dynamic channel model, i.e.

$$c(l + 1) = F_c c(l) + v_c(l)$$

$$\tau(l + 1) = F_\tau \tau(l) + v_\tau(l)$$

where F_c and F_τ are $KM \times KM$ state transition matrices for the amplitudes and time delays respectively whereas $v_c(l)$ and $v_\tau(l)$ are $K \times 1$ mutually independent Gaussian random vectors with zero mean and covariance given by $E\{v_c(i)v_c^T(j)\} = \delta_{ij}Q_c$, $E\{v_\tau(i)v_\tau^T(j)\} = \delta_{ij}Q_\tau$, $E\{v_c(i)v_\tau^T(j)\} = 0 \,\forall i, j$ with $Q_c = \sigma_c^2 I$ and $Q_\tau = \sigma_\tau^2 I$ are the covariance matrices of the process noise v_c and v_τ respectively, and δ_{ij} is the two-dimensional Kronecker delta function equal to 1 for $i = j$, and 0 otherwise.

Using (2-4), the state model can be written as

$$x(l + 1) = Fx(l) + v(l) \tag{3}$$

where
$F = \begin{bmatrix} F_c & 0 \\ 0 & F_\tau \end{bmatrix}$ and $Q = \begin{bmatrix} Q_c & 0 \\ 0 & Q_\tau \end{bmatrix}$ are $2KM \times 2KM$ state transition matrix and covariance matrix, and $v = [v_c^T \ v_\tau^T]$ is the $2KM \times 1$ process noise vector with mean of zero and covariance matrix respectively. The scalar measurement model follows from the received signal of (1) by

$$z(l) = h(\mathbf{x}(l)) + \eta(l) \tag{4}$$

where the measurement $z(l) = r(l)$, and
$h(x(l)) = \sum_{k=1}^{K} \sum_{i=1}^{M} c_{k,i}(l)d_{k,m_l}a_k(l - m_l T_b - \tau_{k,i}(l))$.

The scalar measurement $z(l)$ is a nonlinear function of the state $x(l)$. Given the state-space and measurement models, we may find the optimal estimate of $\hat{x}(l)$ denoted as $\hat{x}(l|l) = E\{x(l)|z^l\}$, with the estimation error covariance

$$P = E\left\{[x(l) - \hat{x}(l|l)][x(l) - \hat{x}(l|l)]^T |z^l\right\}$$

where z^l denotes the set of received samples up to time l, $\{z(l), z(l-1), \ldots, z(0)\}$.

3 Parameter Estimation Using the Divided Difference Filter

For the nonlinear dynamic system model such as above, the conventional Kalman algorithm can be invoked to obtain the parameter estimates [17, 18]. The most well known application of the Kalman filter framework to nonlinear systems is the EKF. Even though the EKF is one of the most widely used approximate solutions for nonlinear estimation and filtering, it has some limitations [17]. Firstly, the EKF only uses the first order terms of the Taylor series expansion of the nonlinear functions which often introduces large errors in the estimated statistics of the posterior distributions especially when the effects of the higher order terms of the Taylor series expansion becomes significant. Secondly, linearized transformations are only reliable if the error propagation can be well approximated by a linear function. If this condition does not hold, the linearized approximation can be extremely poor. At best, this undermines the performance of the filter. At worst, it causes its estimates to diverge altogether. And also linearization can be applied only if the Jacobian matrix exists. However, this is not always the case. Some systems contain discontinuities, others have singularities. Calculating Jacobian matrices can be very difficult.

DDF, unlike EKF, is a sigma point Kalman filter (SPKF) where the filter linearizes the nonlinear dynamic and measurement functions by using an interpolation formula through systematically chosen sigma points. The linearization is based on polynomial approximations of the nonlinear transformations that are obtained by Stirling's interpolation formula, rather than the derivative-based Taylor series approximation [18]. Conceptually, the implementation principle resembles that of the EKF, however, it is significantly simpler because uses a finite number of functional evaluations instead of analytical derivatives. It is not necessary to formulate the Jacobian and/or Hessian matrices of partial derivatives of the nonlinear dynamic and measurement equations. Thus the new nonlinear state filter DDF can also replace the EKF and its higher-order estimators in practical real-time applications that require accurate estimation, but less computational cost. The derivative free, deterministic sampling based DDF outperform the EKF in terms of estimation accuracy, filter robustness and ease of implementation.

3.1 Overview of DDF Algorithm

Consider a nonlinear function, $\mathbf{y} = \mathbf{h}(\mathbf{x})$ with mean $\bar{\mathbf{x}}$ and covariance $\mathbf{P_{xx}}$. If the function $\mathbf{h}$ is analytic, then the multi-dimensional Taylor series expansion of a random variable $\mathbf{x}$ about the mean $\bar{\mathbf{x}}$ is given by the following [18]

$$\mathbf{y} \simeq \mathbf{h}(\bar{\mathbf{x}} + \Delta\mathbf{x}) = \mathbf{h}(\mathbf{x}) + D_{\Delta x}\mathbf{h} + \frac{1}{2!}D_{\Delta x}^2\mathbf{h} + \frac{1}{3!}D_{\Delta x}^3\mathbf{h} + \cdots$$

where $D_{\Delta\mathbf{x}}^i\mathbf{h}$ is the total derivative of $\mathbf{h}(\mathbf{x})$ given by

$$D_{\Delta\mathbf{x}}^i\mathbf{h} = \left(\Delta x_1\frac{\partial}{\partial x_1} + \Delta x_2\frac{\partial}{\partial x_2} + \ldots + \Delta x_n\frac{\partial}{\partial x_n} \right)^i \mathbf{h}(\mathbf{x}) \Bigg|_{\mathbf{x}=\bar{\mathbf{x}}}$$

The first and second order operators can be written as

$$D_{\Delta x}h = \left(\sum_{p=1}^{n} \Delta x_p \frac{\partial}{\partial x_p} \right) h(x) \Big|_{x=\bar{x}}$$

$$D_{\Delta x}^2 h = \left(\sum_{p=1}^{n} \sum_{q=1}^{n} \Delta x_p \Delta x_q \frac{\partial}{\partial x_p \partial x_q} \right) h(x) \Big|_{x=\bar{x}}$$

The second order divided difference approximation of the function is formulated by using the vector form of Stirling's interpolation formula, which is similar to the extension of the Taylor series approximation

$$y \simeq h(\bar{x}) + \tilde{D}_{\Delta x}h + \frac{1}{2!}\tilde{D}_{\Delta x}^2 h$$

where the operators $\tilde{D}_{\Delta x}$ and $\tilde{D}_{\Delta x}^2$ are defined as

$$\tilde{D}_{\Delta x}h = \frac{1}{\gamma} \left(\sum_{p=1}^{n} \Delta x_p \mu_p \delta_p \right) h(\bar{x})$$

$$\tilde{D}_{\Delta x}^2 h = \frac{1}{\gamma^2} \left(\sum_{p=1}^{n} \Delta x_p^2 \delta_p^2 + \sum_{p=1}^{n} \sum_{q=1,p\neq q}^{n} \Delta x_p \Delta x_q (\mu_p \delta_p)(\mu_q \delta_q) \right) h(\bar{x})$$

where γ is an interval of length, taken as $\gamma = \sqrt{3}$ for a Gaussian distribution and δ_p and μ_p denote the partial difference operator and the partial average operator respectively. The second order DDF algorithm is shown in Table 1.

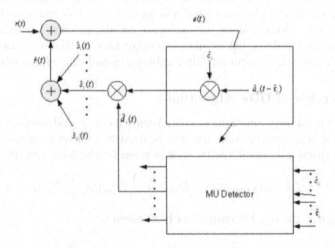

Fig. 1. Multiuser parameter estimation receiver

4   Application to Channel Estimation with Multipath/Multiuser Model

We have simulated a CDMA system with varying number of users and with multipaths using DDF. The delays are assumed to be constant during one measurement. For the state space model we assumed $\mathbf{F} = 0.999\mathbf{I}$ and $\mathbf{Q} = 0.001\mathbf{I}$

Table 1. UKF Algorithm

---

1. Initialization:

$\hat{\mathbf{x}}_k = E[\mathbf{x}_k]$

$\mathbf{P}_k = E[(\mathbf{x}_k - \hat{\mathbf{x}}_k)(\mathbf{x}_k - \hat{\mathbf{x}}_k)^T]$

2. Square Cholesky factorizations:

$\mathbf{P}_0 = \mathbf{S_x}\mathbf{S_x}^T,$

$\mathbf{Q}_k = \mathbf{S_w}\mathbf{S_w}^T,$

$\mathbf{R} = \mathbf{S_v}\mathbf{S_v}^T$

$\mathbf{S}_{x\hat{x}}^{(2)}(k+1) = \frac{\sqrt{\gamma-1}}{2\gamma}\{\mathbf{f}_i(\hat{\mathbf{x}}_k + h\mathbf{s}_{x,j}, \bar{\mathbf{w}}_k) + \mathbf{f}_i(\hat{\mathbf{x}}_k - h\mathbf{s}_{x,j}, \bar{\mathbf{w}}_k) - 2\mathbf{f}_i(\hat{\mathbf{x}}_k, \bar{\mathbf{w}}_k)\}$

$\mathbf{S}_{xw}^{(2)}(k+1) = \frac{\sqrt{\gamma-1}}{2\gamma}\{\mathbf{f}_i(\hat{\mathbf{x}}_k, \bar{\mathbf{w}}_k + h\mathbf{s}_{w,j}) + \mathbf{f}_i(\hat{\mathbf{x}}_k, \bar{\mathbf{w}}_k - h\mathbf{s}_{w,j}) - 2\mathbf{f}_i(\hat{\mathbf{x}}_k, \bar{\mathbf{w}}_k)\}$

3. State and covariance Propagation:

$\hat{\mathbf{x}}_{k+1}^- = \frac{\gamma-(n_x+n_w)}{\gamma}\mathbf{f}(\hat{\mathbf{x}}_k, \bar{\mathbf{w}}_k)$

$+ \frac{1}{2\gamma}\sum\limits_{p=1}^{n_x}\{\mathbf{f}(\hat{\mathbf{x}}_k + h\mathbf{s}_{s,p}, \bar{\mathbf{w}}_k) + \mathbf{f}_i(\hat{\mathbf{x}}_k - h\mathbf{s}_{s,j}, \bar{\mathbf{w}}_k)\}$

$+ \frac{1}{2\gamma}\sum\limits_{p=1}^{n_x}\{\mathbf{f}(\hat{\mathbf{x}}_k, \bar{\mathbf{w}}_k + h\mathbf{s}_{w,p}) + \mathbf{f}_i(\hat{\mathbf{x}}_k, \bar{\mathbf{w}}_k - h\mathbf{s}_{s,p})\}$

$\mathbf{S}_x^-(k+1) = \left[\mathbf{S}_{x\hat{x}}^{(1)}(k+1)\ \mathbf{S}_{xw}^{(1)}(k+1)\ \mathbf{S}_{x\hat{x}}^{(2)}(k+1)\ \mathbf{S}_{xw}^{(2)}(k+1)\right]$

$\mathbf{S}_x^-(k+1) = \left[\mathbf{S}_{x\hat{x}}^{(1)}(k+1)\ \mathbf{S}_{xw}^{(1)}(k+1)\ \mathbf{S}_{x\hat{x}}^{(2)}(k+1)\ \mathbf{S}_{xw}^{(2)}(k+1)\right]^T$

$\mathbf{P}_{k+1}^- = \mathbf{S}_x^-(k+1)(\mathbf{S}_x^-(k+1))^T$

4. Observation and Innovation Covariance Propagation:

$\hat{\mathbf{y}}_{k+1}^- = \frac{\gamma-(n_x+n_v)}{\gamma}\mathbf{h}(\hat{\mathbf{x}}_{k+1}^-, \bar{\mathbf{v}}_{k+1})$

$+ \frac{1}{2\gamma}\sum\limits_{p=1}^{n_x}\{\mathbf{h}(\hat{\mathbf{x}}_{k+1}^- + h\mathbf{s}_{x,p}^-, \bar{\mathbf{v}}_{k+1}) + \mathbf{h}(\hat{\mathbf{x}}_{k+1}^- - h\mathbf{s}_{x,p}^-, \bar{\mathbf{v}}_{k+1})\}$

$+ \frac{1}{2\gamma}\sum\limits_{p=1}^{n_x}\{\mathbf{h}(\hat{\mathbf{x}}_{k+1}^-, \bar{\mathbf{v}}_{k+1} + h\mathbf{s}_{v,p}) + \mathbf{h}(\hat{\mathbf{x}}_{k+1}^-, \bar{\mathbf{v}}_{k+1} - h\mathbf{s}_{v,p})\}$

$\mathbf{P}_{k+1}^{vv} = \mathbf{S}_v(k+1)\mathbf{S}_v^T(k+1)$

$\mathbf{P}_{k+1}^{xy} = \mathbf{S}_{\hat{x}}^{(1)}(k+1)\left(\mathbf{S}_{y\hat{x}}^{(1)}(k+1)\right)^T$

5. Update:

$\mathbf{K}_{k+1} = \mathbf{P}_{k+1}^{xy}(\mathbf{P}_{k+1}^{vv})^{-1}$

$\hat{\mathbf{x}}_{k+1}^+ = \hat{\mathbf{x}}_{k+1}^- + \mathbf{K}_{k+1}(\mathbf{y}_{k+1} - \hat{\mathbf{y}}_{k+1})$

$\mathbf{P}_{k+1}^+ = \mathbf{P}_{k+1}^- - \mathbf{K}_{k+1}\mathbf{P}_{k+1}^{vv}\mathbf{K}_{k+1}^T$

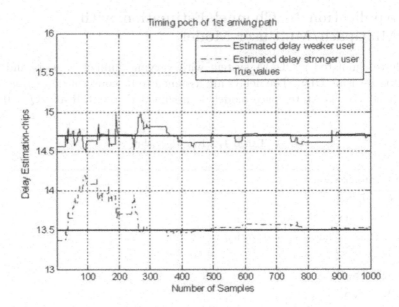

Fig. 2. Timing epoch estimation for first arriving path with a five user-three path(1/2-chip apart) channel model

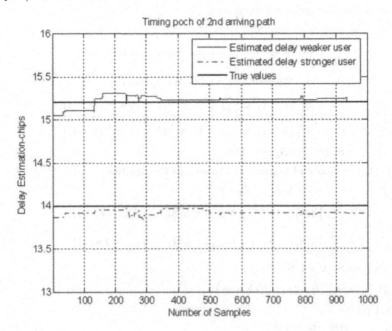

Fig. 3. Timing epoch estimation for second arriving path with a five-user/three-path channel model (with 1/2-chip path separation)

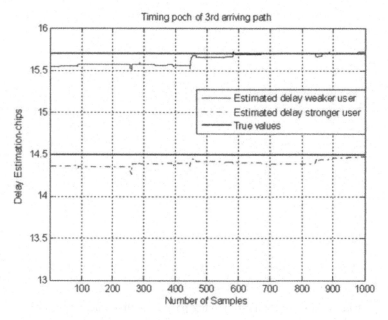

Fig. 4. Timing epoch estimation for third arriving path with a five-user/three-path channel model (with 1/2-chip path separation)

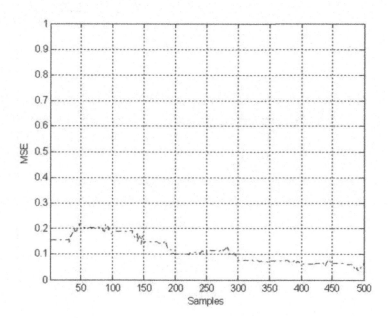

Fig. 5. MSE of the channel coefficients for first arriving path with a ten-user/two-path channel model

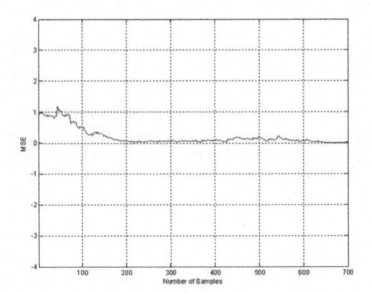

Fig. 6. MSE of the first arriving path in a fifteen user/two path

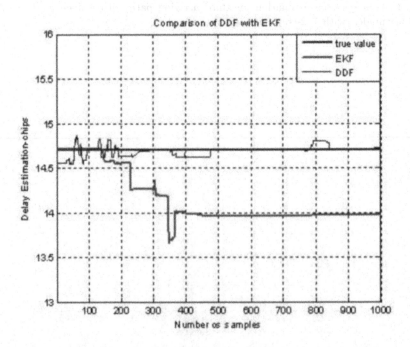

Fig. 7. Comparison of the DDF with EKF in terms of timing epoch estimation for first arriving path with a five-user/three-path channel model (with 1/2-chip path separation

where $\mathbf{I}$ is the identity matrix. We will be considering fading multipaths and multiuser environment with 2, 5 and 10 user scenario. The SNR at the receiver of the weaker user is taken to be of 10 dB. The near far ratio of 20 dB has been assumed with the power of the strong user is $P_1 = 1$ and that of the weak user is $P_1/10$. We note that the data bits,$d_{k,m}$, are not included in the estimation process, but are assumed unknown a priori. In the simulations, we assume that the data bits are available from decision-directed adaptation, where the symbols $d_{k,m}$ are replaced by the $\hat{d}_{k,m}$ decisions shown in Figure 1. We also considered the special case of closely spaced multipaths. Figures 1, 2 and 3 show the timing epoch in a multiuser scenario with three multipaths with the path separation of 1/2 chip. We have considered the case of the weaker user and have compared it with the stronger user. Proposed estimator converges to the close to the true value approximately in 6-8 symbols even in the presence of MAI and is able to track desired user delay even when the paths are closely spaced. Figures (4) show the mean square error for Now if we compare the UKF algorithm [10] with the DDF algorithm, we see that the performance of the two is nearly same. This is demonstrated in fig.5. It is due to the fact that DDF is based on the derivative approximation on Stirling formula whereas UKF is based on Taylor series approximation for the nonlinear function.

5 Conclusion

This paper presented a nonlinear filtering approach for CDMA time delay and channel gain estimation over multipath fading based on the DDF. It was shown that the DDF achieves better performance and enjoys moderate complexity compared to the (linearized) EKF algorithm because of the nonlinear dependency of the channel parameters on the received signals in multiuser/multipath scenarios. A general derivation the processing steps was presented, followed by a specialization to the case of time delay and channel gain estimation for multipath CDMA signals, with particular focus on closely-spaced multipath epochs. The numerical results showed that the DDF is quite robust vis-a-vis near-far multiple-access interference, and can also track a given signal epoch even in the presence of other closely-spaced multipaths (within a fraction of a chip).

References

1. Gilhousen, H.F., et al.: On the capacity of a cellular CDMA system. IEEE Transactions on Vehicular Technology 40(2), 303–312 (1991)
2. Pickholtz, R.L., Milstein, L.B., Schilling, D.L.: Spread spectrum for mobile communications. IEEE Transactions on Vehicular Technology 40(2), 313–322 (1991)
3. Iltis, R.A., Mailaender, L.: An adaptive multiuser detector with joint amplitude and delay estimation. IEEE Journal on Select Areas Communications 12(5), 774–785 (1994)
4. Radovic, A.: An iterative near-far resistant algorithm for joint parameter estimation in asynchronous CDMA systems. In: Proceedings of 5th IEEE Intenational Symposium on Personal, Indoor, Mobile Radio Communications, vol. 1, pp. 199–203 (1994)

5. Ström, E.G., Parkvall, S., Miller, S.L., Ottersten, B.E.: Propagation delay estimation in asynchronous direct-sequence code-division multiple access systems. IEEE Transactions on Communications 44(1), 84–93 (1996)
6. Bensley, S.E., Aazhang, B.: Subspace-based channel estimation for code division multiple access communication systems. IEEE Transactions on Communications 44(8), 1009–1020 (1996)
7. Ström, E.G., Parkvall, S., Miller, S.L., Ottersten, B.E.: DS-CDMA synchronization in time-varying fading channels. IEEE Journal on Select Areas Communications 14(8), 1636–1642 (1996)
8. Latva-aho, M., Lilleberg, J.: Delay trackers for multiuser CDMA receivers. In: Proceedings of IEEE International Conference on Universal Personal Communications, pp. 326–330 (1996)
9. Caffery Jr, J.J., Stüber, G.L.: cOverview of radiolocation in CDMA cellular systems. IEEE Communication Magazine 36, 38–45 (1998)
10. Caffery Jr, J.J., Stüber, G.L.: Nonlinear Multiuser Parameter Estimation and Tracking in CDMA Systems. IEEE Transactions on Communications 48(12), 2053–2063 (2000)
11. Ström, E.G., Malmsten, F.: A maximum likelihood approach for estimating DS-CDMA multipath fading channels. IEEE Journal on Select Areas Communications 18(1), 132–140 (2000)
12. Bhashyam, S., Aazhang, B.: Multiuser channel estimation and tracking for long-code CDMA systems. IEEE Transactions on Communications 50(7), 1081–1090 (2002)
13. Kim, K.J., Iltis, R.A.: Joint detection and channel estimation algorithms for QS-CDMA signals over time-varying channels. IEEE Transactions on Communications 50(5), 845–855 (2002)
14. Lakhzouri, A., Lohan, E.S., Hamila, R., Renfors, M.: Extended Kalman Filter channel estimation for line-of-sight detection in WCDMA mobile positioning. EURASIP Journal on Applied Signal Processing 2003(13), 1268–1278 (2003)
15. Klee, U., Gehrig, T.: Kalman Filters for Time Delay of Arrival-Based Source Localization. EURASIP Journal on Applied Signal Processing 2006(1), 167 (2006)
16. Shunlan, L., Yong, M., Haiyun, Z.: Passive location by single observer with the Unscented Kalman Filter. In: IEEE International Symposium on Microwave, Antenna, Propagation and EMC Technology for Wireless Communications, vol. 2, pp. 1186–1189 (2005)
17. Wan, E.A., Merwe, R.: Kalman Filtering and Neural Networks. In: Adaptive and Learning Systems for Signal Processing, Communications, and Control, pp. 221–280. Wiley, Chichester (2001)
18. Alfriend, K.T., Lee, D.-J.: Nonlinear Bayesian Filtering For Orbit Determination and Prediction. In: 6th US Russian Space Surveillance Workshop, St. Petersburg, Russia, pp. 22–26 (2005)

Author Index